The Technical Resource

for Installing, Configuring,

and Supporting

Microsoft Office

for Windows 95,

Professional Edition

Microsoft®
Office for Windows® 95
Resource Kit

PUBLISHED BY
Microsoft Press
A Division of Microsoft Corporation
One Microsoft Way
Redmond, Washington 98052-6399

Library of Congress Cataloging-in-Publication Data pending.

Printed and bound in the United States of America.

1 2 3 4 5 6 7 8 9   RMRM   0 9 8 7 6 5

Distributed to the book trade in Canada by Macmillan of Canada, a division of Canada Publishing Corporation.

A CIP catalogue record for this book is available from the British Library.

Microsoft Press books are available through booksellers and distributors worldwide. For further information about international editions, contact your local Microsoft Corporation office. Or contact Microsoft Press International directly at fax (206) 936-7329.

PostScript is a trademark of Adobe Systems, Inc. America Online is a registered trademark of America Online, Inc. Apple and Macintosh are registered trademarks of Apple Computer, Inc. AutoCAD is a registered trademark of Autodesk, Inc. dBASE, MultiMate, and Paradox are registered trademarks and Quattro Pro is a trademark of Borland International, Inc. cc:Mail is a trademark of cc:Mail, Inc., a wholly owned subsidiary of Lotus Development Corporation. CompuServe is a registered trademark of CompuServe, Inc. CorelDRAW is a registered trademark of Corel Systems Corporation. Kodak is a registered trademark of Eastman Kodak Company. GEnie is a trademark of General Electric Corporation. HP is a registered trademark of Hewlett-Packard Company. Intel is a registered trademark of Intel Corporation. DisplayWrite and PROFS are registered trademarks of International Business Machines Corporation. 1-2-3, Lotus, and Lotus Notes are registered trademarks of Lotus Development Corporation. MapInfo is a registered trademark of MapInfo Corporation. FoxPro, Microsoft, MS-DOS, Multiplan, PivotTable, PowerPoint, Windows, TipWizard, Visual Basic, Win32, Win32s, and Wingdings are registered trademarks and Rushmore, Visual C++, and Windows NT are trademarks of Microsoft Corporation. NetWare and WordPerfect are registered trademarks of Novell, Inc. RC4 Algorithm is a registered trademark of RSA Data Security, Inc. Harvard Graphics is a registered trademark and HyperShow is a trademark of Software Publishing Corporation. Timex is a registered trademark of Timex Corporation. PC Paintbrush is a registered trademark of Wordstar Atlanta Technology Center. WordStar is a registered trademark of WordStar International Incorporated.

Acquisitions Editor: Casey D. Doyle
Project Editor: Brenda L. Matteson

PUBLISHED BY
Microsoft Press
A Division of Microsoft Corporation
One Microsoft Way
Redmond, Washington 98052-6399

Library of Congress Cataloging-in-Publication Data pending.

Printed and bound in the United States of America.

1 2 3 4 5 6 7 8 9   RMRM   0 9 8 7 6 5

Distributed to the book trade in Canada by Macmillan of Canada, a division of Canada Publishing Corporation.

A CIP catalogue record for this book is available from the British Library.

Microsoft Press books are available through booksellers and distributors worldwide. For further information about international editions, contact your local Microsoft Corporation office. Or contact Microsoft Press International directly at fax (206) 936-7329.

Acquisitions Editor: Casey D. Doyle
Project Editor: Brenda L. Matteson

Contents

Appendixes

Welcome to the Microsoft Office for Windows 95 Resource Kit

The *Microsoft Office for Windows 95 Resource Kit* is written for administrators and MIS professionals. It provides the information required for rolling out, supporting, and understanding Microsoft® Office for Windows® 95. This book is being published both in bound form and on CD, and it is posted in the Microsoft Office Resource Kit forum on the Microsoft Network (MSN). For late-breaking, up-to-date information about Office for Windows 95, MSN is the place to look. MSN has a forum for each of the Office applications, and one for Office for Windows 95, too. For information about accessing MSN, see Appendix F, "Resources."

In the past three to five years, much has changed in terms of how an MIS department treats desktop applications. Five years ago, departmental LANs were sprouting up all over organizations. Individual departments, and even individual users, were deciding which applications they would use. In choosing an application, their primary criterion was the set of tasks the application could do. Today, however, departments are increasingly interested in how well an application allows people within a workgroup to share data.

Two factors have contributed to this change. First, the use of LANs and WANs is much more widespread, and MIS departments are now managing them centrally rather than departmentally. Second, in the autumn of 1993, Microsoft Office 4.0 was launched. Office 4.0 provided much more consistency and ease of use than has been available before in a group of integrated desktop applications. This spurred many organizations to standardize on Office. In standardizing on a single, integrated solution, MIS organizations appreciate the control they have over their departmental desktops, yet they also recognize the importance of supporting and maintaining this software to reap the benefits that standardization provides.

The purpose of this Resource Kit is to provide the information that the MIS professional or administrator needs to support Microsoft Office for Windows 95. This includes planning for deployment of Office for Windows 95, deciding which configurations are best for your organization, and understanding issues regarding migrating from earlier versions of Office or from competitive applications.

What's in the Office for Windows 95 Resource Kit

The following paragraphs describe the contents of the Resource Kit, and there is also a list of conventions used throughout the book. Each part of the Resource Kit begins with a summary of the chapters contained in that part, and the first page of each chapter includes a list of the contents of that chapter.

A Guided Tour to Microsoft Office for Window 95 Use this tour for a quick glance at the new features in Microsoft Office for Windows 95 and in the individual Office applications. By reading this guided tour, network administrators and MIS professionals can learn which features of Office for Windows 95 can reduce the total cost of ownership for personal computers in their organizations.

Part 1, Architecture Provides an overview for MIS managers and technical support personnel of the structure of Office and its applications. Includes details on components shared between applications and the location of these components. Use these chapters as a starting point for troubleshooting any user-related problems or unexpected results in Office applications.

Part 2, Installing Microsoft Office for Windows 95 Provides MIS managers with the details they need for installing Office for Windows 95—including steps for choosing a strategy for installation, such as assembling a planning team and tools and rolling out a pilot project. This part also explains the steps necessary for installing Office on end-users' computers—either directly on a workstation or from a file server on a network. Managers can choose to have employees install their own software, or they can administer individual installations from an administrative installation point on the network. This part explains how to customize the installation process for specific system configurations or user needs. Installation issues specific to particular Office applications are also included. In addition, this part provides techniques for upgrading users' software to the current version of Office, whether a user is upgrading all of Office or one or more of the individual Office applications.

Part 3, Maintaining and Supporting Microsoft Office Provides technical information about customizing and updating users' software and about fine-tuning Office for optimum performance. This part includes a troubleshooting chapter designed to address specific issues that may arise when software is updated.

Part 4, Running Multiple Versions of Office and Using Office in a Workgroup
Presents information that helps MIS managers and technical support personnel when their workgroups include multiple platforms and/or multiple versions of Office applications. This part also includes information about how to take advantage of the workgroup features built into Office, such as setting up corporate forms and templates and integrating Office applications and electronic mail.

Part 5, Switching from Other Applications Provides detailed information about migrating users from other applications (Microsoft or otherwise) to their Office counterparts, such as from WordPerfect® to Word, from Lotus 1-2-3® to Microsoft Excel, from Harvard Graphics® to PowerPoint®, or from dBASE to Microsoft Access. This part includes information about filters that convert documents to the format of the destination Microsoft application, and it explains how Office applications manage documents and data that were created in other applications.

Appendixes Separate appendixes provide detailed references for Setup command line options and file format, registry settings, installed components, items included on the Office Resource Kit CD, system requirements for Office, and resources for technical support.

Conventions

The following conventional terms, text formats, and symbols are used throughout this Resource Kit.

Convention	Meaning
[brackets]	Enclose optional items in syntax statements. For example, [password] indicates that you can choose to type a password with the command. Type only the information within the brackets, not the brackets themselves.
Bold	Indicates the actual commands, words, or characters that you type in a dialog box or at the command prompt.
Italic	Indicates a placeholder for information or parameters that you must provide. For example, if the procedure asks you to type a filename, you type the actual name of a file.
Capitalized_Path\Filenames	Indicates a file system path or registry key—for example, the file Templates\Normal.dot. You can use a mixture of uppercase and lowercase characters when you type paths and filenames, unless otherwise indicated for a a specific application or utility.
Monospace	Represents examples of screen text or entries that you might type at the command line or in the Windows registry.

A Guided Tour to Microsoft Office for Windows 95

This part of the *Office Resource Kit* provides an overview of the new features in Microsoft Office for Windows 95. By reading this guided tour, network administrators and MIS professionals can learn which features of Microsoft Office for Windows 95 can reduce the total cost of ownership for personal computers in their organizations. The tour focuses on five areas:

- Rich support of Windows 95 technologies.
- New and enhanced ease-of-use features so users can focus on their work.
- Improved integration and information sharing among all Microsoft Office for Windows 95 applications.
- How Microsoft Office for Windows 95 enables you to communicate better in an increasingly connected world.
- The ability to build custom business solutions using Office for Windows 95.

A study by Kelley Services found that Microsoft Office 4.*x* users were 37 percent faster and 36 percent more accurate at completing tasks in Microsoft Office for Windows 95, after only 45 minutes of going through a document that guided them through many of the new features.

Another study, completed by Workgroup Technologies, Inc., called Rescue for the Helpdesk: Microsoft Office for Windows 95, looked at what the likely impact on your corporate Helpdesk would be based on upgrading to Office 95. These results are above and beyond the savings gained by upgrading to Windows 95. Their analysis shows that there should be a reduction of Microsoft Office support calls by 35 percent, resulting in a total reduction of all support calls by 3 percent to 7 percent. Much of this is due to the Office 95 Answer Wizard, which is able to help the user through 70 to 85 percent of applications questions, so the user doesn't need to call the Helpdesk. The average company should be able to save $62 per year, per user, due to reduced support costs alone.

For more information on these studies, please call Microsoft Customer Service, at (800) 426-9400 and ask for the Windows 95 and Office 95 Business Value Reports.

Windows 95 Support

Microsoft Office for Windows 95 is designed to take full advantage of the Windows 95 operating system, not only by using key technologies such as the 32-bit architecture and pre-emptive multitasking, but through an interface consistent with that of the operating system.

ScreenTips The previous version of Microsoft Office included an innovative feature called ToolTips to help users navigate through the user interfaces of each application. Now, ToolTips have been taken a step further with the introduction of Screen Tips—providing pop-up information about different elements of the application, such as dialog boxes.

ToolTips ToolTips provide a brief description of the function of a toolbar button. These helpful tips are abundant throughout Windows 95 and all Microsoft Office for Windows 95 applications.

Shortcut menus Office version 4.*x* enabled access to common document functions by clicking the right mouse button. These shortcut menus enable the user to get the most commonly used commands with a simple click of the mouse. Now these shortcut menus are also pervasive throughout Windows 95.

Tabbed dialog boxes Office version 4.*x* also pioneered the use of tabbed dialog boxes to group common commands and functions in a single unified area. Windows 95 uses tabbed dialog boxes as well.

Performance

In the Windows 95 Performance tab, you can see a listing of your processor type, the amount of RAM, and available system resources. With previous versions of Office, it was common to exhaust system resources when operating multiple applications at once—especially applications that were graphic-intensive. With Microsoft Office for Windows 95, the likelihood of running out of system resources is now a thing of the past.

Multi-tasking With Windows 95 and Microsoft Office for Windows 95, you can now enjoy true pre-emptive multi-tasking. For example, you can perform a time-intensive query in Microsoft Access or run a large macro in Microsoft Excel, while at the same time composing a letter in Word or a presentation in PowerPoint.

Multi-threading Multi-threading is related to, but different from, multi-tasking. Multi-tasking is the ability to perform two or more tasks simultaneously in separate programs, while multi-threading is the ability to perform separate tasks within a single program. In Microsoft Office for Windows 95, certain time-intensive tasks can now be handled on a separate thread. For example, printing in PowerPoint and Word is now done on a separate thread, giving you control of your application in a more timely manner while the process of printing your documents is concurrently performed. Similarly, in Microsoft Access, queries are run on a separate thread.

Speed In addition to the performance enhancements available with Windows 95, additional enhancements speed up the applications. The Microsoft Excel development team spent over 20 percent of its development time hand-tuning the recalculation engine to take advantage of the Windows 95 32-bit API. Calculations are now faster and more efficient than ever, as are charting and cut, copy, and paste operations.

Microsoft Access Briefcase Replication

Using the Windows 95 Briefcase, users of Microsoft Access for Windows 95 can work remotely with replicated copies of their databases and then merge those changes back into their master database. In addition, any changes made by the developer in the design master are propagated down to all the replicas. In this way, replication can be used for managing remote changes to data, versioning applications, and balancing network load.

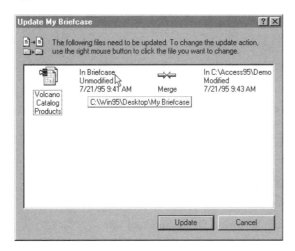

Windows 95 Shortcuts

Shortcut to Microsoft
Access Form

Users of Microsoft Access for Windows 95 can create desktop shortcuts to their database objects simply by dragging and dropping the object to the Windows 95 desktop. Once created, these shortcuts to Microsoft Access objects can be put in mail messages, documents, or other programs that support Windows 95 shortcut technology. Double-clicking on the shortcut opens the database and the object.

Microsoft Office Shortcut Bar

The name of the Microsoft Office Manager (MOM) has been changed to the Office Shortcut Bar to reflect changes in its functionality and increase consistency with Windows 95 terminology. MOM enabled Office 4.x users to launch and switch easily between applications. With the Office Shortcut Bar, users can not only launch and switch between applications, but dock files or applications directly on the Office Shortcut Bar. Users can even create their own toolbars in the Office Shortcut Bar.

Office Shortcut Bar

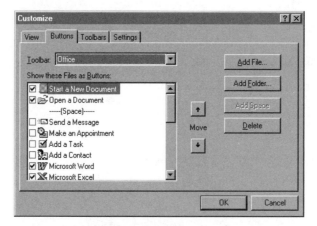

Customizing the Microsoft Office Shortcut Bar

Focus on Your Work, Not Your Software

A key design goal of Microsoft Office for Windows 95 is to help people tap the full potential of their software so they can more easily get their job done. Innovative technologies, such as IntelliSense, and the addition of Schedule+ to the Microsoft Office suite make it easier and faster than ever before to get your work done.

Microsoft Office

Part of allowing people to focus on their work and not their software is consistency across all of the applications they work in. Once a user has learned a task, it is easier to repeat that task in another application if it works the same way. Following are the ease of use features that are consistent across the Office suite.

File Starter

Start a New
Document

The new File Starter dialog box is shared across all applications in Microsoft Office for Windows 95. It provides an easy-to-use solution for retrieving and managing your document templates. Using a familiar tabbed dialog box pioneered in Microsoft Office 4.*x*, you can quickly switch between categories to find the template you want.

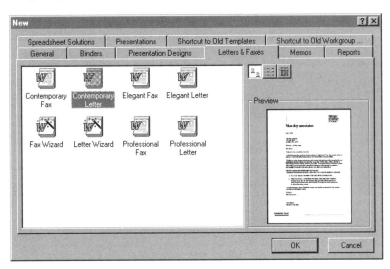

The new File Starter dialog box is shared by all Microsoft Office 95 applications.

Answer Wizard

Twenty five percent of the requests on the Microsoft Wish Line are for features that are already in existing products. To help users explore and get more done with the tools they have available in Microsoft Office for Windows 95, the Answer Wizard was created. The Answer Wizard enables users to ask questions about any Office application in their own words. Not only does it provide quick access to the help topics, but the help you get is better and more task-oriented. The Answer Wizard gives you the help you need to complete tasks faster. For example, suppose a user needs help performing a mail merge in Word 95. They type their question in the Answer Wizard, get back a list of topics pick the one they want, and they're off, with the information they need to complete the task.

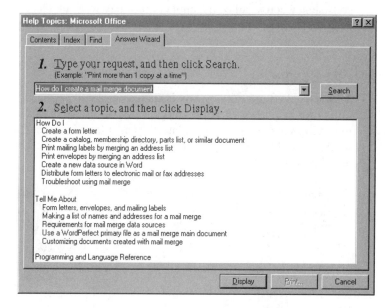

The Answer Wizard in Microsoft Office for Windows 95

Some Help topics are step-by-step answers, which users follow to complete tasks; sometimes, they are interactive answers, with the Answer Wizard doing part of the work for you. For example, if you ask how to print sideways on a page, the answer wizard takes you where you need to go to finish your task.

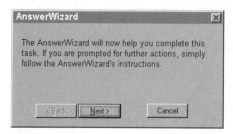

After clicking Next, the Answer Wizard picks the appropriate menu commands to display the product functionality you need to complete the task. In this case, the File menu is activated, and the cursor moves down the menu to the Page Setup command.

The Answer Wizard displays the Page Setup dialog box and provides a Screen Tip instructing you what to do to set the page orientation the way you want it.

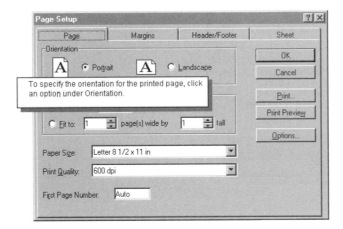

Screen Tip as a result of interactive Answer Wizard answer

The Answer Wizard is available in all of the Office for Windows 95 applications.

New File Open Dialog Box

One of the most common end-user enhancement requests for Office was better integration of file management into document creation. Now Office 95 applications all share a common File Open dialog box with integrated file management capability built-in. The new File Open dialog box uses an interface similar to the Windows 95 Explorer to navigate your hard drive as well as identical document property views. And to rename documents, all you do is click the filename and type a new name. The high degree of consistency between Office and Windows 95 means users can be productive quickly without spending a lot of time learning new tools.

File Open
Button

The File Open dialog box also gives you shortcuts to create a list of favorite places to look for documents and to get to that list.

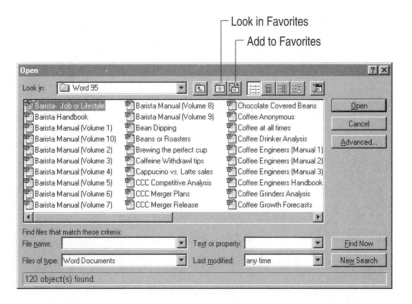

The new File Open dialog box is shared across all Office 95 applications.

And now users can preview their documents before they open them, to check that its the one they want. By clicking the Preview button in the File Open dialog box, the dialog box changes to show a thumbnail view of the document.

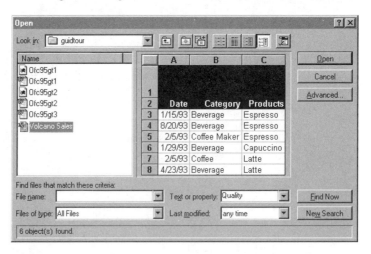

The new File Open dialog box showing a preview of a document

Find Fast Technology

Beyond integrating file management capabilities, Microsoft developers devoted a lot of effort to make it easier for users to find their documents once they create them. Office 4.3 included a powerful feature called FileFind for retrieving documents. However, research indicated that only 34 percent of Office users were taking advantage of this built-in capability.

With this research in mind, Microsoft developed a new interface for retrieving documents and integrated it into the File Open dialog box for easy access. Now, over 98 percent of all the search operations created with the advanced FileFind feature in Office 4.3 can be accomplished from File Open in all Office applications. In addition, Microsoft also developed a new way for users to quickly retrieve and manage documents using the new Fast Find Technology in Office 95, which does full text indexing in a very efficient manner.

AutoCorrect

AutoCorrect, a feature previously only available in Word, is now available in Microsoft Excel, Microsoft Access, and PowerPoint. In addition, the AutoCorrect list is shared between the applications.

Microsoft Word

Microsoft Word continues to focus on creating an intuitive, easy-to-use environment that naturally fits the way people use their word processing application every day. Even though this is a new version of Word, the number of major user interface modifications were minimized to make it easier for users of previous versions of Word to be productive immediately.

Enhanced AutoCorrect

AutoCorrect is an excellent example of a feature in Word 6.0 that demonstrated the Microsoft commitment to making everyday tasks easier than ever before. Since the release of Word 6.0, Word developers have learned a lot about how customers are using AutoCorrect and how it could be improved. With this in mind, the next generation of IntelliSense technology was created with Enhanced AutoCorrect—providing intelligent features that learn from the user.

AutoCorrect Ease-of-Use Improvements Many of the refinements to AutoCorrect are the direct result of observing users working with Word 6.0. For example, users would manually override AutoCorrect changes, so AutoCorrect was enhanced to provide more flexibility. The end result is that AutoCorrect is easier and more natural to use.

Exceptions List   For those times when AutoCorrect does not work the way user wants, it learns from its mistakes automatically, becoming an even better customized tool for creating documents. This Word for Windows 95 feature analyzes situations where the user overrides changes that AutoCorrect makes to the document. Once these changes are identified, they are added to the exceptions list so that AutoCorrect does not make the same mistaken correction twice.

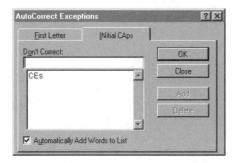

The AutoCorrect Exceptions Dialog Box

Spell-It

Microsoft Word 6.0 for Windows set a new standard for ease of use with innovative features such as AutoCorrect and AutoFormat. Word 95 builds on that tradition with the addition of Spell-It, which automatically spell-checks your document as you type and lets you make corrections on the fly. The spell-checking feature is faster than ever since Word 95 already knows which words are misspelled. For those who prefer to view their spelling errors at the end of their work session, Word 95 also supports the option to not view misspelled words while you work. This option is available on the Spelling tab in the Tools Options dialog box.

TipWizard

Users were first introduced to the TipWizard® in Microsoft Excel 5.0. The TipWizard provides real-time interactive suggestions to help users learn how to use Microsoft Excel while they work on their spreadsheets. Follow-up research indicated that users want more help on getting their tasks done faster and easier, so the new TipWizard in Word 95 focuses primarily on helping users complete their tasks.

The TipWizard automatically provides you with an explanation of the changes it made to your document. To get more information on this feature, click the Show Me button.

The TipWizard toolbar in Word 95

AutoFormat As You Type

Users like to see their document formatting as they type, but many users don't know how to access the extensive formatting capabilities in Word. To make it easier for users to create great-looking documents and provide them with immediate feedback, AutoFormat As You Type was created. AutoFormat As You Type automatically applies formatting to your document for lists, borders, symbols, fractions, and headings, without your hands ever leaving the keyboard.

Microsoft Excel

Microsoft Excel is a very powerful analysis tool. Over the years, the Microsoft Excel development team has also concentrated on ensuring that Microsoft Excel is easy to use so all users can take advantage of that power.

Animation

Providing feedback to the user is just another way that Microsoft Office for Windows 95 enables users to focus on their work, not their software. For example, in Microsoft Excel, when a column or row is deleted, the screen action is animated to let you know what just happened.

AutoComplete

Data entry is one of the most common tasks for spreadsheet users. Often times, they're entering the same data over and over again. AutoComplete not only makes data entry faster, but increases data entry accuracy because the user no longer has to type entries that are duplicates of existing entries. Microsoft Excel finishes the entries for them, based on what's already in the list. Or users can pick from a list instead of typing.

AutoComplete

Pick from list in Microsoft Excel

AutoFilter with Top 10

AutoFilter is a powerful way to extract relevant data from lists of information in Microsoft Excel. Now AutoFilter offers increased filtering capabilities that make it more powerful than ever.

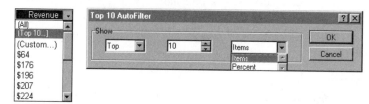

AutoFilter with Top 10

AutoCalculate

AutoCalculate Display in Status Bar

Spreadsheet users often create temporary "scrap" formulas within their spreadsheet to calculate the value of a range of cells, only to immediately delete that calculation once they've seen the result. Often it is done to check values, or see an intermediate value as they build their spreadsheet. AutoCalculate automatically shows this value in the status bar, as a result of selecting the cells that need to be calculated.

Cell Tips

The ability to add notes to a cell has been in Microsoft Excel since version 3. Now, in Microsoft Excel for Windows 95, access to the notes in a cell is easier and faster. When a user points to a cell that contains a note, the note pops up.

Screen Tips

Navigating in large spreadsheets can be tedious. Microsoft Excel makes it much easier with the assistance of Screen Tips to accurately judge your destination within the spreadsheet.

Screen Tip

Mapping

Map Button

Microsoft Office for Windows 95 has added geographic mapping to both Microsoft Excel and Microsoft Access to provide even greater data analysis functionality. Since the DataMap is a shared component in Microsoft Office for Windows 95, it can be used by all applications.

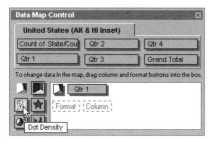

Microsoft Access

New usability features in Microsoft Access include a Performance Analyzer to help you improve your databases; easy, intuitive ways to filter and query your databases; and a Table Analyzer to help you create relational databases from existing non-relational data.

Performance Analyzer

Microsoft Access for Windows 95 includes a Performance Analyzer that examines existing databases and recommends changes to improve application performance. Some of the performance enhancements can be completed automatically, while others are recommended changes or suggestions.

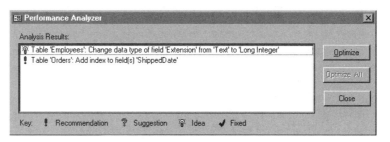

Filter by Form/Datasheet

Microsoft Access for Windows 95 introduces a new way for users to find
information by using a form or datasheet to formulate the query. All forms now
have a new Filter By Form mode wherein users can type the information they are
seeking and Microsoft Access will build the underlying query to deliver just that
data, again in a form view.

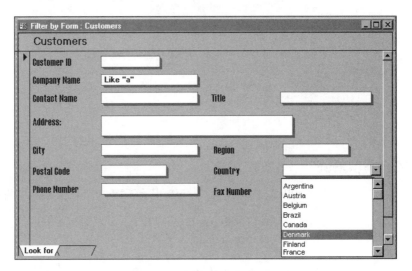

Filter By Selection

Microsoft Access for Windows 95 allows users to quickly locate information on
forms or datasheets by highlighting a selection and filtering the underlying data
based on that selection. Usability testing showed that users often highlight part of
what they are looking for and then search for a way to limit the view of their data
to what they have selected. Filter By Selection does just that.

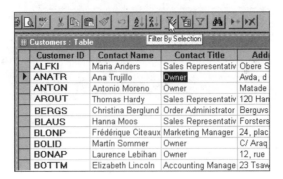

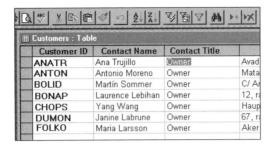

Table Analyzer

The Table Analyzer in Microsoft Access for Windows 95 can intelligently decipher flat file data from a wide variety of data formats, including Microsoft Excel, and create a relational database that stores the original data but avoids all the problems of non-relational data. This normalization process makes a recommendation that users can accept or customize and then splits the original table into relational tables. In this way, new users can harness the power of a relational database without necessarily having to understand the relational database model.

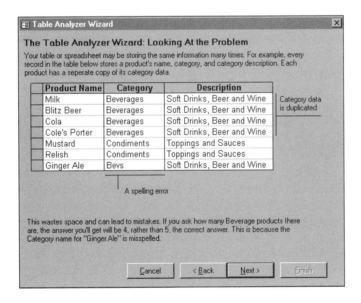

Microsoft PowerPoint

Presentations graphics programs were at one time used only by professionals creating powerful one-to-many presentations. More and more, presentations are being used by business people to deliver a message or communicate news, and are even being used as interactive discussion tools at small meetings. Microsoft PowerPoint enables users to be more effective in creating and giving various presentations, and it also lets users focus on the task at hand and be more effective in their communication.

Screen Tips

Finding a particular slide in a large deck of slides can be difficult. Oftentimes, users would switch to outline view or slide sorter to find a particular slide. With the help of Screen Tips, it's easy now.

Screen Tip

When you scroll through the slides, a Screen Tip appears and tells you not only the slide number, but the title of the slide as well.

Custom Backgrounds

PowerPoint for Windows 95 includes many ways to customize background fills for your presentations so you can maximize the impact of your communication.

Custom Background Options

Textured Fills

Another Custom Fill option in PowerPoint for Windows 95 is textured fills.

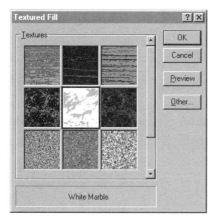

Textured Fill Dialog Box

These images are not full-screen bitmaps, but instead are small, specially designed images that are tiled throughout the slides. Rather than store these images over and over again in all slides, PowerPoint intelligently manages these images and stores the image only once, so your file size remains compact.

Multiple Level Undo and Redo

PowerPoint for Windows 95 now has multiple levels of undo. For example, if you're not sure which background you like better, you can toggle back and forth using the Redo and Undo buttons.

Undo Button   **Redo Button**

Animation Settings

PowerPoint for Windows 95 gives you hundreds of ways to create fancy text builds and animated object builds.

Drive In Effect   **Reverse Build**   **Flying Effect**

With a few mouse clicks anyone can create a presentation with reverse builds (David Letterman-style Top Ten lists), drive-in effects, flying effects, or paragraphs, words, or even characters added one by one. All of these choices make it easier to create a presentation with impact.

Slide Miniatures

When people give presentations, they often distribute paper copies. For presentations with colored text and objects, it's not always easy to know what the hard copy will look like when it's printed in black and white. With PowerPoint for Windows 95, you can always check as you build your slides using the Slide Miniature view option.

Black and White Options

Black and White
Button

To see what your slides will look like in black and white, use Black and White view. Click with the right mouse button on any object to view or change the way it will print in black and white. These options do not change the way the presentation looks in color.

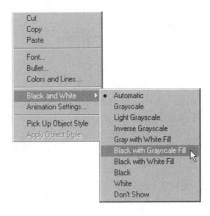

Black and White Shortcut Menu Options

Style Checker

Using IntelliSense technology, PowerPoint can take your presentation and make it look better with the new Style Checker. The Style Checker searches through your presentation and check for spelling, visual clarity, case, and end punctuation.

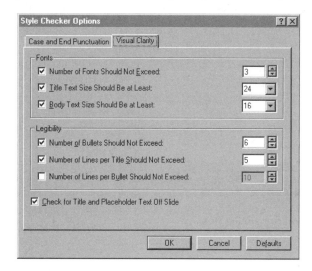

Slide Navigation Options

New navigational and presentation tools in PowerPoint slide show mode are available on a shortcut menu. Click the right mouse button to go to the Slide navigator, and move to any slide in your presentation.

Slide Navigator Shortcut Menu

Meeting Minder

Also on the Slide Navigator shortcut menu is the Meeting Minder—a powerful new tool that is very useful when using a presentation during interactive group meetings. This tool allows the presenter to see their Notes Pages, take minutes of the meeting, or add a list of action items to follow up on after the meeting.

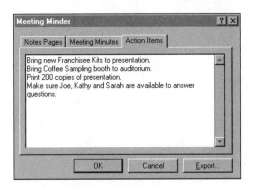

Meeting Minder Dialog Box

Microsoft Schedule+

Once just a great group-scheduling product, Schedule+ has evolved into a powerful time-management application, incorporating task management, group scheduling, and contact management capabilities in one easy-to-use application.

Flexible Views

People have different tastes and preferences in how they manage their schedules and tasks. Schedule+ lets you view your information the way you want to. Choose from the many preset views, or use the view rules to customize the views so you can work the way you want to.

Task and Appointment Management

Task List

Schedule+ lets you easily move appointments within your schedule and also assign time in your day to complete your tasks. There is a detailed task management tab, plus you can drag and drop tasks right onto the calendar.

Meeting Wizard

Meeting Wizard

Arranging a meeting with many colleagues can be a difficult and frustrating task. It's easy with the Schedule+ Meeting Wizard which prompts you through adding required and optional attendees, resources, and a conference room, and even picks the next time everyone is available, based on your criteria.

Timex Watch Wizard

Timex Watch Wizard

With Schedule+ and the Timex® Data Link watch, your appointments and vital information are now as close as your watch.

To Do List

Schedule+ provides the user with a separate area to manage and organize tasks. This view is completely customizable, enabling you to choose which columns (fields) to show, define how they are sorted, and even filter for the tasks you want to see.

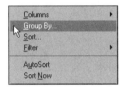

Task Grouping Shortcut Menu

Contact Management

Schedule+ now has new contact management capabilities that let you store important names and address, as well as other key contact information. Schedule+ also has Notes fields for important information about each contact.

Contact Management Tab

Printing Options

Schedule+ includes over 1,500 different ways to print your information. You even have the option to print it in the format of many popular paper planners.

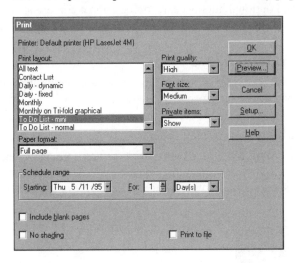

Share Information Easily Between Applications

To make it easier for users to get their work done, Office 95 includes many new features to make sharing information between applications even easier. These features include consistent menus; dragging and dropping from one application to another using the Windows 95 Taskbar; Office Binders to group documents from various applications; integration with the Microsoft Exchange client address book and the Schedule+ contact manager; new Microsoft Access including the Import/Export Wizard, Pivot Table Wizard, and Forms/Reports from Microsoft Excel, Write-up in PowerPoint; plus the Office Compatible program that helps developers create programs that integrate with Office for Windows 95.

Consistent Menus and Toolbars

All of the Office 95 applications have consistent menus and toolbars. In fact, Microsoft Excel, PowerPoint, and Word share eight of nine menus. In addition, each of the Office 95 applications has an updated user interface to take advantage of the new interface of Windows 95.

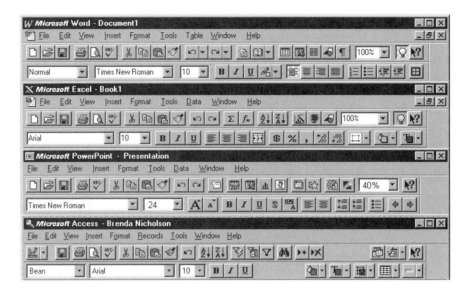

Microsoft Office 95 applications share consistent toolbars and top-level menus.

Drag and Drop Between Applications Using the Taskbar

Microsoft Office 4.0 introduced dragging and dropping OLE objects between applications. One of the most common scenarios was for users to drag a chart from Microsoft Excel to a Word document. Research indicated that while this feature was easy to use, arranging the applications side by side to make it easier to perform the drag and drop operation was cumbersome. Now, users of Microsoft Office for Windows 95 can quickly share information between applications by dragging and dropping to the Windows 95 Taskbar.

The Windows 95 Taskbar

Sharing information between applications using the Windows 95 Taskbar is also another example of how Office 95 takes advantage of the operating system to make it easier to create great documents.

Office Binders

Office Binder Tray

Another common task of office workers is to create compound documents that consist of different document types and files, and are printed out and bound together to form one giant document. This task has been tedious in the past because the files were kept separately, and printed separately, and then needed to be combined by hand to produce the final result. Creating consistent page numbers across all the sections was also a painful exercise. Microsoft Office for Windows 95 has new OfficeLinks technology called the Office Binder that addresses exactly this need.

The Office Binder is an electronic three-ring binder that allows for documents of different types to be included in one file, and for that file to be printed with one command, with consecutive page numbering that spans all of the individual file types.

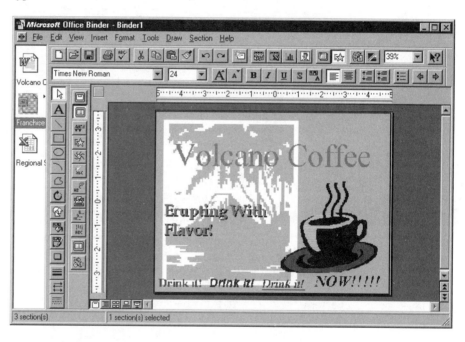

Microsoft Office Binder

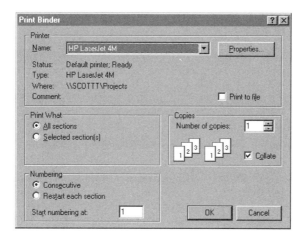

Office Binder Printing Dialog Box

Rearranging the order of the files is easy. You just rearrange them in the Binder until they are in the order you want.

Schedule+ and Address Book Integration

Address Button

Over 50 percent of all word-processing documents created are letters, faxes, or memos. In each of these document types most users have to manually insert address information. To make it even easier to insert and manage address information, Word for Windows 95 uses the Address Book features found in the Microsoft Exchange client for electronic mail that comes in Windows 95. In addition, Word 95 integrates with Microsoft Schedule+ for Windows 95 to store personal contact information. Now, inserting an address into a Word document or even an envelope is as easy as clicking on the toolbar.

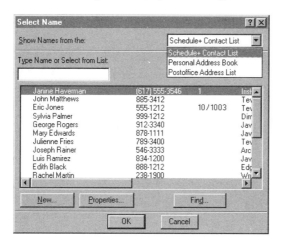

Microsoft Access Import/Export Wizard

Users no longer need to figure out how data is structured to bring it into Microsoft Access 95. The new wizard analyzes the target data and allows the user to decide what and how data should be imported into the database. Depending on the type of file being imported, users can define data types and indices at the time of import.

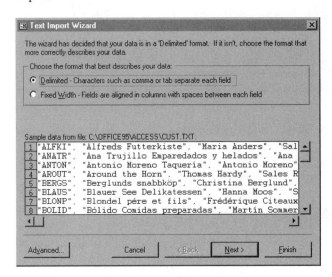

Pivot Table Wizard in Microsoft Access

Microsoft Access for Windows 95 includes a Pivot Table Wizard that walks users through the creation of Microsoft Excel Pivot Tables based on a Microsoft Access table or query. Using this tool, Microsoft Access users can take advantage of one of the great analysis capabilities in Microsoft Excel from directly within Microsoft Access.

Microsoft Access Forms/Reports from Microsoft Excel

Microsoft Excel users now have an easy way to use the advanced reporting and forms capability within Microsoft Access for Windows 95 directly from their Microsoft Excel worksheet. There is a new ISAM driver that allows users to create new tables in Microsoft Access linked to Microsoft Excel sheets—allowing forms, reports, and queries to work against native Microsoft Excel data.

Write-up in PowerPoint

Overhead or projected slides are often only part of a full-impact presentation. Hard copies of the presentation with notes on each slide are often distributed, especially when used in a training or highly informational presentation. Using OfficeLinks technology, the PowerPoint Write-up feature lets you share information easily with Microsoft Word to create handouts of your presentation that have added impact.

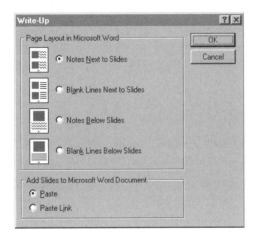

Office Compatible

Office for Windows 95 also extends integration beyond its core components to encompass both Windows 95 and a broad family of Office Compatible applications. The latest edition of the Office Compatible program offers new opportunities for third party software developers to closely integrate their applications with Office for Windows 95. Admission to the program is now free and development tools have been enhanced through the creation of the Office Compatible Advanced Developers Kit. Office Compatible programs can now directly access Office code and tie directly into the latest Office innovations such as the Office Binder. Office Compatible makes it easy for you to develop applications that look and act like Microsoft Office, and makes it easier for users to learn and use a broad range of software.

Communicate in a Connected World

In recent years, the combination of rapidly expanding technologies, such as the Internet, and the proliferation of information, have precipitated a fundamental change in the way we communicate and view document-based information. As we move into the future, the movement from paper-based to electronic documents will continue at an increasingly rapid pace. But just because the world grows increasingly connected should not mean that users need to learn and understand new tools to navigate through the electronic landscape. Microsoft users said they need to edit online, communicate using electronic mail, create documents for the Internet, and post information to advanced workgroup information databases. Not only are these uses important, they should be as easy and familiar as creating a document today.

WordMail

Word now works seamlessly with Exchange, the electronic mail client in Windows 95, to become your electronic mail editor.

Read & Reply

All of the editing, formatting, toolbar access, and automatic features that make Word a great word processor can now be used in e-mail.

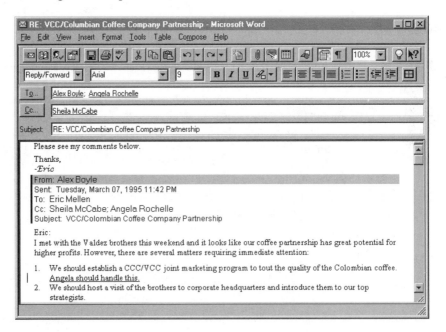

Using Microsoft Word 95 as the Exchange e-mail editor

Revision Marking

Revision marking is a powerful workgroup feature that has been available in Word since version 2.0. In WordMail, revision marks are used as an easy way to identify the changes and comments added by other users.

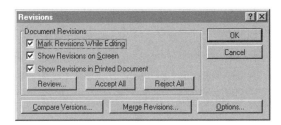

The Word 95 revisions capabilities enable rich workgroup document collaboration.

Highlighter Tool

Another feature requested by many users is to be able to mark or highlight portions of a document to call out the contents for other users. Now in Word 95, you can quickly and easily highlight information in your documents by using the Highlighter toolbar button. You can use this feature in WordMail, or in documents you share in other ways.

The Highlight Tool

Presentation Conferencing

Now you can conduct a meeting across the network, with up to 64 members of your team, using Presentation Conferencing. A wizard steps you through the setup and connection process to get the meeting going painlessly and easily. A set of Stage Manager tools provide extra control and confidence. For example, Slide Meter shows you at a glance whether you're running ahead or behind your rehearsed times. The Slide Navigator gives you a list of slide titles and preview pictures. And you have access to your speaker's notes on your system. This feature can also be used during formal, podium based presentations, as long as there are two computers networked together on the podium. In either case, all your audience sees is your professional presentation.

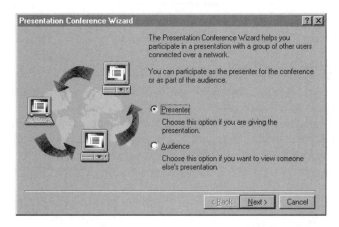

Building Solutions with Microsoft Office

While Microsoft Office is regarded as a powerful suite of desktop applications, Office is also a very powerful development platform for creating custom solutions. Three technologies make Office a compelling solutions platform— powerful applications that expose their functionality as programmable OLE objects, common programming languages, and support for OLE. These technologies work together, allowing the developer to create more powerful applications in less time, while writing less code, and using the software that users already know.

This section summarizes the enhancements made to Microsoft Office for Windows 95 to make development with Microsoft Office even easier.

Powerful Objects, Reusable and Programmable

At the heart of Office Solutions is the functionality provided by the features in the Microsoft Office products. Now you can incorporate even more of these features into your own solutions by using OLE Automation to control the richest sets of programmable objects of any development platform available on the market. In total, Office provides over 300 programmable OLE objects, representing millions of lines of code written by Microsoft in-house developers. By using Office objects, developers can create high-quality custom solutions that deliver more power, with less time required to create the solution. The table below displays existing, new, and improved OLE object model support provided by Office.

Existing	New	Improved
Microsoft Excel Object Model	Microsoft Access Object Model	Data Access Objects
Word Object Model	PowerPoint Object Model	Additional objects to support new features
Microsoft Project Object Model	Schedule+ Object Model	
	Binder Object Model	
	OLE Properties	

Common Programming Languages

While objects allow developers to create custom solutions with less code, some code must still be written for most solutions. Microsoft Office provides a set of common programming languages, based on the technology of the Visual Basic® programming system, that makes it easy for developers to write code to control Office objects. The following table shows existing and new support for common programming languages.

Existing	New
Visual Basic for applications in Microsoft Excel	Visual Basic for applications in Microsoft Access
Visual Basic for applications in Microsoft Project	
Word Basic in Word	

OLE Support

Developers need to create solutions that include data from various Office applications, in the same way that a user might need to create a word-processing document that contains a spreadsheet and a chart. Microsoft Office supports OLE features such as embedding and linking, visual editing, and drag and drop. This built-in integration at the user-interface level allows developers to use objects from different applications together in a single custom solution.

Microsoft Office also supports OLE Automation, which allows developers to use OLE objects from discrete applications together in a single custom solution. OLE Automation Servers are applications that can be controlled by OLE Automation Controllers; OLE Automation Controllers are languages or applications that can control OLE Automation Servers. Developers can combine objects representing data from many different sources into a custom solution, including objects from third party applications that also support OLE, such as the various Office Compatible applications. The following table lists the Office support for OLE Controllers and Servers.

OLE Controllers	OLE Servers
Microsoft Access	Microsoft Access
Microsoft Excel	Microsoft Excel
Microsoft Project	Microsoft Schedule+
	Microsoft Word
	Office Binder
	Office Document Property Object Library
	Microsoft PowerPoint
	Microsoft Project

In addition to the changes listed in this section, there are numerous other enhancements that make developing with Microsoft Office even easier and more efficient than it has been with past versions of Microsoft Office.

P A R T   1

Architecture

Chapter 1, "Microsoft Office Architecture," describes the overall architecture of Office. It emphasizes the components of Office that are shared among the Office applications, and provides an overview of the Office features that help the Office applications run smoothly together.

Chapter 2, "Microsoft Access Architecture," describes the architecture of Microsoft Access, including the Jet Database Engine, library databases, ISAMs, database objects, and how Microsoft Access resolves conflicts.

Chapter 3, "Microsoft Excel Architecture," describes the architecture of Microsoft Excel, including information on workbooks, cell values, formulas, cell formatting, charts, AutoFormats, macros, security, data mapping, and how Microsoft Excel resolves conflicts.

Chapter 4, "Microsoft PowerPoint Architecture," describes the architecture of PowerPoint, including an explanation of presentation templates, design templates, master elements, and how PowerPoint resolves conflicts.

Chapter 5, "Microsoft Schedule+ Architecture," describes the architecture of Schedule+, including information on the differences between running Schedule+ in group-enabled mode versus working alone, how Schedule+ resolves conflicts, and interoperability with Microsoft Exchange.

Chapter 6, "Microsoft Word Architecture," describes the architecture of Word, including detailed information about templates and how they work; how Word resolves conflicts; how to manage styles, AutoText entries, macros, and toolbars; whether components are stored with the template, the document, or the Word application; and how to create wizards and add-ins.

CHAPTER 1

Microsoft Office Architecture

Microsoft Office for Windows 95 teams up with the Windows 95 operating system to implement a method of work that is centered around information rather than applications. Office allows users to create information, then manipulate it with a suite of software tools. Each of these tools is a standalone application in its own right, yet Office integrates their functionality to form a unified work area—like the office metaphor for which it is named.

In This Chapter

Coordination of Applications

Office for Windows 95 coordinates the work of Microsoft Excel, Word, PowerPoint, Schedule+, and Microsoft Access. From a user's point of view, this is apparent in the consistency of the user interface. Menu and command names are standardized, not only in their terminology, but in their order and placement on the screen. If users are already familiar with one Office application, it will be easy for them to use the tools of another application. From an architectural point of view, the Office applications form an integrated whole.

Implementation of OLE   OLE is the basis for integration among the Office applications. Each of the Office applications is written to this standard.

Interoperability with Electronic Mail   Each of the Office applications supports interoperability with a variety of electronic mail systems, including Microsoft Exchange, the mail client installed with Windows 95.

Shared application tools Individual Office applications share tools such as spell checking, Microsoft Graph, Equation Editor, Data Map, and so forth. These tools are provided with the applications whether purchased individually or as part of Office.

Shared code As components of Office, the individual applications in Office share code in Office dynamic link libraries (DLLs). These DLLs provide functionality that is not available when the applications are purchased individually.

Shared services Office adds its own services to the Office applications. For example, the Microsoft Office Shortcut Bar enhances your ability to customize and standardize users' desktops, and Office Binders allows users to manage groups of documents from separate applications as if they were a single publication.

This chapter is to help you better understand these features, in order to better support your users.

Implementation of OLE

OLE is the basis for integration between the Office applications. OLE allows users to drag documents from a folder to an Office Binder or to their Microsoft Exchange Inbox so that the document retains its own properties while it gains the services of the *container* or destination application. OLE treats these compound documents as a single entity, yet maintains the uniqueness of each document.

OLE also allows users to insert data from a source document into a client document—cells from a Microsoft Excel workbook into a Word document, for example. Data can be linked or embedded. A *linked* object is a reference to the source and is updated dynamically with the source data. An *embedded* object is a copy of the source data that can be edited with the tools from the source application; it has no link to the source data. Documents with embedded objects take up more memory than documents with linked objects. This is because embedded objects are copies whereas linked objects are merely references.

OLE Properties

OLE standardizes the way that applications store properties for documents. Office uses a standard set of properties across all applications. In addition, users can define a wide variety of custom properties. Properties are stored with the document file. For details concerning the specifications for properties, see the *OLE Software Developer's Kit*, published by Microsoft Press and available at your local bookstore.

The OLE properties stored with a document are accessible to any application that supports OLE. For example, when a user drags and drops a Microsoft Excel worksheet into a Word document, the user can manipulate the worksheet's properties through Word.

Office applications include the following sets of OLE properties:

Summary information   These properties are standard ones, familiar to users of Office 4.*x* as those that appear in the Summary Info dialog box. More properties have been added in Office for Windows 95 applications.

Document summary information   These properties provide an enhanced set of properties, over and above those found in the Summary Info set.

Custom   These properties are defined by the user with string names rather than property IDs. This allows users to create any property they want with any name they want.

For each of the Office for Windows 95 applications, the Property dialog box includes the following tabs:

- General
- Summary
- Statistics
- Contents
- Custom

Most of the properties that appear on the General, Summary, and Statistics tabs will be familiar to users of previous versions of Office applications. These are the Summary Information properties, with some Document Summary Information properties added.

Properties that appear on the Contents tab are new. These are Document Summary information properties.

Properties that appear on the Custom tab are also new. They are Custom properties that users define themselves.

The following tables show the source for each group of properties, by tab.

General Properties

The following table lists the source for the information displayed on the General tab.

Property	Source
Icon of application that created document	System
Filename	System
Type	System
Location	System
Size	System
MS-DOS name	System
Created	System
Modified	System
Accessed	System
Attributes	System

Summary Properties

The following table lists the source for the information displayed on the Summary tab.

Property	Source
Title	PID_TITLE
Subject	PID_SUBJECT
Author	PID_AUTHOR
Manager	PID_MANAGER
Company	PID_COMPANY
Category	PID_CATEGORY
Keywords	PID_KEYWORDS
Comments	PID_COMMENTS
Template	PID_TEMPLATE

Statistics Properties

The following table lists the source for the information displayed in the Statistics tab:

Property	Source
Created	PID_CREATE_DTM[2]
Modified	System
Accessed	System
Printed	PID_LASTPRINTED
Last saved by	PID_LASTAUTHOR
Revision number	PID_REVNUMBER
Total editing time	PID_EDITTIME
Pages[1]	PID_PAGECOUNT
Paragraphs [1]	PID_PARCOUNT
Lines[1]	PID_LINECOUNT
Words[1]	PID_WORDCOUNT
Characters[1]	PID_CHARCOUNT
Bytes[1]	PID_BYTECOUNT
Slides[1]	PID_SLIDECOUNT
Notes pages[1]	PID_NOTECOUNT
Hidden slides[1]	PID_HIDDENCOUNT
MM clips[1]	PID_MMCLIPCOUNT
Presentation Target[1]	PID_PRESFORMAT
Scale Crop	PID_SCALE

[1] These statistics are made available according to the Office application. For example, Microsoft Excel uses none of these statistics, Word uses Pages, Paragraphs, Lines, Words, and Characters, while PowerPoint uses Slides, Paragraphs, Words, Notes, Hidden Slides, and Multimedia Clips.

[2] The value displayed here is derived from the property ID and not from the system, as on the General property tab. The value on the General tab tells when the document was created on the system and is not necessarily when the document was created absolutely.

Contents Properties

The Contents tab stores names of the different sections in the document (documents in a binder, sheet names in a workbook, slide titles in a presentation, and so forth). The following illustration shows the contents properties of a Microsoft Excel workbook.

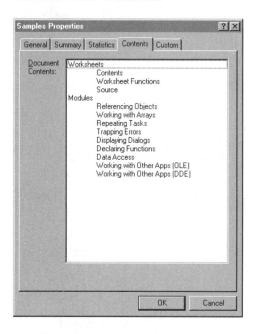

Custom Properties

The Custom tab provides an interface for users to create their own properties, which are either constants stored in the property stream or are linked to some document content, such as PowerPoint text, a Word bookmark or a Microsoft Excel named range. A *property stream* is a predefined part of a structured storage (file) that is used for storing the property data.

Valid property types are number (VT_I4 or VT_R8), date (VT_DATE), boolean (VT_BOOL), and text (VT_LPSTR).

When a property is linked to document content, the user chooses the source for the property value, and this value is displayed in the property list with a linked chain icon next to the entry. If the link source is not available, for example, if the name the link points to has been deleted, the icon changes to a broken chain link, shown in the following example.

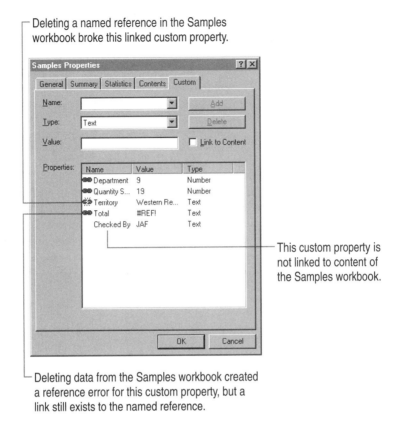

Deleting a named reference in the Samples workbook broke this linked custom property.

This custom property is not linked to content of the Samples workbook.

Deleting data from the Samples workbook created a reference error for this custom property, but a link still exists to the named reference.

User-defined property names are stored separately from other properties so that users cannot create conflicts by naming a Custom property with the same name as a Summary Information or Document Summary Information property. For example, the property Author already exists as a Summary Information property, but a user could create a property named "Author." These names are stored separately in the property list and displayed on separate tabs in the Property dialog box.

In addition, users can hide properties of documents posted to a Microsoft Exchange public folder by using the underscore character as the first character of the property name. For example, a user may want to create a property strictly for selection purposes, such as "EmployeesEarningGreaterthan80k," which the user would never want to appear. The user can make the property invisible in the Microsoft Exchange viewer by including an underscore character as the first character of the string (for example, "_EmployeesEarningGreaterthan80k").

Note The underscore does not cause the Property dialog box to hide properties. Rather, it is an advisory to an application that reads properties, such as the Microsoft Exchange Server, that it should not display the property.

Interoperability with Electronic Mail

The individual Office applications detect whether a Messaging API (MAPI), such as the Microsoft Exchange client, Microsoft Mail, or cc:Mail™, is installed on the system. To determine existence of MAPI, the application checks the DLL32 value of the Registry key Hkey_Local_Machine\Software\Microsoft\Microsoft Office\95\MapiDLL, and uses the DLL specified in this path. If this key does not exist, the application uses the Windows MAPI DLL, Mapi32.dll.

If the Office application detects a 16-bit vendor independent messaging (VIM) system, such as cc:Mail, the application installs a 32-bit DLL that converts MAPI calls to VIM, Mapivi32.dll, and sets the path in the Registry. Mapivi32.dll is a 32-bit DLL. To communicate with the 16-bit VIM mail provider, it requires the 16-bit DLL, Mapivitk.dll. For more information on how 16-bit applications communicate with 32-bit DLLs, see "Porting Your 16-bit Office-Based Solutions to 32-bit Office" in Chapter 12.

If the Office application detects a mail provider, it adds Send and Add Routing Slip commands to the File menu. This allows users to send documents directly from their application, without having to launch their mail software manually.

With the Microsoft Exchange client installed, users can use Word as their e-mail editor (WordMail), and can enable group scheduling by combining the use of Schedule+, the Microsoft Exchange client, and a postoffice. That postoffice can be the local type you install with Windows 95 or any other valid MAPI mail server that supports MAPI 1.0.

Office applications also check for a connection to the Microsoft Exchange Server on the user's system. To determine whether or not a connection to the Microsoft Exchange Server exists, the Office application checks for the Registry key Hkey_Local_Machine\Software\Microsoft\Exchange\Client\Extensions for installed mail providers. If the application finds a value for the Microsoft Exchange Server, it adds the Post To Microsoft Exchange Folder command to the File menu. This allows users to post documents to a public folder.

For more information about the interoperability between Office and electronic mail, see "Interoperability with Electronic Mail" in Chapter 15.

Documents Stored in Microsoft Exchange Public Folders

The Microsoft Exchange public folder can store three main types of items: documents, e-mail messages, and forms. By either dragging and dropping from the file system or by posting a document from an application, users can store documents in a public folder. For more information on public folders, see the documentation that comes with the Microsoft Exchange Server.

Public folders store documents as OLE objects, contained in invisible mail messages. To users, the documents inside a public folder may appear to be a files stored in a file structure on disk. However, Microsoft Exchange public folders treat documents as mail messages, not files. This leads to two major differences between a Microsoft Exchange public folder and a folder in the disk file structure:

- Public folders can have multiple documents with the same name.
- Microsoft Exchange allows more than one person to open and edit a document at the same time, with *optimistic file locking*. With optimistic file locking, if more than one user is accessing the same server, the first user to save the document will have data saved without any messages. When other users go to save the document, Microsoft Exchange issues a warning that the message has been changed by another user, and provides an option for users to lose their changes or to save the document as a new document.

  If each of these users is on a different server, the message is put into a conflict state. The most recently changed version is designated as the master message, and the other messages are attached to it. The master message is marked as being in conflict. When a user opens it, a form shows the different versions and allows a user with Edit All permission to merge the changes.

Note The Microsoft Excel file sharing feature does not work for documents in public folders. This is because Microsoft Excel cannot determine whether more than one person is accessing a document when the document is embedded in a message.

Properties Exchanged with Microsoft Exchange

When users store a document in a Microsoft Exchange public folder, Microsoft Exchange initiates a process to read out the properties from the document, and promote them to be MAPI properties.

There are three different sets of properties that Microsoft Exchange promotes:

- The 18 standard SummaryInformation properties
- The new standard DocumentSummaryInformation
- All of the UserDefinedProperties

After the properties are promoted, they become available in the Microsoft Exchange user interface. With the document highlighted, users can click Properties on the File menu to see the properties. Any user-defined properties that include an underscore as the first character are not displayed in the list of property names in Microsoft Exchange.

Users can search on properties in Microsoft Exchange, using the Advanced button in the Open dialog box, similar to how they search for properties from the Open dialog box in Office applications.

Shared Application Tools

This section discusses tools that are shared by Office applications, such as Microsoft Organization Chart, WordArt, AutoCorrect, Microsoft Graph, and so forth. In a way, these are standalone applications. Most include their own executable (.exe) file, and many include their own dynamic link libraries (DLLs) which must be present for the tool to run. Rather than being components of Office, these tools are included with one or more of the Office applications. For example, Word and PowerPoint share Microsoft Graph whether or not Office is installed on the user's system.

Applications that serve as tools for the Office applications are identified in the Registry, under the Hkey_Local_Machine\Software\Microsoft\Shared Tools keys. The default installation path for most of these tools is the \Program Files\Common Files\Microsoft Shared folder.

Many of these tools are applications that must be run from within an Office application. For example, if users double-click the icon for Graph5.exe in the Windows Explorer, they will get an error message stating that the application must be run from within another program. To run Microsoft Graph, the user must be running Microsoft Word, PowerPoint, Microsoft Excel, or Microsoft Access. Some of these tools are *OLE servers*, which means they are available when users click Object on the Insert menu of any application that supports OLE.

The following table lists the application tools shared by Office applications, the applications that share them, and their default location as Office Setup installs them. For a complete listing of these tools, see Appendix C, "List of Installed Components."

Tool	Applications that share	Default installation location
Art Gallery	Microsoft Access, Microsoft Excel, PowerPoint, Word	\Program Files\Common Files\ Microsoft Shared\Artgalry
Data Access Objects	Microsoft Access, Microsoft Excel	\Program Files\Common Files\ Microsoft Shared\Dao
Data Map	Microsoft Access, Microsoft Excel	\Program Files\Common Files\ Microsoft Shared\DataMap

Tool	Applications that share	Default installation location
Equation Editor	Microsoft Access, Microsoft Excel, PowerPoint, Word	\Program Files\Common Files\ Microsoft Shared\Equation
Graphics Filters	PowerPoint, Word	\Program Files\Common Files\ Microsoft Shared\Grphflt
Microsoft Graph	Microsoft Access, Microsoft Excel, PowerPoint, Word	\Program Files\Common Files\ Microsoft Shared\Msgraph5
Microsoft Info	Microsoft Access, Microsoft Excel, PowerPoint, Word	\Windows\Msapps\Msinfo
Microsoft Query	Microsoft Access, Microsoft Excel, Word	\Program Files\Common Files\ Microsoft Shared\Msquery
Microsoft Organization Chart	Microsoft Access, Microsoft Excel, PowerPoint, Word	\Program Files\Common Files\ Microsoft Shared\Orgchart
Spell checking dictionary[1]	Microsoft Access, Microsoft Excel, PowerPoint, Word	\Program Files\Common Files\ Microsoft Shared\Proof
Microsoft WordArt	Microsoft Access, Microsoft Excel, PowerPoint, Word	\Program Files\Common Files\ Microsoft Shared\WordArt

[1] See the following section for more information about this tool.

Spell Checking Dictionary

The Office applications that implement spell checking all share the same dictionary file, Custom.dic. The default path for this file is the user's \Program Files\Common Files\Microsoft Shared\Proof folder. Customizations that users make to the spelling list by running spell check within an application are saved to this file.

It is possible to create a corporate dictionary, although you cannot share this file across a workgroup due to potential sharing violation problems.

▶ **To create a corporate dictionary file**

1. Open the file Custom.dic in a text editor, such as Notepad.

2. Edit the text file.

3. Save the file and install it to users' local workstations.

4. Edit the users' Registry key Hkey_Local_Machine\Software\Microsoft\Shared Tools\Proofing Tools\ Custom Dictionaries to point to the location of the corporate Custom.dic.

Shared Code

Office applications share code through the Office DLLs. These DLLs allow Office to integrate operations—such as creating a new document and sharing an AutoCorrect list—across all the Office applications. DLLs for Office, for the Office applications, and for shared applications often make calls to other DLLs, including Windows 95 system DLLs, so if another application on a user's system overwrites an existing DLL, Office may not run properly. This section discusses the Office DLLs and lists the DLLs called by the Office application programs.

Office DLLs

The Office DLL primarily responsible for supporting all shared Office components is Mso95.dll. Mso95.dll allows users to create new documents in a way that integrates the Office applications with one another. Mso95.dll also creates a single list of entries that is accessed by AutoCorrect in each of the Office applications. The following section describes these two features that Mso95.dll supports.

Starting a New Document

When users click the Start A New Document button on the Microsoft Office Shortcut Bar, a dialog box appears, showing all available templates. When users double-click a template icon, the Office application associated with the template creates a new, blank document based on the template. By default, the templates shown in this dialog box are from the user's \Msoffice\Templates folder and its subfolders.

Templates that appear on the General tab are stored in the user's Templates folder.

Templates that appear on other tabs are stored in subfolders of the user's Templates folder.

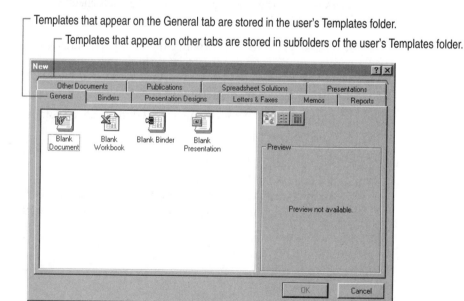

Msoffice\Templates is the default location for templates on users' local computers. Users can modify this setting by clicking Customize on the application control menu of the Microsoft Office Shortcut Bar and then clicking the Settings tab. This tab also allows users to set a location for templates on a network share, by clicking Workgroup Templates location and then clicking Modify.

You can maintain these settings for your users in the Registry key Hkey_Current_User\Software\Microsoft\Microsoft Office\95\FileNew. The path specified in the LocalTemplates key is the User Templates location, and the path specified in the SharedTemplates key is the Workgroup Templates location. For information on customizing these settings during Setup, see Chapter 9, "Customizing Client Installations."

If users have defined both the User Templates and Workgroup Templates locations, the New dialog box displays all available templates from both locations. Templates stored in the root folder of each location appear on the General tab of the New dialog box, and templates stored in subfolders appear on separate tabs. The names of the separate tabs match the names of the subfolders. For information on how to customize the tabs of the New dialog box, see "Supporting Custom Templates" in Chapter 12, "Support and Troubleshooting."

AutoCorrect List

The AutoCorrect feature, formerly available only in Word, allows users to automate corrections to frequently misspelled words and to create abbreviations that are expanded automatically for commonly used text. Because Office applications share an AutoCorrect list, all documents that a user creates in Office will have consistent spellings and stylistic conventions. For example, users can set AutoCorrect to replace the abbreviation "ppt" with "PowerPoint" as they type, and the convention of capitalizing the second "p" is maintained automatically.

Office installs a file containing a default AutoCorrect list, Msoffice.acl, to the user's Windows folder. When the Office application saves the user's personal list, it is stored as *Usernamenn*.acl, where *username* is the user's logon name and *nnn* is a number to further identify the user. You can modify the path for either the default or the user list. If you do this, you must modify the Windows Registry entry that points to this file, as explained later in this section.

When an Office application starts, the AutoCorrect code in Mso95.dll does the following:

1. Loads the .acl file pointed to in the Registry key
   Hkey_Current_User\Software \Microsoft\Microsoft Office\95\AutoCorrect\
   List with the value named by Path.
2. Opens the file pointed to in the Registry key
   Hkey_Local_Machine\Software\Microsoft\Shared Tools\AutoCorrect\List to
   find a default path, if the key/value in step 1 does not exist.

When the user quits the Office application, the AutoCorrect code in Mso95.dll does the following:

1. Saves the AutoCorrect list as *Usernamennn*.acl.

2. Writes the Hkey_Current_User key to point to the user's list file.

Users can modify AutoCorrect entries by clicking AutoCorrect on the Tools menu. These entries are stored in the Registry, in the key Hkey_Current_User\Software\Microsoft\Microsoft Office\95\AutoCorrect\Settings.

Caution   The value of the Hkey_Current_User\Software\Microsoft\Microsoft Office\95\AutoCorrect\Settings key is binary and should not be edited. Modify AutoCorrect entries with the AutoCorrect command on the Tools menu in any Office application.

▶   **To create a customized AutoCorrect list and distribute it to your users**

1. Run an Office application, and modify the default list in the AutoCorrect dialog box.

2. Quit the application, and find the resulting *Usernamennn*.acl file.

3. Store this file where your users can access it.

4. If you want to make this the default list for your users, you can modify users' Registry key Hkey_Local_Machine\Software\Microsoft\Shared Tools\AutoCorrect\List path entry to point to the file.

When users modify the master list and quit an Office application, the default list is stored on the local computer as *Usernamennn*.acl. When users customize their copy of the list, the changes do not affect the master list. To reinstall the original master list, users can delete their customized list and restart the Office application.

DLLs Called by Office Applications

Office applications call DLLs from executable program (.exe) files and application DLLs. This section lists those DLLs that may be called *statically,* when the application starts up in its default state. Other DLLs could be called *dynamically,* controlled by users while running the applications or while running macros, converters, drivers, or add-ins.

The following lists of statically called DLLs are to help you troubleshoot for your users when they start up an application. For example, if a user's Office Binder does not run properly, you could check to see that none of the DLLs associated with Binder.exe have been deleted or overwritten by some other application on the user's system. The lists include DLLs that are called by other DLLs. For example, if an application calls Mso95.dll, the DLLs called by Mso95.dll are also listed in the table.

DLLs Called by Office

Executable files and DLLs associated with Office and its components call DLLs as shown in the following table:

Calling file	DLLs
Binder.exe	Kernel32.dll, Advapi32.dll, User32.dll, Gdi32.dll, Cmdlg32.dll, Shell32.dll, Comctl32.dll, Mso95.dll, Oledlg.dll, Ole32.dll, Msvcrt20.dll, Rpcrt4.dll
Fastboot.exe	Kernel32.dll, User32.dll, Ole32.dll, Msvcrt20.dll, Rpcrt4.dll
Findfast.exe	Gdi32.dll, Kernel32.dll, User32.dll, Ole32.dll, Advapi32.dll, Mso95.dll, Shell32.dll, Comctl32.dll, Msvcrt20.dll, Rpcrt4.dll
Msoffice.exe	Kernel32.dll, User32.dll, Gdi32.dll, Advapi32.dll, Shell32.dll, Comctl32.dll
Msow.exe	Shell32.dll, Ole32.dll, Msvcrt20.dll, Rpcrt4.dll, Advapi32.dll, User32.dll, Kernel32.dll, Mso95.dll, Gdi32.dll, Comctl32.dll
Bdrec.dll	Kernel32.dll, Advapi32.dll, User32.dll, Gdi32.dll, Comctl32.dll, Ole32.dll, Mso95.dll, Shell32.dll, Msvcrt20.dll, Rpcrt4.dll
Commtb32.dll	Gdi32.dll, Kernel32.dll, User32.dll
Docobj.dll	User32.dll, Rpcrt4.dll, Kernel32.dll, Advapi32.dll
Explode.dll	Kernel32.dll, Advapi32.dll, User32.dll, Gdi32.dll, Shell32.dll, Ole32.dll, Msvcrt20.dll, Rpcrt4.dll, Comctl32.dll
Mfcans32.dll	Oleaut32.dll, Ole32.dll, Msvcrt20.dll, Rpcrt4.dll, Kernel32.dll, User32.dll, Advapi32.dll
Mfcuia32.dll	Oledlg.dll, Ole32.dll, Msvcrt20.dll, Rpcrt4.dll, Mfcans32.dll, Kernel32.dll, Oleaut32.dll, User32.dll, Advapi32.dll
Mso95.dll	User32.dll, Gdi32.dll, Advapi32.dll, Shell32.dll, Kernel32.dll, Ole32.dll, Msvcrt20.dll, Rpcrt4.dll, Comctl32.dll
Mso95fx.dll	Kernel32.dll
Mstool32.dll	Advapi32.dll, Kernel32.dll, User32.dll
Openenu.dll	Kernel32.dll
Osbreg.dll	User32.dll, Advapi32.dll, Kernel32.dll

DLLs Called by Microsoft Access

Executable files and DLLs associated with Microsoft Access and its components call DLLs as shown in the following table:

Calling file	DLLs
Msaccess.exe	Msjt3032.dll, Mswng300.dll, Vba232.dll, Mso95.dll, Ole32.dll, Oleaut32.dll, Msvcrt20.dll, Gdi32.dll, User32.dll, Advapi32.dll, Kernel32.dll, Comctl32.dll, Shell32.dll, Rpcrt4.dll, Mpr.dll
Wrkgadm.exe	Comdlg32.dll, Advapi32.dll, User32.dll, Kernel32.dll, Gdi32.dll
Msaccreg.dll	Advapi32.dll, Mpr.dll, Mfcans32.dll, Ole32.dll, User32.dll, Kernel32.dll, Msvcrt20.dll, Rpcrt4.dll, Oleaut32.dll
Msaexp30.dll	User32.dll, Gdi32.dll, Comdlg32.dll, Advapi32.dll, Shell32.dll, Kernel32.dll, Comctl32.dll
Msain300.dll	Msvcrt20.dll, Kernel32.dll, User32.dll
Msau7032.dll	Version.dll, Gdi32.dll, User32.dll, Comdlg32.dll, Advapi32.dll, Msvcrt20.dll, Msjt3032.dll, Oleaut32.dll, Kernel32.dll, Mpr.dll, Ole32.dll, Rpcrt4.dll
Msjrci30.dll	Kernel32.dll
Msjtrclr.dll	Msjt3032.dll, Mswng300.dll, Version.dll, Vbajet32.dll, Gdi32.dll, Msjter32.dll, Mpr.dll, Kernel32.dll, User32.dll, Advapi32.dll, Ole32.dll, Oleaut32.dll, Msvcrt20.dll, Rpcrt4.dll, Msjint32.dll
Oc30.dll	Mfcans32.dll, Msvcrt20.dll, User32.dll, Gdi32.dll, Comdlg32.dll, Advapi32.dll, Ole32.dll, Shell32.dll, Kernel32.dll, Oleaut32.dll, Ole32.dll, Rpcrt4.dll, Comctl32.dll
Soa300.dll	Gdi32.dll, User32.dll, Ole32.dll, Kernel32.dll, Msvcrt20.dll, Rpcrt4.dll

DLLs Called by Microsoft Excel

Executable files and DLLs associated with Microsoft Excel and its components call DLLs as shown in the following table:

Calling file	DLLs
Excel.exe	Mso95.dll, User32.dll, Gdi32.dll, Advapi32.dll, Shell32.dll, Kernel32.dll, Ole32.dll, Xlintl32.dll, Msvcrt20.dll, Rpcrt4.dll, Comctl32.dll
Analys32.xll	Kernel32.dll, Xlcall32.dll
Solver32.dll	Xlcall32.dll, Kernel32.dll, Olecli32.dll, User32.dll
Xlcall32.dll	Kernel32.dll
Xlkey32.dll	Kernel32.dll, User32.dll
Xlkey32.dll	Kernel32.dll, User32.dll

Calling file	DLLs
Xlodbc32.dll	Kernel32.dll, Xlcall32.dll, User32.dll, Odbc32.dll, Msvcrt20.dll, Advapi32.dll
Xlodbc32.dll	Xlcall32.dll, Kernel32.dll, User32.dll, Odbc32.dll, Msvcrt20.dll, Advapi32.dll
Xlqpw.dll	Kernel32.dll

DLLs Called by Microsoft PowerPoint

Executable files and DLLs associated with PowerPoint and its components call DLLs as shown in the following table:

Calling file	DLLs
Powerpnt.exe	Kernel32.dll, Gdi32.dll, User32.dll, Shell32.dll, Advapi32.dll, Comctl32.dll, Ole32.dll, Oleaut32.dll, Msvcrt20.dll, Rpcrt4.dll, Mso95.dll
Graflink.exe	Comctl32.dll, Kernel32.dll, User32.dll, Gdi32.dll, Comdlg32.dll, Advapi32.dll, Version.dll
Autoclip.dll	Kernel32.dll, User32.dll, Oleaut32.dll
Autoclip.dll	Kernel32.dll, User32.dll, Oleaut32.dll, Ole32.dll, Msvcrt20.dll, Rpcrt4.dll
Ghost.dll	User32.dll, Kernel32.dll
Msroute.dll	Kernel32.dll, User32.dll, Gdi32.dll, Advapi32.dll
Pngcomp.dll	Kernel32.dll, User32.dll
Pp4x32.dll	Ole32.dll, Kernel32.dll, User32.dll, Gdi32.dll, Advapi32.dll, Msvcrt20.dll, Rpcrt4.dll
Pp4x32.dll	Ole32.dll, Kernel32.dll, User32.dll, Gdi32.dll, Advapi32.dll, Msvcrt20.dll, Rpcrt4.dll
Ppt7reg.dll	Kernel32.dll, Advapi32.dll
Ppt7reg.dll	Kernel32.dll, Advapi32.dll
Ppttoolr.dll	Kernel32.dll, User32.dll
Ppttoolr.dll	Kernel32.dll, User32.dll
Ppttools.dll	Kernel32.dll, User32.dll, Advapi32.dll, Oleaut32.dll, Ole32.dll, Msvcrt20.dll, Rpcrt4.dll
Presconf.dll	Wsock32.dll, Oleaut32.dll, User32.dll, Kernel32.dll, Advapi32.dll
Ttemb32.dll	User32.dll, Gdi32.dll, Lz32.dll, Kernel32.dll

DLLs Called by Microsoft Schedule+

Executable files and DLLs associated with Schedule+ and its components call DLLs as shown in the following table:

Calling file	DLLs
Schdpl32.exe	Gdi32.dll, Advapi32.dll, Kernel32.dll, User32.dll, Msvcrt20.dll
Datzap32.dll	Kernel32.dll
Mscal32.dll	Msspc32.dll, Shell32.dll, Winmm.dll, Gdi32.dll, Advapi32.dll, Mpr.dll, Kernel32.dll, User32.dll, Msvcrt20.dll, Comctl32.dll
Msscd32.dll	Msspc32.dll, Shell32.dll, Winmm.dll, Gdi32.dll, Advapi32.dll, Mpr.dll, Kernel32.dll, User32.dll, Msvcrt20.dll, Comctl32.dll
Msspc32.dll	Shell32.dll, Winmm.dll, Gdi32.dll, Advapi32.dll, Mpr.dll, Kernel32.dll, User32.dll, Msvcrt20.dll, Comctl32.dll
Mstre32.dll	Msspc32.dll, Shell32.dll, Winmm.dll, Gdi32.dll, Advapi32.dll, Mpr.dll, Kernel32.dll, User32.dll, Msvcrt20.dll, Comctl32.dll
Mstrs32.dll	Msspc32.dll, Mscal32.dll, Shell32.dll, Winmm.dll, Gdi32.dll, Advapi32.dll, Mpr.dll, Kernel32.dll, User32.dll, Msvcrt20.dll, Comctl32.dll

DLLs Called by Microsoft Word

Executable files and DLLs associated with Word and its components call DLLs as shown in the following table:

Calling file	System DLLs
Winword.exe	Wwintl32.dll, Advapi32.dll, Gdi32.dll, Kernel32.dll, Shell32.dll, User32.dll, Ole32.dll, Mso95.dll, Comctl32.dll, Msvcrt20.dll, Rpcrt4.dll
Schdmapi.dll	Oleaut32.dll, Ole32.dll, Msvcrt20.dll, Rpcrt4.dll, Kernel32.dll, User32.dll, Gdi32.dll
Station.dll	Kernel32.dll, User32.dll, Gdi32.dll, Comdlg32.dll, Advapi32.dll, Shell32.dll, Ole32.dll, Oleaut32.dll, Mapi32.dll, Comctl32.dll, Msvcrt20.dll, Rpcrt4.dll
Wordmail.dll	Kernel32.dll, Advapi32.dll, User32.dll, Gdi32.dll, Comdlg32.dll, Shell32.dll, Mapi32.dll, Mfcans32.dll, Ole32.dll, Mpr.dll, Oleaut32.dll, Comctl32.dll, Msvcrt20.dll, Rpcrt4.dll
Wwintl32.dll	Kernel32.dll, User32.dll

DLLs Called by Shared Applications

Executable files and DLLs associated with shared application tools call DLLs as shown in the following tables:

Shared application	Calling file	DLLs
Art Gallery	Artgalry.exe	Mpr.dll, Picstore.dll, Comctl32.dll, Pubdlg.dll, Kernel32.dll, User32.dll, Gdi32.dll, Comdlg32.dll, Advapi32.dll, Shell32.dll, Mfcans32.dll, Ole32.dll, Msvcrt20.dll, Rpcrt4.dll, Oleaut32.dll
	Picstore.dll	Kernel32.dll, Ole32.dll, Msvcrt20.dll, Rpcrt4.dll, User32.dll
	Pubdlg.dll	Kernel32.dll, User32.dll, Gdi32.dll
Data Access Objects	Odbcad32.exe	Odbccp32.dll, Msvcrt20.dll, Kernel32.dll, User32.dll, Advapi32.dll, Gdi32.dll, Comdlg32.dll, Lz32.dll, Version.dll
	Dao3032.dll	Msjt3032.dll, Msjter32.dll, Msjint32.dll, Kernel32.dll, User32.dll, Advapi32.dll, Oleaut32.dll, Mpr.dll, Ole32.dll, Msvcrt20.dll, Rpcrt4.dll
	Dbnmpntw.dll	Kernel32.dll, Msvcrt20.dll, User32.dll
	Ds32gt.dll	Msvcrt20.dll, Kernel32.dll, User32.dll
	Mscpxl32.dll	Msvcrt20.dll, Kernel32.dll, User32.dll
	Msjint32.dll	Kernel32.dll, User32.dll
	Msjt3032.dll	Mpr.dll, Kernel32.dll, User32.dll, Advapi32.dll, Ole32.dll, Oleaut32.dll, Msvcrt20.dll, Rpcrt4.dll
	Msjter32.dll	Msjint32.dll, Kernel32.dll
	Mslt3032.dll	Msjt3032.dll, Kernel32.dll, User32.dll, Advapi32.dll, Oleaut32.dll, Ole32.dll, Msvcrt20.dll, Rpcrt4.dll, Mpr.dll
	Mspx3032.dll	Kernel32.dll, User32.dll, Advapi32.dll
	Msrd2x32.dll	Msjt3032.dll, Kernel32.dll, User32.dll, Advapi32.dll, Oleaut32.dll, Ole32.dll, Msvcrt20.dll, Rpcrt4.dll, Mpr.dll
	Mstx3032.dll	Msjt3032.dll, Kernel32.dll, User32.dll, Advapi32.dll, Oleaut32.dll, Ole32.dll, Msvcrt20.dll, Rpcrt4.dll, Mpr.dll
	Msvcrt20.dll	User32.dll, Kernel32.dll
	Mswng300.dll	Msjt3032.dll, Msjter32.dll, Msjint32.dll, Mpr.dll, Kernel32.dll, User32.dll, Advapi32.dll, Ole32.dll, Oleaut32.dll, Msvcrt20.dll, Rpcrt4.dll
	Msxb3032.dll	Kernel32.dll, User32.dll, Advapi32.dll

Shared application	Calling file	DLLs
Data Access Objects *(continued)*	Msxl3032.dll	Msjt3032.dll, Kernel32.dll, User32.dll, Advapi32.dll, Oleaut32.dll, Ole32.dll, Msvcrt20.dll, Rpcrt4.dll, Mpr.dll
	Odbc32.dll	Msvcrt20.dll, Kernel32.dll, Advapi32.dll, User32.dll
	Odbc32gt.dll	Msvcrt20.dll, Kernel32.dll, User32.dll
	Odbccp32.dll	Msvcrt20.dll, Kernel32.dll, Advapi32.dll, User32.dll, Gdi32.dll, Comdlg32.dll, Lz32.dll, Version.dll
	Odbccr32.dll	Odbc32.dll, Kernel32.dll, User32.dll, Shell32.dll, Advapi32.dll, Gdi32.dll, Comdlg32.dll, Comctl32.dll, Msvcrt20.dll
	Odbcjt32.dll	Odbcji32.dll, Msjt3032.dll, Msjter32.dll, Odbctl32.dll, Odbccp32.dll, Kernel32.dll, Advapi32.dll, User32.dll, Comdlg32.dll, Msvcrt20.dll, Gdi32.dll, Mpr.dll, Ole32.dll, Oleaut32.dll, Rpcrt4.dll, Msjint32.dll, Lz32.dll, Version.dll
	Odbctl32.dll	Kernel32.dll, User32.dll, Msvcrt20.dll
	Oddbse32.dl	Odbcjt32.dll, Odbcji32.dll, Msjt3032.dll, Msjter32.dll, Odbctl32.dll, Odbccp32.dll, Kernel32.dll, Advapi32.dll, User32.dll, Comdlg32.dll, Msvcrt20.dll, Gdi32.dll, Mpr.dll, Ole32.dll, Oleaut32.dll, Rpcrt4.dll, Msjint32.dll, Lz32.dll, Version.dll
	Odexl32.dll	Odbcjt32.dll, Odbcji32.dll, Msjt3032.dll, Msjter32.dll, Odbctl32.dll, Odbccp32.dll, Kernel32.dll, Advapi32.dll, User32.dll, Comdlg32.dll, Msvcrt20.dll, Gdi32.dll, Mpr.dll, Ole32.dll, Oleaut32.dll, Rpcrt4.dll, Msjint32.dll, Lz32.dll, Version.dll
	Odfox32.dll	Odbcjt32.dll, Odbcji32.dll, Msjt3032.dll, Msjter32.dll, Odbctl32.dll, Odbccp32.dll, Kernel32.dll, Advapi32.dll, User32.dll, Comdlg32.dll, Msvcrt20.dll, Gdi32.dll, Mpr.dll, Ole32.dll, Oleaut32.dll, Rpcrt4.dll, Msjint32.dll, Lz32.dll, Version.dll
	Odpdx32.dll	Odbcjt32.dll, Odbcji32.dll, Msjt3032.dll, Msjter32.dll, Odbctl32.dll, Odbccp32.dll, Kernel32.dll, Advapi32.dll, User32.dll, Comdlg32.dll, Msvcrt20.dll, Gdi32.dll, Mpr.dll, Ole32.dll, Oleaut32.dll, Rpcrt4.dll, Msjint32.dll, Lz32.dll, Version.dll

Shared application	Calling file	DLLs
Data Access Objects *(continued)*	Odtext32.dll	Odbcjt32.dll, Odbcji32.dll, Msjt3032.dll, Msjter32.dll, Odbctl32.dll, Odbccp32.dll, Kernel32.dll, Advapi32.dll, User32.dll, Comdlg32.dll, Msvcrt20.dll, Gdi32.dll, Mpr.dll, Ole32.dll, Oleaut32.dll, Rpcrt4.dll, Msjint32.dll, Lz32.dll, Version.dll
	Sqlsrv32.dll	Kernel32.dll, Msvcrt20.dll, User32.dll, Advapi32.dll, Odbccp32.dll, Version.dll, Netapi32.dll, Gdi32.dll, Comdlg32.dll, Lz32.dll, Netbios.dll
	Vbajet32.dll	Msvcrt20.dll, Kernel32.dll
Data Map	Datainst.exe	Mitmdl32.dll, Kernel32.dll, User32.dll, Gdi32.dll, Comdlg32.dll, Advapi32.dll, Shell32.dll, Comctl32.dll
	Datamap.exe	Mitmdl32.dll, Kernel32.dll, Gdi32.dll, User32.dll, Comdlg32.dll, Advapi32.dll, Shell32.dll, Comctl32.dll, Mfcans32.dll, Oleaut32.dll, Ole32.dll, Msvcrt20.dll, Rpcrt4.dll, Mfcuia32.dll,
	Midi10in.dll	Kernel32.dll
	Mitmdl32.dll	Kernel32.dll, Gdi32.dll, User32.dll
	Mo10in32.dll	Kernel32.dll
	Tm10in32.dll	Kernel32.dll
Equation Editor	Eqnedt32.exe	Kernel32.dll, User32.dll, Gdi32.dll, Advapi32.dll, Ole32.dll, Shell32.dll, Comctl32.dll, Msvcrt20.dll, Rpcrt4.dll
Graphics Filters	Msbmp32.dll	Kernel32.dll
	Msgif32.dll	Kernel32.dll
	Msjpeg32.dll	Kernel32.dll
	Msjpeg32.dll	Kernel32.dll
	Mspcd32.dll	Kernel32.dll, Pcdlib32.dll, Gdi32.dll, User32.dll
	Mspcx32.dll	Kernel32.dll
	Mstga32.dll	Kernel32.dll
	Mstiff32.dll	Kernel32.dll
	Pcdlib32.dll	Gdi32.dll, Kernel32.dll, User32.dll
Text Converters	Wpequ532.dll	Kernel32.dll
Microsoft Info	Msinfo32.exe	Version.dll, Kernel32.dll, User32.dll, Gdi32.dll, Advapi32.dll, Shell32.dll, Comctl32.dll
	Imgwalk.dll	Kernel32.dll, User32.dll

Shared application	Calling file	DLLs
Microsoft Query	Msqry32.exe	Qryint32.dll, Kernel32.dll, User32.dll, Gdi32.dll, Comdlg32.dll, Odbc32.dll, Advapi32.dll, Msvcrt20.dll
	Qryint32.dll	Kernel32.dll
Microsoft Organization Chart	Orgchart.exe	Kernel32.dll, User32.dll, Gdi32.dll, Comdlg32.dll, Advapi32.dll, Ole32.dll, Comctl32.dll, Msvcrt20.dll, Rpcrt4.dll
Proofing Tools	Mssp232.dll	Kernel32.dll, User32.dll
	Msth32.dll	Kernel32.dll, User32.dll
	Gram32.dll	Gdi32.dll, Kernel32.dll, User32.dll
	Hyph32.dll	Kernel32.dll, User32.dll
Microsoft WordArt	Wrdart32.exe	User32.dll, Gdi32.dll, Kernel32.dll, Pubole32.dll, Mfcans32.dll, Ole32.dll, Shell32.dll, Advapi32.dll, Comctl32.dll, Oleaut32.dll, Msvcrt20.dll, Rpcrt4.dll
	Pubole32.dll	User32.dll, Gdi32.dll, Kernel32.dll, Advapi32.dll, Ole32.dll, Msvcrt20.dll, Rpcrt4.dll
Visual Basic for applications	Vba232.dll	Ole32.dll, Oleaut32.dll, Gdi32.dll, User32.dll, Msvcrt20.dll, Kernel32.dll, Advapi32.dll, Winmm.dll, Rpcrt4.dll
	Vba32.dll	Ole32.dll, Oleaut32.dll, Gdi32.dll, User32.dll, Crtdll.dll, Mpr.dll, Kernel32.dll, Advapi32.dll, Winmm.dll
	Vbar2132.dll	Ole32.dll, Oleaut32.dll, Gdi32.dll, User32.dll, Msvcrt20.dll, Kernel32.dll, Advapi32.dll, Rpcrt4.dll
Help and Cue Cards	Cuecrd32.dll	User32.dll, Kernel32.dll
	Visx.exe	User32.dll, Kernel32.dll
	Hlp95en.dll	Kernel32.dll, User32.dll, Gdi32.dll

Shared Services

Services that Office adds to the individual Office applications are designed to unify common activities such as creating and opening documents, making appointments, or adding tasks or contacts. In this way, users do not necessarily "run Schedule+" or "start Microsoft Excel." Instead, they go straight to a task, and Office opens the tools necessary to accomplish the task.

In particular, the services that Office provides are the Microsoft Office Shortcut Bar, Office Binders, and the Find Fast utility.

Microsoft Office Shortcut Bar

The Microsoft Office Shortcut Bar is an upgraded version of the Microsoft Office Manager from Office 4.*x*. It is a set of toolbars that users can use to start applications. By default, the Shortcut Bar includes toolbars for Office, Desktop, Programs, Accessories, and the Microsoft Network (MSN) if MSN has been installed on the system.

Users can create their own toolbars, and can include buttons of their choice for creating single-click shortcuts to their most commonly used documents and applications. They can create a shortcut by dropping any file system object (such as files, folders, printers, or the control panel) onto any Shortcut Bar toolbar.

As an administrator, you can also create and distribute custom shortcut toolbars. The toolbars that appear on the Shortcut Bar are *.tbb files stored in \Msoffice\Office\ShortCut Bar on the user's computer. The buttons that appear on the Office toolbar by default are shortcut files in \Msoffice\Office\ShortCut Bar\Office. You can use the Network Installation Wizard to modify the collections of files in these locations on users' computers. For information on using the Network Installation Wizard, see Chapter 9, "Customizing Client Installations."

The folder location for the toolbar you create must also be specified in the Windows Registry. Each toolbar is listed under its own key under the key Hkey_Current_User\Software\Microsoft\Office Shortcut Bar\Toolbars:

```
\Hkey_Current_User\Software\Microsoft\Office Shortcut Bar
    \Position
        \Height
        \Left
        \Top
        \Width
    \Toolbars
        Key: \<path>
        Value: <RGB: 4 bytes> <Buttons> <#Rows: 2 bytes>
```

Each toolbar has a binary value pair where the name of the value is the folder path and the value is set to a null delimited and double null terminated string of the files in that folder and their ordering. Separators can be specified by a hyphen (-) character. The four bytes preceding this list are for the value of the toolbar color. The final two bytes of the value are reserved for the number of rows of buttons last displayed on the toolbar.

For example, if a folder C:\My Documents\Work were listed under Toolbars, then its entry might look like this:

```
[key] c:\my documents\work [value]<rgb-4 bytes>my first file()my second
file()my third file()-()my last file()()<rows-2 bytes>
```

In this case, the toolbar would contain three buttons, then a separator, then the last button; the buttons would correspond to each file and would appear in the order listed. Filenames in the list prefixed with an asterisk (*) are interpreted as hidden, so they will show up in the Customize dialog box, but not on the toolbar.

Office Binders

Office Binders are based on the metaphor of a three-ring binder, where all work that pertains to a single topic can be stored conveniently. Users can store spreadsheets, charts, documents, and presentations together in a binder, where they are saved and opened as a single unit, and can be printed in a single pass, with consecutive page numbering. Users can also disassemble a binder's contents and save each section as its own file.

Binders are OLE containers for embedded document objects. That is, opening a Word document section of a binder activates the Word tools necessary for editing the document, but any changes to the document are not reflected in the source document; likewise any changes to the source document are not reflected in the binder.

For more information about Office Binders, see "Supporting Office Binders" in Chapter 12, "Support and Troubleshooting."

Find Fast Indexer

The Find Fast indexer is a utility provided by Office that allows a user's system to create an index of document files on the local system or on a network share. Find Fast indexes are not seen by users, but are used by Office applications to make file searches faster. Indexes correspond to folders: the name, scope and location of each index matches that of its associated folder.

The indexer and indexes do not greatly tax system resources. The indexer can work in the background as an idle-time process, and indexes are usually less than five percent of the size of the document collection being indexed. For more information about using the Find Fast indexer, see "Finding and Managing Documents within a Workgroup" in Chapter 15.

By default, Setup installs the indexer as the file Findfast.exe in the user's \Msoffice\Office folder, copies a Find Fast shortcut to the \Windows\Start Menu\StartUp folder, and installs Find Fast in the Windows Control Panel. Setup also installs the Find Fast log file, Ffastlog.txt, in the user's \Windows\System folder. The location of the indexer is specified in the Registry key Hkey_Local_Machine\Software\Microsoft\Shared Tools Location, and the location of the log file is specified in the Registry key Hkey_Local_Machine\Software\Microsoft\Shared Tools\Find Fast\95.

Users can access the Find Fast indexer by going to the Control Panel and double-clicking on the Find Fast icon. The Find Fast dialog box allows users to create and delete indexes, to force an update to their index, to suspend indexing, and to see information about their index. By default, the Find Fast indexer creates an index of all Office documents, but users can choose to index whatever type of files they want. For example, they can index only PowerPoint presentations (*.ppt and *.pot files), or they can expand the index to include all files (*.*). Users can also choose the location of the index, such as the \Msoffice folder or the root folder of their hard drive. When the indexer creates an index, it creates the files __ofidx.ffa, __ofidx.ffl, and __ofidx0.ffx in the folder being indexed. Indexes cover all searchable files of a folder, including subfolders. Indexes are updated automatically by default.

Instead of a root-level index, users may elect to create several smaller indexes for each volume that they want to search. Users can create as many indexes as they want, providing corresponding folders don't overlap. That is, the folder of one index cannot contain the folder of another index. Following are some reasons that multiple indexes might be practical:

- The user has multiple hard drives, such as a C and a D drive.

- The user may want to index a Windows for Workgroups share. Because the folder for one index cannot be above or below the folder for another index, the user needs to create several indexes to cover all documents of a drive. For example, if the Windows for Workgroups folder is top-level, the user may want to create additional indexes for each other top-level folder.

- The user creates an index for a share on a NetWare® server. It would be unnecessary for the user to create an index for a Windows 95 or NT file server, as these servers should already be running an instance of the indexer, maintaining an index of server files.

How Indexes are Updated

When the Find Fast indexer creates an index, it produces a single master index that is optimized for speed and size. The Find Fast indexer updates and optimizes the master index as follows:

1. Perform a simple update to produce a sorted term list. The list contains one term for each document that is out of date. Documents are out of date if their current last-saved time stamp differs from the time stamp stored in the index.

2. Periodically merge collections of sorted term lists to produce a shadow index. A shadow index is structured the same as a master index, and is usually much smaller and faster than the collection of term lists it replaces.

3. Periodically merge together all shadow indexes and the previous master index to produce a new master index.

The interval between automatic updates is adjusted automatically by the indexer based on past updates, according to the following rules:

- Update interval initially is two hours.

- If more than 10 files are out of date on the current update, then the update interval is shortened by 15 minutes, down to a minimum of 30 minutes. Files added, deleted, or modified since the last update all count as being out of date.

- If 10 or fewer files are out of date on the current update, then the update interval is lengthened by 15 minutes up to a maximum of 24 hours.

Find Fast Indexer Log

As the Find Fast indexer updates indexes, it logs events and errors in a log file, Ffastlog.txt. Users are not alerted to errors and messages from the indexer. To see these messages, users must click Show Indexer Log on the Index menu in the Find Fast dialog box.

Events in the log file are listed so that the most recent events appear at the beginning of the file. The indexer log is truncated when its size exceeds 20K. When this happens, the log file displays a message that the log has been truncated.

CHAPTER 2

Microsoft Access Architecture

The architecture of Microsoft Access consists of the application, the database container or file, and the database objects, such as tables, queries, forms, reports, macros, and modules. The Microsoft Access application stores components such as menus and toolbars, as well as the Microsoft Jet database engine, and any add-ins written in Visual Basic for applications. The database container stores the database objects, and the database objects store the data itself, as well as OLE custom controls and procedures for extracting and reporting the data. This chapter explains the distribution of data, components, and database objects across the architecture of Microsoft Access.

In This Chapter

Application Layer

The application layer of Microsoft Access controls the user interface and provides an environment for the Jet database engine. In addition, the application layer makes calls to any *library databases,* which are collections of procedures, and *add-ins,* which are Visual Basic programs designed to accomplish specific tasks. When users are running Microsoft Access in a workgroup, their preference settings and security information are stored in a workgroup information file. This section explains the Jet database engine, library databases, add-ins, and the workgroup information file.

Microsoft Access and the Jet Database Engine

Together, Microsoft Access and the Jet database engine form a complete database management system (DBMS). Microsoft Access is the part of the DBMS that is responsible for the user interface and all the ways that users view, edit, and manipulate data through forms, queries, reports, and so forth. The Jet database engine retrieves data from, and stores data in, user and system databases. It is the data manager component of the DBMS.

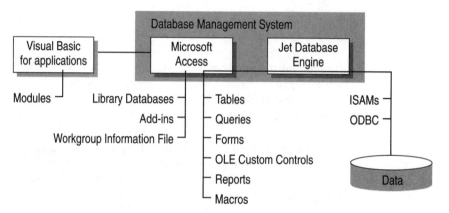

Microsoft Access

Microsoft Access is the container for the user interface and for all application code. It includes all the default settings for menus, toolbars, and database objects. It also includes all the library database files that come with Microsoft Access.

Default Settings   Users can modify the look and behavior of the Microsoft Access user interface in the Options dialog box. Some of these settings are stored in the Windows Registry, while others are stored in the user's workgroup information file, System.mdw. For information about Microsoft Access entries in the Windows Registry, see Appendix B, "Registry Keys and Values." For information about the settings that are stored in System.mdw, see "Workgroup Information File," later in this chapter.

Library Database Files   The library databases that come with Microsoft Access include all the wizards and add-ins, as well as the default System.mdw. For more information about the library databases included with Microsoft Access, see "Library Databases," later in this chapter.

Jet Database Engine

The Jet database engine is a relational database engine that handles all database processing for Microsoft Access and Visual Basic. With Microsoft Access, the Jet database engine can also provide data to Open Database Connectivity (ODBC) client applications.

The Jet database engine is made up of a set of dynamic-link libraries (DLLs):

Jet database engine DLL   The Jet database engine DLL (Msjt3032.dll) is the main program that evaluates and executes requests for data. If the request is for *native* data—data stored in the Microsoft Access Database (.mdb) format—then Msjt3032.dll also handles the reading and writing of the data. However, if the request involves non-native data, then Msjt3032.dll makes calls to either the ODBC Driver Manager DLL (Odbc32.dll) or one of the external ISAM DLLs, as explained later in this section.

Data Access Objects DLL   The Data Access Objects DLL (Dao3032.dll) is the Jet component that provides a developer interface to the Jet database engine. Data Access Objects (DAO) includes a rich, high-level set of objects that insulates developers from the physical details of reading and writing records.

External ISAM DLLs   The Jet database engine provides access to several external Indexed Sequential Access Method (ISAM) format files using a series of installable DLL files. The Jet database engine supports the external ISAM formats shown in the following table.

ISAM format	Supported by DLL
Xbase (dBase and FoxPro)	Msxb3032.dll
Paradox	Mspx3032.dll
Lotus	Mslt3032.dll
Microsoft Excel	Msxl3032.dll
Text	Mstx3032.dll

These DLLs handle the reading and writing of data stored in dBase®, FoxPro®, Paradox®, Lotus, Microsoft Excel, and text file formats.

Library Databases

A library database is a collection of procedures that Microsoft Access makes calls to for specific tasks. Library databases contain code only, and they can be functions that Microsoft Access calls as needed. They do not contain database objects such as forms or tables.

To use library databases, Microsoft Access must have a reference to them. Users make this reference by clicking References in the Tools menu. Library database files have the file extension .mda.

Add-ins

Add-ins are Visual Basic programs that add functionality to Microsoft Access. Add-in files, like library database files, have the file extension .mda. Users can add or remove add-ins from Microsoft Access by clicking Add-ins on the Tools menu and then clicking Add-in Manager.

Add-ins can automate complex or repetitive tasks in Microsoft Access. You can create or customize add-ins for your users. For information about creating add-ins in Microsoft Access, see Chapter 16 of the Microsoft Access book, *Building Applications*.

Microsoft Access has three kinds of add-ins: wizards, builders, and menu add-ins. Wizards and builders are context-specific; they are called into the application when the user wants to do something, such as build a form, create a table, or make a query. Menu add-ins must be called into the application by the Add-in Manager.

Wizards

Wizards allow users to accomplish tasks quickly and easily, without knowing much about Microsoft Access. A wizard is usually a series of dialog boxes that lead a user, step by step, through a complex procedure. The dialog box format helps to limit the user's choices and provides them a defined sequence to follow.

You can create wizards for your own users. Microsoft Access provides direct support for some types of wizards. For example, if you create a wizard to design a specific type of form, your wizard can be installed to appear in the same list as the Microsoft Access Form Wizard. Microsoft Access supports the following kinds of wizards:

- Table and query wizards
- Form and report wizards
- Property wizards
- Control wizards

Builders

Builders are simpler tools than wizards. Builders usually consist of a single dialog box or form that guides the user through the process of constructing an expression or other single data element. The Microsoft Access Expression Builder is an example of this type of add-in.

Microsoft Access supports many kinds of builders automatically. If you create one of the following kinds of builders, it will appear on the list of Microsoft Access builders:

- Property builders
- Control builders
- Expression builders

Menu Add-ins

Menu add-ins are general-purpose mini-applications that accomplish tasks that are not context-sensitive in the way that wizards and builders are. A menu add-in usually operates on multiple objects or on the Microsoft Access application itself. The Microsoft Access Documentor is an example of a menu add-in.

Menu add-ins are supported by the Add-in command on the Tools menu.

Workgroup Information File

In Microsoft Access installations where user and group level security is being used, the user and group information is stored in the workgroup information file, System.mdw. For all Microsoft Access users, this file also stores user-specific preferences such as custom toolbars and other options. The System.mdw file is required for Microsoft Access to start up.

For users to share data, they join a workgroup by using the Workgroup Administrator, Wrkgadm.exe, to specify the System.mdw file on the network share where they want to run Microsoft Access. If a password has been defined, users are required to log on to this account. The shared System.mdw stores passwords for each user.

The System.mdw a user specifies is the file that Microsoft Access uses every time it starts up, until the user specifies some other System.mdw. If a user does not belong to a workgroup and therefore specifies no System.mdw, Microsoft Access uses the System.mdw on the local workstation, with default security settings. The System.mdw that Microsoft Access uses for any given desktop is specified in the Registry setting Hkey_Local_Machine\Software\Microsoft\Access\7.0\Jet\3.0\Engines\Jet, as the string value for SystemDB.

Once users have joined a workgroup and established their settings, they should back up their System.mdw. If the file somehow gets corrupted, the user must re-create it. Users must have a System.mdw to run Microsoft Access.

Database Layer

Data is generally stored in tables in the database, but links can be established to tables in other databases, to data in other file formats (such as Microsoft Excel, dBase, and Paradox), and to ODBC data sources, such as SQL Server. These links are stored in the database container and act like native tables.

Installable ISAMs

Data that is stored separately from the main database is accessed through *lookup tables*, which are Index Sequential Access Method (ISAM) files. Databases created in formats other than Microsoft Access—such as FoxPro, dBase, and Paradox—use ISAMs that are non-native to Microsoft Access. To enable Microsoft Access to work with databases created in these other formats Microsoft Access ships with *installable ISAMs* (IISAMs). Using IISAMs, Microsoft Access treats non-native ISAM data very similarly to how it treats native tables.

IISAMs in Microsoft Access support the following ISAM file formats:

- Microsoft FoxPro, versions 2.0, 2.5, 2.6, and import/export (no linking) for version 3.0
- dBase III PLUS, dBase IV, and dBase V
- Paradox, versions 3.*x,* 4.*x,* and 5.0
- Microsoft Excel, versions 3.0 and 7.0
- Lotus, versions 2.*x,* 3.*x,* and 4.0
- Text files (fixed-width and delimited text files)

Microsoft Access supports two methods of access to external ISAMs: linked tables and direct table opening.

Linked Tables

Linking to tables is the preferred method for accessing external data. Linking to a table from a non-native database attaches the non-native database to the user's current Microsoft Access database. Any changes to the table are reflected in the linked database. Using linked tables, Microsoft Access stores connection information by adding an icon in the database window, so users can readily access the external table again.

The linked table method of accessing external data is preferred, because the data is live and up to date, and because the link works whether the data is coming from a table or query. For example, if the table is moved to a SQL server, the application can still access the data by linking to the table.

Direct Table Opening

The Microsoft Access user interface does not allow users to open an external table directly. Microsoft Access opens external tables directly only through Visual Basic. A developer might use this method to get a value quickly from a table that does not need to be accessed very often in the application.

The disadvantage to using this method for accessing external data is that it ties the application to the data source. For example, if the table is moved to a SQL server, the data is no longer ISAM data, and the application will fail when attempting to read tables directly. For more information, see "Separating the Application from the Data," later in this section.

ODBC Connectivity

Microsoft Access allows users to retrieve data from Open Database Connectivity (ODBC) data sources. The ODBC connectivity standard is typically used to connect to server-based database systems. Microsoft Access includes ODBC drivers for Microsoft SQL Server.

The ODBC standard can also be used to connect to non-server databases and spreadsheets.

As with IISAM data, Microsoft Access can connect to ODBC data sources by linking or opening tables. Microsoft Access also supports SQL Pass-through (SPT) queries for retrieving ODBC data. By using pass-through queries, users work directly with the tables on the server, rather than with linked tables. SPT queries also allow users to run procedures that are stored on the server. The disadvantage of applications that use SPT queries is that they are not portable. For example, an application written for a SQL server will fail if it attempts to access an Oracle server. Users create SPT queries by clicking SQL Specific on the Query menu and then clicking Pass-Through.

Separating the Application from the Data

Microsoft Access applications can be designed to be separate from the data they store. For an example of this type of architecture, see the Northwind Order Entry Application (Orders.mdb) that Setup installs with Microsoft Access. The forms, queries, reports, and other application features are self-contained within Orders.mdb. The database tables, however, are stored in the Northwind database (Nwind.mdb).

This is the preferred method of developing applications in Microsoft Access. Keeping application and database code separate makes both the application and the data easier to maintain. By keeping them separate, you can upgrade a database to future versions of Microsoft Access independently of the custom application. Keeping the application separate from the database also makes it easier for users with different versions of Microsoft Access to use the same data.

Database Objects

Database objects are stored in the database container, which is a file with the extension .mdb. Users can design new objects or open existing ones to work with their database. Database objects are tables, queries, forms, reports, macros, and modules. Each of these is described below.

Tables Tables are containers for storing data that is related in some particular way. Users can define separate tables for each subject on which they wish to keep data, such as employees, invoices, or inventory. Users can enter and modify data in tables directly or through data entry forms, which are described below.

Queries Users retrieve data from the database with queries. Queries are processed by the Jet database engine. The simplest form of queries are *select queries,* where users identify data by category, range, and boolean operators. Microsoft Access displays the results of select queries in *dynasets*, which are tables that are connected to the live data. They may appear to a user to be static tables, but they are actually a dynamic view of the data. When users open a query in Datasheet view, or open a form or print a report that is based on a query, Microsoft Access creates a dynaset using the information currently stored in the database. This allows users to enter and modify data. The changes they make effect the underlying tables in the database itself.

Forms Forms give users a way of entering data into databases, displaying data to the screen, and printing it. Forms can contain text, graphics, data, color, and OLE custom controls. The appearance of a form is controlled by a form template. For more information, see "Form and Report Templates," later in this chapter.

OLE custom controls OLE custom controls (OCXs) are similar to Visual Basic custom controls (VBXs). They are used to add custom functionality to forms and are stored in forms. Microsoft Access 7.0 includes three OLE custom controls: calendar control, spin box, and outline. Additional controls are available from third parties.

Reports Reports present information from a Microsoft Access database so that it is formatted and organized according to the user's specifications. This formatting and organization is controlled by a report template. For more information, see "Form and Report Templates," later in this chapter.

Macros Macros are actions or a set of actions that have been stored to automate tasks. They are associated with the event property of a form, report, section, or control.

Modules   A module is a collection of Visual Basic declarations, statements, and procedures. Users can store related procedures in a single module. Databases can include multiple modules, including global, form, and report modules:

- Global modules can be used throughout the database. Microsoft Access loads them when a user opens a database.

- Form modules are associated with a specific form. Microsoft Access loads them when a user opens the form.

- Report modules are associated with a specific report. Microsoft Access loads them when a user opens the report.

Form and Report Templates

When users create a form or report without using a wizard, Microsoft Access uses a template to define the default characteristics of the form or report. The template determines which sections a form or report will have and defines each section's dimensions. The template also contains all the default property settings for the form.

The default templates for forms and reports are called Normal. However, users can use any existing form or report as a template. Users specify which template they want to use in the Options dialog box. This setting is stored in the workgroup information file, System.mdw, and applies to all databases the user opens or creates. Users can copy or export templates to use them in other databases. Additionally, you can create corporate templates to distribute to your users.

Form and report templates define:

- Whether to include a form or report header and footer.

- Whether to include a page header and footer.

- What the dimensions (height and width) of the sections will be.

- Which control default properties to use. However, templates do not create controls on new forms or reports.

Where Microsoft Access Components Reside

Microsoft Access components are stored with the application or an add-in, on disk, or in the Windows Registry. The following table lists components and where they reside.

Component	Stored
Tables	On disk in the database file (*.mdb)
Queries	On disk in the database file (*.mdb)
Forms	On disk in the database file (*.mdb)
Reports	On disk in the database file (*.mdb)
Macros	On disk in the database file (*.mdb)
Modules	On disk in the database file (*.mdb)
OLE custom controls	In the form or report in which it was created
User passwords	On disk in System.mdw
Permissions for security accounts	On disk in the database file (*.mdb)
Custom toolbar settings	On disk in System.mdw
Custom menu settings	On disk in System.mdw
User preferences, set with Options command on Tools menu[1]	In the Windows Registry
AutoCorrect settings	In the Windows Registry
Custom dictionary	On disk in Custom.dic
AutoFormat styles	In the AutoFormat Wizard
Expression Builder	On disk in Utility.mda
AutoDialer	On disk in Utility.mda
Normal template for forms and reports	On disk in Utility.mda
Zoom Box	On disk in Utility.mda
Save Output As	On disk in Utility.mda

[1] In multi-user environments, the workgroup file (System.mdw) also stores user preferences.

Where Security Settings Are Stored

Security settings are stored differently, depending on how a user is securing the database. Microsoft Access provides two methods of securing a database: setting a password for opening the database, or employing user-level security, which provides flexibility for allowing different users different levels of permission for the various objects in a database.

Password Security With password security, users specify a password from the Security command on the Tools menu. This password is stored with the database, in the .mdb file.

User-level Security With user-level security, System.mdw stores user accounts, the passwords used to verify user's identities, and the groups to which users belong. If users leave a group, they can be removed from the group and no longer have permissions.

The actual permissions for the database objects are stored in the database file. These permissions are associated with each object within the database as defined by the security administrator. Permissions can be assigned to individual users and groups.

For more information about security settings, see Security in on-line help, or see "Security Administration" in the Microsoft Access section of Chapter 15, "Using Workgroup Features and Applications with Office."

How Microsoft Access Resolves Conflicts

Conflicts can arise in Microsoft Access when a database is being replicated, or when more than one user attempts to edit the same record of a database, causing a locking conflict.

Replication Conflicts

During replication setup—for example, when a user drags a database into the Windows 95 Briefcase—the Jet database engine requests Globally Unique IDs (GUIDs) from the operating system that are associated with each row of data in the design master. These GUIDs are then copied into any replica databases. If a row changes in the design master or a replica, a counter is incremented for the row. This makes it easy for Microsoft Access to compare the values of rows, detect that a change has been made, and replicate the changed data to other databases. If the same row is changed in more than one database simultaneously, Microsoft Access selects between them based on the following rules:

- Microsoft Access chooses the database that has the highest value for its counter. That is, the row that has changed most often has a higher counter, because the counter is incremented every time a row is changed.

- If both rows have been changed the same number of times (counters are the same on both rows in both databases), Microsoft Access chooses a database randomly, as the replication logic cannot reasonably know which of the two rows has the correct data.

Regardless of how the data is selected, users who submit the data that is not chosen are told by a Conflict Wizard in Microsoft Access that their data was rejected. Users can then resubmit their change or accept the other data.

Locking Conflicts

If record locking is set to No Locks, there may be locking conflicts when more than one user attempts to edit or save the same record. Users can set record locking by clicking Options in the Tools menu and selecting the Advanced tab.

The No Locks setting allows more than one user to edit a record simultaneously, but the record is locked during the instant when it is being saved. If two users attempt to save changes to the same record, Microsoft Access displays a message to the second user who tries to save the record. This user can then discard the record, copy the record to the Clipboard, or replace the changes made by the other user. Using this option, it is possible for users to write over one another's changes.

For more information about record locking, see "Multiuser Settings" in the Microsoft Access section of Chapter 15, "Using Workgroup Features and Applications with Office."

C H A P T E R   3

Microsoft Excel Architecture

This chapter describes the architecture of Microsoft Excel in terms of its two primary elements: the application and the workbook. A section of the chapter lists Microsoft Excel components and where they are stored within Microsoft Excel, another section describes the architecture of the Microsoft Excel mapping feature, and the chapter concludes with an explanation of how Microsoft Excel resolves conflicting settings.

In This Chapter

Overall Structure

The architecture of Microsoft Excel consists of the Microsoft Excel application and the workbook file. The Microsoft Excel application controls the standard menus, toolbars, and default settings for how workbook files are created, opened, and stored. The workbook file is a collection of sheets: worksheets, chart sheets, and macro sheets. The workbook file also stores workbook-level components, such as passwords, styles, and scenarios. To standardize workbooks and the Microsoft Excel application across your organization, you can save workbooks in formats other than a workbook file. You can save workbooks as templates and as add-ins.

Microsoft Excel Application

Microsoft Excel default settings and paths that are established at setup. These features can be customized after installation for a single user, a workgroup, or across an entire organization.

There are several ways to customize the Microsoft Excel application:

- **Through the user interface, in the Options dialog box** Users can customize Microsoft Excel on their desktop, by clicking Options on the Tools menu. The settings they make here are stored in their Windows Registry.

- **In the Windows Registry** For information on Registry settings for Microsoft Excel, see Appendix B, "Registry Keys and Values."

- **With an Add-In** Another way of customizing Microsoft Excel is to create add-ins. An add-in is a hidden, read-only workbook in which the Visual Basic code has been fully compiled from a source workbook. For a particular workgroup's specific tasks, you could create an add-in that runs as a standalone, customized version of Microsoft Excel. Or, you can create add-ins that provide supplemental functionality to your users' version of Microsoft Excel as installed on their system. For information about creating, maintaining, and distributing add-ins, see Chapter 12 of the *Microsoft Excel/Visual Basic for Windows 95 Programmer's Guide.*

In addition to these methods of customizing Microsoft Excel, you can also customize specific features for your users. Some of these customizations are stored in a separate file on the user's system, as explained in the following list of features:

- **Toolbar Settings and Custom AutoFill Lists** When users modify their toolbar settings, Microsoft Excel stores these settings in the file *Username*.xlb in the user's Windows folder, where *Username* is the Windows 95 logon name of the current user. When users create their own AutoFill lists for filling in a range of cells with a series of data, these lists are also stored in *Username*.xlb.

  You can distribute a common set of custom lists for AutoFill and sorting, or provide custom toolbars for particular tasks at your site. To do so, create the custom lists and custom toolbars in a workbook. Save the workbook, and place the resulting .xlb file on a network share, where users can merge the customizations into their own workbooks by opening the .xlb file with the Open command on the File menu.

Note When custom toolbars are attached to a module in a workbook, they are not stored in the user's \Windows*Username*.xlb file. Instead, they are stored with the workbook that contains the module.

- **Startup and Alternate Startup Folders**   When Microsoft Excel starts, it opens all workbooks, charts, and workspace files stored in the user's Xlstart folder. When a user clicks New on the File menu, the workbook templates listed are those stored in Xlstart. If you want your users to open a workbook automatically when they start Microsoft Excel, move or copy the workbook to this folder. This strategy is especially useful if a workgroup is running Microsoft Excel from a network share, and all users are sharing the same Xlstart folder.

  If users want to start Microsoft Excel with workbooks and templates stored somewhere other than Xlstart (such as a network share), they can specify an alternate startup folder. Users specify an alternate startup folder on the General tab in the Options dialog box. This setting is stored in the Windows Registry.

  You might want to create an alternate startup folder for your users if they have Microsoft Excel installed on individual workstations, each with individual Xlstart folders. By specifying a single alternate startup folder on a network share, you would have a single folder to maintain for any workbooks, charts, or workspace files you want your users to open when they start Microsoft Excel.

- **Default Startup Workbook and Autotemplates**   If users do not specify a startup workbook, Microsoft Excel displays a new, unsaved workbook when they start Microsoft Excel. This startup workbook is derived from the *autotemplate*, a template that opens automatically because it has the reserved filename Book.xlt, and it is stored in the user's Xlstart or alternate startup folder.

  You can specify the default font, formatting, and other options for new workbooks for your users by creating a custom autotemplate. For example, you can create a workbook autotemplate that includes customized headers and footers and your company name or any text, formatting, formulas, and macros that your users want as defaults when creating new workbooks.

  To create a workbook autotemplate, create or open the workbook you want to use as the autotemplate. Click Save As on the File menu, and save the workbook in the template file format, with the name Book.xlt. Distribute this file to your users' Xlstart or alternate startup folder.

  When users click the New button on the Standard toolbar, Microsoft Excel creates a new workbook, based on the autotemplate. The autotemplate also shows up as the Workbook icon on the General tab in the New dialog box when users click New on the File menu or when they click the Start a New Document button on the Microsoft Office Shortcut Bar.

- **Workspace File**   If you want your users to be able to open a group of workbooks in one step, you can create a workspace file for them. A *workspace file* contains information about which workbooks to open, their locations, and their size and position on the screen. The workspace file does not contain the workbooks themselves.

To create a workspace file for your users, open all the workbooks you want to include in the workspace. Size and position them as you want them to appear when the users open the file. Then, click Save Workspace on the File menu. The default name Microsoft Excel gives to the workspace file is Resume.xlw. You may rename the file if you want.

Distribute this file to your users. If you want the workspace file to open automatically each time users start Microsoft Excel, copy the file to the users' Xlstart or alternate startup folder.

Note The workbook names and folder locations are saved with the workspace file. If the files are moved to another location, Microsoft Excel will not be able to find them.

Workbooks

The workbook in Microsoft Excel is analogous to the document in Word, or the presentation in PowerPoint. The workbook is where the data is stored, in the Microsoft Excel file format. Microsoft Excel workbook files have the extension .xls.

Microsoft Excel stores workbook files in the binary interchange file format (BIFF). Workbooks are *compound files*: files that contain a hierarchical system of storages and streams. A *storage* is analogous to a folder, and a *stream* is analogous to a file in a folder. This file format is the OLE implementation of the Structured Storage Model standard.

Fore more information about the Structured Storage Model, see the *OLE 2 Programmer's Reference, Volume One,* and *Inside OLE.* For detailed information about the BIFF file format, see the *Microsoft Excel Developer's Kit.* All of these books are published by Microsoft Press and are available at your local bookstore.

Templates

A *template* is a special workbook used as a pattern to create other workbooks of the same type. Rather than an .xls file extension, templates have the file extension .xlt.

You can create templates for workgroups to maintain consistency. For example, you can create a sales report workbook, save it as a template, and distribute it to a workgroup. Users in the workgroup then create weekly sales reports based on the template or insert sheets from template into their workbook.

Settings saved in a template determine the following characteristics of new workbooks based on that template:

- The number and type of sheets in a workbook
- Page formats
- Cell formats
- Row and column styles
- Text, dates, numbers, formulas, and graphics, such as a company name and logo
- Custom menu commands, macros, and toolbars attached to a module sheet in the template

When users open a template, Microsoft Excel opens an untitled, unsaved copy of the template that contains all data, formatting, formulas, macros, styles, scenarios, and so forth that is contained in the template. The original template file remains unchanged.

To create a template, first create the workbook that includes any text, formats, and formulas your users want, and then click Save As on the File menu. Enter a filename and select the folder, such as a network share, to store the template. In the Save As Type box, select Template. Storing workbook templates in a user's Xlstart or alternate startup folder automatically makes the template available when the user clicks New on the File menu.

Note   Although templates in a user's startup folder are automatically available for creating new workbooks, only the template with the reserved name Book.xlt stored in the startup folder is an autotemplate. When users start Microsoft Excel, click the New button on the Standard toolbar, or click the Start a New Document button on the Microsoft Office Shortcut Bar, the new workbook is based on the autotemplate.

Add-Ins

In addition to saving workbooks as .xls and .xlt files, users can also save workbooks as add-ins. Add-Ins compiled from Microsoft Excel workbooks have the file extension .xla.

You can create custom add-ins to assemble and distribute custom features that, from the user's point of view, act as if they are built into Microsoft Excel itself. For information about creating, maintaining, and distributing add-ins, see Chapter 12 of the *Microsoft Excel/Visual Basic for Windows 95 Programmer's Guide*, published by Microsoft Press and available from your local bookstore.

Note Add-Ins can also be written in C. When compiled, these add-ins have the file extension .xll (similar to .wll files in Word).

Add-Ins Included with Microsoft Excel

Several add-ins are included with Microsoft Excel, although whether or not they are installed on a user's system depends on what kind of installation was chosen during setup, and on which add-ins were selected during a Custom installation. For information about the components installed for each type of installation, see Appendix C, "List of Installed Components."

Users can install additional add-ins by clicking Add-Ins on the Tools menu.

The following table describes the add-ins included with Microsoft Excel. Their default installation folder is \Excel\Library and its subfolders. Some add-ins require a dynamic link library or compiled C add-in in addition to the .xla file, as indicated in the table.

Add-In	Filename	Description
Analysis ToolPak	Funcres.xla, Procdb.xla, Analys32.xll	Adds financial and engineering functions, and provides tools for performing statistical and engineering analysis.
Analysis ToolPak - VBA	Atpvbaen.xla	Adds Visual Basic functions for Analysis ToolPak.
Microsoft Query[1]	Xlquery.xla	Retrieves data from external database files and tables using Microsoft Query.
ODBC	Xlodbc.xla, Xlodbc32.dll	Adds worksheet and macro functions for retrieving data from external sources with Microsoft Open Database Connectivity (ODBC).
Report Manager	Reports.xla	Prints reports that consist of views and scenarios.
Solver	Solver.xla	Calculates solutions to what-if scenarios based on adjustable cells, constraint cells, and optionally, cells that must be maximized or minimized.
Template Utilities	Tmpltnum.xla	Adds utilities used by Microsoft Excel templates.
Template Wizard with Data Tracking	Wztemplt.xla	Creates a template to export worksheet data to a database.
Update Links	Updtlink.xla	Updates links to Microsoft Excel 4.0 add-ins to directly access the new built-in functionality.

Add-In	Filename	Description
View Manager	Views.xla	Saves the current window display as a view and lets users apply their own saved views to see their worksheet in different formats.
AutoSave	Autosave.xla	Saves workbook files automatically.

[1] To use Microsoft Query with Microsoft Excel, users must install the Microsoft Query application, the Microsoft Query add-in, the drivers for the types of data they want to retrieve, and the necessary ODBC files. Users can install these files by clicking Add/Remove Office Programs and selecting the Data Access option. For information about Data Access components, see Appendix C, "List of Installed Components."

Where Components Are Stored

Workbook components are stored on sheets of the workbook. These components include all the contents of all data cells (constant values and formulas), cell formatting, charts, macros, add-ins, and security settings. Security settings can be stored for an entire workbook, as well as for individual sheets.

This section lists the various components of a workbook and explains how each is stored within the workbook.

Constant Values of Cells

Constant values stored in cells can be numeric values, including date, time, currency, percentage, or scientific notation, or it can be text. The way Microsoft Excel displays numbers in a cell depends upon the number format for the cell. This value may differ from the actual value Microsoft Excel stores, which is with 15 digits of accuracy. By default, Microsoft Excel makes calculations based on the stored value (full precision), but users can have Microsoft Excel calculate based on displayed values by selecting Precision As Displayed on the Calculations Tab in the Options dialog box.

If users are getting results from their formulas that appear to be wrong, it may be due to the difference in precision between displayed and stored values. For example, if two cells each contain the value 1.007, and a formula adds them in a third cell, the result is 2.014. If all three cells are formatted to display only two decimal places, the displayed calculation, 1.01+1.01=2.01, appears to be wrong. Similarly, calculating on displayed values, 1.01+1.01=2.02 appears to be correct, but this results in a value that is not as precise as it would be by calculating on stored values.

Caution   Once users switch to calculating on displayed values, Microsoft Excel stores all constant values as their displayed values, and full precision values cannot be restored.

Calculating with precision as displayed:

- Affects all worksheets in the active workbook.

- Does not affect numbers in the General format, which are always calculated with full precision.

- Slows calculation because Microsoft Excel must round the numbers as it calculates.

Formulas

Formulas are a sequence of values, cell references, names, functions or operators that produce a new value from existing values. They are part of the data that is stored with the workbook file. Cell references in a function can be relative, absolute, or mixed references in the A1 style, or row-and-column (R1C1) style; or they can be name references.

Users who use the A1, or R1C1, reference style may experience difficulty with formulas if they reposition or delete cells, as these references refer to data by position. A way to avoid this problem is to reference cells by name.

Name References

Users can use names as references to a cell, a group of cells, a value, or a formula. Name references can be accessible to an entire workbook or restricted to a sheet. When restricted to a sheet, the same name, such as "Profit" can be used to define related cells on different sheets in the same workbook. Book-level names, on the other hand, can refer to cells on one worksheet and be used throughout the workbook, eliminating the need to re-create names for each new worksheet or to type worksheet references in formulas.

When users create book-level names, they simply type the name they are defining in the Name box on the formula bar. When they create sheet-level names, however, they must include the name of the sheet, such as "Sheet1!Profit" in the Name box.

Sheet-level names override book-level names when used on the sheet where they are defined. For example, in a workbook where Profit is defined both as a book-level name and a sheet-level name for Sheet1, if a user enters a formula that uses the name Profit on Sheet1, the formula uses the sheet-level name rather than the book level name.

Scenarios

Scenarios are the Microsoft Excel method of allowing users to pose what-if models in their data. To create a what-if model, users specify a set of *changing cells*, or cells that store hypothetical data under a name. This name is stored with the workbook file.

Scenarios can be sheet-level or book-level. Users can merge scenarios among different sheets in the same workbook and among multiple workbooks. To merge scenarios among workbooks, all the workbooks must be open.

When a user merges scenarios, there may be some duplicate names. "Best Case" and "Worst Case" are common examples. In such instances, Microsoft Excel appends additional information to the duplicate scenario names, such as creation date, creator name, or an ordinal number.

Users can protect scenarios by selecting the Prevent Changes and Hide options in the Add Scenario dialog box. For the protection option to take effect, however, the user must also activate protection for the sheet.

Cell Formatting Styles

Cell formatting is stored separately from the cell data, as a collection of format settings that are saved together as a style. Styles can be copied between cells, changed, or deleted, without affecting the data in the cell.

The following table shows the individual format settings determined by styles.

Setting	Determines
Number	Decimal places, separator, inclusion of dollar sign, style for displaying negative number and other options for formatting different kinds of numbers, such as currency, dates, fractions, and so on.
Alignment	Horizontal, vertical, text orientation, and whether or not text wraps in the cell.
Font	Typeface, style, size, special effects, and color of the text in the cell.
Border	Placement and style of the border of the cell.
Pattern	Shading and color of the cell.
Protection	Whether data in the cell is locked or the formula is hidden. This option does not take effect until the worksheet is protected, which the user can do by clicking Protection on the Tools menu.

Styles are saved with the workbook. Users can copy styles from one workbook to another by clicking Merge in the Style dialog box and then selecting the workbook they want to merge styles from. Both the source and destination workbooks must be open. All styles from the source workbook are merged into the destination workbook. If styles in the destination document have names that match styles being merged, the user is prompted to choose whether or not to overwrite existing styles in the destination workbook.

All cells in all of the sheets of a new workbook are initially formatted with the Normal style. Users can change and store the settings for the Normal style, but the change does not affect any other workbooks unless they merge the new Normal style into another workbook or save the workbook with the new Normal style to a template. If the Normal style has been modified in a user's autotemplate, the default formatting for cells in all new workbooks is the modified Normal style.

Note The default font that the Normal style uses is specified by the Standard Font setting on the General tab in the Options dialog box. This setting is stored in the Registry key Hkey_Current_User\Software\Microsoft\Excel\7.0\Microsoft Excel, as the string value for Font.

Charts

Users create charts based on a range of selected cells on a worksheet. Depending upon which option the user specifies, a chart is stored either on the same worksheet as the cells it is linked to, or it exists as an entire sheet within the workbook. Charts are linked dynamically to data on a worksheet. This means that changes to the data are updated in the chart, and changes to a data marker on the chart are reflected in the linked data cells.

Data markers are the chart symbols (dot, bar, area, slice, and so on) that represent a single data point or value originating from a worksheet cell. Users can modify data markers on the following types of charts only: bar, column, line, stacked, pie, doughnut, and xy (scatter) charts. Data markers on 3-D charts cannot be modified.

Text on the chart is also linked to text in worksheet cells. This text appears as data labels, legend entries, and labels for axis tick-marks. Editing text in the worksheet cells affects text in the charts that are linked to the cells. Users can also edit text in charts, but this breaks the link to the cells on the worksheet.

Microsoft Excel stores charts in the workbook file. Charts sheets can be copied into other workbooks, and charts can be copied and pasted into other workbooks and into other Office applications, such as Word documents and PowerPoint presentations.

AutoFormats for Charts

Instead of formatting chart items individually, users can quickly change the look of a chart using AutoFormat. Microsoft Excel stores AutoFormats as charts on separate chart sheets in a workbook with the reserved filename Xl5galry.xls.

AutoFormats, like cell styles, are a collection of characteristics. Each AutoFormat is based on one of the 14 predefined chart types, and can include a chart subtype, legend, gridline options, data labels, color settings, patterns, and layout. Microsoft Excel includes built-in AutoFormats and also allows users to create custom AutoFormats by selecting User-Defined and clicking Customize in the AutoFormat dialog box.

To create a unified look, you can build a library of custom AutoFormats for workgroups at your site. For example, you can create a series of AutoFormats with a consistent layout and color scheme, designed to be integrated into a PowerPoint presentation. To do this, you create custom AutoFormats in a workbook, and then save the workbook. When you save this file, your custom AutoFormats are stored in Xl5galry.xls.

To make the custom AutoFormats available to your users, do one of the following:

- Copy Xl5galry.xls to each user's Xlstart folder.
- Rename Xl5galry.xls and copy the file to the alternate startup folder defined for each user.

Macros

Macros store Visual Basic code in workbooks, allowing users to automate repetitive or complex tasks. You can create macros for your users, and distribute them in the following ways:

- **As macro sheets** When stored within workbooks, Visual Basic modules are stored on sheets called macro sheets. Users can copy these sheets into their own workbooks.
- **As workbooks** You can create a workbook of custom macros, where each Visual Basic module is its own macro sheet. To make the macro sheets available to users at startup, store the workbook in the users' Xlstart or alternate startup folder. To make the macro sheets automatically available to users at startup, name the file Xl5galry.xls and store it in the users' Xlstart folder.
- **As Add-Ins** You can distribute the macros as a standalone, customized version of Microsoft Excel by saving a workbook as an add-in. To automatically open the add-in for users, copy the file to the users' Xlstart or alternate startup folder.

Security

You and your users can secure specific sheets or entire workbooks, according to how you set Protection options in the Protect Sheet or Protect Workbook dialog boxes. Security settings are stored with the workbook file. The only way to change them is to open the workbook file, modify the protection options, then save the file.

You can also assign passwords at the sheet level or workbook level. Passwords enable users to bypass sheet or workbook protections.

At the sheet level, the following items can be protected:

- **Sheet contents** Protects cells on worksheets or on Microsoft Excel 4.0 macro sheets, as well as items in charts.
- **Sheet objects** Protects graphic objects on worksheets and charts from being moved, edited, resized, or deleted.
- **Scenarios** Prevents changes to the definitions of scenarios on a worksheet.

At the workbook level, the following items can be protected:

- **Structure** Protects the structure of a workbook so sheets can't be deleted, moved, hidden, unhidden, or renamed, and new sheets can't be inserted.
- **Windows** Protects windows from being moved, resized, hidden, unhidden, or closed.

Microsoft Excel Data Map

The Microsoft Excel Data Map supplies six map formats for analyzing geographical data: Value Shading, Category Shading, Dot Density, Graduated Symbols, Pie Charts, and Column Charts. These formats and their uses are described in the Data Map Help (available only when the Data Map server is active). The map formats allow users to spot geographical patterns in their data, and to correlate one data item, such as sales in a city, to another, such as a city's population.

Data Map and OLE

Data Map consists of an OLE mini-server (meaning that it can only be invoked from within an OLE application) and a set of maps for use with the Data Map server. Users can insert a Data Map object in any OLE application. In OLE container applications, such as the Office applications, users can edit the object in place using OLE visual editing. Users can also move or copy Data Map objects between OLE applications using OLE drag and drop.

Regardless of the location of a Data Map object, data for the map must come from either a Microsoft Excel worksheet or a Microsoft Access database. A user can create a map in Microsoft Excel and then drag it to a Word document or PowerPoint presentation, but doing so breaks the link to the data. To update the map in Word or PowerPoint, the user must replace it with an updated copy of the map. Creating a map in Microsoft Excel and embedding the Microsoft Excel file in an Office Binder can also break the link to the data.

Data Map Terminology

Term	Refers to	Example
Map Template	A collection of features, such as political boundaries, cities, airports, and highways. Some map templates contain a feature that consists of points for single data items, such as postal codes. These single-point feature sets are also called *centroid maps*.	US States map template consists of the following features: • U. S. state political boundaries • U. S. major cities • U. S. minor cities • U. S. airports • U. S. interstate highways • Centroid map for five-digit ZIP Codes
Features	A set of political boundaries or physical entities, such as cities, which are in a template.	U. S. state political boundaries.
Data Set	Cell data that is mapped to a map template.	Sales by major U. S. cities in the US States map template.
Geographic data	Cell data that corresponds to names of boundaries and other features, such as cities, in a map template.	The cell data "AL" and "AK" corresponds to the boundary names "Alabama" and "Alaska," respectively, in the US States map template.

The GeoDictionary

All Data Map map files are installed in the \Program Files\Common Files\Microsoft Shared\Datamap\Data folder. Data Map keeps a data dictionary of all installed maps in the file Geodict.dct. The location of the geodictionary is set and maintained in the Registry in the key Hkey_local_machine\Software\Microsoft\ DataMap\Directories, as the text value for MapData.

For Microsoft Excel to have access to a map, the map must be registered in the geodictionary. Therefore, if a user removes a map file from the disk, the geodictionary will still refer to the file, and the user will get error messages when Microsoft Excel attempts to access the file. Similarly, users cannot add new maps simply by adding map files to their disk. Copying map files to the disk does not register the files in the geodictionary.

To add or remove map files, users must use the Data Installer (Datainst.exe), a utility installed with Data Map, usually in the \Program Files\Common Files\Microsoft Shared\Datamap folder. The Data Installer provides an easy, graphical way to add and remove map files to and from the geodictionary. The geodictionary cannot be edited directly by a user, and must be edited using the Data Installer.

Note Removing a map from the geodictionary does not delete the files from the user's disk; you must delete the files manually.

About the Map Files

Data Map map files use the same format as MapInfo® 3.0 files. Each map consists of four to five files. For example, the World Map consists of the following files:

File	Description
World.dat	Binary file. Stores names for all boundaries or points in the map.
World.id	Binary file. Stores information about relationships with other maps.
World.ind	Binary file. Index used for speeding access to the .map file. Only used in large maps.
World.map	Binary file. Stores latitude and longitude for all points which make up all boundaries in the map.
World.tab	Map descriptor file, used for storing version information, a friendly name for the map, and description of the map feature structure.

How Data Map Works

There are three ways to create a Data Map object in Microsoft Excel:

- With a source data range selected
- Without a range selected, on a blank sheet
- By copying an existing Data Map object

When the Data Map object is created, Microsoft Excel checks for a source data range, which is the user's selection. If Microsoft Excel does not find a source data range, it creates a blank Data Map object. If Microsoft Excel finds a source data range, it sends the range to Data Map. Data Map takes a sample from each column of the source data range and attempts to match the sample against all installed map templates.

Each primary map in a template contains a set of labels in the .dat file. These labels correspond to a set of boundaries (such as "Washington," "Colorado," and so on). In order for the user's data to be displayed on a map, Data Map must be able to match geographic data in the user's selection to labels stored in the .dat file.

Data Map attempts to match over 80 percent of the geographic data against an installed map. If this level is attained, Data Map opens the matched map and begins to plot the data.

In some cases, Data Map can match more than one map. For example, "Germany" matches both the World by Country and the Europe by Country maps. In such cases, users are prompted to choose which of the matched maps they wish to use.

If no maps are matched, Data Map disregards the data and prompts the user to choose a map to display.

If the matching process takes more than five seconds, Data Map aborts auto-matching and prompts the user for a map to use.

Once a map is matched, Data Map displays the map and binds the user's data to it. It is possible that Data Map will not recognize some geographic data, either because the data is misspelled or because the user used an unfamiliar variation of a region's name, such as "Mainland China" instead of "People's Republic of China." Data Map displays all unknown labels one by one to help users find an acceptable alternative. The file Mapstats.xls, stored in the \Program Files\Common Files\Microsoft Shared\Datamap\Data folder, contains lists of proper labels for all installed maps, as well as demographic data to compare with your own data.

By default, Data Map plots values in the first column to the right of the geographic data as a Value Shaded format on the map. If Data Map finds multiple records that pertain to the same region, the values are aggregated. These values are usually added, but it is also possible to count and average them.

Data Map can map data on only one template and one map at a time. If a user's selection has labels for regions in more than one map, Data Map matches the greatest amount of geographic data to one map, and reads geographic data that does not match that map as a mismatch. For example, suppose a user's selection includes several U. S. states and the country Japan. Data Map matches the geographic data to the US by State map, but comes up with a mismatch for the label Japan.

Once users have created a Data Map based on a template, they can import data to other maps in the template. For example, suppose the active template is North America. This template contains three maps: US States, Canadian Provinces, and States in Mexico. The user can select geographical data for one of these maps (US States, for example) to create the North America Data Map object, but then the user must import data separately for the Canadian Provinces map and for the States in Mexico map. Data Map cannot map the user's original selection with data for multiple maps; it must map them one at a time.

How Microsoft Excel Resolves Conflicts

Conflicts can arise in Microsoft Excel when files of the same name reside in a user's startup and alternate startup folders, or when the user interface has been customized through macros or Visual Basic code.

Startup and Alternate Startup Folders

Microsoft Excel opens files in a user's Xlstart folder before opening files in the alternate startup folder. If there is a file in the alternate startup folder with a name that matches a file in the user's Xlstart folder, the file in the alternate startup folder is ignored. For example, if Xl5galry.xls exists in both the Xlstart and the alternate startup folder, only the custom AutoFormats defined in \Xlstart\Xl5galry.xls are available to the user.

Customized Toolbars

There are two ways to create customized toolbars in Microsoft Excel.

- **With the Customize command**   Toolbars customized with the Customize button in the Toolbars dialog box are saved in the file *Username*.xlb when the user quits Microsoft Excel. If the user is not logged on, the filename is Excel.xlb

- **With a Visual Basic module**   Toolbars attached to Visual Basic modules are stored in the workbook file.

When a user opens a workbook that has a toolbar attached, the attached Toolbar definitions are saved to the user's .xlb file. These definitions will exist on the user's computer after the user closes or even deletes the workbook. If custom macros are attached to the toolbar and the user tries to implement the toolbar after closing or deleting the original workbook, the user will get an error message stating that Microsoft Excel cannot find the macro. This is because the macro resides with the workbook where the toolbar originated.If users edit the toolbar, their changes do not affect the original toolbar stored with the workbook. When the user reopens the original workbook, Microsoft Excel uses the copy of the toolbar stored in the user's .xlb file rather than reloading the toolbar stored with the workbook. To generate the original version of the toolbar, users can delete the edited copy by selecting it and clicking Delete in the Toolbars dialog box.

For information about modifying Microsoft Excel toolbars with Visual Basic, see Chapter 9 of the *Microsoft Excel/Visual Basic for Windows 95 Programmer's Guide.*

Customized Add-Ins

If an add-in's source workbook contains a reference to another add-in—for instance, a reference to Xlodbc.xla—make sure that when you distribute the add-ins, the referenced add-in is stored somewhere on the user's computer where the calling add-in can find it. You should always store a referenced add-in in the folder that contains the calling add-in. When you compile a source workbook to an add-in, Microsoft Excel stores a hard-coded path to the referenced add-in in the calling add-in. If you move the calling add-in to another computer (for example, when you distribute the add-in to your users) and Microsoft Excel cannot find the file in the hard-coded location, it searches in the following locations, in this order:

- The folder that contains the calling add-in
- The System folder in the Windows folder
- The Windows folder
- The path defined by the Path environment setting (to see the path, type **set** in an MS-DOS® window)

For information about creating, maintaining, and distributing add-ins, see Chapter 12 of the *Microsoft Excel/Visual Basic for Windows 95 Programmer's Guide*.

CHAPTER 4

Microsoft PowerPoint Architecture

PowerPoint architecture consists of three layers: the application, a template, and the presentation. The application provides the default user interface for creating presentations: menus, commands, toolbars, and tools. Templates provide a model for creating new presentations, and contain *master* slides. Master slides govern the default look of every slide in a particular presentation. The presentation file contains the master information, as well as the presentation content, including text, graphics, formatting, multimedia content, and settings such as slide setup and view settings for that particular presentation.

In This Chapter

Application Layer

The application layer in PowerPoint provides the default settings for users to create presentations. Unlike other Office applications, such as Word and Microsoft Excel, users cannot modify the PowerPoint application with macros or Visual Basic modules.

As in Microsoft Excel, users can customize their toolbar settings. And, as in all Office applications, users can set preferences in the Options dialog box. These settings are stored in the Windows Registry. For information on PowerPoint entries in the Windows Registry, see Appendix B, "Registry Keys and Values."

Understanding Templates

The key to understanding PowerPoint architecture is understanding PowerPoint templates. PowerPoint has two kinds of templates:

- Presentation templates
- Design templates

Presentation Templates

Presentation templates are presentations that serve as a pattern for creating new presentations. By basing many presentations on a single presentation template, users can quickly create standard presentations with consistent formatting, graphic elements, and standard text.

For example, a standard company presentation template can save users time by including the company logo, providing a standard slide structure, providing layout for speakers notes and handouts, and providing the basic slide design using standard company colors, fonts, and boilerplate text. With part of the work already done for them, users simply fill in the specific information.

Presentation templates can provide the following:

- **Master elements**   Text, graphics, and other elements that appear on each slide of the presentation. These elements include standard formatting, such as fonts and sizes, bullets, styles, slide backgrounds, and page orientation.
- **Boilerplate elements**   Text, graphics, and other elements such as sound clips, graphs, or charts embedded onto particular slides (rather than appearing on each slide) of the presentation.

These templates are available to users when they specify Start A New Document on the Microsoft Office Shortcut Bar, or when they click New on the PowerPoint File menu. By default, these templates are .pot files stored in \Msoffice\Templates\Presentations. When users run the AutoContent Wizard, they are accessing these templates.

Design Templates

Design templates contain no textual content and no actual slides. Rather, they supply the look of the presentation. They are what is known as Templates in PowerPoint 4.0. Typically, design templates control the color scheme, font selection, bullet style, and overall look of the slides in a presentation.

Design templates consist of master elements only, as defined on the Slide Master and the Title Master. Users can edit design templates, by opening them directly and using Slide Master view. Slide and Title masters are discussed later in this chapter.

These templates are available to users when they click Apply Design Template on the Format menu. When applied to existing presentations, the master elements in the new design template replace the master elements in the presentation. Design templates are .pot files stored in \Msoffice\Templates\Presentation Designs.

Templates Applied to Presentations

In PowerPoint, all presentations are based on a template. When a user creates a new presentation, it initially has the characteristics of the selected presentation or design template. Users can create a new presentation in several ways.

If the user	Available templates are
Clicks New on the File menu in PowerPoint	All presentation and design templates in \Msoffice\Templates folder and subfolders.
Clicks Start A New Document on the Office Shortcut Bar	All Office templates as defined in the User and Workgroup templates locations for the Office Shortcut Bar. PowerPoint presentation templates are on the Presentations tab. Design templates are on the Presentation Designs tab.
Clicks the New button on the Standard toolbar in PowerPoint	Blank design template. The New dialog box does not appear.

The default blank design template is Blank Presentation.pot, which contains default settings for layout, font, and color scheme. Because it is a design template and not a presentation template, it contains no text, only placeholders for text and graphics.

Users can modify a presentation at any time by applying a different design template to an open presentation. The Apply Design Template dialog box allows users to apply a presentation template or a design template to an open presentation. When users apply a presentation template, it is only the master elements that are copied to the presentation. Any text or graphics in the presentation template are not copied.

Master Elements

The master elements defined for slides in a presentation are known collectively as the Slide Master. Users can also define a second type of master, the Title Master, whose default settings are a copy of the Slide Master. Design templates are specialized templates in that they contain *only* master elements.

Slide Masters A Slide Master is the main master for a presentation. Users can edit Slide Masters in master view to control the default placement and style of elements on every slide of the presentation. When users create their presentation, however, they can choose which master elements a slide adheres to or deviates from, and these slides will be exceptions to the master. Slides that are exceptions to the master are not updated if the user defines a new master or applies a new design template.

Title Masters A Title Master is another kind of master that users can define for their presentations. This allows for two consistent yet independent looks in a presentation: one for title slides (opening slide, section dividers, and ending slide, for example), and one for slides that make up the body of the presentation. By default, the characteristics of the Title Master are based on the characteristics of the Slide Master. Users can edit these characteristics by modifying a title slide in Title Master view.

Note The Blank Presentation.pot design template has only a Slide Master defined. Users can create a customized, unique Title Master based on the Slide Master by clicking New Title Master. All other design templates contain both Slide and Title masters.

Predefined Slide Layouts

When users create a new presentation that is based only on a design template, PowerPoint displays the New Slide dialog box, where users choose an AutoLayout for the first slide in their presentation. AutoLayouts are predefined slide layouts that users can apply to any slide in their presentation. The default AutoLayout for the first slide is the Title Slide layout, as shown in the following example.

Default layout for the first slide of a new presentation is the Title Slide AutoLayout.

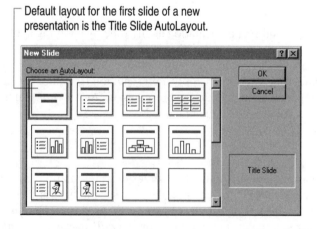

Throughout a presentation, slides that have the Title Slide AutoLayout applied to them are identified as title slides, and their default characteristics are those of the Title Master, which users can modify separately from the Slide Master.

Handout and Notes Masters

Users can also define masters for handouts and for speaker's notes. Design templates do not affect the look of Handout and Notes masters. These masters are stored with the presentation file.

Note The Outline Master, which was available in PowerPoint 4, has been removed for PowerPoint 7.0. Printed outlines follow the format of the Handout Master.

Presentation Layer

The presentation layer is comparable to the document layer of Word. When users create a presentation, all the content and settings associated with the presentation template and design template are copied to the presentation file. For example, changes to a Slide Master in a presentation based on a design template affect the active presentation only, not the design template file. Presentation files store Slide and Title masters, as well as all content that is an exception to the master slides. The presentation file also stores Handout Masters and Notes Masters.

PowerPoint stores presentation files with the file extension .ppt.

How PowerPoint Resolves Conflicts

A slide in a presentation may seem to have many influences converging upon it: presentation templates, design templates, Slide Masters, Title Masters, and layout that a user has specified for a particular slide. In the case of conflicting settings, the setting closest to the slide takes precedence. For example, if a slide's Slide Master is formatted with text in the Arial font on a blue background, but the user specified Times Roman text on a red background for this slide, the user's specifications take precedence over the Slide Master. PowerPoint resolves conflicts in the following order:

1. Settings defined for an individual slide (exceptions to the master)
2. A slide's AutoLayout (slides whose AutoLayout is Title Slide adhere to Title Master settings)
3. Slide Master and Title Master settings
4. Presentation template
5. Design template

There are two ways PowerPoint creates a new presentation:

From a design template In this case, PowerPoint copies all information from the Design Template including Slide and Title master information to the presentation file. From that point on, everything that is added to or modified in the presentation is stored in the presentation file. Changes to the master elements do not affect the Design Template.

From a presentation template In this case, PowerPoint copies all information from the presentation template, including text, graphics, and custom layout, as well as masters for slides, handouts, and notes, to the new presentation file. All modifications are stored in the presentation file. Changes to boilerplate text, master elements, or any other properties of the file do not affect the presentation template.

Slide Setup Default Settings

PowerPoint stores settings such as slide sizing and the page orientation of slides, notes, handouts, and outlines with the presentation file. A new presentation based on this presentation inherits these settings. These settings are the default settings for the layout of a presentation. Users specify them by clicking Slide Setup on the File menu.

CHAPTER 5

Microsoft Schedule+ Architecture

The architecture of Schedule+ is dependent on the existence of a version 1.0 Messaging Application Programming Interface (MAPI 1.0) on the local computer. MAPI 1.0 is available by installing the Microsoft Exchange client from Windows 95. If users have MAPI 1.0 installed, they can run Schedule+ in either stand-alone mode or group-enabled mode. If users do not have MAPI 1.0 installed on their computer, they can run Schedule+ in stand-alone mode only This chapter provides information on how the components of Schedule+ fit together, explains the differences between running Schedule+ in stand-alone or group-enabled mode, and describes how Schedule+ works with the Microsoft Exchange Server.

In This Chapter

Schedule+ Components

On the user's system, Schedule+ consists of the Schedule+ application, the schedule file, and all the schedule items. At the top of the hierarchy is the Schedule+ application, which manages any number of schedule files. Each schedule file contains many items, such as appointments, tasks, contacts, and projects, as shown in the following illustration. In most cases, there is one schedule file for each user, although users can create multiple schedule files for themselves if they want.

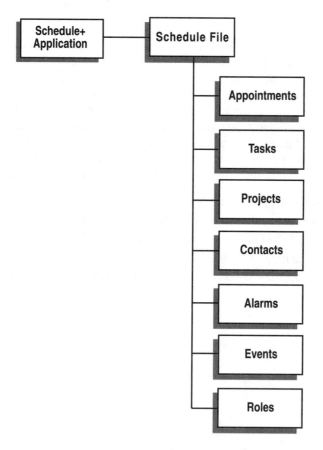

Schedule items are like tables that can be further broken down by property. They all have a structure similar to that shown in the following illustration, where appointment items have properties such as attendees, starting date, starting time, and description, and attendee items have properties such as an attendee's free/busy status and last-received invitation.

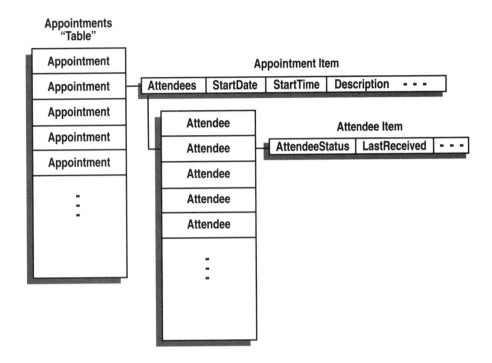

Schedule+ Application

The Schedule+ application consists of the Schedule+ program file Schdpl32.exe and the Schedule+ DLLs. Additional files types installed by Setup for running Schedule+ are listed in the following table:

File extension	Description
.prt	Print layout files
.fmt	Paper format description files
.hlp	Online Help files
.ico	Icon files
.cfg	Mail forms configuration files

Users can customize Schedule+ default settings by clicking Options on the Tools menu. These settings are stored in the Windows Registry. For information about Registry settings for Schedule+, see Appendix B, "Registry Keys and Values." Other ways in which users can customize their Schedule+ application include the following:

- **Time and date settings**   Schedule+ uses time and date settings that are controlled in Windows, under Regional Settings in the Control Panel. Users can customize these settings in Schedule+ and can specify a secondary time zone to use when scheduling meetings across time zones. These custom settings are stored in the Windows Registry.

- **View settings, such as the Tab Gallery or Columns settings**   Users configure these settings by using the commands on the View menu, and the settings are stored in *Username*.vue, where *Username* matches the user's logon name. This file also contains the list of most recently used schedule files. You cannot edit this file directly, as it is binary. However, you can rename it, causing Schedule+ to create a new *Username*.vue file with default settings the next time the user starts Schedule+.

- **OLE automation**   The Schedule+ application can be extended with OLE automation, using an OLE IDispatch interface. For information about developing software that accesses Schedule+, see the documentation that comes with the *Microsoft Solutions Development Kit* or the Microsoft Developer's Network (MSDN). For information about accessing MSDN, see Appendix F, "Resources."

Filters for Importing and Exporting Data

The Schedule+ application includes filters for exporting and importing task, calendar, and contact information to and from other personal information managers, such as Lotus Organizer time management software, Sharp 9600 personal digital assistant, and Timex Data Link watch.

The following table shows the personal information management systems supported by Schedule+ filters. Currently, only the Sharp digital assistants are supported. Filters for the rest of the personal information managers listed will be available free of charge through Microsoft support resources. For information about these resources, see Appendix F.

In addition to the filters listed here, IntelliLink Corporation supplies a translator package that will be available with future updates to Schedule+. In the meantime, you can call IntelliLink at (603) 888-0666 for information on obtaining the translator package and the converters it contains.

Personal Information Manager / File Format	Import/Export
Schedule+ 1.0	Import
ACT! for Windows	Import
ECCO Professional	Import
Lotus Organizer	Import
PackRat 4.1+	Import
Windows Accessories	Import
Sharp 9600	Import/Export
HP 95LX	Import/Export
Sharp 5000/7000/7200	Import/Export
Sharp 7600/7620	Import/Export
Sharp 8000/8200	Import/Export
Sharp 8600/YO-610	Import/Export
Timex Data Link Watch	Export
CSV (comma-separated value file format)	Import/Export
ASCII format	Import/Export
Microsoft Schedule+ 1.*x*	Import/Export
Windows Cardfile and Calendar	Import/Export

The Text Import/Export Wizard allows information to be exchanged with other applications using a comma-delimited (CSV) format, a standard method for transferring text-based information. For example, this provides an easy way to import contact information into Schedule+ for users who currently store their contact lists in Microsoft Excel or Microsoft Access.

Users can also insert contact information into Microsoft Word documents by using the Address Book tool in Word. Word imports the contact information by reading the Schedule+ contact list using OLE automation. In addition to accessing address information for a specific Schedule+ contact through the Address Book, Word can also integrate the entire Schedule+ contact list into a mail merge.

Schedule File

The Schedule file (.scd) contains all appointments, projects, tasks, alarms, events, contacts, and roles for a single user. The first time a user runs Schedule+, Schedule+ creates a schedule file on the user's local drive. If the user is running Schedule+ in group-enabled mode, this file is copied to the user's server after the user has been running Schedule+ for 15 minutes. By default, Schedule+ accesses the local file rather than the user's server file, keeping network traffic to a minimum.

Schedule Items

Items are stored in the user's schedule file, as described in the preceding section. Schedule items are appointments, tasks, projects, contacts, alarms, events, and roles.

Appointments Appointments in Schedule+ are activities that occur within a specific time period. Users create appointments in the Schedule+ Appointment Book, which is visible on the Daily, Weekly, Monthly, or Yearly tab. Appointments can have reminders attached to them, and they can be made to be private, tentative, and recurring. A private appointment is hidden to all users except those to whom a user has granted Owner or Delegate Owner access permission. A tentative appointment does not show up as a busy time slot for a user when others view the user's schedule in their Planner. In other words, when a user schedules a tentative appointment for themselves, they can still be considered free to schedule other appointments. A recurring appointment occurs at regular intervals, such as 10 A.M. every Thursday.

If users are running Schedule+ in group-enabled mode, they can schedule meetings by inviting others to their appointments. The list of possible attendees that appears in the user's Meeting Attendees dialog box comes from the user's address list in the workgroup postoffice, or from the address list supplied by the mail server if your worksite is running Microsoft Mail 3.*x*.

Tasks Tasks are items on a user's To Do list. They can be part of a project, or they can stand alone. Users can assign priorities to their tasks, and they can schedule an end date and a duration for each task.

Projects Projects are groups of tasks. Users can create projects to organize their tasks, although tasks do not need to be associated with a project. Users can assign priorities to projects without affecting the priorities assigned to individual tasks within the projects. Users can designate any project as private, which hides all tasks within the project so that only those users granted Owner or Delegate Owner access permission can view the tasks.

Contacts Contacts are people who users keep track of in a Contact List in their schedule file. The Contact List stores information such as addresses, phone numbers, and user-defined notes. This list is not connected to a user's postoffice address list. Users can assign access permissions to allow other users to view or modify their contact information. Contacts designated as private are visible only to users granted Owner or Delegate Owner access permission.

Alarms   Alarms are reminders that users can set for appointments and tasks. The reminder is a message box that appears at a specified interval before an appointment or at the start of an appointed day if the reminder is associated with a task. Reminders can be accompanied by sound if the user sets this option. The default sound is provided by the file Msremind.wav, but users can use the Control Panel to change this sound to any .wav file on the system. Users can set reminders automatically for each new appointment or task by clicking Options on the Tools menu and then clicking the Defaults tab. They can also set the default reminder time on the Defaults tab. Users can change reminder settings for individual appointments and tasks without affecting their default settings.

Events   Events are activities or special occasions that occur on a specific day but do not fill a block of time on a user's schedule. Examples of events include birthdays, conferences, and trade shows. Users can designate events as annual if the event occurs on the same day every year. Events and annual events do not appear as busy times in the Planner.

Roles   Roles are predefined combinations of access permissions. Users can assign roles to members of their workgroup by clicking Set Access Permissions on the Tools menu. Roles grant access to appointments, contacts, events, and tasks in a user's schedule, as shown in the following table.

Role	Access permissions
None	Cannot read or modify user's schedule. Question mark appears next to user's name in Invite pane of the Schedule+ Planner for free/busy times.
Read	Can read schedule, except for items designated as private.
Create	Can read schedule except for items designated as private; can create new schedule items.
Modify	Can read schedule and can modify existing items, except for items designated as private.
Delegate	Can read schedule and modify existing items, including items designated as private. Can send and receive meeting messages on user's behalf.
Owner	Can read schedule and modify existing items, including items designated as private. Can change access permissions for user's schedule. Can send and receive meeting messages on user's behalf.
Delegate Owner	Can read schedule and modify existing items, including items designated as private. Can change access permissions for user's schedule.
Custom	User sets read, create, and modify permissions separately for appointments, contacts, events, and tasks.

Server Files

When users run Schedule+ in group-enabled mode, Schedule+ creates files on their workgroup server to allow group scheduling. These files include the user's server schedule file, free/busy file, key file, and server files associated with the mail server your worksite uses to support Schedule+.

Server Schedule File   Schedule+ creates the user's server schedule file the first time it synchronizes the user's local .scd file with the server. This initial synchronization creates a copy of the user's local schedule file in the Cal subfolder of the folder that contains the user's postoffice. The name of the file is *hex-ID*.scd, where *hex-ID* is a hexadecimal number that is incremented according to the last entry in the Schedul2.key file, which is also stored in the Cal folder.

Free/Busy Files   Files with the extension .pof contain a user's free/busy information. Schedule+ stores these files in the Cal folder of the user's workgroup postoffice. A single .pof file stores free/busy information for the entire workgroup. If your worksite is running Microsoft Mail 3.*x* with Schedule+, there will be one .pof file for each postoffice participating in schedule distribution. These additional files contain Free/Busy information for users in other postoffices. All users in the workgroup postoffice can be invited to meetings, whether or not they are running Schedule+, and regardless of whether they are running Schedule+ in stand-alone or group-enabled mode. If users are not running Schedule+ or are running Schedule+ in stand-alone mode, a question mark appears next to the their name in the Invite pane of the Schedule+ Planner view.

Key File   Schedule+ creates .key files in the Cal folder of the workgroup postoffice. These files act as a maps to identify which server schedule file belongs to which user in the workgroup. These files contain each user's mailbox name and an eight-digit hexadecimal ID that corresponds to the user's schedule file. Users running Schedule+ 1.0 store their schedules in .cal files, which are mapped by Schedule.key. Users running Schedule+ 7.0 store their schedules in .scd files, which are mapped by Schedul2.key. You can use the utility Dumpkey.exe to display the contents of both .key files.

Mail Server Files   Depending on the mail server you are using at your worksite to support Schedule+, such as Microsoft Mail 3.*x*, you may need to install and set up an administration program, a schedule distribution program, and other utilities. For information about how to set up this software, see the documentation that comes with your mail server.

Running Schedule+ in Stand-Alone Mode

Users can run Schedule+ in stand-alone mode whether or not their system is set up with a postoffice. If a user's system is mail enabled—which means it has a postoffice—Schedule+ asks the user at startup whether the user wants to work in group-enabled mode or alone. If a user's system is not mail enabled, Schedule+ always runs in stand-alone mode.

When users run Schedule+ in stand-alone mode, they can use all the time management features of Schedule+, create contact lists, and manage projects. However, they cannot share any of this information with others in their workgroup nor can they use Schedule+ to schedule meetings with other people, until they run Schedule+ in group-enabled mode.

The first time users run Schedule+ in stand-alone mode, Schedule+ prompts them for whether they want to create a new schedule file or to use an existing one. If users have been working group-enabled, they should use their existing .scd file (or .cal file if their schedule file is in Schedule+ 1.0 format), which is stored in the \Msoffice\Schedule folder by default.

If users choose to create a new schedule file, Schedule+ presents a dialog box for the user to supply a name and location for the file. The default location is the \Msoffice\Schedule folder, and the default name is the user's logon name. If the user's system is mail enabled, the default name of the schedule file is the name of the user's mail profile, as determined by Microsoft Exchange. For more information about creating new profiles in Microsoft Exchange, see "Profiles" in the Microsoft Exchange online help.

Running Schedule+ in Group-Enabled Mode

Before a user can run Schedule+, MAPI 1.0 must be available on the local workstation. Also, the user must have a valid mail account on one of the following platforms:

- **Windows 95 Workgroup Postoffice**   This postoffice is included with Windows 95. It must be accessible by all users in the workgroup. For more information about setting up a Windows 95 workgroup postoffice and configuring the Microsoft Exchange client, see "Using the Microsoft Exchange Client with Microsoft Mail" in Chapter 26 of the *Microsoft Windows 95 Resource Kit*.

- **Microsoft Mail Server**   Microsoft Mail 3.*x* supplies a Schedule+ transport that allows users to share schedules and invite one another to meetings across workgroups. For information about configuring the Microsoft Mail server to run with Schedule+, see the documentation that comes with your server.

- **Microsoft Exchange Server**   The Microsoft Exchange Server includes MAPI drivers that extend the capabilities of the Microsoft Exchange client by providing access to public folders, creating custom forms and shared documents, scheduling meetings with others, managing time and tasks among workgroups, and creating custom electronic forms. For more information about configuring the Microsoft Exchange Server and setting up public folders, see the documentation that comes with the Microsoft Exchange Server.

When users run Schedule+ in group-enabled mode, they can share the following kinds of information between Schedule+ and other messaging or scheduling applications:

- **Meeting requests**   When users make an appointment and invite others, Microsoft Exchange provides a form for sending the meeting request through electronic mail.

- **Free/busy information**   On the Planner tab in Schedule+, a meeting organizer can add specific people to a list of invitees, and then check their availability before scheduling a meeting. Their busy times show up as colored bars in the Planner.

- **Details**   If an invitee has given the meeting organizer permission to view the details of the invitee's schedule, the meeting organizer can use the right mouse button to click on a busy time for that person and view the details of an appointment, such as location, purpose of the meeting, and so forth. Details also include access permissions users can give each other to specific parts of their schedule, such as contacts or tasks.

The first time users run Schedule+ in group-enabled mode, Schedule+ creates a schedule file on the user's local drive, as described earlier for running Schedule+ in stand-alone mode. At a default interval of 15 minutes, Schedule+ copies the user's local schedule files to the server, in the Cal folder of the user's workgroup postoffice folder. Schedule+ synchronizes users' local and server schedule files at regular intervals. Users can configure the synchronization interval by clicking Options on the Tools menu and then clicking the Synchronize tab. Schedule+ also synchronizes schedule files when the user quits Schedule+, and when the user synchronizes the files manually from the Synchronize tab in the Options dialog box.

Note   If users have been running Schedule+ in stand-alone mode, Schedule+ synchronizes their local and server schedule files the next time they run Schedule+ in group-enabled mode.

During users' initial Schedule+ session, their free and busy times are not available on the server until the local schedule file is copied to the server. These users can still be invited to meetings, because their names are in the workgroup's postoffice address book.

Running Schedule+ in group-enabled mode allows users to set access permissions on their schedule, allowing certain users to Read, Create, or Modify appointments and tasks. Users set access permissions by clicking Set Access Permission on the Tools menu. By granting create permission for appointments, users can open each other's schedules and create appointments as needed.

You can grant individuals various combinations of permissions based on the needs at your worksite. For more information about access permissions, see the Schedule+ online help.

When users invite attendees to their meetings, Schedule+ runs the users' mail software automatically. However, when users run Schedule+ in group-enabled mode, Schedule+ adds a button to the standard toolbar with the Microsoft Exchange Inbox icon. This button allows users to run Microsoft Exchange manually from Schedule+, making it easy to correspond with other invitees after reading a meeting request.

How Schedule+ Resolves Conflicts

Conflicts can arise in Schedule+ when the local and server schedule files are being synchronized, when backup server files are created, or during file recovery.

File Synchronization

Schedule+ synchronizes a user's local and server schedule files by merging changes from one file to the other. During the merge, schedule items are merged on a property by property basis. For example, if the text of an appointment is modified in one file and the time is modified in the other file, the appointment will have new text and a new time in the resulting merged file.

Recovered Files

During normal operation, Schedule+ monitors file read and write operations to ensure the user's data integrity remains intact. Data integrity is measured using two methods.

Checksums Each block of data is validated with a checksum. A *checksum* is a calculated value used to test data integrity. If the checksum does not match the recorded value, the operation fails.

Data typing Each data block has a specific type. If the data type of the written file does not match that of the file being read, the operation fails.

If the operation fails on either method, Schedule+ calls an internal recovery function that seeks to prevent further data loss by rebuilding the data file without the damaged data. In recover mode, Schedule+ removes the damaged data and copies the valid data blocks to a new file.

If the damaged file is the local file and the server file is undamaged, the user can synchronize with the server file to merge undamaged data back into the local file. Likewise, if the damaged file is the server file, the user can merge the undamaged local file into the server file. Users can force synchronization by clicking Options on the Tools menu, clicking the Synchronization tab, and then clicking Synchronize Now.

When Schedule+ recovers a damaged file, it stores the recovered file in the user's Temp folder, or if this folder does not exist, in the Windows folder. The filename is Recoverx.scd, where x is a number from 0 to 9. If files Recover0.scd through Recover9.scd exist on the user's computer, Schedule+ continues to overwrite Recover9.scd.

How Schedule+ Works with Microsoft Exchange Server

Schedule+ works with the Microsoft Exchange client for much of its group scheduling capabilities:

- Meeting requests and responses appear as custom forms in the Inbox.
- Meeting attendees are selected from the Microsoft Exchange address book.
- Microsoft Exchange and Schedule+ use the same user list, so there is no need to maintain two different lists.

When combined with a Microsoft Exchange Server, Schedule+ becomes an even more powerful group scheduling platform. In addition to all of the benefits of using just the Microsoft Exchange client:

- Schedule+ adopts the client/server architecture of the Microsoft Exchange Server. You do not need to add anything to Schedule+; the enhancement to Schedule+ is built into the Microsoft Exchange Server.
- Time zone information is stored on each Microsoft Exchange Server so that meeting requests from a user in another time zone are booked at the correct times for their time zone, and free/busy information in the planner view is adjusted for time zone differences.
- Microsoft Exchange Server public folders are used to store free/busy information. Because public folders can be replicated among Microsoft Exchange Servers, this information can easily be shared with others.

- Schedule+ can be incorporated into any public folder application, such as customer tracking, using OLE automation.

- No separate administration is required for Schedule+ on a Microsoft Exchange Server. All of the administrative features of the Microsoft Exchange Server automatically incorporate Schedule+.

Accessing Personal Schedules

Microsoft Exchange stores information in public and private folders. These folders are kept in an information store on a Microsoft Exchange server. The information store is made up of two elements: the public information store, where public folders are located; and the private information store, where private folders are located.

Microsoft Exchange stores users' personal schedules in private folders on their home servers. Each time users change their personal schedules, the Microsoft Exchange private folder is updated to reflect that change. Individual users can delegate access permissions to their personal schedule using the Set Access Permissions dialog box in Schedule+.

When one user tries to access another user's personal schedule in the same site, the following events occur:

- Schedule+ checks to see that the user has the appropriate access permissions to view the personal schedule information.

- If the appropriate permissions are in place, Schedule+ connects to the private information store and logs onto the private folder where personal schedule information is stored.

Accessing Free and Busy Times

Schedule+ free and busy times are stored in a public folder on a Microsoft Exchange server. The Schedule+ Free Busy Information public folder is a hidden folder and can be viewed by choosing the Hidden Recipients command from the View menu in the Microsoft Exchange Administrator program.

The Schedule+ Free Busy Information public folder is created automatically when you install Microsoft Exchange and configure your first site and server. Each time you create a new Microsoft Exchange mailbox, an entry is created in the Schedule+ Free Busy Information public folder for the associated account. By default, each time the users logs in and change the information in their schedule file, their entry in the Schedule+ Free Busy Information public folder is updated to reflect the change. Individual users can prohibit the publication of their free/busy information using the Set Access Permissions dialog box in Schedule+.

The information in the Schedule+ Free Busy Information public folder is available to all other users within a Microsoft Exchange site. When a user invites attendees to a meeting the user scheduling, Schedule+ connects to the public information store on the Microsoft Exchange server that contains the Schedule+ Free Busy Information public folder, logs on to the public folder, and accesses all free/busy information for the attendees.

Sharing Free/Busy Information Between Sites

Schedule+ Free Busy Information can be shared between sites, extending group scheduling functionality to your entire organization. Every Microsoft Exchange public folder is represented by two entries: a directory entry, which records configuration information about the public folder, and an entry in the public information store, which is where the actual content of the public folder is stored.

Each time you create a new site and initiate site replication between the two sites, the directory entry for the Schedule+ Free Busy Information public folder is automatically replicated to the new site. When users in the new site invite users from the original site to a meeting, Schedule+ detects the directory entry for the Schedule+ Free Busy Information public folder, and attempts to connect to the public information store on the Microsoft Exchange server that contains the Schedule+ Free Busy Information public folder.

C H A P T E R   6

Microsoft Word Architecture

Microsoft Word architecture consists of three layers: the Word application, the document, and the template. Each of these layers affects Word documents in a different way. The Word application provides the standard Word menus, commands, and toolbars. Templates serve a dual purpose: they provide a model for creating new documents and also act as a storage container for styles, macros, AutoText entries, and customized Word commands and toolbar settings. The document file contains the text, graphics, formatting, and settings such as margins and page layout for that particular document.

In This Chapter

Template Layer

The key to understanding Word architecture is understanding how the document, template, and application layers interact. Of the three layers, the template is the layer that has the greatest impact on both the document and the application layers.

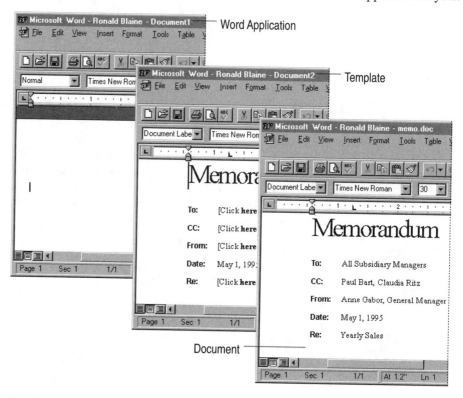

Templates can provide the following:

- Customized menus, toolbars, and keyboard assignments that place frequently used commands on the menus and toolbars, remove unused commands from menus and toolbars, and provide key combinations to quickly carry out commands and macros.

- Macros to automate complicated and repetitive tasks with a single command.

- Boilerplate text and graphics, such as your company's name and logo, in every document based on that template.

- Standard formatting, such as fonts and sizes, styles, margin settings, and page orientation.

- The ability to automatically insert frequently used text and graphics by including specialized AutoText entries.

Impact on Application Layer

Users can customize the Word application with templates. With templates, you can adapt Word menus, toolbars, keyboard assignments, and macros to meet the needs of different types of users or for different types of documents.

For example, you can create a template for new users that has a toolbar with buttons and menus designed to step them through common tasks. More advanced users, who are familiar with the tasks, don't need the extra guidance and can use a template with toolbar buttons that meet their particular needs.

Impact on Document Layer

A template provides a guide or pattern for creating documents. By basing a group of documents on a single template, users can quickly create standard documents, such as letters and memos, with consistent formatting and standard text.

For example, a template for memos can save users time by setting the page margins, inserting the company logo, and providing the text for standard headings, such as "Memo," "To:," and "From:." With part of the work already done for them, users simply fill in the additional text.

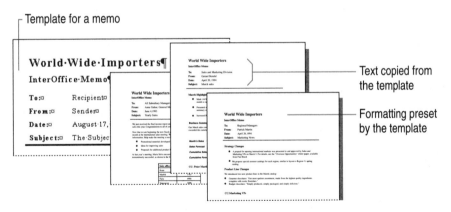

Templates give you a head start in creating the types of documents you work with most often.

Templates Attached to Documents

In Word, all documents are based on a template. When a user creates a new document, it initially has the characteristics of the selected template. A user can create a new document in several ways.

If the user	Available templates are
Clicks New on the File menu in Word	All Word templates and wizards as defined in the user's User Templates location. Word templates have the file extension .dot. Word wizards are specialized templates with the file extension .wiz.
Clicks Start A New Document on the Office Shortcut Bar	All Office templates as defined in the User and Workgroup templates locations for the Office Shortcut Bar. Word templates are on the General, Letters and Faxes, Memos, Reports, Other Documents, and Publications tabs.
Clicks the New button on the Standard toolbar in Word	Normal template. The New dialog box does not appear

Unless users select another template when creating a new document, Word defaults to the Normal.dot template. In addition to Normal, Word comes with templates for the most common types of documents, such as letters, memos, reports, and mailing labels. Users can use the templates as they are or customize them to their own specifications. Users can also create their own templates.

In addition to basing a new document on a template, users can attach a different template to an open document at any time by clicking Templates on the File menu.

Global Templates

Items stored in the Normal template are global—that is, available to all documents. These items include AutoText entries, macros, menu assignments, toolbar button assignments, and keyboard assignments. If a document is attached to a template other than the Normal template, the items stored in that template are available only to documents that are also based on that template.

Document settings and commands specific to only one type of document, such as a fax sheet, are available only to documents based on that template. Other commands and components, such as AutoText entries, that you want available to all documents should be placed in a global template. By using custom and global templates judiciously, your users have a flexible method for creating documents that can be highly customized while adhering to company-wide standards of design.

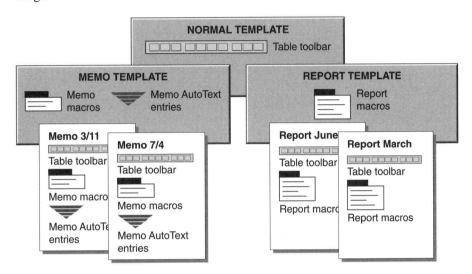

Items stored in the Normal template are available to all of your documents. Items stored in any other template are available only to documents based on that template.

Making Template Items Global

Sometimes users may want to use a macro, toolbar, or AutoText entry from another template. To make these items available to all open documents, you can make a template global. Users can then use the macros, AutoText entries, and customized command settings found in both the global and Normal templates in all their documents. However, styles in the global template are not added to your users' documents; Word continues to use the styles from the template on which the document is based. Customized items in the global template are available for the remainder of the current Word session.

Use the Templates command on the File menu to open a template as a global template.

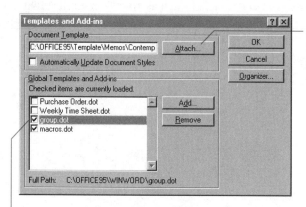

Attaching a template replaces the template currently attached to the document.

Customized items from selected templates are available to all documents. The template attached to each document does not change.

Making Template Items Global at Startup

You may have special toolbar settings or other items stored in a template that you want to make available to users at any time they are using Word. For example, you may have a special corporate or workgroup template that contains special macros and AutoText entries that all users may want to use. Rather than duplicating this information in every copy of the Normal template, you can make this template available globally when a user starts Word.

To load a template globally at startup, make a copy of the template. Store the duplicate in the Startup folder, which is inside the Winword folder (or the folder indicated in the Startup-path entry of the Registry key Hkey_Current_User\Software\Microsoft\Word\7.0\Options). Do not simply move the template from its original folder. Doing so makes the template unavailable when a user creates a new document by clicking New on the File menu.

Storing Templates

The Office Setup program sets default locations for different kinds of documents and Word components: user documents, user templates, spelling dictionaries, clip art, and so forth. Users can change these default locations by choosing Options on the Tools menu. For information about changing these defaults systematically, see "Modifying Client Setup with the Network Admin Wizard Application" in Chapter 9.

Note Changing settings for User Templates and Workgroup Templates in Word changes them for all Office applications. For more information about specifying user and workgroup templates, see "Starting a New Document" in Chapter 1.

User and Workgroup Templates

In a workgroup, there are usually two places where Word templates are stored:

- Templates used by only a few users or that a user may want to customize (such as Normal, because it's always loaded globally) are usually stored in the user's template folder on the user's local hard disk. The default location of these templates is determined by the User Templates setting.

- Templates needed by an entire workgroup or that users do not need to customize are typically stored on a network volume. The default location of these templates is determined by the Workgroup Templates setting.

When creating a new document, templates from both the User Templates folder and the Workgroup Templates folder are listed together in the New dialog box.

By default, Word stores user templates in the Template folder. For workgroup templates, there is no initial default setting. To change the default location, click Options on the Tools menu, and then choose the File Locations tab. Select User Templates or Workgroup Templates from the File Types list, and click Modify. Enter or select the new folder for user templates and for workgroup templates.

Normal Template

At startup, Word looks for the Normal template in the following locations: the user's Template folder, the Winword folder, and the current folder—in that order. If Word cannot find the Normal template, Word uses the standard document and command settings that have been preset by Microsoft. AutoText entries, macros, and command settings the user stored for global use in the Normal template will not be available until the user returns the Normal template to one of the default search locations and then restarts Word.

Note When Word is first installed, there is no Normal.dot file. It is constructed and saved the first time a user exits Word.

How Word Resolves Conflicting Settings

Throughout the discussion of templates, you may have noticed that more than one template can affect the working environment of a document. Each document has access to the macros, AutoText entries, and custom commands and toolbar settings from the attached template, the Normal template, and any global templates. These templates, as well as add-ins or Word itself, may each define a macro or setting in some way that differs from the other templates or add-ins associated with a document. The definition or setting that takes precedence is the one that resides closest to the document. Therefore, Word resolves such conflicts in the following order of priority:

- Template attached to the active document
- Normal template
- Additional global templates
- Add-ins
- Application layer

For example, the style Heading 1 is defined in the Normal template as Arial bold, 18 points, but the document is attached to a template where the style Heading 1 is defined as Times Roman bold, 24 points. Word uses the setting in the attached template, so Text formatted to the Heading 1 style is in Times Roman bold, 24 points.

If several global templates have conflicting settings, Word resolves the conflicts in the order in which they are listed in the Templates And Add-ins dialog box. Templates in the Startup folder appear at the top of the list and have a higher priority. Subsequent ranking on the list is determined by alphabetic order.

Templates in Startup folder show up first in alphabetical order.

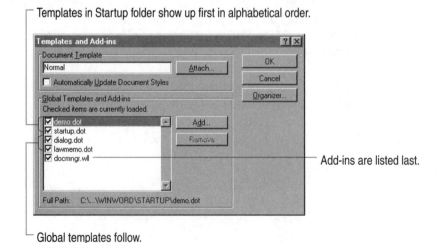

Add-ins are listed last.

Global templates follow.

Where Components Are Stored

The various components of Word, such as styles, macros, default page settings, AutoText entries, AutoCorrect entries, and custom command settings are stored at two levels of Word's three-level architecture. Some components reside strictly at the document level, others reside at the template level, and still others are stored with both the document and the template. Of those components that reside at the template level, some are stored specifically with the Normal or the attached template, while others can also be stored in a global template. The table below shows how components from each kind of template affect the document and what is contained in the document file.

Component	Document file	Attached template	Normal template	Global templates
Document text and graphics	✔			
Boilerplate text and graphics	✔	✔[1]	✔[1, 3]	
Styles	✔	✔[2]	✔[2, 3]	
Default page settings	✔	✔[1]	✔[1, 3]	
AutoText entries		✔	✔	✔
Macros		✔	✔	✔
Custom command and toolbar settings		✔	✔	✔
AutoCorrect formatted text entries			✔[4]	

[1] Copied to the document when first created.

[2] Copied to the document when first created or each time document is opened if the option to automatically update styles is selected.

[3] Applies only to documents attached to the Normal template.

[4] All plain text AutoCorrect entries are stored in the Windows Registry.

Text and Graphics

When a document is first created, Word copies all information from the attached template including boilerplate text and graphics to the document file. From that point on, the text and graphics are saved with the document file. Changes in the boilerplate text and graphics in the template will not affect documents previously created with that template.

Styles

When users create a new document, Word copies styles from the template on which the document is based. No link between template styles and documents styles is made. So, when users change the styles in the document, those changes are saved with the document file. Likewise if users change styles in the template after the document is created, those changes are not automatically reflected in the document.

To automatically update the document styles to match the template, click Templates on the File menu and select the Automatically Update Document Styles check box. Each time a user opens the document, Word copies the styles in the attached template to the document.

Styles and AutoFormat

The AutoFormat command analyzes text in a document and applies styles as appropriate from the styles that have been copied to the document. These document styles originally come from the attached template.

If AutoFormat cannot find an appropriate style among those in the document, it uses the built-in styles provided by Word. These built-in styles allow AutoFormat to format body text, headings, bulleted lists, and other text elements. Users can customize built-in styles in their documents by clicking Style on the Format menu and then clicking Modify. Customizing a built-in style in a user's document has no effect on the original style, because the built-in style is copied to the document by AutoFormat.

The following illustrations show some of the built-in styles you can use to format common text elements.

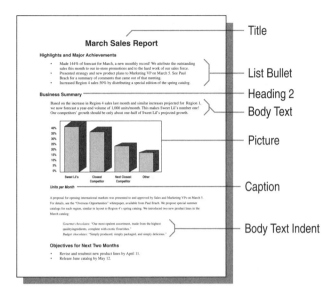

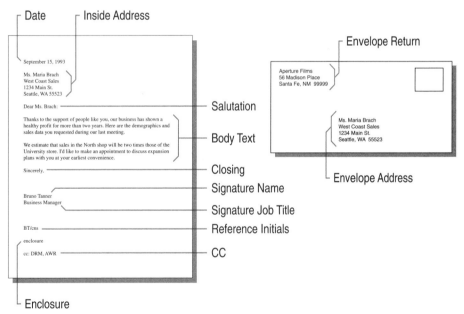

Style Gallery

When users apply styles to text in a document—either by using the AutoFormat command or by applying styles themselves—they can use the Style Gallery command on the Format menu to see how the appearance of the document changes according what template is applied.

Click a template to preview its formatting. Double-click to copy the
selected template styles to your document and close the dialog box.

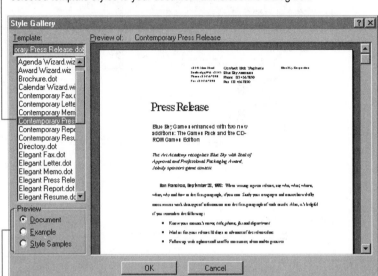

Preview your document, an example document, or samples of styles in a template.

By using the Style Gallery, a user may decide to apply a different template to the
document. When a user chooses to use the styles from another template, Word
copies all styles from the selected template into the document. This has the
following effects:

- A style from the template that has the same name as a style in the document
  replaces the style in the document.

  For example, suppose the Heading 1 style in the template is defined as
  Arial 14-point bold, and the Heading 1 style in the document is defined as
  Times 12-point italic. Word redefines the Heading 1 style in the document
  as Arial 14-point bold. All paragraphs formatted with the Heading 1 style
  are changed to reflect the new style definition.

- Template styles that are not in the document are added to the document.

- Styles unique to the document are not affected.

The Style Gallery command does not attach the selected template to the active
document. Rather, it copies the styles from the selected template to the active
document. The template on which the active document is based remains attached
to the document. To attach a different template to a document, use the Templates
command on the File menu.

Users can also use the Style Gallery to preview their own templates. To create an example document, they select the text in the template and assign it the predefined AutoText entry Gallery Example. This predefined AutoText entry is displayed in the preview box of the Style Gallery when Example is selected.

AutoText

AutoText entries are stored in templates. In order for users to use the AutoText entry in any Word document, store it in the Normal or other global template. If you want to make the AutoText entries available only in documents of the same type as the active document, store them in the template attached to the active document.

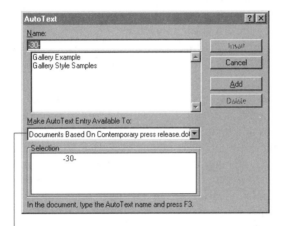

AutoText entries are stored in either the Normal template
or the template attached to the active document.

To add or edit AutoText entries in a global template, you must open the template in a non-global mode. This is because global templates cannot be edited. To open a global template non-globally, you can open it directly (in the File Open dialog box, select Document Templates in the File Of Type box), or open a document to which the template is attached—not a document to which the template has been loaded.

To determine whether a template is attached or loaded into a document, click Templates on the File menu. The template whose name appears in the Document Template box is the attached template, and is editable. The template whose name appears in the Global Templates And Add-ins box is a loaded template and is read-only.

Macros

Word stores macros in templates. When a user creates a new macro, it is stored by default in the Normal template and is available globally. A user can also specify which template a macro should be attached to.

To store a new macro in a template other than Normal, either the template itself or a document attached to the template must be active when the user creates the macro. If users want to create a new macro in a global template, they must open the template itself rather than an attached document. When attached to a document, global templates are read-only.

- To create a new macro using the Macro dialog box, the user selects the existing template name in the Macros Available In box and then clicks Create to open a new macro-editing window.

- To record a new macro, the user selects the existing template name in the Make Macro Available To box in the Macro Record dialog box.

Together, macros and templates can be used to create a highly customized version of Word designed to accomplish a particular task or set of tasks. For example, a group of macros and templates could be designed to automate the creation of forms and other documents a company uses. Because the macros are stored in one or more custom templates, the custom version of Word is relatively simple to distribute; it's just a matter of copying the templates. If the macros are stored in the Normal template instead, it is much more complicated to install the custom version on another machine, which already has its own Normal template.

AutoCorrect

Any AutoCorrect entries that use formatted text, with Formatted Text selected in the AutoCorrect dialog box, are specific to Word, and are stored in the user's own Normal template.

Custom Toolbars, Menus, and Shortcut Keys

By customizing toolbars, menus, and shortcut keys, you can change Word to better suit the needs of your users. For example, you can add frequently used commands and dialog box options to toolbars and menus. And you can remove items users rarely use. You can also customize shortcut key assignments by creating the shortcut keys that work best for your users.

To customize toolbars, menus, and shortcut keys, click Customize on the Tools menu. You can specify whether to store these customizations in the Normal template, an open template, or the template attached to the active document. To make customized settings available in any document, save the settings in the Normal template or to a template that will be made global.

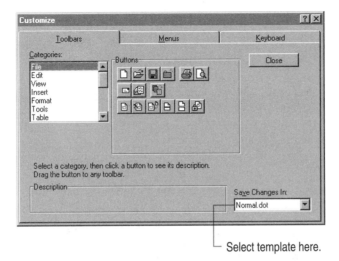

Select template here.

Page Setup Default Settings

Default page settings for the document layout, such as margins, layout, and paper size, are similar to styles. The default settings are saved with a template. Each new document based on that template inherits those default settings from the template. Subsequent changes to the settings in the document reside with the document and are not automatically saved to the template. However, these settings can be stored in the template.

To save settings from the document to the attached template, click Default in the Page Setup dialog box. The changes will be reflected in subsequent documents created from this template.

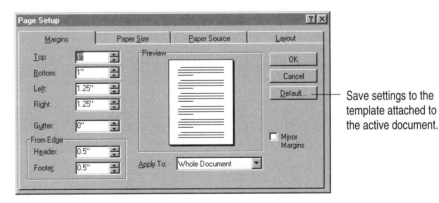

Save settings to the template attached to the active document.

Managing Styles, AutoText Entries, Macros, and Toolbars

Users may want to take advantage of styles, toolbars, macros, or AutoText entries that have already been created in another template. They can use the Organizer dialog box to copy these items between templates. Styles can also be moved between templates and documents.

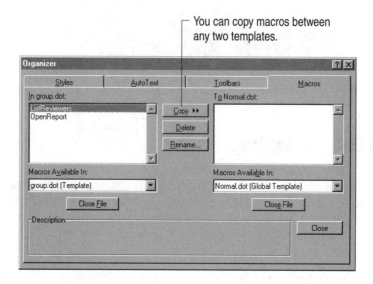

You can copy macros between any two templates.

Users can also use the Organizer to delete or rename styles, AutoText entries, macros, or toolbars. To open the Organizer, click Templates on the File menu and then click Organizer.

Wizards

From a user perspective, a *wizard* is a fast, easy way to create a document—because the wizard does the work. Architecturally, wizards are specialized templates. They are designated with a .wiz extension instead of a .dot extension, and their Type is described as MS Word Wizard rather than MS Word Template. The wizards that come with Word all share a common user interface. The key component of the wizard is the macro or set of macros stored with the template. These macros automate the creation of the document.

Word provides wizards to help users create the following types of documents: agenda, award, calendar, fax cover sheet, legal pleading, letter, memo, newsletter, and resume. Word also includes a wizard to help users create tables. You can create your own wizards to step users through complex tasks specific to your company. For more information about creating your own wizards, see "Creating a Wizard," in Chapter 9 of the *Microsoft Word Developer's Kit.*

Add-ins

Add-ins are programs written in the C programming language. They act like custom commands or custom features you can use in Word. For more information about add-ins, see Appendix C in the *Microsoft Word Developer's Kit.*

You can place add-in commands on toolbars and menus or assign them to shortcut keys, just as you can with Word macros. Architecturally, add-ins fit in at the template layer. They modify toolbars, menu commands, and shortcut keys just like templates.

You can write your own add-ins or obtain them from software vendors. To use an add-in, you must load it into Word. Add-ins are installed and loaded the same way global templates are. Like a template, the add-in program remains available until you quit Word. If you want to load an add-in program automatically each time you start Word, store it in the Startup folder.

Installing Microsoft Office for Windows 95

Chapter 7, "Guide to Deploying Microsoft Office for Windows 95," is written for the administrator who is responsible for corporate implementation of Office for Windows 95. This chapter provides an overview of the significant steps in the deployment schedule, along with a checklist for each step.

Chapter 8, "Installing Microsoft Office," describes the most basic installation process for Microsoft Office for Windows 95. The chapter begins with the installation planning process and installation options, followed by specific procedures for you to follow as you install Office.

Chapter 9, "Customizing Client Installations," explains how to customize the installation process to meet your needs. The Setup program is explained, as is the Network Installation Wizard—the tool you use to customize client setup.

Chapter 10, "Upgrading to Office for Windows 95," covers application-specific issues you'll want to know about as you upgrade your organization to Office for Windows 95. In this chapter, you'll find information about the changes in Office for Windows 95 (also called Office 7.0) and in all of the individual Office applications. This chapter does not contain a list of all the new features; rather, it explains the differences between Office 4.2 applications and Office 7.0 applications, including changes to file formats, macros, menus and shortcut keys, programming, security, and so on.

CHAPTER 7

Guide to Deploying Microsoft Office for Windows 95

This chapter is for administrators responsible for corporate implementation of Office for Windows 95, providing an overview of the significant steps in the deployment schedule.

In This Chapter

Overview of the Process

Microsoft Office for Windows 95 is designed to run on Windows 95 or Windows NT™ 3.51 operating system or higher, so you will also need to evaluate and install Windows 95 or Windows NT 3.51 before you can install Office for Windows 95. This section explains how to get started with the Windows deployment and then how to use this guide to plan and implement your Office deployment.

Microsoft Windows Deployment

The assumption made in this chapter is that there are separate groups within your organization that will review, test, and deploy Windows 95 or Windows NT 3.51. In general, you will have one team that is responsible for upgrading your operating system to Windows 95 or Windows NT, while another team will be responsible for upgrading your applications to Microsoft Office for Windows 95. If the team deploying Office is separate from the team deploying Windows, the Office team can skip those phases that involved Windows evaluation and installation.

The overall process for evaluating, planning, and deploying Microsoft Office for Windows 95 is very similar to the process used for Windows 95 or Windows NT. If you will be deploying Windows along with Office, you will want to consider how your Office configuration will influence your planning and deployment of Windows.

As you are going through the planning process for Windows, then, it is recommended that you work through the Office planning process as well. In particular, the section titled, "Recommended Windows 95 Features," discusses features of Windows 95 that you should consider deploying to assist in your subsequent deployment of Office.

For more information about how to deploy Windows 95, see the *Microsoft Windows 95 Resource Kit*. This book is available from Microsoft Press at 1-800-MS-PRESS and in bookstores. For more information about how to deploy Windows NT, see the *Windows NT Resource Kit*, also available from Microsoft Press.

Microsoft Office Deployment

The deployment process for Microsoft Office for Windows 95 is divided into distinct phases that span everything from evaluating the product, to specifying the preferred client configuration, to pushing the installation from a central network server. The following are the suggested phases of deployment:

- Review and install Windows
- Review Office for Windows 95
- Assemble the planning team and tools
- Specify the preferred client configuration
- Conduct the lab test
- Plan the pilot rollout
- Conduct the pilot rollout
- Finalize the rollout plan

- Roll out Office for Windows 95
- Maintenance and support

In the sections that describe each phase, checklists are provided to describe the tasks for the specific phase.

The following sample illustrates a checklist and how you can use it at your site.

Sample of Checklist Format

Deployment Phase

Task	Team	Start week	Duration
☐ 1: Summary of the task.	Who will work on this task?	When does this task start?	How long will it take to complete?

Following each checklist is expanded information about selected items.

On the CD included with this book is a project plan created in Microsoft Project. It will help step you through the process of creating your custom plan, allowing you to assign specific resources to different tasks. It also helps you see the dependencies and what tasks must happen sequentially, as well as those that can happen in parallel.

The tasks may vary for your particular organization's structure and needs. For the purpose of this guide, individuals performing tasks are grouped in the following teams, which are made up of employees from your organization.

Name of team	Includes
Executive team	Deployment project manager (usually the head of the Information Systems department) and members of the executive committee of the corporation.
Planning team	Deployment project manager, key Installation team members, a representative from the Windows 95 deployment team, and a representative from the Support and Training teams.
Installation team	Technicians and individuals who will be conducting the installation, including a representative from the Windows 95 Installation Team.
Support team	Staff of the Help desk or Support department, and select individuals from the Planning team.
Training team	Individuals responsible for user training.

Review and Install Windows

Before you can deploy Microsoft Office for Windows 95 you need to install Windows 95 or Windows NT on servers and client systems. As part of the planning process for these Windows installations, you need to consider what effect the Office requirements will have.

Recommended Windows 95 Features

For client systems that will be using Windows 95, there are some recommended features of Windows 95 that may be useful in setting up Office initially, and also later on when administering your client systems. The following table lists these features.

These features should be reviewed before deploying Windows 95, and they should be considered during the planning and deployment of Windows 95.

Recommended Windows 95 Features for Office for Windows 95 Client Configurations

Windows 95 feature	Decisions and issues	Reference
☐ **1:** Windows 95 system policies	Choose this feature to restrict the user's ability to use Control Panel options or configure components.	*Microsoft Windows 95 Resource Kit*, Chapter 15, "User Profiles and System Policies"
To restrict access to controls and features	Use the Windows 95 System Policy Editor to define policies at any time.	
☐ **2:** Windows 95 user profiles	Choose this feature to maintain consistent desktop and environment settings on a user-specific basis. Enabling user profiles causes a slight delay during logon.	*Microsoft Windows 95 Resource Kit*, Chapter 15, "User Profiles and System Policies"
To allow multiple users to use a single computer with their own settings or, conversely, to allow personalized settings per user on multiple computers	Options: ☐ Users can control changes to their user profiles and update them as they want. ☐ Administrators can predefine a mandatory profile for specific users, that can only be changed by the administrator.	

1: Windows 95 System Policies

System policies are used to restrict or pre-define the desktop and network functionality on each client computer, including restricting or optimizing Office features and capabilities. System policies make it easy to disable the ability to use peer-sharing services or the ability to use the command prompt from a central location for a large number of users. Similarly, if you want all the users in a workgroup to use a shared folder for Word template files, system policies allow you to set the default template file folder used by Word from a central location.

Enabling policies is done by creating a single file that resides on the server, and thus does not require user intervention on the client computer. For details on the types of restrictions available and for information about how to implement system policies, see Chapter 15, "User Profiles and System Policies," in the *Microsoft Windows 95 Resource Kit*, and Part 3, "Maintaining and Supporting Microsoft Office," in this book.

2: Windows 95 User Profiles

User profiles enable users to use personalized desktop settings each time they log on to a computer. Multiple users sharing a single computer can customize their own desktops and load them at logon time. Conversely, a single user can move between computers using the same profile by storing the profile on the server. An administrator can also take advantage of profiles to require that a mandatory desktop configuration be loaded each time a user logs on. The ability to change profile settings can be controlled by the administrator. For information about how to use user profiles, see Chapter 15, "User Profiles and System Policies," in the *Microsoft Windows 95 Resource Kit.*

User profiles are not needed when only one person uses the computer or when a custom desktop adds no value. By not enabling user profiles, the logon process is shortened slightly, because the system does not need to locate and load the profile.

Install Windows

Before you can install Microsoft Office for Windows 95, you need to have already installed Microsoft Windows 95 or Microsoft Windows NT on your server and client systems. The first step, then, is to work through the deployment process for Windows 95 or Windows NT (or both if you will be using a combination of these operating systems in your configuration).

Review and Install Windows 95 or Windows NT

Task	Team	Start week	Duration
☐ **1:** Acquire the *Microsoft Windows 95 Resource Kit* or the *Microsoft Windows NT Resource Kit* (or both as needed).	Executive, Planning	Week 1	1 day
☐ **2:** Install Microsoft Windows 95 or Microsoft Windows NT (or both as needed) on client and server systems.	Executive, Planning	Week 1	†

† The amount of time necessary to install Windows depends on the version of Windows being installed. See the appropriate *Resource Kit* for details.

1: Acquire the Microsoft Windows Resource Kit

The *Microsoft Windows 95 Resource Kit* and the *Microsoft Windows NT Resource Kit* are technical supplements to the Windows product documentation, written to assist administrators in installing, supporting, and managing Windows on corporate networks. Both are available from Microsoft Press (1-800-MSPRESS) and many larger bookstores.

2: Install Windows 95 or Windows NT

Using the *Microsoft Windows 95 Resource Kit* for Windows 95 or the *Microsoft Windows NT Resource Kit* for Windows NT, the team responsible for deploying Windows needs to install Windows on each client and server system that will be running Microsoft Office for Windows 95 or from which you will be running Office Setup (the Setup program for Microsoft Office for Windows 95 requires windows NT or Windows 95).

Review Office for Windows 95

When Office is implemented, it can yield significant benefits to your organization. The first step in beginning to plan the rollout process is to closely examine the new and enhanced features in Office.

Office is designed to make deployment easy in the corporate environment. By understanding how best to plan and automate the installation process, you can potentially reduce the cost of migration.

Review Office for Windows 95 Features

Task	Team	Start week	Duration
☐ **1:** Read "A Guided Tour to Microsoft Office for Windows 95" or the *Microsoft Office for Windows 95 Evaluation Guide.*	Executive, Planning	Week 1	3 days
☐ **2:** Review the *Microsoft Office for Windows 95 Resource Kit.*	Planning	Week 2	1 day

1: Read about the Office for Windows 95 features

At the beginning of this book is "A Guided Tour to Microsoft Office for Windows 95." This provides a quick summary to many of the new features in Office. For more details, you may want to review the *Microsoft Office for Windows 95 Evaluation Guide,* which provides an overview of Office features and is a guide to evaluating Office in terms of your company's productivity. For a copy of the *Evaluation Guide*, contact Microsoft Customer Service at (800) 426-9400. Ask for part number 098-60004.

2: Review the Microsoft Office for Windows 95 Resource Kit

This book, the *Microsoft Office for Windows 95 Resource Kit*, is a technical supplement to the Office product documentation, written to assist administrators in installing, supporting, and managing Office on corporate networks. Each Planning and Installation team member should obtain a copy of the *Resource Kit* for use during the deployment process.

Assemble the Planning Team and Tools

After the assigned teams complete the review phase and have a general perspective on Office features and benefits, you are ready to assemble the people and tools needed to plan the Office implementation. The tasks for assembling the resources are described in the following checklist.

Assemble the Planning Team and Tools

Task	Team	Start week	Duration
☐ **1:** Assign the project manager (if appropriate; usually this is the head of the Information Systems department).	Planning	Week 1	—
☐ **2:** Select key Planning and Installation team members.	Planning	Week 1	5 days
☐ **3:** Acquire Office.	Planning	Week 1	1 day
☐ **4:** Inventory your client and server hardware and software configurations on the network.	Planning	Week 2	5 days
☐ **5:** Set up a testing lab.	Planning	Week 2	1 day
☐ **6:** Acquire test computers for use as the network server and clients. Choose computer models that are typical of those used in your organization.	Planning	Week 2	5 days
☐ **7:** Install the Microsoft Windows 95 and networking software in the lab to simulate the network environment.	Planning, Installation	Week 2	3 days
☐ **8:** Have the Installation team review product features in "A Guided Tour to Microsoft Office for Windows 95" or the *Office for Windows 95 Evaluation Guide;* also have them study Part 2, "Installing Microsoft Office for Windows 95," in this book.	Planning, Installation	Week 3	3 days
☐ **9:** If needed, send team members to a Microsoft Authorized Technical Education Center for additional training.	Installation, Support, Training	Week 3	3 days

1–2: Assign the Project Manager and Planning Teams

The deployment project manager participates in the Executive team and leads the Planning team. This individual is usually the head of the Information Systems department; however, the executive committee may find another individual to be more appropriate, depending on the organization.

When setting up the Planning team, it is important to include a set of individuals representing the groups involved in the deployment process. This includes people from Corporate Support and Employee Training departments, the Corporate Standards Committee, and key Installation team members. Individuals from the Finance and Accounting group will need to take part in planning and evaluation later on, but need not be assigned to the team for the duration of the process.

4: Inventory Client and Server Hardware and Software Configurations

You'll need to survey a representative sample of your network to compile an inventory of hardware and software used on client and server computers. When this inventory is compiled, you can accurately simulate the organizational environment in the lab. Such a simulation helps you make broad decisions about your organization's computing infrastructure, such as the default desktop configuration.

Software management tools can be used to query computers on the network for their hardware and software configurations. For example, the Microsoft Diagnostics (MSD) tool can run a report describing a computer's specific hardware and settings and put the output in a text file. For more detailed information about a large number of computers on a network, you can use system management programs, such as the Microsoft Systems Management Server, to conduct the inventory. In addition, Systems Management Server allows you to query the database and quickly get information about which equipment is capable of running Office and which equipment might need upgrading.

5–8: Set Up a Testing Lab and Equipment

To effectively evaluate and test the Office installation process, you need to set aside enough physical space and assemble a sufficient number of computers to test everything from Server-Based Setup to hand-tuning options for the local computer. It is important that you comprehensively test and implement all of the key Office features in the lab with all of your business-specific applications before moving to the pilot installation. If you have created custom solutions in Office, you will want to test those as well. Be aware that 32-bit applications cannot call 16-bit DLLs or make calls to the 16-bit Windows API. So, if your applications call special DLLs that you created or make Windows 3.x API calls, you may need to update these calls. In addition, it is important to ensure that basic operating system functions are working before installing Microsoft Office. These functions include:

- Booting successfully
- Connecting to a server
- Printing

9: Send Team Members to a Microsoft Authorized Technical Education Center (Optional)

For information about authorized training offered for Office, call
(800) SOLPROV ((800) 765-7768) for a referral to a local Microsoft Solution
Provider Authorized Technical Education Center (ATEC), or call the Microsoft
Fax Server at (800) 727-3351 and request document number 10000256 for the
location of the Authorized Academic Training Program (AATP) site nearest you.
Microsoft ATECs and Microsoft AATPs offer Microsoft Official Curriculum
delivered by Microsoft Certified Trainers to educate computer professionals on
Microsoft technology.

Specify the Preferred Client Configuration

With the Planning team assembled and educated on Office capabilities, the next
step is to specify the preferred configuration for client computers to be used for
evaluation and testing prior to full implementation. For the purpose of this
discussion, *client computer* refers to any computer running Office.

There are four parts to specifying the client computer configuration:

1. **Research**   Understand the current server and client configurations.
2. **Office Features**   Select which features will be used in the preferred
   configuration on client computers.
3. **Workgroup Features**   Select which features will be used to enable users to
   work together.
4. **Installation Planning**   Decide where Office files will be located and how they
   will be installed. That is, will Office files be installed onto the client
   computer's local hard disk, or will they be installed onto a server and accessed
   remotely by the client computer, or a combination of both?

For any given feature or capability there may be several options to choose from.
Before making a decision, evaluate the features and consider the alternatives—
including whether to use them at all. Then choose the appropriate implementation
based on its performance, functionality, compatibility, and maintainability.

Although you can use other methods to determine the preferred client
configuration, Microsoft recommends that you start from the complete
configuration, which uses all of the most powerful features of Office, and then
work backward to a configuration that may have fewer features but more closely
fits your company's needs. The selected configuration and any modifications will
be rigorously tested in your lab before company-wide implementation.

The following tables list the features and capabilities of the complete configuration and related alternatives, plus the chapters where these features are discussed later in this book. Use this table, checking off the features you plan to implement. To learn more about these features, see the related chapters in this book.

Specify the Preferred Client Configuration

Task	Decisions and issues	Reference
☐ **1:** Research current configuration variables	Catalog your current network and client system configurations for the following: ☐ Hardware configuration ☐ Network topology ☐ Existing configurations to migrate ☐ Multiple platforms ☐ IS Department Policies	See specific references given later in this section
☐ **2:** Select Office standard features	Review the Microsoft Office for Windows 95 feature set and decide which to install for the client	See "A Guided Tour to Microsoft Office for Windows 95" or the *Microsoft Office for Windows 95 Evaluation Guide*
☐ **3:** Select Office workgroup features	Decide which special Office features to install for the client: ☐ Group scheduling with Schedule+ ☐ Using Word as your email editor ☐ Workgroup templates ☐ Sendmail and routing features of MAPI and VIM ☐ Windows 95 Briefcase support, especially for Microsoft Access databases	See specific references given below
☐ **4:** Decide on configuration and installation options	Decide on the following configuration options: ☐ Location of Office files ☐ Installation options ☐ Installation media ☐ Installation method	See Chapter 8, "Installing Microsoft Office"

1: Research Current Configuration Variables

To successfully deploy Microsoft Office for Windows 95, you need to understand your current hardware and software configurations. Your deployment plan will be dictated by your current system environments:

- **Hardware Configuration**   Researching the current hardware configurations in your organization will help you understand the steps that will be necessary to deploy Office. Specifically, you need to check:

  - Minimum Hardware Requirements—To understand what your minimum hardware requirements will be and to decide if any of your computers need to be upgraded, see Appendix E, "System Requirements for Office for Windows 95."

Note   Schedule+ requires a Windows-compatible network and MAPI 1.0-enabled mail server for scheduling and workgroup functionality.

  - Laptops vs. Desktop Computers—Laptop and desktop users have different configurations, including disk space and access to the network. Installation options will need to be selected with the user's specific computer in mind.
  - Network Access—Users without network access will need Office software installed locally from CD or floppy disks. Users with network access can install Office from the network and can share Office files over the network.

- **Network Topology**   The network can be used in two ways for deploying Office for Windows 95: software can be installed on client computers from a network server, and Office applications can be run over the network from a server. You may need to have different configurations for the differing levels of network connectivity within your organization.

  - WAN connections—For client computers connected over a slow-link network, it may not be practical to either install or run Office remotely over the network.
  - Network operating systems in use—You need to consider how your particular network operating system (NOS) affects your plans for deploying Office. Some of the issues include server file sharing methods and client-server permission schemes.
  - Network bandwidth—Understanding your network capacity, as well as the performance expectations of your users, will help you make decisions about Office client configurations. Installing Office over the network and executing Office applications over the network place different demands on network bandwidth, both in terms of response time and length of time connected.

- **Migrating Existing Configurations** For existing users, whether they are users of Office applications or competitive applications, planning for migrating these users is critical. You need to determine if you need to convert existing files, macros, and custom programs, and how to train users. For more information, see Chapter 10, "Upgrading to Office for Windows 95", and Part 5, "Switching from Other Applications."

- **Supporting Multiple Platforms** In many large organizations, users are running Office on a variety of supported platforms. Microsoft has worked to make this as seamless as possible, but because the operating systems are different, and because Office for Windows 95 does include new features, it is important to understand any differences across the platforms.

  For more information about these issues, see Chapter 13, "Running Multiple Versions of Microsoft Office."

- **IS Department Policies** Planning the deployment of Windows 95 and Office for Windows 95 provides a good opportunity to review department policies concerning centralized system configuration control versus individual user control. For information about using batch and push installations to standardize client installations, see Chapter 9, "Customizing Client Installations." For information about using Windows 95 system policies to configure client computers from a central location, see Chapter 11, "Maintaining, Customizing, and Optimizing Office."

2: Select Office Standard Features

By reviewing the feature set of Office, you can determine how best to configure your client computers for the needs of your users. Because you can choose which components of Office are installed, you have a lot of flexibility in tailoring client installations to include the best set of features for your users, while reducing disk space usage. "A Guided Tour to Microsoft Office for Windows 95" or the *Microsoft Office for Windows 95 Evaluation Guide* discusses the Office feature set.

3: Select Office Workgroup Features

There are some workgroup features in Office that you can select to establish how your users will communicate and work together.

- **Group Scheduling with Schedule+** The group calendaring functions of Schedule+ require an underlying mail client, Microsoft Exchange, which is part of Windows 95. The small-business mail system that comes with Windows 95 allows users to exchange mail and meeting requests, through a single post office. Microsoft Exchange can also work with other mail systems as long as the mail system uses a valid MAPI 1.0 driver. Such systems include Microsoft Mail and Microsoft Exchange Server.

For more information about using Schedule+ in workgroup mode, see "Schedule+ Installation Issues" in Chapter 8, "Installing Microsoft Office." For more information about Microsoft Exchange, see Chapter 26, "Electronic Mail and Microsoft Exchange," in the *Microsoft Windows 95 Resource Kit.*

- **Using Word as Your E-mail Editor**   Microsoft Word for Windows 95 can be used to replace the default text editor used in the Microsoft Exchange mail client that is included with Windows 95. This gives the user access to all the Word editing and formatting features from within the Microsoft Exchange client. To use this feature, Microsoft Exchange in Windows 95 must be installed first on the user's computer. Then, when Office is installed, choose the Custom install; WordMail is one of the customization options for Word.

  For more information about using Word in this way, see the section "Mail-Enabling Applications" in Chapter 15.

- **Workgroup Templates**   Users can share template files for Office documents using the Workgroup Template setting in Office. This setting, maintained in each user's registry, specifies a folder in which Office document templates may be stored for users. By defining this to be a folder on a network server, users in a workgroup can have access to a common set of templates. You can use the Windows 95 Policy Editor to define this setting for your users rather than having them set it individually.

  For more information about Workgroup Templates in Office, see "Shared Code" in Chapter 1. For information about using the Windows 95 Policy Editor for remotely setting user registry entries, see "Customizing the User Environment" in Chapter 11.

- **MAPI and VIM**   The Office applications include commands to send and route documents via e-mail. These commands work with Simple MAPI and MAPI 1.0 or greater systems, such as Microsoft Mail 3.*x* and the Microsoft Exchange client included with Windows 95, and with 16-bit VIM-based mail systems such as cc:Mail and Lotus Notes®.

  For more information about setting up mail support in Office, see "Mail-Enabling Applications" in Chapter 15.

- **Briefcase Support**   Microsoft Office for Windows 95 supports the Windows 95 Briefcase, which allows users to synchronize different versions of a file whether or not they are on the same hard disk drive or on the network. Microsoft Access, in particular, provides the capability of doing individual database replication using Briefcase.

  For more information about using Briefcase with Microsoft Access, see Chapter 16, "Microsoft Access Database Replication." For more general information about using Briefcase in Windows 95, see "Using Briefcase for File Synchronization" in Chapter 28 of the *Microsoft Windows 95 Resource Kit.*

4: Decide on Configuration and Installation Options

When you understand the variables in your organization and how they will affect the manner in which you deploy Office, you can decide on the configuration for the preferred client. You will make decisions in the following four areas.

- **Location of Office Files**   When deciding where to place Office files, consider how the client computer will be used and evaluate the benefits of each placement option, including how each option will affect your ability to support these configurations over the long run. Both Windows and Office have the option of being *local* (files are installed onto the client computer's local hard disk) or being *shared* (files are located on a network server and users share those files over the network). Office has the additional option of putting some files on the local hard disk and some files on the server.

- **Installation Options**   There are several basic installation options available in the Office Setup program when Setup is run interactively by the user. You can also create your own customized option if the Setup program is to be run in batch mode using a customized script. For more information, see Chapter 8, "Installing Microsoft Office" and Chapter 9, "Customizing Client Installation."

- **Installation Media**   Office can be installed on a user's computer from the CD or floppy disks, or Office files can be placed on a network server and installed onto client computers over the network. Each option has its own advantages and disadvantages, and they are discussed in detail in Chapter 8, "Installing Microsoft Office."

- **Installation Method**   There are three methods that can be used to perform the installation on the client computers:

    - Interactive—allows the user to make all installation decisions.

    - Batch—provides a preset installation script for the user.

    - Push—initiates the installation for the user without user intervention.

    A complete discussion of all these options can be found in Chapter 9, "Customizing Client Installations."

Conduct the Lab Test

Using the client configuration that you have developed on paper, the people and tools assembled earlier for the Planning team now need to install this configuration in the lab for testing and evaluation. You should install Office on your test system in the same way that you plan to install Office on your users' systems. This means setting up the network installation location on the server and then installing Office on the test client system from the server.

Depending on how the test installation proceeds, it may be necessary to modify the configuration, by either adding or removing selected features. If more than one configuration is being considered, side-by-side evaluations of different configurations can be performed to help determine which one works best.

The tasks in the following checklist apply for each computer used to install a client configuration. For step-by-step instructions on installing and selecting features, see Chapter 8, "Installing Microsoft Office," and Chapter 9, "Customizing Client Installations."

Conduct the Lab Test

Task		Team	Start week	Duration
□	**1:** Use Administrative Setup to install Office files on a server. Make setup choices based on your client configuration. Document any customizations done.	Installation	Week 4	0.5 day
□	**2:** Before running Office Setup, make sure that the client computers meet your company's standards and the Office minimum standards for operation. If not, perform the hardware upgrades now.	Installation	Week 4	1 day
□	**3:** Defragment the hard disks and scan for viruses. Create an MSD report and copy it to a floppy disk.	Installation	Week 4	1 day
□	**4:** Back up and verify key data and configuration files.	Installation	Week 4	0.5 day
□	**5:** Ensure that the current network client software is fully operational and that all important applications operate correctly.	Installation	Week 4	0.1 day
□	**6:** Install Office on the test computers in the lab, using your preferred client configuration.	Planning, Installation	Week 4	2 days
□	**7:** Test the installation: • Can you open, run, and close applications? • Can you use the major Office features, including opening, modifying, saving, and printing documents? • Can you shut down successfully?	Planning, Installation	Week 4	2 days
□	**8:** Optionally, if you have several test computers, compare your old client configuration and your new preferred configuration. How do the two compare in terms of functionality, performance, ease of use, stability, and compatibility with other applications and hardware?	Planning, Installation	Week 5	3 days
□	**9:** If the specified client configuration did not work as expected, modify it, documenting the changes until a working preferred client configuration is installed.	Planning, Installation	Week 5	As required

Conduct the Lab Test *(continued)*

Task	Team	Start week	Duration
☐ **10:** Perform a complete uninstall of Office files (using the uninstall option of Office Setup) on a computer running Office.	Installation	Week 5	1 day
☐ **11:** Evaluate the uninstall process for problems. Make any necessary corrections, and then document the process.	Installation, Planning	Week 5	0.5 day

1: Create the Administrative Installation Server Share

For client systems to install Office over the network, you first create a network installation server share by performing an administrative setup of Office from the Office Installation CD or floppy disk set. You can modify the files in this share to customize the client installations, including whether clients will run Office locally or on the network. For information about creating and customizing a network installation location, see Chapter 8, "Installing Microsoft Office," and Chapter 9, "Customizing Client Installations." Be sure to document how you customize the installation.

2–4: Prepare the Test Site

Preparing the site involves ensuring that the location of each computer, the computer itself, the hard disk, and the data are all ready for Office to be installed. In terms of the physical site, ensure that you have the appropriate network connection hardware. You may require power supplies and surge protectors for your computers, depending on the number of computers used for testing. Also, research and eliminate the potential for problems related to overheating or frequency distortion from the location.

In terms of the computer itself, ensure that it has the enough hard disk space, RAM, and processing capability to run Office. To review the requirements for Office, see Appendix E, "System Requirements for Office for Windows 95."

In addition, run virus detection, disk scanning, and defragmentation programs on the computer to prevent any later problems prior to installation. Although the computer may appear to be operating properly, software upgrades often uncover hardware or software problems, because of the way they read and write data to the hard disk. Checking the computer before installing Office will help you stay focused on issues related to the installation process.

Lastly, when preparing the site, be sure to back up critical data and configuration files for the system, in case the installation fails or you need to revert to the old system for some reason. You should also create a Microsoft Diagnostics (MSD) report and copy it to a floppy disk by running Msd.exe on the hard disk. If you need to automate the restoration, consider using a commercial backup program, instead of copying the files by hand.

5–6: Install Office for Windows 95 on Test Computers

Before setting up Office for the first time, verify that the computer's existing network is fully operational. Then use Chapter 8, "Installing Microsoft Office," to help you install and configure Office correctly. Chapter 9, "Customizing Client Installations," includes instructions on how to automate the installation process using batch scripts. Take note of which options you want to pre-define in the setup batch script.

7–9: Test the Installation

After you have set up a computer with Office, you will need to run a variety of tests to ensure that it runs correctly and that you can still perform all of your usual tasks. Use your own testing methodology or test the following to verify correct system operation:

- Open, run, and close Office applications.
- Use the major Office features, including opening, modifying, saving, and printing documents.
- Open existing files in the new Office applications.
- If the client is using shared components on the network, such as spell-checking, exercise these functions.
- If the client is using a shared Windows installation, exercise standard Windows functions such as printing.
- Shut down completely.

In addition to ensuring that the preferred client configuration works as expected, you may also want to conduct additional testing of optional software features and components. This can help you determine whether you are running Office optimally. For this kind of testing, conduct side-by-side evaluations on two computers, changing individual features on each one, to determine the following:

- Performance in terms of responsiveness and throughput for local disk and network actions.
- Ease of use for performing common tasks.
- Stability of the two computers under stress.
- Compatibility with applications and hardware.

10–11: Test the Uninstall Process

Having thoroughly tested the preferred network client, completely remove Office from one of the test computers to restore the previous client configuration, and document the process. Office files are removed by rerunning Office Setup and selecting the Uninstall option.

Plan the Pilot Rollout

A previous phase helped to determine the best client configuration for Office. In this phase, appointed teams will determine the best methods for automatically installing the specified configuration for a pilot or trial rollout. Planning for this pilot program involves creating the automated installation process, determining the logistics of testing, and preparing a training plan for users.

Automating the installation is a key step in reducing the cost of migration. By creating a batch script with predetermined answers for installation questions, the installation process can run from start to finish without user intervention. It is also possible to push the installation from the server, so that you can install Office on an individual personal computer without ever touching the computer. This automation work is done in the lab, prior to conducting the pilot rollout.

Plan the Pilot Rollout

Task		Team	Start week	Duration
☐ **1:**	Use Administrative Setup to install Office files on a server. Customize this installation based on your client configuration.	Planning, Installation	Week 6	2 days
☐ **2:**	Create and test an automated installation by creating a batch script to pre-define settings for Setup. Document the key parts of the batch script that vary by installation.	Planning, Installation	Week 6	3 days
☐ **3:**	Determine and test how you will push the installation from the server without having to touch the client computers (see Chapter 9, "Customizing Client Installations").	Planning, Installation	Week 6	2 days
	Options:			
	▪ Modify login scripts on the server.			
	▪ Use management software such as Microsoft System Management Server.			
	▪ Send a batch file that runs Office Setup as an embedded link in an electronic mail message.			
☐ **4:**	Document the process for the rest of the Installation team.	Planning, Installation	Week 6	1 day

Plan the Pilot Rollout *(continued)*

Task		Team	Start week	Duration
☐ **5:**	Evaluate the Office installation process for opportunities to upgrade or improve your organization's existing technology infrastructure. For example, a system management software tool can help you administer computers on the network more easily, and it can help with the push installation process.	Planning, Executive	Week 6	2 days
☐ **6:**	Document the logistics of the pilot installation. This includes the total time for installation, the purchase of new software or tools, selection of the pilot user group, and scheduling of specific installations.	Planning, Installation	Week 7	3 days
☐ **7:**	Prepare a memo for your users to clearly explain how the installation process will affect their daily work schedule and describe the differences they will see after the installation is completed.	Planning	Week 7	1 day
☐ **8:**	Establish a support plan for the pilot user group. This includes a contact name and phone number for assistance, a short list of the top questions and answers, and troubleshooting tips.	Planning, Support	Week 7	3 days
☐ **9:**	Prepare a user training course (or hire a training vendor to prepare one). Use the *Getting Results with Microsoft Office* manual to jump-start your training efforts.	Planning, Support, Training	Week 5	10 days
☐ **10:**	Set up the lab or classroom with computers for hands-on training.	Training	Week 6	5 days

1: Install the Source Files for Setup

You need to designate a network server that will be used as the source for installing Office over the network during the pilot rollout. Then use administrative Setup to install Office source files on the server.

You must make choices based on your client configuration, including whether client computers will run a shared copy of Office from the server, or run Office locally from the hard disk.

For step-by-step instructions, see Chapter 8, "Installing Microsoft Office." Document any changes to this process.

2: Automate the Installation

To automate the installation, create a batch script and create a push installation process.

With a batch script you can perform a hands-free installation, so that the user need not respond to any prompts or even touch the computer during Office Setup.

When you run Administrative Setup to install source files on the server, you also create a default setup script. You can specify whether the Office source files on the server will be used to set up Office to run locally from a single computer or to run a shared copy from the server for client computers that require a shared installation.

In addition, you can modify this script to customize how installed clients are configured. You may also want to manually add other files to the shared folder on the server, such as custom templates or forms, so that client computers are fully configured when Office is installed.

For more information, see Chapter 9, "Customizing Client Installations."

3: Create the Push Installation Process

Creating a push installation process involves doing some additional work on the server. This includes editing the login script for the user, or sending a link in electronic mail to a batch file that runs Office Setup. System management software such as Microsoft Systems Management Server can also be used to start the installation centrally.

For more information, see Chapter 9, "Customizing Client Installations."

4–7: Document the Logistics of a Pilot Installation

Part of the planning for a pilot installation includes determining the timing and the process for pilot installation, choosing the pilot user group, and communicating to the group about the pilot rollout.

Even though you are just testing the installation process, the first pilot sets the tone and presents an example of the final rollout, so it is important that you are completely prepared with all aspects of the rollout. You'll need to determine the time it will take for installation, the personnel, the tools needed to facilitate the process, and the overall schedule.

Estimates of the installation time should be based on an individual computer installation; be sure to schedule the computer downtime for each user. Also, in obtaining tools for the pilot rollout, you may want to include management or debugging software that can help automate the installation.

It's important to choose a pilot user group that is interested in and capable of being the first test case. For example, choosing a pilot group that is close to a schedule deadline on a project, or a group that is traditionally slow in adopting new technology is likely to increase the difficulty of the pilot installation.

Another step at this stage is informing users about the pilot rollout plan. You can use a videotape presentation, an interoffice memo, or a company meeting as the means for communicating with users about the rollout. Regardless of the form used, the message must explain the benefits to users in moving to Office, and describe the overall plan and process by which each group or department will make the move. This makes it easier for your users to plan for and accept the migration to Office as part of their schedules.

8: Develop the Support Plan

Similar to the training plan, the support plan must be in place the first day you begin performing Office installations. The quality of support available during the pilot rollout will be seen as an indicator of the quality of the rollout as a whole.

Staff the Support team for your pilot rollout with some of your best technicians dedicated solely to the pilot group for the first few weeks. The assigned technicians should carry pagers or be available by phone at all times, to give immediate assistance to users.

Track the volume of support calls during the pilot to gauge what effect rolling out Office 95 will have on your support staff. You may want to be able to plan for additional staffing as you roll it out, or use this information to determine the rollout schedule.

9–10: Develop the User Training Plan

The interface for Microsoft Office for Windows 95 has not changed greatly since Microsoft Office 4.*x*. In addition, the new user assistance model and tools make it easier for a user to learn the product without having to go through formal training. Therefore, you may not even have to setup up formal training classes for users of Microsoft Office 4.*x*.

For those users who do not have experience with Microsoft Office 4.*x*, the first steps in developing a training plan are to acquire a training lab, set up computers in the lab, and appoint a team member as instructor. The instructor will be responsible for creating and testing the training program. If in-house resources are not available, use a vendor to develop and conduct the training.

There are numerous training approaches and a variety of tools you can use. After creating and testing the program, schedule training sessions to occur immediately before the installation date. This will ensure that users retain most of what they learn by putting it to use immediately. It is also important that they are trained before they actually must use the software. You may want to conduct this training while user computers are being upgraded.

Conduct the Pilot Rollout

The goal of the pilot program is to test your automated installation in everyday use among a limited group of users (for example, between 15 and 50). This process will help to identify problems that may impede or delay the deployment process, and to determine what resources you will require for the final, company-wide rollout. The pilot rollout will also set the tone for the rest of the deployment process; a successful pilot rollout will help other installations run smoothly by stimulating the cooperation and enthusiasm of your organization's users.

Conduct the Pilot Rollout

Task	Team	Start week	Duration
☐ **1:** Select a pilot user group that is willing and able (particularly in terms of their workload) to handle the installation process.	Planning	Week 6	2 days
☐ **2:** Train the users.	Training	Week 7	2 days
☐ **3:** Back up the test computers.	Installation	Week 7	3 days
☐ **4:** Perform the installation in the same manner that you expect to install Office throughout the company.	Installation	Week 8	10 days (assuming non-push installation on 50 machines)
☐ **5:** Have your technicians on-site for the initial installations to document the process and problems, and to support the users. Have other technicians monitor time and all measurable factors in the installation process.	Support	Week 8	10 days
☐ **6:** Ensure that all computers are "up and running" as expected. Document areas in which the installation, training, or support can be improved.	Planning, Installation, Support	Weeks 8–9	As steps 4 and 5 take place
☐ **7:** Survey members of the pilot user group about their satisfaction with the installation process and take feedback on what could have been done better.	Planning	Week 9	3 days
☐ **8:** Continue to monitor the pilot installation for a week or more to ensure that everything continues to run smoothly.	Support, Planning	Week 10	5 days
☐ **9:** If the pilot program did not run smoothly or user feedback was poor, conduct additional pilot installations until the process works well.	Planning, Installation	Week 11	See "Plan the Pilot Rollout"

4: Simulate the Installation Process

The schedule for the pilot rollout should simulate—on a smaller scale—the schedule of the final rollout. As you conduct the pilot rollout, you may find that certain tasks take more or less time than expected, that some tasks need to be added, or that some tasks can be avoided. Modify the pilot rollout schedule to account for such changes, and use the revised pilot schedule for projecting the final rollout timetable.

5: Test Office for Windows 95 Performance and Capabilities

In addition to the technicians responsible for conducting the pilot installation, extra technicians should be assigned to measure, observe, and test the installation. By tracking the time per installation, handling problems that arise, and identifying areas for improvement or automation, these individuals help ensure the success of both the pilot and final rollouts.

In addition, after Office is installed, these technicians test system capabilities, such as remote administration, for proper operation and monitor the client computers for performance, stability, and functionality, highlighting any inconsistencies with the lab configuration.

7–9: Survey and Adjust Based on User Feedback

The final part of the pilot rollout involves surveying the users to gauge their satisfaction and proficiency with the new installation and to evaluate the level of training and support provided. Test users' proficiency by having them perform a few common tasks or use several of the new features in Office. For example, have these users register their survey results in an Access application on the server.

Finalize the Rollout Plan

The results of the pilot installation provide the basis for developing a final plan for rollout. Using the actual time and resource requirements from the smaller-scale pilot rollout, teams make projections for time and resources, corresponding to the company-wide scope of the final rollout. If additional resources are required, these should be identified and acquired at this time. In addition, company policies and standards regarding computer and network use should be updated in accordance with the Office implementation.

Finalize the Rollout Plan

Task	Team	Start week	Duration
☐ **1:** Determine your rollout goals—specifically the number of computers on which you will install Office and the time expected for completion.	Planning, Executive	Week 11	1 days
☐ **2:** Budget the resources, in terms of personnel and tools, required to meet your goals.	Planning	Week 11	1 days
☐ **3:** If necessary, present and obtain approval for the resources and the rollout process.	Executive, Planning	Week 11	2 days
☐ **4:** Hire and train the extended Installation and Support teams and purchase the additional software or tools needed.	Training, Installation, Support	Week 11	5 days
☐ **5:** Update the company's hardware and software standards lists.	Planning	Week 11	2 days
☐ **6:** Update the company's policies and practices manuals or guidelines for use of computers and the network.	Planning	Week 11	2 days
☐ **7:** Before beginning the installation, notify your users that company standards and policies for computer use will be enforced and that they must bring their computers into compliance. Alternatively, you could give them a plan on how you will help them get into compliance.	Planning	Week 11	1 day
☐ **8:** Create a registration template or worksheet that lists the specific configurations and uses of each computer. Be sure to leave room to document any system problems or deficiencies that require further attention.	Installation	Week 12	1 day
☐ **9:** Post the updated registration template to a central network location.	Installation	Week 12	1 day

2–4: Document, Budget, and Carry Out the Logistics

As you prepare for final rollout, estimate the length and scope of the overall installation process. Also plan for all tools needed to complete the process within the stated time frame. If necessary, propose a formal budget for the company-wide implementation and present it to management for approval. Your budget should include the costs for personnel and additional resources, such as systems management software.

After obtaining approval (if necessary), purchase the resources required to facilitate the installation. If you need additional staff, be sure to hire experienced and qualified individuals for the team, and train them completely before starting the project.

Complete your training, communication, and staffing plans for the final rollout at this time.

5–7: Update the Policies and Practices Guidelines

Before beginning final rollout, update all company policies regarding the use of the network and computers by employees. In addition, update the corporate standards lists for software usage so that you can bring all computers up to compliance during the installation process.

8–9: Create and Post the Registration Template

A registration template is used to create a central database for monitoring the progress of the rollout and document any areas requiring further action. As you prepare for final rollout, create the template using appropriate database management software, include configuration information for every computer and user in the company, and place the template on the server. Then, as Office is installed during final rollout, the Installation team fills in the template for each computer and user, indicating if any additional upgrading is needed. The team can then use the template to track open items following the rollout and to measure actual progress against original objectives.

Roll Out Office for Windows 95

After the extensive research, planning, testing, and analysis performed in the previous phases, the final step in the deployment process is rolling out the Office installation to your entire organization.

Roll Out Office for Windows 95

Task	Team	Start week	Duration
☐ **1:** Set up the distribution servers by using the administrative Setup and configuring any system policy files.	Installation	Week 12	3 days
☐ **2:** Customize the server installation by modifying the setup script and by adding or removing the appropriate files.	Installation	Week 12	2 days
☐ **3:** Notify the users of the upcoming installation.	Planning	Week 12	1 day
☐ **4:** Train the users on Office.	Training	Week 13	As required
☐ **5:** If needed, upgrade the hardware on the client computers and remove any software not complying with company policy.	Installation	Week 13	As required
☐ **6:** If needed, back up critical data and configuration files on the client computers.	Installation	Week 13	As required
☐ **7:** If needed, defragment the client hard disks.	Installation	Week 13	As required
☐ **8:** Optionally, you can temporarily reset the user password and ID for each computer, to allow your technicians easy access to the client computer and ensure that the logon scripts and environment operate correctly.	Planning	Week 14	As required

Roll Out Office for Windows 95 *(continued)*

Task	Team	Start week	Duration
☐ **9:** Ensure that the client computers are fully operational.	Installation	Week 14	As required
☐ **10:** Prepare the client computers for the push installation process: edit the logon scripts; run the management software; or send the batch file for setup to the user by electronic mail.	Installation	Week 14	As required
☐ **11:** Initiate the installation by having the user log on, double-click the batch file, or use whatever mechanism you have created for triggering the installation process.	Installation	Week 15	As required

Maintenance and Support

Now that you have rolled out Microsoft Office for Windows 95, there will be a continuing need to maintain, update, and support your users. For specific ongoing help in keeping your users productive with Office, continue using this book, especially Part 3, "Maintaining and Supporting Microsoft Office," Part 4, "Running Multiple Versions of Office and Using Office in a Workgroup," Part 5, "Switching from Other Applications," and Appendix F, "Resources."

C H A P T E R   8

Installing Microsoft Office

This chapter describes the most basic installation process for Microsoft Office for Windows 95. Because there is a lot of flexibility in the installation process, the chapter begins with the installation planning process and installation options, and is followed by specific procedures for you to follow as you install Office.

If your Office setup needs to be customized, the next chapter, "Customizing Client Installations," covers how to alter Office Setup to customize the installation process for your specific needs.

In This Chapter

Installation Planning

Before beginning the process of installing Office on your users' computers, you need to make some decisions about the installation and plan the process. There are a number of options to choose from in the following main areas.

Decision	Description
1. Location of Office files	**Where Office files are installed**
Local hard disk	All files are installed on user's local hard disk.
Server	Files are shared on the network server.
Both	Some components are installed locally, and some are shared on the server.
Shared Windows	Used with any of the above options, system files are installed in a shared Windows environment.

Decision	Description
2. Installation options	**Which Office files are installed**
Typical	Installs common Office files.
Compact	Installs minimum Office files.
Custom	User selects which Office files to install.
Run from CD	Leaves some files on CD to save disk space.
3. Installation media	**Where Office files are coming from**
Physical media	Floppy disks or CD.
Network	Central network share.
4. Installation method	**How the installation is done**
Interactive	User runs Setup interactively.
Batch	Setup runs unattended.
Push	Setup is initiated without user intervention.
5. Application-specific installation issues	Issues that affect what must already be installed, such as a mail system, and what you install for the individual Office applications.

Some of these decisions affect others. For instance, if client installations are from physical media, then all files must be installed locally and the only installation method available is interactive.

Location of Office Files

When deciding where to place Office files, consider how the client computer will be used and evaluate the benefits of each placement option, including how each option will affect your ability to support these configurations over the long run.

Both Windows and Office have the option of being *local* (files are installed on the client computer's local hard disk) or being *shared* (files are located on a network server and users share those files over the network).

Consider the following as you make this decision:

- **Performance**   What is the performance on the client computer when executing Windows or Office software? Executing Windows software and Office applications locally is generally faster than executing them over the network.
- **Disk space**   How much local disk space is available on the client computer for Office software? Sharing software from a server reduces the disk space needed on a client computer's local hard disk, while it increases the need for disk space on the server.

- **Maintenance and support** How do you install new software in your organization and how are updates to Windows or Office software distributed to users? Software on a server can be maintained and updated more easily than software on client computers.

- **Availability** Is Windows and Office software available when the user needs it? Software installed locally is always available to the user, while software shared from a server is available only when the network is up and the server is running.

Client computers can be configured to run under any combination of these environments:

	Local Windows, local Office	Shared Windows, shared Office	Shared Windows, partially shared Office[1]
Performance	Best overall	Lowest overall	Compromise for Office, lowest for Windows
Disk space	Highest local usage, lowest server usage	Lowest local usage, highest server usage	Split between client and server computers
Maintenance/ support	No central control complicates task	Simplifies control for both Office and Windows	Simplifies control for Windows
Availability	Always available	Depends on both Office and Windows servers	Depends on both Office and Windows servers

[1] Executables for Office are local, other support files are on the server

Office software can be split between the server and client computers, or between the local hard disk and the CD, providing even more options for distributing disk space and managing the software.

Windows Installed Locally vs. Shared

This decision is made when you deploy Windows. If Windows is installed locally, all Windows software is on the client computer's local hard disk. When Windows is shared, you put the common Windows files on a network server and only user-specific data files are stored on the local hard disk.

Office can be installed under either environment. Some files included with Office are system-level files, and they are installed in the Windows folders. If Office is installed in a shared Windows environment, those files are shared from the Windows server and the space required by Office on the local hard disk is reduced, even if Office itself is installed locally.

Whether Windows is local or shared has a bearing on the amount of available disk space for Office as well as overall performance of the client computer. It also has a bearing on maintenance and support, as Windows software installed once on a central server is easier to control than software installed on each user's computer.

For more information about making this decision for Windows 95, see Chapter 4, "Server-Based Setup for Windows 95," in the *Microsoft Windows 95 Resource Kit.*

Using Windows 95 system policies is an alternate way to control the Windows environment even if the Windows software is installed locally on users' computers. For information about using Windows 95 system policies to configure client computers from a central location, see "Customizing the User Environment" in Chapter 11.

Office Installed Locally vs. Shared

If Office is installed from floppy disk, the only choice is to install all files locally and place them on the client computer's local hard disk. If Office is installed from CD, the user has the choice of installing all files on the local hard disk or installing some files locally and leaving the rest on the CD to be accessed as needed. This reduces the local disk space needed for Office.

If you install Office from a network server, you can leave some or all of the Office files on the server and put only some of the files on the local hard disk. This can be done regardless of whether Windows is local or shared.

InstallationTypes

There are several basic installation types available in the Office Setup program when Setup is run interactively by the user. You can also create your own customized type if the Setup program is to be run in batch mode using a customized script.

Typical and Compact For these two types, a predefined set of Office features is installed. The Typical type installs the most commonly used Office components, while the Compact type installs only the minimum files needed to run Office, and uses the least amount of disk space.

Custom The third type gives the user a list of all available Office components and the user can select which options are installed.

Run from CD When installing from CD, a fourth type is available, which leaves some files on the CD to be accessed directly from there rather than copying them to the local hard disk.

Using the tools available on the CD supplied with this book, you can also create a customized Setup script in which you define the features to be installed on the client computer. Setup is run in batch mode using this script, with no interaction by the user, and the components are installed as you defined them. For more information, see Chapter 9, "Customizing Client Installations."

Installation Media

Office can be installed on a user's computer from the floppy disks or CD, or Office can be placed on a network server and users can install Office from there.

Floppy disks Floppy disks do not need special hardware (such as a CD-ROM drive or networking hardware), but they require the installer to be physically present at the computer during installation.

CD The CD contains additional files not available on the floppy disks and a special CD installation option allows the user to leave some files on the CD to reduce local disk space usage. But a CD requires a CD-ROM drive and it requires the installer to be physically present at the computer during installation.

Network Installing over the network simplifies the distribution of Office to users, and it provides additional options for sharing files among users. But installing over the network requires network access during installation, and, if files are shared, continuous network access while Office is being used.

An alternative to installing Office directly on client computers from physical media is to perform an administrative installation that copies the Office files on a network server. Users then install Office directly from the server. In this case, you can customize the installation process by modifying the Setup script that users will be executing on the server.

Installation Method

After decisions have been made regarding the client configuration, there are three methods that can be used to install Office on the client computers.

Interactive The interactive method means users run Setup and choose the installation options they want. This is the only method that can be used if Office will be installed from physical media.

Batch The batch method involves creating a customized Setup script that pre-defines all the installation options for the user. When Setup is run using the script, installation occurs with no interaction with the user.

If you have a custom installer program that you use in your organization for installing software and tools on client computers, you may be able to add the installation of Office to the installer's list of software. Using the Setup batch capability, you can define a command line for Setup that installs Office with the client options you've chosen. Using Microsoft Mail, you can create a message with a Windows package object that contains a link to the setup batch script. The script will run when the user double-clicks the object in the mail message.

To completely automate the installation process, use batch scripts with push installations.

Push   A *push* installation of Office is an installation that is run on a user's computer without user intervention. You can do this by editing a user's logon script to launch the installation process when the user logs on to the network, or by using a tool such as Microsoft Systems Management Server to perform the installation on remote-user computers.

Application-Specific Installation Issues

Some Office applications have special installation requirements that you need to consider before completing your overall Office installation plan. If you intend to install these applications, this section will help you understand these requirements before you continue with your Office installation.

You need to also read the Ofreadme.txt and Network.txt files included with Office to be sure you understand the latest updates and issues associated with installing and running Office.

Electronic Mail-Enabled Applications

Because Office Setup automates the installation of electronic mail support, you should install and set up any email client software on user systems before installing Office. For example, if a user wants to use Word as their email editor, the Windows Exchange client must be installed before Office or Word Setup is run. If Exchange is installed after Office, Office or Word must be reinstalled.

If users have more than one email client, Setup asks during client installation which client the Office applications should use.

For more information about how to install and configure mail-enabled applications, including using Word as your email editor, see "Interoperability with Electronic Mail" in Chapter 15.

Microsoft Access

If you are using Microsoft Access to link Paradox data on a network at the same time as users of Paradox, you must be sure to define a unique Paradox user name in the registry.

The ParadoxUserName entry is in the Windows registry folder \\Hkey_Local_Machine\Software\Microsoft\Jet\3.0\Engines\Paradox. When Setup asks the user for a user name and organization name, Setup puts the user name in this registry key when Office is installed. If the user does not specify a user name when asked by Setup, or if Setup is run with the **/q** command line option to run without user interaction but without the **/n** option to specify a user name, then Setup puts the organization name into this registry key.

There must not be more than one user registered with the same Paradox user name on the same network, so it is important to specify a unique user name during Office Setup.

Microsoft Schedule+

From the administrator's point of view, setting up Schedule+ is somewhat different from setting up other Microsoft Office applications. Most setup and configuration issues for using Schedule+ in workgroup mode are taken care of as part of the process of setting up a postoffice that can be accessed by the Windows 95 Exchange client, or happen automatically when a user logs on to Schedule+ in workgroup mode for the first time.

Installation Requirements

Using Schedule+ in workgroup mode requires Windows 95, and the Windows 95 Exchange client connected to a MAPI-compliant postoffice. The postoffice can be one of the following:

- Windows Messaging System (WMS) workgroup postoffice provided with Windows 95 or Windows for Workgroups 3.*x*.

- Workgroup postoffice provided with Windows NT 3.*x*.

- Microsoft Mail Server 3.*x* postoffice.

- Microsoft Exchange Server postoffice (available after the release of Windows 95).

- Any mail server or messaging service provider for which the vendor has provided a valid MAPI 1.0 driver and transport specification.

Note   Schedule+ for Windows 95 runs only in stand-alone mode on Windows NT 3.51. When Microsoft Exchange Server is available, it will include a Windows NT Exchange client that allows Schedule+ to be used in workgroup mode.

To make using Schedule+ as straightforward as possible, set up the postoffice and configure the Exchange client before Schedule+ is started for the first time. If the Exchange client is installed as part of the Windows 95 process but is not yet connected to a valid postoffice, users see the following dialog box when they start Schedule+.

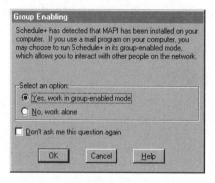

Note This dialog box also appears on workstations where the Microsoft Mail 3.*x* client is installed. Because Schedule+ 7.0 requires the Exchange client for workgroup mode, Schedule+ 7.0 can only be used in stand-alone mode on a Microsoft Mail client workstation. Users who are working with Schedule+ 7.0 in stand-alone mode should click No, Work Alone and Don't Ask Me This Question Again before clicking OK.

For more information about the Exchange client setup process, and on how to specify a postoffice after the Exchange client has already been installed, see Chapter 26, "Electronic Mail and Microsoft Exchange," in the *Microsoft Windows 95 Resource Kit.*

Using Schedule+ in Stand-Alone Mode

No special intervention by the administrator is required for Schedule+ to be used in stand-alone mode. The first time Schedule+ is started, a new schedule (.scd) file is created for the current user in the Windows folder of the local computer.

Using Schedule+ with a Windows 95 Workgroup Postoffice

The recommended steps for setting up Schedule+ for use with the Windows Messaging System (WMS) postoffice provided with Windows 95 are as follows:

1. Set up the workgroup postoffice on a computer where all users in the workgroup will have access.

2. Install Windows 95 on the user machine and specify the Windows 95 workgroup postoffice during the Exchange-client phase of setup.

For more information about how to set up a Windows 95 workgroup postoffice and configure the Exchange client, see "Using the Microsoft Exchange Client with Microsoft Mail" in Chapter 26 of the *Microsoft Windows 95 Resource Kit.*

Note Installing Microsoft Exchange on a computer with Schedule+ 1.0 disables the workgroup functions of Schedule+ 1.0. If Windows 95 is installed using interactive setup, and if the Exchange client is on the list of installed options and Schedule+ 1.0 is present, the user sees a message that Schedule+ 1.0 can no longer be used in workgroup mode, and asking if they want to continue anyway. The default answer is Yes.

The first time a user starts Schedule+, a schedule file is created on the user's local computer just as in stand-alone mode. At the next synchronization interval, the local .scd file is copied to the Cal folder on the workgroup postoffice server. Synchronization takes place by default every 15 minutes, and also when quitting Schedule+. The user can also force synchronization to take place by clicking Synchronize Now on the Synchronize tab in the Options dialog box.

The fact that a workgroup postoffice user's schedule file is not copied to the server until the user logs on for the first time means that that user's free and busy times and schedule details cannot be read until they start Schedule+ at least once. A user whose local schedule file has not yet been copied to the server can still be invited to meetings, because their name is present in the postoffice address book. However, a question mark displays next to the user's name in the Invite pane of the Schedule+ Planner view.

Using Schedule+ with a Microsoft Mail Server

From the client perspective, the steps in setting up Schedule+ 7.0 to work with a Microsoft Mail version 3.*x* server are the same as those described in the previous section.

On the server side, the Schedule+ 1.0 administration program (Adminsch.exe) that is distributed with Microsoft Mail Server can still be used to administer most postoffice-related Schedule+ functions. The only comands that do not work are the Adminsch.exe commands for deleting archive information and deleting inactive Schedule+ schedule files. Schedule+ 7.0 schedule files have a .scd extension which the Schedule+ 1.0 admin program does not recognize.

Caution Running the server clean-up commands of the Schedule+ 1.0 administration program on Schedule+ 7.0 schedule files can damage the files.

An update to the Adminsch.exe program that fixes this limitation may be available at a later date through the Microsoft Product Support Quick-Fix Engineering (QFE) program.

Using Schedule+ with Other MAPI Servers

To use Schedule+ for Windows 95 with other MAPI 1.0 mail servers, set up the postoffice first and then install Windows 95 and the Exchange client, as recommended above.

For information about how to best configure the MAPI server for use with Schedule+, see the documentation that comes with your server.

Upgrading to Microsoft Exchange Server

A next-generation client-server messaging system known as Microsoft Exchange Server will be available from Microsoft after the release of Windows 95. Microsoft Exchange Server provides advanced electronic mail, scheduling, groupware applications, and custom application development. Microsoft Exchange Server includes MAPI drivers that extend the capabilities of the Windows 95 Microsoft Exchange client. For example, when Microsoft Exchange is connected to an Exchange Server, you can access a replicated public folder, create custom forms and shared documents, schedule meetings with others, manage time and tasks, and create custom electronic forms for use in business.

Microsoft Exchange Server requires a computer running Windows NT Server version 3.51 or higher. It also includes a built-in X.400 gateway, plus support for SMTP and for Microsoft Mail for Intel® and Apple® Macintosh® computers. For more information about Microsoft Exchange Server, contact your Microsoft sales representative.

Microsoft Word

Not all converters are installed with Word in a Typical or Compact Office installation. To ensure that you get the converters you need, install Office using the Custom installation type and select the converters you want. You can reinstall Office later to add or remove converters as your needs change.

For a list of converters installed with each installation type, see Appendix C, "List of Installed Components."

Client Installation from Physical Media

If you have decided to use physical media, either floppy disks or CD, to install Office on each client computer:

- The user or whoever performs the installation must be physically present at the user's computer.
- Office files are installed on the user's local hard disk or, if installing from CD, the user can install some components on the local hard disk and access the rest directly from the CD.

- The user chooses what components will be installed and the name of the top-level folder.
- Setup is run interactively.

Client Installation from Floppy Disks

To install from floppy disks, you need to either purchase a copy of the product for each user, or, if you have multiple licenses and a large number of users, you can copy the floppy disks to a network file server. Users can then run Setup from the server. Setup functions the same as if it had been run from the floppy disks except that it will not prompt the user to insert each floppy disk.

The advantage of copying the floppy disks to a server over creating a normal administrative installation point is that this method takes less server disk space because the files are compressed. However, it is much less flexible and provides little opportunity for customization. For information about creating an administrative installation point, see "Client Installation Over the Network" later in this chapter.

The procedures in this section cover both installing from floppy disk and from the server.

▶ **To install from floppy disks**

1. Insert Disk 1 into the disk drive.

2. In Windows 95 Explorer, switch to drive A, and then double-click Setup, or click Run on the Start menu and type **a:\setup**

   In Windows NT, double-click Setup.exe in File Manager or click Run on the Program Manager File menu and type **a:\setup**

3. Follow the instructions on the screen. If needed, give instructions to your users about what to do on each screen for your organization. Users can get help while running Setup by pressing F1 or choosing the Help button.

4. Select the installation type: Typical, Compact, or Custom.

   For Typical and Compact, the components installed are predefined. For a list of files installed for these two installation types, see AppendixC, "List of Installed Components." For the Custom installation type, the user chooses which of the Office components to install, and, for some components, can also change the default destination folder.

Use the next procedure if you have multiple licenses and want to copy the disks to a server so users can install from there. The following example uses an MS-DOS batch file for copying all the disks to a folder on a file server. You could also enter the equivalent command line for Extract.exe in the Run command in the Windows 95 Start menu or in the Run command in the File menu of the Windows NT Program Manager.

▶   **To copy floppy disks to a file server**

For this example, assume the floppy disk drive is drive A: and the file server folder in which you want to copy the Office files is X:\disks.

1. Create a folder on your file server:

```
mkdir x:\disks
```

2. Copy all the files from disk 1 to a subfolder called disk1.

```
mkdir x:\disks\disk1
copy a:\*.* x:\disks\disk1
```

3. Use Extract.exe (which you copied to X:\disks in step 1) to copy each subsequent disk to additional subfolders. To do this, create two batch files:

   - Create X:\disks\copydisk.bat:

```
echo Insert disk #%1 in drive A
pause
mkdir x:\disks\disk%1
a:
for %%I in (*.*) do x:\disks\disk1\extract /c a:\%%I
↪ x:\disks\disk%1\%%I
x:
```

   Given a disk number in the command line (%1), this batch file prompts you to insert the disk into drive A, creates the corresponding subfolder under X:\disks, and then copies the cabinet file from the disk to the subfolder.

   - Create X:\disks\copyall.bat:

```
@echo off
call x:\disks\copydisk.bat 2
call x:\disks\copydisk.bat 3
call x:\disks\copydisk.bat 4
```

   ...and so on, for each disk in the floppy disk set. This batch file calls the previous batch file once for each disk.

   - Run X:\disks\copyall.bat and insert each floppy disk as prompted. This creates a complete set of subfolders under X:\disks for all the disks in the set.

4. Make X:\disks available to users of the file server.

Users can now connect to the file server in folder X:\disks, run Setup.exe from the Disk1 subfolder, and proceed as if they were running Setup directly from the floppy disk set. Instead of prompting for each floppy disk, Setup goes to each subfolder of X:\disks to find the next set of files.

For more information about the floppy disk format and the Extract.exe program, see "Copying Disks and Extracting Files Manually" later in this chapter.

Client Installation from CD

To install from CD, you need to either purchase a copy of the product for each user, or, if you have multiple licenses, you can copy the CD to a server. The procedures in this section cover both cases.

If you have a large number of users, and you have a single Office CD with multiple licenses, you can share the CD on a network server or you can copy the files from the CD to a server. Users can then run Setup from the server. Setup functions the same as if it has been run from the CD except that if you copy the files to the server, users will not have the Run From CD installation option.

The advantage over creating a normal administrative installation point is that this method takes less server disk space, because the shared component files are not duplicated. However, it is less flexible and provides less opportunity for customization. For information about creating an administrative installation point, see "Client Installation Over the Network" later in this chapter.

▶ **To install from CD**

1. Insert the Office CD into the drive.

2. In Windows 95 Explorer, switch to the CD drive, and then double-click Setup, or click Run on the Start menu and type *drive***:\setup** where drive is the the CD-ROM drive letter.

   In Windows NT, double-click Setup.exe in File Manager or click Run on the Program Manager File menu and type *drive***:\setup**

3. Follow the instructions on the screen. If needed, give instructions to your users about what to do on each screen for your organization. Users can get help while running Setup by pressing F1 or choosing the Help button.

4. Select the installation type: Typical, Compact, Custom, or Run From CD.

   For Typical and Compact installation types, the components installed are predefined. For a list of files installed for these two installation types, see Appendix C, "List of Installed Components."

   For the Custom installation type, the user chooses which of the Office components to install, and, for some components, can also change the default destination folder.

   For the Run From CD installation type, a predefined small set of components is installed on the user's hard disk while most of the files are left on the CD and run from there. For a list of which files are installed on the disk and which are left on the CD, see Appendix C, "List of Installed Components."

Use the next procedure if you have multiple licenses and want to copy the CD to a server so users can install from there. For this example, assume the CD disk is in drive D and the file server folder to which you want to copy the Office files is X:\disks.

▶ **To copy CD contents to a file server**

1. Create a folder on your file server:

```
mkdir x:\disks
```

The server must have enough space to hold the entire contents of the CD. For Microsoft Office Standard for Windows 95, this is about 95 MB; for Office Professional, it is 126 MB.

2. Copy all the files from the CD to the x:\disks folder. You can use the MS-DOS XCOPY command to copy the entire folder hierarchy:

```
xcopy d:\ c:\disks\ /s /e /v
```

3. Make x:\disks available to users of the file server.

Users can now connect to the file server in folder X:\disks, run Setup.exe, and proceed as if they were running Setup directly from the CD. Setup detects that Setup is not running from a CD and presents only the Typical, Compact, and Custom installation types.

Client Installation Over the Network

If you have decided to have your users install Office over the network, you and your users will be involved in a two step process:

1. You must create the *administrative installation point*—the set of folders that will hold all the Office software, residing on a file server to which users can connect.

2. Users will perform client installations—running Setup from the administrative installation point to install Office software on their computers.

Creating an administrative installation point is different from just copying files from the floppy disks or CD to a server. Some or all of the Office component files can be shared from the administrative installation point reducing the disk space used on user computers. The shared Office components, such as Spelling Checker and ClipArt Gallery, can be installed to a different folder or even a different server to allow for more flexibility in sharing Office components. Also, you can modify the administrative installation point to customize how users install Office. For details on how to customize an administrative installation point, see Chapter 9, "Customizing Client Installations."

While you use Setup.exe to create the administrative installation point, and users use the same Setup.exe to install Office, it is run in a different way for each task. To avoid confusion in the discussion below, these two modes will be referred to as follows:

- To create the administrative installation point, you run Setup.exe from the physical media with the **/a** command line option. This is called *administrative Setup* and is run once to create the administrative installation point.

- To perform a client installation, a user runs Setup.exe from the administrative installation point without the **/a** command line option. This is called *client Setup* and is done every time a user wants to install Office on his or her own computer.

Creating the Administrative Installation Point

There are two steps to creating an administrative installation point. First, you need to select the server and prepare it, making sure there is enough disk space and that it's free from viruses. Second, you install the Office software on the server.

Preparation

The administrative installation point contains two primary folders:

- **Main Office Folder**   The first folder is for the main Office application files, such as Winword.exe and Excel.exe. The default folder name is \Msoffice.

  If your users will be sharing these main Office files over the network rather than installing them locally, this is the folder they will use to access those files.

- **Shared Applications**   The second folder is for the shared application files, such as Msspell.dll (Spelling Checker) or Artgalry.exe (ClipArt Gallery). The default folder name is \Msapps. The shared applications are those tools that are used by more than one Office application. The shared components include: Spelling Checker, WordArt, Organizational Chart, Microsoft Graph 5.0, MS Info, Clip Art Gallery, graphics filters, text converters, and Microsoft Excel sheet converters.

  If your users will be accessing these shared component files over the network rather than installing them locally, this is the folder they will use to access those files. For more information about this option, see "Client Installation" later in this chapter.

When you perform an administrative installation, Setup asks for the location of these two folders. They don't have to be on the same disk or even on the same file server. But you do need to share these folders on the network so that users have read access to both of them. You can either create a single server share that contains both folders, or you can create two separate shares, on one server or even on separate servers, with one share for each folder.

Later, during client installation, users will access these folders as you have defined them here: they will connect to the main Office folder to run client Setup, and they will be asked to identify the shared applications folder during Setup.

To prepare the administrative installation point, use the following check list:

☐ Pick the location of the administrative installation point.

   ☐ Make sure that there is sufficient disk space. Office Standard needs about 125 MB for the administrative installation, Office Professional needs about 170 MB.

   ☐ You need read, write, delete, and create permissions to use these folders while doing the administrative installation.

☐ At the administrative installation point, before beginning the installation procedure:

   ☐ Make sure that all folders are empty. If a previous version of Office exists, delete all of it; move any custom templates you want to save.

   ☐ All users sharing applications or running shared Windows from this server must be logged off.

   ☐ Lock all folders to network user access during the administrative installation.

   ☐ Disable virus detection software to prevent erroneous virus detection triggers as Setup writes into various executable files.

☐ The computer on which you will be running Setup.exe must be running Windows 95, Windows NT Workstation 3.51 or later, or Windows NT Server 3.51 or later.

☐ Either before or after running administrative Setup, share the folder that contains the main Office applications and the folder that contains the shared applications. Users need read access only to these folders.

☐ If users will be running in a server-based Windows environment, after running administrative Setup, run client Setup once on the same server-based Windows environment that your Office users will be using. During the first client installation, Setup will place some files, such as shared applications, in the server-based Windows folders for all users to share. You will need write and create permissions to the server-based Windows folders. Subsequent client installations will not need write access to the shared Windows folders because the shared applications will already be there.

Installing the Software

After you have the administrative installation point prepared, do the following to install Office software in those folders.

▶ **To create the administrative installation point**

1. If you are installing from floppy disks, insert Disk 1. If you are installing from CD, insert the CD.

2. In Windows 95, click Run on the Start menu and then type **setup /a**

   In Windows NT, click Run in the Program Manager or File Manager File menu and type **setup /a**

   Note Because you must use the /a command line option to run Setup in administrative mode, you have to type the command to start Setup rather than double-clicking Setup.exe.

   ---

3. When asked, type your organization's name.

   When users install from this installation point, Setup will use the organization name you type here as the organization name for each user.

4. Setup will next verify the product number.

   If you are installing from CD, enter the product ID printed on the CD package.

   If you are installing from floppy disks, Setup generates a unique product ID and displays it for you.

5. Setup will ask for the destination folder for Office. If necessary, change the folder name to the name of the folder where you want the main Office files to reside.

6. Setup will next ask for the destination folder for the shared applications. If necessary, change the folder name to the name of the folder where you want the shared application files to reside.

7. Setup will ask for the server and path for the shared applications folder. Type the exact path that users will have to type when they connect to it to install Office.

   You can specify whether the shared applications folder is referenced with a drive letter or with a UNC path (UNC stands for Universal Naming Convention and refers to the \\servername\sharename syntax used for defining servers and shared areas on the server for LAN Manager-compatible networks). If you select the Drive Letter option, the drive letter in the Drive box is used for connecting to the location of the shared files.

Setup will try to verify the server by connecting to it as specified. If it cannot connect, you'll see an error message. This error can occur for several different reasons. The following table explains what to do in each case to correct the error.

Cause	Correction
Misspelled server or share name.	Click Edit and correct the name.
Share not yet created.	Click Continue and remember to create the share before users will need it.
You are running directly on the server and you cannot connect to a local share on the server (many network operating systems will not allow this).	Click Continue; you can verify the share later from another computer on the network.
The UNC path does not work for some other reason.	Click Continue; be sure to verify that the share is accessible before telling users to install from this server.

8. Setup will ask how shared applications are to be installed by the end user. The option you choose will determine whether the user can choose how to install the shared applications, or whether you make that choice for them. The options are:

- **Server**   Shared applications remain on the server and users access them over the network. Users running client Setup do not get a choice, even if they are running Setup interactively.

- **Local Hard Drive**   Shared applications are installed on the user's local hard disk. Users running client Setup do not get a choice.

- **User's Choice**   Users running client Setup choose between Server and Local Hard Drive installation options when they run client Setup.

9. Setup will check for available disk space on the server and then copy all the Office files from the floppy disks or CD to the administrative installation point.

Users can now run client Setup from this administrative installation point and install Office on their computers. Based on the responses you provided while setting up the administrative installation point, you have customized the installation process: When a user runs client Setup from the administrative installation point, Setup will either install Office on the user's local hard disk, or it will configure the user's system to run Office remotely from the server, or it will give the user the choice of running locally or on the server.

This level of customization is generally sufficient for many installations, but there are more elements of the client installation process that you can customize. For a description of all the ways you can modify the administrative installation point to customize client installation, see Chapter 9, "Customizing Client Installation."

Client Installation

Now that you have created the administrative installation point, users can connect to that location, run client Setup, and install Office. This section describes the client installation process.

In the following installation procedure, client Setup is interactive, which means the end user answers questions. Client Setup can also be run in a batch mode, which means the answers to setup questions come from client Setup script files rather than the user. You customize these scripts to provide the appropriate responses. For information about customizing the client Setup process, see Chapter 9, "Customizing Client Installation."

When a user installs from an administrative installation point, client Setup needs to know where to put the main Office application files and the shared application files.

This section describes the client installation process, highlighting the important decision points, but doesn't give all the details of the client installation process.

▶ **To install on the client computers**

1. Connect to the administrative installation point and access the folder containing the main Office application files.

2. From this folder, run Setup.exe.

3. Setup asks for the user's name and uses the organization name you entered when you created the administrative installation point.

4. Setup verifies the product ID.

5. Setup then asks for the destination folder for Office.

   The folder specified here can be on the local hard disk or it can be a network drive to which you have read, write, create, and delete permissions. Even if the software is not going to be installed locally but will be accessed from the server, Setup still creates a folder with some user-specific files in it.

6. If you chose to allow users to select where shared applications are installed, the user selects one of the following:

   - **Server**   This option leaves the shared application files on the server and you run the files over the network.

   - **Local Hard Drive**   This option installs shared application files locally on your hard disk.

   Whether this option was pre-selected during the creation of the administrative installation point or the user selects it, Setup does the following:

   - If the option is Server, Setup configures the client system to point to the server share defined during administrative installation (the server location of the shared applications folder).

   - If the option is Local Hard Drive, Setup asks for a folder name and copies the shared application files to that folder.

7. Setup asks for the installation type. There are four types:

   - **Typical**   A predefined subset of components are installed representing the most commonly used features of Office.

   - **Compact**   A predefined subset of components are installed representing the minimal set of files that deliver basic Office features.

   - **Custom**   The user selects some or all Office components to be installed.

   - **Run From Network Server**   The main Office application files are left on the server and run from the network.

   For a complete list of the options installed for each installation type, see Appendix C, "List of Installed Components."

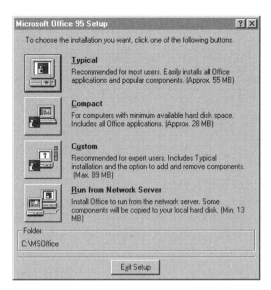

If Compact is selected, Setup displays the list of Office applications with check boxes. The user can choose which applications are to be installed by setting or clearing the check box for a particular application. The list consists of:

- Office Binder and Shortcut Bar
- Microsoft Excel
- Microsoft Word
- Microsoft PowerPoint
- Microsoft Schedule+
- Microsoft Access (Office Pro only)

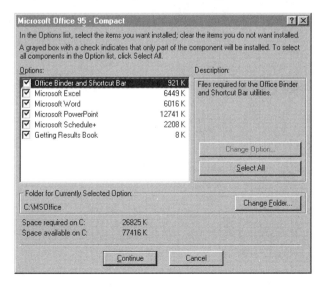

The subcomponents installed with each application are predetermined for the Compact installation type and are defined to provide the basic functions of Office using a minimum amount of disk space.

If Custom is selected, Setup displays a series of lists so you can choose which components to install. The first list contains the main Office components:

- Office Binder & Shortcut Bar
- Microsoft Excel
- Microsoft Word
- Microsoft PowerPoint
- Microsoft Access (Office Professional only, not in Office Standard)
- Microsoft Schedule+
- Office Tools
- Converters, Filters, and Data Access
- Getting Results Book

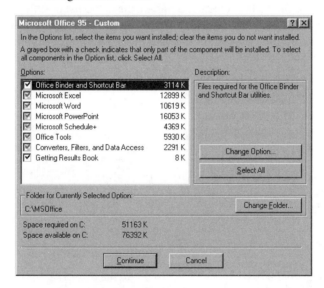

For each of these components, the user can click Change Option to view the list of subcomponents within the component. For example, selecting Microsoft Word and clicking Change Option displays the list:

- Microsoft Word Program Files
- Online Help
- Wizards, Templates, and Letters
- Proofing Tools
- Address Book

- Word Mail
- Dialog Editor
- Text Converters

Each of these subcomponents may also have more subcomponents—if so, Change Option is enabled when the component is selected. The user can continue to walk through all the components for Office choosing which ones to install.

For each component displayed in the list, the check box will be in one of three states:

- **Checked**   All subcomponents of this component will be installed.
- **Clear**   No subcomponents of this component will be installed.
- **Gray**   Some, but not all, of the component's subcomponents have been selected to be installed; click Change Option to see and change the selected subcomponents.

The Select All button allows the user to select all the components displayed in the dialog box along with their subcomponents.

For some components, you can change the folder where that component is installed. If the folder can be changed, the Change Folder button is available.

8. If you are running Windows NT, Setup asks for the Program Group for the application icons.

Setup checks for available disk space, and starts copying files. If Setup determines that there is not enough disk space for all the components chosen, you have two choices.

- If you used the Custom installation option, you can specify a different destination folder for some components to install them on another hard disk. Even if you change the folder for every component, Setup will still install some files in the original Office folder you specified.
- Exit Setup and restart, specifying an Office folder on a different hard disk.

Installation Issues

This section describes the format used on the floppy disks and how to extract files from the disks if you need to do so manually. It also describes the product identification method used by Microsoft; explains compliance checking, which verifies that the user has an appropriate older version of Office or competitive product installed before installing Office as an upgrade; and covers the licensing options available from Microsoft.

Copying Disks and Extracting Files Manually

With the exception of the Setup disk (Disk 1), your Microsoft Office disks use a format called DMF (Distribution Media Format). DMF increases the capacity of a 3.5-inch floppy disk, reducing the number of disks needed to install your application and therefore speeding up the installation process.

> **Warning** Because DMF has been only recently developed, many existing disk examination or copying utilities do not recognize DMF and can corrupt the DMF disk. For more information, see "DMF Disk Issues" later in this section.

What Is DMF?

Microsoft Office 3.5" floppy disks are created using a recently developed compression and disk creation technology that reduces the number of floppy disks needed to install Office. The three parts to the new technology are Diamond, Quantum, and DMF.

Diamond A disc layout tool used by Setup that combines multiple files into a single *cabinet* (CAB file) or across multiple cabinets on separate disks. Extract.exe is the tool used for extracting and decompressing a single file from a Diamond cabinet, or for copying Diamond disk images from floppies to the network; it cannot put new or changed files back into a cabinet. Extract.exe is described later in this section.

Quantum New compression algorithm used by Diamond.

DMF Distribution Media Format is essentially a method of storing 1.68 MB of data on a high density 3.5" floppy disk. Because DMF reduces the gap between sectors, there is no way to write to a DMF floppy disk using standard disk copying tools without damaging the floppy disk.

Disk 1 of a DMF disk set is always a normal, 1.44 MB read/write disk so it can be handled using normal disk utilities such as the MS-DOS COPY command.

To create or copy a DMF disk, the DiskWrite utility is used. For Select customers, DiskWrite is available on the Select CD. For MOLP customers and corporate accounts with disk duplication rights, DiskWrite is available on a fulfillment CD from Microsoft.

DMF has no effect on Setup functionality and is used only for storing software when put on floppy media.

DMF Disk Issues

Because of the way DMF modifies the disk at the sub-sector level, a DMF disk cannot be handled in the same way as a standard MS-DOS disk. Here are some of the issues to keep in mind:

- Many existing utilities such as Norton Disk Doctor, Microsoft ScanDisk, MS-DOS DiskCopy, and Microsoft Windows Copy Disk do not recognize DMF. You should not use disk utilities to examine a DMF formatted disk, as these utilities can corrupt the DMF disk.

- You cannot copy DMF formatted disks using MS-DOS DiskCopy or Microsoft Windows Copy Disk. You must use the tool Extract.exe.

- Because the DMF format reduces the gap between sectors on a disk, low-quality or older disk drives may have trouble reading the disk.

- Any utility, or computer virus, that writes an MS-DOS type of master boot record on the disk will render any DMF data on the disk unusable.

Using Extract.exe

The preferred method for placing Office files on a network server from which users can run client Setup is to create an administrative installation point. For more information, see "Client Installation Over the Network" earlier in this chapter. But if you need to copy the Microsoft Office disks to a network server or other permanent storage drive, you can use the copy switch (**/c**) with the Extract.exe utility on Disk 1 to copy the Microsoft Office installation files to the target location.

To see a list of and help about the Extract command options, type **extract /?**

For example, after creating a folder called C:\Disks on your hard disk for the Microsoft Office files, copy all the files on Disk 1 to that folder. Because Disk 1 does not use DMF, you can use the standard MS-DOS Copy command, copy a:*.* c:\disks. Switch to drive A and type the following command to copy the rest of the disks to the folder C:\disks:

```
FOR %I IN (*.*) DO C:\DISKS\EXTRACT /C A:\%I C:\DISKS\%I
```

A cabinet (.cab) file includes many files stored as a single file. If you need only a single file that is contained in one of the cabinet files, you may search for it using the **/d** switch with Extract.exe. After you find the file, you can use Extract.exe again to make a copy of the file in the new location.

The file setup.inf is a disk information file for Setup that describes the contents of each disk. For a description of the format of this file, see Appendix A, "Setup Command Line Options and File Format."

Here are some examples of how to use the Extract command to find and extract files from a cabinet file.

To	Type this command
List all files in the cabinet file Disk1.cab.	**extract /d a:\disk1.cab**
List all EXE files in Disk1.cab.	**extract /d a:\disk1.cab *.exe**
Extract a file named Any.exe from Disk1.cab and copy it to the current folder. If the file spans more than one disk, Extract.exe will prompt you to enter the second disk.	**extract a:\Files.cab any.exe**
Extract Any.exe from Disk1.cab and copy it to c:\Office.	**extract a:\files.cab /l c:\office any.exe**

Product Identification

The product ID for Office is the unique identifier for each license of Office. The complete product ID consists of 20 digits and is handled slightly differently depending on the media used to install Office.

Floppy Disk

A portion of the product ID is stamped on the floppy disks at manufacturing time and a portion is generated at the time the software is installed from the floppy disks. The complete ID is stamped into the Office main executable files on the user's hard disk (Winword.exe, Excel.exe, Msaccess.exe, Powerpnt.exe, and Schdpl32.exe).

If multiple installations are done from the same set of floppy disks, a different product ID is generated for each installation and is associated with the license for that particular installation. Each product ID consists of a common root (the first 15 digits) that were stamped on the floppy disk at manufacturing time. This common root identifies each installation as coming from the same floppy disk set.

When installing from floppy disks, Setup keeps track of the number of different installations performed from the same floppy disk set and displays a warning if the legal number of installations is exceeded. Selecting Remove All from Setup will not decrement the installation counter. If you hold multiple licenses, you can use a command line option for Setup to specify the number of licenses you have. For more information about this option, see Appendix A, "Setup Command Line Options and File Format."

CD

CDs aren't stamped at manufacturing time as floppy disks are, so a portion of the product ID is printed on the CD package; the user running Setup will be asked to enter that portion manually during the installation process. The ID is stamped into the Office main executable files on the user's hard disk ((Winword.exe, Excel.exe, Msaccess.exe, Powerpnt.exe, and Schdpl32.exe).

Select CD

When installing Office from a Select CD (from the Select customer program), the user is not prompted to enter any product ID information. A portion of the ID is stamped on the CD and includes the product code and a Select ID. The remainder of the total product ID is generated at the time the software is installed and is unique for each installation. Multiple client installations of Office from a single Select CD have a common root in the product ID that identifies each installation as coming from the same Select CD.

Network

Every installation done from the administrative installation point is given a unique, 20-digit product ID with a common root (the first 15 digits). The ID is stamped into the Office main executable files on the user's hard disk (Winword.exe, Excel.exe, Msaccess.exe, Powerpnt.exe, and Schdpl32.exe).

Compliance Checking

Microsoft Office for Windows 95 is available as an upgrade for those who have a previous version of Office, or for those who are moving to Office from a competitive product. If you purchase Microsoft Office for Windows 95 as an upgrade, client Setup performs a *compliance check* to verify that the upgrade is being installed in accordance with the upgrade agreement. It verifies that you have an appropriate older version or competitive product installed before it proceeds with the upgrade installation.

The verification procedure is performed according to a table defined by Microsoft for each specific upgrade and that may vary for each application, for each version, and for each language depending on international competitive markets. The table consists of a defined list of products and product versions that satisfy the compliance check, along with a *signature* for each product that defines how Setup can tell if the product is installed.

The signature can consist of one or more of the following items:

- Product files, including a filename, size, and folders to search. The signature can indicate whether to search one or more default folders only, or to search the entire disk.
- INI file entries, including an .ini filename, key, and value.
- Registry entries key and value.

At the beginning of the client installation process, Setup works through this table, examining the client computer for indications that at least one of the products on the list is installed. The first product it finds satisfies the search and Setup proceeds with the installation. If the table instructs Setup to search the entire disk, Setup display a message to this effect and lists the products it is looking for.

If no products are found from the list, Setup stops and give the user a chance to insert the installation floppy disk for a complying product so that it can be verified. If the user doesn't have such a disk, Setup ends and does not install the upgrade. In some cases, the compliance checking table for an upgrade may specify that Setup can continue without finding a compliant product, in which case Setup displays a warning and then continues with the upgrade. This depends on how Microsoft defined the compliance checking rules for a specific product upgrade.

The following list shows the products that are searched for by the initial release of the upgrade version of Microsoft Office for Windows 95, US version.

Presentation Graphics

Aldus Persuasion v 2.*x* and 3.0 for Windows

Harvard Graphics 1.0, 2.0, and 3.0 for Windows

Harvard Graphics 2.3 and 3.0 for DOS

Lotus Freelance 1.*x* and 2.*x* for Windows

Lotus Freelance 4.0 for DOS

PowerPoint 4.0 or earlier

WordPerfect Presentations 2.0 and 3.0 for Windows

WordPerfect Presentations 2.0 for DOS

Word Processors

Ami Pro 1.0, 1.01, 1.1, 1.1B, 1.2, 2.0, 3.0, 3.01, and 3.1 for Windows

Display Write for DOS 1.0, 1.1, 2.0, and 2.1

First Choice for DOS 1.01

Legacy for Windows 1.0

Lotus Manusc for DOS 1.0

Word Processors *(continued)*

Lotus Manusc for DOS 2.1

Mass 11 6C

Multimate 1.0 and 4.0

Multimate for DOS 1.0, 3.3, 3.6, and 4.0

Prof Write+ for Windows 1.0

ProfWrite for DOS 1.0

Q&A for DOS 1.0

Samna Word for DOS IV

Sprint for Windows 1.01

Volks W III for DOS 1.0

Word for Dos 2.0, 3.0, 4.0, 5.0, 5.5, and 6.0

Word for Windows 1.0, 1.1, 2.0c, 6.0, and 6.0c

WordPerfect 5.1, 6.0, 6.0A, and 6.1 for Windows

WordPerfect* 4.0, 4.1, 4.2, 5.1, and 5.2 DOS

Wordstar 1.0, 1.5, and 2.0 for Windows

Wordstar 2000 for DOS 3.0, 3.5, and 6.0

Wordstar for DOS 1.0, 1.5, 5.5, 6.0, 7.0, and 7.0 Upgrade

Wordstar Pro for DOS 1.0 and 4.0

XyWriteIII+ for DOS 3.06, 3.52, and 3.56

Spreadsheets

Lotus 1-2-3 for Windows 1.0, 4.0, 4.01, and 5.*x*

Lotus for DOS 1-2-3 2.01, 2.2, 2.3, 3.1, and 4.0 Upgrade, 3.4 and 3.4A

Microsoft Excel 3.0, 4.0, 4.0a, 5.0, 5.0a, and 5.0c

Multiplan all versions

Quattro Pro for DOS 1.0, 2.0, 3.0, 4.0, and 5.0

Quattro Pro for Windows 1.0, 5.0, and 6.0

Quattro Pro Special Ed. 1.0

Supercalc for DOS 3.1, 3.2, 4, 5.1, and 5.5 B

Databases

Alpha Five

Approach for Windows 2.1

Clipper 5.01

Clipper 5.02c, 5.02b, 5.02a, and 5.02

Clipper 5.2 DOS

Databases *(continued)*

Dateease 1.1, 4.5, and 4.53 Exec

Dbase 1.0, 1.1, and 1.5

dBASE 5.0 DOS

dBASE 5.0 WIN

Dbase IV 2.0

FileMaker Pro 2.0 and 2.1 WIN

FoxPro 2.0 DOS

FoxPro 2.5, 2.5a, 2.5b, and 2.6 DOS

FoxPro 2.5, 2.5a, 2.5b, and 2.6 WIN

FoxPro 2.6 WIN

Microsoft Access 1.0, 1.1, and 2.0

Microsoft Office Std (all Windows versions including Office 95 Std)

Paradox 1.0, 3.0, 3.5, and 3.5 Update, 4.0 and 4.5

Paradox 5.0 DOS

Paradox 5.0 WIN

Powerbuilder 3.0

Q&A 2.0 and 3.0 DOS

Q&A 4.0 Win (Checking for Q&A or QAWrite)

R:Base 2.11, 3.0, 3.1, and 4.0

R:Base 3.1, 4.0 , 4.5, and 4.5+

Superbase for Windows 4.1.3

Superbase4 1.2 and 1.3 WIN

Suites

Borland Office

Microsoft Office (all Windows versions)

Microsoft Works (all Windows versions)

Perfect Office

Smart Suite

Contact Microsoft Product Support for additional help with specific upgrading situations.

Licensing

Each user must have a Microsoft Office license, no matter how your users install Office. One license is provided with each retail package of Microsoft Office.

If you don't want to purchase a complete copy of Office for every user, you can purchase a License Pak. Each License Pak allows you to make and use one additional copy of Office. You don't need to store extra copies of Office or the documentation, and it's less expensive than purchasing a retail package. For quantities of 13 licenses or more, ask your reseller about the Microsoft Open, Variable, and Enterprise licensing options.

Client Installation Example

The following example demonstrates how an administrator can prepare and perform a basic installation of Office. For this example, no customization is needed. If you need to customize setup, see Chapter 9, "Customizing Client Installations."

Corporation 1 is a mid-sized publishing firm that has just purchased licenses to upgrade their 100 users to Windows 95 and Office for Windows 95. The users are well-trained and usually install their own software, although the internal support group can assist them if needed. The administrator believes that all the machines have sufficient hard disk space. Users have had training on the features of Office for Windows 95 and understand the features of Office enough to know what components they should install. As the software was purchased through a volume license agreement, each user does not have a copy of Office disk, and the administrator wants to avoid the time and cost of distributing physical media.

The administrator decides to create an administrative installation point on a central file server, and then the users can run the Office Setup program from there.

Steps for Installation

- Install Office for Windows 95 on the server using administrative Setup.
- Inform the users that Office is available for installation, and set a deadline for the upgrade.
- Distribute installation instructions to users including the path to the administrative installation point.
- Confirm that users completed the installation process.

CHAPTER 9

Customizing Client Installations

The flexibility available in the standard Setup process—installing from physical media or from the network, choosing which components to install, running the applications locally or from a server—is sufficient for many situations. But there are cases in which it is beneficial to customize the client installation process. The tools available to customize client installation are discussed in this section.

In This Chapter

About the Setup Program

The Setup program is general-purpose application that receives all of its instructions from a set of tables that describe what files are to be installed and how that installation is to occur. Even portions of the user interface in Setup are governed by these tables.

There are two primary table files used by Setup.exe:

Filename	Description
Setup.stf	Setup table file (called the STF file). This file contains the sequence of instructions Setup is to follow for performing the installation. It specifies when and where files are to be copied, what registry entries are to be created, and it defines the general logical flow of the installation process.
Setup.inf	Setup disk information file (called the INF file). This file contains detailed descriptions of all the files included in the product. The STF file uses the disk information file to describe what product files are to be installed.

These two files are initially designed to produce the standard Office client installation process. By making small, careful modifications to these files, you can alter the behavior of client Setup and create a customized client installation process.

> Warning Do not modify either of these files with a standard text editor. These are tab-delimited files that rely heavily on positional parameters, and they can be easily damaged by modifying them with anything other than the tools described here.

For a complete description of the contents and format of these files, see Appendix A, "Setup Command Line Options and File Format."

What Can Be Customized

There are two basic types of modifications you can make to customize the client installation. You can:

- Change default values in the Setup table file. By doing this, you can modify the following values:
    - Installation type to use during batch mode (Typical, Compact, Custom, Run From Network Server).
    - Specific modules to be installed during batch mode.
    - Default destination folders to use for Office and its components.
    - Default responses to Yes/No questions.
    - Default settings for application options.
    - Default Program groups to use for application icons.
    - Default working folder of Program group icons.
    - Default program group icons.
- Add new entries to the table file or disk information file so Setup will perform the following additional tasks during client installation:
    - Create additional registry settings.
    - Install additional files that are not Office files.

The most common method for creating customized client installations is to create an administrative installation point and modify the client Setup files there. The Setup table file and disk information file reside in the same folder as the Setup.exe program. Using the tools described in this chapter, you can modify these files directly on the server. Then, users who install Office from that folder will be running the custom client installation that you designed. The majority of this chapter assumes that you will customize a network installation in this way.

Customizing Physical Media

Besides customizing a network installation, it is also possible to do some customization for users installing Office from the physical media, although the preparation for this is generally more difficult. The technique is different depending on whether you will be using the floppy disk set or CDs. These techniques are covered briefly here before discussing network installations in the remainder of this chapter.

Floppy Disk

There is very little customization you can do for users installing from the floppy disk set. The Setup table file is compressed inside the cabinet file on disk 1, and so is inaccessible for customization. While the disk information file on disk 1 is not compressed and can be modified, there is only one possible way to customize Setup, and that is to cause Setup to install additional files that are not Office files during installation. For a description of the cabinet file, see "Copying Disks and Extracting Files Manually" in Chapter 8, "Installing Microsoft Office."

You can add additional files to the installation by adding another disk to the floppy disk set, and modifying the disk information file to add entries for the files on that disk. Because you cannot modify the table file, you will need to add these extra entries into the disk information file in a file group that the table file already refers to and installs. The added files will be installed into the same folder as the other files in this group.

Once you have a modified version of the disk information file, and your extra disk, you need to make these available to users along with the rest of the standard Office disks. If users will be installing from the physical media itself, you need to replace disk 1 of each set with your modified version. If you have put the disk images on a network server, you can replace the disk information file on the server and add a new subfolder for the extra disk. For a description of putting disk images on a network server see "Client Installation from Floppy Disks" in Chapter 8 "Installing Microsoft Office." For a description of the disk information file format, see Appendix A, "Setup Command Line Options and File Format."

Note   The Network Installation Wizard application described in the following section *cannot* be used with a floppy disk set because the Setup table file is inaccessible.

CD

Because the files on the CD are not compressed, you have access to both the Setup table file and the disk information file and can modify them using the tools described in this chapter. However, because a CD is read-only, you won't be able to write modified files back to the original CD.

If you have the ability to duplicate CDs, and you have multiple user licenses for Office, you can create a new Office installation CD with your modified Setup files and duplicate this CD for your users.

If you have put the CD image on a network server, you can modify the Setup files on the server, and then users installing Office from that location will be using your customized files. For a description of putting the CD image on a network server see, "Client Installation from CD," in Chapter 8, "Installing Microsoft Office."

The following section describes the use of the Network Installation Wizard application to modify the Setup files on an administrative installation point. These same techniques, however, can be used to customize a CD or a CD image on a network server. You use the Network Installation Wizard to modify the Setup table file and disk information file on the root folder of the CD or CD image.

Modifying Client Setup with the Network Installation Wizard

The Network Installation Wizard is a tool designed to modify the table and disk information files for the version of client Setup used in Office for Windows 95. The tool is included on the CD provided with this book. For the latest information about the Network Installation Wizard, check the folder containing the Wizard on the CD. You can install and run the wizard from the initial screen that appears when the CD starts.

The purpose of the Network Installation Wizard is to allow you to change the default values for items in the STF file. If the user will be performing a client installation in batch (non-interactive) mode, client Setup will perform the installation using the default values you specified. If the user will be installing in interactive mode, the values you set with the Network Installation Wizard will be presented to the user as the default responses during installation.

To best understand what the Network Installation Wizard is doing and the modifications you can make, you should be familiar with the basic client installation process for Office. If you haven't already done so, read "Client Installation" in Chapter 8, "Installing Microsoft Office."

Starting the Network Installation Wizard

After the initial startup screen, the Network Installation Wizard asks for the name of the Setup table file to modify. Specify setup.stf from the folder containing the main Office application files. While the Network Installation Wizard is reading the file, which can take several minutes, it displays the following message:

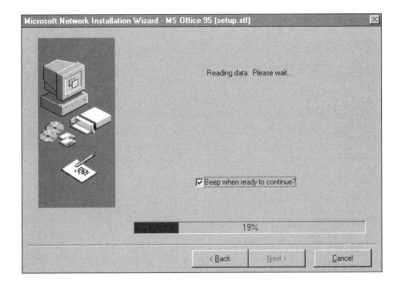

The Network Installation Wizard then steps through dialog boxes that are similar to the dialog boxes a user sees when running client Setup to install Office. As with other wizards in Office, you step through the process by clicking the Next button to proceed to the next screen. Clicking the Back button, when available, takes you back to the previous screen. You can quit the Network Installation Wizard by clicking Cancel.

Naming the Default Folder for the Office Main Application Files

You can change this folder name by deleting the name and typing a new name, or by clicking the Browse button and selecting the appropriate folder.

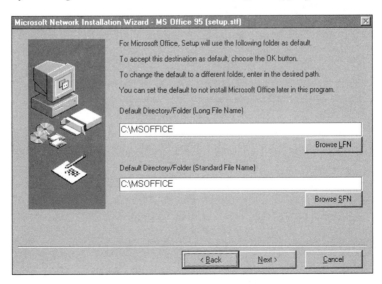

If the user will be running client Setup in batch mode, the folder named here will be used by Setup for the application files. If the user will be running client Setup interactively, this folder will be presented as the default folder.

Location of Shared Applications (Server, Local Hard Drive, User's Choice)

This is the same dialog box used when creating the administrative installation point. This setting determines if the user will have a choice of installing the shared applications locally or running them from the server, or if you make that choice for them. If users will be installing in batch mode, with no user interface, you need to select Server or Local Hard Drive because User's Choice doesn't make sense in batch mode.

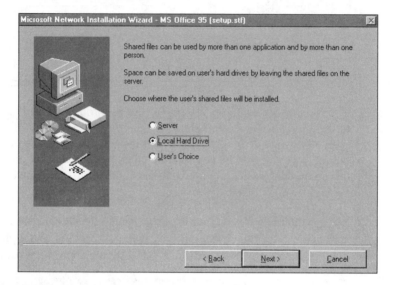

The three choices are:

- **Server**   Shared applications will be left on the server and users will access them over the network. Users running client Setup will not get a choice.

- **Local Hard Drive**   Shared applications will be installed onto the user's local hard disk. Users running client Setup will not get a choice.

- **User's Choice**   Users running client Setup will be asked to choose between Server and Local Hard Drive installation types when they run client Setup.

If you select Server, a second dialog box comes up for you to specify the location of the shared applications. This is similar to the dialog box in administrative setup mode and defines the path to the server share and the folder path on that share.

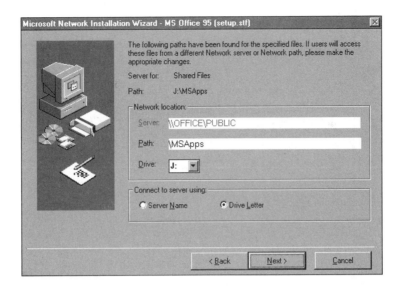

The Connect To Server Using option allows you to specify whether you want the location of the shared applications to be defined with a drive letter or with a UNC (Universal Naming Convention; refers to the \\servername\sharename syntax used for defining servers and shared areas on the server for LAN Manager-compatible networks) path.

When you click Next, the Network Installation Wizard attempts to connect to the server to verify it. If any errors are encountered, the Network Installation Wizard will ask if you want to use the path as specified. To continue and leave the path as is, click Yes; to change the path, click No.

The following table shows some reasons why the verification might fail and what you can do to fix it.

Cause	Correction
Misspelled server or share name.	Click No and correct the name.
Share not created yet.	Click Yes. Remember to create the share before users will need it.
You are running on the server and you cannot connect to a local share on the server (many network operating systems will not allow this).	Click Yes. You can verify the share later from another computer on the network.
UNC path does not work for some other reason.	Click Yes. Be sure to verify that the share is accessible before telling users to install from this server

Choose the Installation Type

Select the installation type to use when running Setup in batch mode. The type you select here will have no effect if the user runs in interactive mode.

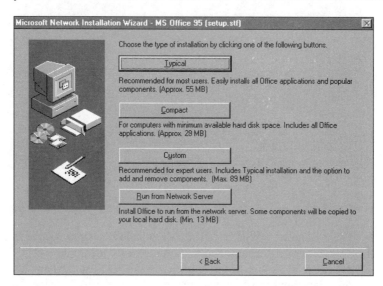

If you select Custom, the Network Installation Wizard will display the list of available installation options in a manner similar to the way they would be presented to an end user running client Setup in interactive mode.

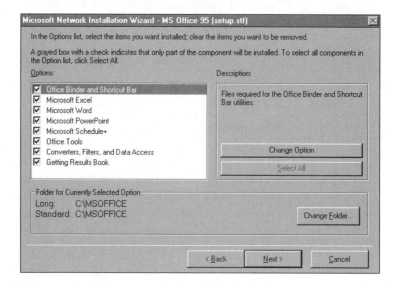

Each of the components listed may also have more subcomponents—if so, the Change Option button is enabled when the component is selected, and the user can click Change Option to see and change the subcomponents. The user can continue to walk through all the components for Office choosing which ones to install.

For each component displayed in the list, the check box will be in one of three states:

- **Checked**   All subcomponents of this component will be installed.

- **Clear**   No subcomponents of this component will be installed.

- **Gray**   Some, but not all, of the component's subcomponents have been selected to be installed; click Change Option to see and change the selected subcomponents.

Use the Select All button to select all the components displayed in the dialog box along with their subcomponents.

If the STF file is to be used in batch mode, the check box for a particular option determines whether the option will be installed when client Setup is run: a checked option will be installed, an option with the check box cleared will not.

If the STF file is to be used in interactive mode, the state of the check boxes in this dialog box represent the default settings that will be presented to the user. For example, if the check box is cleared for the Office Tools, that check box will be clear when the user runs client Setup interactively and views the options for the Custom installation type.

With the Change Folder button you can modify the default folder for the selected option, as shown in the following illustration.

The Standard File Name field defines the MS-DOS 8.3 filename (an eight-character filename followed by a three-character extension, which denotes the file type). You must define a standard filename for the folder. If you also enter a different name in the Long File Name field, this will define the long filename associated with the folder.

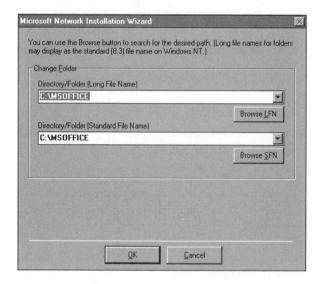

Clicking the Directory/Folder arrow displays the following special path options:

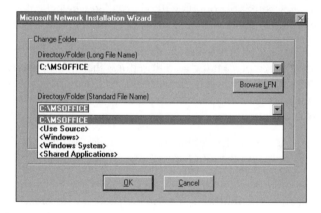

These options are:

- **Use Source**   Folder from which Setup is being run.
- **Windows**   Location of the Windows folder as defined on the user's computer.
- **Windows System**   Location of the Windows System folder as defined on the user's computer.
- **Shared Applications**   Folder containing the Office shared applications.

You can also type a folder name.

Additional Options You Can Modify

The additional options include yes/no Setup questions for which you can specify default answers, setting the links to applications, a place to list other files and registry settings you want as part of the Setup process, and specific Office options, such as the path to templates.

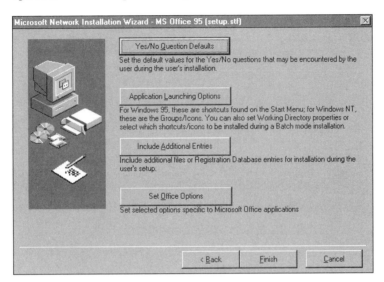

The available option groups are:

Yes/No Question Defaults   Lists all the Yes/No questions in the table file so you can change their default answers.

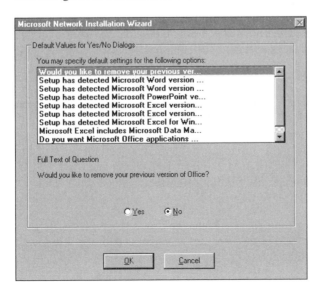

Selecting a specific question and clicking Yes or No sets the default answer for that question.

Application Launching Options   Lists the program links that can be created by client Setup so you can choose whether to install a specific link. You can also modify the working folder for a particular link and choose what Startup folder or program group the link is to be installed into.

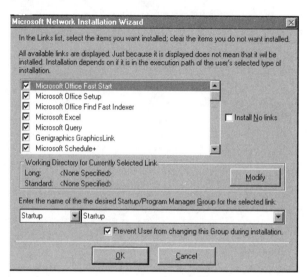

The program links listed are all the links defined in the Office Setup table file, but not all the links will necessarily always be installed. The links that are actually installed during a particular installation depend on the options selected and a number of environmental factors that affect Setup's execution path through the table file. Clearing a check box in this list, however, will guarantee that under no circumstances will that particular link be installed.

The Install No Links check box clears the check boxes for all links in the list.

If you select a link in the list and click Modify, you can change the working folder defined for the program link. The working folder for an application is the default folder used for creating new files or browsing for existing files. Some applications explicitly define the folder to be used for certain types of files (for example, Word defines a specific folder to be used for template files), in which case the working folder is used only for those files that have no other folder explicitly defined for them.

In the Startup/Program Manager Group box, you can define the Startup group (for Windows 95) or the Program Manager group (for Windows NT) in which any links will be created.

Include Additional Entries   Allows you to add files and registry settings to the Office installation process.

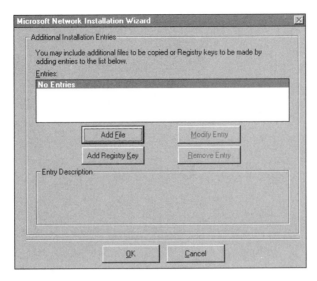

Click Add File to select a file to be added to the set of files installed by client Setup. This can be any file. After you identify the file, you can set the folder into which this file will be copied during the installation process. In addition, the file will need to be copied into the Custom subfolder in the administrative installation point. The Network Installation Wizard gives you the option of copying the file into the Custom folder immediately or letting you copy it later.

Click Add Registry Key to define a registry key and value:

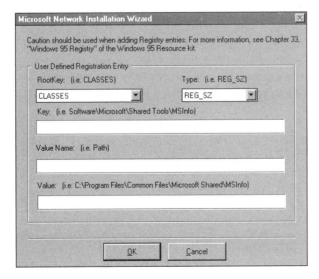

Set Office Options   Lists the selected Office options so you can review and modify them.

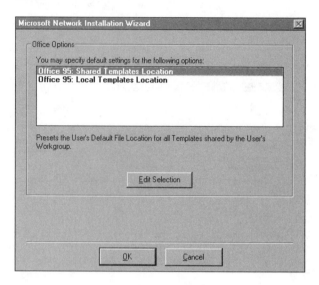

Note   The list of Office Options that are available in the Network Installation Wizard may be different from that shown in the preceding illustration.

You can change any of these options by selecting the option and clicking the Edit Selection button. There are 3 types of options, and they are each modified differently:

- **Folder or Location**   The Edit Selection button displays the dialog box for changing the working folder.
- **Yes/No Option**   The Edit Selection button displays the question so you can set the default answer for the option.
- **Registry Values**   The Edit Selection button displays a dialog box in which you set the value used in the registry for this option.

Finishing the Network Installation Wizard

When you click Finish in the Additional Options dialog box, the Network Installation Wizard writes the modified version of the STF file into a new file. This may take a minute or two, and the Network Installation Wizard displays a progress bar until it is finished.

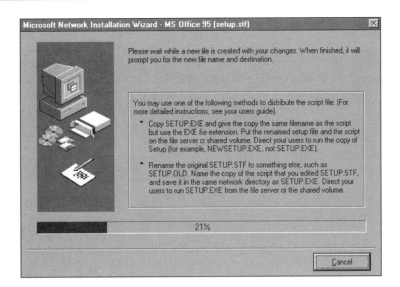

Giving Users Access to the Modified STF File

When you have successfully modified the Setup table file and disk information file, you need to place them so that users running client Setup will use your modified files and not the original ones.

Setup looks for the table file in the same folder as the Setup.exe file. It looks for a file with the same filename as Setup.exe but with an .stf extension. For example, if a user runs c:\msoffice\setup.exe, it will look for a table file with the name c:\msoffice\setup.stf.

Setup finds the disk information file through the table file that contains a reference. When the Network Installation Wizard creates a new table file, it inserts the name of the associated disk information file.

Note   Because the name of the disk information file is defined in the table file, you cannot rename the disk information file after you've created the new table file with the Network Installation Wizard.

You can get Setup to use your modified Setup files by doing one of the following:

- Rename the standard Setup.stf file to something else and name your modified file Setup.stf. When users run Setup.exe, Setup will use your modified table file. For example, if you created a table file from the Network Installation Wizard with the name Newsetup.stf, then rename Setup.stf to something else and rename Newsetup.stf to Setup.stf:

```
rename setup.stf setupold.stf
rename newsetup.stf setup.stf
```

A client installation is initiated by running the original Setup executable:

```
setup.exe
```

- Create a copy of Setup.exe under a new name that corresponds to the name of your modified table file, and then have your users run the copy of Setup.exe. For example, if your modified table file has the name Newsetup.stf, then copy Setup.exe to Newsetup.exe:

```
copy setup.exe newsetup.exe
```

A client installation is initiated by running the copy of Setup:

```
newsetup.exe
```

This copy of Setup will look for a table file with the name Newsetup.stf.

- Use the Setup **/t** command line option to instruct Setup to use your modified table file. For example, if your modified table file has the name Newsetup.stf, then a client installation can be initiated with the following command:

```
setup.exe /t newsetup.stf
```

For an explanation of all the available Setup command line options, see Appendix A, "Setup Command Line Options and File Format."

Once you have configured your Setup executable and your modified table file and disk information file, there are three ways to initiate a client installation of Office: interactive, batch, and push.

Interactive Installations

Users connect to the Office server and run Setup using the executable and command line you have configured. Setup will run interactively, prompting the user for installation information. Modifications you have made to the Setup table file will be used as default responses to user prompts.

Batch Installations

Setup can run in a quiet mode in which the user is not prompted for information, and default responses from the table file are used instead. By customizing the table file and then creating a batch file with the appropriate command line options, you can cause Setup to run without interacting with the user.

Assuming you have a modified table file named Newsetup.stf, an example command line for Setup might be:

```
setup.exe /t newsetup.stf /q1
```

This will run Setup using the modified table file, displaying only progress indicators to the user. The **/q1** option directs Setup to run with no user intervention. For an explanation of all the available Setup command line options, see Appendix A, "Setup Command Line Options and File Format."

By placing this command line into a batch file that the user can run, you can create a simple mechanism for users to launch a client installation.

A special mechanism for distributing a batch Setup command to users is by using electronic mail. You can create a Windows Package Object that contains the network path to Setup.exe. The following example is for Microsoft Mail specifically, but any mail client that allows the insertion of Windows Package objects can be used.

▶ **To create a package object in Microsoft Mail**

1. In Microsoft Mail, compose your message and then click Insert Object on the Edit menu.

2. Under Object Type, select Package, and then click OK.

3. In the Object Packager, click Command Line on the Edit menu.

4. Type the full path to Setup.exe on the network server, and then click OK. For example, you might type:

   ```
   g:\msoffice\setup.exe /t newsetup.stf /q
   ```

   or, using a UNC path:

   ```
   \\dragon\public\msoffice\setup.exe /t newsetup.stf /q
   ```

5. To attach a Setup icon, click the Insert Icon button.

6. To locate Setup.exe on the network where your edited STF file is located, click Browse.

7. To use the icon in Setup.exe, click OK.

8. Click OK again.

9. To add a label to the package object, click Label on the Edit menu.

10. Type the label, for example, "Double-click here to install Office." and click OK.

11. In Object Packager, click Update on the File menu.

12. On the File menu, click Exit.

If the network supports UNC path names, users who receive the email message can double-click the Setup script icon to install Office over the network. If the network does not support UNC path names, you will need to use a drive letter in the Package Object command line and the user will need to have the specified drive letter mapped correctly before running the package.

Push Installations

A special case of a batch installation is a *push* installation. In a push installation, you configure the client installation to be initiated automatically without the need for user intervention. This can be done by putting the Setup command line in the user's system login script; the installation will be initiated the next time the user logs on to the network. You may want to use a batch file that prompts the user before installing, giving the user the chance to postpone the installation if it's inconvenient.

Another push installation method is using a network administration tool such as the Microsoft System Management Server. Microsoft System Management Server can be used to distribute an Office installation package to your users, and execute the package with or without user interaction. Although Microsoft System Management Server doesn't directly support shared applications at the time of the release of Microsoft Office for Windows 95, it is possible to create a shared environment while using Microsoft System Management Server.

There are two levels of sharing that can be done with Microsoft Office. Users can install all the main Office components (such as Word and Excel) on their local hard disk but run the shared components (such as Spelling and ClipArt Gallery) from a network server. Or users can install Office using the Run From Network Server installation type and run all Office components from a network server. The technique for creating each of these sharing environments within the Microsoft System Management Server system varies and are discussed separately.

How Microsoft System Management Server Distributes Office

The following steps give an overview of how Microsoft System Management Server handles packages and how to distribute Office using it.

1. Create an administrative installation point for Office (run setup /a to a server location).

2. In the Microsoft System Management Server Administration program, create a package using the Office PDF file that references the administrative installation point. For more information, see "Creating the Microsoft Office Package" later in this chapter.

3. Instruct Microsoft System Management Server to distribute the package to selected user computers.

4. Microsoft System Management Server will pick up all the files in the MSOffice folder on the administrative installation point and copy them to one or more Microsoft System Management Server distribution servers that service the selected users.

5. When users run the package on their computer, Microsoft System Management Server runs Setup from the copy of MSOffice residing on the distribution server. All the main and shared Office components are accessed from this server.

The service performed by Microsoft System Management Server is to copy the Office files to a server that has been designed to service a set of users. If the users install Office onto their local hard disk, the work of Microsoft System Management Server is completed and the user has successfully installed Office.

However, if you want users to share some or all of the Office components, there are more steps for you to take.

Sharing MSApps Components

As described in Chapter 8, "Installing Microsoft Office," when you create an administrative installation point, you define where the shared MSApps folder will be placed on the network and this location is written into the Setup.stf file. When a user installs Office to run shared components from this MSApps folder, the MSApps location defined in the Setup.stf file is written into the user's registry.

Microsoft System Management Server will distribute the Office installation package to whatever distribution server is defined for a particular user, but it will not change the shared MSApps location defined in the STF file. This means that even though a particular package may be sent to multiple distribution servers, all users of that package will share the same MSApps network location definition.

If you want different groups of users to share different MSApps folders, you first need to place copies of the MSApps folder on the servers you want to use for this purpose. You can do this by performing multiple administrative installations, creating the MSApps folder on the different servers, or you can do one administrative installation and copy the MSApps folder to the other servers.

Once you have the MSApps folder on different servers, you can give users access to the appropriate MSApps location in one of two ways: using drive letter mapping and creating one Microsoft System Management Server package, or using UNC paths and creating multiple packages.

Drive Letter Mapping with One Package

By mapping the same drive letter in every user system to the appropriate MSApps server, you need only one Microsoft System Management Server package for all users.

▶ **To use drive letter mapping to define multiple MSApps locations**

1. During administrative Setup (setup /a) of Office, specify the location of MSApps to be a certain drive letter, for example, drive letter H.

2. Copy the MSApps folder, with subfolders, to multiple servers, creating the same folder structure on each server.

3. On each user's system, map that drive letter to the server containing the MSApps folder appropriate for that user.

4. Create a single Microsoft System Management Server package for Office using the administrative installation point you created. For information about creating this package, see "Creating the Microsoft Office Package" later in this chapter.

5. Distribute this package to all users.

6. When each user installs Office using the package, Setup will define the drive letter you specified to be the location of the MSApps folder, and that drive letter will be mapped to the server appropriate for each user.

UNC Paths with Multiple Packages

If you are using UNC paths to specify the location of the MSApps folder, or if you are using drive letters but cannot define a single drive letter for all users and all MSApps servers, then you need to create a different Microsoft System Management Server package for each MSApps location.

One option is to perform multiple administrative installations and create a separate Microsoft System Management Server package for each installation. During each administrative installation, you specify a different network location for MSApps so that each package will install Office with a different MSApps location. You then distribute the appropriate package to those users who need to use a particular MSApps location.

The other option is to perform one administrative installation and make multiple copies of the Setup.stf file, one for each MSApps location. The location of the MSApps folder is defined in the Setup.stf file at the time you do the administrative installation. By using the Network Installation Wizard, you can modify the MSApps definition in each Setup.stf file to point to a different network location. You then create multiple Microsoft System Management Server packages using the same MSOffice folder, but substituting the appropriate Setup.stf file each time.

▶ **To use multiple STF files to define multiple MSApps locations**

1. Run administrative Setup (setup /a) of Office.

2. Copy the MSApps folder, and all subfolders, to multiple servers.

3. Make copies of the Setup.stf file (found in the MSOffice folder), one copy for each MSApps location.

4. Run the Network Installation Wizard on each Setup.stf file.

5. In the dialog box in which you define the location of the MSApps folder, specify for each Setup.stf file a different MSApps location.

6. Copy one of these Setup.stf files into the MSOffice folder.

7. Create a Microsoft System Management Server package for Office using the MSOffice folder. For more information, see "Creating the Microsoft Office Package" later in this chapter.

8. Send this package to those users who will be using the MSApps location defined in the Setup.stf file.

9. Repeat steps 6 to 8 for each Setup.stf file.

Sharing MSOffice Components

Although Microsoft System Management Server doesn't provide any special support for sharing applications, it is possible for users to share the main Office applications on the distribution server from which the Office installation package was executed.

When Microsoft System Management Server sends the MSOffice package to a distribution server, it places the entire MSOffice folder and subfolders in an internal location on the distribution server. When the user package is executed on a user system, Setup is run from within this copy of MSOffice. If the user selects the Run From Network Server installation type, Setup will install Office so that the user will share the Office executables from this location on the distribution server.

If you elect to have your users share the Office executables in this way, it is important that you make sure that you leave the package on the Microsoft System Management Server distribution server and don't delete it.

This technique can be combined with the previous information about sharing MSApps to give you all the sharing options available in Office with the Microsoft System Management Server.

Creating the Microsoft Office Package

Microsoft Office for Windows 95 includes a sample Package Definition File (PDF) for use with System Management Server: Off95std.pdf in the Office Standard product or Off95pro.pdf in the Office Pro product. The PDF file has command definitions in it for the standard types of client setup: Typical, Compact, Custom, Complete (the same as Custom but with all options selected), and Workstation (called Run From Network Server in Setup). Each of these command definitions contains a Setup command line that will cause Setup to run in batch mode with the specific installation type (except for Custom for which Setup is run interactively).

For example, the command line for Typical is:

```
CommandLine=setup.exe /q1 /b1
```

The **/q1** option directs Setup to run with no user interaction, and the **/b1** option directs Setup to use the first installation type (Typical). For an explanation of all the available Setup command line options, see Appendix A, "Setup Command Line Options and File Formats." When this command is run from this System Management Server package, Setup automatically installs Office using the predefined options for the Typical installation type.

Using the Packages window in the System Management Server Administrator, you can create a new command in the Office package that will run your custom command line for Setup. Use the following procedure to add your command to the Office PDF.

▶ **To add custom commands to the Office PDF**

1. Open the Packages window.

2. On the File menu, click New.

3. In the Package Properties dialog box, click Import.

4. In the file browser, select the appropriate PDF file (Off95std.pdf or Off95pro.pdf) that is included with Office. It is located in the administrative installation point in the folder containing the main Office application files.

5. In the Package Properties dialog box, click Workstation if you want to install Office on the user's local hard disk.

6. In the Setup Package dialog box, specify the location of the administrative installation point for Office as the source folder.

7. To define the new command line, click New.

8. In the Command Name box, type a name for the new command.

   For example, type **Install Office**

9. In the Command Line box, type the command to run your custom Setup.

   For example, to run Setup.exe from the administrative installation point with the modified Newsetup.stf file, in quiet mode, type
   setup.exe /t newsetup.stf /qt

10. To indicate that no user input is required to run the package, select the Automated Command Line check box.

    If you will be installing on Windows NT, you can also select the System (Background) Task check box to indicate that you want the package to run in the background.

11. In the Supported Platforms box, select the appropriate platforms: Windows 95, Windows NT, or both.

12. Click OK and then click Close.

13. You can now create a Run Command On Workstation job to distribute this package.

For more details on creating or modifying packages, for information about distributing packages, and other options available in System Management Server, see the System Management Server documentation.

Client Customization Installation Example

The following example shows how the administrator would prepare and perform a custom installation of Office. The Setup script customizations are described in detail to show examples of how the Network Installation Wizard can be used to customize a network installation.

This is by no means the only possible Office configuration, but this example should help in understanding the scope of what types of installations are possible.

The users at corporation X can be divided into three main groups:

- **Marketing**   The marketing group is responsible for advertising and promotional materials, as well as presentations.

- **Sales**   The sales team uses laptop computers that they can connect to the network, and they work off-line most of the time.

- **Everyone else**   The majority of the user population use their computers primarily for word processing and electronic mail.

The administrator would like to conserve local hard disk space wherever possible, and ensure a consistent desktop within each of the three user groups. The users don't typically install their own software.

The administrator decides to do the following:

- For most of the users, run Office from a server-based setup on the network.
- For the marketing team, because of their need for quick performance, install Office directly on their local hard disks by running client Setup using the Typical installation type.
- For the laptop users, install the main components of Office on their local hard disks, and leave those components they use less frequently (such as Clipart) on the server so they can access them as needed.
- Use batch installation scripts, creating a separate Setup script for each group.
- Push the installation by using network logon scripts to launch Setup in batch mode with the correct script for each group.

Steps for Installation

- Install Office for Windows 95 to the server using administrative Setup.
- Create three custom setup scripts.
- Edit the system logon script, adding commands to run Setup with the appropriate Setup files. Add a command to prompt the user if you want to allow the user to overrule the installation process.
- Inform users that when they log on the network the next day, they will experience a delay as Office 95 is loaded for the first time.
- Wait for each user to log on and have Setup run automatically.
- Confirm the setup scripts ran properly.

Installation Customization

To customize the installation for each of these three groups, the administrator will create three custom Setup scripts:

- Script A for Marketing that performs a Typical install to the local hard disk.
- Script B for Sales that installs the minimum components of Office to the local hard disk, and creates a Run From Server installation for the other components.
- Script C for the rest of the user population that installs Office using the Run from Server installation type.

After Office has been installed on the administrative installation point using administrative Setup, the custom scripts are created by running the Network Installation Wizard, opening the standard Setup script, making the appropriate modifications in the dialog boxes, and then saving the changes into three separate files.

The steps for creating the three custom scripts are as follows.

▶ **To create Script A with the Network Installation Wizard**

This is a simple script modification, setting defaults for the Office folder, the location of shared files, and the installation type.

1. Run the Network Installation Wizard and open the standard Setup script file, Setup.stf.

2. Set the default user folder for the main Office application files.

3. Select Local Hard Drive as the location of shared files.

4. Select the Typical installation type.

5. If you want to set additional options, click Yes/No Question Defaults, Application Launching Options, Include Additional Entries, or Set Office Options.

6. After the Network Installation Wizard has created the new script file, save it to a unique name, for example, Script_a.stf.

▶ **To create Script B with the Network Installation Wizard**

This procedure is similar to the procedure for creating script A, except that it specifies that shared files will be run from the server, and specifies Compact installation type.

1. Run the Network Installation Wizard and open the standard Setup script file, Setup.stf.

2. Set the default user folder for the main Office application files.

3. Select Server as the location of shared files.

4. Specify the network path to the server containing the shared Office files.

5. Select the Compact installation type.

6. If you want to set additional options, click Yes/No Question Defaults, Application Launching Options, Include Additional Entries, or Set Office Options.

7. After the Network Installation Wizard has created the new script file, save it to a unique name, for example, Script_b.stf.

▶ **To create Script C with the Network Installation Wizard**

This procedure is similar to the procedure for script B, except that it specifies that both the main Office files and the shared files will be run from the server.

1. Run the Network Installation Wizard and open the standard Setup script file, Setup.stf.

2. Set the default user folder for the main Office application files.

3. Select Server as the location of shared files.

4. Specify the network path to the server containing the shared Office files.

5. Select the Run From Server installation type.

6. If you want to set additional options, click Yes/No Question Defaults, Application Launching Options, Include Additional Entries, or Set Office Options.

7. After the Network Installation Wizard has created the new script file, save it to a unique name, for example, Script_c.stf.

After the custom Setup scripts have been created, the next step is to modify the logon scripts of each set of users to run the appropriate setup script. Do this by adding commands to connect to the Office server, and then adding the following command to run Setup with the appropriate custom script file.

```
setup /qt /t filename
```

Replace *filename* with the name of your custom script file.

The **/qt** option makes Setup run in batch mode with no user interface. The **/t** option specifies what script file to use, for example, **/t** setup_a.stf for the Marketing group.

The administrator can use other command line options such as **/n** to specify the user name. For a description of command line options, seee Appendix A, "Setup Command Line Options and File Format."

C H A P T E R   1 0

Upgrading to Office for Windows 95

In this chapter, you'll find information about the changes in Office for Windows 95 (also called Office 7.0) and in all the Office applications. This chapter does not contain a list of all new features, but rather explains the differences between Office 4.2 applications and Office 7.0 applications, including changes to file formats, macros, menus and shortcut keys, programming, security, and so on.

For information about switching from applications other than Office 4.2 applications, such as Microsoft FoxPro, Lotus 1-2-3, Word for MS-DOS, or WordPerfect, see Part 5, "Switching From Other Applications."

In This Chapter

Upgrading to Microsoft Office for Windows 95

When you upgrade from a previous version of Microsoft Office:

- Any custom button that was created for the Microsoft Office Manager (MOM) in Office 4.x is included in the new Office Shortcut Bar. The custom button is located on the Old Office toolbar.

- If you have a network template location, you may need to specify this location. Using the right mouse button, click the Office Shortcut Bar. Click Customize, click the Settings tab, and set the Workgroup Templates location to your network template path.

- Office Binders, a new feature of Microsoft Office for Windows 95, provides a means of combining different types of documents into a single storage unit. A binder stores documents created by different applications by embedding them into a single file. Office Binders cannot be accessed by any application in Office 4.*x* or earlier.

- All applications in Office for Windows 95 run unmodified on Windows NT version 3.51 or later.

- If you or a user wrote a custom Office solution that accesses 16-bit DLLs or calls APIs from 16-bit Windows, this custom Office solution must be updated to run with Office for Windows 95, which requires 32-bit DLLs and APIs. For more information, see "Porting Your 16-Bit Office-Based Solutions to 32-Bit Office" in Chapter 12.

The following sections provide information about upgrading to the Office Shortcut Bar and on how electronic mail functions are handled in the Office applications if you are now using the Microsoft Exchange client, which is provided with Windows 95.

Upgrading Previous Versions of Microsoft Office Manager

In Office 95, the Office Shortcut Bar replaces the Microsoft Office Manager from Office 4.*x*. Toolbars in the Office Shortcut Bar actually represent a view onto a folder in the file system. Each item on a toolbar represents a file in that folder.

When upgrading from Office 4.*x*, Setup creates an Old Office toolbar based on the existing Office 4.*x* Office Manager settings in the Msoffice.ini file. The button arrangement is preserved. Setup creates shortcuts for each button, preserving the path and working folder information. Setup does not preserve the placement of the old Office Manager when upgrading.

Setup transfers buttons, menu items, and settings from Office 4.*x* as follows:

Item	Windows 95	Windows NT
Office Applications	Microsoft Access, Microsoft Excel, PowerPoint, and Word buttons are transferred using paths to the new Office installation.	Microsoft Access, Microsoft Excel, PowerPoint, and Word buttons are transferred using paths to the new Office installation.
Program Manager	Not transferred.	Transferred as is.
File Manager	Transferred as a shortcut to Windows Explorer.	Transferred as is.
Control Panel	Transferred as a shortcut to Control Panel.	Transferred as is.
Print Manager	Transferred as a shortcut to the Printers folder.	Transferred as is.

Item	Windows 95	Windows NT
Task Manager	Not transferred.	Transferred as is.
Find File	Transferred as a shortcut to the Office Open dialog box.	Transferred as a shortcut to the Office Open dialog box.
Run	Not transferred.	Not transferred.
Screen Saver	Transferred as a shortcut to the Office 95 version of Screen Saver.	Transferred as a shortcut to the Office 95 version of Screen Saver.
menu items	Not transferred.	Not transferred.
Button size	Not transferred.	Not transferred.
Show Title Screen at Startup	Not transferred.	Not transferred.

Toolbars on the Office Shortcut Bar

You can create and modify toolbars by either working directly with the Office Shortcut Bar or by adding folders to the Shortcut Bar. By storing shortcuts in the toolbar folders, you can rely on Windows 95 to track changes in the location of files. Folders for blank toolbars and some default toolbars are stored in *the MS Office root*\Office\Shortcut Bar\ folder. By default, this folder has an Office subfolder with the default items for the Office toolbar. Other toolbars may represent folders elsewhere in the system.

Using the Toolbars tab in the Customize dialog box, you can add the following toolbars to the Office Shortcut Bar, or you can create your own. To see a list of available toolbars, click with the right mouse button on the background of any toolbar.

Source folder path	Toolbar name	Contains buttons for
toolbar root folder\Office	Office	Office 95 applications
toolbar root folder\QuickShelf	QuickShelf	Bookshelf QuickShelf
windows folder\Favorites	Favorites	Favorites folder
windows folder\Desktop	Desktop	Windows 95 desktop
windows folder\Start Menu\ Programs	Programs	Windows 95 Start menu
windows folder\Start Menu\ Programs\Accessories	Accessories	Windows 95 accessories such as Paint and Calculator
toolbar root folder\ Old Office	Old Office	Applications on user's Office 4.*x* toolbar
toolbar root folder\MSN	MSN	Microsoft Network forums

Default Configurations for the Office Shortcut Bar

How Setup configures the Office Shortcut Bar depends on platform or computer speed. The default options for the different platforms and speeds are listed in the following table.

Option \ Environment	Windows 95 640x480	Windows 95 800x600+	Windows NT 640x480	Windows NT 800x600+
Large Buttons	off	off	off	off
Show Tooltips	on	on	on	on
Always on Top	on	on	on	on
Auto Hide	off	off	off	off
Auto Fit (title bar)	on	off	on	on
Docked location	top	right	top	top
Smooth fill	off	off	off	off
Show title screen	on	on	on	on
Standard color	off	off	off	off

Option \ Environment	"Fast" PC (All)	"Slow" PC (All)	16 Colors
Animate Toolbar	on	off	N/A
Use Gradient Fill	on	off	off
Sound	on	off	with sound card

Note On VGA (640x480) systems and all Windows NT systems, the Office Shortcut Bar docks to the top of the screen. For higher resolutions, it docks to the right.

Upgrading Previous Versions of Microsoft Mail

The Microsoft Exchange client can provide all electronic mail functions of applications currently relying on Microsoft Mail 3.2. If your application sends or receives electronic mail messages (such as the Send command on the Word File menu), the Microsoft Exchange client processes the message traffic. The Microsoft Exchange client also processes any application macro statements that send or receive mail messages.

For information about how Windows 95 upgrades users of Microsoft Mail to the Microsoft Exchange client, see Chapter 26, "Electronic Mail and Microsoft Exchange," of the *Microsoft Windows 95 Resource Kit*.

Upgrading to Microsoft Access for Windows 95

Each new version of Microsoft Access includes improvements designed to help users develop more powerful, intuitive, and flexible database applications. For the most part, Microsoft Access 7.0 is compatible with its predecessors; however, in a few cases new features can conflict with existing macros and code.

Microsoft Access 7.0 can open databases from previous versions without conversion to maintain backward compatibility, or can convert them to Microsoft Access 7.0 format. The first part of this section will help you decide whether to convert existing Microsoft Access 1.*x* and 2.0 databases to Microsoft Access 7.0, or whether to open them in their existing format.

The latter part of this section is mainly for developers who have database applications written in Microsoft Access 1.*x* or 2.0 and want to modify or update their applications for use with Microsoft Access 7.0. It explains what changes in Microsoft Access 7.0 can affect your existing applications, and how you can modify objects or Visual Basic for applications code in a converted Microsoft Access 1.*x* or 2.0 application to avoid conflicts in Microsoft Access 7.0.

File Formats

There are three options for using Microsoft Access 1.*x* and 2.0 databases in Microsoft Access 7.0:

- Convert the database
- Open the database in its existing format
- Create a front-end application database linked to table data from the previous version

If all users of a shared Microsoft Access 1.*x* or 2.0 database have upgraded to Microsoft Access 7.0, then convert that database to Microsoft Access 7.0 format.

The last two options apply to situations where all users of a shared database will not be upgraded to Microsoft Access 7.0 simultaneously.

Converting Databases

Converting previous version databases provides full access to all of the new features available in Microsoft Access 7.0. After a database is converted, it cannot be opened from older versions of Microsoft Access, and cannot be converted back to a previous version's format. Before converting a database to Microsoft Access 7.0 format, make sure that anyone who needs to use the database has Windows 95 or Windows NT version 3.51 or later and Microsoft Access 7.0 installed on their computer.

Important If your database contains Access Basic code, you should fully compile your database in Microsoft Access 1.*x* or 2.0 before you convert it. If you are converting a 1.*x* application, open a module in Microsoft Access 1.*x* and click Compile All on the Run menu. If you are converting a Microsoft Access 2.0 application, open a module in Microsoft Access 2.0 and click Compile All Modules on the Run menu.

Important In a secure workgroup, you must meet the following requirements or conversion will not succeed:

- You must join the workgroup information file that defines the user accounts used to access the database or that was in use when the database was created.
- Your user account must have Open/Run and Open Exclusive permissions for the database object.
- Your user account must have Modify Design or Administer permissions for all tables in the database, or you must be the owner of all tables in the database.
- Your user account must have Read Design permission for all of the objects in the database.

After you convert a secured database, you should also convert the workgroup information file used with it. For more information about converting secured databases and workgroup information files, see "Converting a Secured Database" later in this section.

▶ **To convert a database**

1. Make a backup copy of the database you're going to convert until you're comfortable working with the version 7.0 database. If you're going to convert a database with linked (attached) tables, make sure these tables are still in the folder that the database you are converting refers to.

2. If the database you're going to convert is open, then close it. If the database is located on a server or shared folder, make sure that no one else has it open.

3. On the Tools menu, point to Database Utilities, and then click Convert Database.

4. In the Database to Convert From dialog box, select the database you want to convert, and then click Convert.

5. In the Convert Database Into dialog box, type a new name (without the .mdb extension) for the version 7.0 database file, or select a different location if you want to keep the same name, and then click Save.

Important A Microsoft Access 7.0 table can contain up to 32 indexes. Very complex tables that are a part of many relationships may exceed the index limit, and you won't be able to convert the database that contains the tables. Microsoft Access 7.0 creates indexes on both sides of relationships between tables. If your database won't convert, open it in the version it was created with, and then delete some relationships and try to convert the database again.

Converting OLE Object Fields to Microsoft Access 7.0 Format

When converting databases, you have the option to convert OLE Object fields to Microsoft Access 7.0 format. While this will slow down the conversion process considerably, performance will be faster for OLE Object fields in the converted database. If you don't select this option, the contents of OLE Object fields will be converted to the new format whenever a record containing an OLE object is updated and saved. To convert OLE Object fields when converting a database, select the Convert OLE check box in the Database To Convert From dialog box.

Converting a Secured Database

The *workgroup information file* is a database file that stores the user names, passwords, and group accounts for a workgroup. In previous versions, a workgroup information file was referred to as just a "workgroup" or as the "system database." The workgroup information file is also used to store user preference information defined by each user with the Options command on the Tools menu.

By default, the Setup program for Microsoft Office and Microsoft Access creates a new workgroup information file named System.mdw in the folder where Microsoft Access is installed. If a user is not participating in a secure workgroup, retain this file and do not convert the workgroup information file from the previous version. User preference information from the previous version file will be lost, but can be redefined using the Options command on the Tools menu.

In a secure workgroup, all users share the same workgroup information file. Generally a single file is copied to a network location and the file is shared from there. However, it is also possible to distribute copies of the same file to each user and share it that way. In Microsoft Access 7.0, the location of the workgroup information file is specified in the Windows registry in the \\Hkey_Local_Machine\Software\Microsoft\Access\7.0\Jet\3.0\Engines\Jet key. In Microsoft Access 2.0, its location is specified in Msacc20.ini. In both cases, the value that identifies the workgroup information file is named SystemDB.

If any member of a secure workgroup that was defined with a previous version will not be upgraded to Microsoft Access 7.0, have all Microsoft Access 7.0 users in that workgroup use the Workgroup Administrator to join the workgroup information file created by the previous version. Do not convert any databases shared by all users of that workgroup. These databases can be opened in their existing format as described later in this section. Users of Microsoft Access 7.0 can use workgroup information files and secure databases in previous version formats. However, users of previous versions of Microsoft Access cannot use workgroup information files or databases in Microsoft Access 7.0 format.

If all members of a secure workgroup that was defined with a previous version will be upgraded to Microsoft Access 7.0, convert all databases used by that workgroup and their workgroup information file. To convert a database that has security implemented, the user converting the database must be logged on as a member of the Admins group of the workgroup of the database to be converted. This makes sure that security cannot be broken.

Converting Previous Version Workgroup Information Files

If all members of a secure workgroup that was defined with a previous version will be using Microsoft Access 7.0, you should also convert their workgroup information file before they need to use it. While Microsoft Access 7.0 can use workgroup information files from previous versions, additional memory is required to do so. Performance is improved if you convert the workgroup information file.

There are two ways to convert a workgroup information file:

- If you know the exact, case-sensitive user names, group names, and personal IDs used to create the accounts in the workgroup, use the Workgroup Administrator to create a new workgroup information file and re-create all users and groups. All users will have the ability to view their group memberships. This is a new feature in Microsoft Access 7.0 which is only available when a workgroup information file has been created using the Workgroup Administrator from Microsoft Access 7.0.

- If you do not have the information to re-create user and group accounts, convert the workgroup information file to Microsoft Access 7.0 format using a method similar to converting a database. However, if you do this, only members of the Admins group will have the ability to view their group memberships.

▶ **To re-create a workgroup information file from a previous version of Microsoft Access using the Workgroup Administrator**

1. Start the Workgroup Administrator and create a new workgroup information file.

2. Start Microsoft Access, point to Security on the Tools menu, and then click User And Group Accounts.

3. Click the Users tab and re-create the user accounts from the previous version workgroup. You must type the exact, case-sensitive user names and personal IDs.

4. Click the Groups tab and re-create any group accounts in addition to the default Users and Admins groups. You must type the exact, case-sensitive group names and personal IDs.

5. Click the Users tab and add users to the appropriate groups.

6. Remove the Admin user from the Admins group.

7. Click the Change Logon Password tab, and define a password for the Admin user to activate the Logon dialog box.

8. Click OK to close the Users And Groups dialog box

   Exit Microsoft Access, and then re-start it and log on as a member of the Admins group, and then use the Users And Groups command to define a password for this account.

At this point, the user and group accounts will be re-created, and only the member of the Admins group you logged on as in step 9 and the default Admin user have passwords. You may want to define passwords for other accounts, or you can have those users log on and define their own passwords. As long as you entered the exact, case-sensitive names and personal IDs in steps 3 and 4, all user and group accounts will have the same permissions as the accounts in the previous version workgroup.

▶ **To convert a workgroup information file from a previous version of Microsoft Access using the Convert Database command**

1. If you are using the file you want to convert, use the Workgroup Administrator to join another workgroup.

2. Make sure that no other users are using the workgroup information file by having them quit Microsoft Access or join another workgroup.

3. Start Microsoft Access without opening a database. On the Tools menu, point to Database Utilities, and then click Convert Database.

4. In the Files Of Type box, select Library Databases (*.mda), select the workgroup information file you want to convert, and then click Convert.

5. Type a new name for the Microsoft Access 7.0 workgroup file, or select a different location if you want to keep the same name.

6. In the Files Of Type Box, select Workgroup Information Files (*.mdw), and then click Save.

7. Use the Workgroup Administator to join the converted workgroup information file.

Note In Microsoft Access 7.0, new workgroup information files have a .mdw extension by default. In previous versions, workgroup information files have a .mda extension. The .mdw extension uniquely identifies workgroup information files and keeps them from showing up in dialog boxes for library database (*.mda) files. However, you can use the Workgroup Administrator to join or create workgroup information files with .mda extensions.

Opening a Database in its Existing Format

In some cases, not all users will be updated to Microsoft Access 7.0 simultaneously. In this case, open the database in the current version format instead of converting it. Opening the database keeps the format intact so it can be shared by users of different versions of Microsoft Access. When a Microsoft Access 7.0 user opens a Microsoft Access 1.x or 2.0 database, the user can browse the database, add, delete, or modify records, but not switch into Design view on any objects. To modify the design of existing objects or to add new objects, the database must be opened with the version of Microsoft Access used to create it.

Microsoft Access 7.0 users can open Microsoft Access 1.x or 2.0 databases without conversion by clicking Open Database on the File menu and then specifying the database filename. The first time a previous version database is opened, Microsoft Access 7.0 displays the Open/Convert dialog box. Click Open to open the database and retain the previous version file format.

If the database contains forms, reports, and modules, Microsoft Access 7.0 needs to create separate copies of these objects and their Access Basic code so that they can be run under Visual Basic for applications. This information is stored in a hidden table named MSysModules. Depending on the size of the forms, reports, and modules in the database, the addition of the MSysModules table can as much as double the size of the file.

Microsoft Access 7.0 will not display the Open/Convert dialog box the next time the database is opened unless a change has been made to Access Basic code in modules, forms, or reports with the previous version. If any change has been made to Access Basic code, you must perform the process over again.

For other considerations when running applications developed in Microsoft Access 1.x and 2.0, see the "Macros" and "Upgrading Access Basic to Visual Basic for Applications" sections later in this section.

Creating an Application Database Linked to the Previous Version Table Data

Opening a database in its existing format as described in the previous section places limitations on Microsoft Access 7.0 users, increases the size of the database, and requires additional memory, particularly when running Access Basic code. As an alternative, you can split the database into a Microsoft Access 7.0 front end application database that contains all objects other than tables and then link (attach) this database to a shared back end database in the previous version format that contains the tables.

In general, it is good practice for developers to keep application code and objects in a separate database from the tables. This allows administrators to convert a copy of the application database to Microsoft Access 7.0 format while leaving the database containing tables in the previous version format until all users have upgraded to Microsoft Access 7.0. In this way, the converted copy of the application database gains all the features and functionality of Microsoft Access 7.0, yet the database containing tables is still available to all users.

Many developers using previous versions of Microsoft Access organize shared databases as front end/back end applications. If this is the case, simply convert a copy of the front end database and distribute that to all Microsoft Access 7.0 users. If the current database hasn't been split in this fashion, you can do so using the previous version and then convert the front end database. Yet another alternative is to create a new blank database in Microsoft Access 7.0. To import all objects but tables into the database, point to Get External Data on the File menu, and then click Import. To then link the tables from the previous version database, click Link Tables on the Get External Data submenu.

Replicated Databases

Previous versions of Microsoft Access do not have the capability to replicate a database; therefore, earlier versions of Microsoft Access cannot use replicated databases created with Microsoft Access 7.0. Microsoft Access 1.x and 2.0 databases can be replicated, however, if they are first converted to Microsoft Access 7.0 format. For more information about database replication, see Chapter 16, "Microsoft Access Database Replication."

Database Properties

Microsoft Access 7.0 employs the standard set of properties common to all Office for Windows 95 documents. These database properties are parallel to document properties in the other Office applications, and should not be confused with the properties of objects, such as tables, forms, and reports within the database itself.

These properties are new in Microsoft Access 7.0, and are not supported by earlier versions of Microsoft Access. To view or set database properties, open the database, and then click Database Properties on the File menu.

Following is a list of the new standard properties in Microsoft Access 7.0:

- **General**

  Type (Windows 95 specification, not file extension)

  Location (Windows 95 location, not pathname)

  Size (number of bytes)

  MS-DOS Name (8.3 filename)

  Created (Date/time)

  Modified (Date/time)

  Accessed (Date/time)

  Attributes (Read-only, Archive, Hidden, System)

- **Summary**

  Title

  Subject

  Author

  Manager

  Company

  Category

  Keywords

  Comments

  Template (this property and the Save Preview Picture check box aren't used by Microsoft Access and are always disabled)

- **Statistics**

  Created (Date/time)

  Modified (Date/time)

  Accessed (Date/time)

  Printed (Date/time)

  Last Saved By (user name)

  Revision Number

  Total Editing Time

- **Contents**

  Database Contents (lists names of all Table, Query, Form, Report, Macro, and Module objects)

- **Custom**

  Microsoft Access 7.0 also provides the user with a method of defining custom properties for the database. These properties can be used to identify a file when using the Advanced Find features in the Open dialog box. The Link To Content check box on the Custom tab in the Properties dialog box isn't used by Microsoft Access and is always disabled.

Wizards and Templates

The Microsoft Access 7.0 Report Wizard, Form Wizard, and AutoFormat commands provide names and formatting that are similar to Microsoft Word and Excel AutoFormats and templates. The Microsoft Access 7.0 Database Wizard functions similarly to a template in that it provides pre-defined choices used to create new databases. Microsoft Access 7.0 also allows users to select from a number of other add-ins and wizards, which function like templates in that they present themselves as pre-defined choices when the user creates a new table, query, and some properties and controls.

Previous versions of Microsoft Access allow users to customize wizards; however, there is no way to convert these customizations to Microsoft Access 7.0 format. Any customization of Microsoft Access 7.0 wizards must be performed using the commands available in the Microsoft Access 7.0 wizards themselves.

The only feature called a template in the Microsoft Access user interface is the set of defaults used when creating a form or report without using a wizard (Blank Form or Blank Report). A form or report template determines which sections a form or report will have and defines each section's dimensions. The template also contains all the default property settings for the form or report and its sections and controls.

A form or report template is set using the Options command on the Tools menu on the Forms/Reports tab. The Normal template is the default template for both forms and reports. Any existing form or report can be used as a template by entering its name. All templates from previous versions of Microsoft Access are supported in Microsoft Access 7.0, but cannot be used until the previous version files are converted to the new format.

Macros

In most cases, macros defined in previous versions run in Microsoft Access 7.0 for both converted databases and databases opened in their existing format. However, a previous version macro that uses the **SendKeys** action won't function properly if the arguments refer to menu commands or dialog box options that have changed. For suggestions on alternatives to using the **SendKeys** action, see "SendKeys Key Combinations" later in this section.

If you open a Microsoft Access 1.*x* or 2.0 database in Microsoft Access 7.0, the arguments for the **DoMenuItem** action in macros in this database will be mapped to the appropriate menus and menu commands in Microsoft Access 7.0. However, a previous version macro that uses the **DoMenuItem** action will fail if the arguments refer to menu commands that have been removed or whose function has changed.

The following macro actions are new to Microsoft Access 7.0.

- **SetMenuItem**

  This action allows you to modify the state of a custom (user-defined) menu bar for the current window. For example, you can dim a menu item to make it unavailable. For more information, search Microsoft Access Help for "SetMenuItem action."

- **Save**

  This action saves either the currently selected database object or a specified database object. For more information, search Microsoft Access Help for "Save action."

- **Save argument for the Close action**

  The Save argument allows you to determine whether an object is saved when it's closed, or if the user will be prompted to decide.

Macro Actions and Methods of the DoCmd Object

Some macro actions work differently in Microsoft Access 7.0 than in previous versions. These changes can affect macros or code developed in version 1.*x* or 2.0 using the **DoCmd** statement to carry out Microsoft Access actions. The following actions have changed:

The CopyObject Action

If the current database is specified as the destination database argument for the CopyObject action, the copied object doesn't show up in the database immediately. To view or use the copied object, the database must be closed and reopened.

The TransferSpreadsheet Action

Microsoft Access 7.0 cannot import Microsoft Excel version 2.0 spreadsheets or Lotus 1-2-3 version 1.0 spreadsheets. If a converted database contains a macro that provides this functionality in Microsoft Access version 1.*x* or 2.0, converting the database changes the Spreadsheet Type action argument to Microsoft Excel version 3.0 (if it was originally specified as Microsoft Excel version 2.0), or causes an error if it was originally specified as Lotus 1-2-3 version 1.0 format.

The TransferText Action

If the TransferText action was used to export a query in the prior version, and the query contains two or more fields which have the same name, the fields must be renamed in the query before the query can be exported using this action. To rename a field in query, display the query in Design view.

The TransferText and TransferSpreadsheet Actions

In Microsoft Access 7.0, an SQL statement cannot be used to specify data to export using the TransferText action or the TransferSpreadsheet action. Instead of using an SQL statement, you must first create a query and then specify the name of the query in the Table Name action argument.

Changes to Menus and Shortcut Keys

The following sections list changes to menu and shortcut keys. Changes to menu commands may affect previous version macros that use the SendKeys action or DoMenuItem action. For more information, see "Macros" earlier in this section.

New or Renamed Menu Bars

There is a new menu bar: Filter By Form.

In addition, the Module menu has been renamed Visual Basic.

New or Renamed Menus

The following menus are new in Microsoft Access 7.0, and are not supported by Microsoft Access 2.0, although many commands in these menus exist in Microsoft Access 2.0.

- Insert
- Tools

The Macro menu in Microsoft Access 2.0 is renamed the Run menu in Microsoft Access 7.0.

Commands

The following commands have changed from Microsoft Access 2.0 to Microsoft Access 7.0. Some have been moved to another menu location, and work exactly as they did in Microsoft Access 2.0. Some commands have been modified, and some commands have been removed. In nearly all cases, the function performed by removed commands is handled in some other way by Microsoft Access 7.0. For example, on the Edit menu on the Module menu bar, Find Next and Find Previous no longer exist as commands, because that function is handled by the Find dialog box in Microsoft Access 7.0.

Commands are listed according to the menu under which they appear in Microsoft Access 2.0.

File Menu

Commands on the File menu depend on the active object, as listed below.

Active object	Command change
No Database Open	Compact Database moved to Tools menu, Database Utilities command.
	Convert Database moved to Tools menu, Database Utilities command.
	Encrypt/Decrypt Database moved to Tools menu, Security command..
	Repair Database moved to Tools menu, Database Utilities command.
	Run Macro moved to the Tools menu, where it is renamed Macro.
	Add-ins moved to the Tools menu and only shows when a database is open.
Database Window	Close Database renamed Close and uses the Ctrl+W shortcut keys.
	New removed; New submenu commands moved to the Insert menu, where AutoForm and AutoReport are appended to the list of objects.
	Rename moved to Edit menu.
	Output To replaced by Save As/Export.
	Import moved to submenu of Get External Data.
	Export replaced by Save As/Export
	Attach Table renamed Link Tables and moved to submenu of Get External Data.
	Import/Export Setup removed; now a function of the Import Text and Export Text wizards.
	Print Setup replaced by Page Setup.
	Print Definition replaced by Tools menu, Analyze submenu, Documentor command.
	Any commands listed for the active object above this object that are available when this object is active; see the changes above.

Active object	Command change
Relationships	Close uses a new shortcut key combination: CTRL+W.
	Save Layout replaced by Save.
	Any commands listed for the active objects above this object that are available when this object is active; see the changes above.
Table Design, Query Design	Save As replaced by Save As / Export.
	Output To replaced by Save As / Export.
	Any commands listed for the active objects above this object that are available when this object is active; see the changes above..
Datasheet view: Table, Query, or Form	Save Table, Save Query, and Save Form replaced by Save.
	Save Query As and Save Form As replaced by Save As. Save As added to Table Datasheet menu.
	Save Record moved to the Records menu.
	Any commands listed for the active objects above this object that are available when this object is active; see the changes above.
Form view	Save Form replaced by Save.
	Save Form As replaced by Save As.
	Other commands, see menus above.
Filter/Sort	Any commands listed for the active objects above this object that are available when this object is active; see the changes above.
Form Design	Save As Report is available only on shortcut menu for a Form in the database container
	Any commands listed for the active objects above this object that are available when this object is active; see the changes above..
Report Design	Sample Preview moved to the View menu, where it is renamed Layout Preview.
	Any commands listed for the active objects above this object that are available when this object is active; see the changes above.
Macro window	Any commands listed for the active objects above this object that are available when this object is active; see the changes above.

Active object	Command change
Module window	Load Text replaced by Import submenu or Get External Data.
	Save Text replaced by Save As Text.
	Any commands listed for the active objects above this object that are available when this object is active; see the changes above.

Edit Menu

Commands for the Edit menu depend on the active object, as listed below.

Active object	Command change
Database Window	Relationships moved to the Tools menu.
Table Design	Insert Row moved to the Insert / Row.
	Set Primary Key changed to a toggle named Primary Key.
Query Design	Undo All removed.
	Insert Row moved to Insert / Row.
	Insert Column moved to Insert menu, where it is renamed Column.
Datasheets: Table, Query, or Form	Undo Current Field replaced by Undo Current Field/Record.
	Insert Object moved to Insert menu, where it is renamed Object.
	Links replaced by OLE/DDE Links
Form Design, Report Design	Tab Order moved to View menu.
	Any commands listed for the active objects above this object that are available when this object is active; see the changes above.
Module	Delete replaced by Clear.
	Find Next removed, included in Find dialog box.
	Find Previous removed, included in Find dialog box.
	New Procedure moved to Insert menu, where it is renamed Procedure.

View Menu

Commands for the View menu depend on the active object, as listed below. For all View menus, the Options command has moved to the Tools menu.

Active object	Command change
Database Window	Tables moved to submenu of Database Objects.
	Queries moved to submenu of Database Objects.
	Forms moved to submenu of Database Objects.
	Reports moved to submenu of Database Objects.
	Macros moved to submenu of Database Objects.
	Modules moved to submenu of Database Objects.
Table Design	Table Properties replaced by Properties.
Form Design, Report Design	Palette removed; Palette functions are available on Formatting toolbar.
	Control Wizards removed; still available as button in the Toolbox.
Module	Split Window moved to Window menu.
	Procedures replaced by Object Browser.
	Next Procedure removed.
	Previous Procedure removed.
	Immediate Window replaced by Debug Window.
	Calls removed; still available on Visual Basic toolbar.

Relationships Menu

The following commands on the Relationships menu have changed:

- Add Table replaced by Show Table.
- Remove Table replaced by Hide Table.
- Create Relationship removed.

Query Menu

The Join Tables command has been removed.

Format Menu

Commands on the Format menu depend on the active object, as listed below.

Active object	Command change
Datasheets	Gridlines removed; more functions available through Cells command.
Form Design	Apply Default replaced by AutoFormat.
	Change Default replaced by Set Control Defaults.
	Page Header/Footer moved to View menu.
	Form Header/Footer moved to View menu.

Records Menu

The following commands on the Records menu have changed:

- Go To moved to the Edit menu.
- Quick Sort replaced by Sort.
- Edit Filter/Sort replaced by Filter.
- Allow Editing removed.

Macro Menu

The Macro menu has been replaced by the Run menu, and the Run command has been replaced by Start.

Run Menu

The following commands on the Run menu have changed:

- Compile Loaded Modules replaced by Compile All Modules.
- Step Into replaced by Step In.
- Modify Command$ removed.

Window Menu

The Tile command has been replaced by Tile Horizontally and Tile Vertically.

Help Menu

The following commands on the Help menu have changed:

- Contents removed.
- Search replaced by Microsoft Access Help Topics.
- Cue Cards removed.
- Answer Wizard added.
- The Microsoft Network added.
- Technical Support moved to a button on the About Microsoft Access dialog box.

Shortcut Menus

Clicking with the right mouse button on the following areas of the Access window brings up a shortcut menu of commands. Listed here are the changes that have been made to Microsoft Access 7.0. Shortcuts not listed here perform as they do in Microsoft Access 2.0.

Toolbars

The Microsoft command has been removed. Users can use the Microsoft Office Shortcut Bar to switch between applications.

Database Container: Objects

Clicking with the right mouse button on a database object (table, query, form, report, macro, or module) in the database container displays a shortcut menu that differs from Microsoft Access 2.0 as follows:

- Commands removed:

  Output To, Send, Help (all objects), and Print from Macro shortcut menu

- Commands added:

  Open for tables, queries, and forms; Preview for reports; Run for macros; Design, Cut, Copy, Create Shortcut, and Properties for all database objects.

  The Create Shortcut command is available on a shortcut menu only. It is not programmable using the DoMenuItem macro action.

Database Container: In List Control

This shortcut menu does not exist in Microsoft Access 2.0. Clicking with the right mouse button within the list control, but not on an object, displays the following shortcut menu:

- View. This command displays a sub-menu of the following commands:

  Large Icons

  Small Icons

  List

  Details

- Arrange Icons. This command displays a sub-menu of the following commands:

  by Name

  by Type

  by Created

  by Modified

  Auto Arrange

- Line Up Icons
- Import/Link
- Relationships

Database Container, Outside List Control

Clicking with the right mouse button outside the list control, but not on an object, displays a shortcut menu that differs from Microsoft Access 2.0 as follows:

- Commands removed:

  Help

- Commands added:

  Startup, Database Properties

- Commands changed:

  Attach Table replaced by Link Tables, Export replaced by Save As/Export.

Form View

Clicking with the right mouse button in the background or title bar of a form displays a shortcut menu that differs from Microsoft Access 2.0 as follows:

- Commands removed:

  Find, Edit Filter/Sort, Help

- Commands added:

  Filter By Selection, Filter Excluding Selection, Filter By Form

- Commands changed:

  Show All Records replaced by Remove Filter/Sort

Filter/Sort Window

Clicking with the right mouse button in the background or title bar of the Filter/Sort window displays a shortcut menu that differs from Microsoft Access 2.0 as follows:

- Commands removed:

  Help

- Commands added:

  Clear Grid

Filter By Form Window

This shortcut menu does not exist in Microsoft Access 2.0. Clicking with the right mouse button in the background or title bar of the Filter By Form window displays the following shortcut menu:

- Apply Filter/Sort
- Delete Tab
- Clear Filter
- Load From Query
- Save As Query

Quick Filter Control Fields

Clicking with the right mouse button on a control field in the Quick Filter window displays the following shortcut menu:

- Build
- Zoom
- Cut
- Copy
- Paste

Form Design

Clicking with the right mouse button on the titlebar of a form in the Form Design window displays a shortcut menu that differs from Microsoft Access 2.0 as follows:

- Commands removed:

  Help

- Commands added:

  Tab Order

Macros

Clicking with the right mouse button on the titlebar of the Macros Design window displays a shortcut menu that differs from Microsoft Access 2.0 as follows:

- Commands removed:

  Help, Print Definition

Table Design

Clicking with the right mouse button in the upper pane of the Table Design window displays a shortcut menu that differs from Microsoft Access 2.0 as follows:

- Commands removed:

  Help

- Commands changed:

  Build replaced by Field Builder, Set Primary Key replaced by Primary Key toggle

Table and Form Datasheets

Clicking with the right mouse button on the titlebar of the Table Datasheet and Form Datasheet windows displays a shortcut menu that differs from Microsoft Access 2.0 as follows:

- Commands removed:

  Find, Edit Filter/Sort, Help

- Commands added:

  Filter By Selection, Filter Excluding Selection, Filter By Form, Unfreeze All Columns

- Commands changed:

  Show All Records replaced by Remove Filter/Sort, Show Columns replaced by Unhide Columns

Query Datasheet

Clicking with the right mouse button on the title bar of the Query Datasheet window displays a shortcut menu that differs from Microsoft Access 2.0 as follows:

- Commands removed:

  Find, Help

- Commands added:

  Filter by Selection, Filter Excluding Selection, Filter by Form, Unfreeze All Columns

- Commands changed:

  Show All Records replaced by Remove Filter/Sort, Show Columns replaced by Unhide Columns

Table, Query and Form Datasheets: Column Header

Clicking with the right mouse button on a column header in the Table Datasheet, Query Datasheet, or Form Datasheet window displays a shortcut menu that differs from Microsoft Access 2.0 as follows:

- Commands removed:

  Help

- Commands changed:

  Quick Sort Ascending replaced by Sort Ascending, Quick Sort Descending replaced by Sort Descending

Relationships Window

Clicking with the right mouse button on the titlebar or background of the Relationships window displays a shortcut menu that differs from Microsoft Access 2.0 as follows:

- Commands removed:

  Help

- Commands changed:

  Add Table replaced by Show Table, Save Layout replaced by Save

Shortcut Keys

The following shortcut keys represent changes in Microsoft Access 7.0 from previous versions:

Shortcut key	Function
F1	Invokes the Answer Wizard, not Help Contents as in previous versions.
F7	Spelling
SHIFT+F10	Shortcut menu
CTRL+W	File menu, Close command
CTRL+TAB	Next tab (for tabbed windows)
SHIFT+CTRL+TAB	Previous tab (for tabbed windows)

Upgrading Access Basic Code to Visual Basic for Applications

Microsoft Access 7.0 uses Visual Basic for applications instead of Access Basic, which was used in previous versions of Microsoft Access. In most respects, Visual Basic for applications is identical to Access Basic, and Microsoft Access makes most necessary conversions to your code automatically when you convert your database.

However, the conversion process makes some changes to your code that you need to be aware of, and there are some changes that you must make to your code for your application to run successfully in Microsoft Access 7.0.

Handling Calls to 16-bit DLLs and Windows 3.x APIs

Microsoft Access 1.x or 2.0 applications that make calls to the 16-bit Windows 3.x API or other 16-bit DLLs must be modified in order to run correctly when converted to Microsoft Access 7.0 format. To update the application, code must be modified to make calls to the 32-bit equivalent of the 16-bit DLLs. Specifically:

- For applications that make calls to custom 16-bit DLLs, a developer must provide a 32-bit compatibility layer (a *thunking* layer) for the 16-bit DLL, or else the DLL source code must be recompiled into a 32-bit version of the DLL.

- For applications that make calls to 16-bit Windows 3.x API functions or subroutines, a developer must edit the application code to replace the calls with appropriate calls to the Windows 95 API.

For more information, see "Porting Your 16-bit Office-Based Solutions to 32-bit Office" in Chapter 12, "Support and Troubleshooting."

Passing Uninitialized Strings to DLL Functions That Don't Accept a Null

To pass a value to a DLL function that doesn't accept a **Null** value for the argument, the variable must be explicitly set to the empty string ("") before passing it to the DLL. For example:

```
Declare Function MessageBox Lib "user32" Alias "MessageBoxA" (ByVal _
hWnd As Long, ByVal lpText As String, ByVal lpCaption As String, _
ByVal wType As Long) As Long

Function DisplayMessage()

Dim strEmpty As String
Dim strNull As String

strEmpty = ""
' The following line of code runs.
Debug.Print MessageBox(0, strEmpty, "Empty", 0)

' The following line of code generates an error.
Debug.Print MessageBox(0, strNull, "Null", 0)
End Function
```

CurrentDB versus DBEngine(0)(0)

In your Visual Basic for applications code, use the **CurrentDb** function instead of DBEngine(0)(0) to return the value of the object data type that refers to the current database. The **CurrentDb** function creates another instance of the current database, while DBEngine(0)(0) refers to the open copy of the current database. Using DBEngine(0)(0) limits your ability to use more than one variable of type Database which refers to the current database.

The DBEngine(0)(0) syntax is still supported, so Microsoft Access doesn't change your code during the conversion process. However, making this modification to your code will avoid possible conflicts in a multiuser environment.

The CurDir Function

The **CurDir** function works differently than it did in version 1.*x* or 2.0 due to the way that all programs interact with Windows 95. Because each program has its own current folder, setting the current folder in Windows 95 by double-clicking on an icon doesn't affect the current folder in Microsoft Access. The **CurDir** function in Microsoft Access 95 always returns the current path.

Assigning an OLE Object to a String Variable

If you manipulate OLE Objects or other binary data in your code, you should use an array of bytes to store binary data. In previous versions of Microsoft Access, you assign OLE Objects or other binary data less than 64K in size to string variables when you needed to manipulate the objects or data in code. You also assign the data returned by the **GetChunk** method to string variables. Code written like this will fail in Microsoft Access 7.0, because Visual Basic for applications uses the Unicode character set internally.

Unicode encodes characters as 16-bit values (2 bytes), whereas ANSI characters are 8-bit (1 byte) values. Thus all strings that appear to be, for example, three characters, "abc", are actually six bytes internally in Unicode. This will cause problems when using the **Len** function, which returns the number of characters, not the number of bytes.

Data Access Objects (DAO) code translates between ANSI and Unicode based on the type of the field that is being written to. For example, if it's writing to a long binary field, it won't translate the incoming data; otherwise, it will.

For example, the following code will no longer work:

```
TestString$ = MyRecordset!PictureField.GetChunk(0, 40)
FldLength = MyRecordset!PictureField.FieldSize()
If Len(TestString$) <> FldLength Then Stop
```

This code no longer works because **Len** returns the number of characters, whereas FieldSize returns the number of bytes. Because TestString is a string, the **Len** function assumes that the number of characters is the number of bytes divided by 2, which returns the wrong number. Because MyRecordset!PictureFld is a **Long Binary** value, Visual Basic for applications returns the actual number of bytes, not the number of characters. If it was a **Text** value, Visual Basic for applications would return the character count.

Visual Basic for applications supplies a **Byte** data type and new byte functions such as **LenB**, **LeftB**, and **RightB**. You should store binary data in an array of bytes instead of a string variable, and you should use the byte functions to manipulate that data.

Declare DDE Channels as Variant or Long

If you use **DDEInitiate** to open a DDE communication channel, you can declare the variable that stores the channel number, which is a **Long** value, as either a **Variant** or a **Long** value. In previous versions of Microsoft Access, the channel number was an **Integer** value, so you must modify any declaration statements in your code that create variables of type **Integer** to store the channel number.

String Conversion Fails if String Contains a Percent Sign

You cannot assign a string containing a percent sign (%) to a variable or a field that has a numeric data type. For example:

```
Dim intX As Double
    intX = "10"     ' This works.
    intX = "10%"    ' This returns an error.
```

Performing Macro Actions using the DoCmd Object

To perform macro actions from code in Microsoft Access 7.0, use the **DoCmd** object. This replaces the **DoCmd** statement that you used in previous versions of Microsoft Access to perform a macro action. To perform actions using the **DoCmd** object, you invoke methods of the object.

For this reason, you now use the **.** (dot) operator instead of a space between the **DoCmd** object and the action you want to perform. However, you pass arguments to a method of the **DoCmd** object in the same way that you passed arguments to actions in Microsoft Access 1.*x* and 2.0. For example, to perform the OpenForm action, use the following code:

```
DoCmd.OpenForm "Orders"
```

When you convert a database, Microsoft Access automatically converts any **DoCmd** statements and the actions that they perform in your Access Basic code to methods of the DoCmd object by replacing the space with the **.** (dot).

The hWnd Property

If you use the hWnd property in your code to pass a window handle of a form or a report to a Windows routine, you should pass the value directly to the routine, for example:

```
If Not IsZoomed(Screen.ActiveForm.hWnd) Then
    DoCmd.Maximize
EndIf
```

Because the value of the hWnd property can change while a program is running, you should not assign the value of this property to a variable.

Also, in previous versions of Microsoft Access, the hWnd property of a form or report was an **Integer** value. In Microsoft Access 7.0, the hWnd property is a **Long** value. You must change your code to accept a **Long** value.

DAO Property Objects versus Access Property Objects

You cannot use an object variable in your code to refer to a **Category** property object. The **Category** property is no longer supported for **Form**, **Report**, and **Control** objects.

For example, the following code, which worked in Microsoft Access 2.0, will not work in Microsoft Access 7.0:

```
Sub DisplayCategory()
    Dim prp As Property
    Set prp = Forms!Orders.Properties(0)
    MsgBox prp.Category
End Sub
```

The Parent Property

In Microsoft Access 7.0, if you use the **Parent** property of a control in code or in an expression on a form or report, it returns the **Form** or **Report** object that contains the control. For example, if CategoryID is a text box on the Categories form, `Forms!Categories![CategoryID].Parent` returns a reference to the Categories form. There are two exceptions: for attached labels, the **Parent** property now returns the control the label is attached to, and for controls in an option group, it now returns the option group control.

In previous versions of Microsoft Access, you could only use the **Parent** property of a control to get the name of the form or report that contained a control. You can still use this type of reference in Microsoft Access 95, (with the exceptions of the attached label control and controls in an option group). For example, `Forms!Categories!CategoryID.Parent.Name` returns the name of the Categories form, but not the Categories **Form** object.

Calling Code in Microsoft Access Wizards

If code in your Microsoft Access 1.*x* or 2.0 applications calls procedures that were located in Microsoft Access wizards, after you convert your application you must establish a reference from your application to the wizard database that contains the procedures that you call. You can establish a reference to the wizard database using the References command on the Tools menu in the Module window. For more information about establishing references, see Chapter 12, "Using Library Databases and Dynamic-Link Libraries," in *Building Applications with Microsoft Access for Windows 95*.

In Microsoft Access version 2.0, there was no distinction between wizards and libraries, so their global code was always available to the current database. In Microsoft Access 7.0, wizards and other add-ins are no longer treated as libraries. In addition, because wizards may change a great deal from one version of Microsoft Access to the next, you may need to rewrite some of your code to adapt to the changes after upgrading to a new version of Microsoft Access.

For procedures that are no longer available in the Microsoft Access wizards, such as the AutoDialer, use the capabilities added to Utility.mda, a special library database that is provided with Microsoft Access. A reference to this library is automatically added when you convert a database to Microsoft Access 7.0.

Handling OLE Automation Errors

If you have error-handling code to deal with errors that are returned by an OLE Automation server, that code may need to be modified. Previous versions of Microsoft Access returned a single error for all OLE Automation errors (error number 2763). In Microsoft Access 7.0, Visual Basic for applications returns the same error that the OLE Automation server gives in the error information returned to the OLE container. Thus, you can now make your error-handling code specific to the actual error that the OLE Automation server returns. For more information about error handling and determining the exact errors returned by an OLE Automation server, see Chapter 8, "Handling Run-Time Errors," in *Building Applications with Microsoft Access for Windows 95*.

Microsoft Access Errors and the Error Function

In Microsoft Access 7.0, you can no longer use the **Error** function to return a description of Microsoft Access errors. For example, the following reference will not work.

```
Error(2450)
```

In Microsoft Access 7.0, the **Error** function returns strings for Visual Basic for applications errors, or for the last error stored in the **Err** object, but not for Microsoft Access errors, with one exception. If a Microsoft Access error actually occurs, you can get the error description by passing the value of the **Err** object to the **Error** function, as follows:

```
Error(Err)
```

Exclamation Point versus Dot Operator When Referencing DAO Objects

If you used the **.** (dot) operator syntax when referring to **Recordset**, **Dynaset**, **Table**, or **Snapshot** objects in applications created in previous versions of Microsoft Access, you must modify those references to use the **!** (exclamation point) operator syntax. Or, if you want to continue using the **.** (dot) operator syntax, you must establish a reference to the Microsoft DAO 2.5/3.0 Compatibility Library in the References dialog box. The References dialog box is available from the Tools menu in the Module window.

Note   When a previous version database is converted or opened in its existing format, Microsoft Access 7.0 automatically establishes a reference to the Microsoft DAO 2.5/3.0 Compatibility Library for that database. New databases created with Microsoft Access 7.0 default to using the Microsoft DAO 3.0 Object Library. For more information about DAO Object libraries, see "DAO Object Libraries" later in this chapter.

In Microsoft Access version 2.0, you can use either the **!** (exclamation point) operator syntax or the **.** (dot) operator syntax on all collection lookups and references when manipulating data access object collections. In Microsoft Access 7.0, you can use only the **!** (exclamation point) operator syntax when referencing **Recordset** objects. For example, you can use `rstOrders!CompanyID` to refer to the CompanyID field in the **Recordset** rstOrders, but you cannot use `rstOrders.CompanyID` to refer to that field.

For all other object types, use the **!** (exclamation point) operator syntax. For example, you can use `dbs.Containers!Forms`, but `dbs.Containers.Forms` causes an error.

Converted Custom Controls

If your application contains custom controls that were set up in Microsoft Access 2.0, you may need to insert the **ByVal** keyword in front of arguments that are passed to event procedures called from custom control events, for example:

```
Sub ChangeMonth_Click(ByVal intCurrentYear as Integer)
```

To determine whether an argument needs to be passed by value, click Compile All on the Run menu in module Design view. If you receive an error message that the event procedure declaration does not match description of an event having the same name, you need to insert the **ByVal** keyword in front of the argument:

Because type checking of arguments is improved in Microsoft Access 7.0, new event procedures created for custom controls automatically have the **ByVal** keyword inserted when it is needed.

Referring to Forms and Controls in the Debug Window

When you are testing and debugging code, you must fully qualify all references to objects that you use in the Debug window, unless you have suspended execution in a form or report module. This means that in the Immediate pane of the Debug window, you need to use `Forms!Categories![CategoryID]` to refer to the CategoryID control on the Categories form in Form view, instead of just `CategoryID`, even when the Categories form is the current form.

Also, you cannot use the **Me** keyword from the Debug window to refer to an object on a form or report when that form or report is in Design view unless you have suspended the execution of code in a form or report.

Visual Basic for Applications Functions Not Supported in Expressions

The following six Visual Basic for applications functions can no longer be used in expressions outside of a user-defined **Sub** or **Function** procedure:

EOF	**Loc**
FileAttr	**LOF**
FreeFile	**Seek**

If you need to use one of these functions in an expression outside of a procedure, you can call the function from within a user-defined function that you call from the expression.

Line Numbers in Visual Basic for Applications Procedures

You cannot assign line numbers greater than 65529 to statements in your Visual Basic for applications procedures. If your converted Microsoft Access application contains line numbers greater than 65529, you must modify them to fall within the acceptable range.

The Next and Previous Procedure Buttons

The Next Procedure and Previous Procedure buttons that were on the Module window toolbar in previous versions are not available in Microsoft Access 7.0. If you convert a database with a custom toolbar that contains one of these buttons, you will not receive an error, but the buttons will not do anything when clicked.

Scoping and Object Naming Features

Visual Basic for applications introduces several changes to scoping rules that affect the names that are used for your objects and procedures. The following sections detail these issues and provide guidelines.

Modules and Other Objects with the Same Name

Do not name modules names that will conflict with form or report names as they appear in the Object Browser. For example, if a form is named Orders, it appears as Form_Orders in the Object Browser. Therefore, do not preface a module name with Form_ or Report_ or it will appear to be a form or a report in the Object Browser

If a module in an application created with a previous version of Microsoft Access doesn't follow the naming rules described above, Microsoft Access automatically changes the name of the module to conform to those rules. For example, a module named Form_Orders in a Microsoft Access version 1.*x* or 2.0 database would be converted to a module named Form1_Orders.

Modules and Procedures with the Same Name

A procedure can have the same name as a module. However, to call that procedure from an expression anywhere in an application, the expression must use a fully qualified name for the procedure, including both the module name and the procedure name. For example:

```
IsLoaded.IsLoaded("Orders")
```

Procedures and Controls with the Same Name

If a procedure is called from a form, and that procedure has the same name as a control on the form, the procedure call must be fully qualified with the name of the module it resides in. For example, to call a procedure named PrintInvoice() which resides in a standard module named Utilities when there is also a button on the same form named PrintInvoice, the fully qualified name `Utilities.PrintInvoice()` must be used to call the procedure from a form or form module.

Controls with Similar Names

Two or more controls cannot have names that differ only by a space or a symbol. For example, there cannot be a control named [Last_Name] and a control named [Last Name] or a control named [Last+Name].

DAO Object Libraries

Microsoft Access 7.0 includes new DAO objects, methods, and properties that replace those in earlier versions. While Microsoft Access 7.0 is compatible with all previous DAO code, future versions of Microsoft Access may not provide support for some older objects, methods, and properties. The following sections help you take advantage of the backward-compatibility features in Microsoft Access 7.0, and also help you create new applications and modify current applications to be prepared for conversion to future versions of Microsoft Access.

Using Backward Compatibility Features

If you want to continue to use the old versions of DAO objects, methods, and properties in your application, you must first establish a reference to the Microsoft DAO 2.5/3.0 Compatibility Library. You can do this using the References command on the Tools menu in the Module window. The Microsoft DAO 2.5/3.0 Compatibility Library provides complete backward compatibility with all preceding versions of Microsoft Access, so that your code functions and compiles correctly. A reference to this version of the library is added to previous version databases when you convert them to Microsoft Access 7.0 format. Unless you make modifications to your code, you should not remove this reference.

The Microsoft DAO 3.0 Object Library does not include the old objects, methods, and properties, and is selected by default whenever you create a new database. To make sure that your new Microsoft Access application only uses the current methods, only reference the DAO 3.0 Object Library. If your application only references the DAO 3.0 Object Library, you won't have to distribute the Microsoft DAO 2.5/3.0 Compatibility Library when you distribute your application to other users.

Tip If you want to verify that your application only uses the objects, methods, and properties in the Microsoft DAO 3.0 Object Library, you can remove the reference to the DAO 2.5/3.0 Compatibility Library, make sure that the Microsoft DAO 3.0 Object Library is referenced, and then recompile your application by clicking Compile All on the Run menu in Module design view. If your application recompiles without errors, you no longer need to maintain the reference to the Microsoft DAO 2.5/3.0 Compatibility Library, and you can be sure that your application will work with the next version of DAO.

For more information about establishing references, see Chapter 12, "Using Library Databases and Dynamic-Link Libraries," in *Building Applications with Microsoft Access for Windows 95.*

Preparing for Conversion to Future Versions

The following table provides you with a list of objects, methods, and properties that are not included in the Microsoft DAO 3.0 Object Library, as well as the features that have been provided to replace them. You can use the new items in the second column to modify code written in earlier versions of Microsoft Access, so that your application will be prepared for conversion to future versions of Microsoft Access, when the items in the first column will no longer be available.

Functionality not present in DAO 3.0	Recommended DAO 3.0 replacements
FreeLocks	**Idle** method of **DBEngine** (not needed for Microsoft Access 7.0 databases)
SetDefaultWorkspace	**DefaultUser/DefaultPassword** properties of **DBEngine** object
SetDataAccessOption	**IniPath** property of **DBEngine**
Database.**BeginTrans**	*Workspace*.**BeginTrans**
Database.**CommitTrans**	*Workspace*.**CommitTrans**
Database.**Rollback**	*Workspace*.**Rollback**
Database.**CreateDynaset**	*Database*.**OpenRecordset** of type **dbOpenDynaset**
Database.**CreateSnapshot**	*Database*.**OpenRecordset** of type **dbOpenSnapshot**
Database.**OpenTable**	*Database*.**OpenRecordset** of type **dbOpenTable**
Database.**DeleteQuerydef**	**Delete** method of the **QueryDefs** collection
Database.**ExecuteSQL**	*Database*.**Execute** method and *Database*.**RecordsAffected** property
ListFields method of **Table**, **Dynaset** and **Snapshot** objects	*Recordset*.**Fields** collection
Database.**ListTables**	*Database*.**TableDefs** collection
Table.**ListIndexes**	*TableDef*.**Indexes** collection
Database.**OpenQueryDef**	*Database*.**QueryDefs** collection
QueryDef.**CreateDynaset**	*QueryDef*.**OpenRecordset**
QueryDef.**CreateSnapshot**	*QueryDef*.**OpenRecordset**
QueryDef.**ListParameters**	*QueryDef*.**Parameters** collection
Dynaset object	Dynaset-type **Recordset** object
Table object	Table-type **Recordset** object

Functionality not present in DAO 3.0	Recommended DAO 3.0 replacements
Snapshot object	Snapshot-type **Recordset** object
CreateDynaset method of **Dynaset** and **QueryDef** objects	*Recordset*.**OpenRecordset** with **dbOpenDynaset** parameter
CreateSnapshot method of **Dynaset** and **QueryDef** objects	*Recordset*.**OpenRecordset** with **dbOpenSnapshot** parameter

New Style of Constants

If you use predefined or intrinsic constants in your code, you can now find these constants listed in the Object Browser dialog box in the Microsoft Access for Windows 95 library, the Visual Basic for applications library, the Microsoft DAO Object Library, and the Microsoft DAO 2.5/3.0 Compatibility Library.

There are two sets of constants in Microsoft Access 7.0. The constants that are available in Microsoft Access 1.*x* and 2.0 are still available in Microsoft Access 7.0. To view these constants in the Object Browser window, click the Microsoft Access For Windows 95 library in the Libraries/Databases box, then click OldConstants in the Modules/Classes box. Although the old style constants listed under OldConstants are supported, they are not mapped to new style constants. They may not be included in future versions of Microsoft Access.

The following constants are included in Microsoft Access 2.0 to provide backward compatibility with Microsoft Access 1.*x*.

```
DB_UNIQUE
DB_PRIMARY
DB_NONULLS
DB_PROHIBITNULL
DB_IGNORENULL
DB_TABLE
DB_QUERYDEF
DB_OPTIONINIPATH
DB_BINARY
```

In Microsoft Access 7.0, the new set of constants have been renamed to be consistent with other Microsoft applications, such as Visual Basic and Microsoft Excel. To view these constants in the Object Browser, click the Microsoft Access For Windows 95 library in the Libraries/Databases box, then click Constants in the Modules/Classes box.

SendKeys Key Combinations

If Microsoft Access 1.*x* or 2.0 code or macros use **SendKeys** statements or the SendKeys action to fill in dialog boxes or choose commands from menus, changes in some dialog boxes and menus may require recoding the statement or action. For example, the Add-ins submenu has been moved from the File menu to the Tools menu, and the previous Import and Attach Table commands on the File menu have changed to Import and Link Tables commands on the Get External Data submenu. Because changes like this are likely to occur for each new version of Microsoft Access, avoid using the **SendKeys** statement or action to carry out commands and fill in dialog boxes.

Here are some tips to avoid using the **SendKeys** statement or action:

- Before using the **SendKeys** statement or action to carry out a menu command, check for an equivalent macro action or Visual Basic for applications method. Most commands that are commonly carried out in a macro or procedure have an equivalent action or method.

- If a menu command doesn't have an equivalent action or method, use the **DoMenuItem** action rather than the **SendKeys** statement or action to carry it out. When running a **DoMenuItem** action, Microsoft Access 7.0 remaps menu commands that have moved to different menus. Generally, a **DoMenuItem** action defined in a previous version will fail only if the menu command has been removed or if its function has changed.

- Avoid using the **SendKeys** statement or action to set options in the Options dialog box. New versions of Microsoft Access are likely to have new and changed options, so the code in your **SendKeys** statement or action could easily break. Instead, use the new **GetOption** and **SetOption** methods.

- If using the **SendKeys** statement to carry out an action, consider declaring constants for the values in the **SendKeys** statement. Defining keystrokes as constants makes updating code less work in the future.

Converting Libraries and Add-ins

Add-ins or library databases created with a previous version of Microsoft Access must be converted to Microsoft Access 7.0 format before they can be used with Microsoft Access 7.0 databases. Just as when converting Microsoft Access 1.*x* and 2.0 databases, changes may need to be made to the objects and code in library databases and add-ins to make sure that they function correctly in Microsoft Access 7.0.

Referencing and Loading Library Databases

Before using a library in Microsoft Access 7.0, a reference must be established to the library database from each application that uses it. For more information about library databases and establishing references, see Chapter 12, "Using Library Databases and Dynamic-Link Libraries," in *Building Applications with Microsoft Access for Windows 95.*

A library database should only contain Visual Basic for applications code, which can then be called from any application that maintains a reference to that library. In previous versions of Microsoft Access, a library database is loaded at startup by creating an entry in the Libraries section of an .ini file. Most of the information that was previously stored in an .ini file is now stored in the Windows registry. However, there is no need to create a Windows registry key set to use a library database; establishing a reference is sufficient.

An add-in may contain objects in addition to Visual Basic for applications code. You must create a Windows registry key to use the objects in your add-ins.

Circular References Between Libraries

In previous versions of Microsoft Access, libraries could *contain circular references*, meaning, that procedures in library A could call procedures in library B, and procedures in library B could also call procedures in library A. Visual Basic for applications does not support circular references, therefore they cannot be used in Microsoft Access 7.0. User-defined libraries, created under previous versions, that contain circular references must be modified to eliminate the circular references before they can be used in Microsoft Access 7.0.

If you create a reference from Library A to Library B using the References dialog box, and then try to create a reference from Library B to Library A, you will get an error message.

Custom Add-ins Menu Behavior

If you create a custom menu bar that includes an Add-ins submenu, Microsoft Access automatically adds all of the items that appear on the Microsoft Access Add-ins submenu.

In Microsoft Access 2.0, the Add-ins submenu is on the File menu. In Microsoft Access 7.0, the Add-ins submenu is on the Tools menu. To get the items that appear on the Microsoft Access 7.0 Add-ins submenu to appear on a custom Add-ins submenu, move the custom Add-ins submenu to the Tools menu.

Security

Microsoft Access for Windows 95 includes the following new security features:

- Database password protection
- Integration of the Security Wizard
- Password caching
- AllowBypassKey method
- Hiding objects in the Database window
- Changing a workgroup information file from the command-line

Two of these features, Database Password Protection and Password Caching, may raise some concerns when used in a multiuser setting. By default, any user can set a database password that will lock all other users out of a database. Password caching stores the last user name and password entered if the Microsoft Access Logon dialog box has been activated. This can compromise security—the user doesn't have to re-enter the user's name and password the next time they log on —and can cause complications for users that need to log on using more than one user name. For more information about all of these features, and for details on how to address the potential problems with database passwords and password caching, see "Workgroup Features for Microsoft Access" in Chapter 15.

Interoperability

Microsoft Excel for Windows 95 allows users to create a Microsoft Access form or report, or to convert their spreadsheet to a Microsoft Access database. These commands rely on OLE Automation to move data from Microsoft Excel to Microsoft Access, and to run the appropriate action in Microsoft Access. All three commands are on the Data menu in Excel.

- **Convert To Access**

  This command creates a new database or opens an existing database, and then runs the Import Spreadsheet Wizard to import data from the Microsoft Excel spreadsheet. The data is moved to Microsoft Access; no link is established between the spreadsheet and the Microsoft Access database. This feature can only be used to convert to Microsoft Access 7.0 databases.

- **Access Form**

  This command calls the Microsoft Access Form Wizard with the necessary information for the Form Wizard to automatically connect to the Microsoft Excel list.

- **Access Report**

  This command calls the Microsoft Access Report Wizard with the necessary information for the Report Wizard to automatically connect to the Microsoft Excel list.

Upgrading to Microsoft Excel for Windows 95

This section explains the differences between Microsoft Excel for Windows 95 and Microsoft Excel version 5.0. The file formats are completely compatible, so upgrading to Microsoft Excel 7.0 is relatively straightforward. There are some new capabilities in Microsoft Excel 7.0, such as the Data Map and the Data Access Object programming interface, that are not available to Microsoft Excel 5.0 users. These issues are covered in the following sections.

Microsoft Excel 7.0 uses the system registry to store configuration data. Microsoft Excel 5.0 uses a combination of .ini files and the system registry. If you have customized the Microsoft Excel 5.0 Excel.ini values, these customized values are not migrated to Microsoft Excel 7.0 registry values during installation.

File Formats

Because the file formats for Microsoft Excel 5.0 and 7.0 are completely compatible, files created in Microsoft Excel 5.0 can be opened directly in Microsoft Excel 7.0 and vice versa.

The following standard document properties are available in both Microsoft Excel 5.0 and Microsoft Excel 7.0:

- Title
- Subject
- Author
- Keywords
- Comments
- Name of Application
- Attributes

The following standard document properties are only used in Microsoft Excel 7.0. If a Microsoft Excel 7.0 file is opened in Microsoft Excel 5.0 and then saved, these standard document properties are lost

- Last Saved By
- Created
- Modified

The following standard document properties are displayed in the Microsoft Excel 7.0 Properties dialog box, but are not used by Microsoft Excel 7.0:

- Template
- Revision Number
- Total Editing Time
- Printed

Microsoft Excel 7.0 contains a set of extended document properties. If a Microsoft Excel 7.0 file is opened in Microsoft Excel 5.0 and then saved, the extended document properties are lost. The following list contains the extended document properties:

- Manager
- Company
- Category

Microsoft Excel 7.0 also provides an interface to define custom document properties (the Custom tab in the Properties dialog box). A custom property can obtain its value from a link to a worksheet cell. (To establish the link, you must define a name first.) If a Microsoft Excel 7.0 file is opened in Microsoft Excel 5.0 and then saved, the custom document properties and the links are lost.

Templates

Microsoft Excel 7.0 contains a new set of built-in templates. All of the new Microsoft Excel 7.0 templates work with Microsoft Excel 5.0, unless they use the new Template Wizard. Any template created in Microsoft Excel 7.0 can be opened by Microsoft Excel 5.0. The only loss of function that occurs is if the new template contains a toolbar that includes template-oriented buttons. If you open a template containing a toolbar that includes these buttons in Microsoft Excel 5.0, the toolbar will not appear. All Microsoft Excel 5.0 templates work in Microsoft Excel 7.0.

In Microsoft Excel 5.0, templates are stored in the Xlstart folder. In Microsoft Excel 7.0, the built-in templates are stored in a folder called Spreadsheet Solutions under \Msoffice\Templates. Custom templates in Microsoft Excel 7.0 are stored in the \Msoffice\Templates folder. The New dialog box displays all custom templates, as well as templates stored in the Microsoft Excel 5.0 Xlstart folder, on the General tab, and the built-in templates on the Spreadsheet Solutions tab.

Microsoft Excel 7.0 templates can save information in a database that tracks key cells from each document made from the template. In an expense report, for example, one might be interested in tracking the employee's name, the date of travel, and the amount reimbursed for each form. If a Microsoft Excel 5.0 user attempts to save a file created from a Microsoft Excel 7.0 template, the data will not be saved into the database, but the user will be able to save the file.

Chart Formats

When you upgrade to Microsoft Excel 7.0, your custom chart autoformats aren't automatically saved. You must manually copy the files.

▶ **To copy Microsoft Excel 5.0 autoformats**

1. Before upgrading, copy Xl5galry.xls from your Excel\Xlstart folder to another location on your hard disk.

2. Upgrade to Microsoft Excel 7.0.

3. Copy the saved Xl5galry.xls file into the Microsoft Excel 7.0 Xlstart folder.

Macros

Because the file format for Microsoft Excel 7.0 is compatible with Microsoft Excel 5.0, Microsoft Excel 5.0 users can open and run macros created in Microsoft Excel 7.0.

There are some new Microsoft Excel 7.0 macro features that will not work in Microsoft Excel 5.0. Use the following procedure to identify those features that will not work in Microsoft Excel 5.0. For more information, see Visual Basic online Help.

▶ **To find out which macro features will not work in Microsoft Excel 5.0**

1. Start Microsoft Excel 7.0 and create a new workbook.

2. Insert a new Visual Basic macro module.

3. On the Tools menu, click References.

4. Select the Microsoft DAO 3.0 Object Library.

5. To display the Object Browser, press F2.

6. In the Libraries box, select DAO.

The objects, methods, and properties that are displayed cannot be used in Microsoft Excel 5.0.

In addition, the following objects, methods, and properties cannot be used in Microsoft Excel 5.0:

- AutoCorrect object
- Application.Cursor property
- Workbook.CustomDocumentProperties property
- Workbook.MultiUserEditing property
- Workbook.OnSave property
- UserInterfaceOnly parameter of Workbook/sheet.Protect method

Menus and Shortcut Keys

The following Microsoft Excel 5.0 commands have changed in Microsoft Excel 7.0:

File Menu
- The Find File command has been removed. The options found through the Find File command on the Open menu in Microsoft Excel 5.0 are now in the Open command on the File menu.
- The Summary Info command has been renamed Properties.
- A command called Shared Lists has been added.
- A command called Print Area has been added.

Insert Menu
- A command called Map has been added.
- A command called Object has been added.

Format Menu
A new item called Background has been added to the Sheet command.

Tools Menu
A new command called AutoCorrect has been added.

Data Menu
- A new command called Template Wizard has been added. This command appears only if you have installed the Template Wizard With Data Tracking. This is installed with the Typical installation option.
- Four new commands have been added for the Access Links feature: Access Form, Access Report, Convert To Access, and Get External Data. These commands appear only if you have installed Access Links. This is installed with the Typical installation option.

Help Menu

The Help menu has been redesigned.

Shortcut Keys

- The shortcut key for the Repeat command on the Edit menu has changed from F4 in Microsoft Excel 5.0 to CTRL+Y in Microsoft Excel 7.0. However, F4 will work in Microsoft Excel 7.0, for backward compatibility.

- The shortcut key for the Go To command on the Edit menu was changed from F5 in Microsoft Excel 5.0 to CTRL+G in Microsoft Excel 7.0. However , F5 will work in Microsoft Excel 7.0, for backward compatibility.

- ALT+DOWN ARROW activates the AutoComplete Pick List in Microsoft Excel 7.0. The list contains all completion values for the selected column sorted alphabetically.

Viewing a Data Map in Microsoft Excel 5.0

When you create a data map on a worksheet using Microsoft Excel 7.0 and then save the workbook, Microsoft Excel stores both an OLE object and a bitmap representation of the map. Because of the stored bitmap, a Microsoft Excel 5.0 user can open the file and view the data map. However, the Microsoft Excel 5.0 user cannot double-click the data map to edit it.

The Microsoft Excel 5.0 user can edit the data from which a data map was created, and then save the workbook. The data map will be updated automatically when the workbook is opened in Microsoft Excel 7.0.

Upgrading to Microsoft PowerPoint for Windows 95

This section contains information pertaining to the transition from PowerPoint 4.0 to PowerPoint 7.0. It explains differences between PowerPoint 4.0 and PowerPoint 7.0 file formats, issues that users upgrading to PowerPoint 7.0 need to keep in mind, and examines some of the differences that users will immediately notice.

File Formats

Because of both the new features and the underlying changes made to the architecture of PowerPoint itself, there are differences between the file formats of PowerPoint 4.0 and PowerPoint 7.0.

Reading Older Files into PowerPoint 7.0

PowerPoint 7.0 will read PowerPoint files from PowerPoint 2.0 through 4.0.

Converting Older Files into PowerPoint 7.0 Format

To convert files created with previous versions of PowerPoint, open the file in PowerPoint 7.0, choose the Save As command on the File menu, and select Presentations in the Save As Type list.

Note If you want to convert a large number of files to PowerPoint 7.0 format, the Microsoft Office Resource Kit CD includes a conversion utility called BatchConvert.exe that you can use to convert multiple files at once. As you run the utility, you can specify a new destination and extension for the converted files.

Reading PowerPoint 7.0 Files in PowerPoint 4.0

PowerPoint 7.0 files cannot be directly opened and saved in PowerPoint 4.0. There are two ways for PowerPoint 4.0 to read PowerPoint 7.0 files.

- In PowerPoint 7.0, save files in PowerPoint 4.0 format. The PowerPoint Viewer, which must be installed to save in PowerPoint 4.0 format, converts the files for you.

- In PowerPoint 4.0, install a filter to open PowerPoint 7.0 files.

To save in PowerPoint 4.0 format, use the Save As command on the File menu, and select the PowerPoint 4.0 option. Behind the scenes, PowerPoint 7.0 launches the PowerPoint Viewer, which then saves the file in PowerPoint 4.0 format. When you save in PowerPoint 4.0 format, any PowerPoint 7.0-specific features and effects are lost.

About the PowerPoint Viewer

The PowerPoint Viewer shipped with the initial release of PowerPoint 7.0 is a 16-bit version similar to the one provided with PowerPoint 4.0, and runs on both Windows 95 and Windows 3.1. The 16-bit Viewer allows you to view presentations created by PowerPoint 4.0 or PowerPoint 7.0, but does not support some of the new PowerPoint 7.0 online presentation features, such as object builds, two-color shaded fills, and textured fills.

To install the Viewer, choose Add/Remove Office Programs from the Office Shortcut Bar menu. For custom installation scripts, make sure that the Viewer application is specified for installation on machines where sharing files between versions of PowerPoint is important.

Note An updated 32-bit version of the PowerPoint Viewer application will be available after PowerPoint 7.0 ships. The new version will support all of the new PowerPoint 7.0 online presentation features. To obtain a copy, contact Microsoft Customer Service, download it from the Microsoft Network, the Microsoft forum on CompuServe®, or Microsoft Select. For more information, see the list of resources in Appendix F, "Resources."

Embedded Fonts Are Not Saved

The PowerPoint Save As dialog box includes the Embed TrueType option that saves the fonts used in the presentation along with the file when the check box is selected. The Viewer does not support this, so you must make sure that the fonts you need are available on the destination computer. In addition, when you save PowerPoint 7.0 files in PowerPoint 4.0 format, fonts cannot be embedded because the Viewer is used to implement the file conversion.

About the Installable Filters

Installable filters that you can use to open PowerPoint 7.0 files are available on the Microsoft Office Resource Kit CD for both the Windows and Macintosh versions of PowerPoint 4.0.

- For the Windows version of PowerPoint, the Vsetup program is provided, which installs the filter to PowerPoint 4.0. Simply copying the filters to users' machines will not work. The Vsetup program must be used to install them.

- For the Macintosh version of PowerPoint, you can simply copy the filter to the PowerPoint folder.

Note Installable filters for the PowerMacintosh version of PowerPoint 4.0 will be available by the end of 1995. To obtain them, contact Microsoft Customer Service, download it from the Microsoft Network, the Microsoft forum on CompuServe, or Microsoft Select. For more information , see the list of resources in Appendix F, "Resources."

Some Macintosh Features Not Supported

When sharing presentations between PowerPoint 7.0 and PowerPoint 4.0 for the Macintosh, Publish and Subscribe is not supported, nor are QuickTime features.

Sharing PowerPoint 7.0 Files With PowerPoint 3.0 Users

You can save PowerPoint 7.0 files in PowerPoint 4.0 format, but you cannot directly save them in PowerPoint 3.0 format. Instead, you need to use the Save As command in PowerPoint 7.0 to save in PowerPoint 4.0 format, then open the presentation in PowerPoint 4.0 and save it again in PowerPoint 3.0 format. Of course, PowerPoint 7.0 features and effects that are not supported in PowerPoint 3.0 are lost in the transition process.

Differences Between PowerPoint 7.0 and PowerPoint 4.0 Files

PowerPoint 7.0 files opened in PowerPoint 4.0 retain their PowerPoint 7.0–specific attributes, but any effects that are not supported in PowerPoint 4.0 are not displayed.

PowerPoint 7.0 files that are saved in PowerPoint 4.0 format lose any PowerPoint 7.0–specific features. This section identifies features particular to PowerPoint 7.0, and what happens to them in PowerPoint 4.0.

Builds

In PowerPoint, progressive disclosure of items on a slide, one item at a time, is called a *build*. Only bulleted-list builds will continue to work when a PowerPoint 7.0 presentation is saved in PowerPoint 4.0 format. All other types of PowerPoint 7.0 builds are ignored.

Interactive Buttons

Using the Interactive Settings command on the Tools menu, graphic objects in PowerPoint 7.0 can become *interactive buttons* that you can use to branch to other slides or other presentations, or to open other OLE applications. When you save a presentation containing interactive buttons in PowerPoint 4.0 format, only the graphic itself is saved. Any interactivity that has been applied using entries in the Object Action box in the Interactive Settings dialog box is lost in the transition.

Headers and Footers

PowerPoint 4.0 does not have a Header And Footer command, as does PowerPoint 7.0. However, headers and footers in PowerPoint 7.0 are preserved when you save a presentation in PowerPoint 4.0 format.

Graphics

The following table outlines the specific mapping from PowerPoint 7.0 features to PowerPoint 4.0.

Black and white view in PowerPoint 7.0 is translated to a regular full-color representation in version 4.0, according to the specifics outlined in the following table.

PowerPoint 7.0 feature	PowerPoint 4.0 conversion	Comments
Semi-Transparent Object Fill	Solid	PowerPoint 4.0 displays the solid color that would be seen if the Semi-Transparent check box is cleared in PowerPoint 7.0.
Automatic Fill	PowerPoint 4.0 default fill color	
Two-Color Shaded Fill	Plain shaded	PowerPoint 7.0 color #1 maps to non-black PowerPoint 4.0 color. If black, maps to PowerPoint 7.0 color #2.
Preset Shaded Fill	None	No fill applied.
Textured Fill	Default fill color	Matches whatever shaded fill exists in the object. If none, maps to default fill color.
Background Pattern	None	No pattern applied.
Background Texture	None	No texture applied.
Background Picture	Picture Object	Picture object is placed on slide and sized to fill the slide.
Line: Automatic Color	PowerPoint 4.0 default line color	
Line: Arrows (New Styles)	Closest equivalent	The line points in the same direction.

Document Properties

The following standard set of document properties is found in both PowerPoint 4.0 and PowerPoint 7.0:

- Title
- Subject
- Author
- Keywords
- Comments

- File Name (MS-DOS Name)
- Directory (Location)
- Template
- Slides

PowerPoint 7.0 contains an extended set of standard document properties. If a PowerPoint 7.0 file is saved in PowerPoint 4.0 format, the extended document properties are lost.

The following extended set of document properties is found only in PowerPoint 7.0:

- Manager
- Company
- Category
- Type
- Location
- Size
- Created
- Modified
- Accessed
- Attributes (read-only, archive, system, hidden)
- Printed
- Last Saved By

- Revision Number
- Total Editing Time
- Paragraphs
- Words
- Bytes
- Notes
- Hidden Slides
- Multimedia Clips
- Fonts Used
- Presentation Designs
- Slide Titles

PowerPoint 7.0 also provides the user with a method of defining custom properties for the presentation. These custom properties are found on the Custom tab in the Presentation Properties dialog box. If a PowerPoint 4.0 user saves a file from PowerPoint 7.0 containing custom properties, the custom properties are lost.

Templates

Although the set of templates shipped with PowerPoint 7.0 have been updated and new content has been added, all PowerPoint 7.0 templates will work with PowerPoint 4.0 and vice versa. You will need to install the filters described earlier to open PowerPoint 7.0 templates in PowerPoint 4.0.

For more information, see Chapter 4, "Microsoft PowerPoint Architecture."

Changes to Menus and Shortcut Keys

The following lists show the PowerPoint 7.0 menu and shortcut key items that have changed or are new since PowerPoint 4.0:

File Menu

- Find File command removed. Enhanced Find File features are is now found in the Open dialog box on the File menu.

- Summary Info command removed. The information is now in the Properties dialog box.

Edit Menu

- Repeat command added, with the shortcut key CTRL+Y.

- Go To Property command added, which takes you to the assigned custom property fields.

View Menu

- Outline Master command replaced with Title Master command.

- The Handout Master command now also determines the layout of outlines.

- Black And White command added, which displays the presentation in black and white, approximating the way the presentation will print on a non-color printer.

- Slide Miniature command added, which displays a color thumbnail view of the current slide (useful when editing in Black and White view when the slide is displayed at a high zoom percentage).

Insert Menu

- Date command and Time command replaced by the Date And Time command.

- Movie command added to insert an AVI video clip.

- Sound command added to inset a sound file.

Format Menu

- Presentation Template command replaced by the Apply Design Template command.

- Pick A Look Wizard command removed and replaced by slide templates and color schemes.

- Slide Background command replaced by Custom Background command, which applies colors, patterns, fills, or pictures to the slide background.

- Slide Footer command added in the Slide View and Slide Sorter View.

- Notes Header and Footer command added in the Notes View.

Tools Menu

- Transition command replaced by the Slide Transition command.

- Build command replaced by the Build Slide Text command. Object builds are now possible using the Animation Settings command.

- Play Settings command replaced by the Animation Settings command.

- AutoCorrect command added.

- AutoClipArt command added.

- Interactive Settings command added, which assigns actions to occur when an object is clicked.

- Presentation Conference command added.

- Write-Up command added.

Window Menu

New Window command added.

Help Menu

- Contents, Search For Help On, and Index commands replaced by the Microsoft PowerPoint Help Topics command and the Answer Wizard command.

- Quick Preview command and Cue Cards command were removed.

- The Microsoft Network command was added to give you quick access to the Microsoft Network, if you have a modem.

- Technical Support command was removed; the information is now available by clicking the Tech Support button in the About Microsoft PowerPoint dialog box.

Upgrading to Microsoft Schedule+ for Windows 95

This section contains information about how Schedule+ 1.0 (.cal) files are converted to Schedule+ 7.0 (.scd) files when a user starts Schedule+ 7.0 for the first time.

Upgrading Existing Calendar Files

When Schedule+ 7.0 is run for the first time, it searches for the path to an existing Schedule+ 1.0 calendar (.cal) file on the user's local machine in the following locations:

- Schedule+ 1.0 .ini file

- For mail-enabled clients, the current user's profile entry:

  `HKey_Current_User\Software\Microsoft\Windows Messaging Subsystem`
  `\Profiles\[name of profile]\5363686564756c65506c7573322e3000\`

- The Schedule+ registry entry:

  `HKey_Current_User\Software\Microsoft\Schedule+\Application`

If a Schedule+ 1.0 file is found, the user is asked if they want to use the existing information. If the answer is yes, data from the Schedule+ 1.0 calendar file is imported into Schedule+ 7.0. The server version of the 1.0 file is also converted to the new format at the next update interval, usually 15 minutes after logon.

However, if an existing .cal file is not found, the following dialog box appears:

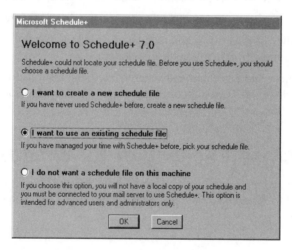

Users can choose to work with a new file, or use a standard file-open dialog box to specify the location of an existing 7.0 file.

Users can also choose to work with a Schedule+ file on the server only. However, this is not usually required. One exception is where a resource schedule file needs to be accessed by multiple delegates. In this case, individual copies of the schedule file on each delegate's workstation are not needed.

Administrators can update resource calendar files (for resources such as conference rooms) by logging on with Schedule+ 7.0 under the name of the resource. However, in most cases this shouldn't be required, because Schedule+ 7.0 can read free/busy times from Schedule+ 1.0 files, and free/busy times is usually the only kind of data required from resource calendar files. However, if a resource calendar has information that needs to be managed by a delegate, known as an *assistant* in Schedule+ 1.0, or schedule details that need to be viewed by others, then the calendar file should be converted to Schedule+ 7.0.

Menus and Shortcut Keys

The menu structure of Schedule+ for Windows 95 has changed from Schedule+ 1.0 to make it more consistent with other Microsoft Office applications. The following table summarizes where Schedule+ 1.0 menu commands can now be found in Schedule+ 7.0:

Schedule+ 1.0 commands on this menu	Now found on this Schedule+ 7.0 menu
File	File and Options (turn off reminders)
Edit	Edit
Appointments	Edit, View, and Insert
Tasks	Edit, View, and Insert
Options	Tools and View (status bar, display options)
Help	Help
Window	[none]

Upgrading to Microsoft Word for Windows 95

This section addresses issues when upgrading from or coexisting with earlier versions of Word for Windows or the Macintosh. Word for Windows 95 will run unmodified in Windows NT version 3.51 or later.

Word and the Office Resource Kit CD-ROM include several tools to help you convert or share files with other word processor applications. For a complete list of file and graphics converters supported by Word 7.0, see Chapter 20, "Switching to Microsoft Word."

Upgrading from Word 6.0 for Windows or the Macintosh

Because the file formats of Word 7.0 and Word 6.0 are almost completely compatible, upgrading to Word 7.0 is relatively straightforward. There are some new capabilities in Word 7.0, such as the Spell-It and text highlighting features, that are not available to Word 6.0 users. These issues are discussed in the following sections.

Most .ini files and their associated entries have been moved to the registry. The exceptions are Msfontmap.ini and Mstxcnv.ini.

If a user has customized any Word 6.0 .ini entries that are moved to the registry in Word for Windows 95, these customized entries are lost when upgrading to Word for Windows 95 File Formats.

Word 7.0 files can be directly opened and saved in Word 6.0. However if a Word 7.0 file is saved in Word 6.0, any text highlighting will be lost.

If you or a user have updated a computer to PowerPoint for Windows 95 or Publisher for Windows 95, but have not updated to Word for Windows 95 on that computer, PowerPoint or Publisher will attempt to install the 16-bit converters, and will display an error message.

Word 7.0 contains a highlighting feature that marks text in a variety of colors, like a highlighting pen. If you open a Word 7.0 file in Word 6.0, you won't see the highlighting; if you then save the file in Word 6.0, the highlighting is lost. As long as you don't save the file in Word 6.0, the highlighting will show again when you next open the file in Word 7.0.

The following standard set of document properties is found in both Word 6.0 and Word for Windows 95:

- Title
- Subject
- Author
- Keywords
- Comments
- File Name (now labeled MS-DOS Name)
- Directory (now labeled Location)
- Template
- Created
- Last Saved (now labeled Modified)

- Last Saved By
- File Size (now labeled Size)
- Revision Number
- Total Editing Time
- Last Printed (now labeled Printed)
- Pages
- Words
- Characters
- Paragraphs
- Lines

Word 7.0 contains an extended set of standard document properties. If a Word 7.0 file is saved in Word 6.0, the extended document properties are lost. The following extended set of document properties is found in Word for Windows 95:

- Type
- Accessed
- Attributes
- Manager

- Company
- Category
- Bytes
- Document Contents

Word 7.0 also provides the user with a method of defining custom properties for the document. These custom properties are on the Custom tab in the Properties dialog box. If a Word 6.0 user saves a file with these custom properties, they are lost.

When you save a document in Word 6.0 for the Macintosh, data associated with the Macintosh-only Publish/Subscribe feature is stored in the file. This data is ignored when you open the document using Word 7.0 on either Windows 95 or Windows NT. However, when you save the file using Word 7.0 on Windows 95 or Windows NT, the Macintosh-specific data is preserved in the file.

If you have to convert a large number of files to Word 7.0 format, use the macros in the Convert template included with Word 7.0. You can also use the Convert template's macros to convert Word 7.0 files to another format.

Templates

Although the set of templates shipped with Word 7.0 has grown, all Word 7.0 templates work unchanged with Word 6.0 and vice versa. Word 7.0 stores all templates in a common office folder, \Msoffice\Templates.

If you or your users have designed custom templates, Word 7.0 will upgrade the existing Word 6.0 template folder. Office Setup will create a shortcut to your Word 6.0 template folder in the new Office templates folder.

Macros

Most Word 6.0 macros run unchanged in Word 7.0. The only exception is Word 6.0 macros that call 16-bit DLLs, which will produce errors in Word 7.0. These macros must be rewritten with declare statements that call 32-bit DLLs with similar functionality. 16-bit Word add-in libraries (WLLs) must also be rewritten and recompiled. For more information, see "Porting Your 16-bit Office-Based Solutions to 32-bit Office," in Chapter 12, "Support and Troubleshooting."

Word 7.0 macros that have been rewritten with 32-bit DLLs and WLLs will still open in Word 6.0, but these macros will not run properly. Any new statements will show up as "Unrecognized_Statement###" where the ### corresponds to the tokenized number of the macro statement.

When rewriting macros, use APPINFO$ to figure out what version of Word is in use and what operating system (platform) it is running on. This way, macros can be made to work on all versions and all platforms of Word 6.0 and 7.0.

Menus and Shortcut Keys

The following Word 6.0 menu items have changed in Word 7.0.

File Menu

- Find File command removed. Enhanced Find File functionality is now found in the Open dialog box on the File menu.

- Summary Info command removed. The information is now in the Properties dialog box.

Help Menu

- Contents, Search For Help On, and Index commands replaced by the Microsoft Word Help Topics command and the Answer Wizard command.

- Quick Preview command and Cue Cards command have been removed.

- The Microsoft Network command has been added to give you quick access to the Microsoft Network, if you have a modem.

- Technical Support command has been removed. The information is now available by clicking the Tech Support button in the About Microsoft Word dialog box.

Upgrading from Word Version 2.x for Windows

The file formats for Word 2.x and Word 7.0 differ. However, you can directly open and save Word 7.0 files in Word 2.x if you've installed the Word 2 converter included on the Office Resource Kit CD-ROM. Using this converter makes it easier for groups of users with different versions of Word to share files. For installation instructions, see Appendix D, "Contents of the Office Resource Kit CD."

Converting Between Word 7.0 and Word Version 2.x

Word 7.0 reads all previous formats of Word for Windows directly. This section discusses problems or limitations that may arise when converting Word 7.0 documents into Word 2.0 format, either by saving as Word for Windows 2.0 format or by reading the Word for Windows 7.0 document into Word 2.0.

In the following table, "Yes" means the feature exists in both products and is converted from one product to the other. "No" means it exists in both products but is not completely converted between the two. "Not supported" means the feature is not supported in one of the products or is not converted completely between products.

Feature	Word 7.0 to Word 2.0	Comments
Character Formatting		
Superscript/Subscript	Not supported	This property is emulated with raised/lowered character formatting.
Expand/Condense	Yes	Word 7.0 supports finer control of this property. The value is rounded to the closest value Word 2.0 supports.
Underline	Yes	Dotted-underline formatting not supported in Word 2.0
Kerning	Not supported	
Paragraph Formatting		
Borders, shading	See comment	Word 7.0 has more borders and shading options than Word 2.0. Word 7.0 borders are mapped to the closest value available in Word 2.0.
Other Features		
Cell borders, shading	See comment	Word 7.0 has more borders and shading options than Word 2.0. Word 7.0 borders are mapped to the closest approximation in Word 2.0.
Fields	See comment	Word 7.0 has additional fields and field switches. These are preserved in conversion along with the current results. If these fields are updated, the results may be lost. Reopening the file in Word 7.0 and updating the fields will restore the result.
Drawing layer	No	All drawn objects are lost.
Form fields	See comment	Results of text fields are displayed. Other form fields and bar code fields have no result to display.
Styles	See comment	Word 2.0 allows only 223 user-defined styles. Style numbers greater than 223, and style references to them, are not retained, although the formatting is.
Endnotes	Yes	All footnotes and endnotes are retained, but they are merged into one continuous stream.
Bullets/Numbering	Yes	Automatic bullets and numbers are converted to plain text.
Character styles	No	Style definitions are lost, although formatting is retained.
Bar tabs	No	

Feature	Word 7.0 to Word 2.0	Comments
Other Features *(continued)*		
Mail merge	See comment	When opening Word 7.0 documents in Word 2.0, mail merge documents (main documents, header sources, and data sources) lose their association with each other. This association can be restored by running Print Merge again.
Master documents	No	Master documents lose the contents and association with the subdocuments. Subdocuments are automatically converted into separate files if you save as Word 2.0. Reading in Word 7.0 files will only convert the master document.
Revision marks	See comment	Multiple author and/or color revision marks convert to single color.
Variable-width columns	Not supported	Variable-width columns are mapped to equal-width columns.
Bookmarks and references	See comment	Word 7.0 allows greater flexibility in naming bookmarks. These are converted as closely as possible along with the corresponding references.
Page numbering	See comment	Word 7.0 has more page numbering options than Word 2.0. These are mapped to the closest alternative in Word 2.0.

Upgrading from Word version 4.0 or 5.x for the Macintosh

This section contains information pertaining to sharing files between Word 5.x for the Macintosh and Word 7.0, or upgrading from Word 4.0 or 5.x for the Macintosh to Word 7.0.

Sharing Documents Between Word 7.0 and Word version 5.x for the Macintosh

The file formats for Word 5.x and Word 7.0 differ. However, you can directly open documents created with Word 7.0 for Windows or Word 6.0 for Windows or Word 6.0 for the Macintosh in Word 5.x if you've installed the Word 6.0 Converter. Using this converter makes it easier for groups of users with different versions of Word to share files. If a complete installation of Word 6.0 exists on the same Macintosh computer as Word 5.x, the converter is available for installation and use with Word 5.x. If not, you can obtain the converter from several online sources. For more information, see Appendix F, "Resources."

After you've obtained the converter, see the installation instructions that are included with the converter. Word 4.0 cannot use the converter. In Word 7.0, save documents you want to share with Word 4.0 users in Word 4.0 for the Macintosh format.

Converting Between Word 7.0 and Word version 4.0 or *5.x* for the Macintosh

Word 7.0 reads Word 4.0 and 5.*x* for the Macintosh file formats directly. Word 7.0 also fully supports long filenames. If your workgroup shares files between Macintosh computers and computers running Windows, you do not need to change document filenames.

In the following table, "Yes" means the feature exists in both products and is converted from one product to the other. "No" means it exists in both products but is not completely converted between the two. "Not supported" means the feature is not supported in one of the products or is not converted completely between products.

Feature	Word 7.0 to Word for the Macintosh	Word for the Macintosh to Word 7.0	Comments
Character Formatting			
Outline	Not supported	See comment	Converted to normal text in Word 7.0.
Shadow	Not supported	See comment	Converted to normal text in Word 7.0.
Superscript/ Subscript	See comment	Yes	Word 7.0 superscript/subscript is different from previous versions of Word. This property is emulated using raised/lowered character formatting.
Kerning	No	Not supported	
Expand/ Condense	See comment	Yes	Word 7.0 supports finer control of this property. This value is rounded to the closest value that Word for the Macintosh supports.
Paragraph Formatting			
Borders/Shading	See comment	Yes	Word 7.0 has more options for borders and shading than Word for the Macintosh, including color. These are mapped to the closest Word for the Macintosh value available.
Columns			
Columns	Yes	Yes	Line Between not converted.
Variable-width columns	See comment	Not supported	Variable-width columns are mapped to equal-width columns in Word for the Macintosh.

Feature	Word 7.0 to Word for the Macintosh	Word for the Macintosh to Word 7.0	Comments
Columns (*continued*)			
Page formatting	See comment	See comment	Page formatting for Word for the Macintosh documents is stored in the Macintosh print record. On export, the converter is unable to create a print record.
Page orientation	No	Yes	
Page size	No	Yes	
Paper source	No	Yes	
Section Formatting			
Line numbering (Start At *number*)	No	Not supported	
Vertical alignment (top, centered, justified)	No	Not supported	
Other Features			
Annotations	See comment	Yes	Annotations are retained when converting to Word for the Macintosh version 5.1; otherwise, annotations are converted to footnotes.
Fields (FILENAME)	No	Not supported	
Graphics	See comment	Yes	When converting from Word 7.0 to Word for the Macintosh version 5.x, graphics are retained, provided the conversion is performed from within Word for the Macintosh. When converting to Word for the Macintosh version 4, an empty graphics frame is created in the Word for the Macintosh document.
Language	No	Not supported	
Revision marks	No	Not supported	Character formatting indicating revised text is retained.
Subdocuments (INCLUDE field)	See comment	Not supported	If the RetainInclude flag is set to Yes in the [MacWordConv] section of Mstxtcnv.ini, then the include field will be converted; however, any path information in the field will be lost. Otherwise the latest result is inserted in the Word for the Macintosh document and the INCLUDE field is lost.

Feature	Word 7.0 to Word for the Macintosh	Word for the Macintosh to Word 7.0	Comments
Other Features *(continued)*			
Master documents	No	Not supported	Master documents lose the contents of the subdocuments and the references, but all the subdocuments are converted (at the same time as the master document) into separate documents.
Cross-references and bookmarks	No	Not supported	
Object linking and embedding	Yes	Yes	OLE objects may be edited after conversion, providing the OLE server is available on the target platform.
Drawing layer	No	Not supported	
Cell borders/ shading	See comment	Yes	Word 7.0 has more options for borders and shading than Word for the Macintosh, including color. These are mapped to the closest Word for the Macintosh value available.
Fields (Form and bar code fields)	See comment	Not supported	Results of text form fields are retained. Other fields have no result that can be displayed.
Styles	See comment	See comment	Word for the Macintosh allows only 255 defined styles. Style definitions numbered greater than that are omitted, along with any references to them. All formatting is preserved, however.
Character styles	No	Not supported	Character style definitions are lost. All formatting is retained.
Bullets/ Numbering	See comment	Not supported	Automatic bullets/numbers are converted to plain text.
Endnotes	See comment	Not supported	All footnotes and endnotes are retained, but they are merged into one continuous stream.
Page numbering	See comment	Yes	Word 7.0 has more page numbering options than Word for the Macintosh. These are mapped to the closest alternative.
Extended characters	See comment	See comment	Some ANSI extended characters have no Macintosh character set equivalent, and vice versa. If the equivalent character is not available, it is replaced by the underscore (_) character. Equivalent characters available in fonts such as Symbol or Wingdings® can be used to replace lost characters following conversion. Characters available in the unique symbol sets of Microsoft TrueType fonts are retained, provided that the same font is available on both platforms.

PART 3

Maintaining and Supporting Microsoft Office

Chapter 11, "Maintaining, Customizing, and Optimizing Office" contains information on maintaining your Microsoft Office for Windows 95 installation on an ongoing basis: specifically, how to update your Office installation with new Microsoft releases, customize user environments, and tune user systems for optimum performance.

Chapter 12, "Support and Troubleshooting" covers support issues for the Office applications. It also includes information on customizing templates in Office so your users can follow whatever corporate standards exist for creating documents. Also in this chapter is information about porting 16-bit Office-based solutions to 32-bit.

CHAPTER 11

Maintaining, Customizing, and Optimizing Office

This chapter contains information about maintaining your Microsoft Office for Windows 95 installation on an ongoing basis; specifically how to update your Office installation with new Microsoft releases, customize user environments, and tune user systems for optimum performance.

In This Chapter

Updating Software

After the initial release of Microsoft Office for Windows 95, Microsoft may, from time to time, release software updates for Office. If you decide to update your users' computers with a new version, the process of installing the update is very similar to the way in which Office was installed originally.

While installing the updated software, you can simply update the software using the same configuration or you can change the way your client systems are configured. For instance, you may want to change whether shared applications are installed on the user's local hard drive or shared on the network. Either way, the steps you need to follow are outlined below.

Updating Office — Keeping the Same Configuration

Updating the Office software on client computers without changing client software configurations is a simple process.

Warning You cannot update an Office installation using the standalone product versions of Office applications (Microsoft Access, Microsoft Excel, PowerPoint, Schedule+, or Word). To update Office software, you need to use an updated version of the Microsoft Office product.

Installing from CD or Floppy Disks

If your users originally installed Office from CD or floppy disks, they can install the Office update the same way.

▶ **To update Office from CD or floppy disks**

1. Close all Office applications.

2. Run Setup.exe from the CD or floppy disk 1.

3. Follow the instructions on the screen.

Installing from the Network

If your users originally installed Office from an administrative installation point on a network server, the process for updating users involves two steps: updating the Office administrative installation point on the network from which Office was installed originally, and then running Setup from the user computers to update the user systems.

▶ **To update the Office administrative installation point**

1. Have all users log off the server. Users must not access the server during the update and all files should be closed.

2. Completely delete the existing Office folder structure. When Office was installed, two directories were created: one for the main Office files (default name is \MSOffice) and one for shared application files (default name is \MSApps). Both of these directories, including all the files and subdirectories under them, must be deleted.

   If you have placed any workgroup documents, templates, or other custom files in either of these directories, move the files before deleting these directories. After the installation is complete, you can move the files back into the Office folder structure. If you have customized the Setup.stf file, do not copy this file into the updated Office folder—customize the Setup.stf file that is included with the updated version of Office instead.

3. Run Setup.exe from the CD or floppy disks with the **/a** option to install the new version of Office into the same directories as the previous version.

```
setup /a
```

4. When asked where the shared applications are to be installed, specify the location the same way you did when installing Office previously. If you specified that the shared applications will be accessed with a drive letter, specify the same drive letter again. Or if you specified the location with a UNC path, use the same path again.

After the administrative installation point is updated, user computers can be updated.

▶ **To update user computers**

1. Close all Office applications.

2. Run Setup.exe from the main Office folder on the administrative installation point.

3. Follow the instructions on the screen.

As during the original installation of Office, you can have users run Setup.exe themselves, or you can automate the process using the techniques described in Chapter 9, "Customizing Client Installations."

Adding Microsoft Access to Office Standard

If you purchased the Standard version of Office and you want to add Microsoft Access to your Office installation, you need to purchase the Professional version of Office. The standalone Microsoft Access product cannot be used to update a Microsoft Office installation. After you purchase Office Professional, follow the same steps given earlier for updating Office software.

Updating Office—Changing the Configuration

While updating Office software, you can take the opportunity to change the way Office is configured on your network. With your original installation, user computers may have been configured so that all Office software is located on the user's local hard disk, or so that some or all of the Office components are shared on a network server. While installing an Office update, you can change this configuration. For example, you may have upgraded your network servers and would now like users to run the Office shared applications from a network server rather than having them stored on their local hard disks.

Changing your Office configuration is a two-step process. First, you need to create or update your administrative installation point with updated software and with new configuration options. Second, users must uninstall Office and reinstall it to get the new version.

If your users originally installed Office from the CD or floppy disks, you need to create an administrative installation point on a network server from which users can install Office. For instructions on creating an administrative installation point, see Chapter 8, "Installing Microsoft Office."

If you have an existing administrative installation point, you need to update it.

▶ **To update the Office administrative installation point**

1. Have all users log off the server. Users must not access the server during the update and all files should be closed.

2. Select a new network server location for the update. Office Setup will need to create the administrative installation point in a clean folder (no pre-existing files). You cannot delete the existing Office folder structure yet because users must use the current Setup program to remove their existing Office installations.

3. Run Setup.exe from the CD or floppy disks with the **/a** option to install the new version of Office into the new directories on the server.

   ```
   setup /a
   ```

4. In response to prompts from Setup, enter any new configuration information, such as where the shared applications will be located.

Because configuration information is being changed, your users will next need to remove their existing version of Office and then install the new version.

▶ **To update user computers**

1. Close all Office applications.

2. Run Setup.exe from the same location it was run originally.

3. Click Remove All.

4. When Setup completes, connect to the new administrative installation point and run Setup.exe from the main Office folder.

5. Follow the instructions on the screen.

As during the original installation of Office, you can have users run Setup.exe themselves, or you can automate the process using the techniques described in Chapter 9, "Customizing Client Installations." Using these techniques, you can automate the removal of the existing version of Office, and the installation of the updated version of Office. To automate removal, use the **/u** Setup command line option; for more information, see Appendix A, "Setup Command Line Options and File Format."

Customizing the User Environment

Windows 95 system policies are used to restrict or predefine the desktop and network configuration on each client computer, including restricting or optimizing Office features and capabilities. System policies are defined by the administrator in a central network location, then Windows 95 client computers automatically use these system policies to update or modify local registry settings. For example, if you want all the users in a workgroup to use a shared folder for Word template files, use system policies to set the default Word template file folder from a central location.

Enabling policies involves creating a single file that resides on a server. A template file of Office policies is included with the *Resource Kit* CD. After installing the template file, you can modify it by running the Windows 95 System Policy Editor.

For details on how to implement system policies, see Chapter 15, "User Profiles and System Policies," in the *Microsoft Windows 95 Resource Kit*.

▶   **To read and edit the Office policies template**

1. Run the System Policy Editor.

2. Choose the mode you want to use: Registry or Policy File.

   In Registry mode, you edit the contents of the registry directly, and changes are reflected immediately.

   In Policy File mode, you create or modify system policies for future implementation.

3. In the System Policy Editor, make sure that that all policy files are closed.

4. On the Options menu, click Template.

5. Click Open Template and select the Office template file.

6. Click Close to return to the System Policy Editor.

7. Edit the policy, as needed.

Optimizing Microsoft Access for Windows 95

Depending on your computer's configuration and your working environment, there may be several things you can do to improve the performance of Microsoft Access or your database. The optimal settings in the categories listed below can vary with the type of computer on which you run Microsoft Access.

Using the Performance Analyzer

The place to start when you want to optimize the performance of a Microsoft Access database is with the Performance Analyzer. You can use the Performance Analyzer to analyze a whole database or just selected objects in a database. The Performance Analyzer can even make some changes for you automatically if you want.

▶ **To run the Performance Analyzer**

1. Open the database you want to optimize.

2. On the Tools menu, point to Analyze, and then click Performance.

3. In the Object Type list, click the type of database object you want to optimize.

   To view a list of all database objects at once, click All.

4. In the Object Name list, select the database objects to optimize.

   To select all database objects of that type, click Select All.

5. Repeat steps 3 and 4 until you have selected all the objects you want to optimize, and then click OK.

A list of three kinds of performance suggestions is displayed: Recommendations, Suggestions, and Ideas. When you click an item in the list, information about the proposed optimization is displayed below the list. Microsoft Access can perform Recommendation and Suggestion optimizations for you. You must perform Idea optimizations yourself.

- To perform specific Recommendation or Suggestion optimizations, click the optimization you want performed, and then click Optimize.

- To perform all Recommendation or Suggestion optimizations, click Optimize All.

- To perform an Idea optimization, click that optimization, and then follow the instructions displayed in Suggestion Notes.

Optimizing Your System to Run Microsoft Access

In addition to running the Performance Analyzer, the following suggestions can help you optimize the performance of Microsoft Access and your computer itself.

- Use the Add-in Manager to uninstall wizards, builders, and other add-ins you don't need. This reduces memory consumption and load time of Microsoft Access.

- Make more memory available by closing applications that you aren't using.

- Increase RAM on your computer. Microsoft Access requires a minimum of 12 MB, but additional RAM improves performance.

- If you have less than 16 MB of RAM, don't use any of your RAM for a RAM disk.

- Occasionally delete unnecessary files, compact your databases, and then defragment your hard disk with the Windows System Tools Disk Defragmenter.

- In most cases, the default virtual memory setting used by Windows should perform optimally. However, in some situations adjusting virtual memory parameters can improve performance. If you've already tried deleting unnecessary files, and you still have a performance problem, try changing the drive used for virtual memory if:

    - You don't have much disk space available on the drive that is currently being used for virtual memory and another local drive with space is available.

    - Another local drive is available that is faster than the current drive (unless that disk is heavily used).

    You also might get better performance by specifying that the disk space available for virtual memory cannot be less than 25 minus available RAM. You may want to specify more if you are running several large applications.

    To change Windows virtual memory parameters, in Windows Control Panel, double-click the System icon, click the Performance tab, click the Virtual Memory button, and then click Let Me Specify My Own Virtual Memory Settings. Then specify a different hard disk, or enter a value in the Minimum box that is no less than 25 minus your available RAM.

- When using databases that other users don't have to share, install Microsoft Access and all your databases on your hard disk drive rather than on a network server.

- If you have a wallpaper (full-screen background) bitmap on your Windows desktop, replace it with a solid color or pattern bitmap, or no bitmap at all.

In addition to the above suggestions, you may want to adjust Jet settings in the Windows registry. Settings in the Jet section of the Windows registry control how the Microsoft Jet database engine uses memory in some of its operations. The Jet database engine provides default settings that usually give the best performance for most common database operations. However, depending on what kind of operations your application performs and how much memory is available at any given time, you may be able to improve performance by adjusting these settings.

Tip   Keep in mind that the optimum value for a setting can change from computer to computer, and can even change on an individual computer depending on how much memory is available at any given time. You'll need to experiment with these settings to find out what works best, using a system that's as much like your typical user's system as possible.

The following Jet settings have the most significant impact on performance:

- **MaxBufferSize**   The MaxBufferSize setting controls the maximum size of the Jet database engine's *internal cache* (the cache the Jet database engine uses to store records in memory), measured in kilobytes. The Jet database engine reads data in 2K pages, placing the data in the cache. After the data is in the cache, Microsoft Access can use it wherever it's needed—in tables, queries, forms, or reports.

  The default setting is 512K; you can set it to any value from 18 to 4096. For computers with minimal memory (8 MB), consider setting MaxBufferSize to a value less than 512K to free more memory for other Microsoft Access operations. For high-memory machines, try increasing the MaxBufferSize setting. This enables the Jet database engine to read more records into its memory cache, which minimizes time-consuming reading of the hard disk.

- **ReadAheadPages**   The ReadAheadPages setting controls the number of 2K data pages the Jet database engine reads ahead when doing sequential page reads. A sequential page read occurs when the Jet database engine detects that data in a current read request is on a data page adjacent on the hard disk to the data page of the previous request.

  The default setting is 16; you can set it to any value from 0 to 31. A setting of 0 causes the Jet database engine to not read ahead pages during sequential scans of data. The dynamics for this setting are similar to MaxBufferSize: a low setting frees up memory for other operations; a high setting uses more memory but enables the Jet database engine to quickly access more records in operations performed on sequential records. The ReadAheadPages setting is more efficient immediately after you compact the database because compacting makes all data pages contiguous.

Values for the default settings are not entered in the Windows registry by Setup. To use values different from the default settings, add values in either of the following Windows registry keys:

\\Hkey_Local_Machine\Software\Microsoft\Jet\3.0\Engines\Jet

\\Hkey_Local_Machine\Software\Microsoft\Access\7.0\Jet\3.0\Engines\Jet

When entered under the first key, these settings affect the performance of all programs using the Jet database engine on the computer (Microsoft Access 7.0, Microsoft Excel 7.0, Microsoft Visual Basic 4.0, Visual C++™ 4.0, and perhaps others). When entered under the second key, these settings override settings in the first key and affect only the performance of Microsoft Access. For information about all registry entries, see the Microsoft Access section of Appendix B, "Registry Keys and Values."

Note   When you change Jet database engine settings in either key, you must quit and then restart Microsoft Access for the new settings to take effect.

Optimizing Table Performance

You'll achieve the best performance results by following these guidelines for table design.

- Design tables without redundant data. A well-designed database is a prerequisite for fast data retrieval and updates. If existing tables contain redundant data, you can use the Table Analyzer Wizard to split your tables into related tables to store your data more efficiently.

- Choose appropriate data types for fields. You can save space in your database and improve join operations by choosing appropriate data types for fields. When defining a field, choose the smallest data type or FieldSize that's appropriate for the data in the field.

- Create indexes for fields you sort, join, or set criteria for. You can make dramatic improvements in the speed of queries by indexing fields on both sides of joins, or by creating a relationship between those fields and indexing any field used to set criteria for the query. Finding records through the Find dialog box is also much faster when searching an indexed field.

- Indexes take up disk space and slow adding, deleting, and updating records. In most situations, the speed advantages of indexes for data retrieval greatly outweigh these disadvantages. However, if your application updates data very frequently, or if you have disk space constraints, you might want to limit the number of indexes.

- In a multiple-field index, use only as many fields in the index as necessary.

Optimizing the Performance of Linked Tables

Although you can use linked tables as if they're regular Microsoft Access tables, it's important to keep in mind that they aren't actually in your Microsoft Access database. Each time you view data in a linked table, Microsoft Access has to retrieve records from another file. This can take time, especially if the linked table is on a network or in an SQL database.

If you're using a linked table on a network or in an SQL database, follow these guidelines for best results:

- View only the data you need. Don't page up and down unnecessarily in the datasheet. Avoid jumping to the last record in a large table. If you want to add new records to a large table, use the Data Entry command on the Records menu to avoid loading existing records into memory.

- Use filters or queries to limit the number of records that you view in a form or datasheet. This way, Microsoft Access can transfer less data over the network.

- In queries that involve linked tables, avoid using functions in query criteria. In particular, avoid using domain aggregate functions, such as **DSum**, anywhere in your queries. When you use a domain aggregate function, Microsoft Access retrieves all of the data in the linked table to execute the query.

- If you often add records to a linked table, create a form for adding records that has the DataEntry property set to Yes. When you open the form to enter new data, Microsoft Access doesn't display any existing records. This property setting saves time because Microsoft Access doesn't have to retrieve all the records in the linked table.

- Remember that other users might be trying to use an external table at the same time you are. When a Microsoft Access database is on a network, you should avoid locking records longer than necessary.

Optimizing SQL Database Performance

If you're connecting to an external SQL database table, you'll achieve the best performance results by using linked tables whenever possible instead of tables you open directly. Linked tables are considerably faster, more powerful, and more efficient than directly opened tables.

You can only open tables directly using Visual Basic code, so this is not pertinent if you are accessing SQL server data using the Microsoft Access user interface.

Following are additional guidelines for improving performance:

- Retrieve and view only the data you need. Use restricted queries to limit the number of records that you retrieve, and select only the columns you need, so Microsoft Access can transfer less data over the network. Don't use updatable result sets, if you're not updating the data. You can prevent data from being updated when using a form by setting the form's RecordSet property to Snapshot. Also don't page up and down unnecessarily in the data, and avoid jumping to the last record in a large table—the Data Entry command on the Records menu is the fastest way to add new records to a table.

- Use a cache. If the data most recently retrieved from the server will be requested again while the application is running, it's faster to fetch a single large chunk of data (many rows) from a cache than to fetch many individual rows. Microsoft Access forms and datasheets automatically use a cache.

- Avoid using queries that cause processing to be done locally. When accessing external data, the Jet database engine processes data locally only when the operation cannot be performed by the external database. Query operations (as defined by the SQL commands used to implement them) performed locally include:

  - WHERE clause restrictions on top of a query with a DISTINCT predicate.

  - WHERE clauses containing operations that cannot be processed remotely, such as user-defined functions that involve remote columns. Only those parts of the WHERE clause that cannot be processed remotely will be processed locally.

  - Joins between tables from different data sources. For best performance, join only indexed columns. Having joins between tables from different data sources doesn't mean that all of the processing occurs locally. If restrictions are sent to the server, only relevant rows are processed locally.

  - Joins over aggregation or the DISTINCT predicate.

  - Outer joins containing syntax not supported by the ODBC driver.

  - DISTINCT predicates containing operations that cannot be processed remotely.

  - ORDER BY arguments if the remote data source doesn't support them.

  - ORDER BY arguments containing operations that cannot be processed remotely.

  - Multiple-level GROUP BY arguments, such as those used in reports with multiple grouping levels.

  - GROUP BY arguments on top of a query with a DISTINCT option.

- GROUP BY arguments containing operations that cannot be processed remotely.

- Crosstab queries that have more than one aggregate or that have an ORDER BY clause that matches the GROUP BY clause.

- TOP or TOP PERCENT predicate.

Optimizing Multi-User Performance

The following suggestions can help you optimize the performance of databases that are used in a multiuser environment.

- Put only the tables on a network server, and keep other database objects on users' computers. The database's performance is faster because only data is sent across the network. You can separate the tables from the other database objects by using the Database Splitter. To split a database, make a backup copy of the database, and then use the Database Splitter command on the Add-ins submenu of the Tools menu.

- Choose an appropriate record locking method. The default setting is No Locks. To set the record locking method, use the Options command on the Tool menu, and then click the Advanced tab. There are three locking methods to choose from.

  - **No Locks** Microsoft Access does not lock the records being edited. When a user tries to save changes to a record that another user has also changed, Microsoft Access displays a message giving options of overwriting the other user's changes to the record, copying the user's version of the record to the Clipboard, or discarding the changes. This strategy ensures that records can always be edited, but it can create editing conflicts between users.

  - **Edited Records** Microsoft Access locks the record being edited, so no other user can change it. It might also lock other records that are stored nearby on the disk. If another user tries to edit a record that is locked, Microsoft Access displays an indicator in the other user's datasheet. This strategy ensures that users can always finish making changes that they've started. It is a good choice if you don't have editing conflicts often.

  - **All Records** Microsoft Access locks all records in the form or datasheet (and underlying tables) being editied for the entire time it is being edited, so no one else can edit or lock the records. This strategy is very restrictive, so choose it only when you know only one person needs to edit records at any one time.

- Avoid locking conflicts by adjusting the following settings. To adjust these settings, use the Options command on the Tool menu, and then click the Advanced tab.

  - **Update Retry Interval**   Sets the number of milliseconds after which Microsoft Access automatically tries to save a changed record that is locked by another user. Valid values are 0 through 1,000 milliseconds. The default setting is 250.

  - **Number of Update Retries**   Sets the number of times Microsoft Access tries to save a changed record that is locked by another user. Valid values are 0 through 10. The default setting is 2.

  - **ODBC Refresh Interval**   Sets the interval after which Microsoft Access automatically refreshes records that are accessed using ODBC. Valid values are 1 through 3,600 seconds. The default setting is 1500.

  - **Refresh Interval**   Sets the number of seconds after which Microsoft Access automatically updates records in Datasheet or Form view. Valid values are 1 through 32,766 seconds. The default setting is 60.

Note   When Microsoft Access refreshes the current datasheet or form, it doesn't reorder records, add new records, or remove deleted records. To view these changes, you must requery the underlying records for the datasheet or form.

Optimizing Query Performance

There are several things you can do to make queries run faster. In addition to using the Performance Analyzer to analyze specific queries, consider the following ideas.

- You can index fields on both sides of joins, or create a relationship between those fields and index any field used to set criteria for the query.

Note   The Microsoft Jet database engine automatically optimizes queries that join a Microsoft Access table on your hard drive and an ODBC server table (typically some kind of SQL server table) if the Microsoft Access table is small and the joined fields are indexed. In these cases, Microsoft Access improves performance by requesting only the necessary records from the server. Make sure that tables you join from different sources are indexed on the join fields.

- When defining a field in a table, choose the smallest data type or FieldSize that's appropriate for the data in the field. Also, give fields you use in joins the same or compatible data types.

- When creating a query, don't add fields that you don't need, and clear the Show check box for selection criteria fields whose data you don't want Microsoft Access to display.

- Avoid calculated fields in nested queries. If you add a query that contains a calculated field to another query, the expression in the calculated field slows performance in the top-level query. For example, suppose this is Query1:

```
SELECT Format$(Field1)As TempField FROM Table1
```

  Query1 is nested in the following query, Query2:

```
SELECT * FROM Query1 Where TempField = 100
```

  Nesting Query1 in Query2 causes optimization problems due to the expression Format$(Field1) in Query1. For best performance, use calculated fields only in the top-level query of nested queries. If that's not practical, use a calculated control on the form or report that's based on the query to show the result of the expression instead of nesting the query.

- When grouping records by the values in a joined field, specify Group By for the field that's in the same table as the field you're totaling (calculating an aggregate on). For example, if your query totals the Quantity field in an Order Details table and groups by OrderID, specify Group By for the OrderID field in the Order Details table, not the OrderID field in the Orders table.

- For greater speed, use Group By on as few fields as possible. As an alternative, use the **First** function where appropriate. For more information about the **First** function, search Microsoft Access Help Topics or ask the Answer Wizard.

- If a totals query includes a join, consider grouping the records in one query and then adding that query to a separate query that performs the join. This improves performance in some queries.

- Avoid restrictive query criteria on calculated and nonindexed columns whenever possible. For more information, see "Optimizing Criteria Expressions in Queries Using Rushmore Technology" next in this section.

- If you use criteria to restrict the values in a field used in a join, test whether the query runs faster with the criteria placed on the "one" side or the "many" side of the join. In some queries, you get faster performance by adding the criteria to the field on the "one" side of the join instead of the "many" side.

- Use field sorting judiciously, especially with nonindexed fields.

- If your data doesn't change often, use make-table queries to create tables from your query results. Use the resulting tables rather than queries as the basis for your forms, reports, or other queries.

- Avoid using domain aggregate functions, such as the **DLookup** function, in a query to access table data. Instead, add the table to the query or create a subquery.

- If you are creating a crosstab query, use fixed column headings whenever possible. For more information about sorting or limiting column headings in crosstab queries, search Microsoft Access Help Topics or ask the Answer Wizard.

- Use the **Between...And**, the **In**, and the equal (=) operators on indexed columns. This helps optimize queries. For more information, see "Optimizing Criteria Expressions in Queries Using Rushmore Technology" in the following section.

Optimizing Criteria Expressions in Queries Using Rushmore Technology

Rushmore™ is a data-access technology that permits sets of records to be queried very efficiently. With Rushmore, when you use certain types of expressions in query criteria, your query will run much faster.

Simple Expressions

Microsoft Access can optimize simple expressions in the Criteria row of the query design grid or in a WHERE clause in an SQL SELECT statement. A simple optimizable expression can form an entire expression or can appear as part of an expression.

A simple optimizable expression takes one of the following forms:

Indexed field Comparison operator Expression

  –Or–

Expression Comparison operator Indexed field

In a simple optimizable expression:

- *Indexed field* must be a field on which an index is constructed.

- *Comparison operator* must be one of the following: **<, >, =, <=, >=, <>, Between, Like, In**.

Note For best results, the comparison value in an expression using the **Like** operator must begin with a character, not a wildcard character. For example, you can optimize **Like** "m*" but not **Like** "*m*".

- *Expression* can be any valid expression, including constants, functions, and fields from other tables.

Examples of Simple Optimizable Expressions

If you have created indexes for the LastName, Age, and HireDate fields in an Employees table, the following are simple optimizable expressions:

```
[LastName]="Smith"
[Age]>=21
#12/30/90#<[HireDate]
Employees.[LastName]=Customers.[LastName]
[LastName] IN ("Smith", "Johnson", "Jones")
[Age] BETWEEN 18 AND 65
```

If you have a multiple-field index on the LastName, FirstName fields, the following expression is optimizable:

```
((([LastName])="Smith") AND ((([FirstName])="Pat")
```

The SQL SELECT statement for the following COUNT(*) query is Rushmore optimizable if there are indexes on the LastName and FirstName fields. This query counts the number of employees who are not named Pat Smith:

```
SELECT Count(*)
FROM Employees
WHERE (Employees.[LastName] <> "Smith") AND (Employees.[FirstName] <>
➡ "Pat")
```

Complex Expressions

Microsoft Access can also optimize complex expressions made by combining simple expressions with the **AND** or **OR** operators.

A complex optimizable expression takes one of the following forms:

Simple Expression AND *Simple Expression*

   –Or–

Simple Expression OR *Simple Expression*

An expression created with a combination of simple optimizable expressions is fully optimizable. If one of the simple expressions is not optimizable and the two expressions are combined with **AND**, the complex expression is partially optimizable. If one of the simple expressions is not optimizable and the two expressions are combined with **OR**, the complex expression is not optimizable.

The following rules determine query optimization when combining simple expressions in query criteria.

Expression	Operator	Expression	Query result
Optimizable	AND	Optimizable	Fully optimizable
Optimizable	OR	Optimizable	Fully optimizable
Optimizable	AND	Not optimizable	Partially optimizable
Optimizable	OR	Not optimizable	Not optimizable
Not optimizable	AND	Not optimizable	Not optimizable
Not optimizable	OR	Not optimizable	Not optimizable
—	NOT	Optimizable	Not optimizable
—	NOT	Not optimizable	Not optimizable

You can also use parentheses to group combinations of simple expressions. The preceding rules also apply to combinations of expressions grouped with parentheses.

After you've combined simple optimizable expressions into complex expressions, these complex expressions can, in turn, be combined to form even more complex expressions that will be optimizable according to the preceding rules.

Examples of complex optimizable expressions

These examples assume that you have created indexes for the LastName and HireDate fields, but not the MiddleInitial or FirstName fields. The following table lists examples of combined simple expressions and the extent to which the result is optimized.

Expression	Expression type and operator	Query result
[LastName]="Smith" AND [Hire Date]<#12/30/90#	Optimizable AND Optimizable	Fully Optimizable
[LastName]="Smith" OR [Hire Date]<#12/30/90#	Optimizable OR Optimizable	Fully Optimizable
[LastName]="Smith" AND [MiddleInitial]="C"	Optimizable AND Not Optimizable	Partially Optimizable
[LastName]="Smith" OR [MiddleInitial]="C"	Optimizable OR Not Optimizable	Not Optimizable
[FirstName]="Terry" AND [MiddleInitial]="C"	Not Optimizable AND Not Optimizable	Not Optimizable
[FirstName]="Terry" OR [MiddleInitial]="C"	Not Optimizable OR Not Optimizable	Not Optimizable

Additional Notes on Rushmore Optimization

- The **COUNT** (*) function is highly optimized for queries that use Rushmore.
- If the index is descending and the comparison operator is other than equal (=), the query cannot be optimized.

- Rushmore queries will work with Microsoft Access tables, as well as with Microsoft FoxPro and dBASE tables (.dbf files). You cannot use Rushmore with ODBC data sources, because Microsoft Access sends these queries to the ODBC data source instead of processing them locally.

- You can optimize multiple-field indexes if you query the indexed fields in the order they appear in the Indexes window, beginning with the first indexed field and continuing with adjacent fields (up to and including 10 fields). For example, if you have a multiple-field index on LastName, FirstName, you can optimize a query on LastName or on LastName and FirstName, but you cannot optimize a query on FirstName.

Optimizing Filter Performance

If the lists in fields in the Filter By Form window take too long to display or they aren't displaying values from the underlying table, you can set filtering options to change these behaviors. By setting filter options, you can prevent the lists from displaying the underlying table's field values, display field values on the list for certain types of indexed or nonindexed fields only, or change the record limit that determines if the list displays a field's values.

You can perform this optimization for all tables, queries, and forms in the database, or for specific combo box or list box controls in forms.

Tip If you use the same nonindexed field repeatedly to filter records, consider indexing it before changing the following settings. This will improve filtering and other search operations on the field.

To optimize Filter By Form performance for all tables, queries, and forms, use the Options command on the Tool menu, select the Edit/Find tab, and then set the Filter By Form Defaults according to the performance you want to achieve:

- If the list of values takes too long to display in nonindexed fields only, try limiting the lists to indexed fields. You can do this by clearing the check boxes for Local Nonindexed Fields and ODBC Fields.

- If the lists take too long to display in indexed fields, also clear the Local Indexed Fields check box because there are too many records in the indexes for the lists to display quickly.

- If lists aren't displaying the values from indexed or nonindexed fields, check under Show List Of Values In to make sure that the appropriate boxes are selected, or try increasing the number in the box Don't Display Lists Where More Than This Number Of Records Read so that it's greater than or equal to the maximum number of records in any nonindexed field in the underlying table.

How many records Microsoft Access reads depends on whether or not the field is indexed. If the field is indexed, Microsoft Access reads only the unique values, not all the values in a field. If the field isn't indexed, Microsoft Access reads all the values in the field. If the number of records it reads is more than the maximum it's allowed to display, Microsoft Access doesn't display the values for that field on the list. Consequently, you need to change the setting to a number greater than or equal to the maximum number of records in any nonindexed field in the underlying table.

When Microsoft Access is able to display the list in a field, it only shows the unique values, even for a nonindexed field.

To optimize Filter by Form performance for a specific field in a table or query, display the table or query in Design view, display the property sheet for the field, and then set the FilterLookup property. To optimize a specific combo box or list box on a form, display the form in Design view, display the property sheet for combo box or list box, and then set the FilterLookup property.

- If the lists take too long to display in nonindexed fields only, try limiting the lists to indexed fields. You can do this by setting the property to Database Defaults, and then use the Options command on the Tool menu. On the Edit/Find tab, select the Local Indexed Fields check box and clear the Local Non-Indexed Fields and Remote check boxes.

- To prevent a list from ever displaying, regardless of the database defaults, set the FilterLookup property to Never.

- To force a list to display, regardless of the database defaults, set the FilterLookup property to Always.

- If lists aren't displaying the values from indexed or nonindexed fields, make sure that the FilterLookup property for each field is not set to Never. If it isn't, display the Option dialog box, and verify that the boxes under Show List Of Values In are checked. If they are, try increasing the number in the Don't Display Lists Where More Than This Number Of Records Read box so that it's greater than or equal to the maximum number of records in any nonindexed field in the underlying table.

Optimizing Find and Replace Performance

For the fastest searches when using the Find or Replace commands on the Edit menu, search for whole field values or the first character within a single indexed field. If you search the same nonindexed field repeatedly, index the field.

Optimizing Form and Subform Performance

There are several things you can do to make your forms run faster. In addition to the tips listed below, you can use the Performance Analyzer to analyze specific forms in your database. For information about using the Performance Analyzer, see "Using the Performance Analyzer" earlier in this section.

- Avoid overlapping controls.
- Use bitmaps and other graphic objects sparingly.
- Convert unbound object frames that display graphics to image controls.
- Use black-and-white rather than color bitmaps.
- Close forms that aren't being used.
- If the underlying record source includes many records and you want to use the form primarily to enter new records, set the DataEntry property of the form to Yes so that the form opens to a blank record. If you open a form with all records showing, Microsoft Access has to read in each record before it can display the blank record at the end of the recordset. If the form is already open, you can click the Data Entry command on the Records menu to switch to Data Entry mode.
- Base subforms on queries rather than tables, and include only fields from the record source that are absolutely necessary. Extra fields can decrease subform performance.
- Index all the fields in the subform that are linked to the main form.
- Index any subform fields used for criteria.
- Set the subform AllowEdits, AllowAdditions, and AllowDeletions properties to No if the records in the subform won't be edited.

Optimizing List Box and Combo Box Performance

There are several things you can do to make list boxes and combo boxes run faster:

- Base the list box or combo box on a saved query instead of an SQL statement. If you use a wizard to create the list box or combo box, Microsoft Access automatically sets the RowSource property of the control to an SQL statement. To change the RowSource property to a saved query, click the Build button next to the RowSource property. In the SQL Builder window, click Save on the File menu and type a name for the query. When you close the SQL Builder window, click Yes when Microsoft Access asks if you want to update the property.
- In the query specified in the RowSource property, include only fields that are absolutely necessary. Extra fields can decrease performance.

- Index the first field displayed in the combo box or list box.

- Index any fields used for criteria.

- In combo boxes, set the AutoExpand property to No if you don't need the fill-in-as-you-type feature.

- Create a default value for combo boxes if the AutoExpand property is set to Yes. If there is no default value, the combo box tries to find a null value in the list to match the value in the combo box. To use the first row of data as the default value, use the following syntax:

```
=[combobox].ItemData(0)
```

- The first non-hidden column in a combo box should have a Text data type instead of a Number data type. To find a match in the list, Microsoft Access converts a numeric value to text. If the data type is Text, Microsoft Access doesn't have to do this conversion.

- Don't create list boxes or combo boxes based on data from linked tables if the data won't change. It's better to import the data into your database, in this case.

- For information about optimizing the Filter By Form performance of a list box or combo box, see "Optimizing Filter Performance" earlier in this section.

Optimizing Report and Printing Performance

Here are some suggestions for speeding up report and printing performance:

- Set only the properties that need to be set. Setting a property always uses processor time. You may want to check the value of a property before you set it.

- If you're updating data in a form or control, use the **Requery** method rather than the Requery action to update the data. The performance of the **Requery** method is significantly faster than the Requery action. For information about using the **Requery** method, search Microsoft Access Help Topics, or ask the Answer Wizard.

- For fast printing, use few graphic objects on forms and reports. Lines, bordered controls, and opaque controls on a form or report are treated as individual bitmaps. Forms and reports that contain these or other graphic objects can print more slowly than forms and reports without graphic objects. For faster printing on non-laser printers, delete some or all of the graphic objects from the form or report. If you use a laser printer, be sure the FastLaserPrinting property for the form or report is set to Yes.

- Use the Image control to display bitmaps. Because this optimization technique both improves the speed and reduces the size of your application, use it whenever possible. If an OLE object does not need to be activated, use the Image control instead of an object frame control. Object frame controls are actual windows and use significant system resources, but the Image control doesn't use nearly as many resources.

Optimizing Visual Basic for Applications Performance

In general, you can do more to improve the speed of your code by choosing more efficient algorithms than by implementing particular coding tricks. However, certain techniques can help you write more efficient code.

- Use variables to refer to properties, controls, and data access objects. If you refer more than once to the value of a property or control on a form, or to a data access object or its property, create object variables and refer to the variables rather than using full identifiers. This approach is especially effective for speeding up a looping operation on a series of properties, controls, or objects.

- Use the **Me** keyword for form references within an event procedure. When you make form references within an event procedure, use the **Me** object variable to refer to the form. This restricts the search for the form to the local name space.

- Use the **IIf** function judiciously. Avoid using the **IIf** function if either of the return expressions takes a long time to evaluate. Microsoft Access always evaluates both expressions. It's often more efficient to replace the **IIf** function with an **If...Then...Else** statement block.

- Use string functions when appropriate. Use the $ functions (for example, the **Str$** function) when working with strings and the non-$ functions when working with the **Variant** or other data types. This will make your operations run faster, because Microsoft Access won't need to perform type conversions.

- Use the **Integer** or **Long** data type for math when the size and type of numbers permit. The **Variant** data type, though more flexible, uses more memory and processor time as it translates between data types. The following table ranks the numeric data types by calculation speed.

Numeric data types	Speed
Integer, **Long**	Fastest
Single, **Double**	Next-to-fastest
Currency	Next-to-slowest
Variant	Slowest

- Use dynamic arrays and the **Erase** or **ReDim** statement to reclaim memory. Consider using dynamic arrays instead of fixed arrays. When you no longer need the data in a dynamic array, use either the **Erase** statement or the **ReDim** statement with the **Preserve** keyword to discard unneeded data and reclaim the memory used by the array. For example, you can reclaim the space used by a dynamic array with the following code:

```
Erase intArray
```

While the **Erase** statement completely eliminates the array, the **ReDim** statement used with the **Preserve** keyword makes the array smaller without losing its contents.

```
ReDim Preserve intArray(10, conNewUpperBound)
```

Erasing a fixed-size array does not reclaim the memory for the array; it simply clears out the values of each element of the array. If each element was a string, or a **Variant** data type containing a string or an array, then erasing the array would reclaim the memory from those strings or **Variant** data types, not the memory for the array itself.

- Use specific object types. References to objects and their methods and properties are resolved either when an application is compiled or when it runs. To improve execution speed, resolve references to objects when the application is compiled, rather than while the application is running. This is especially important if you're working with OLE Automation objects or separate instances of Visual Basic.

When working with OLE Automation objects, instead of using a **Variant** data type or the generic **Object** data type, declare objects as they are listed in the Modules/Classes box in the Object Browser. This ensures that Visual Basic recognizes the specific type of object you're referencing, allowing the reference to be resolved when you compile.

- Replace procedure calls with inline code. Although using procedures makes your code more modular, performing each procedure call always involves some additional work and time. If you have a loop that calls a procedure many times, you can eliminate this overhead by removing the procedure call and placing the body of the procedure directly inline within the loop. If you place the same code inline in several loops, however, the duplicate code increases the size of your application. It also increases the chance that you won't remember to update each section of duplicate code when you make changes.

- Use constants whenever possible. Using constants makes your application run faster. Constants also make your code more readable and easier to maintain. If your code has strings or numbers that don't change, declare them as constants. Constants are resolved once when your program is compiled, with the appropriate value written into the code. With variables, however, each time the application runs and finds a variable, it needs to get the current value of the variable. Whenever possible, use the intrinsic constants listed in the Object Browser rather than creating your own.

- Use bookmarks for fast relocation. Use bookmarks instead of the **FindNext** method or some other means to return to a particular record. Using the **Bookmark** property, you can write a procedure to find a target record, store its bookmark value in a variable, move to other records, and return to the original record by referring to the bookmark. For more information about the **Bookmark** property, search the online index for "Bookmark property," or ask the Answer Wizard.

- Use the Find methods on indexed fields. Find methods are much more efficient when used on a field that is indexed.

- Open add-in databases for read-only access. If your application includes add-ins and doesn't need to write to them, load the add-in databases for read-only access rather than for read/write access. Because a locking information file (.ldb) doesn't need to be maintained when the add-in database is opened as read-only, the database loads and runs faster.

- Compile modules before saving them and before distributing an application. This decreases the time it takes to load the module when the application calls a procedure that resides there. To compile all procedures in all modules in the current database, click Compile All Modules on the Run menu in the Module window.

- Consider reducing the number of procedures and modules. While your application runs, each called procedure is placed in its own public block of memory. Microsoft Access incurs some overhead in creating and managing these blocks. You can save some of this overhead by combining short procedures into larger procedures.

- Organize the modules in an application. Visual Basic for applications loads modules on demand—that is, it loads a module into memory only when your code calls one of the procedures in that module. If you never call a procedure in a particular module, Visual Basic for applications never loads that module. Placing related procedures in the same module causes Visual Basic for applications to load modules only as needed.

- Eliminate dead code and unused variables. As you develop and modify your applications, you may leave behind dead code—entire procedures that are not called from anywhere in your code. You may also have declared variables that are no longer used. Review your code to find and remove unused procedures and variables; for example, **Debug.Print** statements.

To search for references to a particular variable, use the Find command on the Edit menu. Or, if you have **Option Explicit** statements in each of your modules, you can quickly discover if a variable is used in your application by removing its declaration and running the application. If the variable is used, Visual Basic for applications will generate an error. If you don't see an error, the variable was not used.

If your application has places in which the contents of a string variable or a **Variant** data type containing a string isn't needed, assign a zero-length string ("") to that variable. If you no longer need an object variable, set that variable to **Nothing** to reclaim the memory used by the object reference.

You can also use compiler directives and conditional compilation to ignore portions of code based on constant values that you specify. For more information about debugging Visual Basic for applications code, see Chapter 7, "Debugging Visual Basic Code," in *Building Applications with Microsoft Access for Windows 95*.

- Consider stripping comments from applications. Because comments in code use memory, consider stripping the comments from an application if the application contains many lines of commented code. Before distributing the application, save the code to a text file. Make a copy of the text file and strip out the comments. Then load the stripped code back into the application database. Retain the text file that contains the commented code for your reference and future development work.

Optimizing Microsoft Excel for Windows 95

There are several techniques you can use to optimize Microsoft Excel for size and speed. In general, size optimizations decrease both the amount of memory required and the amount of disk file space required. Speed optimizations usually occur when you modify worksheets so that the recalculation engine in Microsoft Excel can work more efficiently.

To optimize for size, if a worksheet contains links to large ranges on external documents, it may require a large amount of disk space and take a long time to open. To prevent this, clear the Save External Link Values check box on the Calculation pane in the Options dialog box.

To optimize for speed:

- Don't select the Precision As Displayed check box on the Calculation tab in the Options dialog box unless you really need it.

  When Precision As Displayed is off, Microsoft Excel stores the full precision of a number in memory, and displays the number of digits specified by the formatting.

When Precision As Displayed is on, Microsoft Excel performs a math operation on every cell, which rounds the number. The operation forces the precision of the number stored in memory to be equal to the number of decimal places in the cell number format. When Precision As Displayed is on, calculation is slower than when it is turned off.

- If you use complicated IF functions on a worksheet, recalculation is much faster if you replace them with VLOOKUP or HLOOKUP functions.

- Try to avoid using the functions INDIRECT, CELL, OFFSET, RAND, NOW, TODAY, INFO, INDEX, ROWS, COLUMNS, or AREAS. Formulas that contain these functions, and dependents of those formulas, must be recalculated every time there is a calculation, because their results may change even if their precedent cells have not changed. If you must use these functions, try to avoid having other calculations depend on their results.

- Try to avoid using user-defined functions and names that are complex expressions. These are recalculated more slowly than the equivalent formula in a cell.

- If your worksheets contain a large number of pictures (bitmaps), you can speed up scrolling by selecting the Show Placeholders option for objects on the View tab in the Options dialog box. If users want to switch quickly, you can assign the following two Visual Basic procedures to custom buttons.

```
Sub ViewObjectPlaceholders()
    ActiveWorkbook.DisplayDrawingObjects = xlPlaceholders
End Sub

Sub ViewObjects()
    ActiveWorkbook.DisplayDrawingObjects = xlAll
End Sub
```

- If you have large worksheets that take a long time to recalculate, consider setting the Manual option on the Calculation tab in the Options dialog box. Whenever you make a change to the worksheet that necessitates recalculation, Microsoft Excel displays the word Calculate in the status bar. You can continue to change the worksheet and when you're finished, press F9 to recalculate manually.

- If your users' computers have less than 6 MB of RAM, consider adding more.

- Consider setting your users' monitors to use only 16 or 256 colors. If they are writing reports and working with spreadsheets, they may need only 16 to 256 colors, so they can switch to a video driver that supports a lower resolution and fewer colors. They can always switch back if there is no change in performance or if your work requires additional video capabilities.

Note If you have one of the newer video cards that contains a Windows accelerator chip set, you may find that Windows runs just as fast with 16 million colors as with 256 colors.

Optimizing Microsoft PowerPoint for Windows 95

If your users include video clips in their presentations, there are two things they can do to enhance performance:

- Video clips embedded in a presentation should be stored in the \MSOffice\Powerpnt folder.
- To minimize contention among palette colors, slides containing video clips should have a minimum of colors, including special effects like two-color shaded fills.

Optimizing Microsoft Schedule+ for Windows 95

This section discusses ways to speed the Schedule+ start-up process, and improve overall performance.

Optimizing the Schedule+ Start-up Process

When used in group-enabled mode, Schedule+ should be configured to work primarily from the local copy of the schedule file. This is the default, and is set on the Synchronize tab in the Options dialog box. Working primarily from the local file speeds the start-up process; operations such as logging on to the messaging server can take place during idle time.

However, Schedule+ files for resources such as conference rooms should be run primarily from the server to avoid the possibility of double booking.

If Schedule+ is used in stand-alone mode by a single user, the program can be started with the /U command-line option to specify the user name. This bypasses the user-name dialog box and reduces program start-up time.

Archiving Out-of-Date Information

For best performance, Schedule+ files should contain no more that 6 to 12 months of data. By default, users are prompted to archive outdated information every three months. Users can also use the Archive command on the File menu to archive outdated information at any time. Creating an archive deletes the information from the current schedule file.

Optimizing Microsoft Word for Windows 95

The following issues affect overall Word performance. You can control some of these issues at setup, but other issues must be addressed at each user's system.

- If your users' computers have less than 6 MB of RAM, consider adding more. Add more RAM especially if they work with large documents (50 pages or more) or documents that include many graphics.

- Set your users' computer to use the correct video driver for faster screen display. They may not need the highest resolution video driver and the up to 16 million colors their video drivers support. Additional color support in a video driver can dramatically decrease the speed of screen updates when your users scroll or update graphics.

- Consider setting your users' monitors to use only 16 or 256 colors. If they are writing reports and working with spreadsheets, they may need only 16 to 256 colors, so they can switch to a video driver that supports a lower resolution and fewer colors. They can always switch back if there is no change in performance or if your work requires additional video capabilities.

Note If your users use one of the newest video cards that are designed to accelerate Windows, they may find that Windows runs just as fast with 16 million colors as with 256 colors.

- Set your users' computer to use fewer fonts, or to use a font organizing utility. The more fonts installed in Windows, the slower Windows and Word start because both programs read the entire font list at startup. Furthermore, when Word needs to perform some complex actions, fonts use additional memory and file resources.

To speed up printing, try the following:

- If your users print large documents that take several minutes to print, disable any screen savers during the print job, or switch to a blank screen saver. Animated screen savers use computer processor time that you can allocate to a print job. For more information, see your user's screen saver Control Panel program or documentation.

- If your users don't need to continue working while Word is printing, turn off the Background Printing option in Word. This option allocates processor time to Word during a print job so they can continue working while Word is printing, but this means less processor time is available for printing. To turn off Background Printing, click Options on the Tools menu. On the Print tab, clear the Background Printing check box.

CHAPTER 1 2

Support and Troubleshooting

This chapter covers issues for the Office applications that will help you support your users. It also includes information about customizing templates in Office so your users can follow the standards that exist in your organization for creating documents.

Also in this chapter is information about porting 16-bit Office-based solutions to 32-bit.

In This Chapter

Supporting Microsoft Office

This section includes information for supporting and customizing templates for your organization, creating shortcuts on the Office Shortcut Bar to access the Microsoft Network, and supporting Office Binders.

Supporting Custom Templates

Office 95 has several features that make it easy to create files based on templates. When a user clicks the Start A New Document button on the Office Shortcut Bar or clicks New on the File menu in any Office application, the New dialog box is displayed. This dialog box has tabs listing templates available for the application, or in the case of the Office Shortcut Bar, for all documents. When the user selects a template, a new document is created with the attributes of the template. When the user subsequently saves this document, the user is prompted to name it, and the template remains intact.

You can customize the templates presented in several ways. You can:

- Create templates customized for your site and add them to any of the tabs in the New dialog box.
- Add tabs to the dialog box to help users find the customized templates.
- Use shortcuts to add templates stored on network shares to the dialog box. If you have a set of shared templates used within a workgroup, you can designate a workgroup template location for inclusion in the New dialog box.

The following sections explain how to add templates to the New dialog box and customize this dialog box to help users find the templates they need.

Adding Custom Templates

To add a template to the New dialog box, copy it to the appropriate subfolder of the Templates folder within the Office folder. Templates added directly to the Templates folder are listed on the General tab in the New dialog box. The General tab is usually reserved for blank documents.

Office creates the following tabs for the New dialog box by default:

Letters & Faxes	Other Documents	Presentation Designs
Memos	Spreadsheet Solutions	Binders
Reports	Presentations	Databases
Publications		

Whenever possible you should add your templates to one of these categories. The Other Documents tab is provided as a location for miscellaneous templates.

To add a template stored in another folder or on a network share, create a shortcut to the template in the Templates folder. For more information about creating shortcuts, see the Windows 95 documentation or online help.

If you want to list the template on one of the other tabs in the New dialog box, copy it to the subfolder of the Templates folder that has the same name as the tab you want. For instance, you can copy a memo template used in your company to the Memos folder, so that it appears on the Memos tab.

You can create special-purpose templates that run programs other than the Office applications by setting up entries in the Windows registry. For information about creating these entries, see "Template Settings in the Windows Registry" in Appendix B, "Registry Keys and Values."

Adding Tabs to the New Dialog Box

In most cases, using the existing tabs is sufficient, but you can add tabs to the New dialog box if you need them to identify and organize your templates.

To add a tab to the dialog box, create a subfolder in the Templates folder. Give the subfolder the name you want shown on the tab. Then copy your templates to the subfolder.

For a subfolder to be available as a tab in the dialog box, it must contain at least one template. When a user clicks New on the File menu from an application, the New dialog box displays a tab for each subfolder of the Templates folder that contains at least one template for that application. Clicking the Start A New Document button from the Office Shortcut Bar displays tabs for all subfolders that contain at least one template for any Office application.

If the folder that you want to be available as a tab is on a network share or other folder, create a shortcut to the folder within the Templates folder.

Note Only folders and folder shortcuts directly under the Templates folder appear as tabs. Templates stored in subfolders all appear on the same tab as the parent folder. For example, if you create a folder named Company Forms within the Templates folder, and Company Forms has subfolders that contain templates, all of these templates appear on the Company Forms tab in the New dialog box.

Setting the Workgroup Templates Location

In addition to the Templates folder, you can specify an additional folder location for shared templates used within a workgroup. Templates in this folder and its subfolders become icons and tabs in the New dialog box, along with the templates and folders on the user's local hard disk. Subfolders with the same name in both locations are merged; for example, if both the local Templates folder and the Workgroup Templates folder have subfolders named Memos, all of the templates in both subfolders appear on the Memos tab in the New dialog box. Templates stored directly in the Workgroup Templates folder appear on the General tab in the New dialog box.

Local templates override templates in the Workgroup Templates location. If a template file has the same name in both locations, the New dialog box presents the file from the user's local disk instead of the workgroup version.

▶ **To set the Workgroup Templates location**

1. Using the right mouse button, click the Office Shortcut Bar, and then click Customize.

2. Click the Settings tab.

3. Under Item, select Workgroup Templates location, and then click Modify.

4. Type the path to the network share designated for shared templates, or click Browse to search for the share.

5. Click OK.

Note The setting for the User Templates location is required. Do not delete this setting when you add a Workgroup Templates location.

Using the Office Shortcut Bar with Microsoft Network Shortcut Files

Users who create shortcuts to Microsoft Network forums on the desktop cannot add these shortcuts to the MSN toolbar by dragging and dropping. Links to MSN forums are .mcc files, but dragging them onto the toolbar creates a .lnk file, which does not appear on the MSN menu in the user's applications.

Instead, have the user copy the .mcc file to the MSN toolbar folder. The default location for this folder is Office\Shortcut Bar\MSN within the Office installation folder. For information about registry settings affecting toolbars and their locations, see "Office Shortcut Bar Settings in the Windows Registry" in Appendix B.

Supporting Office Binders

Office binders provide a means of combining different types of documents into a single storage unit. Documents in a binder preserve their order, open and save together, print together, and are stored as a single file. Each document becomes a section of the binder and can be manipulated using the original application via OLE in-place editing. If needed, a binder can be broken apart into separate documents.

Binders allow users to print the collection of documents, in sequence, with consecutive page numbers, as long as headers or footers are set in each document to print page numbers and the initial page number is not reset within an individual document.

Users create new binders from the Office Shortcut Bar or by using the New Binder command on the File menu. Users add sections to binders by dragging and dropping documents from the file system or by using the commands on the Section menu. The Binder menus provide commands to reorder, rename, and delete sections.

Office Binder includes templates to help you assemble common sets of business documents such as client billings, proposals, and presentations. These templates are stored in the Binders folder of the Template folder.

Note If you have previously installed a Beta copy of Office 95, such as the Office Preview Program, make sure that you and all your users completely remove the early copy of Office and then install Office 95 before you create or use Office Binders.

The following sections provide information to help the administrator support users of Office Binders.

Required Files

The following DLLs and other files support the Office Binder capability.

Filename	Location	Purpose
Docobj.dll	*Windows folder*\System	Provides document object capability
Explode.dll	*Office folder*\Office	Provides unbind capability
Bdreg.dll	*Windows folder*\System	Supports binder registration
Mso95.	*Windows folder*\System	

Binder Documents, Templates, and Wizards

Binders use the following file extensions:

Extension	File type
.obd	Binder document
.obt	Binder template
.obz	Binder Wizard, a binder template that includes macros

There is no difference in file format among the three file types above, only the extensions and icons are different to indicate how the files are used. A binder file with the .obt extension uses the binder template icon; files with the .obz extension have the Binder Wizard icon.

To create a template from a binder document, users can save the binder as a template using the Save As command on the File menu, or just rename the file to change the extension from .obd to .obt. To create a new binder based on a template, use the New Binder command on the File menu. Saving the binder does not overwrite the template. To edit the template itself, you must use the Open command on the File menu in Office Binder.

You can create binder templates based on sets of documents in use in your organization. You can add your own templates to the files installed on users' computers by editing the setup scripts your organization uses. For information about custom setup scripts, see Chapter 9, "Customizing Client Installations."

Use a wizard to tell users how to use a template or provide information they'll need to complete the project.

▶ **To create a wizard for an Office Binder template**

1. Write macros that gather information from, or give information to, users of the template. Set up the macros to run whenever the template is opened.

2. Save the macros.

3. Place the document containing the macros in a binder document by dragging its icon into the binder, and then click the icon in the binder to make it the active document.

4. Save the binder document as a template.

Note You can edit macros only in the original document before you place it in the binder. Create, debug, and test your macros first, and then assemble the binder. The macros run when the document containing them is opened.

Binder Templates in the Office Value Pack

If your system uses A4 paper size, you can take advantage of a set of binder templates designed to use your paper size. Run the Setup program for the Office Value Pack to install these templates.

Editing Binder Sections

Users edit a document in a binder by clicking its icon on the left side of the Binder window. The binder then activates the application originally used to create the document. Because the documents in the binder are OLE objects contained in the binder frame, the application menus are combined with the Binder menus. The Binder File menu replaces the application File menu, and the application file-based commands are not available. Other commands that would normally appear on the application File menu appear on the Section menu.

In most Office applications, the Help menu includes the selections from both the Binder Help menu and the application Help menu.

Users who prefer to edit a document in its own window, similar to OLE 1.0-style object editing, can use the View Outside command on the Section menu. Using View Outside provides the usual menus for the application, without the binder selections.

Binder Security

No password protection is available for binders. When a document that is password protected is added to a binder, the binder prompts for the password. However, after the document becomes a binder section, the password protection is lost.

To protect a binder from changes, you can place it on a read-only network share. Users can open and view the binder on the read-only share, but cannot make changes to it or its sections.

Binder-Compatible Applications

For an application to produce documents that can be included in binders, the application must implement the Microsoft document objects interfaces in addition to OLE 2.0. Currently Word 7.0, Microsoft Excel 7.0, and PowerPoint 7.0 documents can be included in binders.

Developers of third-party applications who want to create documents that can be placed in binders must do three things:

- They must participate in the Office-compatible program. For more information about this program, contact Microsoft Customer Support.

- They implement OLE 2.0 in-place editing.

- They must support the required document objects interfaces.

For files that don't support document objects and OLE 2.0, drag and drop, insertion as a section, and dropping the document icon on a binder file in the Windows Explorers are not possible.

Unbinding into Separate Files

Users can break a binder up into its component document files using the Unbind command on the shortcut menu. This command creates a separate file for each binder section, using the section name as the filename. The files are copies of the sections and are stored in the same folder as the binder. The original binder remains intact.

Note   The Unbind command is not available under Microsoft Windows NT.

Users can also save a copy of an individual binder section in a separate file using the Save As File command on the Section menu.

Using Office Binder to Simplify Collaborating on Documents

Briefcase, a file synchronization program included with Windows 95, can transform Office Binder into a multi-user authoring tool. By using Briefcase and Office Binder together, different users can work on different sections in a binder while keeping the other sections current.

▶ **To use a binder with the Briefcase**

1. Place a binder file on the network where others can access it.

2. Instruct those using the binder to copy it to their local Briefcase. Each person can then open the copy of the binder in his or her Briefcase and work on individual sections. For more information about Briefcase, see Windows online Help.

3. Each person working on the binder can update his or her copy by clicking Update All on the Briefcase menu. This command copies the individual's work to the binder on the network, and copies any changes in the network copy of the binder to that person's personal Briefcase.

Note This command is not available under Microsoft Windows NT.

Normally, Briefcase is installed only with laptop configurations of Windows 95.

▶ **To install Briefcase**

1. In the Control Panel, click Add/Remove Programs.

2. Click the Windows Setup tab.

3. In the Components box, click Accessories and then click Details.

4. In the Components box, click Briefcase.

You can also edit your organization's setup script for Windows 95 to include Briefcase as part of all installations. For details, see the *Microsoft Windows 95 Resource Kit*.

Briefcase Reconcilers Keep Files Synchronized

The Briefcase allows for reconciliation of the original file and the file in the Briefcase, updating either file with the most recent version. While the standard reconciliation handler for Windows 95 does this on a file basis, the Office Binder reconciler updates at the section level.

The binder reconciler examines the time stamps on the corresponding sections of the two binders and determines when each was edited. The options possible are:

Section that changed	Reconciliation
Neither	None.
Section in the Briefcase	Section in the Briefcase is copied over the section in the original file.
Section in the original file	Section in the original file is copied over the one in the Briefcase.
Both sections	Reconciler for the application used to create the section is used to merge changes between both sections. If no reconciler is available for that application, the user is prompted to make the decision.

Currently, Microsoft Access 7.0 is the only Office application that provides its own Briefcase reconciler support. Office-compatible third party applications may provide reconciliation handlers; see the documentation for your application for information.

Troubleshooting Binder Problems

The following sections provide information to help the administrator solve problems that users of Office Binders may encounter.

Problems with Printing

Users can print a whole binder, an individual binder section, or a group of sections. The application that created each section does the printing for the section. The binder dispatches each section in sequence, passing control to the originating application for each section and receiving control back as each section finishes printing. The result is a single print job.

The Print Binder dialog box, displayed by the Print command on the File menu, lets users make print settings that apply to the entire binder. In some cases the originating application for a section can override these settings. For example, if a Word document resets page numbering to page 1, that section starts printing at page 1 regardless of the starting page number for the binder. The originating application controls page layout, including orientation, margins, headers, and footers. For page numbers to print, the user must include them on the page in the originating application.

Print preview is not available for binders or individual sections.

The following are solutions for common printing problems.

Binder too large to print

Possible Cause Being collections of documents, binder files can grow quite large. Because a binder is printed as a single print job, it can become too large for the print spooling system.

Solution If a binder is too large to print in one job, print it in sections. Use the Selected Section(s) option in the Print Binder dialog box to print smaller groups of sections, or use the Print command on the Section menu to print one section at a time. Consecutive page numbering should be correct, provided the binder is correctly set up to print with consecutive page numbers.

Page numbers don't print

Possible Cause Page numbers are not enabled for each section in the application that created the document.

Solution In each section, make sure that page numbers are in place in the header or footer. For example, if the section is a Microsoft Excel workbook, the user can use the Page Setup command on the Section menu to add a header or footer that includes the page number.

Wrong page numbers print

Possible Cause When the user selects consecutive page numbering, the binder passes the start page number to the application for the first section. When the section is finished printing, it passes the number of pages printed and the last page number printed back to the binder. The binder passes the next page number to the application for the next section, and continues dispatching until all sections are printed.

If the user resets the page numbering explicitly in the originating application, the binder uses that page number instead of the number passed from the preceding section. For example, if you reset the first page in a Word document to page 1, the binder does not override this setting.

Solution To locate a section that is resetting page numbering, you can print each section individually in sequence, using the Print command on the Section menu, and see how each section is numbered.

Problems with Email

Possible Cause Because binder files often grow quite large, sending them through electronic mail may not be feasible, depending on the limitations of your mail system.

Solution Consider alternative ways to distribute a large binder file: place it on a network share, post it to a public folder, or use the Unbind command on the shortcut menu to place the sections in separate files that you can mail or distribute individually.

Controlling File Size

Binders that contain many document files can easily become quite large. To maintain the best possible performance for large binder files, users should use the Save As command from time to time to save the binder as a new file, and delete the old binder file. Doing so defragments the binder file and can reduce its size.

Problems with Linked Objects

Binders do not support external OLE links. You can embed but not link documents in binders. You can, however, create links between two sections of the same binder.

Problems Opening a Binder File or Section

If you are having problems opening a Binder file or section, load the binder, then unbind it into separate files using the Unbind command on the shortcut menu. If that doesn't work, open the individual files. If you identify a problem section, delete that section from the binder.

Problems with Macros Stored in a Section

Users can record and run macros in individual sections by using the macro language for the originating application. Users cannot, however, edit macros that are stored within the sections while the document is in the binder. To edit a macro, save the section to a file using the Save As File command on the Section menu. Edit the macros in the file, and then reincorporate it into the binder.

Problems with Spell Checking

Spell checking across an entire binder is not provided. To spell check a binder, activate and spell check each section individually.

Commands Unavailable on Windows NT Systems

With the Windows NT 3.1 shell, the Unbind command is not available, and the Briefcase reconciler for binders is not available because Windows NT does not include the Briefcase feature. As an alternative to the Unbind command, users can use the Save As File command on the Section menu to save each section out to a file.

Supporting Microsoft Excel

This section describes common problems you or your users may encounter with Microsoft Excel 7.0.

File is locked when you save or close a shared file

Possible Causes

- The file you are saving or closing is open in Microsoft Quick View. Quick View is an application that ships with Microsoft Windows 95 that you can use to view a document without opening it in the application that was used to create the document. When a non-shared file is open in Microsoft Excel, you cannot open the same file in Microsoft Quick View, because the file is locked by Microsoft Excel. However, when a shared file is open in Microsoft Excel, the file is not locked (to allow for sharing) and can be viewed in Microsoft QuickView.

- You opened a shared file in Microsoft Excel, and then set the file attributes to read-only while the file is still open.

Solution

To avoid receiving an error message that the file is locked when you save or close a shared file in Microsoft Excel, you must close the file in QuickView.

Open command without SHIFT opens template for editing

When you open a template file (.xlt), the file is opened for editing, even if you do not hold down the SHIFT key. This behavior is different from earlier versions of Microsoft Excel. In earlier versions of Microsoft Excel, when you open a template file without holding down SHIFT, a copy of the template was opened, rather than the template file itself. This change in Microsoft Excel 7.0 is consistent with the way templates act in Microsoft Word.

To create a new worksheet, chart, macro, or workbook file based on a template file in Microsoft Excel 7.0, do the following:

1. On the File menu, click New.
2. Click either the General tab or the Spreadsheet Solutions tab.
3. Click the template file.

Issuing the Shared Lists command results in an error message

The error message "Can't access read-only document *filename.xls*" appears when you click the Shared Lists command on the File menu. The Shared Lists dialog box does not open, and you cannot show the Conflict History in the file when you click Shared Lists on the File menu.

Possible Cause   The file is open as read-only and you cannot change the status of the Multi-User Editing feature. When you change the status of the Multi-User Editing feature in a file, Microsoft Excel requires that you then save the file. When a file is open as read-only, you cannot display the Shared Lists dialog box.

Solution   Although you cannot display the Shared Lists dialog box in a read-only file, you can display the Conflict History by running the following procedure in a Visual Basic module:

```
Sub Conflict_History()
' In the following commands, replace BOOK1.XLS
' with the name of the file that is open read-only
Workbooks("BOOK1.XLS").Activate
Workbooks("BOOK1.XLS").ShowConflictHistory = True
    End Sub
```

The Conflict History is a worksheet that contains information—such as Date, Time, Cell Location, and Value—about conflicting cells in the workbook. Conflict history is created when more than one person edits the same file. To display the Conflict History, do the following (the file must be open with read-write protection):

1. On the File menu, click Shared Lists.

2. Click the Editing tab.

3. Select the Show Conflict History check box. A Conflict History worksheet is inserted in your workbook with the information about the conflicting cells on the worksheet.

Save As Type box contains only the Excel Workbook option

Possible Cause   You selected the Allow Multi-User Editing check box in a workbook that has not been saved or is saved in a file format other than Microsoft Excel workbook. This is by design, as you cannot share a file in Microsoft Excel unless it is saved in the Microsoft Excel workbook file format. Additionally, you cannot save a file in Microsoft Excel to a file format other than Microsoft Excel workbook and still maintain the Allow Multi-User Editing feature.

Solution   Save the file as a Microsoft Excel workbook file.

Save As dialog box saves the file without multi-user editing

When you save a file that has the multi-user editing feature turned on, this feature may not be turned on in the saved file. This occurs when you use the Save As command on the File menu to save the file, and you change either the file format or the filename. If you change the file format, the multi-user editing feature is not turned on in the new file, because you can only share a Microsoft Excel Workbook file. If you change only the filename, the multi-user editing feature is not turned on in the new file. This behavior is by design, because normally, when you save a shared file, you do so to make your own local copy. Therefore, the multi-user editing feature is not saved to the new copy of the file.

Saving a shared workbook causes unexpected results

You see the Conflict Resolution dialog box when you save a shared workbook and the mouse pointer changes to an hourglass; when this happens, Microsoft Excel may or may not appear to have stopped running.

Changes you made to the shared file conflict with the changes saved in the same file by another user. When a conflict occurs, the Conflict Resolution dialog box appears, asking how you want to resolve the conflicts. If you click the Use All Remaining Changes From My Session button or the Use All Remaining Changes From The Other Session button, the conflicts are resolved without prompting you for each conflicting cell. If there are many changes to resolve, this process can take a long time, perhaps as long as a few minutes. If you choose one of the Use All Remaining Changes buttons, there is no indication that Microsoft Excel is processing any changes while the conflicts are being resolved. If you press CTRL+ALT+DELETE to display the Close Program dialog box, the text "Not responding" follows Microsoft Excel in the list of programs.

Solution   Switch to another application in Windows while Microsoft Excel resolves the conflicts in the workbook. Windows 95 allows you to work in another application while your original application is processing in the background.

The Save As dialog box does not replace an existing file if it is currently open by another user

When you save a shared workbook using the Save As command, you get a message that the filename already exists and you are asked whether you want to replace the existing file. If you use the Save As method in a Visual Basic for applications procedure to save a shared workbook, you see a message asking if you want to replace the existing file.

This behavior occurs as expected when you save a file to the same location and with the same name as an existing file. However, when you are editing a shared file, this message is misleading because another user may be editing the file. In this case, if you answer Yes to replace the existing file, you are not truly replacing the file. You are still prompted with the Conflict Resolution dialog box if a change you made conflicts with a change saved in the workbook by another user. The Save As dialog box does not replace an existing file if it is currently open by another user.

Solutions

When you use a Visual Basic for applications procedure to save a shared workbook, you must use the Save As command if you want to use the Conflict Resolution argument to determine whose changes to accept in case of a conflict. When you use the Save command instead of the Save As command, you cannot use command arguments to specify information about the workbook, such as any of the following: the filename, whose changes to accept in case of a conflict, whether to save the file exclusively, and so on.

- Click Yes in the dialog box asking if you want to replace the existing file. This method saves the file the same way it does if you click Save on the File menu. The Conflict Resolution dialog box will still appear if there is a conflict with a change you made to the workbook.

- If you are not using a Visual Basic procedure to save the shared workbook, click Save on the File menu, instead of Save As, to avoid receiving this message when you save a shared workbook.

In Microsoft Excel, when you share a workbook, you may make a change to the workbook that conflicts with a change that another user has made to the workbook. The conflicting change appears in the Conflict Resolution dialog box, and also appears on the Conflict History worksheet box when a conflict occurs. A conflict occurs when you enter data in a cell that has already been used. When this occurs, the Conflict Resolution dialog box appears and notifies you that you made a change that conflicts with a change made by another user who has already saved the workbook. The type of change that causes the Conflict Resolution dialog box to appear is displayed in the Your Changes On Sheet box and the Conflicting Changes By box in the Conflict Resolution dialog box, and in the Change column on the Conflict History worksheet. The following list shows the change type values that can appear in these locations.

- Cell Change
- Sheet Rename
- Range Move
- Sort Cells

Commands and features unavailable in a shared workbook

When you use the shared lists feature, some of the commands and features that you normally use in your workbook are not available. This behavior is by design, because of the way that a shared file is saved. For example, you cannot change cell formatting in a shared workbook. The following information describes the features and commands that are not available while you are editing a shared workbook.

The following table contains the menu commands that are unavailable (dimmed) in a shared workbook:

Menu	Command
File	Properties
Edit	Delete Sheet
	Links
	Object
Insert	Worksheet
	Chart (submenu items dimmed)
	Macro (submenu items dimmed)
	Function
	Name (submenu items dimmed)
	Picture
	Map
	Object
Format	Cells
	AutoFormat
	Style
Tools	Scenarios
	Protection (submenu items dimmed)
Data	Subtotals
	Table
	Group And Outline (submenu items dimmed)
	PivotTable®

You cannot use any of the buttons on the Formatting, Forms, Drawing, and Chart toolbars in a shared workbook.

On the Standard Toolbar, the AutoSum, Function Wizard, ChartWizard, Map, and Format Painter buttons are disabled.

Formulas   When you enter a formula on a worksheet in a shared workbook, you receive a message that new or copied formulas won't be saved while the file is being shared. You can turn this message off to prevent it from repeating on the current computer for the current session.

Objects   You cannot select any objects on a worksheet in a shared workbook, including OLE objects, drawing objects, and dialog box controls.

Visual Basic Modules   You cannot edit Visual Basic for applications modules in shared mode; however you can run a macro on a module sheet in a shared workbook. If you record a new macro in a shared workbook, the macro is recorded in a new workbook. In the Record New Macro dialog box, the New Workbook option is selected by default. This Workbook option is unavailable in a shared workbook.

Chart Sheet or Dialog Sheet   Although you can select a chart sheet or dialog sheet in a shared workbook, you cannot select any of the items on the chart or custom dialog box.

Macro Sheet   You can select a macro sheet in a shared workbook. However, because commands on a macro sheet generally begin with an equal sign (=) (as when you enter a formula), you receive an error message. You can run a macro from a macro sheet in a shared workbook.

Unable to insert a cell not in a shared workbook

You cannot insert a cell note in a worksheet when the workbook you are using is shared. When you use the shared lists feature, the Note command on the Insert menu is available and you can enter text in the Text Note box in the Cell Note dialog box. However, this text is not saved in a cell note, and the error message that a cell cannot be inserted appears. Clicking OK closes both the error message and the Cell Note dialog box without saving the entered text.

New sort order in Microsoft Excel 7.0

In Microsoft Excel 7.0 and Microsoft Excel 5.0 for Windows NT (32 bit), the order used for sorting is different from that used for Microsoft Excel 5.0 for Windows and the Macintosh (16 bit). This occurs because Windows 95 and Windows NT use a sort order different from the Microsoft Windows version 3.x operating system. The differences in sorting are described in the following sections.

Special Characters The following table displays the differences in the sort order of special characters.

Microsoft Excel 7.0 Microsoft Excel 5.0 for NT	Microsoft Excel 5.0 for Windows and the Macintosh
-	!
!	#
#	$
$	%
%	&
&	(
(	)
)	
	+
,	,
.	-
?	.
@	=
\	?
^	@
_	\
+	^
=	_

Extended Characters When you sort extended characters (used, for example, in international versions) in Microsoft Excel 5.0 for Windows NT or Microsoft Excel 7.0, the international characters are sorted as US English alphabetic characters. In Microsoft Excel 5.0 for Windows or the Macintosh, extended characters are sorted before alphabetic characters. The following table displays some of these differences.

List	Result in Microsoft Excel 7.0 and 5.0 for NT	Result in Microsoft Excel 5.0 for Windows or the Macintosh
A1: b	A1: b	A1: ë*
A2: ë*	A2: *	A2: b
A3: f	A3: f	A3: f

* Lowercase e with the Umlaut character (ALT+0235)

List	Result in Microsoft Excel 7.0 and 5.0 for NT	Result in Microsoft Excel 5.0 for Windows or the Macintosh
A1: a	A1: a	A1: â**
A2: â**	A2: â**	A2: ê***
A3: e	A3: b	A3: a
A4: ê***	A4: e	A4: b
A5: b	A5: ê***	A5: e

** Lowercase a with the Caret character (ALT+0226)

*** Lowercase e with the Caret character (ALT+0234)

Case Sensitive   When you select the Case Sensitive check box in the Sort Options dialog box (Ascending order, Top To Bottom), in Microsoft Excel 5.0 for Windows NT and Microsoft Excel 7.0, your list is sorted with the lowercase entries at the top of the list. Under the same conditions in Microsoft Excel 5.0 for Windows, the list is sorted with the uppercase entries at the top of the list. The following table displays some of the differences.

List	Result in Microsoft Excel 7.0 and 5.0 for NT	Result in Microsoft Excel 5.0 for Windows or Macintosh
A1: A	A1: a	A1: A
A2: AAA	A2: A	A2: a
A3: a	A3: AAA	A3: AAA
A1: Add	A1: add	A1: ADD
A2: ADd	A2: Add	A2: ADd
A3: ADD	A3: ADd	A3: Add
A4: add	A4: ADD	A4: add

DataMap objects do not automatically update

DataMap is a new OLE object included with Microsoft Excel 7.0 that allows a geographical representation of data. Unlike other objects, such as charts, DataMap objects do not automatically update when associated data is changed, due to the potentially prohibitive amount of time required to update DataMap objects associated with large amounts of data.

Solutions

- Manually update by activating the object and clicking the Update button.

- Programmatically update through a Visual Basic for applications procedure. The following example outlines a Microsoft Excel Visual Basic for applications macro that updates a DataMap object on a worksheet.

```
Sub Update_DataMap_Object()
'Assign DataMap Object Name to a Variable
MapName = "Picture 1"
'Update DataMap Object
ActiveSheet.OLEObjects(MapName).Object.Refreshmap
End Sub
```

You receive the error message "A column of data in your selection must contain geographical data" when creating a DataMap object based on ZIP Codes

Possible Cause

A column of non-formatted zip codes is selected and you insert a DataMap object.

Solution

Format the numeric postal codes (zip codes) with the special ZIP Code number format. This format is designed to prevent the possible misinterpretation of numeric data as ZIP Codes.

DataMap Objects Are Programmatically Limited

The only Visual Basic command available for DataMap Objects is the RefreshMap command. This command updates a DataMap Object on a worksheet. The following example illustrates the use of the RefreshMap command:

```
ActiveSheet.OLEObjects("Picture 1").Object.
```

You receive the error message "You must select cells from the workbook *workbook name*" when using the Template Wizard

When you use the Template Wizard to create a template, if the name of the workbook from which you create the template contains an apostrophe character ('), you receive this error message. In Microsoft Excel, the apostrophe character is reserved for use in references. This problem does not occur if the name of the template or the database that you create using the Template Wizard contains an apostrophe character. However, as a general rule, to avoid problems with linking, you should not use the apostrophe character in a workbook or worksheet name in Microsoft Excel.

Solution

Rename your workbook to a name that does not contain an apostrophe, and then use the Template Wizard to create a template from this file.

Array formulas return #NUM error value

Possible Cause

You are using an array greater than 5458 elements in a function. The maximum array size is 5458 elements (approximately 75 rows by 75 columns) in Microsoft Excel 7.0. In Microsoft Excel 3.0, 4.0, and 5.0, the maximum is 6553 elements. In Microsoft Excel 7.0, the maximum array size is still 64K, as it is in earlier versions of Microsoft Excel. However, because Microsoft Excel 7.0 is a 32-bit application and uses 12-byte data types (instead of 10-byte data types found in the 16-bit versions of Microsoft Excel), the maximum array size in Microsoft Excel 7.0 holds fewer elements than the earlier versions of Microsoft Excel. The following is a list of some of the functions in Microsoft Excel that use arrays:

- LINEST()
- MDETERM()
- MINVERSE()
- MMULT()
- SUMPRODUCT()
- TRANSPOSE()
- TREND()

Solution

Recalculate your function with a smaller array.

Microsoft Excel 5.0 file size larger after saving in Microsoft Excel 7.0

If you open and save a file in Microsoft Excel 7.0 that you created in Microsoft Excel 5.0, the file size increases by 4 to 6K. Even though Microsoft Excel 7.0 uses the same file format as Microsoft Excel 5.0, this occurs because of an optimization in Microsoft Excel 7.0 that allows Microsoft Excel to save files faster than in the previous version. When you create and save a file in Microsoft Excel 7.0, the file is not necessarily larger than the equivalent file that you create and save in Microsoft Excel 5.0.

Run-time error 438: Object doesn't support this property or method

When you use a Visual Basic for applications procedure to create an Office Binder OLE Automation object, and you edit a Microsoft Excel worksheet object in the Binder, you may receive the error message that the object doesn't support the property or method.

Possible Cause

This error message occurs when you edit a Microsoft Excel worksheet object in a Binder using OLE Automation if you attempt to access a single sheet (such as a worksheet) or an item on a single sheet (such as a cell value) from outside the Application object without using the Parent object. This occurs because the Microsoft Excel object is a worksheet, even though the section in the Binder is a workbook.

Solution   Use the Parent object to access a Microsoft Excel workbook object, and then use the property or method of the Worksheet object as in the following example: The following command adds a worksheet to section 1 (a Microsoft Excel workbook) in the Binder MyBinder:

```
MyBinder.Sections(1).Object.Parent.Worksheets.Add
```

Supporting Microsoft PowerPoint

This section describes supporting some new features in PowerPoint, including the AutoContent Wizard, the Pack and Go Wizard, using and managing ClipArt in PowerPoint and other applications, customizing the style checker, and setting up self-running presentations. At the end of this section are common issues you or your users may encounter with PowerPoint 7.0.

The AutoContent Wizard

The AutoContent Wizard creates a presentation and suggests an agenda for a variety of different topics, such as "Communicating Bad News" and "Reporting Progress." Some topics are only available after clicking the Other button in the AutoContent Wizard. For many topics, the Wizard asks questions about presentation length, style, type of output, printing, and customization. When you click the Finish button, the Wizard creates a pre-formatted presentation with a suggested agenda based on the selected topic. Each slide includes suggestions about when, where, and how to present the information. You simply replace the tips with the content of your presentation.

Note The starter presentation templates used by the AutoContent Wizard are stored in the \MSOffice\Templates\Presentations folder. You can also access them using the New command on the File menu, or the Start a Document button on the Office Shortcut Bar.

You can create new AutoContent templates for your users and make them available through the wizard by storing them in the \MSOffice\Templates\Presentations folder. Make sure to save the presentation in template format. Choose the Save As command on the File menu and select the Presentation Templates option in the Save As Type list. To access these templates in the AutoContent Wizard, click the Other button when the Wizard displays a list of presentation types to choose from. The Select Presentation Template dialog box appears, which displays the contents of the Presentations folder.

When you use the Other button to select a custom template, the subsequent steps in the Wizard that provide options regarding length, style, and output are not displayed. Thus, the only element that the AutoContent Wizard is able to control in a custom template is the creation of the title slide.

If you want a custom title slide, make sure you create one when you create a template for use with the AutoContent Wizard. If you don't, the Wizard automatically inserts one for you, formats it using the default title slide format, and applies the master formatting to the background. If you want a custom look for the title slide, include one in the template and format it the way you want. Because the title slide already exists, a new one is not inserted. Custom title slide text entered in the AutoContent Wizard is added to the existing title slide without disturbing the formatting.

The Pack And Go Wizard

Presentations are frequently created and then given on different computers, sometimes by different people. The Pack and Go Wizard assembles all the files required to give the presentation and ensures that they're all bundled together. The Wizard clones the presentation, copying the presentation file and all of its source files to a destination selected by the user.

Tip You can pack multiple presentations by holding down CTRL while selecting files in the Pack and Go Wizard's Browse dialog box.

Here's how the Pack and Go Wizard works:

- When packing the active presentation, the Pack and Go Wizard saves a copy of the presentation to the Windows\Temp folder. If the presentation has not yet been saved, it is saved as "Untitled.ppt."

- The temporary copy of the presentation is loaded into memory. (If the Other Presentations option is selected in the Wizard, the original file is loaded into memory.) If your presentation contains links to two or more files with the same name but stored in different folders, the Wizard renames the second and subsequent files using the Windows GetTempFileName API function. This is done because all files packed by the Pack and Go Wizard are unpacked together in the same folder at the destination.

- If the Embed TrueType Fonts option is selected in the Wizard, a flag is set in the presentation to embed the fonts. The font embedding code is identical to the code used when Embed TrueType Fonts is selected in the Save As dialog box.

- If the Package Links option is selected, the Wizard looks through the presentation for linked files. When a linked file is found, that file is copied to the Temp folder and the link source is reset accordingly in the presentation. Because both the presentation and the link source are in the same folder when the link source is reset, the link is preserved after the files are moved to another folder.

- If the Wizard detects an embedded Media Player object, the user is asked to browse for the linked file. (Embedded Media Player object links are not maintained by OLE. The Wizard must ask for user intervention to identify the source.)

- The presentation is saved to the folder used as the temporary folder (for example, Windows\Temp), ensuring that the original presentation remains untouched. If the original presentation was stored in the temporary folder, the new copy will overwrite it. All files that are copied to the temporary folder automatically overwrite existing files of the same name.

Note The location of the temporary folder is normally specified in the Autoexec.bat file, if one exists. By default, Windows 95 sets \Windows\Temp as the temporary folder.

- If the Include PowerPoint Viewer option is selected, the Wizard checks to see which version of the PowerPoint Viewer is installed. The latest version of the Viewer will always be packed with the presentation. When you unpack the Viewer, you don't need to worry about installing an older version over a newer version; the Wizard checks for this.

- The PNGSetup.ex_ file is copied to the destination disk and renamed to PNGSetup.exe. PNGSetup.exe is used to unpack the presentation.

- A function in the PNGComp.dll file is called to create a cabinet file on the destination disk. Cabinet files are compressed files that are designed to span multiple disks. Each cabinet file is the same size, and the size is calculated based on the amount of space remaining on the destination disk at the time the first cabinet file is created. Thus, when packing to floppy disks, the space remaining on Disk 1 will determine how much space is used on all subsequent diskettes. If the user is packing to a hard disk or network location, only one cabinet file is created, and the size limit is determined by the remaining space on the disk. Make sure, when packing to floppy disks, that Disk 1 is clean, to ensure that the minimum number of disks are necessary.

- In addition to the presentation, linked files, and the PowerPoint Viewer files, the Wizard also packs a text file called Playlist.lst that contains the names of all the presentations that were packed. This list is used to run the slideshow feature from the PNGSetup program. (This playlist file has no relationship with the playlist files used with the 16-bit Viewer.)

- Once all files are copied into the cabinet files, the temporary files are removed from the Temp folder and the working copy of the presentation is removed from memory. The Pack and Go Wizard always leaves PowerPoint in the same state as when it started.

Note An updated 32-bit version of the PowerPoint Viewer application will be available after PowerPoint 7.0 ships. The new version will support all of the new PowerPoint 7.0 electronic presentation features. To obtain a copy, contact Microsoft Customer Service, download it from the Microsoft Network, the Microsoft forum on CompuServe, or Microsoft Select. For more information, see the list of resources in Appendix F, "Resources."

Setting Up a Packed Presentation

To give a presentation that has been packed with the Pack and Go Wizard, the user must first decompress the packed presentation and its linked files. The Pack and Go Wizard provides a setup program to decompress the presentation files and install them to a specified directory.

▶ **To unpack a presentation**

1. Insert the disk containing PNGSetup.exe, or navigate to PNGSetup.exe in the destination folder.

2. Double-click PNGSetup.exe

3. Specify a destination folder for the unpacked presentation. If the folder doesn't exist, PNGSetup will create it.

4. If PNGSetup detects that PowerPoint or the PowerPoint Viewer is installed when the presentation is unpacked, it offers the option of running the slideshow immediately. If you choose this option, PNGSetup launches the slideshow and shows each presentation (if more than one was packed) in sequence.

Removing an Unpacked Presentation

To remove the presentation from the computer when you're finished with it, delete the folder to which it was unpacked. Except for the Viewer files, all files installed by the Pack and Go Wizard are installed to this folder.

Note If any objects in a packed presentation have Interactive Settings applied, these settings will be preserved, but any programs that are specified in the Run Program edit box in the Interactive Settings dialog box will not be packed with the presentation. The user must ensure that these programs are installed on the destination system.

Clip Art in PowerPoint

Microsoft ClipArt Gallery 2.0 is an OLE tool that ships with Microsoft Office. You activate the ClipArt Gallery by clicking the Clip Art command on the Insert menu in PowerPoint, or by clicking the Object command on the Insert menu and double-clicking Microsoft ClipArt Gallery in the Object Type list. ClipArt Gallery displays graphics stored in Picture Store files. By default, the Microsoft ClipArt Gallery application is installed in the \Program Files\Common Files\Microsoft Shared\Artgalry folder. By default, the Picture Store files are installed in the MSOffice\Clipart\Pcsfiles folder.

The version of PowerPoint supplied on floppy disks includes a selection of clip art spanning a variety of categories. The version of PowerPoint supplied on CD provides additional clip art in the Office Valupack directory.

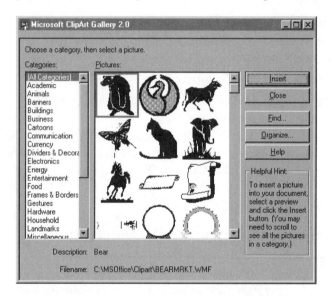

Using Clip Art in Other Applications

ClipArt Gallery .psc file images are not necessarily available in individual graphic formats, such as Windows Metafile (.wmf) or Tagged Image File Format (.tif). Therefore, it might not be possible to directly insert ClipArt Gallery images into Office documents by clicking Picture on the Insert menu. To access, view, and insert graphic images from the .pcs files, you must insert the image as an object from the ClipArt Gallery. On the Insert menu, click Object. In the Object Types list, choose Microsoft ClipArt Gallery. Select the image you want, and click OK.

You can also copy a ClipArt Gallery image already inserted into one document and paste it into another document.

Managing the Clip Art Gallery

Click the Organize button in the ClipArt Gallery dialog box to display the Organize dialog box. Here you can add or update pictures in the gallery. When you add art to the gallery, a thumbnail sketch is created and added to the category of your choice. With the Add Pictures button, you can specify particular art files to add. Many formats are recognized, including .wmf, .tif, .eps, and .bmp, as well as .cag (ClipArt Gallery 2.0 database format) and proprietary formats such as CorelDRAW® and Kodak® Photo CD, among others. The Update Pictures button searches your computer for readable picture files, and updates the gallery to include all the pictures it finds. This button is generally not a good choice if you have artwork installed that you don't want to include in the gallery.

Note The CD releases of Microsoft Office and PowerPoint include a ValuPack directory containing additional clip art you can install using the methods described above (the floppy-disk release of PowerPoint includes a separate CD with similar contents). You can install the files from the Clipart folder onto your hard disk, or you can conserve space by leaving the clip art files on the CD. If you install the clip art files on your hard disk, you must copy both the .pcs and .cag files to the same folder. If you decide to leave the art on CD, you need to insert the CD when you insert clip art from the Office ValuPak.

To change the categories in which pictures appear in the gallery, to create new categories, or to change the text description of pictures in the gallery, click the right mouse button on the thumbnail image in the ClipArt Gallery dialog box and click the Picture Properties command. To delete a picture, click the Delete Picture command. To Delete or rename the categories themselves, click the right mouse button on the category name in the Choose A Category list and click the Edit Category List command.

Note When you add or remove pictures in the ClipArt Gallery, information such as category, thumbnail sketch, and description is updated in the master clip art database file, named Artgalry.cag, located in the Windows directory.

Installing ClipArt Gallery 2.0 Over ClipArt Gallery 1.0

Previous Versions of ClipArt Gallery created *.idx* and *.thm* database files, containing index information, category information, and thumbnail art used by the ClipArt Gallery to locate and organize the actual clip art files. ClipArt Gallery 2.0 creates a single database file to accomplish the same objectives, identified by the extension .cag. If you install ClipArt Gallery 2.0 over a previous version, the .idx and .thm files are merged into the new .cag file, and then they are deleted.

Note When you install PowerPoint 7.0 over PowerPoint 4.0, settings in the Artgalry.ini file used by ClipArtGallery 1.0 are transferred to the Windows registry, to be used by ClipArt Gallery 2.0.

Relocating and Renaming .Cag Files

By default, each user's .cag database file is named Artgalry.cag, and is created in the user's \Windows folder. You can specify where the ClipArt Gallery creates this file by adding a new string value in the Windows registry, to the following key:

```
HKEY_LOCAL_MACHINE\Software\Microsoft\ClipArt Gallery\2.0
```

The string value name should be "Database", and the value should be a string containing the full path and filename for the ClipArt Gallery database file. For example, setting this value to "C:\Program Files\Common Files\Microsoft Shared\Artgalry\My Database.cag" would cause ClipArt Gallery to call the database "My Database.cag," and to store it in the same folder with the ClipArt Gallery application. If you choose to customize this property, you should ensure that the folder you specify exists, is writable, and is exclusive to the user (i.e. not shared). This value must be set before ClipArt Gallery is launched for the first time.

Installing Clip Art on a Server

To conserve hard-disk space on users' machines, the ClipArt Gallery .pcs files (installed in the Msoffice\Clipart\Pcsfiles folder), and any additional art files you want to add to the gallery, can be installed on a network server. The .cag files created by the ClipArt Gallery must be stored on the local machine, or in a private user directory on the server. These files cannot be shared.

Some clip art packages come pre-indexed with their own .cag files. For example, the Cartoons package on the PowerPoint ValuPak CD includes two files: Cartoons.pcs and Cartoons.cag. When this package is imported into the ClipArt Gallery, the .cag file is merged with the user's master .cag file, then deleted from the hard disk. Until a .cag file is merged, it must be stored with the associated clip art images. If you do not want the ClipArt Gallery to delete the .cag file after importing it (if it is stored on a server where other users need access to it, for example), simply make the folder where they are stored read-only.

For information about setting up a custom installation, see Chapter 9, "Customizing Client Installations."

Optimizing Custom Artwork for the ClipArt Gallery

You can add custom artwork such as company logos to the ClipArt Gallery. Use the following guidelines when creating art for the ClipArt Gallery:

- Use a vector graphic format such as .wmf (preferred) or .cgm. These formats are readily scalable and have transparent backgrounds, allowing the art to "float" when placed on a colored background. Don't use raster graphic formats such as .bmp or .tif. These formats save background pixels as well as the main body of the art, causing a "white box" effect when placed on a colored background.

- Make sure that you use colors that work well on all the computer displays used in your workgroup. For example, if the lowest-common-denominator is 16-color VGA, optimize the art for that display format.

- When art is added to the ClipArt Gallery, a thumbnail is created for display in the ClipArt Gallery dialog box. This thumbnail uses the display settings of the computer that is used to add the clip art to the gallery.

How AutoClipArt Works

The AutoClipArt command on the Tools menu suggests specific clip art you can add to a presentation, based on the text contained in the presentation. This feature uses a search mechanism that looks at every word in the presentation and finds any matches against a master list of concepts that PowerPoint stores internally. If a match is found, AutoClipArt suggests one or more pieces of clip art for each slide in the presentation that contains text matching the internal concept list. The following guidelines apply to AutoClipArt:

- You must first run the ClipArt Gallery and import the *PowerPoint Popular Clip Art* package, which is supplied with PowerPoint, before AutoClipArt will work.

- The presence of the AutoClipArt feature is indicated by the appearance of the AutoClip key in the following Windows registry location:

  ```
  HKEY_CURRENT_USER\Software\Microsoft\Office\PowerPoint\7.0\Addins
  ```

- AutoClipArt uses the value stored in the following key in the Windows registry to locate clip art files on disk.

  ```
  HKEY_CURRENT_USER\Software\Microsoft\Office\PowerPoint\7.0\AutoClipArt
  ```

- AutoClipArt requires the Microsoft ClipArt Gallery version 2.0, whose presence is indicated by the appearance of the following Windows registry key:

  ```
  HKEY_LOCAL_MACHINE\Software\Microsoft\ClipArt Gallery\2.0
  ```

For more information about the Windows registry, see Appendix B, "Registry Keys and Values."

Making You Own Art Available to AutoClipArt

By adding concept keywords to images you add to the ClipArt Gallery, you can make them available for AutoClipArt searches. To do so, activate the ClipArt Gallery, click the Organize button, and then click the Picture Properties button. Type the concept keywords into the Description box. Follow these guidelines for adding concept keywords:

- You can add multiple concept keywords to each piece of clip art.

- The first entry you type in the Description box should be a space character. For example, if you type "war" as the first entry in the Category box for a piece of art, AutoClipArt might suggest the picture when searching for the keyword "reward." Adding a space before the word (" war") ensures that the search would use only the entire word.

- You must type a single space character between each concept keyword.

- Do not use punctuation.

- Use only valid concept keywords, which are listed in the file named "AutoClipArt Concepts.txt" in the \Documentation\PowerPoint folder on Office Resource Kit CD. Keywords other than those listed here are not recognized.

Customizing the Style Checker

You can specify a number of different style and punctuation preferences that the PowerPoint Style Checker can look for when reviewing a presentation. For example, you can specify that all body text should end with a period (or with any other character). If the Style Checker finds a body text item that does not end with a period, you can have the Style Checker add one automatically.

To set these options, click Style Checker on the Tools menu and click the Options button. The settings in the Style Checker Options dialog box are preserved in the Windows registry. For more information about the specific registry settings, see Appendix B, "Registry Keys and Values." These options can also be set during installation using an installation script. For more information, see Chapter 9, "Customizing Client Installations."

Setting Up Self-Running Presentations

Presentation kiosk is a term used to describe a special presentation implementation where a presentation runs in an unattended setting, such as a trade-show booth or an information desk. Presentation kiosks can be interactive, if allowing the audience to have access to the keyboard is acceptable, but you can also hide the keyboard and mouse to prevent interaction and possible disruption of the presentation.

The keys to creating a presentation kiosk are using the slide timing and presentation looping features. You can set options for kiosk presentations so that the slides change automatically and the presentation repeats continuously. First, click the Rehearse Timings button on the Slide Sorter toolbar in Slide Sorter view. This starts the slide show with the Rehearsal dialog box visible, shown in the following illustration.

With the Rehearsal dialog box visible, go through your presentation slide by slide and click the Next button (with the right-pointing arrow) when you want to advance to the next slide. PowerPoint records the amount of time the slide was displayed. Be sure to allow plenty of time to read the entire slide. When you have gone through the entire presentation, PowerPoint returns to Slide Sorter view, where the timings you recorded appear below the corresponding thumbnail for each slide.

Tip   In the Rehearsal dialog box, instead of waiting for the time to elapse for each slide, you can type the amount of time you want in the edit box.

Next, choose Slide Show from the View menu, click the Use Slide Timings and Loop Continuously Until ESC options, so that the presentation will repeat indefinitely. Click OK to start the slide show, and then press ESC. Then save the presentation. This way, the options you set in the Slide Show dialog box are preserved in the presentation file.

Creating a Special Shortcut Icon

You can create a duplicate PowerPoint shortcut icon that will automatically start PowerPoint and launch a slideshow with no further user interaction. This can be handy for presentation kiosks where you want to allow audience interaction using the keyboard.

Tip   For interactive kiosks, set up the kiosk computer with the special shortcut icon displayed in the center of the screen and hide the taskbar. Click the Windows Start menu, choose the Settings, Taskbar command, and click the Auto Hide option. Give the icon a name like "Double-click to start." Then, if an audience member somehow shuts down the program, getting the kiosk up and running again is no problem.

First, you should create a duplicate PowerPoint program icon to use specifically for this purpose.

▶ **To create a shortcut icon that automatically starts a slideshow**

1. In the MSOffice\Powerpnt folder, select the PowerPoint program icon (Powerpnt.exe) and click the right mouse button to display the shortcut menu.

2. Click Create Shortcut.

   A new icon appears, entitled "Shortcut to Powerpnt." Rename it using the Rename command on the shortcut menu.

3. Click the right mouse button on the new shortcut icon and click Properties on the shortcut menu.

   In Windows NT, click Properties on the File menu.

4. Click the Shortcut tab.

5. In the Target edit box, after the path string, type a space then **/s** and then type the name and path of the presentation file you want to start. For example, the complete string should resemble the following:

   ```
   C:\MSOffice\Powerpnt\Powerpnt.exe /s c:\My Documents\MyKiosk.ppt
   ```

   In Windows NT, edit the string in the Command Line edit box.

6. Click OK.

After you create the special shortcut, double-clicking the icon or choosing it from the Start menu starts PowerPoint directly in slideshow view and starts the indicated presentation. All evidence of the PowerPoint program, including the user interface and the startup logo screen remain hidden. Clicking the ESC key in this mode not only stops the presentation, but also exits PowerPoint.

The Special Slide Show File Type

Another way to directly launch a presentation is to rename the three-character extension of a presentation file. When you change the extension from .ppt to .pps, and then click the presentation file, the presentation launches directly into a slide show.

Using Batch File Lists

You can create a batch file list if you want to show more than one presentation at a time. The presentations listed there are displayed as one continuous slide show without interruptions. This feature can be useful with kiosks, allowing you to string together different groups of presentations for different audiences.

To create a batch file list, start Microsoft Word, Notepad, or any other word processor. Type the filenames of each presentation you want to show on a separate line. Then, save the document as a text file, but give it a .bat extension, and save it in the same folder along with the presentations it opens.

To use the batch file list, click Open on the File menu in PowerPoint, and double-click the batch file list document.

Using Playlists With The 16-Bit Viewer

You can also use batch files with the 16-bit PowerPoint Viewer (shipped with PowerPoint 4.0 and the initial release of PowerPoint 7.0). Instead of naming the text files using .bat extensions, use the .lst extension instead. The files are otherwise identical to batch files described above.

To use a playlist with the PowerPoint Viewer, double-click it in the Windows Explorer, select the playlist file, and click the Show button.

Note   An updated 32-bit version of the PowerPoint Viewer application will be available after PowerPoint 7.0 ships. The new version does not support playlists. To obtain a copy of the updated Viewer, contact Microsoft Customer Service, download it from the Microsoft Network, the Microsoft forum on CompuServe, or Microsoft Select. For more information, see the list of resources in Appendix F, "Resources."

PowerPoint Command-Line Startup Switches

The following startup switches can be added to end of the Target string in the Windows 95 Properties dialog box (or the Command Line box in Windows NT) to cause specific things to happen whenever you start PowerPoint. In each case you must type a space before and after the switch, followed by the full path to a file.

/s	Starts PowerPoint in Slide Show view and runs the specified presentation or presentations. For more information, see "Using Batch File Lists" earlier in this section.
/p	Prints the specified presentation.
/n	Creates a new presentation using the specified presentation as a template.
/i	Creates a new presentation by inserting the slides of the specified presentation

Files Created Using Beta Releases of PowerPoint 7.0

Because PowerPoint 7.0 uses a file format that is different from that of previous versions of PowerPoint, and because the file format itself underwent incremental changes throughout the beta release cycle, you might experience problems with presentations created with a beta release of PowerPoint 7.0. Problems are more likely to occur in a presentation that was created in one beta version of PowerPoint, and then edited and saved in later beta releases. Some problems that might indicate a file-format problem include the following:

- Embedding Word tables produces unpredictable results.
- In Outline view, selecting, dragging, or reordering slides sometimes produces unpredictable results.

- In Notes view, slide images disappear or are incorrect.
- In Notes printouts, slide images are incorrect.
- When printing, bullets are repeated on a particular slide.

To alleviate these problems:

- Everyone in your workgroup should be using the final release version of PowerPoint 7.0. Do not allow a person who has the final release and another who is still using a beta version to work on the same presentation. This can cause file corruption, to the extent that the file may not even open in PowerPoint 7.0.
- If you notice unusual behavior with presentations that were created using beta versions of PowerPoint 7.0, create the files again using the final version. When you do so, you can copy embedded objects and paste them into the new presentation, but don't copy entire slides or groups of slides.

PowerPoint 7.0 Printing Issues

Printing in PowerPoint is somewhat different from printing in the other Office applications. Specifically, PowerPoint:

- Uses landscape mode by default.
- Uses large text by default.
- Allows gradient fills.
- Allows layering of graphics.
- Allows recoloring of graphics on-the-fly (recolor picture, black and white view).
- Allows scaling of documents on the fly (scale to fit paper).
- Positions output on the page starting at the center of the paper and working outwards in all directions.

Slides print individually, but fail if all printed together

This problem usually occurs with a particular presentation file rather than all presentation files.

Possible Causes
- Insufficient printer memory.
- Insufficient disk space.
- Timeout problem.

Solutions
- Check for old temporary files and delete them.
- Use an emulation printer driver.
- Clean up disk space by deleting old files and defragmenting.

- Change the Windows 95 spooler settings.
- Reduce printing resolution.
- Switch HPPCL/Raster mode.
- Print to a file and copy the file to the printer.

Certain slides don't print at all

This problem usually occurs with a particular presentation file rather than all presentation files.

Possible Causes
- Corrupted graphic/OLE object.
- Corrupted font.
- Incorrect printer driver.

Solutions
- Copy problem slides to new presentation to see if they print.
- Select or clear the Black And White check box in the Print dialog box.
- Use an emulation printer driver.
- If there something about that specific slide, such as the composition or content that is unique and causing the problem, try reformatting the slide.

Complex slides don't print

This problem usually occurs with any presentation files containing complex slides.

Possible Causes
- Insufficient printer memory.
- Insufficient disk space.
- Timeout problem.
- Bad emulation printer driver.
- Corrupted graphic that is commonly used (such as a logo).
- Driver has a problem with landscape printing.
- Hardware problem (printer or cable).

Solutions
- Free disk space and remove old temporary and spool files.
- Print using a different printer driver.
- Print to a different printer.
- Switch printer cables.
- Print to a file and copy the file to the printer at the command prompt.
- Look for common graphics that are used in all affected slides.
- Copy the slide to another application, such as WordPad, and then try to print from there.

All slides don't print

This problem usually occurs with any presentation file, rather than just one.

Possible Causes
- Printer is not connected correctly.
- Inappropriate or corrupt printer driver.
- Insufficient disk space.
- Hardware problem (printer or cable).

Solutions
- Print from another application such as WordPad.
- Print a portrait mode slide from PowerPoint.

Other applications don't print, either

When you cannot print in any application:

Possible Causes
- Printer not connected correctly.
- Inappropriate or corrupt printer driver.
- Hardware problem (printer or cable).

Solutions
- Print a Windows 95 test page.
- Use the Print Troubleshooter in Windows 95 or the Print Troubleshooter included on the *Office Resource Kit* CD.

Whole slide image is too large or too small

This problem usually occurs with all presentation files.

Possible Causes
- Slide Setup is incorrect.
- You used the Scale To Fit Paper command.
- Corrupt graphic/OLE Object (particularly an EPS file).

Solutions
- Check PowerPoint configuration.
- Check Slide contents (does removing any specific element clear this up?)
- Make sure that you have the current or best printer driver.

Whole slide image is in the wrong place

This problem usually occurs with all presentation files.

Possible Causes
- Printer has uneven unprintable regions (Deskjet 550, 560c).
- Printer driver reports center of page in the wrong place (Epson Stylus, Tektronics 200i).
- Printer driver is set up for wrong paper size.

Solutions
- Select or clear the Scale To Fit Paper check box in the Print dialog box.
- Print to legal size paper and trim off unwanted excess.
- Use an emulation printer driver.

Portions of the slide image are in the wrong place

This problem usually occurs with all presentation files.

Possible Causes
- Corrupted graphic or OLE Object (often an EPS graphic).
- Corrupted font.
- Insufficient printer memory.
- Communications problem (for example, timeout or a bad cable).

Solutions
- Copy the slide to a blank presentation to check for a corrupted object on the slide master.
- Replace fonts.
- Print to a different printer.
- Use a different driver.
- Adjust the Windows 95 spooler settings.
- Adjust the Windows 95 printer driver settings.

Graphic prints incorrectly or not at all

This problem usually occurs with all presentation files.

Possible Causes
- Corrupt graphic.
- Printer Driver issue.
- Display Driver issue.

Solutions
- Print the graphic from another application.
- Use an updated driver or an emulation driver.
- Use standard VGA display.
- Adjust the Windows 95 spooler settings.
- Adjust the Windows 95 printer driver settings.

Text prints incorrectly or not at all

This problem usually occurs with all presentation files.

Possible Causes
- Corrupt font.
- Incompatible font.
- Font substitution causing unexpected output.
- Font not available to printer.

Solutions
- Print the text from another application.
- Reinstall the font from the original location.
- Make sure that the printer driver provides the font to the printer.
- Make sure that the display driver doesn't prohibit the font from getting to the printer.

PowerPoint 7.0 OLE Troubleshooting

Here are some troubleshooting tips you can use when you encounter problems working with embedded objects or OLE servers.

Problem is PowerPoint-Specific

Make sure that the problem is application-specific by trying other OLE applications (such as other Office applications).

Check the registry Make sure that the application is properly registered in the Windows registry. PowerPoint will reregister when launched, if it finds a problem with the current registration.

Compel Office to reregister This is more effective than compelling PowerPoint to self-register alone. To do this, run Office Setup using the Run command on the Windows Start menu with the /y switch (type **setup /y**). This starts Setup maintenance mode. After selecting Reinstall, Setup rewrites all the registry keys for the last installation.

Compel PowerPoint to self-register Delete the key for the .ppt extension from Hkey_Classes_Root, and then launch PowerPoint.

Maximize resources Minimize other system variables such as memory usage and background tasks.

Problem Is Not PowerPoint-Specific

Determine whether the problem is application-specific by trying other OLE applications (such as other Office applications).

Check the registry   Make sure that the application is properly registered in the Windows registry. Windows 95-compatible applications will reregister if run from outside of an application. Double click to reregister the application.

Try alternative approaches   If the application has a toolbar button or a specific menu item associated with it, try those methods. If they don't work, try using the Object command on the Insert menu. If the object doesn't appear, it is not registered. If it appears, but does not work, it is improperly registered. If it appears and works using the Insert command, but does not work using the toolbar or menu, it is partially improperly registered and re-registration should fix it.

Check the path to the OLE server   Check the path of the server in Hkey_Classes_Root. Trace the path to make sure that the OLE server executable is found.

Delete the server key   Delete the key for the server from Hkey_Classes_Root. If necessary, remove and reinstall the server application itself. This should refresh all the files associated with the server. You must uninstall all of the applications that are registered as clients while uninstalling the OLE server application. Then reinstall them all. Otherwise, the OLE server application will not be completely uninstalled.

Problem Affects All OLE Applications

If none of your OLE functionality works from any OLE application, the problem may be with Windows. Call Windows product support or check your Windows technical documentation.

Word-to-PowerPoint Interoperability

Here are some tips that may be useful when you encounter problems inserting OLE objects from Word onto a PowerPoint slide.

Inserting a Word table doesn't work

- Make sure that Word is installed and properly registered.
- Make sure that Word objects (not tables) can be inserted.
- Make sure that registration is complete.

Inserting Word objects will not work

Try inserting a Word object into another application. If that doesn't work, Word is not properly registered.

Word objects in PowerPoint cannot be edited

- If the object is linked, make sure that the linked object is available and the link is correct. Use the Links command on the Edit menu.

- If the object is embedded, make sure that Word is properly registered and available. (The Document Object command appears on the Edit menu if a Word object is embedded.)

PowerPoint-to-Word Interoperability

Here are some tips that may be useful when you encounter problems inserting OLE objects from PowerPoint into a Word document.

Write-Up doesn't work

- Make sure that Word 7.0 is installed and registered.

- Make sure that you can put PowerPoint objects into Word without Write Up. If you cannot, reregister PowerPoint and Word.

Report-It doesn't work

- Make sure that Word 7.0 is installed and registered. If it is not installed, your presentation is exported to WordPad instead.

- Make sure that you can put PowerPoint objects into Word without Report-It. If you cannot, reregister PowerPoint and Word.

Copying and pasting a slide doesn't work

Make sure that PowerPoint is correctly registered.

Inserting an object in PowerPoint doesn't work

Make sure that PowerPoint is correctly registered.

PowerPoint objects in Word cannot be edited

- If the object is linked (check to see if the Links command on the Edit menu is active), make sure that the linked object is available and the link is correct.

- If the object is embedded (check to see if the Object command on the Edit menu is active) make sure that PowerPoint is properly registered and available.

Microsoft Excel-to-PowerPoint Interoperability

Here are some tips that may be useful when you encounter problems inserting OLE objects from Microsoft Excel onto a PowerPoint slide.

Inserting a Microsoft Excel worksheet doesn't work

- Make sure that Microsoft Excel is installed and properly registered.
- Make sure that Microsoft Excel objects (other than worksheets from the toolbar) can be inserted.

Inserting Microsoft Excel objects will not work

- Make sure that Microsoft Excel is installed and properly registered.
- Make sure that Microsoft Excel worksheets can be inserted using the Insert Microsoft Excel Worksheet button on the Standard toolbar. Microsoft Excel objects in PowerPoint cannot be edited.
- If the object is linked (check to see if the Links command on the Edit menu is active), make sure that the linked object is available and the link is correct.
- If the object is embedded (check to see if the Object command on the Edit menu is active), make sure that Microsoft Excel is properly registered and available.

PowerPoint-to-Microsoft Excel Interoperability

Here are some tips that may be useful when you encounter problems inserting OLE objects from PowerPoint into a Microsoft Excel workbook.

Copying and pasting a slide doesn't work

Make sure that PowerPoint is correctly registered.

Inserting a PowerPoint object doesn't work

Make sure that PowerPoint is correctly registered.

PowerPoint objects in Microsoft Excel cannot be edited

- If the object is linked (check to see if the Links command on the Edit menu is active), make sure that the linked object is available and the link is correct.
- If the object is embedded (check to see if the Object command on the Edit menu is active), make sure that PowerPoint is properly registered and available.

Supporting Microsoft Schedule+

This section contains information about possible Schedule+ user questions.

For information about the support implications of using Schedule+ 7.0 with Schedule+ 1.0, and with different mail servers and gateways, see Chapter 13, "Running Multiple Versions of Microsoft Office."

Additional support issues are discussed in the Schedule+ readme file, Screadme.txt, located in the Microsoft Office Schedule+ folder.

Using Schedule+ with a Microsoft Mail 3.*x*/PROFS Gateway

PROFS® users connected to Schedule+ via a Microsoft Mail 3.*x*/PROFS gateway receive formatted meeting requests from Schedule+ 1.0 users. However, because of enhancements made to the Schedule+ 7.0 meeting request form, Schedule+ 7.0 meeting requests are transmitted to PROFS users as a plain text email message.

An update to the gateway software that fixes this limitation may be available at a later date through the Microsoft Product Support Quick-Fix Engineering (QFE) program.

Schedule+ 7.0 and the Timex Data Link Watch

Schedule+ 7.0 supports downloading schedule data to the Timex Data Link watch on Windows 95 only. The current release of Schedule+ 7.0 running on Windows NT does not support the Timex Data Link watch downloader.

Timex Data Link watch users can download text with international characters (for example, ê or Ç) to the watch. Due to physical limitations of the watch display, however, accented characters will download as their non-accented equivalent (for example, ê will download as e and Ç will download as C).

Calibrating the Timex Data Link Watch Manually

If a user is unable to download data consistently, or does not hear the watch's confirming beep when lines are displayed on the workstation screen during the download process, the display may need to be calibrated manually.

▶   **To manually calibrate the workstation display for Timex Data Link downloading**

1. On the File Menu, click Export, and then click Timex Data Link Watch.

2. Answer the Export Wizard questions and click Finish.

3. In the Export To Watch dialog box, hold down the CTRL key and click Cancel. The Manual Calibration dialog box appears.

4. In the manual calibration dialog box, click OK. Adjust the spacing between the lines on the screen with the UP ARROW and DOWN ARROW keys. When the watch starts beeping at regular intervals, press ENTER to begin the data download process.

Supporting Microsoft Word

This section describes common problems you or your users may encounter with Word 7.0.

General Troubleshooting Tips

The cause of many Word issues can be isolated and/or corrected by performing a few standard procedures described below.

Isolate the Problem   When possible, try to isolate whether the problem exists in all cases or just in a specific case. For example, does the problem happen with all Word documents, or with just one document? Do you receive error messages when you try to convert any type of word processing document, or only when you try to convert a specific type of document? Are all inserted graphics printing incorrectly, or just one graphic? Answering the "all or one" question will help you determine whether it's a system or Word problem, or if the single document or portion of a document is at fault.

Start Word without Loading templates or Add-ins   You can start Word without loading any global templates, add-ins, or settings. On the Windows Start menu, click Run, type **winword /a** and then click OK.

If the problem disappears when you start Word this way, the problem may be in your Normal.dot template, another global template, or one of the WLLs loading from the Startup folder.

Rename Normal.dot   There are times when the Normal.dot template, which is the global template that comes with Word, may become corrupt, and adversely affect Word. Try quitting Word and then renaming this file to Normal.old. Restart Word as you normally would. Word will not locate the Normal.dot file and will revert to the original settings stored in the application program. If the problem does not reappear, it is likely that a setting, macro, or some problem in the Normal.dot template is causing the problem.

Tip   If the problem is corruption in Normal.dot, you can copy macros, styles, and AutoText entries to a new Normal.dot by using the Organizer. On the File menu, click Templates, and then click Organizer.

Use Standard VGA Video Display   Incompatible or corrupt third-party video drivers can create problems in Word. Display problems are an obvious symptom of this, but there are other problems that can be caused by a corrupt or incompatible video driver, such as printing problems, system stops, or even out-of-memory error messages when trying to start Word. Switching the video driver to the standard VGA video driver is a quick way to determine if it's a video driver problem.

If switching to another video driver works, it may be necessary either to reinstall the third-party video driver or to update the incompatible driver to the latest version. Switching to standard VGA most often won't be an acceptable fix, but it can provide a temporary workaround until you can reinstall the original video driver or obtain an update.

Use the Latest Video and Printer Drivers   Word is very printer and display-centric. Word polls both the printer and video drivers for information more extensively than most Windows applications. As a result, other applications may not exhibit a particular problem, while Word does. Third-party video and printer drivers, as well as some of the printer drivers distributed by Microsoft, are updated fairly frequently. Updating your drivers to the latest versions will often correct display, printing, and other system-related problems. For information about obtaining updated video and printer drivers from Microsoft, see Appendix F, "Resources."

Try using WordPad   When a problem is encountered in Word, it is wise to see if the problem is a more global Windows problem, so you don't waste all your time focusing on it as a Word-specific problem. WordPad is an excellent application in which to test problems you encounter in Word, whether they are printing, screen display, or other issues. While other applications such as Microsoft Excel may also be good test applications, WordPad is an excellent choice because it is more similar to Word than most Windows applications. Microsoft Excel, for example, isn't as concerned about printer driver information as is either Word or WordPad. So, if you can, use WordPad as a test application.

Specific Troubleshooting Areas

Word cannot open a document

Follow the suggested solutions in the order listed until the problem is solved.

Possible Causes
- The document is not on a properly formatted disk.
- The document is not in a format that Word supports.
- Not enough free disk space is available.
- The document has been corrupted.

Solutions
- If working with a document on a floppy disk that is not properly formatted for Windows, go back to the source of the document and copy it to a properly formatted disk.
- If the document is not in a format that Word supports, see if Word or *the Office Resource Kit* CD-ROM includes a converter and install it. For more information, see Chapter 20, "Switching to Microsoft Word." If no converter is available for the document's format, go back to the originating application and save the document in a format that Word supports.
- If not enough free disk space is available, free some. Try emptying the recycle bin, moving old, unused files to floppy disks, or deleting old, unused programs.
- If you still cannot open the document, check to see if the document is corrupt. Try opening it in the originating application if other than Word 7.0. If the originating application can open the document, resave it and try opening it in Word 7.0 again. If the originating application is Word 6.0 or Word 7.0, see "Determine if a document is damaged" later in this section.

Word cannot save a document

Follow the suggested solutions in the order listed until the problem is solved.

Possible Causes
- Not enough free disk space.
- The document is really a template.

Solutions
- If not enough free disk space is available, free some. Try emptying the recycle bin, moving old, unused files to floppy disks, or deleting old, unused programs.
- If the document is really a template, select all the contents of the document and paste it into a new document, and then save the new document.

When importing, Word fails to convert a graphic correctly

Follow the suggested solutions in the order listed until the problem is solved.

Possible Cause   The graphics filter Word needs is not installed.

Solutions
- If the graphics filter Word needs is not installed, install it. For more information, see Chapter 20, "Switching to Microsoft Word." If no filter is available for the graphic format, go back to the originating application and save the graphic in a format that Word supports.
- Try opening the graphic in the originating application. If the originating application cannot open the graphic, the graphic file may be damaged.
- Instead of opening the graphic with the Open command on the File menu, try inserting the graphic with the Picture command on the Insert menu.
- Try copying the graphic in the originating application and pasting it into Word.

Determine whether a document is damaged

If you experience any of the following symptoms when working with a document, it is possible the document is damaged. Follow the Solutions in the order listed until the problem is solved.

Tip When troubleshooting what appears to be document corruption, it is important to first rule out the possibility that it is not document corruption at all, but rather some unusual formatting or document setting. Save the document in RTF format or copy and paste all but the last paragraph mark into a new document.

Symptoms include:

- Incorrect document layout and formatting, unreadable characters on the screen, error messages during processing, Word stops running when you load or view the document.
- You are unable to save the document.

Possible Causes
- Word add-ins or other programs are interfering with Word.
- The template attached to the document is corrupted.
- The active printer driver is interfering with Word.
- The current video display is interfering with Word.

Solutions
- Check the paragraph, character, section and style formatting.
- Disable add-ins.
- Disable terminate-and-stay-resident (TSR) programs and third-party software, particularly font driver packages.
- Attach the document to a different template.
- Switch to a different printer driver.
- Change the video display to standard VGA.
- Try working with the document on another computer.

If none of these Solutions corrects the problem, it's likely that the document is damaged. See "Recover a damaged document in Word" in the following section.

Recover a damaged document in Word

Follow the suggested solutions in the order listed until the problem is solved.

Possible Causes
- Word was interrupted while saving the document.
- The document became corrupted while stored on disk.

Solutions

- If you can open the damaged document, save it in RTF format, close the document, then open the RTF document, and save that in Word format.

- If you can open the damaged document, highlight a small portion of the document and copy it to a new document based on the Normal template. If this portion of the document responds normally, switch back to the original document and copy another portion to the new file. Repeat this process until an error occurs. At that point, you have isolated the problem to a specific part of the document. Recreate that part of the document in the new file.

- If you cannot open the damaged document in Word, try opening it in WordPad. Start WordPad, click the Open button, and in the Files Of Type box, make sure that Word for Windows 6.0 is selected. (Word 6.0 and Word 7.0 have the same file format.) If you can open the document in WordPad, save it in RTF format and then try opening that in Word 7.0.

- If you cannot open the damaged document in WordPad, try opening it in Notepad. Start Notepad, then click Open on the File menu. In the Files Of Type box, make sure that All Files is selected. The document will open with gibberish characters at the top of the document, followed by your unformatted text, followed by more gibberish characters. Copy the unformatted text out of Notepad and paste it into a new Word document based on the Normal template.

- Write a macro that opens the document, turns off screen updating and change other display options that might affect the document, as follows.

▶ **To create a macro to open a possibly corrupted document**

1. On the Standard toolbar, click New.

2. On the Tools menu, click Macro.

3. In the Macro Name box, type **screen**

4. Click Create.

5. In the macro editing window, click between the Sub Main line and the End Sub line.

6. Type the following:

```
ScreenUpdating 0
FileOpen.Name = c:\docs\mydoc.doc
ViewNormal
ToolsOptionsView.DraftFont = 1, .PicturePlaceHolders = 1
ToolsOptionsGeneral.Pagination = 0
ScreenUpdating
```

7. On the File menu, click Close, and then click Yes when prompted to keep changes to the macro Global:Screen.

8. On the Tools menu, click Macro.

9. Click Screen, and then click Run.

10. If the document opens, click Save As on the File menu.

11. In the Save File As Type box, select Rich Text Format.

12. In the File Name box, give the file a new name, and click Save.

Word 7.0 cannot complete a macro that Word 6.0 or earlier could complete

If your workgroup uses a custom macro that calls a 16-bit Windows application programming interface (API) or 16-bit Windows dynamic-link library (DLL), you will have to rewrite the macro for Word 7.0, which is a 32-bit application.

Possible Cause   A 16-bit WordBasic macro calls a 16-bit Windows API or 16-bit Windows DLL.

Solution   Rewrite your 16-bit WordBasic code to make Win32® API calls when the WordBasic code is executed from 32-bit Word. For more information, see "Porting Your 16-bit Office-Based Solutions to 32-bit Office" later in this chapter.

Word prints a document, but incorrectly

Follow the suggested solutions in the order listed until the problem is solved.

Possible Causes
- Various settings in Word don't match your printer's options.
- Out-of-date or corrupt printer or video driver.
- Problems with fonts.

Solutions
- If the printed output is missing graphics or underlines, make sure that Word is not set to print draft output. On the Tools menu, click Options and then click the Print tab. Clear the Draft Output check box. If a graphic is still missing from the printed output, see "When importing, Word fails to convert a graphic correctly" earlier in this section.
- If the printed output is missing portions of text or individual letters, make sure that the text is not formatted as hidden text or as the color white.
- Create a new document in Word with just one line of text. Try printing this document. If it prints correctly, return to your original document and carefully check its formatting. If it still doesn't print properly, the document may be damaged. See "Determine whether a document is damaged" earlier in this section.
- Start WordPad and try to print the document from WordPad.
- Change the video settings to standard VGA.
- Turn off background printing in Word. On the Tools menu, click Options, and then click the Print tab. Clear the Background Printing check box.

- Use a printer font. On the Edit menu, click Select All, and then choose a font from the Font box on the Formatting toolbar that has a printer symbol beside it. If this corrects the problem, you may have a problem with the fonts you were originally using.

- Rename Normal.dot and then restart Word.

- Verify that you have the correct printer driver installed and it is set as the default.

- Disable TSRs and third-party software, particularly font driver packages.

- If you're using a font cartridge, turn your printer off, remove the cartridge, and turn your printer back on.

- Double-click Printers in the Windows Control Panel, and then double-click the printer you are using. In the Properties dialog box, click the Fonts tab, and then click Print TrueType As Graphics. For this option, you need about 300K of free memory per page. Some printers such as dot matrix, DeskJet, and BubbleJet do not support this option.

- The problem may be hardware related. Try removing any switch boxes, using a new printer cable, and, if you are on a network, connecting the printer locally. If this doesn't fix the problem, you may have a mechanical problem with the printer, the port connection on your printer, or the port connection on your computer.

Word cannot print a document

Follow the suggested solutions in the order listed until the problem is solved.

Possible Causes

- Word does not have the correct paper size or paper source settings specified for the printer you are using.

- The printer does not have enough memory.

Solutions

- If an error message prints or appears on the computer screen, follow the instructions it contains.

- Check the paper size and paper source settings in Word. On the File menu, click Page Setup. Check the settings on the Paper Size and Paper Source tabs.

- Reset the printer to clear the printer buffer.

- Restart the print queue by selecting Printers in the Windows Control Panel, double-clicking the printer you are using, and then clicking Resume Printing on the Document menu.

- Clear the print queue by selecting Printers in the Windows Control Panel, double-clicking the printer you are using, and clicking Cancel Printing on the Document menu.

Page faults in Word

This section describes page faults in Word 7.0 running under Windows 95, which are comparable to General Protection (GP) faults in Word 6.0 running under Windows 3.*x*. Follow the Solutions in the order listed until the problem is solved.

Possible Causes

- Something unexpected has happened within the Windows environment, typically an improper memory address. For example, an application or a Windows component might read or write to a memory location that has not been allocated to it (memory that it does not own), potentially overwriting and corrupting other program code in that area of memory.

- Parameters that are not valid have been passed between applications and the Windows environment. Invalid parameters can cause invalid instructions to be executed, resulting in page faults. This is usually the result of the application's internal program code incorrectly passing specific data that could not be correctly interpreted by Windows or a Windows-based application.

Solutions

- Change the video display to standard VGA.

- Switch your printer driver to another compatible printer driver, or temporarily switch it to the Generic\Text Only printer driver.

- Temporarily remove any items located in the Windows Startup folder.

- Start Word without loading any global templates, add-ins, or settings. On the Windows Start menu, click Run, type **winword /a** and then click OK.

- Temporarily remove all templates and add-ins from the Word Startup folder.

- Quit Word, then delete the following key in the registry: \Hkey_Current_User\Software\Microsoft\Word\7.0\Data and then restart Word. For information about using the Registry Editor, see Appendix B, "Registry Keys and Values."

- Use the Find command on the Windows Start menu to locate any AutoSave files (look for "*.asd"). If you find any files with the .asd extension, rename the extension. This prevents Word from loading the AutoSave file when it starts.

- Use the Find command on the Windows Start menu to locate any AutoCorrect files (look for "*.acl"). If you find any files with the .acl extension, rename the extension. This prevents Word from loading the AutoCorrect file when it starts.

- Try removing Word through the Add/Remove programs icon in the Windows Control Panel, and then reinstalling Word.

Registry Settings and .Ini Files

Some Office for Windows 95 applications continue to use.ini files, even though they operate based on settings in the Windows registry. For backward compatibility, Office applications allow the use of the /ini command line option. Except for Word, Setup does not migrate .ini settings from previous versions of the applications when Office for Windows 95 is installed. Leftover .ini files have no effect on Office for Windows 95 applications.

When Setup installs Word 7.0 onto a system with a previous version of Word, everything in Winword6.opt and Winword6.ini is registered in the user's Hkey_Current_User registry keys. All shared components currently registered in the user's Win.ini (text converters, filters, proofing tools, and so forth) are registered in the Hkey_Local_Machine registry keys.

The following table lists Office applications, whether they use .ini files or the registry only, and information about how the applications use existing .ini files.

Application	Registry or .ini Files	Use of existing .ini files
Office	Registry only.	When upgrading previous versions of Office, buttons included in Msoffice.ini are migrated to the Old Office toolbar.
Microsoft Access	Registry only.	None.
Microsoft Excel	Registry only.	None.
Microsoft PowerPoint	Registry only, except where compatibility with PowerPoint 4.0 and other 16-bit applications requires use of .ini files. For example, PowerPoint 7.0 to PowerPoint 4.0 translator entries are stored in an .ini file.	None.
Microsoft Schedule+	Registry only.	Schedule+ 7.0 reads the Schedule+ 1.0 .ini file the first time it runs to find existing .cal file, migrates the .cal file to an .scd file, and sets registry entry for LocalPath.
Microsoft Word	Registry and .ini files.	Msfntmap.ini and Mstxtcnv.ini are not made into registry entries.

Long Filenames

When users transfer a file from an Office for Windows 95 application to a previous version and then back to the original application, the long filenames supported by Windows 95 may or may not be preserved. Each application handles preservation of long filenames slightly differently.

Microsoft Access   Microsoft Access does not preserve long filenames, as users cannot open Microsoft Access 7.0 database files in a previous version of Microsoft Access and then move them back to version 7.0.

Microsoft Excel   When opening a Microsoft Excel 7.0 workbook in Microsoft Excel 5.0, the older version of Microsoft Excel cannot update links or find link sources. However, when the workbook is opened again in Microsoft Excel 7.0, the long filename is preserved, and links are preserved and can be updated normally.

Microsoft PowerPoint   When opening a PowerPoint 7.0 file using the Macintosh installable filters, the Windows 95 long filenames are preserved.

When using the Save As command in PowerPoint 7.0 to save a file in PowerPoint 4.0 format, a dialog box appears, prompting the user for a new filename. The user must consider the destination platform of the file when naming it. For example, if the file is destined for PowerPoint 4.0 running on Windows 95 or the Macintosh, long filenames are supported. If the file will be used in PowerPoint 4.0 for Windows 3.x, a long filename will be truncated, so the user might want to create an 8.3 filename, to avoid confusion.

Microsoft Schedule+   Schedule+ does not preserve long filenames, as users cannot open a Schedule+ 7.0 schedule file in a previous version of Schedule+.

Microsoft Word   In Word, the long filename of the document itself is not preserved when the file is modified in Windows 3.x, then reopened in Windows 95. However, document names in links are updated, and the links still work.

Porting Your 16-Bit Office-Based Solutions to 32-Bit Office

The introduction of 32-bit Microsoft Windows 95 (and Windows NT) brings 32-bit Office applications into common use and results in users switching their Microsoft Office files, macros, and solutions to the 32-bit versions. This section assists you in porting solution code—that is, code written in the Microsoft Excel macro language (XLM), WordBasic, Visual Basic for applications, or Access Basic—to 32-bit versions of Office running on 32-bit operating systems.

Changes to your existing code are required if your 16-bit Office solution (including Microsoft Access or Microsoft Project) calls a 16-bit Windows application programming interface (API) or 16-bit Windows dynamic-link library (DLL), and you are porting that code to a 32-bit Office application (again, including Microsoft Access 95 or Microsoft Project 95).

Porting your solution code is necessary because 16-bit API calls and 16-bit DLL calls (referred to in this section simply as API calls) do not execute correctly when the solution code containing those calls is run in a 32-bit Office application. This section applies to solution code that uses APIs in the following products: Microsoft Access, Microsoft Excel, Microsoft Project, and Word for Windows.

Note   16-bit solutions ported to 32-bit Windows are not affected. For example, existing 16-bit Office solutions, 16-bit Visual Basic, and 16-bit FoxPro applications, even if they call 16-bit APIs, will run just fine on Windows 95 or Windows NT. It is only when users want to run solutions code that includes 16-bit API calls on a 32-bit application that porting is required.

Solution providers and corporate developers face an important task in ensuring that their Microsoft Office-based solutions run successfully under Windows 95 and Windows NT.

The rule they must follow is this: neither a 32-bit compiled application nor solution code called from a 32-bit Office application can make direct 16-bit API or DLL calls. In addition, neither a 16-bit compiled application nor solution code called from a 16-bit application can make direct 32-bit API or DLL calls. This inability to make calls back and forth between 16-bit and 32-bit layers occurs in both the Windows 95 and Windows NT environments because of their advanced flat-memory-model management systems, as well as the way in which they load DLLs.

To prepare for Office 95, you must change your solution code to make Win32 API calls when the solution code is executed from 32-bit Office applications. If this is not possible (for example, you don't have access to the source code of the DLL), you must change the solution code to *thunk* through an intermediate DLL to make the 16-bit API call. Updating solution code to support Win32 API calls is a relatively simple mechanical process. A more significant task is to write code that is operating-system--independent (that is, so the solution code will run on both 16-bit and 32-bit Office applications). This section discusses both of these tasks, as well as other 16-to-32–bit API issues you may need to handle.

Note Although you must update API calls when porting solution code to 32-bit operating systems, you do not need to change code that uses OLE Automation or dynamic data exchange (DDE). All OLE and DDE code will continue to work regardless of whether the applications are 16-bit or 32-bit. OLE and DDE insulate automation calls, so all combinations of containers (clients) and servers (16/16, 16/32, 32/16, and 32/32) work under Windows 95 and Windows NT.

How This Section Is Organized

What you need to know depends on your situation; therefore, this section is organized in terms of complexity, from the easier issues to the more complex ones.

- "Which API Should Your Solution Code Call?" is a quick overview of which API you should be using, according to your application needs.

- "Calling the Win32 API" describes what an API is and discusses the issues involved in converting existing 16-bit API calls to Win32 API calls, finding Declaration statements, and testing the Declare statements.

- "Writing a Single Code Base for 16-bit and 32-bit Office Applications" supplies code samples for writing solution code that will run on both a 16-bit and 32-bit Office application.

- "Determining Whether a 32-bit Application Is Running" describes how to determine whether your Office application is 16-bit or 32-bit and how to select the appropriate 16-bit or 32-bit API call.

- "Recompiling DLLs" tells you what you need to do to make the DLL and solution code work on Windows 95 and Windows NT if your solution code calls a custom DLL.

- "Thunking" tells you how, if you cannot recompile your DLLs, you can add an intermediate DLL.

- "Advanced Programming Topics" explains: translating C-API declarations to Visual Basic or Visual Basic for applications.

Which API Should Your Solution Code Call?

When you write solution code for your own use, you write it for the version of the Office application you have and for your own operating system. Distributing this solution to others means that you have to make it also work on their computers, which may use different versions of Windows and Office applications than you used when you wrote it. While the operating system isn't an issue, whether the Office application is 16-bit or 32-bit is important. The following table shows that the application, and not the operating system, determines which API you use in porting your solution code.

Microsoft product	Windows 3.*x*	Win32s	Windows NT	Windows 95
16-bit applications	16-bit API	16-bit API	16-bit API	16-bit API
32-bit applications	N/A	32-bit API	32-bit API	32-bit API

Note Microsoft Office (including 32-bit Microsoft Access and 32-bit Microsoft Project) products do not run on Win32s®, but because Microsoft FoxPro does, the Win32s column was added to show that FoxPro programmers should use the same rules for choosing the API. Also, Win32s, Windows NT, and Windows 95 do not have identical sets of API calls. For more information, see the Win32 SDK documentation in the Development Library (in particular, see the Compatibility Tables in the *Win32 Programmer's Reference*, Vol. 5).

Calling the Win32 API

To write calls to the Win32 API, you must do the following:

- Understand what Windows API calls are.
- Understand the differences between 16-bit and 32-bit Windows APIs.
- Use Win32api.txt to find the correct **Declare** statement.
- Test an API **Declare** statement.

What Is an API Call?

An API call in C, Visual Basic, or other languages places a series of values (parameters) at a location in memory (the stack) and then requests the operating system or DLL to execute a function (the procedure call) using the values provided. The function reads the values (call stack) and executes its function code using those values or the data that the values point to. If a result is returned, it is placed at another location (return register) for the calling application to use. This is shown in the following illustration. To ensure accuracy, the number of bytes of data on the stack is verified before and after the procedure is called. The message "Bad DLL calling convention" appears when the wrong number of bytes are on the stack.

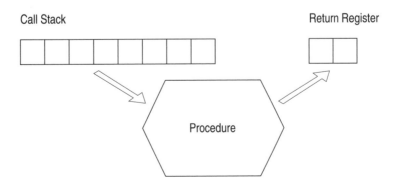

Call Stack

Return Register

Procedure

In practical terms, Windows API calls are how applications request services (screen control, printers, memory) from the operating system. There are approximately 300 API calls in Windows 3.0, over 700 API calls in Windows 3.1, and over 1,000 API calls in Windows 95. These API calls are packaged in executables and DLLs found in the Windows folder—User.exe, Gdi.exe, and one of the following KERNEL files: Krnl286.exe, Krnl386.exe, or Kernel32.dll.

To call an API from your solution code, use these four steps:

1. Identify the file containing the API.
2. Determine the parameters required by the API.
3. Create a **Declare** statement for the API.
4. Call the function with valid parameters.

The following is a simple example for the **GetVersion** API call that obtains the version of Windows that is running. The **GetVersion** API call is located in KERNEL under 16-bit Windows and does not use any parameters (so the **Declare** statement has empty parentheses). The following **Declare** statement is written for 16-bit Windows for use by Visual Basic for applications:

```
Declare Function GetVersion Lib "KERNEL" () As Long
```

By comparison, here is the same function as it would be used by an Office 95 application running on 32-bit Windows:

```
Declare Function GetVersion Lib "KERNEL32" () As Long
```

Although the Windows API name stays the same, the location of the API has changed to KERNEL32. Because you are calling from a 32-bit application, you must make a 32-bit API call. The parameter data type, on the other hand, did not change (it remained a **Long**). In general, the function parameters will change more and require more attention than the parameters of the return value. Understanding the differences between 16-bit API calls and 32-bit API calls is essential to porting your solution code to Windows 95.

What Are the Differences Between a 16-Bit and a 32-Bit Windows API?

As shown in the previous example, most 32-bit Windows API calls have the same name or a very similar name to the 16-bit API calls. In fact, the documentation may show the same arguments, with the only apparent difference being the library name change from KERNEL to KERNEL32. However, the code must handle changes in addition to the name change:

- Case-sensitivity
- Unicode or ANSI options
- Change of parameter data type (shown in the previous example)

These bulleted items can require subtle changes in the **Declare** statements that are not always easy to identify.

Case sensitivity

The first issue in moving to 32-bit Windows API calls is case sensitivity in the name of the function. API calls under 16-bit Windows are not case sensitive and work if you enter the function name as GetVERSION, GeTvErSiOn, or getversion. In other words, in 16-bit Windows the following statements are equivalent:

```
Declare Function GetVersion Lib "KERNEL" () As Long
Declare Function GeTvErSiOn Lib "KERNEL" () As Long
```

API calls under 32-bit Windows are case-sensitive for the function call and must be correctly entered in the **Declare** statement. In other words, the following statements are not equivalent in 32-bit Windows:

```
Declare Function GetVersion Lib "KERNEL32" () As Long
Declare Function GeTvErSiOn Lib "KERNEL32" () As Long
```

The easiest way to handle this change is to always use the **Alias** control word. The contents of an **Alias** string map to the actual API call name (which is case sensitive), but the function name used in code, which appears between "Function" and "Lib," is not case sensitive and will not change if you type it different ways in your code or use the same name for variables or procedures. Using the **Alias** control word, the GetVersion function (32-bit Windows) would be entered as:

```
Declare Function GetVersion Lib "KERNEL32" Alias "GetVersion" () As Long
```

Now the case of API names won't matter when writing code: as long as you spelled and typed the function name correctly in the **Alias** string and you spell the function name in code the same way as in the **Declare** statement, the function will be mapped by Visual Basic or Visual Basic for applications back to the correct **Declare** function automatically.

Note The **Alias** control word is the single most important thing you can use in preparing to switch to 32-bit operating systems because it means you will only have to change the contents of the **Declare** statement and not every instance of the function being called in your code.

Unicode or ANSI Options

Both Windows NT and Windows 95 have two API interfaces. One interface is based on the American National Standards Institute (ANSI) character set, where a single byte represents each character. The other interface was created for the Unicode character set, where two bytes represent each character. All 16-bit Windows operating systems and applications use the ANSI character set. All 32-bit versions of Windows added Unicode to allow foreign language characters to be represented. C programmers handle this by setting a flag in their **include** file (*.h). The flag causes hundreds of macros throughout the C **include** files to select the correct Unicode or ANSI functions.

All western language versions of Office products use ANSI for Visual Basic for applications code. Therefore, programmers using current versions of Visual Basic for applications or macro languages will always use the ANSI version of the API call. When using the Win32api.txt file, this choice is made for you. For more information about this file, see "Change of Parameter Data Type," next in this section.

To distinguish the ANSI version from the Unicode version, the ANSI version adds an "A" to the end of the API name, and the Unicode version adds a "W". W is for wide, as in the width of the bytes provided for characters. The name of an API call includes the characters A and W at the end of the API name only if the API requires parameters with string (character) data types.

The Win32 SDK documentation in the Development Library does not record the permutations of the name of the API call. The documentation gives only the name of the root function and its library name. The actual name of the API in the library can be one of three possibilities:

- **MyAPICall**, which uses no character strings in the call.
- **MyAPICallA**, which uses ANSI character strings in the call.
- **MyAPICallW**, which uses Unicode character strings in the call.

To understand the differences, see the following diagram showing the amount of data the API expects to find on possible call stacks for an example function (the 16-bit version is padded because 16-bit Windows always pads the stack to 16 bits).

The three possible declarations for **MyAPICall** are shown next, formatted to make comparison easier. All of the statements use the **Alias** control word so that the function name used in code (MyAPICall) does not have to change even if the name of the function called is appended with an "A" or a "W":

```
'16 bits
Declare function MyAPICall Lib "MYDLL.DLL" Alias "MyAPICall" (
    ByVal hwndForm As Integer,
    ByVal lpstrCaption$,
    ByVal hAccKey As String,
     ByVal iMagicNumber As Integer
    ) As Integer
'32-bit ANSI
Declare function MyAPICall Lib "MYDLL32.DLL" Alias "MyAPICallA" (
    ByVal hwndForm As Long,
    ByVal lpstrCaption$,
    ByVal hAccKey As String,
    ByVal iMagicNumber As Long
    ) As Long
'32-bit UNICODE * For illustration only.
Declare function MyAPICall Lib "MYDLL32.DLL" Alias "MyAPICallW" (
    ByVal hwndForm As Long,
    ByVal lpstrCaption$,
    ByVal hAccKey As String,
    ByVal iMagicNumber As Long
    ) As Long
```

Any one of these declarations would add the function **MyAPICall** to your application; you can only have one **MyAPICall** function.

Note   This code sample introduces the **ByVal** keyword, which enables you to pass Visual Basic parameters to a API function by value. *By Value* is the default for functions written in C and is therefore the default for Windows API calls. The reason you must use **ByVal** is Visual Basic and Visual Basic for applications default to **ByRef** (*By Reference* which passes a pointer to the value rather than the value itself) which is not what API calls expect. **ByVal** can also be used to convert a Visual Basic string to a null-terminated C string. **ByVal** is included in the Declare statements in Win32api.txt so you will know when to use it, but for more information about **ByVal**, see the MSDN article Q110219 "How to call Windows API from VB," or published references such as "The Visual Basic Programmer's Guide to the Windows API" by Dan Appleman, published by Ziff-Davis Press.

Change of Parameter Data Type

The easiest way to learn what the new required parameter data types are for 32-bit API functions is to have somebody else give them to you. Included on the *Office Resource Kit* CD is a Visual Basic declaration file called Win32api. All you need to do is copy the appropriate API **Declare** statement from Win32api.txt into your source code.

Another source of information is the *Win32 Programmer's Reference* on the MSDN Development Library CD, which is discussed in "Advanced Programming Topics" later in this section. This reference may occasionally be required to resolve questions about the inclusion or exclusion of **ByVal** in the declaration or the need to put parentheses around the actual value passed.

If you use the *Win32 Programmer's Reference*, however, you must be careful to properly convert C to Visual Basic data types. For example, don't mistake a C **int** for a Visual Basic for applications **Integer**. Many Windows data types and Visual Basic **Integer** data types are no longer the same size, as shown in the following table. It is critical to remember that the sizes of many API parameters have changed, and you must not assume they are the same.

Visual Basic data types	Size of variable	16-bit Windows data types	32-bit Windows data types
Integer	2 bytes	**int, short, WORD, HWND, HANDLE, WCHAR**	**short, WCHAR**
Long	4 bytes	**long, LPSTR**	**int, long, HANDLE, HWND, LPSTR**

Finally, whether you use Win32api.txt or the *Win32 Programmer's Reference*, judicious use of the **Alias** control word may assist you with changing parameter data types by allowing existing 16-bit *code* (italicized to point out that code does not include the **Declare** statement, which must change to point to a 32-bit API) that calls the API to be left unchanged. The **ByVal** control word and automatic type conversion in Visual Basic, Access Basic, WordBasic, and Visual Basic for applications change the size of parameters for you in many cases (**Integer** to **Long**, for example). Alternatively, type conversion will extend integers with a sign (+/-) that may lead to incorrect long parameters and cause overflows on conversion from **Long** to **Integer**. Again, the best solution is to check Win32api.txt or the *Win32 Programmer's Reference* to get the correct functions.

What Types of Errors Can Occur with an API Declare Statement?

After you create a **Declare** statement, it may not work. While there are many mistakes possible in a **Declare** statement, the following are the most common errors:

Error 453: Function is not defined in specified DLL   Either you misspelled the function name or you have a problem with case in the function name. Functions are case-sensitive in Win32; they are not case-sensitive in 16-bit Windows.

Error 48: Error in loading DLL   Usually, this error is caused by having the wrong size or arguments, but may also occur for some of the reasons described under Error 53.

Error 53: File Not Found   Windows checks the loaded libraries for matches, and if the DLL is not loaded, it will attempt to load the DLL from disk. Many functions available in the 16-bit Windows on Windows (WOW) layer on a Windows NT system are not available directly from Windows NT. Calling the 16-bit Windows and Win32 **GetProfileString** function from a 16-bit and a 32-bit solution will give a confusing set of error messages. The 16-bit application call will find KERNEL and fail to find KERNEL32, while the 32-bit application will find KERNEL32 and fail to find KERNEL. The general cause of this error is a mismatch of calls and environment. The solution is to write code that works in both 16-bit and 32-bit environments.

Writing a Single Code Base for 16-Bit and 32-Bit Office Applications

If your users are running both 16-bit and 32-bit versions of Microsoft Excel, should you put the 16-bit API call or the 32-bit API call in your solution? Microsoft Excel is not like Visual Basic version 4.0, which allows conditional compilation of code into executables, but instead runs solution code in workbook files which may be opened in either the 16-bit or the 32-bit version. The solution is that you put both the 16-bit API call and the 32-bit API call inside an **If...Then...Else** control structure.

With 32-bit applications using the same solution code as 16-bit applications, you do not know which API to call in the solution code. Your code must determine whether the application is a 16-bit one or a 32-bit one. How does the code answer the following questions:

- Microsoft Access: Is the host application 16-bit Microsoft Access 2.0 or earlier (make 16-bit API calls), or 32-bit Microsoft Access for Windows 95 (make 32-bit API calls)?

- Microsoft Excel: Is the host application 16-bit Microsoft Excel 5.0 or earlier (make 16-bit API calls) or 32-bit Microsoft Excel 5.0 for Windows NT or 32-bit Microsoft Excel for Windows 95 (make 32-bit API calls)?

- Microsoft Project: Is the host application 16-bit Microsoft Project 3.0 (make 16-bit API calls) or 32-bit Microsoft Project version 4.0 or later (make 32-bit API calls)?

- Word for Windows: Is the host application 16-bit Word 6.0 or earlier (make 16-bit API calls) or 32-bit Word 6.0 for Windows NT or Word for Windows 95 (make 32-bit API calls)?

If you make the wrong API call, an error will occur. The solution code must determine whether the application is a 16-bit application or a 32-bit application, so it can make the appropriate call.

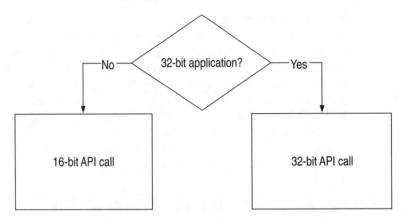

The solution is to put every API call into a *wrapper*—a Visual Basic procedure or a Microsoft Excel 4.0 macro. This wrapper routine checks the "bitness" of the application and selects the appropriate API call. Place these wrappers in separate modules so that your code can be easily reused. Some API calls (for example, **GetPrinterDriveDirectory** and **GetWinMetaFileBits**) are not available in all 32-bit operating environments, which means that the structure of an API wrapper can become as complex as this:

```
Function MyAPICall$(ByVal Args)
    If Engine32() Then
        'Select is rarely needed
        Select Case OS32() 'Based on GetVersionEx API
        Case 0 'Win32s
            ....
        Case 1 'NT 3.1
            ....
        Case 2 'NT 3.5
            ....
        Case 3 'Windows 95
            ....
        End Select
    Else '16-bit
        ....
    End If
End Function
```

An API wrapper this complex is the exception and not the rule.

Compiled languages, such as FoxPro and Visual Basic, build 16-bit or 32-bit application executables. The executable targets either 16-bit API calls or 32-bit API calls. You can determine the appropriate API calls while building the application. You can select the calls either by having all the 16-bit declarations in one file and all the 32-bit declarations in another file and manually switching them in a project, or by using the **#IF... #ELSE...** directives and conditional compilation supported by Visual Basic 4.0. If you must support Visual Basic 3.0 and Visual Basic 4.0 applications concurrently, separate files may reduce code maintenance. If you support FoxPro, you will have no problem using 16-bit API calls from compiled 32-bit FoxPro solutions because the **RegFN** functions will automatically thunk from the 32-bit layer to the 16-bit layer if needed.

Compiled 32-bit languages may require some minor differences in API calls depending on the 32-bit operating system. For example, developers must program context menus differently for Windows 95 than for Windows NT.

Determining Whether a 32-Bit Application Is Running

In the previous section, writing application independent code was covered by adding code for both 16 and 32-bit scenarios. However, you still need to determine in source code whether the application is a 32-bit application or a 16-bit application without doing any API calls. You cannot do an API call because you do not know if a 16-bit API call or a 32-bit API call will work. The following code will determine if the application is a 32-bit application.

Note The **Application.OperatingSystem** property in Microsoft Excel and Microsoft Project does not return the version of Windows you have installed, but the layer of Windows that the application is running on, for example, the 16-bit subsystem in Windows NT.

Microsoft Excel 5.0, Microsoft Excel 95, Microsoft Project 4.0, Microsoft Project 95

```
Function Engine32%()
    If instr(Application.OperatingSystem,"32") then Engine32%=True
End Function
```

Word 6.0, Word 95

```
Function Engine32
    If Val(GetSystemInfo$(23)) > 6.3 Or Len(GetSystemInfo$(23)) = 0 Then
    ➥ Engine32 = - 1 Else Engine32 = 0
End Function
```

Microsoft Access 1.1 or higher

```
Function Engine32% ()
If SysCmd(7) > 2 Then Engine32% = True
End Function
```

Putting It All Together

For examples of code for particular applications, you should consult the Microsoft Developers Network (MSDN), and find the article entitled "Corporate Developer's Guide to Office 95 API Issues." For information about connecting to MSDN, see Appendix F, "Resources." The following simple example may help you understand some issues.

```
Declare Function GetTickCount32 Lib "KERNEL32" Alias "GetTickCount" ()
➡ As Long
Declare Function GetTickCount16 Lib "USER" Alias "GetTickCount" ()
➡ As Long

Function GetRightTickCount() As Long
If Engine32%() Then
    GetRightTickCount = GetTickCount32()
Else
    GetRightTickCount = GetTickCount16()
End If
End Function
```

The **GetTickCount** API has the same name for both 16-bit Windows and 32-bit Windows, so you must use an **Alias** control word to change the function name in at least one of the **Declare** statements. In the previous example, the names in both **Declare** statements were changed, to GetTickCount32 and GetTickCount16. Next, depending on the application's bitness, **GetTickCount** is mapped to the correct API function name (GetTickCount32 or GetTickCount16) and its associated API call. In this example, **GetTickCount** in your code will be mapped to GetTickCount32 (in the GetTickCount function), which is mapped to **GetTickCount** in KERNEL32, when Engine32% is True.

Word Sample Declare-method Solution

Word has a different **Declare** format and syntax. The Word solution is more complex because you cannot place both the 16-bit and 32-bit **Declare** statements in the same macro. The solution is to create three macro libraries: **APICALL16** and **APICALL32**, that contain the **Declare** statements for each operating environment, and a 16-bit/32-bit interoperability macro, **APICALLS**.

First, create a macro library called **APICALL16**. This macro contains all the 16-bit API **Declare** statements.

```
 'This is APICALL16 -- all 16-bit Declare statements are placed here.
Declare Function GetTickCount16 Lib "USER" Alias "GetTickCount"()
➡ As Long
Function GetTickCount
GetTickCount = GetTickCount16
End Function
```

Second, create a macro library called **APICALL32**. This macro contains all the 32-bit API **Declare** statements.

```
'This is APICALL32 -- all 32-bit Declare statements are placed here.
Declare Function GetTickCount32 Lib "KERNEL32"() Alias "GetTickCount"
➥ As Long
Function GetTickCount
GetTickCount = GetTickCount32
End Function
```

Third, create a macro library called **APICALLS**. This macro contains **Engine32** and the procedures your solution code will call.

```
'This is APICALLS -- no Declare statements may be in this macro.
Function Engine32
Engine32 = 0
If Val(AppInfo$(2)) > 5 Then
   OS$ = GetSystemInfo$(23)
   If Val(OS$) > 6.3 Or Len(OS$) = 0 Then Engine32 = - 1
End If
End Function


Function GetTickCount
If Engine32 Then
   GetTickCount = APICall32.GetTickCount
Else
   GetTickCount = APICall16.GetTickCount
End If
End Function
'Other API function calls are placed here.
```

You can now call this function from your solution code. You must preface your calls with **APICALLS**. For example:

```
Sub MAIN
MsgBox Str$(APICalls.GetTickCount)
End Sub
```

▶ **To convert Word solutions to run on 16-bit and 32-bit products**

1. Create a new module called **APICALLS**.
2. Create the **Engine32** function in **APICALLS.**
3. Create a new module called **APICALL16**.
4. Locate all the 16-bit **Declare** statements in the solution and move them to **APICALL16**.
5. Create a new module called **APICALL32**.
6. Create the equivalent 32-bit **Declare** statements and put them to **APICALL32**.

7. Using the template above, create functions for each API in each of the three macro libraries.

8. Add **APICALLS** before all calls to the API in your solution code.

9. Test each function.

This process allows existing calls in other modules to be left untouched. After the developer defines and tests these macros, the developer can add them to Normal.dot and reuse the macros in other solutions so as to cut conversion time.

Recompiling DLLs

This section has so far focused on the issue of updating Windows API calls— but the issues for solution code that calls 16-bit DLLs that you have bought, developed, or simply used is exactly the same. The developer must change all 16-bit DLL **Declare** calls in solution code to 32-bit calls. This requires creating a 32-bit version of the DLL (at least) and possibly changing the **Declare** statement (in Microsoft Excel 4.0 macros, the **Register** function).

This also means a separate DLL must exist for both the 16-bit application and the 32-bit application. For file management, the name of the 32-bit DLL should include "32" at the end. The developer must recompile the DLL as a 32-bit Ansi.dll. The parameters passed to the DLL must use the **stdcall**-passing protocol to talk to 32-bit Visual Basic for applications, instead of the **PASCAL**-passing protocol used with 16-bit Windows. Place the calls for the 16-bit and 32-bit versions of the DLL in a wrapper similar to the API wrapper described previously.

For information about recompiling applications, see Chapter 1, "Porting 16-bit Code to 32-bit Windows," in *Programming Techniques* from the Visual C++ 2.1 documentation in the Development Library, or see your C compiler documentation.

Thunking

When you do not have the source code of a DLL, your solution is to use *thunking* to port your solution to Windows 95. Thunking enables direct 16-bit and 32-bit calls but requires much more work than simply changing the Windows API call. If you cannot change or recompile the 16-bit DLL, you must write a new 32-bit DLL wrapper to access the 16-bit DLL. The 32-bit application calls to this 32-bit wrapper DLL, which then calls the original 16-bit DLL.

Thunking allows parameters to be pushed correctly on the stack, enables a DLL of a different bitness to load in your process, and converts memory addresses from **offset** (32-bit) to **segment::offset** (16-bit). This means, however, there are some issues even if you do the thunking work. For example, pointers to pointers to memory locations require additional work in 16-bit and 32-bit scenarios.

There are different ways to thunk depending on your operating system. Windows 95 and Windows NT thunk differently. For an overview of thunking across the Windows platforms and pointers to more information about thunking, see "Diving into the Requirements for the Windows 95 Logo" in the Development Library.

Advanced Programming Topics

Most developers writing solution code know the C language, and the following information is provided to assist them in using their knowledge of C to create Declare statements for Visual Basic and Visual Basic for applications using the tools they already have.

Working from C Declarations

Apart from the API location changing (from KERNEL to KERNEL32), the main issue in moving from 16-bit API calls to 32-bit API calls is the change in the size of parameter data types. Some background information may help you understand what has changed and why. Windows 3.0 was designed for the Intel 80286 CPU, where the hardware handles data two bytes at a time or in 16-bit words. Windows 95 was designed for later CPUs, where the hardware can handle data four bytes at a time or in 32-bit words. The following list shows how Visual Basic represents an **Integer** versus how Windows represents an **int**:

- **Integer** and **int** are each two bytes in the 16-bit Windows operating system and in 16-bit Microsoft Excel, Visual Basic, Microsoft Access, Word for Windows, and Microsoft Project.

- **Integer** is two bytes in 32-bit Microsoft Excel, Visual Basic, Microsoft Access, Word for Windows, and Microsoft Project, the same as in the 16-bit versions of these products.

- **int** is four bytes in the 32-bit Windows operating systems, Windows 95, and Windows NT.

To illustrate how this change of size can change a call, recall the fictional **MyAPICall** API used earlier. The **MyAPICall** call needs the handle to the application's window (HWND), a string, a character, and an integer to be placed on the stack. In C, the function would be:

```
int MyAPICall (HWND hwndForm, LPSTR lpstrCaption, TCHAR tchAccKey,
➥ int iMagicNumber)
```

Each parameter has two parts: the data type (**HWND**, **LPSTR**, **TCHAR**, **int**) and the field name (**hwndForm**, **lpstrCaption**, **tchAccKey**, **iMagicNumber**). Each data type requires a specific number of bytes to represent it. Each field name has some odd-looking characters as a prefix—these characters (known as Hungarian notation) indicate the data type, such as **int** or **lpstr**.

Windows has many data types that API calls use as parameters. The following table shows some of the more significant data types used by Windows 95 API calls. Many Windows data types use the C data type of **int**. When **int** changed from 16-bits to 32-bits, the related Windows data types also changed.

C data type	Windows 3.x; Windows for Workgroups 3.x (16-Bit)	Win32s, Windows NT, and Windows 95 (32-Bit)
unsigned int, UINT, int	2 bytes	4 bytes
short	2 bytes	2 bytes
long	4 bytes	4 bytes
char, CHAR	1 byte	1 byte
WORD	2 bytes	2 bytes
Handle (hWnd, hDC, hMenu)	2 bytes	4 bytes
LPSTR	4 bytes	4 bytes
WCHAR	2 bytes	2 bytes
TCHAR (ANSI or Unicode)	1 byte	1 or 2 bytes
POINT	4 bytes	8 bytes

Thus, converting our **MyAPICall** API call from C, the declarations for **MyAPICall** using Visual Basic for applications, Access Basic, or WordBasic would be as follows (formatted to make comparison easier):

```
'16 bits
Declare Function MyAPICall Lib "MYDLL.DLL" Alias "MyAPICall" (
    ByVal hwndForm As Integer,
    ByVal lpstrCaption As String,
    ByVal hAccKey As String,
    ByVal iMagicNumber As Integer
    ) As Integer
'32 bits
Declare Function MyAPICall Lib "MYDLL32.DLL" Alias "MyAPICall" (
    ByVal hwndForm As Long,
    ByVal lpstrCaption As String,
    ByVal hAccKey As String,
    ByVal iMagicNumber As Long
    ) As Long
```

A final tool you may find useful is the following table that maps C language declaration data types to their Visual Basic equivalents.

C language declaration	Visual Basic equivalent	Call with
Boolean	**ByVal** B **As Boolean**	Any **Integer** or **Variant** variable
Pointer to a string (LPSTR)	**By Val** S **As String**	Any **String** or **Variant** variable
Pointer to an integer (LPINT)	I **As Integer**	Any **Integer** or **Variant** variable
Pointer to a long integer (LPDWORD)	L **As Long**	Any **Long** or **Variant** variable
Pointer to a structure (for example, LPRECT)	S **As** Rect	Any variable of that user-defined type
Integer (INT, UINT, WORD, BOOL)	**ByVal** I **As Integer**	Any **Integer** or **Variant** variable
Handle (32 bit, HWND)	**ByVal** H **As Long**	Any **Long** or **Variant** variable
Long (DWORD, LONG)	**ByVal** L **As Long**	Any **Long** or **Variant** variable
Pointer to an array of integers	I **as Integer**	The first element of the array, such as I(0)
Pointer to a void (void*)	V **As Any**	Any variable (use **ByVal** when passing a string)
Void (function return value)	**Sub** Procedure	n/a
NULL	**As Any**	ByVal 0&
Char (TCHAR)	**ByVal** Ch **As String**	Any **String** or **Variant** variable

Using the Win32 Programmer's Reference

The two primary sources for Win32 API information are the *Win32 Programmer's Reference* and a list of Microsoft-supplied Win32 **Declare** statements for Visual Basic, such as Win32api.txt. The Development Library contains a listing with explanations of the entire Win32 API set in the *Win32 Programmer's Reference*. For more information about the Development Library, see "Microsoft Developers Network," in Appendix F.

Frequently Asked Questions

Automated answers to common questions, solutions to technical problems, and tips are available at no cost, 24 hours a day, 7 days a week, by telephoning Microsoft FastTips at (800) 936-4100. These tips change frequently to respond to the most common issues.

P A R T   4

Running Multiple Versions of Office and Using Office in a Workgroup

Chapter 13, "Running Multiple Versions of Microsoft Office," explains what you need to know when you are supporting either different versions of Office running on Windows, or have platforms other than Windows in your organization.

Chapter 14, "Coexistence with Microsoft Office for the Macintosh," summarizes the issues around sharing documents or upgrading your organization from Office for the Macintosh to Office for Windows 95. These issues are all mentioned elsewhere in this book, but are pulled together here for your convenience.

Chapter 15, "Using Workgroup Features and Applications with Office," covers those issues and features you need to know about when your users are sharing documents throughout the organization. Included in this chapter is managing documents in your organization using the Find File feature, setting up and using electronic mail to exchange documents, using ODBC (Open Database Connectivity) and external data in Office applications, plus information about specific new workgroup features in the Office for Windows 95 applications. These new features include Shared Lists in Microsoft Excel, PowerPoint Presentation Conferencing and exchanging content with Microsoft Word, using Word Viewer, using the Word Internet Assistant, and creating a document library.

Chapter 16, "Microsoft Access Database Replication," explains everything you need to know about distributed computing database replication with Microsoft Access. This chapter assists you in planning, creating, and administering replicas of your database.

C H A P T E R   1 3

Running Multiple Versions of Microsoft Office

This chapter covers the issues you and your users need to know when you use multiple versions of Microsoft Office in a workgroup environment and share data bases, documents, and schedules from multiple versions.

Because binders are a new feature in Office for Windows 95, users of Office for the Macintosh and Office 4.*x* for Windows cannot open binders directly. If your Office 95 users are using binders and they need to share the contents, they should first unbind them (make separate files of the sections) by clicking the binder with the right mouse button and then clicking Unbind on the shortcut menu. The users of Office 4.*x* can then work with the individual files.

In This Chapter

Running Multiple Versions of Microsoft Access in a Workgroup

Here are some issues to consider when you use two versions of Microsoft Access in a workgroup environment.

Microsoft Access 2.0 (16-bit) and Microsoft Access 7.0 (32-bit)

The following sections describe the issues you will encounter when your users share databases between 16-bit Microsoft Access 2.0 and 32-bit Microsoft Access 7.0.

Database Files

To maintain backward compatibility, Microsoft Access 7.0 can open databases from earlier versions without conversion. However, users of earlier versions cannot open database files created with Microsoft Access 7.0. For more information about file compatibility, see "Sharing Microsoft Access Databases Across Versions" later in this chapter.

Workgroup Information Files

Microsoft Access 7.0 can use workgroup information files created in Microsoft Access 2.0. In Microsoft Access 2.0, a workgroup information file is called a workgroup or a system database, and by default it is named System.mda. The only reason to do this is if a Microsoft Access 7.0 user needs to use a secured Microsoft Access 2.0 database. Use the Workgroup Administrator to join a previous version workgroup information file.

If all users of a secured database have upgraded to Microsoft Access 7.0, that database and the workgroup information file used with it should be converted to Microsoft Access 7.0 format to take advantage of all of the features Microsoft Access 7.0 provides. For information about converting databases and workgroup information files, see "Converting Databases" in the Microsoft Access section of Chapter 10.

Access Basic and Visual Basic Programming Issues

When opening a database in Microsoft Access 2.0 format for the first time, Microsoft Access 7.0 creates a hidden system table named MSysModules that contains copies of all forms, reports, and modules in the database. MSysModules is used to maintain compatibility between the new implementation of Visual Basic for applications used in Microsoft Access 7.0 and the Access Basic code used in Microsoft Access 2.0. This process needs to be repeated any time the code is changed using Microsoft Access 2.0. For more information, see "Opening a Database in its Existing Format" in the Microsoft Access section of Chapter 10.

There might be some changes that need to be made to Access Basic code for it to work when run under Microsoft Access 7.0. See "Upgrading Access Basic Code to Visual Basic for Applications" in Part 2 for additional information.

Microsoft Access 1.x (16-bit) and Microsoft Access 7.0 (32-bit)

All of the issues described for Microsoft Access 2.0 also apply to opening and running a Microsoft Access 1.0 or 1.1 database using Microsoft Access 7.0. The following issues apply only to opening and running Microsoft Access 1.x databases with Microsoft Access 7.0.

Updating Query Fields

Using Microsoft Access 7.0, you can update the data in some fields in multiple-table queries that you cannot update using Microsoft Access 1.*x*. For example, in a query that includes fields from a Customers table and an Orders table (where one customer can have more than one order), you cannot update fields from the Customers table using Microsoft Access 1.*x*. Using Microsoft Access 7.0, you can update fields from the Customers table in most situations. This makes your queries and the forms based on them less restrictive. If you don't want users to update these fields in a form, use Microsoft Access 1.*x* to set the Locked property to Yes for form controls that are bound to the fields.

Combo Boxes and List Boxes

For combo boxes and list boxes that have their RowSource property set to a table or a query, Microsoft Access 7.0 displays data in the rows of the combo or list box using the format defined for the data in the Format property of the underlying field. Microsoft Access 1.*x* doesn't use the Format of the underlying field.

Backquote Character (`) in Object Names

If an object name in a Microsoft Access 1.*x* database includes a backquote character (`), you cannot open that object using Microsoft Access 7.0 or convert the database to Microsoft Access 7.0 format. Use Microsoft Access 1.*x* to rename it first. After renaming the object, you must also change references to that object in your queries, forms, reports, macros, and modules for them to work correctly. You can use the Documentor command on the Analyze submenu of the Tools menu to find occurrences of the old name in your references.

Validation Rules for Tables

Enhanced validation rules for fields and records make your data safer, but come with new restrictions on what elements you can include in a rule. Rules in Microsoft Access 1.*x* databases that conflict with these restrictions cannot be converted.

In Microsoft Access 7.0, validation rules you set for fields and records in a table protect your data regardless of how it's entered or modified: whether by using a datasheet or form, imported data, action queries, or Visual Basic. When you use a form with its own validation rules, the form's validation rules are applied in addition to validation rules set for the table the form is based on.

In most cases, this enhanced validation doesn't change the way your database works at all. If you have the same validation rule set for both a field in a table and a control on a form that's bound to that field in a Microsoft Access 1.*x* database, after converting the database you can delete the rule set for the control if you want—your form works the same whether you change it or not.

If your Microsoft Access 1.*x* database validation rules contain elements not allowed in Microsoft Access 7.0, the rules aren't converted to Microsoft Access 7.0 format. When Microsoft Access encounters invalid validation rules while converting your version 1.*x* database, it creates the ConvertErrors table in the converted database with information to help you fix the rules.

Visible Property

In Microsoft Access 1.*x*, setting a control's Visible property to No makes the control invisible in Form view and also hides its column in Datasheet view. In Microsoft Access 7.0, the Visible property doesn't hide its column in Datasheet view. In Microsoft Access 7.0, if you want to hide a column, use the Hide Columns command on the Format menu.

Sharing Microsoft Access Databases Across Versions

This section discusses issues to consider when users run multiple versions of Microsoft Access in a workgroup or on a single computer and want to share databases from different versions.

Opening a Database using Different Versions of Microsoft Access

This section describes what happens when you open a database using two different versions of Microsoft Access. The following list describes the file compatibility between Microsoft Access 1.*x* or 2.0 and Microsoft Access 7.0 database files.

- Files created in Microsoft Access 1.*x* or 2.0 can be opened directly with Microsoft Access 7.0. The user can browse the database, add, delete, or modify records, but not switch into Design view on any objects. To modify the design of existing objects or to add new objects, the database must be opened with the version used to create the it. For more information about opening earlier version databases with Microsoft Access 7.0, see "Opening a Database in its Existing Format" in the Microsoft Access section of Chapter 10.

- Files created in Microsoft Access 7.0 cannot be opened with Microsoft Access 1.*x* or 2.0. If a Microsoft Access 1.*x* or 2.0 user attempts to open a Microsoft Access 7.0 database, they will see a message that the database cannot be opened because it may not be a Microsoft Access database or because the file is corrupt. For this reason, Microsoft Access 7.0 and users of earlier versions can only share the same database as long as it is stored in the earlier version format.

- Tables in Microsoft Access 1.*x* or 2.0 databases can be linked (attached) to Microsoft Access 7.0 databases. Linking earlier version tables may provide better performance than opening the Microsoft Access 1.*x* or 2.0 database directly. Linking earlier version tables also allows Microsoft Access 7.0 users to take advantage of all of the features available in that version. For more information, see "Creating an Application Database Linked to the Previous Version Table Data" in the Microsoft Access section of Chapter 10.

- Tables in Microsoft Access 7.0 databases cannot be linked (attached) to Microsoft Access 1.*x* or 2.0 databases.

Saving a Database to Earlier Versions of Microsoft Access

Microsoft Access 7.0 cannot create database files in earlier version formats. However, tables from a Microsoft Access 7.0 database can be exported to existing Microsoft Access 2.0 and 1.*x* database files. Only tables can be exported; you cannot export other database objects.

To export Microsoft Access 7.0 tables to an earlier version database, open the database you want to export from, select the table you want to export in the database window, and then use the Save As/Export command on the File menu to select the database to export to.

Running Multiple Versions of Microsoft Access on a Single System

Here are some issues to consider when planning to install and use two different versions of Microsoft Access on the same Windows 95 or Windows NT 3.51 computer. All of the issues noted in the previous sections also apply to running multiple versions of Microsoft Access on a single system.

You can install and run the16-bit versions of Microsoft Access (version 1.*x* or 2.0) and the 32-bit version (version 7.0) on the same computer. All versions of Microsoft Access can be run at the same time, but only Microsoft Access 7.0 can open databases created with all versions.

Important   When installing more than one version of Microsoft Access on the same computer, install Microsoft Access 7.0 last so that it is used by default when opening Microsoft Access database files using My Computer or Windows Explorer. If you install a previous version after installing Microsoft Access 7.0, that version will be used when opening databases with My Computer or Windows Explorer, and you'll see an error message if you try to open a Microsoft Access 7.0 database.

Selecting Which Version to Use When Opening a Database

Use this technique to select which version of Microsoft Access to use when opening a database using My Computer or Windows Explorer. Otherwise, when you open a database it is opened in the last version of Microsoft Access you installed. This technique works only in Windows 95.

▶ **To select which version of Microsoft Access to use when opening a database**

1. In My Computer or Windows Explorer, find the Microsoft Access 2.0 application.

2. In another window, display the Windows\SendTo folder.

3. Using the right mouse button, drag the Microsoft Access 2.0 application to the SendTo folder. On the shortcut menu, click Create Shortcut(s) Here.

4. Repeat step 3 for the Microsoft Access 7.0 application.

5. In the SendTo folder, rename the two Microsoft Access shortcuts so you can identify them.

6. To specify which version of Microsoft Access to use when opening a database, use the right mouse button to click the database. On the shortcut menu, point to Send To, and then click the version you want.

Note Microsoft Access 7.0 databases can be opened only with Microsoft Access 7.0. If you try to open a Microsoft Access 7.0 database with a previous version (2.0 or 1.x), you'll see an error message and the database will not open.

Running Multiple Versions of Microsoft Excel in a Workgroup

This section discusses issues to consider when you use multiple versions of Microsoft Excel in a workgroup environment and share workbooks from multiple versions.

Opening a Workbook from Earlier Versions

In Microsoft Excel 7.0, you can open files created in Microsoft Excel 2.1 or later. All files from Microsoft Excel 2.1 or later have type and version information encoded in the file so that Microsoft Excel can automatically determine the type of file and the version it was created in.

The types of files that can be opened from these earlier versions of Microsoft Excel include the following:

- Worksheets (filename extension .xls)
- Charts (filename extension .xlc)
- Macro sheets (filename extensions .xlm and .xla)
- Workspaces and workbooks (filename extension .xlw)

Saving a Workbook to Earlier Versions

Because the Microsoft Excel 5.0 and 7.0 save files in the same format, there is no need to save to another version when moving between these two versions. Users of Microsoft Excel 7.0 can save files to these earlier versions of Microsoft Excel:

- Version 2.1, which can save single worksheets, charts, and macro sheets only
- Version 3.0, which can save single worksheets, charts, and macro sheets only
- Version 4.0, which can save single worksheets, charts, and macro sheets and can also save version 4.0 workbook format

Whenever you save to an earlier version, data associated with new features is not saved. Microsoft Excel displays a message when it detects that data associated with new features may be lost because of saving to an earlier version.

Sharing Microsoft Excel Workbooks Across Platforms and Versions

Because Microsoft Excel is a true cross-platform application program, users on different operating system platforms or on different versions of the product can work on the same workbook without encountering compatibility problems.

Note This section discusses platform and version issues for Microsoft Excel workbooks. This material is not related to the Shared Lists feature that is new to Microsoft Excel 7.0.

Microsoft Excel 5.0 (16- and 32-bit) and Microsoft Excel 7.0 (32-bit)

The following sections describe the issues you encounter when your users share workbooks between Microsoft Excel 5.0 and Microsoft Excel 7.0.

Workbook Files

Because Microsoft Excel 5.0 and 7.0 save files in the same format, files created in Microsoft Excel 5.0 can be opened directly in Microsoft Excel 7.0, and files created in Microsoft Excel 7.0 can be opened directly in Microsoft Excel 5.0.

Microsoft Excel 7.0 files include two features that Microsoft Excel 5.0 does not recognize: OLE Custom Properties and password-style edit boxes in custom dialog boxes. The Microsoft Excel 5.0 user can open a file that contains these features, but if the file is saved in Microsoft Excel 5.0, the OLE Custom Properties and password-style dialog box formatting is lost.

Document Properties

The following standard set of document properties is retained in both Microsoft Excel 5.0 and 7.0:

- Title
- Subject
- Author
- Keywords
- Comments
- Name of Application
- Attributes

The following standard set of document properties is only used in Microsoft Excel 7.0:

- Last Saved By
- Created
- Modified

The following extended set of document properties is supported in Microsoft Excel 7.0, in addition to the preceding standard document properties:

- Manager
- Company
- Category

The following standard set of document properties is displayed in the Microsoft Excel 7.0 Properties dialog box, but is not used by Microsoft Excel 7.0:

- Template
- Revision Number
- Total Editing Time
- Printed

The Microsoft Excel 7.0-only set of standard document properties and extended document properties is lost if the file is saved in Microsoft Excel 5.0.

Microsoft Excel 7.0 also gives the user a way to define custom properties for the workbook, using the Custom tab in the Properties dialog box. These properties can be linked to the values of cells that are named ranges. These custom document properties are lost if the file is saved in Microsoft Excel 5.0.

Data Map Feature

When you create and save a data map in Microsoft Excel 7.0, Microsoft Excel saves both an OLE object and a bitmap representation of the map. Because of the stored bitmap, a user can open the file and view the data map in Microsoft Excel 5.0. However, the Microsoft Excel 5.0 user cannot double-click the data map to edit it.

The Microsoft Excel 5.0 user can edit the data from which a data map was created, and then save the workbook. The data map is updated automatically when the workbook is opened in Microsoft Excel 7.0.

Shared Lists Feature

When a Microsoft Excel 7.0 user selects the Allow Multi-User Editing option in the Shared Lists dialog box for a workbook, users of Microsoft Excel 5.0 can open the workbook only as a read-only file. When a Microsoft Excel 5.0 user attempts to open the workbook, Microsoft Excel displays the Password dialog box, although no password will work.

Visual Basic Programming Issues

When you write cross-version programs in Visual Basic or in Visual Basic for applications, some objects, properties, and methods that exist in Microsoft Excel 7.0 do not exist in Microsoft Excel 5.0. For a complete list of changes to Visual Basic for Applications in Microsoft Excel 7.0, see VBA online Help. Also refer to "Upgrading Macros" in the Microsoft Excel section of Chapter 10 in this book.

To create completely version-compatible code in Visual Basic for Applications, you should write and test in Microsoft Excel 5.0 or write code that checks the version number and then branches to the appropriate code for that version.

You can write platform-independent Visual Basic code in a workbook and then create an add-in from the source workbook. This add-in can run with both the Windows and Macintosh platforms even though you created it on only one of the platforms. Performance of the add-in may suffer, however, when it runs on the platform on which it was not created. To ensure maximum add-in performance, move the source workbook to the other platform and then create the add-in again.

Sending Workbooks to Either Microsoft Excel 5.0 or 7.0

If you have users running both versions of Microsoft Excel on the same machine, use the following technique to decide which Microsoft Excel version you want to use to open a workbook. Otherwise, when you open a Microsoft Excel workbook, it opens in the last version of Microsoft Excel you installed. This technique works only in Windows 95.

▶ **To open a document in Microsoft Excel 5.0 or Microsoft Excel 7.0**

1. In My Computer or Windows Explorer, find the Microsoft Excel 5.0 application.

2. In another window, display the Windows\SendTo folder.

3. Using the right mouse button, drag the Microsoft Excel 5.0 application program to the SendTo folder. On the shortcut menu, click Create Shortcut(s) Here.

4. Repeat step 3 for the Microsoft Excel 7.0 application.

5. In the SendTo folder, rename the two Microsoft Excel shortcuts so you can identify them.

6. To specify which version of Microsoft Excel to use to open a Word document, use the right mouse button to click the document. On the shortcut menu, point to Send To, and then click the Microsoft Excel version you want.

Microsoft Excel 5.0 for the Macintosh and Microsoft Excel 7.0 (32-bit)

Because the file format for Microsoft Excel 5.0 for the Macintosh is identical to the file format used in Microsoft Excel 5.0 for Windows 3.1, the information in the preceding section also applies to Microsoft Excel 5.0 for the Macintosh.

When you save a workbook on the Macintosh, data associated with the Macintosh-only Publish/Subscribe feature is stored in the file. This data is ignored when you open the workbook using Windows 95 or Windows NT. However, when you save the file on Windows 95 or Windows NT, the Macintosh-specific data is preserved in the file.

Microsoft Excel 4.0 or Earlier (16-bit) and Microsoft Excel 7.0 (32-bit)

The upgrade from Microsoft Excel 4.0 to Microsoft Excel 5.0 includes several major architectural changes, many new features, and significant changes to the file format. Although you could use the Microsoft Excel 4.0 file format as a lowest common denominator, this would eliminate the ability to save data from the more powerful analysis tools, and may actually result in larger files and lower performance in some cases. Because of these factors, upgrading from Microsoft Excel 4.0 to Microsoft Excel 7.0 is highly recommended.

Running Multiple Versions of Microsoft Excel on a Single System

If you are running Windows 95, you can run Microsoft Excel 5.0 and Microsoft Excel 7.0 on the same computer, as long as they are installed in different folders. Use the Windows Send To command on the shortcut menu to control the version in which the file is opened, as described earlier in this section.

Do not run the two 32-bit versions of Microsoft Excel (version 5.0 for Windows NT and version 7.0 for Windows 95) on the same computer. These two versions are incompatible because changes were made to the OLE automation object library and to the DLLs for Visual Basic for applications. The shared Visual Basic DLLs and the object libraries are neither forward-compatible nor backward-compatible between the two 32-bit versions. In this case, you should upgrade from Microsoft Excel 5.0 for Windows NT to Microsoft Excel 7.0. When you upgrade to Microsoft Excel 7.0, performance improvements include reduced time to start Microsoft Excel, faster recalculation, faster saving, faster list searching, and faster printing.

Running Multiple Versions of Microsoft PowerPoint in a Workgroup

This section discusses issues relating to the coexistence of PowerPoint for Windows 95, PowerPoint 4.0 for Windows 3.1, and PowerPoint 4.0 for the Macintosh within the same workgroup. In general, information in this section about PowerPoint 4.0 holds true for both the Windows 3.1 and Macintosh versions. Issues particular to the Macintosh version are noted separately.

Note You might experience problems in when using PowerPoint 7.0 to work with presentation files that were originally created using a beta release of PowerPoint 7.0. For more information, see "Supporting Microsoft PowerPoint," in Chapter 12.

PowerPoint 4.0 (16-bit) and PowerPoint 7.0 (32-bit)

There are considerable differences between the file formats of PowerPoint 4.0 and PowerPoint 7.0. However, with the help of filters and converters, files can be exchanged freely among versions and platforms.

- PowerPoint 7.0 reads PowerPoint files from PowerPoint versions 2.0 through 4.0 for both Windows 3.1 and the Macintosh.

- PowerPoint 4.0 reads PowerPoint files from PowerPoint 7.0. (Requires the installation of special filters in PowerPoint 4.0.)

- PowerPoint 7.0 files opened in PowerPoint 4.0 retain their PowerPoint 7.0-specific attributes, but new features and effects that are not supported in PowerPoint 4.0 are not displayed.

- PowerPoint 7.0 features and effects are lost when you use the Save As command to save a presentation in PowerPoint 4.0 format.

Note For more information about the PowerPoint Viewer and the installable filters for PowerPoint 4.0, see "Upgrading to PowerPoint for Windows 95" in the Microsoft PowerPoint section of Chapter 10.

The following describes features particular to PowerPoint 7.0, and what happens to them in PowerPoint 4.0.

Builds In PowerPoint, progressive disclosure of items on a slide, one item at a time, is called a *build*. Only bulleted-list builds will continue to work when a PowerPoint 7.0 presentation is saved in PowerPoint 4.0 format. All other types of PowerPoint 7.0 builds are ignored.

Graphics PowerPoint 7.0 includes a lot of new graphic features and effects that have no equivalents in PowerPoint 4.0. These effects are, in most cases, converted to a similar effect in PowerPoint 4.0. For more information, see "Differences Between PowerPoint 7.0 and PowerPoint 4.0 Files" in the Microsoft PowerPoint section of Chapter 10.

Saving PowerPoint 7.0 Files in PowerPoint 4.0 Format

To save in PowerPoint 4.0 format, use the Save As command on the File menu, and select the PowerPoint 4.0 option. Behind the scenes, PowerPoint 7.0 launches the PowerPoint Viewer, which then saves the file in PowerPoint 4.0 format.

Note When designing custom setup scripts, make sure that the PowerPoint Viewer is installed on all computers whose users must be able to share presentations with PowerPoint 4.0 users.

Embedded Fonts Are Not Saved The Save As dialog box in PowerPoint includes an Embed TrueType option that, when selected, saves the fonts used in the presentation along with the file. The Viewer does not support this, so you must make sure that the fonts you need are available on the destination computer. In addition, when you save PowerPoint 7.0 files in PowerPoint 4.0 format, fonts cannot be embedded because the Viewer is used to implement the file conversion.

Long Filenames   When using the Save As command in PowerPoint 7.0 to save a file in PowerPoint 4.0 format, a dialog box appears, prompting you for a new filename. You'll need to take into consideration the destination platform of the file when you name it. For example, if the file is destined for PowerPoint 4.0 running on Windows 95 or the Macintosh, you can use a long filename. If the file will be used in PowerPoint 4.0 for Windows 3.1, a long filename will be truncated, so you might want to limit the filename to eight letters to avoid confusion.

When opening a PowerPoint 7.0 file using the Macintosh installable filters, the Windows 95 long filenames are preserved.

Opening PowerPoint 7.0 Files in PowerPoint 4.0

Installable filters are available on the Microsoft Office Resource Kit CD for both the Windows and Macintosh versions of PowerPoint 4.0. After the filters are installed, you can open PowerPoint 7.0 files in either the Windows or Macintosh version of PowerPoint 4.0. A setup program is provided which performs the necessary installation procedure to add the filters to PowerPoint 4.0. Simply copying the filters to users' machines will not work. The setup program must be used to install them.

When opening a PowerPoint 7.0 presentation, new features such as object builds and two-color fills will not be displayed in PowerPoint 4.0, but will still be available when the file is opened in PowerPoint 7.0, provided the presentation is not saved in PowerPoint 4.0.

Note   If you want to convert a large number of files to PowerPoint 7.0 format, the Microsoft Office Resource Kit CD includes a conversion utility called BatchConvert.exe that you can use to convert multiple files at once.

Some Macintosh Features Not Supported   When sharing presentations between PowerPoint 7.0 for Windows 95 and PowerPoint 4.0 for the Macintosh, Publish and Subscribe is not supported, nor are QuickTime features.

Note   Installable filters for the PowerMacintosh version of PowerPoint 4.0 will be available by the end of 1995. To obtain them, contact Microsoft Customer Service, download it from the Microsoft Network, the Microsoft forum on Compuserve, or Microsoft Select. For a list of resources, see Appendix F, "Resources."

Sharing Presentations from Earlier Versions of PowerPoint

PowerPoint 7.0 can open presentations created in versions 2.0 through 4.0 of PowerPoint. However, PowerPoint 7.0 can only save files in version 7.0 or 4.0 format. Filters allowing users to open PowerPoint 7.0 files are only available for installation in PowerPoint 4.0.

To share PowerPoint 7.0 files with PowerPoint 3.0 users, you need to use the Save As command in PowerPoint 7.0 to save in PowerPoint 4.0 format, then open the presentation in PowerPoint 4.0 and save it again in PowerPoint 3.0 format. Of course, PowerPoint 7.0 features and effects that are not supported in PowerPoint 3.0 are lost in the transition process.

Document Properties

The following standard set of document properties are found in both PowerPoint 4.0 and PowerPoint 7.0:

- Title
- Subject
- Author
- Keywords
- Comments

- File Name (MS-DOS Name)
- Directory (Location)
- Template
- Slides

The following extended set of document properties are found only in PowerPoint 7.0:

- Manager
- Company
- Category
- Type
- Location
- Size
- Created
- Modified
- Accessed
- Attributes (read-only, archive, system, hidden)
- Printed
- Last Saved By

- Revision Number
- Total Editing Time
- Paragraphs
- Words
- Bytes
- Notes
- Hidden Slides
- Multimedia Clips
- Fonts Used
- Presentation Designs
- Slide Titles

PowerPoint 7.0 also provides the user with a method of defining custom properties for the presentation. These custom properties are defined and accessed on the Custom tab in the Presentation Properties dialog box.

Templates

Although the set of templates shipped with PowerPoint 7.0 have been updated and new contents have been added, all PowerPoint 7.0 templates work with PowerPoint 4.0 and vice versa. You need to install the filters described earlier to open PowerPoint 7.0 templates in PowerPoint 4.0.

For more information about templates, see Chapter 4, "Microsoft PowerPoint Architecture."

Running Multiple Versions of Microsoft Schedule+ in a Workgroup

This section summarizes the issues relating to using Schedule+ 1.0 and Schedule+ 7.0 together in a workgroup. The implications of using different Schedule+ versions with Microsoft Mail server, Microsoft Exchange Server, or other mail servers are also included.

In a workgroup, users of Schedule+ can exchange three different types of information, either among themselves or with users of other scheduling or messaging applications:

- Meeting requests. These are the forms that Microsoft Exchange provides for sending meeting requests via email.

- Free/busy information. On the Planner tab in Schedule+, a meeting organizer can add names to a list of invited people or resources, and then check each one's availability before scheduling a meeting. Busy times show up as colored bars in the Planner.

- Details. If someone on the invited list has given the meeting organizer permission to view the details of their schedule, the meeting organizer can click using the right mouse button on a busy time for that person and read whatever information has been entered for that appointment, such as location, purpose of the meeting, and so on. Individuals can also give each other permission to access specific parts of their schedule, such as contacts or tasks.

The type of information that can be exchanged depends on the Schedule+ version and the type of mail server used. The following diagram summarizes the ways in which Schedule+ 7.0 works with different platforms and mail servers, and with Schedule+ 1.0.

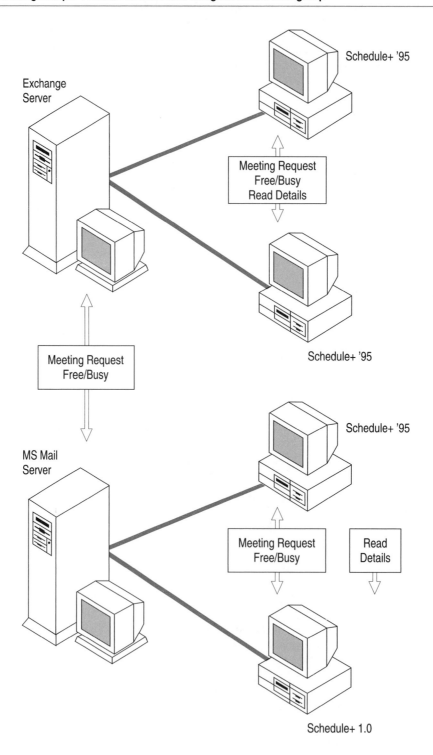

Microsoft Exchange Server

Schedule+ for Windows 95 is fully supported on a Microsoft Exchange server. Within the same Exchange server site, all the workgroup features of Schedule+ are available: users can send and receive meeting requests, display free and busy times for other users, and read the details of someone else's schedule, assuming that they have permission to do so.

Between Exchange Server sites, users can access free and busy information as long as site replication has been established between the sites. Schedule details can be shared if both sites are connected with a site connector and users can be authenticated by a server in the other site.

Note   Schedule+ 1.0 is not supported on an Exchange server.

Microsoft Mail Server

Microsoft Mail Server can be used with Schedule+ for Windows 95 and Schedule+ 1.0. Users can exchange meeting requests and display free and busy times. Schedule+ 7.0 has read-only access to the details of Schedule+ 1.0 calendar files, but Schedule+ 1.0 cannot read the details of files created under Schedule+ 7.0.

Windows 95 Workgroup Postoffice

Schedule+ 7.0 can be used with the Windows Messaging System (WMS) that comes with Windows 95. Users on the same postoffice can exchange meeting requests, read free and busy times, and share detail information. To exchange Schedule+ information with users on different Windows 95 workgroup postoffices, an upgrade to the fully-featured version of Microsoft Mail Server is required.

Schedule+ on Other Servers

In conjunction with the Microsoft Exchange client, Schedule+ 7.0 can be used with other mail servers for which a valid MAPI driver has been written. Schedule+ uses the driver for sending and receiving meeting requests with other users.

Schedule+ 7.0 can exchange meeting requests with other Schedule+ 7.0 users across the Internet via the Exchange client.

Meeting requests can be exchanged between Schedule+ 7.0 and other messaging applications when no MAPI driver is provided. However, the meeting requests will appear as text in a message, instead of in the custom form that the Microsoft Exchange client provides. Users of cc:Mail, for example, receive meeting requests from Schedule+ 7.0 users in the form of a plain-text message.

Access to free and busy information and schedule details requires that the MAPI driver vendor provide a way for the Schedule+ files to be administered on their system. A transport specification, provided in the *Exchange Developer's Kit*, gives vendors the ability to specify for their administration modules where Schedule+ can find users' server files on their system for free/busy lookup and calendar access. The transport is a simple text file that resides on a server and maps the mail address of a user to the location of that user's Schedule+ file.

Communicating between Exchange Server and Other Servers

Schedule+ users on Exchange server can exchange meeting requests and free/busy information with Schedule+ users on Microsoft Mail.

Postoffice files from Microsoft Mail are passed to the free/busy gateway component of the Microsoft Mail Connector by the Schedule Distribution program. The free/busy gateway breaks up the post-office files and creates separate messages with each user's free/busy information. These separate messages are placed in the free/busy public folder on the Exchange Server.

In the other direction, the free/busy gateway combines the separate messages in the free/busy public folder on the Exchange server into a single post-office file, which is then passed to the Cal folder on the Microsoft Mail Server.

Schedule+ users on Exchange server and PROFS users can exchange meeting requests, as well as access both free/busy and details information for each other. Schedule+ users on Microsoft Mail can exchange meeting requests and free/busy information with PROFS users.

Running Multiple Versions of Microsoft Word in a Workgroup

This section discusses issues to consider when you run multiple versions of Word in a workgroup or on a single computer.

Sharing Word Documents Across Platforms and Versions

Because the file formats for Word 6.0 and Word 7.0 are fully compatible, files created in Word 6.0 can be opened directly into Word 7.0, and likewise, files created in Word 7.0 can be opened directly into Word 6. Word 7.0 can also open files created in these earlier versions of Word:

- Word 2.*x* for Windows
- Word 3.*x* through 6.0 for MS-DOS
- Word 4.0, 5.0 and 5.1 for the Macintosh.
- Word 6.0 for the Macintosh (file format identical to Word 7.0 file format)

If your users will share documents between versions of Word other than versions 6 and 7, they may have to use the file format converters available through the Save As command on the File menu. Be sure to include these converters in the network installations you run, as most file format converters are not installed in the Compact installation. For more information, see Part 2, "Installing Microsoft Office."

Word 7.0 can save files to these earlier versions of Word:

- Word 2.*x* for Windows
- Word 3.*x* through 6.0 for MS-DOS
- Word 4.0, 5.0, and 5.1 for the Macintosh
- Word 6.0 for the Macintosh (file format identical to Word 7.0 file format)

Whenever you save to an earlier version, data associated with new features will not be saved. When Word detects that data associated with new features may be lost on save, it displays a message.

Word 6.0 (16-bit) and Word 7.0 (32-bit)

You can install and run 16-bit Word 6.0 and 32-bit Word 7.0 on the same computer. You can also run both of these versions of Word at the same time.

File Format

Both the 16-bit version, Word 6.0, and 32-bit version, Word 7.0, save files in the same format. However, Word 7.0 includes some features that Word 6.0 does not recognize: extended properties, highlighting, and Spell-It background spelling. The Word 6.0 user will have no problem when opening a file that contains these features. However, if a Word 6.0 user opens and saves a file, the extended properties, highlighting, and Spell-It background spelling information will be lost.

When opening a Word 7.0 document on any platform using Word 6.0 (running on Windows 95, Windows 3.1, Windows NT, or the Macintosh), the attributes of the Word 7.0 document that Word 6.0 users will not see are:

- Additional document properties (summary information). Word 6.0 recorded summary information in the Summary Info dialog box (Summary Info command, File menu). Word 7.0 can record more information about the document in the Document Properties dialog box (Properties command, File menu).

- Any highlighting done with the Highlighting button on the Formatting toolbar.

- Any background spelling work done by the Spell-It feature. When the document is opened in Word 7.0 again, however, the background spelling is done again.

If the user closes the Word 7.0 document without saving it in a Word 6.0 or other format, then all document attributes are preserved and will appear when the document is opened in Word 7.0. If, however, the user saves the Word 7.0 document in a Word 6.0 or other format, the Word 7.0 additional document properties and highlighting are lost.

Document Properties

The following standard set of document properties are retained in both Word 6.0 and Word 7.0:

- Title
- Subject
- Author
- Keywords
- Comments
- File Name (labeled MS-DOS Name in Word 7.0)
- Directory (labeled Location in Word 7.0)
- Template
- Created
- Last Saved (labeled Modified in Word 7.0)

- Last Saved By
- File Size (labeled Size in Word 7.0)
- Revision Number
- Total Editing Time
- Last Printed (labeled Printed in Word 7.0)
- Pages
- Words
- Characters
- Paragraphs
- Lines

The following document properties are used only in Word 7.0:

- Type
- Accessed
- Attributes
- Manager

- Company
- Category
- Bytes
- Document Contents

Word 7.0 also provides the user with a method of defining custom properties for the document. These custom properties are found on the Custom tab in the Properties dialog box.

Word 6.0 for the Macintosh and Word 7.0 (32-bit)

Because the file format for Word 6.0 for the Macintosh is identical to the file format used by Word 6.0 for Windows, the issues in the preceding section also apply to Word 6.0 for the Macintosh.

When you save a document on the Macintosh, data associated with the Macintosh-only Publish/Subscribe feature is stored in the file. This data is ignored when you open the document using Word on either Windows 95 or Windows NT. However, when you save the file using Word on Windows 95 or Windows NT, the Macintosh-specific data is preserved in the file.

Word 6.0 for Windows NT (32-bit) and Word 7.0 (32-bit)

The two 32-bit versions of Word, Word 6.0 for Windows NT and Word 7.0 for Windows 95, cannot coexist on the same system.

When you upgrade from Word 6.0 for Windows NT to Word 7.0, performance improvements will include reduced time to start Word, faster scrolling, faster saving, faster finding and replacing, and faster printing.

Word 2.x or Earlier (16-bit) and Word 7.0 (32-bit)

The upgrade from Word 2.x to Word 7.0 includes several major architectural changes, many new features, and significant changes to the file format. Although you could use the Word 2.x file format as a lowest common denominator, this would eliminate the ability to save the features found in later versions of Word. However, you can directly open and save Word 7.0 files in Word 2.x if you've installed the Word 2.x converter included on the Office Resource Kit CD-ROM. For more information, see "Upgrading from Word Version 2.x for Windows" in the Word section of Chapter 10.

Running Multiple Versions of Word on a Single System

If you have users running both versions of Microsoft Word on the same machine, use the following technique to control which version of Word is used when you open a document from outside Word. Otherwise, when you open a Word document it will appear in the last version of Word you installed. This technique works only in Windows 95. All of the issues noted in the preceding section apply as well to running multiple versions of Word on a single system.

▶ **To open a document in Word 6.0 or Word 7.0**

1. In My Computer or Windows Explorer, find the Word 6.0 application.

2. In another window, display the Windows\SendTo folder.

3. Using the right mouse button, drag the Word 6.0 application to the SendTo folder. On the shortcut menu, click Create Shortcut(s) Here.

4. Repeat step 3 for the Word 7 application.

5. In the SendTo folder, rename the two Word shortcuts so you can identify them.

6. To specify which version of Word to use to open a Word document, use the right mouse button to click the document. On the shortcut menu, click Send To, and then click the Word version you want.

Important When installing more than one version of Word on the same computer, install Word 7.0 last so that Word 7.0 is used by default when opening Word files from My Computer or Windows Explorer. If you install a previous version after installing Word 7.0, that version will be used when opening Word files.

C H A P T E R   1 4

Coexistence with Microsoft Office for the Macintosh

If your organization includes a mixed platform of personal computers running Microsoft Office for Windows 95 and Macintosh computers running Microsoft Office for the Macintosh, your users can continue working together and sharing documents. This chapter summarizes the issues when sharing documents or upgrading your organization from Office for the Macintosh to Office for Windows 95. Most of these issues are mentioned elsewhere in this book, but pulled together here for your convenience.

In This Chapter

Microsoft Office Binders

Users of Office for the Macintosh cannot open binders directly. To make the contents of a binder available to these users for viewing and editing, first unbind the binder (make separate files of the sections) in Office for Windows 95. To do this, use the right mouse button to click the binder and then click the Unbind command on the shortcut menu. Users can then work with the individual files.

Microsoft Access

There is no Macintosh version of Microsoft Access; however, it is possible to exchange or share data in the following ways:

- Microsoft Access for Windows 95 can save data from tables, queries, and all or selected portions of datasheets to Rich Text Format; to Microsoft Excel versions 3.0, 4.0, 5.0, and 7.0; and to Text (fixed-width and delimited formats). These file formats can be opened by users of Office for the Macintosh version 4.2 and later. Microsoft Access for Windows 95 can also save formatted data from forms and reports to these same formats, except for Microsoft Excel format, where data can be saved only to version 5.0 and 7.0 formats. To save data to other file formats, use the Save As/Export command on the File menu.

- Microsoft Access for Windows 95 can save (export) data from tables to a variety of database formats using the Save As/Export command on the File menu. For more information, search Microsoft Access Help Topics or ask the Answer Wizard.

- Microsoft Access for Windows 95 and Microsoft FoxPro for the Macintosh versions 2.5 or 2.6 can share data on a network server. To do so, your network must be using Microsoft Windows NT Advanced Server, Novell NetWare, or some other network operating system that allows computers running Windows 95 and the Macintosh operating system to share data on a file server. When using Microsoft Windows NT Advanced Server, you must be running Windows NT Services for the Macintosh and Macintosh computers must be running AppleTalk. As long as you are using a network that is configured to share files on a file server, you can put FoxPro 2.*x* data files (.dbf) and index files (.ndx, .idx, or .cdx) on the network server and then use front ends created with Microsoft Access for Windows 95 and Microsoft FoxPro for the Macintosh to share the data. To share the data from a Microsoft Access front end, link the data using the Link Tables command on the Get External Data submenu of the File menu.

- It is also possible to share data using ODBC drivers. There is no ODBC driver to share data stored in Microsoft Access database format (.mdb) that will run on the Macintosh; however, ODBC drivers are available for data in FoxPro and SQL Server formats. When sharing data using an ODBC driver, Macintosh computers must be running AppleTalk or TCP/IP network protocols. For more information about using ODBC data, see "ODBC and Client/Server Operations" in Chapter 15, "Using Workgroup Features and Applications with Office."

Microsoft Excel

In general, information about Microsoft Excel 5.0 holds true for both the Windows 3.1 and Macintosh versions, with exceptions noted. For details about file and feature differences between Microsoft Excel 5.0 and Microsoft Excel 7.0, see "Upgrading to Microsoft Excel for Windows 95," in Chapter 10, "Upgrading to Office for Windows 95."

When you save a workbook on the Macintosh, data associated with the Macintosh-only Publish and Subscribe feature is stored in the file. This data is ignored when you open the workbook using Windows 95 or Windows NT. However, when you save the file in Windows 95 or Windows NT, the Macintosh-specific data is preserved in the file.

You can write platform-independent Visual Basic code in a workbook and then create an add-in from the source workbook. This add-in can run on both the Windows and Macintosh platforms even though you created it on only one of the platforms. Performance of the add-in may suffer, however, when it runs on the platform on which it was not created. To ensure maximum add-in performance, move the source workbook to the other platform and then create the add-in again.

Microsoft PowerPoint

In general, information about PowerPoint 4.0 holds true for both the Windows 3.1 and Macintosh versions, with exceptions noted. For details about file and feature differences between PowerPoint 4.0 and PowerPoint 7.0, see "Upgrading to PowerPoint for Windows 95," in Chapter 10, "Upgrading to Office for Windows 95."

Reading PowerPoint 7.0 Files in PowerPoint 4.0 for the Macintosh

PowerPoint 7.0 files cannot be directly opened and saved in PowerPoint 4.0 for the Macintosh. There are two ways for PowerPoint 4.0 for the Macintosh to read PowerPoint 7.0 files.

- In PowerPoint 7.0, save files in PowerPoint 4.0 format. The PowerPoint Viewer, which must be installed to save in PowerPoint 4.0 format, converts the files for you.

  To save in PowerPoint 4.0 format, use the Save As command on the File menu, and select the PowerPoint 4.0 option. Behind the scenes, PowerPoint 7.0 launches the PowerPoint Viewer, which then saves the file in PowerPoint 4.0 format. When you save in PowerPoint 4.0 format, any PowerPoint 7.0-specific features and effects are lost. Embedded fonts are also not saved because the Viewer does not support saving the fonts used in the presentation along with the file. Make sure the fonts you need are available on the destination computer.

- In PowerPoint 4.0 for the Macintosh, install a filter to open PowerPoint 7.0 files. Installable filters for PowerPoint 4.0 for the Macintosh are available on the Microsoft Office Resource Kit CD. To use the filter, copy it to the PowerPoint folder on the Macintosh.

When sharing presentations between PowerPoint 7.0 and PowerPoint 4.0 for the Macintosh, Publish and Subscribe is not supported, nor are the QuickTime features.

Note Installable filters for the PowerMacintosh version of PowerPoint 4.0 will be available after PowerPoint 95 ships. To obtain them, contact Microsoft Customer Service, download it from the Microsoft Network, the Microsoft forum on CompuServe, or Microsoft Select. For more information, see the list of resources in Appendix F, "Resources."

Sharing PowerPoint 7.0 Files With Macintosh PowerPoint 3.0 Users

You can save PowerPoint 7.0 files in PowerPoint 4.0 format, but you cannot directly save them in PowerPoint 3.0 format. Instead, you need to use the Save As command in PowerPoint 7.0 to save in PowerPoint 4.0 format, open the presentation in PowerPoint 4.0 and save it again in PowerPoint 3.0 format. Of course, PowerPoint 7.0 features and effects that are not supported in PowerPoint 3.0 are lost in the transition process.

Long Filenames

When opening a PowerPoint 7.0 file using the Macintosh installable filters, the Windows 95 long filenames are preserved.

When using the Save As command in PowerPoint 7.0 to save a file in PowerPoint 4.0 format, a dialog box appears, prompting you for a new filename. If the file is destined for PowerPoint 4.0 on the Macintosh, you can use a long filename.

Microsoft Word

In general, information about Word 6.0 holds true for both the Windows 3.1 and Macintosh versions, with exceptions noted. For details about file and feature differences between Word 6.0 and Word 7.0, see "Upgrading to Word for Windows 95" in Chapter 10, "Upgrading to Office for Windows 95."

When you save a document in Word 6.0 for the Macintosh, data associated with the Macintosh-only Publish/Subscribe feature is stored in the file. This data is ignored when you open the document using Word 7.0 on either Windows 95 or Windows NT. However, when you save the file using Word 7.0 on Windows 95 or Windows NT, the Macintosh-specific data is preserved in the file.

Upgrading from Word version 4.0 or 5.*x* for the Macintosh

The file formats for Word 5.*x* and Word 7.0 differ. However, you can directly open documents created with Word 7.0 for Windows or Word 6.0 for Windows or the Macintosh in Word 5.*x* if you've installed the Word 6.0 Converter. Using this converter makes it easier for groups of users with different versions of Word to share files. If a complete installation of Word 6.0 exists on the same Macintosh computer as Word 5.*x*, the converter is available for installation and use with Word 5.*x*. If not, you can obtain the converter from several online sources. For more information, see Appendix F, "Resources." After you've obtained the converter, see the installation instructions that are included with the converter. Word 4.0 does not support the converter. In Word 7.0, save documents you want to share with Word 4.0 users in Word 4.0 for the Macintosh format.

Converting Between Word 7.0 and Word 4.0 or 5.*x* for the Macintosh

Word 7.0 reads Word 4.0 and 5.*x* for the Macintosh file formats directly. Word 7.0 also fully supports long file names. If your workgroup shares files between computers running Windows 95 and Macintosh computers, you do not need to change document file names.

In the following table, "Yes" means the feature exists in both products and is converted from one product to the other. "No" means it exists in both products but is not completely converted between the two. "Not supported" means the feature is not supported in one of the products or is not converted completely between products.

Feature	Word 7.0 to Word for the Macintosh	Word for the Macintosh to Word 7.0	Comments
Character Formatting			
Outline	Not supported	See comment	Converted to normal text in Word 7.0.
Shadow	Not supported	See comment	Converted to normal text in Word 7.0.
Superscript/Subscript	See comment	Yes	Word 7.0 superscript/subscript is different from previous versions of Word. This property is emulated using raised/lowered character formatting.
Kerning	No	Not supported	
Expand/Condense	See comment	Yes	Word 7.0 supports finer control of this property than does Word for the Macintosh. This value is rounded to the closest value that Word for the Macintosh supports.
Paragraph Formatting			
Borders/Shading	See comment	Yes	Word 7.0 has more options for borders and shading, including more colors, than Word for the Macintosh. These options are mapped to the closest Word for the Macintosh value available.
Columns			
Columns	Yes	Yes	Line Between not converted.
Variable-width Columns	See comment	Not supported	Variable-width columns are mapped to equal-width columns in Word for the Macintosh.
Page Formatting			Page formatting for Word for the Macintosh documents is stored in the Macintosh print record. On export, the converter is unable to create a print record.
Page orientation	No	Yes	
Page size	No	Yes	
Paper source	No	Yes	
Section Formatting			
Line numbering (Start At #)	No	Not supported	
Vertical alignment (top, centered, justified)	No	Not supported	
Other Features			
Annotations	See comment	Yes	Annotations are retained when converting to Word for the Macintosh 5.1; otherwise, annotations are converted to footnotes.

Feature	Word 7.0 to Word for the Macintosh	Word for the Macintosh to Word 7.0	Comments
Other Features *(continued)*			
Fields (FILENAME)	No	Not supported	
Graphics	See comment	Yes	When converting from Word 7.0 to Word for the Macintosh version 5.*x*, graphics are retained, provided the conversion is performed from within Word for the Macintosh. When converting to Word for the Macintosh 4.0, an empty graphics frame is created in the Word for the Macintosh document.
Language	No	Not supported	
Revision marks	No	Not supported	Character formatting indicating revised text is retained.
Subdocuments (INCLUDE field)	See comment	Not supported	If the RetainInclude flag is set to Yes in the [MacWordConv] section of Mstxtcnv.ini, the include field will be converted, but any path information in the field will be lost. Otherwise the latest result is inserted in the Word for the Macintosh document and the INCLUDE field is lost.
Master Documents	No	Not supported	Master documents lose the contents of the subdocuments and the references, but all the subdocuments are converted at the same time as the master document into separate documents.
Cross-references and bookmarks	No	Not supported	
Object linking and embedding	Yes	Yes	OLE objects may be edited after conversion, providing the OLE server is available on the target platform.
Drawing layer	No	Not supported	
Cell borders/shading	See comment	Yes	Word 7.0 has more options than Word for the Macintosh for borders and shanding, including more colors. These options are mapped to the closest Word for the Macintosh value available.
Fields (Form and bar code fields)	See comment	Not supported	Results of text form fields are retained. Other fields have no result that can be displayed.
Styles	See comment	See comment	Word for the Macintosh allows only 255 defined styles. Style definitions numbered greater than that are omitted, along with any references to them. All formatting is retained, however.
Character Styles	No	Not supported	Character style definitions are lost. All formatting is retained.

Feature	Word 7.0 to Word for the Macintosh	Word for the Macintosh to Word 7.0	Comments
Other Features *(continued)*			
Bullets/Numbering	See comment	Not supported	Automatic bullets/numbers are converted to plain text.
Endnotes	See comment	Not supported	All footnotes and endnotes are retained, but they are merged into one continuous stream.
Page Numbering	See comment	Yes	Word 7.0 has more page numbering options than Word for the Macintosh. These options are mapped to the closest alternative.
Extended Characters	See comment	See comment	Some ANSI extended characters have no Macintosh character set equivalent, and vice versa. If the equivalent character is not available, it is replaced by the underscore (_) character. Equivalent characters available in fonts such as Symbol or Wingdings can be used to replace lost characters following conversion. Characters available in the unique symbol sets of Microsoft TrueType fonts are retained, provided that the same font is available on both platforms.

Substituting Fonts for Documents Converted from Word for the Macintosh 4.0

Font mapping for Word for the Macintosh 4.0 files is different from font mapping for Word for the Macintosh 5.*x* and other converters. Macintosh Word 4.0 stores font information in document files by the Macintosh System font numbers. These numbers can be assigned by the user to arbitrary fonts installed in the Macintosh System by the user. This means that character font information in the converted Word for the Macintosh files can be different for every user and the converter may not make the correct font conversion.

Note An application note titled "Mac Font Font-Mapping Utility," which enables identification of the Macintosh System font numbers and matching font names on your Macintosh computer, is available from Product Support Services. For information about contacting Product Support Services, see Appendix F, "Resources."

When opening Word for the Macintosh 4.0 documents in Word 7.0, fonts with numbers greater than 128 are mapped to font names with the following syntax: "Font*font number*", so font number 2001 and 2001 would become "Font2000" and "Font2001" respectively.

Font Mapping Dialog Box

The Word for the Macintosh converter has an option to determine whether a dialog box will be displayed to locate the font-mapping file. This behavior is controlled using the FontDialog setting in the [MacWordConv] section in the Mstxtcnv.ini file. If FontDialog is "yes" or is blank, dialog boxes for user-defined font-mapping files for Word for the Macintosh version 4.0 files are used. If FontDialog is "no," dialog boxes for user-defined font-mapping files for Word for the Macintosh version 4.0 files are not used.

Format of a Word for the Macintosh 4.0 Font-Mapping File

The font-mapping file, Mac_font.dat, consists of a series of entries in the following format:

```
Winfontname;MacFont#[FontFamilyID]
```

The semicolon is required. There can be an arbitrary number of spaces between *Winfontname*, the semicolon, *MacFont#,* and *FontFamilyID*. Each entry must appear on its own line. There can be an arbitrary number of blank lines between entries.

Winfontname

The *Winfontname* is the name of the Windows font that will be replaced in Word for the Macintosh by the associated *MacFont#* when converting to a Word for the Macintosh 4.0 document from Word 7.0. If a *Winfontname* has more than one associated *MacFont#*, then the last *MacFont#* to be associated with the *Winfontname* will be used when converting from RTF to a Word for the Macintosh 4.0 document.

For example, if the following entries appear in the font-mapping file being used in the conversion from Word 7.0 to Word for the Macintosh:

```
Arial;2
Arial;3
```

then all characters in the Arial font will be given font number 3.

If a Word 7.0 font isn't specified in the font-mapping file, then font number 2 (New York) will be used in the Word for the Macintosh document.

MacFont#

The *MacFont#* is the number of the font that will appear in the Word for the Macintosh document in place of the associated Winfontname when converting from Word 7.0 to a Word for the Macintosh 4.0.

For example, if the following entries appear in the font-mapping file being used in the conversion from Word 7.0 to Word for the Macintosh:

```
Arial;3
Arial-Narrow;3
```

then all characters in the Arial or Arial-Narrow font will be given font number 3.

CHAPTER 15

Using Workgroup Features and Applications with Office

This chapter covers those issues and features you need to know about when your users are sharing documents throughout the organization. Included in this chapter is managing documents in your organization using the Find File feature, setting up and using electronic mail to exchange documents, using ODBC (Open Database Connectivity) and external data in Office applications, plus information about specific new workgroup features in the Office for Windows 95 applications. These new features include Shared Lists in Microsoft Excel, PowerPoint Presentation Conferencing and exchanging content with Microsoft Word, using Word Viewer, using the Word Internet Assistance, and creating a document library.

In This Chapter

Finding and Managing Documents within a Workgroup

In Office 4.*x* applications, users could search for documents with the Find File command on the File menu. In Office 95, full text searching is integrated directly into the Open dialog box of all Office applications, so finding files is much simpler and faster.

The Find Fast utility included with Office 95 creates an index of all Office document types (for example .doc and .xls files) on a local, shared or network drive. The index includes information about document content and properties. The Find Fast utility can take advantage of multitasking under Windows 95 and Windows NT to update its indexes automatically in the background, so no user action is required. Searching with a Find Fast index is much faster than searching without one; searching speed can decrease by as much as 100 times with an index.

If your workgroup stores documents on a network or shared drive, they can share the same index of the documents on the drive. The user that creates, updates or deletes an index on a network drive must have write permission on that drive.

The index files created by the Find Fast utility are stored in the same location as the files indexed. The index files are hidden and have the extension pattern .ff*. The index files typically require about 7 percent of the space of the text component of the documents they index, or about 1 percent to 3 percent of the total document size. Documents created with Office 95 applications produce a more efficient index/document size ratio than do documents created with previous Office applications.

Note The Find Fast utility is not associated with the Find command on the Windows Start menu. The Find command on the Windows Start menu searches only by filename; the Find Fast utility allows for searches by filename and content.

Find Fast Service for Windows NT

Microsoft Office includes a Find Fast utility designed to run on an end user's computer. This indexer builds indexes that make content and property searches from the Open dialog box in any Office applications at least 100 times faster.

The Office Resource Kit CD includes a version of the Find Fast indexer called Find Fast NT that is packaged for use as an NT service. Included in the Office Resource Kit CD is a Setup program that copies the Find Fast NT program and related files and makes the necessary registry entries. This Setup program also calls a custom action to create an NT service for Find Fast. For installation instructions, see Appendix D, "Contents of the Office Resource Kit CD."

Find Fast NT runs directly on a Windows NT computer. This allows you to index documents on a Windows NT computer without increasing network traffic or taking up resources on users' computers.

Find Fast NT runs without a user logon and has admin privileges to access the files of the Windows NT server on which it is running. This means that Find Fast NT does not have user privileges and consequently, cannot be used to create or update non-local indexes over the network.

Find Fast NT is typically used by system administrators to schedule the creation and automatic updating of indexes on an NT server.

The Find Fast NT user interface is identical to that of the regular Find Fast utility for single-user computers. Find Fast NT allows the same control over the folders and document types to be indexed.

Find Fast NT does not create indexes automatically. A system administrator with admin privileges on the NT server must create indexes manually. The steps for creating an index in Find Fast NT are identical to those followed in the Find Fast utility for single-user computers.

▶ **To create an index**

1. In the Windows NT Control Panel, double-click Find Fast NT.

2. On the Index menu, click Create Index.

3. Follow the instructions on your screen.

Indexes created by the Find Fast utility for single-user computers and by Find Fast NT are identical. The index is stored in hidden files (with the filename extension ".ff*") in the uppermost folder included in the index. A single index is used by all Office users who have at least read permission to search the folder covered by an index or any of its subfolders. The index files typically require about 7 percent of the space of the text component of the documents they index, or about 1 to 3 percent of the total document size.

Office applications automatically use the indexes, when available, whenever a user conducts a search in the Open dialog box. Therefore, it is very important to keep indexes built by Find Fast NT up to date. Otherwise, as the indexed files change, the indexes become out of date and searching gradually slows down. Also, search results may be initially inaccurate until the Open dialog box completes background indexing.

Note Find Fast NT should never be installed on the same computer as the Find Fast utility for single-user computers that ships with Office. Find Fast NT is not meant to be run on the same computer as the Find Fast utility for single-user computers. Find Fast NT is designed to run on NT computers, whereas the Find Fast utility is designed for single-user workstations.

What happens if users install both Find Fast NT and the Find Fast utility for single-user computers on the same computer anyway? Usually only Find Fast NT will run. There are two possible scenarios to consider, which are described in the following section.

Installed Find Fast NT, then Installed Find Fast Utility for Single-User Computers

Setup will attempt to schedule the creation of indexes with root-level coverage on local drives. The attempt to create root-level indexes will fail if indexes are already present on local drives. This is typically the case if Find Fast NT is already running.

Setup will also attempt to start the Find Fast utility for single-user computers. If Find Fast NT is already running, the start of the Find Fast utility for single-user computers will fail because only one Find Fast can run at one time on a single computer. If Find Fast NT is not currently running, then the Find Fast utility will run.

Finally, Setup will create an entry for Find Fast in the Startup group so that the Find Fast utility for single-user computers starts as a background utility at startup. However, Find Fast NT is typically configured as an NT service that starts with each startup of the NT computer.

In the Control Panel, users will see both a Find Fast icon and a Find Fast NT icon. Clicking either icon will reference the same registry key (Hkey_Local_Machine\Software\Microsoft\Shared Tools Location\FindFast), which, after completion of the setup of the Find Fast utility for single-user computers, now points to Findfast.exe. Any attempt to launch this program will fail.

To fix this problem, uninstall the Find Fast utility for single-user computers using the same Office Setup program that was used to initially install it. If Office Setup is not available, try the following:

- In the Registry Editor, modify \Hkey_Local_Machine\Software…\Shared Tools Location\FindFast to point to Ffastnt.exe (usually in …\Msoffice\Office\F(astnt.exe).
- Delete FindFast.cpl from the Windows\System32 folder.
- Delete all references to Find Fast single-user from the Windows Startup folder.

Installed Find Fast Utility for Single-User Computers, Then Installed Find Fast NT

After Setup restarts the computer, Find Fast NT will be the first to run, thus blocking execution of the Find Fast utility for single-user computers. Find Fast NT Setup deletes all references to the Find Fast utility for single-user computers from the Windows Startup folder to avoid conflicts.

Again, users will see both a Find Fast icon and a Find Fast NT icon in the Control Panel. Because Find Fast NT was the last to install, its registry settings are in effect. Selecting either icon will attempt to start Find Fast NT. If the user does not have admin privileges, this attempt will fail.

Remote Administration

Find Fast NT does not support remote administration. Commands used to create, update, or delete an index and all other Find Fast NT commands must be issued from the Find Fast NT Control Panel running locally on the NT server. The indexing log, with status on recent indexing tasks, is saved in Ffastlog.txt (in the Windows\System folder) and can be accessed remotely (in NotePad, for example).

Security Issues for the Find Fast Utility

As a general rule, it's more efficient in terms of disk space, index time, and search time to work with a single large index, even at the root level, rather than with several smaller indexes. However, this introduces some security implications:

- Everyone with read permission to the index should at least have read permission for all documents covered by the index.

- If a remote user attempts to update an index remotely from the Find Fast utility, this user should have write permission to all documents covered by the index. In any case, remote updates are not necessary if Find Fast NT is running on the server.

- Users of shared network drives will be unable to access an index in a parent folder. When creating an index, use the In And Below box in the Create Index dialog box to avoid these security and share problems.

Setting Up Automatic Indexing

All users share the same indexes for network servers. It is important to keep the indexes up-to-date, otherwise search results will become inaccurate. By default, Find Fast NT, like the Find Fast utility, is set to update indices automatically.

▶ **To update an index automatically**

1. On Windows Start menu, point to Settings, and then point to Control Panel.

2. Double-click Find Fast.

3. Select the index you want to work with.

4. On the Index menu, click Update Index.

5. Make sure the Continue to update automatically box is checked.

Selecting the Types Of Files You Want Indexed

When you create an index, you select what types of files you want indexed.

▶ **To select file types for indexing**

1. On Windows Start menu, point to Settings, and then click Control Panel.

2. Double-click Find Fast.

3. On the Index menu, click Create Index.

4. Under Index For Documents In And Below, select the drive and folder that contain the documents you want indexed.

5. In the Of Type box, select the file types you want indexed. To index all possible file types, select All Files. The Find File utility will then index all the file types listed in the Of Type box, plus file types for which you have installed converters for Office applications such as the WordPerfect converter installed with Word.

Interoperability with Electronic Mail

This section covers electronic mail compatibility and other workgroup features of Office.

Mail-Enabling Applications

The Office applications include commands to send and route documents via e-mail. These commands work with simple MAPI systems as well as MAPI 1.0 or greater, such as Microsoft Mail 3.*x* and the Microsoft Exchange client included with Windows 95, and 16-bit VIM-based mail systems including cc:Mail and Lotus Notes. This section describes how Office Setup mail-enables the applications, how to configure Word as the user's e-mail editor, and how to use the mail commands from within the applications.

Note 16-bit VIM support is not available on Windows NT systems.

Setting Up Mail Support

Because Office Setup automates installation of e-mail support, you should install and set up e-mail client software on user systems before installing Office. If users have more than one e-mail client, they can designate during setup which client the Office applications should use.

The following files are used for e-mail support:

Filename	Location	Installed by	Purpose
Mapi32.dll	*Windows*\System	Windows 95 (Microsoft Exchange client)	Provides 32-bit MAPI support
Mapivi32.dll	*Windows*\System	Office 95	Provides mail support for 16-bit VIM systems
Mapivitk.dll	*Windows*\System	Office 95	Communicates with the 16-bit VIM provider

32-bit MAPI and 16-bit VIM support can coexist on one system, but the Office applications can be enabled to use only one system, as follows.

Office Setup detects whether Vim.dll, a component of the cc:Mail or Lotus Notes Mail client software, is installed on the user's system. If so, Setup installs Mapivi32.dll and Mapivitk.dll. If Setup also detects Mapi32.dll, indicating that a MAPI mail provider is present, Setup prompts the user to specify which mail system to use.

When it installs VIM support, Setup adds a registry entry to specify which DLL to use for e-mail functions by the Office applications. If you change or upgrade your mail system after installing Office, you can create an installation script to install or remove the files listed in the table above, and modify the registry entry on the user's system to enable the support for the new e-mail system. For more information about registry entries, see Appendix B, "Registry Keys and Values." For more information about creating an installation script, see Chapter 9, "Customizing Client Installations."

Setting Up WordMail Support

Users of the Microsoft Exchange client can use Microsoft Word as their e-mail editor. Word as the e-mail editor (WordMail) makes the Word editing and formatting features available for composing e-mail, while maintaining compatibility with other plain-text e-mail systems.

WordMail requires a minimum of 8MB of memory to run, but 12MB is recommended. Both the Microsoft Exchange client default mail editor and WordMail create messages in Rich Text Format (RTF), which are generally somewhat larger than plain-text files.

The Microsoft Exchange client must be installed first, before installing WordMail. Word can be used as editor only with the Microsoft Exchange client, not with other e-mail client software. If you upgrade a system to use the Microsoft Exchange client after installing Office, and you've already specified that WordMail be installed, the only thing you have to do to enable it is to launch Exchange and click WordMail Options on the Compose menu. Select the Enable Word as E-mail Editor check box to use Word as your e-mail editor.

Otherwise, you must add the WordMail capability by running the Office Setup program. WordMail is included in the Custom/Complete installation, as an option under Microsoft Word, and is not included in Typical and Compact installations.

After installation when Exchange is already present, WordMail is enabled automatically. To disable WordMail after installation, use the WordMail Options command on the Compose menu in the Microsoft Exchange client, and clear the Enable Word As E-mail Editor check box.

WordMail does not support custom extensions (add-ins). If you install custom extensions to the Microsoft Exchange client, you must disable WordMail (clear the Enable Word As E-mail Editor check box) to use the extensions.

Note Schedule+ meeting requests and undeliverable message reports are plain text. These messages do not use WordMail regardless of the option setting.

Setting Up E-mail Templates

By default WordMail uses the Email.dot template when composing messages. This template provides the styles for message headers and also provides shortcut key functions.

By changing this template, you can customize the feel and appearance of the message headers, forward and reply headers, fonts, and default message text to suit your site's needs. If you want to set up customized WordMail templates for your site, base them on a copy of Email.dot so as not to lose the basic characteristics provided by this template. For example, if you want to customize the WordMail toolbars, you can do so from Word, by writing a macro in Email.dot or in a customized copy of this template.

Using Word to Compose and View Mail

WordMail gives e-mail users access to the majority of Word features, including formatting, autocorrect, spell checking, and macros. The highlighter tool is particularly useful to mark areas of interest in long messages and replies.

A few Word features are unavailable in WordMail:

- The New and Save All commands are not included on the File menu. Use the Compose command from the Microsoft Exchange client to start a new WordMail message. Because each message is in its own window, Save All is not needed.

- The Templates command is not included on the File menu. To change the template used for WordMail messages, use the WordMail Options command on the Compose menu in the Microsoft Exchange client. Users cannot change the template for a message after they open or start composing the message.

- The Add Routing Slip and Post To Exchange Folder commands are not included on the File menu. Users can post documents directly from the Microsoft Exchange client, or create a document in Word and then route or post it.

- Print preview is not available. If users need to preview a WordMail message, they can paste the message into a regular Word document to view it before printing. The message headers (name, address, and subject lines) are always printed. If users want to preserve the pagination in a message, they can set a page break at the beginning of the message text, so that the headers print on a separate page.

- The MailMerge and Envelopes And Labels commands are disabled on the Tools menu. Users who want to use WordMail messages in mailings can copy the message into a separate Word document.

- The Customize command is disabled on the Tools menu. To change the WordMail toolbars, work in Word and write a macro in Email.dot or in a customized copy of the Email.dot template.

- The Window menu commands are not included, because each WordMail message has its own window. Users who want to view the message in split windows can copy the message to a separate Word document.

Sending Messages Between WordMail and Other Mail

Both Microsoft Exchange and WordMail save the mail file in Rich Text Format (RTF). For compatibility with other mail clients and editors, WordMail messages are saved in both RTF and plain text. Recipients who do not have WordMail, such as users of Microsoft Mail or cc:Mail, receive the plain text version.

In the conversion to plain text, special characters, such as a registered trademark symbol, are converted to the nearest plain text representation, such as "(R)". The same is true of bulleted and numbered lists. Tables become a tab-delimited list. Hidden text is not displayed. Revision marks and annotations remain in your message. WordMail templates are lost. Attachments remain in the message. If the message is then sent back to WordMail from the plain-text system, all of the special characters remain plain text.

The standard editor for the Microsoft Exchange client supports some but not all of the RTF features available in WordMail. If e-mail is sent from WordMail to a user running Microsoft Exchange client but not using WordMail, most of the rich text format is preserved, although there are some exceptions. Tables are displayed as tab-delimited text. Borders and shading are not displayed. Colors such as those used for revision marks are displayed, but may be a different color. If e-mail is then returned from a Microsoft Exchange client to WordMail, nothing is lost from the original mailing as the mail remains in RTF format.

Using the Mail Commands

When mail-enabled as described previously, Word, Microsoft Excel, and PowerPoint all provide Send and Add Routing Slip commands on the File menu. Microsoft Access provides only the Send command; users of Microsoft Access who want to route information can first export it to one of the other Office applications. The Send command launches the e-mail client software and creates a new message that includes the document as an attachment. The Add Routing Slip command displays a routing slip dialog box in which the user enters and orders the recipients, and can add an accompanying message.

When Office is installed on a system that has the Microsoft Exchange client and Microsoft Exchange Server access, the applications also have the Post To Exchange Folder command on the File menu. As for routing, Microsoft Access does not have this command but users can export data to another Office application for posting. The post command allows the user to place a copy of a document directly in a public folder so that other users can access it. For more information, see the documentation for Microsoft Exchange Server.

Users who convert to WordMail from the standard Microsoft Exchange client editor should be made aware of some differences in its commands and behavior:

- To set the priority, read receipt, and similar options, use the Properties button.
- Print preview is not available in WordMail.
- Running a regular Word session at the same time as a WordMail session can cause some confusion. Because one executable supports both sessions, if the user opens a dialog box such as Options in the regular session, the WordMail session does not respond to commands until the user closes the dialog box.

Using Address Books

Word and WordMail allow users to pick addresses from the MAPI Personal Address Book (PAB) or the Schedule+ Contact List. The Insert Address button on the standard toolbar provides a list of either the first few names in the address book or the names most recently selected by the user, and also provides access to the address book browser.

The content and layout of the inserted address are determined by the autotext entries NameLayout and AddressLayout. You can modify these AutoText entries to conform to the addressing requirements of your local e-mail system.

The following properties identify the fields in the address book:

PR_TITLE

PR_GIVEN_NAME

PR_SURNAME

PR_STREET_ADDRESS

PR_POSTAL_ADDRESS

PR_POSTAL_CODE

PR_STATE_OR_PROVINCE

PR_POST_OFFICE_BOX

PR_DISPLAY_NAME

PR_EMAIL_ADDRESS

PR_ADDRTYPE

PR_COMPANY_NAME

PR_DEPARTMENT_NAME

PR_COUNTRY

PR_BUSINESS_FAX_NUMBER

PR_BUSINESS_TELEPHONE_NUMBER

PR_BUSINESS2_TELEPHONE_NUMBER

PR_ASSISTANT

PR_ASSISTANT_TELEPHONE_NUMBER

PR_PAGER_TELEPHONE_NUMBER

PR_CELLULAR_TELEPHONE_NUMBER

PR_HOME_FAX_NUMBER

PR_HOME_TELEPHONE_NUMBER

PR_PRIMARY_FAX_NUMBER

PR_PRIMARY_TELEPHONE_NUMBER

PR_OFFICE_LOCATION

PR_LOCALITY

PR_LOCATION

The default NameLayout and AddressLayout AutoText entries are as follows, where | means "or," braces enclose alternatives, and \r means carriage return.

NameLayout:

```
{<PR_GIVEN_NAME> <PR_SURNAME> | <PR_DISPLAY_NAME>}
```

AddressLayout:

```
{{<PR_GIVEN_NAME> <PR_SURNAME> | <PR_DISPLAY_NAME>}\r}
{{<PR_STREET_ADDRESS>\r}
{{<PR_LOCALITY>}{, <PR_STATE_OR_PROVINCE> <PR_POSTAL_CODE>}\r}
{<PR_COUNTRY>\r}
| <PR_POSTAL_ADDRESS>\r}
```

The address book capability has the following limitations:

- For users to have access to the MAPI PAB, MAPI support, such as that provided by the Microsoft Exchange client, must be installed on the users' systems.

- The Schedule+ Contact List is a feature new to Schedule+ 7.0. Schedule+ 1.0 users must upgrade to the new version to be able to set up a Contact List.

- The address book capability is not available on Windows NT.

Working with Notes/FX

The Office applications support Lotus Notes/FX 1.0 and 1.1 through extensions to OLE. Although no capability to post directly to a Notes database is provided, users can embed documents created by Office applications, including Office Binders, in a database. Users can open and modify the embedded documents. When the user issues a File Update command from within the document or closes and saves the Notes message, the changes are written to the Notes database.

Each Office application exposes a set of properties listed on the General, Summary, and Statistics tabs in the Properties dialog box to Notes/FX. In addition, any custom properties that you create beginning with PROP_ are exposed to Notes/FX. You can set properties for Notes/FX in a document using the Properties command on the File menu. Use the Custom tab to define properties you want to make available for Notes/FX.

Office Setup automatically installs Notes converters in the Notes folder. The Microsoft Excel, PowerPoint, and Word converters each register the file Mscthunk.dll in the Notes.ini file so that it is available in the converters list in the Notes client. A helper file, _msimp32.dll, is also installed in the Notes folder. These files are rich text field converters. Microsoft Excel and Word call the text converters Excel32.cnv and Mswrd632.cnv respectively, in the regular shared components folder.

The text converters only allow for importing text into Notes. Microsoft Excel also has view import (_ixls.dll) and export (_xxls.dll) converters that are installed in the Notes program folder.

Note   Notes/FX support is not available on Windows NT.

Working with Microsoft Exchange Server

In addition to e-mail support, Microsoft Exchange Server allows users to post documents to public folders for sharing with other workgroup members. To enable posting capability, users must install the Microsoft Exchange client included with Microsoft Exchange Server, and then install Office. When installed in this order, the command Post To Exchange Folder is added to the File menu for each application. Public folders are available only when the user has access to a Microsoft Exchange Server system.

Users can post documents directly from the Office applications to any public folders for which they have permissions.

▶ **To post an Office document to a public folder**

1. Log in to your Microsoft Exchange server.

2. Open the document that you want to share with other Microsoft Exchange users.

3. On the File menu, click Post To Exchange Folder.

4. Select the public folder to receive the document.

For information about setting up Microsoft Exchange Server and making public folders available to users, see the documentation accompanying the Microsoft Exchange Server software. For more information about working with public folders, see "Interface with Microsoft Exchange" in Chapter 1.

Custom Properties and Views

Using Microsoft Exchange Server, you can create custom views of the information stored in public folders. Custom views allow you to select what details are displayed about the stored information, and in what sequence. For Office documents, custom views can make use of the properties stored with each document. You can create custom properties for use in your custom views. For example, a view could list information about all documents associated with a particular project using a custom Project Name property.

To create and use custom views, you need to install the enhanced Microsoft Exchange client provided with the Microsoft Exchange Server. This version of the client software provides some additional capabilities to supplement the basic functionality provided in the client software included with Windows 95. For information and details, including instructions for creating custom views, see the documentation accompanying Microsoft Exchange Server. For more information about standard and custom properties, see "Implementation of Properties" and "Sources of Properties" in Chapter 1.

Working with Microsoft Mail

Microsoft Mail 3.*x* clients have the following limitations:

- They cannot use WordMail. In a mixed e-mail environment, WordMail messages from other users are delivered to Microsoft Mail clients as plain text.

- They cannot post documents to public folders from within the Office applications. This capability requires the Microsoft Exchange Server and client software.

Working with Lotus Notes Mail and cc:Mail

Lotus Notes Mail or cc:Mail clients have the following limitations:

- They cannot use WordMail. In a mixed e-mail environment, WordMail messages from other users are delivered to these clients as plain text.

- They cannot post documents to public folders. This capability requires the Microsoft Exchange Server and Client software.

For information about installing support for Lotus Notes Mail and cc:Mail, see "Mail-Enabling Applications" earlier in this chapter.

Working with Other Mail Systems

Because Microsoft Exchange is the message editor used on the Microsoft Network (MSN), WordMail replaces the standard MSN read and compose note when the user enables WordMail.

With Windows 95, any user with a modem has access to Internet electronic mail using MSN. Similarly, because Windows 95 includes CompuServe mail capability for Microsoft Exchange, any user who has a CompuServe account can use the Microsoft Exchange client, and WordMail, to receive and compose e-mail.

For information about MSN connectivity and e-mail Internet access, see chapters 29 and 30 in the *Microsoft Windows 95 Resource Kit*, respectively.

Supporting Mailing, Routing, and Posting

The new WordMail and Office Binder features may increase the e-mail traffic on your network. Both Microsoft Exchange and WordMail messages are somewhat larger than plain-text messages. This is true especially if your environment mixes WordMail and plain-text e-mail clients, because plain-text clients receive both plain text and Rich Text Format versions of messages from WordMail users. WordMail messages are slightly larger than Microsoft Exchange messages, but are actually smaller than a Word document sent as an attachment to an e-mail message. Office Binder files easily grow quite large and can result in large messages if mailed.

Provide the following guidelines to your users to encourage optimal use of network resources:

- When one copy of a document can be passed from one recipient to another, encourage users to route the document instead of mailing a separate copy to each recipient.

- Let users know the maximum message size accepted by your e-mail system, and explain what happens when they exceed this size.

- Encourage users to consider alternatives to mailing large documents. Users can copy large documents to a network share and mail links to the shared file using the Windows Package application. If your site has Microsoft Exchange Server, users can post large documents to public folders. Alternatively, users can share their computer or a folder on their computer over the network.

ODBC and Client/Server Operations

In a client/server application, you store your data in remote tables on a database server, such as Microsoft SQL Server, instead of in local tables in your Microsoft Access database. Your Microsoft Access database, the client, sends queries and updates to the server and retrieves the data it needs. A client/server application takes advantage of the processing power available to both the client and database server components.

By contrast, in a file server application, data simply resides on a network file server; transactions with the data are handled no differently than the reading and writing of any other file on the network, and all processing is performed locally.

Developing, optimizing, and maintaining client/server applications is a complex subject. This section briefly describes what Open Database Connectivity (ODBC) is and how it allows you to interact with a large variety of Structured Query Language (SQL) data sources. The reasons to adopt a client/server approach are covered, as are the issues involved in converting an existing an Microsoft Access application to a client/server application. For more information about developing client/server applications using Microsoft Access, see *Building Applications with Microsoft Access for Windows 95.*

Open Database Connectivity (ODBC)

Providing data access to the large variety of database applications can be very complex. Applications that use the ODBC standard, such as Microsoft Access and Microsoft Excel, ease this burden by using a vendor-neutral means of accessing database management systems (DBMS). Microsoft has gained very broad support for ODBC, which allows you to access a broad variety of data sources.

ODBC provides many significant benefits by providing an open, standard way to access data.

- ODBC allows users to access data in more than one data storage location (for example, more than one server) from within a single application.

- ODBC allows users to access data in more than one type of DBMS (such as DB2, ORACLE, DEC RDB, Apple DAL, dBASE, and Microsoft SQL Server client-server database management system) from within a single application.

- ODBC greatly simplifies application development—it is now easier for developers to provide access to data in multiple, concurrent DBMSs.

- ODBC is a portable application programming interface (API), enabling the same interface and access technology to be a cross-platform tool.

- ODBC insulates applications from changes to underlying network and DBMS versions. Modifications to networking transports, servers, and DBMSs will not create problems for current ODBC applications.

- ODBC promotes the use of SQL—the standard language for DBMSs.

- ODBC allows corporations to protect their investments in existing DBMSs and to protect developers' acquired DBMS skills. ODBC also allows corporations to continue to use existing diverse DBMSs, while developing applications using other systems that are more appropriate to the task at hand.

How ODBC Works

ODBC defines an API. Each ODBC application uses the same code, as defined by the API specification, to talk to many types of data sources through DBMS-specific drivers. A *driver manager* sits between the applications and the drivers. In the Microsoft Windows operating system, the driver manager and the drivers are implemented as dynamic-link libraries (DLLs). The following illustration outlines the process.

ODBC Architecture

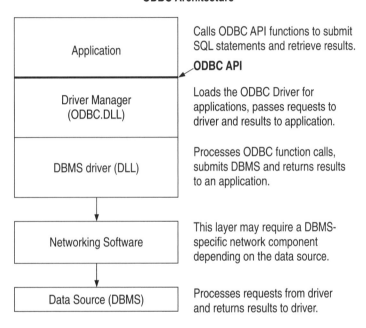

Application	Calls ODBC API functions to submit SQL statements and retrieve results.
ODBC API	
Driver Manager (ODBC.DLL)	Loads the ODBC Driver for applications, passes requests to driver and results to application.
DBMS driver (DLL)	Processes ODBC function calls, submits DBMS and returns results to an application.
Networking Software	This layer may require a DBMS-specific network component depending on the data source.
Data Source (DBMS)	Processes requests from driver and returns results to driver.

The application calls ODBC functions to connect to a data source, send and receive data, and disconnect. The driver manager provides an application with information such as a list of available data sources, loads drivers dynamically as they are needed, and provides argument and state transition checking. The DBMS driver, developed separately from the application, sits between the application and the network. The driver processes ODBC function calls, manages all exchanges between an application and a specific DBMS, and may translate the standard Structured Query Language (SQL) syntax into the native SQL of the target data source. All SQL translations are the responsibility of the driver developer.

Applications are not limited to communicating through one driver. A single application can make multiple connections, each through a different driver, or multiple connections to similar sources through a single driver. To access a new DBMS, a user or an administrator simply installs a driver for the DBMS. The user doesn't need a different version of the application to access the new DBMS. This is a tremendous benefit for end-users, and it also translates into significant savings in support and development costs.

Using ODBC Data in Microsoft Office for Windows 95 Applications

ODBC data is available to Microsoft Office applications in the following ways:

- In Microsoft Access for Windows 95, by importing from or linking to ODBC data sources using the commands on the Get External Data submenu on the File menu. Microsoft Access can also export to available ODBC data formats using the Save As/Export command on the File menu.

- In Microsoft Excel for Windows 95, when building PivotTables using the PivotTable command on the Data menu, and with Microsoft Query using the Get External Data command on the Data menu.

- When creating custom applications in either Microsoft Access or Microsoft Excel using Visual Basic for Applications and Data Access Objects (DAO) code.

The next section covers using Microsoft Access to create a client/server application. For more information about using Microsoft Excel and Microsoft Query to access ODBC data, see "Using External Data with Microsoft Excel for Windows 95" later in this chapter.

Reasons to use Client/Server Architecture

The three primary reasons for adopting client/server architecture for database applications are:

- **Enterprise-wide access to corporate information**   As computers become smaller, more powerful, and more usable, information is more widely distributed across a corporate enterprise in an increasing number of formats. Client/server technology provides the links to access and manipulate data regardless of its location or storage format.

- **Upsizing multi-user file server database applications**   Client/server applications provide improved performance, security, and reliability. Database application solutions can grow and become more complex over time. Client/server architecture provides a way to scale up a database application when it becomes larger and more complex and must support more users and a higher volume of transactions.

- **Downsizing mainframe and minicomputer database applications**   The managers and developers of many mainframe database applications move their applications to client/server architecture to take advantage of Graphical User Interface (GUI) processing. Microsoft Access provides an ideal environment for developing user-driven systems. At the same time, Microsoft Access provides many powerful features for interacting with external data sources. Also motivating this change is the reduced cost of new back-end servers. Downsizing, however, is a more difficult and a much slower migration process. As such, the seamless integration from the mainframe world to the client/server world is a priority. When this level of integration is achieved, client/server applications enhance and add value to existing mainframe-based processes.

Upsizing a Microsoft Access File Server Application to a Client/Server Application

A high-level summary of steps involved in migrating from a file server to a client/server environment include:

- Create the server database.
- Establish your ODBC data source using the ODBC Administrator.
- Document your existing Microsoft Access database.
- Export each table to the server database.
- Add server-based integrity constraints: validation rules, default values, and referential integrity.
- Add the indexes to the server tables with the necessary attributes.
- Link the server tables.

The remainder of this section explains the above steps in more detail. For full details on these procedures and information about optimizing a client/server application, see Chapter 18 in *Building Applications with Microsoft Access for Windows 95*.

To ensure your Microsoft Access applications scale up easily to a client/server database, certain practices are recommended:

- Do not embed spaces in your table names because most servers cannot support them. During export, Microsoft Access will replace spaces with underscores in the name but then references to those fields in queries, forms, reports, expressions, and Visual Basic code will fail.

- Create a *name-mapping query* if your application has tables and fields with names with embedded spaces. A name-mapping query is a query saved as the original table name that includes spaces, but it points to the server table without spaces. You can also alias column names using the convention "Field Name: FIELD_NAME" in the query result column field.

- Be consistent in the use of the case of your object names. Some SQL servers are case-sensitive, but Microsoft Access default behavior is case insensitive.

- When using programatic access, do not use the **Recordset** type of table to manipulate remote objects; always use the **Dynaset** type instead. Tables linked using the Link Tables command automatically use Dynasets.

Creating the Server Database

The method for creating a server database depends on the SQL server software you are using. For details, see your SQL server documentation. If you have an existing SQL database you want to use as the basis for your client/server application, you can export or link tables from Microsoft Access after you have defined this database as an ODBC data source.

Defining Your ODBC Data Source

Use the 32bit ODBC icon on the Windows Control Panel to define your ODBC data source. The 32bit ODBC icon will only be available if you installed the SQL Driver when installing Office or Microsoft Access for Windows 95. Before you can specify a data source, you must have the appropriate ODBC driver for your database server installed. You can see what ODBC drivers are available on a computer by double-clicking the 32bit ODBC icon in the Control Panel, and then clicking the Drivers button. The Office Setup program, and the Setup programs for stand-alone versions of Microsoft Access and Microsoft Excel include the Microsoft SQL Server driver and support files for the 32bit ODBC Control Panel option. If the 32bit ODBC icon is not available in the Control Panel, re-run Setup, click Add/Remove, and from the Data Access option, make sure the Microsoft SQL Server Driver option is selected.

The Data Access option of the Office Setup program also provides a set of additional ODBC drivers. In the Microsoft Access for Windows 95 Setup program, these drivers are called the Microsoft Office Desktop Drivers. These drivers are not used by Microsoft Access itself which uses its own built-in drivers, but can be used by other programs that support ODBC, such as Microsoft Excel and Microsoft Query, to use data in the following formats:

- Microsoft Access
- Microsoft Excel
- Microsoft FoxPro
- dBASE
- Paradox
- Text (fixed-width and delimited text files)

If you are using an SQL database server other than Microsoft SQL Server, contact the vendor of that product to find out about the availability of an ODBC driver for that product. ODBC drivers are also available for data formats other than SQL servers. For example, there is an ODBC driver for Lotus Notes databases. Contact the vendor of the product whose data you want to access for information about the availability of an ODBC driver.

Important   Microsoft Office for Windows 95 applications can only use 32-bit versions of ODBC drivers. If a previous version of a Microsoft Office application, such as Microsoft Access 2.0, was installed on a computer, older 16-bit versions of ODBC drivers may still be present. If you want to use the ODBC drivers available with Microsoft Office for Windows 95 applications, re-run Setup and install the drivers you need. Similarly, other applications written for Windows 3.*x* may have installed older 16-bit versions of ODBC drivers. Contact the vendor of the product whose data you want to access for information about the availability of a current 32-bit version ODBC driver.

Documenting Your Existing Microsoft Access Database

Indexes, validation rules (also referred to as business rules, domain integrity rules, or database-specific rules), default values, and referential integrity rules are not created when Microsoft Access exports tables to a client/server database. After exporting, you need to define the indexes, validation rules, and default values on the server tables themselves. If permissions vary for users of the database, you'll need this information, too. You can print a very comprehensive list of the properties of the tables in your .mdb file by opening the database with Microsoft Access and then using the Documentor command on the Analyze submenu of the Tools menu.

Exporting Microsoft Access Tables to the Server Database

Creating the structure of a complex, multi-table, client/server database can be a tedious and time-consuming process. Microsoft Access table export features can speed up this process greatly. Export each table to the server database, using the Export/Save As command on the File menu.

There are trade-offs to consider when exporting data. Microsoft Access exports each row one row at a time. This ensures that your exported data adheres to all the server-based rules, but is significantly slower with very large tables than using server-based, bulk-copy routines.

If your tables contain a few thousand records or less, it is usually faster to export the tables from the Microsoft Access database to the server database, rather than using bulk-copy programs, such as BCP for SQL Server, with text files. If you do use a batch copy program to load your tables on your server, you can test data type and field size consistency before running the batch copy program by exporting at least one record from each table to the server using Microsoft Access.

Most migrations to client/server operation are done in two phases: test and production. To limit the number of records used for the test phase, write a select query in Microsoft Access and then export data from that query.

Adding Server-Based Validation Rules

Validation rules aren't exported with a table. You can create triggers or rules on the server table that enforces your rules, or you can define form-level validation rules in your Microsoft Access forms instead. Using form-level rules is easier, but not as reliable because invalid entries are rejected only by the form, not by the server table itself. A *trigger* is a piece of code residing on the server that executes an SQL statement prior to the occurrence of a specified event, such as INSERT, DELETE, or UPDATE. If you're using a server-based trigger, be aware that many Visual Basic functions, such as the **DatePart** or **Format**, may have no equivalent on your server.

Adding Default Values and Enforcing Referential Integrity

Most client/server DBMSs provide a default value property. Otherwise, you need to use stored procedures to set default values for fields whose value is not supplied during the append process. If you need to emulate the Required property of fields in Microsoft Access tables, you can use the NOT NULL command in the definition of your SQL table. If the server database does not support ANSI SQL reserved words, you'll need to write stored procedures to enforce referential integrity and perform cascading updates and deletions. None of the rules and stored procedures you create will be visible to Microsoft Access; if your applications violate the rules, your application will receive an error message from the server.

Adding Indexes

Add the indexes to the server tables with equivalent attributes to those in the Microsoft Access database, for example, PrimaryKey, No Duplicates, or No Nulls. Microsoft Access cannot update a table that does not have a unique index.

In Microsoft Access 2.0 or later, dynaset-type record sets support server-based primary key generation from triggers. In earlier versions, as the primary key was generated during an insert, the record set cursor would act as if the record has been deleted because it no longer was in the same location. Microsoft Access now re-fetches the record, keeping the record set up to date. This is particularly significant because many developers use the convenient AutoNumber field (called a Counter field in previous versions) to generate their primary keys. The equivalent of the Microsoft Access AutoNumber field data type seldom is found in client/server DBMSs, yet it can be critical to your application.

This improvement allows you to create an INSERT trigger on the server table that increments the integer value of a field each time a new record is appended to the table. The Transact-SQL statement to create the equivalent of an AutoNumber field is:

```
CREATE TRIGGER add_customer_id ON dbo.customers
FOR INSERT AS
UPDATE dbo.customers
SET inserted.Customer_ID = (SELECT MAX(Customer_ID)
FROM dbo.customers) + 1
WHERE dbo.customers.customer_ID IS NULL
```

When you use a trigger to create the AutoNumber field equivalent, you will not see the generated value in a bound control until you complete the appending process for the record.

Linking Server Tables

Use the Link Tables command on the Get External Data submenu of the File menu to link tables in the server database. When you link a table, Microsoft Access stores a copy of the table's structure in your Microsoft Access database's system tables. This allows you to build queries, forms, and reports as if the linked table is part of your database.

After linking, relationships between tables need to be established using the Relationships window. This establishes the default join conditions and types used when building new queries.

Any operation in Datasheet view that is permissible for a native Microsoft Access table can generally be performed for tables linked by ODBC. In Design view, you can set the values of the Format, InputMask, and Caption properties. All other properties of linked tables are read-only.

Renaming Linked Tables   When Microsoft Access links a remote table, it prefixes the default table owner ID of SQL Server to each table name. The period separator between the owner ID and the table name is replaced by an underscore, because periods in table names are not permitted by Microsoft Access. By doing so, the names of linked tables no longer correspond to the original table names in your .mdb file. The simplest way to correct this is to rename your tables to their original names after linking.

Using External Data with Office for Windows 95

This section explains how to use external data with Microsoft Access for Windows 95 and Microsoft Excel for Windows 95.

Using External Data with Microsoft Access for Windows 95

Microsoft Access is extremely flexible in its ability to handle data from a variety of sources. External data falls into two categories: Indexed Sequential Access Method (ISAM) and Open Database Connectivity (ODBC). The ISAM data sources are the traditionally IBM PC-based database formats. These include Microsoft FoxPro, Paradox, Microsoft Access, and others. The ODBC data sources are typically SQL (Structured Query Language) server tables, such as Microsoft SQL Server tables; however, Microsoft Access can use other ODBC data sources as long as a 32-bit, Level 1-compliant ODBC driver is installed for that data source.

Microsoft Access can either import or link external data. Importing reads the external data and creates a new table in the current Microsoft Access database. The original data is unchanged. Linking leaves the external data in its current location and format, and stores a link to that data in the current Microsoft Access database. When a table from another database is linked, it performs like a native, local table. Users can create queries, forms, and reports that use the external data, combine the external data with the data in Microsoft Access tables, and even view and edit the external data while others are using it in the original application. It makes sense to use this approach as an alternative to importing if the external data you want to use is also being updated by software other than Microsoft Access.

Even if all the data you want to use is in Microsoft Access format, you might find it advantageous to link to external data. By splitting the application (forms, reports, queries, temporary tables) from the rest of the data, you can ease the support burden of distributing your application. Additionally, network traffic is reduced because forms, reports, and queries are run locally on each workstation instead of across the network as when the entire database is run from a shared location.

There are two methods of accessing external data: using the commands on the Get External Data submenu on the File menu, or using Visual Basic for applications code.

External Data Sources

Microsoft Access can use data from any of the following external data sources:

- Databases created by applications that use the Microsoft Jet database engine (Microsoft Access, Microsoft Excel, Microsoft Visual Basic)
- Open Database Connectivity (ODBC) databases such as Microsoft SQL Server 4.2 and higher
- Paradox 3.*x*, 4.*x*, and 5.*x*
- Microsoft FoxPro 2.0, 2.5, and 2.6 (and 3.0, to import but not link)
- dBASE III, dBASE IV, and dBASE 5.*x*
- Lotus WKS, WK1, and WK3 spreadsheets
- Microsoft Excel 3.0, 4.0, 5.0, and 7.0 worksheets
- Text files

To access external data, applications that use the Microsoft Jet database engine use one of several installable ISAM drivers or the Microsoft SQL Server driver. If you chose Typical installation when you installed Microsoft Access, you don't have these drivers installed. To install the appropriate driver for the external database you want to access, run Setup again, click the Add/Remove button, select the Data Access check box in the Options list box, and then click Change Option and select the drivers. If you haven't installed Microsoft Access and want to make sure you have the correct drivers installed, run Setup, click the Custom button, select the Data Access check box in the Options list box, and then click Change Option and select the drivers. The only ODBC driver that is supplied with Microsoft Access is the Microsoft SQL Server driver. To access ODBC data other than Microsoft SQL Server tables, you must obtain a 32-bit version of the appropriate ODBC driver from the vendor of that data format, and install that driver.

Network Access Requirements

To link or directly open an external table on a network, you must be able to connect to the network and have use of:

- The server and share (if applicable) on which the external database is located. Server and share access are established through network permissions. For information about setting up network permissions, see your network product manuals.

- The external table. Table access permissions, if any, are established using the security features of the external database. Depending on how security has been defined, you might need to get the appropriate passwords, or you might need to have a network administrator grant you the appropriate permissions to use the external table. For information about setting up access permissions, see your external database product manuals.

When specifying the database name for a database on a network drive, you can either:

- Indicate a fully qualified network path (if your network supports it) in the format *server**share**path*. For example:

  ```
  \\FOXPRO\DATA\AP
  ```

- Establish a connection to the network drive first, and then specify the path using the network drive letter instead of the server and share name. For example, if you use drive F: to connect to \\FOXPRO\DATA, you would specify the database path for the AP database on that share as follows:

  ```
  F:\AP
  ```

Performance Guidelines

Although you can use external tables just as you use Microsoft Access tables, it's important to keep in mind that they're not actually in your Microsoft Access database. As a result, each time you view data in an external table, Microsoft Access retrieves records from another file. Performance is optimal if you link tables instead of opening them directly, and if you retrieve and view only the data you need. For example, it's a good idea to use restrictive queries to limit the number of returned records so you don't have to scroll up and down unnecessarily.

For more information about improving performance, see "Optimizing Microsoft Access for Windows 95" in Chapter 11.

Windows Registry Settings

When you install Microsoft Access or external database drivers, the Setup program writes associated entries to various keys in the Windows registry. The Setup program writes a set of default values for each installed ISAM engine in a subkey of the Hkey_Local_Computer\Software\Microsoft\Jet\3.0\Engines key. It also writes a set of host-application specific values for each ISAM engine in the Hkey_Local_Computer\Software\Microsoft\Access\7.0\Jet\3.0\Engines key, and in a similar key for other host applications that use the Jet database engine. These multiple registrations allow each host application to run a separate instance of the Jet database engine. If a host-specific registration omits particular values, these settings default to the values registered in the Microsoft\Jet\3.0\Engines key.

Another set of registration settings are provided in the Microsoft\Jet\3.0\ISAM Formats key of the Windows registry. This key contains a subkey for each of the specific data formats supported by a particular ISAM engine.

Although the Setup program writes intelligent defaults for the Windows registry entries, your particular environment or preferences might require you to change entries. For information about all registry entries, see the Microsoft Access section of Appendix B, "Registry Keys and Values."

Note   When you change your initialization settings, you must quit the application and then restart it using the Microsoft Jet database engine for the new settings take effect.

Case Sensitivity

Unlike searches on databases that use the Jet database engine, searches on external databases may be case-sensitive. However, searches aren't case-sensitive in the following cases:

- For Paradox data, if the CollatingSequence entry in the Jet\3.0\Engines\Paradox key of the Windows registry is set to International, Norwegian-Danish, or Swedish-Finnish.

- For FoxPro or dBASE data, if the CollatingSequence entry in the Jet\3.0\Engines\Xbase key of the Windows registry is set to International.

- For ODBC data, if the server is configured not to be case-sensitive.

In addition, if a search is made across more than one data source type, the case sensitivity depends on the collating sequences of the databases in which the query is stored.

Unsupported Objects and Methods

When using Visual Basic for applications code, some data access objects and methods are intended for use only on databases created using the Microsoft Jet database engine, such as databases created by Microsoft Access, Microsoft Visual Basic, and Microsoft Excel. These data access objects and methods aren't supported for use with external databases in other formats. Unsupported data access objects include:

Container

Document

QueryDef

Relation

Unsupported methods include:

CompactDatabase

CreateDatabase

CreateField (if the table has existing rows)

CreateQueryDef

RepairDatabase

In addition, the following transaction processing methods are supported only if the external database supports transactions:

BeginTrans

CommitTrans

Rollback

Troubleshooting

The following information addresses problems you may encounter when accessing an external data source.

Connection Problems

If you have trouble connecting to an external data source, first check your connection to the network. Make sure you have access to:

- The server and share (if applicable) on which the external database is located.
- The external table.

Other things to check include the following:

- Can you connect using another product or a different user account and password?
- Have you exceeded the connection limits on the server?
- Does the server have enough space?
- Does the connection information match the case sensitivity of the server?

If you've checked the items in the preceding lists and you still cannot connect, contact your external database vendor.

Temporary Space

When you query a database, Microsoft Access creates temporary indexes on your local hard disk, even if the database is on an external network device. Temporary space requirements can vary from a few thousand bytes to several megabytes, depending on the size of the external tables being queried.

Temporary space is allocated from the folder indicated by the TEMP environment variable, typically the \Windows\Temp folder. If your system has not defined a TEMP environment variable, the current Microsoft Access root folder is used. If the TEMP environment variable points to an invalid path or if your local hard disk doesn't have sufficient space for these temporary indexes, your application may perform unpredictably if Windows and Microsoft Access run out of resources.

Using External Data with Microsoft Excel for Windows 95

In Microsoft Excel for Windows 95, your users can also use data from external sources. The Microsoft Query application and the Microsoft ODBC Functions Add-in assist you in constructing SQL instructions to extract and summarize information from a variety of database formats. Using the PivotTable Wizard, you can set up complex database queries and build detailed summary reports without having to write any SQL code. Using the Template Wizard with Data Tracking, you can create a template to export data to an external database.

There are five ways to use external data with Microsoft Excel:

- **Microsoft Query**   This is a graphical application used to retrieve and organize data from a variety of data sources. Use it if you want to display and manipulate data before you bring it into Microsoft Excel. You can also initiate a Dynamic Data Exchange (DDE) conversation between Microsoft Excel and Microsoft Query using Visual Basic for applications to create custom applications that use Microsoft Query to access external data. For example, you can send DDE commands to Microsoft Query using the **LinkExecute** method in Visual Basic for Applications code.

- **The Microsoft Query Add-in**   This is an add-in macro that adds the Get External Data command to the Data menu so that you can run Microsoft Query from within Microsoft Excel. It is possible to use Microsoft Query as a stand-alone application (by running the Msqry32.exe program), or by using DDE commands in Visual Basic for applications code; however, the most common method is using the Get External Data command in Microsoft Excel.

- **Microsoft Open Database Connectivity (ODBC) Functions Add-in**   This is used to retrieve data directly from external data sources using Microsoft ODBC. This add-in provides Data Access Objects (DAO) functions that are used in Visual Basic for applications code to create custom Microsoft Excel applications that access ODBC data sources. These functions interact directly with database drivers without using Microsoft Query.

- **The PivotTable Wizard**   This is an interactive worksheet table you use to summarize large amounts of data. It is called a *PivotTable* because you can rotate its row and column headings around the core data area to give you different views of the source data. The PivotTable Wizard uses Microsoft Query to access external data and create a dynamic crosstab table of the results.

- **The Template Wizard with Data Tracking Add-in**   This creates a template and a database from a Microsoft Excel workbook. You select the cells that will be used as the template and the wizard links them to a database in the format you select. After the wizard creates the template, you can share the template with users in a workgroup to update a shared database. Each time users enter data in the template, it will be exported to the database.

The types of data you can retrieve depend on the open database connectivity (ODBC) drivers you install to work with Microsoft Query and Microsoft Excel. An ODBC driver is a system dynamic-link library (DLL) that allows ODBC-enabled applications such as Microsoft Query and Microsoft Excel to access specified data sources and retrieve data created in another format, such as dBASE. For more information about ODBC and how it works, see "ODBC and Client/Server Operations" earlier in this chapter.

You can access and retrieve data using drivers for the following types of data, which are available in Microsoft Excel for Windows 95:

- Microsoft FoxPro (versions 2.0 and 2.5)
- Microsoft Access (versions 1.x, 2.0, and 7.0)
- Paradox (versions 3.x, 4.x, and 5.x)
- dBASE (versions III, IV, and 5)
- Microsoft SQL Server (versions 4.2 and higher)
- Microsoft Excel (versions 3.0, 4.0, 5.0, and 7.0)
- Text (fixed-length and delimited formats)

If you performed a Compact or Typical installation, the ODBC drivers listed will not be available. Re-run the Microsoft Office or Microsoft Excel Setup program to install ODBC drivers. You can also use other 32-bit, Level-1 compliant ODBC drivers that are not supplied with Microsoft Office to access additional data sources. For information about whether a 32-bit, Level-1 compliant version ODBC driver is available for the data source you want to access, contact the vendor of that data format. For information about the installation of drivers other than those that are supplied with Microsoft Office, see the documentation for that driver.

Workgroup Features for Microsoft Access

Microsoft Access workgroup features fall into two areas: Security Administration and Multiuser Settings. The section on Security Administration covers the methods of regulating access to the information and design of a database. The section on Multiuser Settings covers how Microsoft Access works when databases are shared between members of a workgroup, such as how conflicts are handled if two users try to edit the same record at the same time.

Security Administration

Microsoft Access security is not used exclusively in workgroup situations. For example, security can be used to control access to data in a database that resides on a single computer and is not shared by any other user. However, the most common application is in workgroup situations.

The first section describes the difference between the two kinds of security Microsoft Access provides, how to use the new database password feature, and some concerns about using it in a multiuser environment. This is followed by in-depth information about the Microsoft Access user-level security model, how to use the User-Level Security Wizard, and how to address common security scenarios. The final section describes other security enhancements added to Microsoft Access for Windows 95.

User-Level Security vs. Share-Level Security

Microsoft Access security supports two kinds of security: *user-level security* and a simple form of *share-level security* (defined later in this section). The kind of security you use depends on your requirements.

User-Level Security

Unlike most other personal computer-based database programs, Microsoft Access provides user-level security as its primary form of security. In a user-level system, users must have security accounts defined before they can use secured databases. Users' identities are verified when they start Microsoft Access by logging on with a password. Database administrators or object owners grant permissions, such as Read Data or Modify Design, to specific users and groups to regulate access to specific objects. Different users can have different permissions for the same object, hence users or groups can have different *user-levels* with respect to that object.

By contrast, in share-level security systems, passwords are associated directly with objects, not with users or groups. Passwords act as gateways to the objects, and determine the kind of actions that can be performed. Any user who knows a particular password can perform the actions that password allows.

For example, suppose you have a Salary table, and that you have two groups of users on your system: Managers, who you want to allow to update the table, and Payroll personnel, who you want to allow to view but not update the table. In a user-level system, such as Microsoft Access, you assign update permissions to the Managers group and read permissions to the Payroll group. You then make sure that the users logging onto your system are enlisted in the appropriate groups. Users can manage their own passwords, and their passwords are only used to verify their identity when logging on, rather than having any direct connection to their permissions.

To establish the same kind of security using a share-level security system, you would assign two passwords to the Salary table: a read-only password and a read-write password. You would then tell all managers the read-write password, and all the members of your payroll department the read-only password. Whenever a user needs to access the table, the user enters that password and is granted the kind of access provided by that password.

If you've never built or administered a user-level security system before, the important thing to remember is that there's no such thing as a permission for an object that exists all by itself—permissions for objects are always granted to users and groups. In a Microsoft Access database, it doesn't make sense to say, "the Salary table has Read Data permissions" because no user or group is specified. It does make sense to say "the Managers group has Read Data permissions for the Salary table."

Share-Level Security: Database Password Protection

For many users and situations, user-level security in Microsoft Access is too complex and provides more control than is required. There are many situations where users would prefer to simply assign a single password to control who can open a database. This simple form of share-level security was added to Microsoft Access for Windows 95. Whenever the database is opened after assigning a database password, the Password Required dialog box is displayed; if the user knows the password, the database will be opened. Only one password can be assigned to open the database, and no distinction can be made between read/write versus read-only access. If you want to do more than just limit who can open the database, user-level security is required.

If user-level security has been defined and a database password is added, all user-level security remains intact. That is, user-level permissions will still be required to perform any actions on objects. Adding a database password in addition to user-level security does not provide any added security, and is not really the way the feature is intended to be used. It is meant to be a simple alternative to user-level security.

To define a database password, open the database. On the Tools menu, point to Security and click Set Database Password. Supply and verify the password in the dialog box provided. After it is defined, the password is encrypted and stored with the database to which it applies. When a database password is set, all users must supply a password to open the database. Any user who knows the password can change the password or remove it.

Note A password can be set when the database is opened in shared mode (the default mode), even when other users have the database open. However, in this case, the new password won't affect those users until they close the database and open it again. If you work in an environment where users don't turn off their computers at night, they may never close the database. If this is the case, open the database in exclusive mode (set the Exclusive check box in the Open dialog box) so you can ensure that no one is using the database when you add the database password. After setting the password, close the database to make it available again.

After a password is set for a database, the menu command changes to Remove Database Password. Selecting this option displays the Remove Database Password dialog box. Entering the correct password sets the password property to null which turns off share-level security for the database.

Setting a database password only controls whether a user can open the database. If you need to maintain security for individual objects within the database, you need to define user-level security instead.

Caution If any user sets a password and then loses it or forgets it, no user can gain access to the database no matter what their user-level authority is. The form of encryption Microsoft Access uses to hide the database password is extremely secure and is virtually impossible to break. For this reason, make sure that any user that sets a database password, keeps a copy of the password in a secure off-site location.

To provide strict control over who can set a database password, use the User-Level Security Wizard to define user-level security as described later in this section, and then, for users or groups who you don't want to set database passwords, remove the Administer permission on the Database object. To prevent a database from being password-protected, you must remove the Administer permission for that database.

In a more casual environment, you can prevent a database password from being set without setting up a complete user-level security system that requires logging on. To do this, use the User And Group Permissions command on the Security submenu to remove Administer permission for the Admin user and the Users group (and any other users or groups that may have been defined). When defined like this, it is possible for any user to use the User And Group Permissions command to getback the Administer permission, but well-meaning users would have no reason to do so.

User-Level Security Model

The information in this section covers the Microsoft Access user-level security model in detail.

When Do I Need User-Level Security?

Three primary reasons to use user-level security are:

- To prevent users from inadvertently breaking applications by changing code or objects on which the application depends.

- To protect sensitive data in a database.

- To protect the intellectual property of developers' code in Microsoft Access applications.

How Does User-Level Security Work?

User-level security in Microsoft Access functions as follows: Administrators or object owners grant sets of permissions to specific users or groups for specific database objects. The set of permissions granted to the user or group determines that user's or group's user-level which determines how that user or group can access that specific object. When a user starts Microsoft Access in a secure environment, the user logs on, usually with a password. The password verifies that the user is who the user claims to be. Microsoft Access then checks and stores in memory a record of all the groups to which that user belongs. Every time the user tries to perform an action on an object, such as open a form, browse a table, or modify a query, Microsoft Access checks to see if the user, or any of the groups to which the user belongs, has the necessary permissions to do so. If so, Microsoft Access performs the action, if not, Microsoft Access displays a message that the user doesn't have the permissions to perform the requested operation, and the operation fails.

When is User-Level Security Turned On?

Microsoft Access user-level security is always turned on—that is, every time a user performs any action, Microsoft Access first checks to make sure the user has permissions to perform that action. However, most Microsoft Access users never realize they are logging on and never see a security-related message. The illusion that user-level security is not turned on is created by granting full permissions for all objects, by default, to the Users group, which includes all users. Then each user is automatically logged on under a default user account, named Admin, without displaying a logon dialog box. Until a developer or administrator takes explicit action to expose the security subsystem, most users will never notice that it exists. This allows Microsoft Access to be extremely secure, with no backdoor modes of operation, but still keeps security virtually invisible to users who don't need it. This can also be used to implement security without explicitly requiring users to log on. For more information, see "Securing Your Database Without Requiring Users To Log On" later in this section.

Where is User-Level Security Information Stored?

Microsoft Access stores its security information in two different places. User and group information is stored in the workgroup information file that was current when those users and groups accounts were defined using the User And Group Accounts command on the Security submenu of the Tools menu. An administrator or user specifies the current workgroup information file before starting Microsoft Access by running the Workgroup Administrator application. The Workgroup Administrator can also be used to create new workgroup information files. When Microsoft Access 7.0 starts, it determines the current workgroup information file by reading the SystemDB value in the Windows 95 registry in the \\Hkey_Local_Computer\Software\Microsoft\Access\7.0\Jet\3.0\Engines\Jet key. For Microsoft Access 2.0, this is determined by reading the SystemDB value in Msacc20.ini.

A workgroup information file is a database that stores user and group account names, which users belong to which groups, logon passwords for individual users (encrypted), and the internal Security ID (SID) for each user and group. The options available using the User And Group Accounts command change this data in the workgroup database. The preferences users set with the Options command on the Tools menu are stored for each user account. A single workgroup information file can be used to store the user and group account information used to access as many databases as you want.

The default workgroup information file that is created by Setup when installing Microsoft Access is named System.mdw. An identical copy of the default file can be recreated at any time by re-installing Microsoft Access and providing the same name and company name that was used for the original installation. If you need to ensure the absolute security of your system, you should create a new workgroup information file before defining security accounts.

All the permissions that users and groups have for the objects in a database are stored in the database itself. After a user's identity and group membership have been established by checking the logon strings against data in the workgroup information file, all permission checking is done against system tables within the user database. The User And Group Permissions command on the Security submenu of the Tools menu affects only data in the open database, not the workgroup information file. Permission and ownership information set by running the User-Level Security Wizard affects only the new database created by that process.

Logging On

Each user and group account has an associated Security ID (SID). The SID is a computer-generated, non-readable binary string that uniquely identifies the user or group. When a user logs on, Microsoft Access looks in the MSysAccounts table of the workgroup information file for a user of the same name, which is case insensitive. If a user with the same name is found, it then validates the password which is case sensitive. If the password matches, the SID of the user is retrieved and saved in an internal structure. The password is only used to validate the user when logging on. It has no other effect on security.

By default, as Microsoft Access starts up it first attempts to log on as the default user Admin with a blank password. If this logon attempt fails, the Logon dialog box is displayed. If a user name and password is specified on the command line (using the /User and /Pwd command line options), Microsoft Access first tries to log on using that user name and password. However, entering a user name and password from the command line is not a recommended practice as it would compromise the security of the system; it is generally used as a convenience when testing a secured database. After a user logs on, the user's SID is retrieved. Then the SIDs of all groups to which that user belongs are retrieved and saved in the same internal structure. These SIDs are used for all subsequent security operations within Microsoft Access.

Microsoft Access for Windows 95 has added the ability to integrate with Windows 95 password caching policies. For more information about caching policies, see "Password Caching" later in this chapter.

The following flowchart represents the logon sequence from the first time a user installs Microsoft Access.

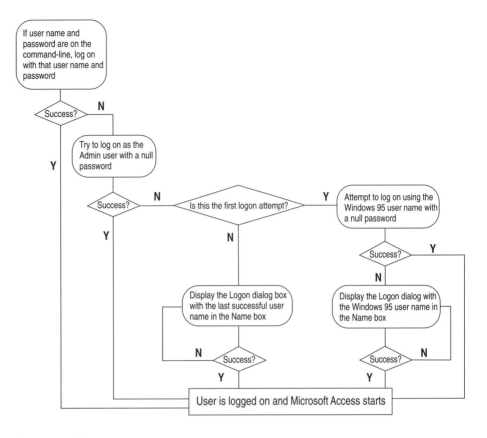

Users and Groups

Each user can belong to one or more groups. Users and groups share the same namespace; you cannot have both a group and user with the same name. User and group accounts are not stored in individual databases; they are stored in the workgroup information file. For more information about workgroup information files, see "Where is User-Level Security Information Stored?" earlier in this chaper.

Each user and group account is uniquely identified by a Security Identifier, or SID. SIDs are the only user information that Microsoft Access checks when deciding whether or not a user has permissions to perform an operation on an object. When you create a new user or guest account, you are prompted for a user name, and a Personal ID (PID). Note that the PID is not the password. The user name and PID are sent to an encryption procedure that generates the SID for that account. The PID is a variable length, alphanumeric string. The SID that Microsoft Access generates from the user name and PID is a 128-bit number. If you send the same two keys again to the encryption program, you will get the same SID. This gives you the ability to recreate user accounts if your system database becomes corrupted.

Microsoft Access defines one default user: the Admin user account, and two default groups: Users and Admins. Understanding how the SIDs of these default accounts are generated helps you understand how the security works.

Admin User

The Admin user is the default user account. If someone is using Microsoft Access and not logging on, they are using the Admin account. The Admin account has no particular administrative abilities. because most users are logged in as the Admin user without ever knowing it, and because all users by default have permissions to objects they create, any objects that are owned by the Admin user or to which the Admin user has explicit permissions are unsecure. You can think of the Admin account as the DefaultUser account, or for those familiar with Windows NT security, as the Everybody account.

The Admin user's SID is identical across all installations of Microsoft Access and any other applications that use the Microsoft Jet Database Engine to access .mdb database files, including applications such as Microsoft Visual Basic and Microsoft Excel. Even if no one in a workgroup is using the Admin account because a password has been set for it, all objects owned by the Admin user, or to which the Admin user has explicit permissions are still open to anyone using their own copy of Microsoft Access or another application that uses Microsoft Jet. So make sure the Admin user has no explicit permissions and owns no objects. The easiest way to do this is to use the the User-Level Security Wizard to secure a database.

By default, the Admin account doesn't receive any permissions for new objects. However, when any user creates an object, that user's account is automatically granted full permissions for this object, and becomes the owner of that object. Because all users in unsecured environments log in as Admin, the Admin account usually owns a lot of objects and has a lot of permissions. When you need to secure your database, use the User-Level Security Wizard to remove those permissions.

Users Group

The Users group is the default group. All users belong to the Users group. Any permissions that are assigned explicitly to the Users group are available to all users in all installations of Microsoft Access. If you ever need to unsecure an object, simply assign permissions for that object to the Users group.

The Users group's SID is identical across all installations of Microsoft Access and any other applications, such as Microsoft Visual Basic and Microsoft Excel, using the Microsoft Jet Database Engine to access .mdb database files.

By default the Users group gets full permissions on all newly created objects. This is the main mechanism that Microsoft Access uses to hide security from the majority of users who don't need it. The easiest way to remove this permission from all objects in a database is to use the User-Level Security Wizard.

Admins Group

Users who are members of the Admins group are the true administrators of a workgroup. They manage user and group membership, and have the power to clear users' passwords. There must always be at least one member of the Admins group.

The Admins group of the workgroup information file in use when the database was created gets full permissions by default on all new objects in a database. The Admins group's right to change permissions cannot be revoked through the Microsoft Access user interface. Even if you uncheck the Administer privileges check box in the Permissions dialog box for the Admins group for an object, the permission remains. It is therefore very important to know and keep track of which workgroup information file was in use when the database was created.

Because the Admins group is invested with superuser capabilities, understanding how the Admins group SID is created is key to understanding the security model. In Microsoft Access 2.0 and 7.0 the Setup program uses the user's name and the company name as seeds for the Admins group's SID. Because these two strings are available from the Help menu, it is critical that users implementing security use the Workgroup Administrator to create a new Admins group with a secure SID.

The Workgroup Administrator will prompt for a Name, a Company Name, and a Workgroup ID. It uses these strings as encryption seeds to generate the Admins group SID. It is very important to record these three case sensitive strings in a secure, off-site location. If the workgroup information file is ever destroyed or corrupted beyond repair, you can generate a new Admins group with an identical SID by running the Workgroup Administrator and entering the same exact strings. If you are a member of this re-created Admins group you will be able to grant yourself permissions on all objects that were created when the old workgroup information file was in effect.

Summary of Default User and Group Accounts

The SID of the Admins group account is unique across workgroups, but the SIDs of the other two default accounts, the Admin user and the Users group, are identical across all installations of Microsoft Access. Permissions assigned to the Admins group are secure, but permissions assigned to the Admin user or the Users group are available to anyone with a copy of Microsoft Access and any other applications using the Microsoft Jet Database Engine to access .mdb database files, such as Microsoft Visual Basic and Microsoft Excel.

Creating Your Own Users and Groups: SIDs, PIDs, and Passwords

Members of the Admins group create new user and group accounts. They determine which users are members of which groups. Microsoft Access identifies each user by the user's SID.

Because each user account is identified by its SID, it's important to record user and group names and their PIDs in a safe place. If you ever need to recreate the workgroup information file, you will need the name and PID of each user and group. If you try to recreate a user or group with the user name or group name and a different PID, you will get a different SID and thus not have the access privileges the user name or group previously had.

After a user account has been created, users can modify their own passwords. Passwords have no effect on the user's SID or permissions. They simply identify the user account to Microsoft Access. There is no built-in password aging in Microsoft Access, although it is possible to write a subroutine to monitor password aging with Visual Basic for applications and Data Access Objects (DAO) code.

The easiest way to administer permissions in a workgroup is to create new groups and assign permissions to the groups, rather than to individual users. Then you can change individual users' effective permissions by adding or deleting the users from the groups. Most workgroups only require three or four groups to give them the permission control that they need, and it's much easier to maintain permissions for three or four groups than for fifty or a hundred users.

The CurrentUser Function and Duplicate User Names

The CurrentUser function in Visual Basic for applications returns the name of the current user. This is not the same as the SID. It is possible for two users in different Workgroup information files to have the same user name but different SIDs, because when their accounts were created, different PIDs were fed to the SID generating program and different SIDs were created. Watch out for this problem if you using the CurrentUser function to log user activity.

Permissions

Explicit permissions are those permissions granted directly to a user; no other users are affected. *Implicit* permissions are those permissions granted to a group; all users who are members of a group get the permissions assigned to that group.

When a user attempts to perform an operation on an object, that user's security level is determined by the least restrictive of the permissions explicitly assigned to that user and the permissions implicitly assigned to the groups to which that user belongs. For example, if User1 has no explicit permissions on the Orders table but belongs to the Clerks group, which has Read Data permission on the Orders table, User1 will be able to read the data in the table. If User1 is removed from the Clerks group and doesn't belong to another group with permissions on the Orders table, User1 will be denied any access to the Orders table.

Permissions can be changed for an object by:

- Members of the Admins group of the workgroup information file in use when the database was created.
- The owner of the object.
- Any user who has Administer permission on the object.

Even though users may not currently be able to perform an action, they may be able to grant themselves permissions to perform the action. This is true if the user is a member of the Admins group of the workgroup information file in use when the database was created, or if the user is the owner of an object.

The user who creates an object is the owner of that object. You can change the ownership of an object using the Users And Group Permissions command on the Security submenu of the Tools menu, or you can re-create the object. To re-create the object, you do not have to start from scratch. You can make a copy of the object, or import it or export it to another database.

Note This procedure doesn't change the ownership of queries whose **RunPermissions** property is set to Owner's. You can change ownership of a query only if you are the query owner, or if its **RunPermissions** property is set to User's.

If you want to secure an entire database, you can create a new database, which establishes your ownership of the database itself, and then import all of the objects into the new database which transfers the ownership of all of the objects. This is part of the process that the User-Level Security Wizard performs for you.

Viewing Permissions

You can view a user's permissions for an object using the Tools|Security|User And Group Permissions command. However, when doing so, you only see the user's explicit permissions. To view a user's implicit permissions, you must view the permissions of each group to which the user belongs. Using the Microsoft Access user interface, there's no way to see the union of all the user's explicit and implicit permissions for an object. In other words, you cannot select a user and see in one place whether that user can perform an action on an object. You need to look at the user's account and the groups to which the user belongs as well. You can print a report of all the users and the groups to which each user belongs using the Print Users And Groups button in the User And Group Accounts dialog box.

Database-Level Permissions

In Microsoft Access, there are three database level permissions: Run/Open, Open Exclusive, and Administer.

Run/Open Permission: Keeping Users from Opening a Database   The Run/Open permission gives you a simple, clean way to lock unauthorized users out of a database entirely. However, users cannot be prevented from creating new objects in a database that they can open.

Open Exclusive Permission: Keeping Users from Opening in Exclusive Mode

The Open Exclusive permission is used to prevent users from locking each other out of a shared database by opening it for exclusive access. This is less of a problem when using Microsoft Access for Windows 95 because it opens databases in shared mode by default, whereas previous versions open databases in exclusive mode by default. However, this may be a significant issue if some of your users are still using previous versions of Microsoft Access and are sharing those databases with Microsoft Access for Windows 95 users. In either case, you can prevent users from locking other users out of a database without setting up a complete security system requiring users to log on. To do so, revoke the Open Exclusive permission for all users and groups, including the Admin user and the Users group. After this is done, users starting Microsoft Access under the default Admin account won't be able to open the database exclusively. Microsoft Access will detect that they don't have this permission, and will automatically open the database as shared. If you don't choose to set up users and groups with logon IDs, it is possible for users to use the User And Group Permissions command and grant themselves this permission, but well-meaning users would have no reason to do so.

Administer Permission: Keeping Users from Setting a Database Password, Replicating a Database, or Changing Startup Properties   In Microsoft Access for Windows 95, the Administer permission has been extended to apply to the database object. In previous versions, the Administer permission only applies to objects within the database. When applied to the database object, the Administer permission controls access to the following areas:

- Setting a database password
- Replicating a database
- Startup properties and the AutoExec startup macro

By default, all users (the default Admin user and all members of the default Users group) have the Administer permission for the database. You need to set up user-level security to revoke this permission. You can prevent users from setting a database password and locking out other users by revoking this permission. For more information about database passwords, see "Share-Level Security" earlier in this chapter. The Administer permission is also required to convert a database for replication. For information about database replication, see Chapter 16, "Microsoft Access Database Replication."

Finally, the Administer database permission allows the user to change the startup properties set using the Startup command on the Tools menu, such as the startup form or the Use Access Special Keys check box that controls special keys such as the ability to hold down the SHIFT key to bypass startup properties and the AutoExec macro. The Administer permission also controls whether a user can edit the AutoExec startup macro. Additionally, you can grant the Administer permission for the database object, and revoke the Administer permission for all objects within the database, to a user. This allows that user to set these administration-level properties without assigning that user to the Admins group, which would confer full permissions on all objects.

Ownership

Ownership is an important part of the Microsoft Access security model. The SID of the user who creates an object is the owner of the object. The object owner always has permission to assign permissions to that object, even if someone with Administer privileges has revoked explicit permissions for that object. Unlike the administer privileges of the Admins group, this irrevocability is enforced by the Microsoft Jet Database Engine, not the Microsoft Access user interface. Therefore it cannot be revoked through DAO code; it can only be transferred to another user.

There are two ways to transfer ownership of a object. The first is to change the owner using the Change Owner tab in the User And Group Permissions dialog box. The second is to recreate the object. This is usually accomplished by importing it or exporting it into a new database. If you want to secure an entire database, this is the easiest way to transfer the ownership of all the objects. The simplest way to transfer ownership of an entire database and all the objects within it is with the User-Level Security Wizard. You can also transfer ownership of one or more objects by importing, exporting, or copying and pasting. To re-create an object, the person doing the importing, exporting or copying and pasting must have permissions to read the object and its data, if the object is a table or query.

Caution   As already mentioned, the Admin user has the same SID in all workgroup information files. It is therefore critical to security that the Admin user not own any objects. If it does, anyone who has Microsoft Access who can open the database can give themselves permissions to those objects. To see who owns an object, open the Change Owner tab in the User And Group Permissions dialog box.

The RunPermissions Query Property

Microsoft Access queries have a property called RunPermissions, available through the query property sheet. This property determines whether Microsoft Access uses the query user's permissions or the owner's permissions when checking the security permissions for each of the source tables in a query.

This property is really a user interface construct that maps to the "WITH OWNERACCESS OPTION" clause of the SQL property of the query. This very powerful feature allows you to build secure views of your data that can provide row- and column-level security for your users.

For example, suppose you have a secure database with an Employees table and a separate Salary table. Using the RunPermissions property, you can build views of the two tables that allow one group to view, but not update the salary column, another to be able to view and update the salary column, and a third to only view the salary column if salary is less than a certain amount.

Only the owner of a query can save it if the RunPermissions property is set to Owner's. Even members of the Admins group of the workgroup information file in use when the database was created cannot save a query created by another user if the RunPermissions property is set to Owner's. Anyone with Modify Definition permissions on the query can set the RunPermissions property to User's and successfully save the query.

Either a user or a group can own an object. Because only the owner of a query with the RunPermissions property set to Owner's can save changes to that query, groups can be set as the owners to aid in group development environments. Create a Developers group, use the Change Owner dialog box to change the owner of the queries to this group, and then add all your programmers to the Developers group. Then any member of the Developers group can edit the query and save changes.

Using RunPermissions Queries to Prevent Users From Viewing Table Designs

For Microsoft Access to display a table or query, it needs to know field names and other field properties such as Format and Input Mask. So for a user to read and display the data in a table or query, that user must also have permissions to read the design of the table or query. That's why selecting the Read Data Permission check box in the User And Group Permissions dialog box automatically selects the Read Design check box as well. If you don't want your users to see your table or query definitions, you can use the RunPermissions property of queries to restrict their access to this information.

▶ **To prevent users from viewing the design of the tables or queries on which a form is based**

1. Remove all permissions to the sensitive source tables or queries for the users or groups that you want to restrict.

2. Build a new query that includes all the fields you want to include from your sensitive tables or queries. By omitting a field, you exclude access to that field. Similarly, you can define criteria for your query to limit access to a certain range of values.

3. Make sure you or a secure group owns the new query.

4. Set the RunPermissions property of the new query to Owner's.

5. Grant appropriate data permissions for the new query to the users and groups who you want to be able to update data but not view the table's design. This usually means Read Design, Read Data, Update Data, Delete Data, and Insert Data.

6. Base your forms and reports on the new query.

Your users can update data in the source tables or queries through forms based on the new query. However, they won't be able to view the design of those tables or queries. If they try to view the design of the new query, they will receive a message that they don't have permissions to view the source tables or queries.

Encryption

Encryption is separate from Microsoft Access security. It is used to prevent someone using a file or disk editor from reading or writing data directly to an .mdb file, and bypassing the Microsoft Jet Database Engine.

Everything in a Microsoft Access .mdb file is encrypted. Microsoft Access uses the RC4™ algorithm from RSA Data Security Inc. for database encryption. Microsoft Jet reads and writes all data one page at a time. Pages are 2K in size. At the level that encryption is being done, there is no notion of what is on the page, only that there's 2K of data that needs to be encrypted and written, or read and decrypted.

If a database isn't encrypted, it would be possible for a very knowledgeable person to use a disk editor to read the SID of the database owner or the SID of the Admins group in use when the .mdb was created. Given that SID, they could assume ownership of the database. If you encrypt your database, you prevent this from happening. The User-Level Security Wizard encrypts databases as part of the process of securing them.

Only the owner, or creator, of a database, or a member of the Admins group of the workgroup information file in use when the database was created, can encrypt or decrypt it. To encrypt a database, either use the User-Level Security Wizard or start Microsoft Access without opening a database and then use the Encrypt/Decrypt Database command on the Security submenu of the Tools menu.

Due to the overhead of encrypting and decryption, an encrypted database will run approximately 10–15 percent slower than a database that is not encrypted. Also, encrypted files cannot be compressed by stand-alone programs such as PKZip or by disk compression programs such as Microsoft DriveSpace.

Using the User-Level Security Wizard and Common Security Scenarios

The Microsoft Access User-Level Security Wizard provides the easiest way to secure databases. In previous versions, the Security Wizard was only available as an Add-in. In Microsoft Access 7.0, the User-Level Security Wizard has been re-written and is available using the User-Level Security Wizard command on the Security submenu of the Tools menu. The Security Wizard allows you to choose which database object types to secure—tables, queries, forms, reports, macros or modules. The selected object types are secured by revoking all permissions from all user and group accounts except that of the user running the wizard.

Note The User-Level Security Wizard will only secure databases created by Microsoft Access 7.0. Microsoft Access 1.*x* or 2.0 databases must be converted using the Convert Database command on the Tools menu before they can be secured using the User-Level Security Wizard.

The following sections describe common security scenarios and how to address them.

Scenario 1: Securing an Existing Database with the User-Level Security Wizard

You need to secure a database that was created while the developer was logged on as the default Admin user. A unique workgroup information file was not created in advance, and thus any user accounts that were created will be vulnerable. The following procedure assumes that the Logon dialog box has not be activated and that you are logged on as the default Admin user.

▶ **To secure an existing database**

1. If you haven't done so before, create a secure workgroup information file using the Workgroup Administrator. Write down the Name, Organization, and Workgroup ID strings that you enter and store them in a safe place. You will need these strings if you ever need to re-create your workgroup information file.

2. On the Tools menu, point to Security and click User And Group Accounts.

3. Create a new user account to be the owner and adminstrator of the database, and then add that user to the Admins group.

4. Click the Change Logon Password tab for the Admin user and define a password for the Admin user. This will cause the Logon dialog box to appear the next time you start Microsoft Access.

5. Quit Microsoft Access and restart it, logging on as the new user created in step 3.

6. Use the User And Group Accounts command to remove the Admin user from the Admins group.

7. Open the database you want to secure.

8. On the Tools menu, point to Security and click User-Level Security Wizard.

9. Select the check boxes for the object types you want to secure and then click OK.

   The Security Wizard creates a new encrypted database, exports all the objects from the current database, and secures the selected object types by revoking permissions for all users other than the user created in step 3. The original database isn't changed in any way. The wizard re-creates any links to tables and table relationships in the new database as well.

10. Create your own users and groups using the User And Group Accounts command on the Security submenu. Assign appropriate permissions to the group accounts, and then add individual users the appropriate groups using the User And Group Permissions command on the Security submenu. Typical permissions might include Read Data and Update Data permissions for tables and queries, Insert Data or Delete Data permissions if you want users to be able to add or delete records, and Run/Open permission for forms and reports.

The new database is now secure. The only people who can use the objects in the new database are those to whom you gave permissions in step 10 and anyone who is a member of the Admins group of the workgroup information file in use when you ran the User-Level Security Wizard.

Scenario 2: Removing Security from a Secured Database

You need to make a secured database open to all users of Microsoft Access. The SIDs of the Admin user and the Users group are the same in all workgroup information files. By giving permissions for an object to the Users group and the Admin user, you unsecure that object for all users.

▶ **Removing security from a secured database**

1. Make a backup of the database.

2. Start Microsoft Access, log on as someone who has Administer permissions for all the objects in the database, and then open the database.

3. Use the User And Group Permissions command on the Security submenu to give the Users group full permissions for all objects in the database.

4. Use the User And Group Permissions command on the Security submenu to give the Admin user full permissions for all objects in the database.

5. Quit Microsoft Access and restart it, logging on as the Admin user, and then use the User And Group Accounts command on the Security submenu to change the password for the Admin user to null (blank). This will turn off the Logon dialog box.

Your database is now completely unsecured. Anyone who can open the database has full permissions for all the objects in it.

Scenario 3: Securing an Application with a Split Application Database and Data Database

You need to secure a database that uses a split frontend/backend architecture. Your data is in stored in Data.mdb, and your code, forms, reports, and other objects are in Application.mdb, along with linked tables pointing to tables in Data.mdb. You want to secure both databases and distribute them to your users. When they install Application.mdb, you want them to be able to re-link to the tables in Data.mdb, based on network share name that will be kept in Data.mdb, and you don't necessarily know the name of this share when you are securing the databases. For more information about split databases, see "Splitting Databases" later in this section.

▶ **To secure an application with a split architecture**

1. Follow the steps to secure a database using the User-Level Security Wizard for both databases.

2. Grant your users the permissions you want them to have for the tables in Data.mdb (Read Data, Update Data, Insert Data or Delete Data). You can either grant users permissions directly for the tables in Data.mdb or you can leave those tables completely secured, and perform all access using RunPermissions queries stored in Application.mdb.

3. Make sure your users have Run/Open permissions on Data.mdb. This is required even if you are using RunPermissions queries.

4. In Application.mdb, grant your users Modify Design permissions for the linked tables.

5. When the users first install the Application.mdb file, have them run the Linked Table Manager command on the Add-ins submenu of the Tools menu to refresh the links to the tables in the new location of Data.mdb.

For more information about RunPermissions queries, see "Using RunPermissions Queries to Prevent Users From Viewing Table Designs" earlier in this chapter.

Because the users have Modify Design permissions for the linked tables, they can reset the connect string to them if the file system location of Data.mdb ever changes. However, they won't be able to make any modifications to the design of the real tables in Data.mdb.

Scenario 4: Securing Your Database Without Requiring Users To Log On

If you want to secure some objects, such as your modules, in a database, but you don't care about granting different permissions to different classes of users, you can secure your application without making your users log on.

▶ **To secure your database without requiring users to log on**

1. Follow the steps to secure a database using the User-Level Security Wizard.

2. While logged on as a member of the Admins group, assign the permissions that you want to be available to all users to the Admin user.

3. Confirm that the Admin user is not a member of the Admins group. This prevents users who are logged in as Admin from granting themselves further permissions.

4. Clear the password from the Admin user.

Users will be able to open your database without logging on and will be able to perform all actions you granted to the Admin user in step 2.

Now you need a way to perform administrative duties such as setting permissions and assigning users to groups. Because you have removed the Admin user from the Admins group, you won't be able to perform these actions when logged on as Admin. And because the Admin user has no password, the Logon dialog box won't be displayed. You'll need to log on as a member of the Admins group to perform these duties.

To perform administrative duties, you can either reactivate the logon procedure and log on as a member of the Admins group, or you can define a shortcut and use the /Pwd and /User command-line options to specify your password and user name when starting Microsoft Access. If you choose to keep this shortcut on your computer, rather than deleting it and recreating the command line each time, you'll have to make sure your computer is physically secure, because someone could copy the user name and password strings arguments from the shortcuts command line and gain access to your system.

Scenario 5: Configuring a Remote Workgroup so that On-Site Administrators can Manage User Accounts Without Gaining Permissions to Objects

You have a multiuser application developed in Microsoft Access that will be administered by users at a remote site. You want to lock up code and other objects to protect intellectual property, and to prevent users from inadvertently breaking the application. Different users at the sites have permissions to different forms in the database because they are authorized to perform different duties. You don't want to manage individual user accounts yourself because you are not on-site and they change frequently. You want to grant remote administrators the ability to manage user accounts without giving them access to code and the design of objects.

▶ **To give permissions to manage accounts but not to access code and the design of objects**

1. Using the Workgroup Administrator, create a secure workgroup information file. This will be the master workgroup file for your database.

2. Log on with this workgroup and follow the steps to secure the database using the User-Level Security wizard.

3. Create your own custom groups that correspond to the different levels of permissions that you want your remote users to have. Write down the exact names of these groups (case sensitive) and the Personal ID you use to create them. You will need these strings later.

4. Assign the appropriate permissions to these groups. Don't grant Administer permissions to anything; just grant the permissions that are necessary for users to run the application and perform their appropriate functions. At minimum, this would probably be Run/Open for the database, forms, reports, and macros; and Read Data and Update Data for tables and queries. You may also want to grant Insert Data and Delete Data permissions for tables and queries to allow users to add and delete records.

5. Use the Workgroup Administrator to create a new workgroup information file that you will distribute with the application. Make sure you use different strings for the Name, Company Name, and Workgroup ID, than the corresponding strings you used for the master workgroup file.

6. Log on under the workgroup file created in step 5 and recreate the same groups created in step 3, using the identical case-sensitive names and the same Personal IDs.

7. Create a user account for your remote administrator to use, and add it to the Admins group of the workgroup file you created in step 5.

8. Remove the Admin user from the Admins group, and put a password on the Admin user. This will cause the Logon dialog box to be displayed, and will make the administrator account created in step 7 the effective administrator of the new workgroup file.

9. Distribute the workgroup file created in step 5 with your database application. Make sure that users use the Workgroup Administrator to join this workgroup information file.

The administrator account created in step 7 will be able to create new user accounts, reset passwords, and add users to the groups that you have already created. As users are added to these groups, they will automatically gain the permissions that you assigned to these group accounts in step 4. This is because the SIDs of the group accounts are identical in both workgroup information files. However, the SIDs of the Admins group in the two workgroups are different.

These SIDs are generated from the strings fed into the Workgroup Administrator, and you used different strings in step 5. Because the database was originally secured under the master workgroup information file, not the file created in step 5, the Admins group in the master file has ultimate permission setting privileges over all the objects in the database. So while the administrator account you created in step 7 can add and delete users from the groups you created, that account does not have any special privileges to the other objects, and therefore cannot see or modify the design of any of the objects to which you haven't granted permissions.

Converting Previous Version Secure Databases to Version 7.0

The conversion process preserves all previously defined security. The same issues apply as for converting databases without security. For more information, see "Converting Databases" in the Microsoft Access section of Chapter 10. There are additional issues regarding converting previous version workgroup information files (called workgroups or system databases in previous versions). For more information, see "Converting Previous Version Workgroup Information Files" in the Microsoft Access section of Chapter 10.

Other Security Enhancements

In addition to database password protection and the integration of the Security Wizard, Microsoft Access for Windows 95 includes the following enhancements.

AllowBypassKey Method

The AllowBypassKey method allows a developer to disable the user's ability to hold down the SHIFT key when starting an application. When this property is set to **True** (the default), if the user holds down SHIFT when starting an application, settings made with the Startup command on the Tools menu are ignored and the AutoExec macro does not run. This allows users to display the database window and make whatever changes that they have permissions to make. Users who have the Administer permission for a database can change the AllowBypassKey property for their account. The only way to be sure that a user cannot hold the SHIFT key to start your application and bypass the Startup command settings and the AutoExec macro is to set the AllowBypassKey property to **False** and remove the Administer permission for the database for that account. Whoever is the owner of the database will be able to change these settings even if that user has not been granted the Administer permission for the database.

Hiding Objects in the Database Container

Hidden is a new property for all objects that allows you to hide database objects in the database window. This property is available on the property sheets of all database objects. A new user preference, Show Hidden Objects, is found on the View tab in the Options dialog box and allows you to display hidden objects. When hidden objects are shown in the database window, they appear with a dimmed icon.

Changing a Workgroup Information File from the Command-Line

Microsoft Access 7.0 provides a new command-line option, /wrkgrp, that allows you to change to a different workgroup information file when starting Microsoft Access. You can use this parameter when using the Run command on the Start menu, or in the Target text box of a shortcut. Use this command-line option in this format:

```
Msaccess.exe <databasename> /wrkgrp <workgroup>
```

where *databasename* is the full pathname of the database you want to open (optional) and *workgroup* is the full pathname of the workgroup information file you want to use.

Multiuser Settings

Several options and settings in Microsoft Access affect how a Microsoft Access database application functions in a multiuser environment. These settings, are described in the following sections.

Database Open Modes

There are three ways to affect how a database is opened in Microsoft Access:

- When you start Microsoft Access you can include a database name on the command line and either the /Excl or /Ro parameter to open that database in exclusive or read-only mode, respectively.

- You can select or clear the Exclusive check box when using the Open Database dialog box. To open read-only, select the database in the Open Database dialog box, click the Commands And Settings button, and then click Open Read Only.

- You can change the default database open mode using the Options command on the Tools menu, changing the Default Open Mode For Databases setting under the Advanced tab. The setting can be Exclusive for single-user access or Shared for multiuser access to the database.

Tip In Microsoft Access 1.*x* and 2.0, using the Options command on the View menu and setting the Default Open Mode set only the default behavior, which the user can still override. The same holds true for Microsoft Access 7.0, where this setting is available using the Options command on the Tools menu. Because the introduction of Microsoft Access 2.0, you can prevent a user or group from opening a database in exclusive mode by removing the OpenExclusive permission of the database for that user or group. This only works if user-level security has been defined for the workgroup.

The Refresh Interval

Using the Options command on the Tools menu, you can also set the refresh interval. Microsoft Access automatically checks the recordsets of open forms and datasheets to see whether changes have occurred at the frequency set by the refresh interval. The default refresh interval is 60 seconds, which may be too long for some applications. If you set the refresh interval to too small a value, however, you may create excessive network traffic. Finding the proper setting for your application may require some experimentation. In general, the smaller the network, the smaller you can set the refresh interval without adverse effect.

You can override the default refresh interval in your applications by using the Refresh method, the Requery method, or the Requery action. Record refreshes— either automatic refreshes by Microsoft Access using the refresh interval or manual refreshes using the Refresh method—are faster than Requeries. New records added by other users, however, appear only after a Requery (method or action), and records deleted by other users vanish from your copy only after a Requery. However, all the values in the fields of deleted records are replaced with the string "#DELETED" when the record is refreshed.

In most cases, you should use the Requery method rather than the almost-equivalent Requery action. The method reruns the query that's already in memory, while the action reloads it from disk. The exception to this rule is when you have used DAO to modify the underlying query definition. You should then use the Requery action to reload the QueryDef from disk.

Tip Even if you leave the refresh interval very high, Microsoft Access automatically refreshes the current record whenever a user attempts to edit it. The benefit of a shorter refresh interval lies chiefly in giving quicker visual feedback when someone else has locked or changed a record while you are viewing it.

Locking Options

To provide concurrent access to records by multiple users, Microsoft Access locks records. But unlike some other databases, Microsoft Access doesn't lock individual records; instead it locks a 2K (2048 bytes) page of records. The advantage of page locking is that there's less overhead and generally better performance over true record locking when performing operations that affect many records. Unfortunately, this also means that Microsoft Access usually locks more records than you would like. This is especially an issue when you employ pessimistic locking (which is defined later in this section) because this type of record locking allows users to keep records locked for long periods of time.

In a multiuser environment you can open recordsets in one of three different modes:

- **No Locks** This is often called *optimistic locking* and is the default setting. With the No Locks setting, the page of records that contains the currently edited record is locked only during the instant when the record is being saved—not during the editing process. This allows for concurrent editing of records with fewer locking conflicts.

  For forms and datasheets, two or more users can edit the same record simultaneously. If two users attempt to save changes to the same record, Microsoft Access displays a message to the user who tries to save the record second. This user can then discard his or her record, copy his or her record to the Clipboard, or replace the record changed by the other user.

  For reports, no records are locked while the report is previewed or printed. Except if a report is printing data from Memo or OLE Object fields, in which case that record will be locked until Microsoft Access is finished reading the Memo or OLE Object field's data.

  For queries, no records are locked while the query is run. Except for action queries, where all records will be locked until the action query is finished.

- **Edited Record** As soon as a user begins to edit a record, the page containing the currently edited record is locked until the changes are saved. This is known as *pessimistic locking*.

- **All Records** This setting causes all the records in the entire recordset to be locked at once. You won't find this option very useful except when doing batch updates or performing administrative maintenance on tables.

  For forms, all records in the underlying table or query are locked while the form is open in Form view or Datasheet view.

  For table and select query datasheets, all records are locked until the datasheet is closed.

  For reports, all records are locked while the report is previewed or printed.

For action queries, all records are locked while the query is run.

Although users can read the records, no one can add, delete, or edit any records until the form or datasheet is closed, the report has finished printing, or the query has finished running.

You can set the default record locking behavior for most objects that access recordsets on the Advanced tab in the Options dialog box. These defaults affect the following objects:

- Table datasheets
- Select query datasheets
- Crosstab query datasheets
- Union query datasheets
- Update queries
- Delete queries
- Make-table queries
- Append queries
- Forms
- Reports

If the default is set to No Locks, it will be ignored for Update, Delete, Make-table, and Append queries, because records must be locked (either Edited or All Records settings) during these operations. Additionally, all records must be locked when using a Data-definition queries.

You can set record locking behavior for individual forms, queries, or reports by opening the object in Design view and setting the RecordLocks property. This allows you to override the default setting made using the Options command on the Tools menu.

Whether you set locking behavior using the Options command on the Tools menu or by setting the RecordLocks property, when the data comes from an Open Database Connectivity (ODBC) database, the Microsoft Access setting is ignored (equivalent to No Locks). All locking for linked ODBC tables, such as Microsoft SQL tables, is determined by the ODBC server application.

Choosing a Locking Strategy

The following list of advantages and disadvantages will help you decide which locking strategy is best for your particular application.

The advantages of pessimistic locking (Edited Record setting) are:

- It is simple for the developer.
- It prevents users from overwriting each other's work.
- It may be less confusing to the user than optimistic locking.
- It works well for small workgroups or where users are not likely to be editing the same record.

The disadvantages of pessimistic locking are:

- It will usually lock multiple records; how many depends on the size of the records.
- When a user is at the end of a table and thus has locked the last page, other users may be prevented from adding new records.
- It is not recommended where lots of users will be editing the same records or where lots of users will be adding new records at the same time.

The advantages of using optimistic locking (No Locks setting) are:

- It is simple to use.
- It allows more than one user to edit the same record at the same time. (In some cases, this may be a disadvantage.)
- It is less likely to lock other users out of records.

The disadvantages of using optimistic locking are:

- It may be confusing to the user when there's a write conflict.
- Users can overwrite each other's edits.

Unless you have a compelling reason to use pessimistic locking, you should consider optimistic locking. In most applications, you don't want your users prevented from being able to edit or—even worse—add new records for potentially long periods of time. If you decide to use pessimistic locking in your forms, you will have to teach your users to recognize and deal with locked records.

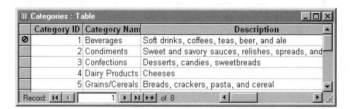

Under pessimistic locking, users are locked out of being able to change a record that is on the same page as a record being edited by another user. (Note the slashed-O icon in the record selector.)

On the other hand, you employ optimistic locking in your forms, you will have to teach users how to deal with the Write Conflict dialog box.

Under optimistic locking, users may encounter the Write Conflict dialog box when attempting to save a record that has been changed by another user.

Tip If you have set the RecordSelector property of a form to No, the slashed-O icon does not appear when a record is pessimistically locked. Microsoft Access beeps at the user, but other than this audible signal, users won't have any clue as to why they cannot edit the values in the record. No trappable error is generated, either. Thus, it's important to leave the RecordSelector property set to Yes when using pessimistic locking with bound forms.

In some applications you may need to use both strategies on different forms. For example, in an inventory application you must ensure that the QuantityOnHand column is pessimistically locked so that salespeople don't try to post a sale beyond QuantityOnHand without invoking back-order processing. On the other hand, you might use optimistic locking on a vendor address form, as it's unlikely that two change-of-address requests for the same vendor will be given to two different users for posting at the same time.

Forcing Access to Lock Individual Records

You can force Microsoft Access to lock individual records by creating record sizes that are larger than half a page—that is, larger than 1024 bytes. This works because Microsoft Access won't begin storing a new record on a partially filled page if it cannot fit the entire record on that page. This strategy wastes a lot of disk space and increases network traffic. However, if you decide to use pessimistic locking and absolutely must have record locking, you may want to consider this technique.

Estimating Record Size

You can estimate the size of your records by using the following table and summing the size of each column:

Column datatype	Storage size
Byte	1 byte
Integer	2 bytes
Long Integer	4 bytes
Single	4 bytes
Double	8 bytes
Currency	8 bytes
AutoNumber (depends on FieldSize)	Long Integer = 4 bytes; Replication ID = 16 bytes
Yes/no	1 bit
Date/time	8 bytes
Text	variable
Memo	14 bytes
OLE	14 bytes

The contents of memo and OLE-type columns are stored elsewhere in the .mdb file, so you only need to count the overhead for their address pointers. Text columns present the greatest problem for estimating record size because they're variable-length fields. Microsoft Access uses 1 byte per actual stored character. Zero-length strings use 1 byte; null strings use 0 bytes.

You also have to account for overhead, which includes the following:

- Seven bytes per record for record overhead.
- One byte variable-length column overhead for each text, memo, and OLE column.
- One additional byte for every 256 bytes of the total space occupied by all text, memo, and OLE datatype columns.
- One byte fixed-column overhead for each yes/no, byte, integer, long integer, counter, single, double, and date/time column.

Note The above numbers can only be used to estimate the record size.

The easiest way to pad a record to exceed 1024 bytes is to create one or more dummy text columns in the table with default values that are 255 characters long. For example, if you estimated your record size to be at least 130 bytes (considering the minimal size of any text fields), you would calculate the needed dummy fields as follows:

- Bytes you will need to pad = (1025 - 130) = 895 bytes.
- Each whole dummy text field would occupy (255 + 2 bytes overhead) = 257 bytes.
- So you would need three completely-filled dummy fields (257*3=771) of 255 x's plus one partially-filled dummy field of (895 - 771 - 1 overhead byte) = 123 x's.

Don't place these dummy columns on your forms. Whenever a new record is created, Microsoft Access will automatically create a record with the four x-filled dummy fields, which forces it into record-locking mode.

Splitting Databases

No matter which locking scheme you use, you are still left with the fact that Microsoft Access puts everything (that is, data, forms, reports, queries, macros, and code) in a single database by default. Performance can suffer considerably because every time an object, such as a form, is used, it must be sent across the network to the user. In a production setting, where nothing but the data stored in tables is being changed, much of this network traffic is unnecessary.

You can eliminate this unnecessary traffic by splitting the database into an application database (sometimes referred to as a *front-end* database) and a data database (sometimes referred to as a *back-end* database). Install the data database, with tables only, on the file server and a copy of the application database, containing all other objects, on each workstation. From each copy of the application database, use the Link Tables command on the Get External Data submenu of the File menu to link the set of tables in the data database.

If your database is in Microsoft Access 7.0 format, you can use the Database Splitter command on the Add-ins submenu of the Tools menu to split your database and link tables in a single operation.

Tip If your network supports Universal Naming Convention (UNC) format, use the UNC pathname to specify the path to linked tables using this format: *\\server\share\path\Filename.ext*. If you specify the path to a linked table using a mapped drive letter, the link to the table will break if another user opens that copy of the application database and the network drive is not mapped or is mapped to a different letter on that user's computer.

There are several advantages and disadvantages to splitting your databases.

The advantages are:

- Performance, especially user-interface performance, is improved considerably.
- You can create temporary tables on each workstation and not worry about naming and locking conflicts for temporary objects.
- Splitting the database makes the updating of applications easier because the data and application are kept separate. Changes to the application can be made off site and easily merged back into the application database without disturbing the data.

The disadvantages are:

- Microsoft Access ignores referential integrity between local and remote tables. Fortunately, Microsoft Access enforces any referential integrity constraints you've established between individual tables in the remote database.
- Microsoft Access hard-codes the paths to linked tables. This means that if you move the data database, you have to delete and re-link all linked tables.

Managing Linked Tables

Because Microsoft Access hard codes linked table paths, their use requires extra maintenance for you. If you move the data database with linked tables, you have to delete and re-link those tables. Use the Linked Table Manager command on the Add-ins submenu of the Tools menu to automate the process.

Other Multiuser Issues

This section covers additional issues you might encounter when using a multiuser database with Microsoft Access.

Correctly Backing Up Multiuser Databases

To back up a multiuser database correctly, make sure that you have exclusive access to the database. If you back up a database while others are using it, you risk producing a damaged backup database. If you open such a backup database, you might receive an error message that the database is corrupted. If you repair and compact the database, the data in the database might be truncated.

The only way to ensure the integrity of your backup database is to open a static copy of the database. To do so, you must have exclusive access to all the tables in the database at the same time. After you have exclusive access to the database, you can copy or export the database, and then archive it.

Microsoft Access Locking and Novell NetWare

When using data from a server back end, Microsoft Access uses the locking facilities provided by that back end. The defaults in NetWare 3.*x* and 4.*x* allow a single workstation to have 500 locks at any given time. This results in a limit of 1 MB of data that Microsoft Access can deal with in a single transaction. Because Microsoft Access tries to lock every record involved in either an update or a delete query before actually carrying out the update or delete, it is quite possible to encounter this limit on a moderately large database.

When using Microsoft Access with a NetWare 3.*x* or 4.*x* server back end, it is recommended that you increase the number of locks available to avoid encountering the lock limit. To increase the number of locks available, enter the following commands at the file server console or in your Autoexec.ncf file:

```
set maximum record locks per connection = 10000
set maximum record locks = 200000
```

The first parameter is the most locks any single connection can have, and the second is the most the entire server can keep track of. These values (10,000 and 200,000, respectively) are the maximums that NetWare can accommodate. Microsoft Access can handle a transaction of up to 20 MB of data when you set the maximum record locks per connection to 10,000.

There is an error in the NetWare 3.11 that can result in a server *abending* (abnormally ending) if the lock limit is exceeded when Microsoft Access is running certain queries or otherwise requesting a large number of locks. If you are still using NetWare 3.11, it is highly recommended that you download the latest NetWare 3.11 patch file which is available on CompuServe in the NOVFILES download area. You will need to load two of the Netware Loadable Modules (NLM) from this file, either directly from the server console or by adding the following commands to your Autoexec.ncf file:

```
load patchman.nlm
load ttsfix.nlm
```

This problem is specific to NetWare version 3.11 and has been fixed in later versions of NetWare.

Workgroup Features for Microsoft Excel

The new Shared List feature allows multiple users to open a workbook and make changes to it at the same time. Uses of Shared Lists include inventory control tracking lists and consolidation of data from multiple users into the same workbook.

A workbook that has been made a Shared List can be saved to a network or shared drive location; users use the Open command on the File menu to open the file, and then enter or edit data, and save and close the file as they would any other file. The word "Shared" is appended to the filename in the Title bar, similar to the way in which "Read-Only" is appended to a filename that is opened as a read-only file.

If two or more users edit a Shared List during the same session, changes made to the same workbook cell are presented to the users for resolution. This conflict resolution occurs when the file is saved by the users. The first user to save the file sees no conflict—the save occurs normally. The second user to save the file sees the Conflict Resolution dialog box. This dialog box displays the sheet name, cell location, and editing change made by the user, as well as the date, time, content of the conflicting data, and name of the user who entered the conflicting data. The second user saving the file must resolve all conflicts before the file can be saved.

A log of the resolved conflicts is maintained in a Conflict History sheet and placed as the final sheet of a Shared List. This sheet is only visible to the user if the user has selected the Show Conflict History check box on the Editing tab in the Shared Lists dialog box. While entries made to the Conflict History sheet are locked, this log can be autofiltered. If a Shared List file is later saved as an exclusive workbook under another filename, or any user makes the file exclusive by clearing the Allow Multi-User Editing check box on the Editing tab in the Shared Lists dialog box, the Conflict History sheet is discarded from the exclusive workbook.

Using Shared Lists on a Network

File locking on a Shared List file can occur when one user is completing the actions required in the Conflict Resolution dialog box and another user attempts to open or save the Shared List at the same time. Microsoft Excel displays a message telling the user who is attempting to open or save the Shared List file, that the file is being used and that the user should try again later.

File locking can also occur if one user saves a Shared List back to an exclusive state while other users have the workbook open. When the remaining users attempt to save, a message will notify them that the file is an exclusive file and can no longer be saved in shared mode. If users of a Shared List file want to have a copy of the Shared List separate from other users, they should save a copy of the Shared List file to another filename. This will maintain the shared mode of the original workbook and the integrity of the Conflict History log; however, changes made to the user's exclusive version will not appear in the original Shared List file.

The number of users who can use a Shared List depends on the access limitations set on the network.

Because of the nature of allowing multiple users to open, edit, and save to the same workbook simultaneously, the following features are disabled when working in a Shared List:

- Formatting cells
- Inserting partial rows or partial columns
- Inserting or deleting worksheets
- Defining or creating names
- Creating and modifying dialog boxes
- Modifying menus
- Creating and formatting charts
- Creating PivotTables
- Creating or modifying outlines
- Drawing
- Modifying styles
- Protection
- Activating OLE objects
- Saving formula entries
- Modifying macro sheets

Worksheet functions and formulas can be entered in a Shared List file. However, the user will be notified that the formula can be entered for calculation purposes but not saved.

Existing macros can be run, but macros cannot be recorded or written into a Shared List file. If you run a macro that includes an operation not supported by a Shared List file, the macro will stop, and a message will be displayed.

New Shared List Visual Basic Properties

The Visual Basic for applications interface for Shared List introduces new properties for the workbook object. These can be found in the Microsoft Excel Visual Basic Reference section of Microsoft Excel online help.

Workgroup Features for Microsoft PowerPoint

In PowerPoint, you can import an existing outline to create a new presentation or add an outline to an existing presentation. You can import outlines from Microsoft Word or another word processor. PowerPoint can read outline files in RTF (rich text format) and plain text formats. Users can create presentations from Word documents created by co-workers, as well as export the content of their presentations for use by others in the workgroup. The Presentation Conferencing feature allows a user to give an onscreen presentation for up to 64 other PowerPoint 7.0 users connected to the same local area network.

Exchanging Content Between PowerPoint and Word

Several features in PowerPoint make it easier than ever for your users to reuse existing information without retyping or reformatting.

Report-It   This button on the PowerPoint Standard toolbar exports the text from the current presentation slides to Word as an outline, using Word heading styles. Slide titles become Heading 1 text, and subordinate bullet items become Heading 2, Heading 3, and so on, up to Heading 6. Clicking the Report-It button starts Word and exports the active presentation.

Write-Up   This command on the PowerPoint Tools menu exports an entire presentation to Word. Slide images are created as embedded objects or links in Word, and text from Notes pages associated with each slide is placed adjacent to or below the slide images, at the user's discretion. Slide images and notes are placed in Word tables, with several optional layouts.

Note   Write-Up links only the slide images in the Word document it creates. Notes Pages text content is not linked.

Exporting Black & White Slide Images   PowerPoint provides the Black and White View feature, which renders the current slide view in black and white, optimizing colors and patterns for printing on a black-and-white printer, and allows you to adjust for any problems before printing. Slide images you export to Word using the Write-Up feature normally appear in color. If you want to export black and white slide images for optimium black and white printing, click the B&W View button on the PowerPoint Standard toolbar (or the Black and White commmand on the View menu) before choosing the Write-Up command.

Slides From Outline and Slides From File   The Slides from Outline command on the PowerPoint Insert menu allows you to specify a file created by a word-processing program from which PowerPoint extracts the outline structure and creates a new slide show. The Slides From File command on the Insert menu allows you to specify a file created by PowerPoint or other presentation programs, from which PowerPoint extracts slides.

PowerPoint imports up to 9 heading levels. Heading 1 becomes the Slide title, Headings 2 through 6 become slide bullet item levels 1 though 5. Any heading levels below 6 are imported as level 5 bullet items. Body text and heading levels lower than 9 are ignored.

Meeting Minder Using the Meeting Minder command on the PowerPoint Tools menu, you can record minutes of a meeting for each slide, read and enter text on notes pages for each slide, and record action items that are placed on a new slide inserted at the end of the presentation.

The Meeting Minder includes an Export button, which sends the text you enter for meeting minutes and action items to Word. When you export from the Meeting Minder to Word, a new Word document is created and headed with the name, time, and date of the presentation, followed by headings for minutes and action items. Minutes are recorded on a per-slide basis and include sub-heads for each slide to which minutes have been added. Action items are listed in one place for the entire presentation.

PowerPoint Presentation Conferencing

PowerPoint 7.0 includes a new command on the Tools menu called Presentation Conference. With this feature, a user on one computer can control multiple instances of PowerPoint 7.0, up to 64 networked computers plus the controlling computer.

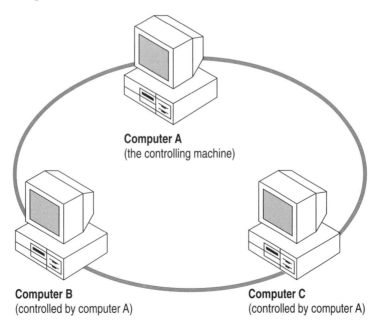

Computer A
(the controlling machine)

Computer B
(controlled by computer A)

Computer C
(controlled by computer A)

Computers on the same LAN, each with TCP/IP installed

This diagram illustrates a simple, three-computer presentation conferencing scenario. Computer A, located in Oregon, controls the presentation. Computer B in California and Computer C in Ireland are presentation nodes being controlled. Although all the computers must be connected to the same LAN, they need not be in proximity. Computer A sets up the links to computers B and C, and then launches the slide show using the Presentation Conference Wizard. In the wizard, the presenter (computer A) enters the computer names of computers B and C, indicates the control components to display on computer A during the conference (Meeting Minder, Slide Meter, and so on), and initiates the slide show on all three machines. Besides changing slides, the presenter (computer A) can review notes, create action items, monitor the time, and get private previews of other slides. However, computers B and C show only an apparently smooth-running and uninterrupted slide show.

Presentation Conferencing requires the following:

- Each computer must be connected to the same network. Remote connection via modem is not supported.
- Each computer must enable file sharing. (Click Settings, click Control Panel, click the File and Print Sharing button on the Configuration tab, and select the checkbox labeled "I want to be able to give others access to my files.")
- Each computer must have PowerPoint 7.0 installed.
- Each computer must be connected to the same LAN.
- The TCP/IP network protocol must be installed on each computer. Presentation Conferencing uses the Winsock API.

The controlling computer can display and use the following controls, which are not visible on any of the other computers:

- Slide Navigator
- Slide Miniature
- Meeting Minder
- Slide Meter
- Stage Manager Toolbar

Starting a Conference

First, the presenter needs to know the network identification of each computer that will be participating in the conference. You must gather this information from each audience member before you begin. To find a computer's name, click the Windows 95 Start button, point to Settings and click Control Panel, double-click the Network icon, and click the Identification tab.

Tip You can use the Save List and Open List buttons in the Presentation Conference Wizard to save and reuse lists of audience computer names, called Conference Address Lists. These files are saved in the My Documents folder by default, and are given the .cfl file extension. You can save multiple address lists for different audience groups.

Each user who wants to participate in the conference must also choose the Presentation Conference command, select the Audience option, and must click the Finish button in the Presentation Conference Wizard before the presenter does. All audience members must complete this sequence before the presenter can start the conference. After the conference is under way, no new audience members can join the conference.

About the Local Presentation Files

When the connection is made, each presentation node copies the presentation file from the host computer into its Windows\Temp folder, named with the standard temporary-file naming scheme. The presentation opens as an untitled presentation on each of the audience members' computer. At the end of the conference, the presentation remains open on each computer. If the file is closed, the temporary file is discarded. The audience member can, however, save the presentation instead of discarding it, so make sure not to leave information you don't want to share in your slides or notes pages.

The Presenter's Control Panel

When running a presentation conference, the presentation control panel is used by the presenter to control many aspects of the presentation using the mouse.

The controls available on the control panel are:

Control Panel Section	Control	Description
Slides	Next Slide	Advances to the next non-hidden slide.
	Previous Slide	Goes back to the previous non-hidden slide.
Screen Controls	Pen	Activates the pen for drawing on slides. Drawings appear on audience computers when the presenter releases the mouse button after each drawing.
	Erase Annotations	Erases on-screen drawings on all computers.
	Black Out Screen	Blacks out the screen. Button remains depressed until presenter clicks it again.

Control Panel Section	Control	Description
Tools	View Meeting Minder	Launches the Meeting Minder.
	View Slide Navigator	Launches the Slide Navigator.
	View Slide Timer	Launches the Slide Timer.
	Send Slide button	Sends the Action Items slide to the audience.
End Show button		Ends the slide show.

Using the Pen for Whiteboard Meetings

Using slides with plain backgrounds (or a blank slide) and the Presentation Conferencing feature, you can conduct a *whiteboard* meeting, in which each audience member can, in turn, make comments using onscreen drawing. Using the pen, the presenter can draw directly on slides. Each audience member can also use the pen to draw on slides during a presentation. Each pen annotation is broadcast to all other audience members as soon as the mouse button is released.

Playing OLE Objects During Conferences

Objects, such as sound or video clips that play when double-clicked, will play on the presenter's computer, but not on the audience computers. Similarly, if you double-click embedded static objects such as drawings or graphs to activate the OLE server application for editing, the action is not displayed on audience computers.

However, sound effects applied to build sequences using the Animation Settings command will play on audience computers, provided the computers are equipped with the necessary hardware and software to play sounds.

Workgroup Features for Microsoft Word

This section describes tools your workgroup can use to more easily share and manage Word documents easier.

Distributing Documents with Word Viewer

Word Viewer is a scaled down version of Word that displays and prints Word documents, but does not allow editing. With Word Viewer, anyone in your workgroup or organization that does not have Word can view and print Word documents. Word Viewer does not require you to take additional steps to get your source documents into a distributable and readable format. Word Viewer users get the same page fidelity, viewing and printing options as regular Word users.

There are two Word Viewer applications for different operating systems. Both are included on the Office Resource Kit CD-ROM. For installation instructions, see Appendix D, "Contents of the Office Resource Kit CD." The two Word Viewer applications are:

- Word Viewer for Windows 95 and Windows NT 3.51. This is a full 32-bit application and fully supports Word 7.0 documents.

- Word 6.0 for Windows Viewer. This is a 16-bit application and runs under Windows 3.1, Windows 95, and Windows NT 3.51. However, it does not have the Word 7.0 look and feel and can only read files that follow the MS-DOS 8.3 file naming convention. Any highlighting done with the Highlighting button in Word 7.0 will not be visible when the document is viewed with the 16-bit Viewer.

Word Viewer users can:

- Open any document created in Word for Windows, version 2.0 or later, and Word for the Macintosh, version 4.0 or later.

- View a document in Normal, Outline, Page Layout, or Full Screen view.

- Print a document with the same fidelity as is provided in Word.

- Copy text or graphics out of a document.

- View annotations previously made to a document.

- Activate embedded OLE objects in a document. However, the user cannot save changes made in the object after the OLE server has been closed.

Word Viewer users cannot:

- Cut text out of or paste text into a document.

- Save any changes to a document.

- Use Word Viewer with the Internet Assistant to browse hyperlinked documents.

- Update fields, except for the FILLIN field. However, changes made with the FILLIN field cannot be saved because Word Viewer cannot save changes to a Word document.

- Create, modify, or run macros.

- Create annotations.

- Use revision marks.

- Display pictures in documents created in Word for the Macintosh.

- Display linked pictures.

> **Tip** To achieve higher fidelity in your documents when they are viewed on other systems with Word Viewer, use TrueType fonts and embed them in the document. In Word, click Options on the Tools menu. Click the Save tab, and select the Embed TrueType Fonts check box. If possible, also select the same printer driver that your Word Viewer users have access to.

Word Viewer is freeware; you can distribute it freely to any number of Windows users. Versions of Word Viewer for MS-DOS, the Macintosh, and other operating systems are not available.

Create, Share and Explore Documents on the World Wide Web with Internet Assistant

Internet Assistant is a free add-on program that enables users of Word for Windows 95 and Windows NT 3.51 to share information on the World Wide Web, a global network of servers on the Internet. Internet Assistant allows your workgroup to use the familiar interface in Word to create documents for the World Wide Web in Hypertext Markup Language (HTML). Internet Assistant has Web browsing capabilities built in, so users can test hyperlinks as they write as well as retrieve information from the World Wide Web without ever leaving Word.

Another great use of Internet Assistant is to create webs of linked Word documents on a local area network. Even if your workgroup does not have Internet access, individuals can still create and browse through Word documents that include links to other documents, including documents with embedded OLE objects. This makes Internet Assistant and Word a great combination for in-house document libraries. For more information about using Internet Assistant to link documents on a local area network, see "Creating a Document Library in Your Organization" later in this chapter.

Browsing with Internet Assistant

With an Internet connection and Internet Assistant for Word, you can connect to and browse the World Wide Web. Users on a local area network can also use Internet Assistant to browse through or create linked documents on a local area network. You also have access to the most popular Internet services because Internet Assistant comes with built-in support for the key Internet protocols: HTTP, FTP, and Gopher. Internet Assistant does not directly support Internet e-mail, however.

Browsing the World Wide Web requires an existing Internet connection via a server (or proxy), or a dialup SLIP/PPP account. The software and hardware to make this connection is not included with Internet Assistant. You must obtain Internet connectivity from an Internet service provider.

Editing with Internet Assistant

Internet Assistant is designed to make it easy for users to create documents for the World Wide Web even if they have never done so before. Internet Assistant lets users automatically convert Word documents to HTML, the standard format for the World Wide Web. Users who want to apply their own HTML styles to documents they create from scratch can do so simply by applying styles in Word. Internet Assistant also installs a unique toolbar that makes it easy to create hyperlinks in either Word or HTML documents and insert horizontal borders and graphics.

Note Internet Assistant creates HTML documents, while Microsoft SGML Author for Word converts between Word text styles and SGML tags. Internet Assistant is not suitable for full SGML authoring.

Internet Assistant gives you the option of creating Internet documents in either Word native format or HTML format. Word native format allows you to fully benefit from the rich formatting capabilities in Word so documents can include multiple columns, text wrapped around graphics, and OLE embedded objects. HTML format does not support these advanced features.

Installing and Distributing Internet Assistant

Internet Assistant is freeware; you can distribute it freely to any number of Windows users.

Note The 16-bit version of Internet Assistant supports only Word 6.0a and 6.0c. The 32-bit version of Internet Assistant, described here, supports Word 7.0.

Internet Assistant is available from several sources. Depending on where you obtain Internet Assistant, it may be in the form of a single compressed, self-extracting file, or it may be in the form of a Setup program and several other files. You can obtain Internet Assistant from any of these sources:

- On the Microsoft Home Page of the World Wide Web. To access the Microsoft Home Page, connect to the Internet and use the following URL:

  HTTP://WWW.MICROSOFT.COM

- On CompuServe, GEnie™, and Microsoft OnLine. You can find Internet Assistant in the Microsoft Software Library.

- From the Microsoft Download Service (MSDL), which you can reach by calling (206) 936-6735. This service is available 24 hours a day, 7 days a week. The highest download speed available is 14,400 bits per second (bps). For more information about using the MSDL, call (800) 936-4100 and follow the prompts.

For more information, see Appendix F, "Resources."

▶ **To install Internet Assistant**

1. Obtain Internet Assistant from one of the sources noted above.

2. If you obtained the self-extracting file, double-click it to extract the contents of the file.

3. Run the Internet Assistant Setup program.

For detailed instructions on using Internet Assistant, install Internet Assistant and refer to the Help and sample documents that are included.

Creating a Document Library in Your Organization

In addition to using Internet Assistant to browse and author for the World Wide Web, you can use Internet Assistant to create a local library of linked Word documents on a local area network. Users equipped with Internet Assistant and Word can author and browse these documents saved in Word format.

For example, your workgroup could have its own home page in the form of a Word document with hotlinks to other documents. If your workgroup has Internet access, these documents could include links to documents on the World Wide Web as well as documents stored on a local area network. Because the Internet Assistant supports the document format in Word, you can use all of the Word formatting and page layout features and OLE embedded objects.

CHAPTER 16

Microsoft Access
Database Replication

Microsoft Access provides MIS professionals and database administrators with a powerful, new tool for distributed computing: database replication. Using the database replication feature, database administrators can reproduce a database in a way that enables two (or more) end users to work on their own replica of the database at the same time. Once created, the replicas can be located on different computers, in different offices, or even in different countries, and the replicas will stay synchronized with one another. The replicas are synchronized on a user-defined schedule or on demand through network sharing, or modem dial-up communication. This chapter assists you in planning, creating, and administering replicas of your database.

In This Chapter

Why Replicate Databases?

In an ideal world, all the users in your organization would have access to centralized databases, so that everyone could work with the most complete and up-to-date data available. All users would be connected 24 hours a day, seven days a week. And your organization would have a totally fault-tolerant network that stretched to each satellite office around the world.

However, chances are your organization does not have the financial resources and staff to create an ideal world. Some of your workers are probably on the road more than they are in their office. Your corporate network might not be available all the time nor are all your satellite offices connected to it. Your centralized database might become corrupted at some time or the central server might fail.

To help overcome the real-world challenges of centralized data and decentralized workers, Microsoft Jet database engine provides you with database replication tools that can address at least six majjor issues in distributed computing:

- Sharing data among offices
- Sharing data among dispersed users
- Limited access to server data
- Distributing software application updates
- Load balancing
- Backing up data

Each of these replication applications is described further in this section.

Share Data Among Offices

More and more companies are establishing satellite offices outside their immediate geographic area. The new offices can be hundreds—or even thousands—of miles away from the location of the corporate network. Companies with limited resources find it too expensive to install a wide area network (WAN) that is available full-time to connect the various offices. The less expensive alternative is to supply each office with its own copy of the corporate database, which then can be accessed locally.

Database replication can be used to create the replicas of the corporate database (for example the names, addresses, and special handling of media contacts around the world) to send to each satellite office. Read-only replicas can easily be distributed to all offices whenever the database administrator wants to send out changes to the database. However, if the remote locations also need to be entering data into their replicas, those replicas can be synchronized with the replica at corporate headquarters. At the same time that the replicas are synchronizing corporate level information, an individual replica can maintain local tables that contain information not propagated to the other replicas in the set. A replica could, for example, be used to update the list of local media contacts, synchronize that list with the corporate list for general mailings, and yet maintain a strictly local list of media events in the immediate geographic area.

Share Data Among Dispersed Users

More and more companies are also confronted with the problem of dispersed users. Dispersed end users cannot be directly connected into an organization's network because their job requires them to be mobile. Companies with limited resources cannot afford wireless LANs to keep field staff (for example, sales people) in constant touch with the database. The less expensive alternative is to supply each field staff person with a copy of the relevant database to carry with him or her on a laptop computer.

Without database replication, a salesperson in the field might have to rely on *file synchronization*, in which the dates and times of files are compared and the later file overwrites the earlier file. File synchronization is not sophisticated enough to recognize or handle parallel modifications to multiple copies of the same file. Whichever file was modified last becomes the winner and the changes in the other file are lost. With database replication, however, the new information being entered into any replica of the database while a salesperson is out of the office can be synchronized anytime the salesperson establishes an electronic link with the corporate network. As part of his or her workday routine, a salesperson can dial into the network when he or she gets to the hotel room, synchronize the replica, and always be working on the most current version of the database.

Make Server Data Accessible

Many companies traditionally place their data into large, centralized databases located on mainframe computers and have limited the access to that data for management or security control. With the growing trend toward decentralization and "right-sizing," corporate information services managers are realizing the need to share more data across administrative and operating units.

Introducing a second server with its own copy of the database helps to alleviate the burden and improve response time. However, a second server also introduces the challenge of keeping the two copies of the database synchronized. If the two copies do not have to be in up-to-the-minute synchronization, database replication can inexpensively balance the load. With database replication, you can reproduce the database on two servers. One group of users—for example, claims adjusters—query one server, while another group of users—for example, service representatives—query the second server.

Using replication to balance loads across multiple servers works well in applications where end users query the database for decision rules, guidelines, price lists, historical data, template information, and other read-only or otherwise stable data. These applications don't need to have data updated in real time, but do need to have data updates as soon as practical. The database administrator determines the schedule for synchronizing the replicas and can adjust that schedule to meet changing user demands. Although replication provides less centralized administration of the database, it offers greater flexibility in combining access to centralized data with access to local data and objects.

Distribute Application Updates

The major focus of database replication is to easily distribute data to end users. However, database replication is also useful to database administrators for distributing updates to a software application. If the application is embedded in the database (as with Microsoft Visual Basic for applications modules), then replicating the database automatically replicates not only the data in the data tables but also the application routines or modules. If you make changes to the design of the database, the changes are transmitted during the next synchronization exchange; you don't have to distribute complete new versions of the software.

Backup Data

At first glance, database replication might appear to be very similar to copying a database. However, while replication makes a complete copy of the database initially, thereafter it simply synchronizes that replica's objects with the original objects at regular intervals. This copy can be used to back up data if the original database is destroyed. Furthermore, users at any replica can continue to access the database during the entire backup process.

Database replication, then, provides automatic data backup for each of the replicas in the replica set. Replicas are synchronized either at scheduled intervals or when a user demands it. Instead of using a separate copy or backup program for maintaining backup copies on different computers or at different facilities, automatic backup can be made an integral part of the database.

Replication Is Not Always the Best Solution

Although database replication can help solve many of the problems inherent in distributed database processing, it is important to recognize the situations in which replication is not the best solution. Applications that process a large number of transactions or that require up-to-the-minute data consistency might be better served by a centralized database.

Large numbers of record updates at multiple replicas   Applications that require frequent updating of existing records at different replicas are likely to experience a larger number of record conflicts than are applications that simply insert new records into a database. The greater potential for two changes to the same record (although different fields within the record) during synchronization would result in more record conflicts and require more time for someone to manually resolve those conflicts.

Data consistency is critical   Applications that rely on information being correct at all times, such as funds transfer and airline reservations, usually use a transaction method. While transactions can be processed within a replica, there is no support for processing transactions across replicas.

Tools for Implementing Replication

There are four sets of tools for implementing database replication in your organization.

- **Briefcase replication**   Windows 95 allows users to use replication when they drag a file into their Briefcase. If the file is a Microsoft Access for Windows 95 database, the file is converted to a replicated database with the Design Master remaining at the source and a replica placed in the Briefcase. As described above, the user can take their replica with them into the field and later synchronize the changes on their laptops replica with changes made to the Design Master.

- **Microsoft Access for Windows 95 replication**   Microsoft Access for Windows 95 provides users replication commands directly from the Access Tools menu while they are working in their database. Users can point to Replication on the Tools menu and have a choice of creating a replica, synchronizing their replica with another replica in the set, or resolving synchronization conflicts. Microsoft Access for Windows 95 also supports database replication when run under Microsoft Windows NT 3.51.

- **Replication Manager utility**   If you need to manage a large number of replicas, support laptop users who are not always connected to a network, create replicas of more than one database, set the schedules for synchronizing replicas, or have tools for troubleshooting errors, you can use the Replication Manager program provided in the Microsoft Access Developer's Toolkit. The Replication Manager provides a visual interface for converting databases, creating replicas, viewing the relationships between replicas, and setting the properties on replicas. The Microsoft Replication Manager also runs under Microsoft Windows NT 3.51.

- **Replication through DAO programming**   Several of the functions of Briefcase replication are available to developers and MIS support staff through data access object (DAO) programming. For more information on programming database replication into custom applications, see Chapter 19, "Using Database Replication" in *Building Applications with Microsoft Access for Windows 95*. If you have third-party developers providing database programs to your organization, they might use DAO programming to add replication functions to their existing applications.

Because organizations differ in which of the four tools they use to implement database replication, the remainder of this chapter addresses the concepts, planning, implementation, and troubleshooting issues that are common across all four sets of tools. The next section begins the discussion by introducing concepts that might be new to or different from the way your organization is currently sharing data.

Architecture of Database Replication

The successful and efficient use of database replication begins with understanding the architecture and operation of each component in the replication process. Microsoft Jet database engine replication has four major components:

- Nonreplicable database
- Replica set
- Members of the replica set
- Transporter

Each component is described in detail in this section.

Nonreplicable Database

Microsoft Jet databases are not replicable until they are converted into a replicable form. To create replicas of an existing Microsoft Jet database, you can use one of the following methods:

- Drag the database file into the Briefcase.
- Point to Replication on the Microsoft Access Tools menu and click Create Replica.
- Use the Convert Database To Replica command on the File menu in Replication Manager.

Depending on which of these three methods you use, If you use Replication Manager to convert your database, the Convert Database to Replica wizard will ask you a series of questions about the database to be converted and the replica set being created.

Important If you protect a database with a database password, you prevent replicas from synchronizing with each other. Before you begin using replication, remove any database password protection from the database you will be making replicable. Setting user permissions does not interfere with replica synchronization.

During the conversion process your original *filename*.mdb file is enhanced through the addition of several system fields, system tables, and replication properties (described later in this chapter). The enhanced database file becomes the Design Master for the replica set and retains all of the functionality it had before conversion. During conversion, you are also asked if you want to make a backup copy of the original database file. The backup copy is named *filename*.bak and is placed in the same folder as the original file. If you opt to make a backup copy, you should use it only if you ever need to create a new replica set. If some users of your database file will continue to use it in its nonreplicated form, make a copy of the database file for them before converting it to a replicable database.

Note   Replicated databases are not readable by Microsoft Access versions 1.*x* or 2.*x*.

Replica Set

Converting a nonreplicable database into a replicable database creates a *replica set*. When you first convert your nonreplicable database into a replicable database, your replica set typically has only one member—the Design Master for the set. If you do not specify a replica set name at the time the database is converted, the Microsoft Jet database engine uses the filename as the default set name. As you create replicas from the Design Master (or, later, from other replicas), you add members to the set. The new replicas are named *machinename1-setname*, *machinename2-setname*, *machinename3-setname*, and so forth, where *machinenamex* is the name of your computer as seen by other users on the network. Thus, the Design Master and all subsequent replicas comprise the replicated database and the replica set. Furthermore, the Design Master and all the replicas in the new, distributed database have a unique identity and the ability to communicate with and update one another.

Each replica set is independent from all other replica sets, and replicas in different sets can never communicate or synchronize with each other. You should never attempt to create replicas from the original, nonreplicable database file. The result would be a new replicated database and a new replica set. Instead, create additional replicas from an existing member of the replica set.

When you convert a nonreplicable database into a replicable database, the Jet database engine:

- Adds new fields to each existing table in your database.
- Adds new tables to your database.
- Adds new properties to your database.
- Changes the behavior of AutoNumber fields.
- Increases the physical size of your database file.

Each of these changes is described in this section.

New Fields

During the conversion of a database into a replicable form, the Microsoft Jet database engine first looks at the existing fields in a table to determine if any field uses both the AutoNumber data type and ReplicationID field size. The ReplicationID AutoNumber is a 16-byte value that appears in the following format:

```
{1234AB87-2314-7623-0000012340506801}
```

If no field uses that data type and field size, the Jet database engine adds the s_Guid field which stores the ReplicationID AutoNumber that uniquely identifies each record. The ReplicationID AutoNumber for a specific record is identical across all replicas.

During the conversion process, the Jet database engine also adds the fields s_Lineage, and s_Generation to each table in the database. The s_Lineage field is a binary field that contains the IDs of replicas that have updated a record and the last version created by each of those replicas. The s_Generation field stores information regarding groups of changes. An additional field is also added for every memo or OLE object in a table. The s_Guid, s_Lineage, and s_Generation system fields may or may not be visible, depending on whether the System Objects check box on the View tab of the Options command on the Tools menu is selected or cleared.

Note All of the new fields in a replicated table are accessible only by Microsoft Access and cannot be directly manipulated by the user or developer. However, these fields can be viewed when you are resolving data conflicts.

New Tables

The Jet database engine adds several new tables to the database during the conversion process. Most of these tables are system tables, which are not normally visible to users and cannot be manipulated by developers. The following table describes the four tables of interest to you as a database administrator.

Name	Description
MSysSidetable	Identifies the tables that experienced a conflict and the name of the sidetable that contains the conflicting records. This table is visible only if a conflict has occurred between the user's replica and another replica in the set.
MSysErrors	Identifies where and why errors occurred during data synchronization.
MSysSchemaProb	Identifies errors that occurred while synchronizing the design of the replica. This table is visible only if a design conflict has occurred between the user's replica and another replica in the set.
MSysExchangeLog	Stores information about exchanges that have taken place between replicas.

To view these four tables and the other system tables, select the System Objects check box on the View tab of the Options command on the Tools menu in Microsoft Access.

New Properties

The Microsoft Jet database engine adds new properties to your database when it becomes replicable: **Replicable**, **ReplicaID**, **DesignMasterID**. The **Replicable** property is set to "T", indicating the database is now replicable. Once the property is set to "T", however, it cannot be changed. Setting the property to "F" (or any value other than "T") returns an error message. The **ReplicaID** is a 16-byte value that provides the Design Master or replica with a unique identification.

The **DesignMasterID** property can be used to create a replica the new Design Master for the replica set. This property should be set only at the current Design Master. Under extreme circumstances—for example, the loss of the original Design Master—you can set the property at the current replica. However, setting this property at a replica, when there is already another Design Master, might partition your replica set into two irreconcilable sets and prevent any further synchronization of data.

Warning   Never create a second Design Master in a replica set. The existence of a second Design Master can result in the loss of data.

The Jet database engine allows developers to append and set two new properties on the individual tables, indexes, forms, reports, macros, and modules in a database: **KeepLocal** and **Replicable**. The **KeepLocal** property can be set to "T" prior to converting a database into a replicable form to keep the object from being copied to the other replicas in the set. After the database is converted, the **Replicable** property can be set to "T" to make a local object replicated. These two properties are described in more detail later in this chapter.

Changes the Behavior of AutoNumber Fields

When you convert a nonreplicable database to a replicated database, the AutoNumber fields in your tables change from incremental to random. All existing AutoNumber fields retain their values, but new values for inserted records are random numbers. Random AutoNumber fields are not meaningful because they aren't in any particular order and the highest value isn't on the record inserted last. When you open a table with a random AutoNumber key, the records appear in the order of ascending random numbers, not in chronological order. With random AutoNumber fields, it is possible for two different records to be assigned the same value. If this happens, updates could be made in incorrect records. If you experience such problems, consider using the s_Guid field as the primary key. Because all numbers in the s_Guid field are unique, each record will have a different AutoNumber.

Before you convert your nonreplicable database into a replicated database, determine if any of your applications or users rely on the order and incremental nature of the AutoNumber field. If so, you can use an additional Date/Time field to provide sequential ordering information.

Increases in the Physical Size of Your Database

The addition of three new fields during the conversion process imposes two limitations on your tables. First, Microsoft Jet database engine allows a maximum of 2048 bytes in a record, of which at least 48 bytes are used by replication. The total number of bytes now available in a record in a replicated table is

>   2048 bytes
> - (16 byte Guid value)
> - (4 bytes * the number of long value fields)
> - (4 bytes for the generation)
> - (24 bytes for Guid and generation indexes)
> - (4 bytes * the number of replicas that have ever made changes to the record)
> = number of bytes now available

Second, Microsoft Jet database engine allows a maximum of 255 fields in a table, of which at least three fields are used by replication. The total number of fields now available in a replicated table is

>   255 fields
> - (3 system fields)
> - (1 field * the number of long value fields)
> = number of fields now available

Few well-designed applications use all the available fields in a table or characters in a record. However, if you have a large number of Memo fields or OLE object fields in your table, you need to be aware of your remaining resources.

In addition to decreasing the available number of characters and fields, Microsoft Jet database engine replication also imposes a limitation on the number of nested transactions allowed. Whereas you can have a maximum of seven nested transactions in a nonreplicable database, a replicated database can have a maximum of six nested transactions.

Members of the Replica Set

When a nonreplicable Microsoft Jet database is converted into a replicable database, the database file by default becomes the Design Master for the newly created replica set. The number of members in the replica set grows as replicas are created from either the Design Master or existing replicas. Similarly, the number of members in the replica set decreases as individual replicas are deleted.

Design Master

The Design Master for the replicated database, *machinenameX-setname,* contains a complete set of objects from the original, nonreplicable database (*filename*.mdb). If you use the Replication Manager to create replicas, you can use the Create Replica wizard to determine which objects in the database will be included in the new replica. For example, you may want the replica at a satellite office to contain all the data tables except for Salaries and all reports except Bonuses. Neither the Briefcase nor the Create Replica command in Microsoft Access allow you to select specific objects to be included.

Microsoft Jet database engine allows only a single Design Master in a database so that users at multiple replicas cannot make conflicting changes to the database's structure, objects, or design. Any changes to the design of the database, or to any of the replicated tables, forms, queries, reports, macros, and modules in the database can be done only in the Design Master. If the Design Master is erased or corrupted, you can make a replica the new Design Master; but there must be only one Design Master at a time. You can make a replica the new Design Master by using one of the following methods:

- Using Microsoft Access to open the replica you want to make the new Design Master. Point to Replication on the Microsoft Access Tools menu and click Synchronize Now. Select the current Design Master as the member to synchronize with, and check the box that says "Make *filename* the Design Master."

- Using Microsoft Replication Manager to open the replica you want to make the new Design Master. On the Tools menu, click Designate New Design Master.

Although the Microsoft Jet database engine allows only a single Design Master and prohibits any changes to the structure of the database except in the Design Master, the Replication Manager allows you to determine whether the data in each replica can be changed. At the time a replica is created, it is given either read-write or read-only privileges. A user of any replica with read-write privileges can update the information in the database and that information will update the same records in all other replicas in the database. A user of a replica with read-only privilege cannot make changes to the replicated data but can make changes to local tables or other local objects.

Replicas Can Be Created From Other Replicas

Although changes to the design of the database can be made only at the Design Master, replicas can be made from the Design Master or any existing replica in the set. In fact, the only way for new copies of the database to be included in the replica set is for them to be created from an existing replica. Once created, all new replicas become part of the replica set; and once removed, they can never rejoin the replica set. A replica is automatically removed from the set if it does not synchronize with another replica in the set within the retention period.

Local Customization

End users can customize the replica used at their location. The user can attach additional tables, develop additional objects, and create links to other data tables. However, the Microsoft Jet database engine recognizes that the locally produced attachments and objects are for local use only and will not transport them to the other replicas during an exchange. Only changes to the objects created by the Design Master and specifically designated as replicated are exchanged with other replicas. Thus, the user can share data and objects with other replicas while customizing database functions, components or appearance.

Transporter

For database replication to be useful, it is not enough for there just to be multiple replicas of the same database. The replicas must communicate with one another to stay synchronized. *Synchronization* is the act or process of making the replicas identical, both in terms of the data they contain and how they are designed. As changes are made to the existing records in one replica, those changes are communicated to each of the other replicas that have that same record. Similarly, as new records are added or old records deleted from one replica, those additions and deletions are communicated to each of the other replicas in the replica set. If you use the Briefcase or Microsoft Access to synchronize your replicas, the Jet database engine is the program that handles the direct exchange of information between replicas.

If you use Replication Manager, a separate utility—called the *Transporter*—keeps track of all the changes to a replica and exchanges the updated information with other replicas. Using the Replication Manager, each replica must have a Transporter assigned to it.

Note Although you can have more than one Transporter assigned to the same replica, there is no benefit from the arrangement, and it is not recommended.

A communication link between replicas can be *direct,* if on the same computer; *network*, if on the same or connected network; or *drop box*, a location where the updated records can be left by the sending Transporter for the receiving Transporter, accessible through the network file system.

The Transporter, replica, and application may or may not all reside on the same computer. For example, in a workgroup setting, where members of a workgroup share a common replica among themselves, the replica might be on a server while the applications could reside at each workgroup computer. The Transporter might run at the server or it could be on the local administrator's computer. One case where the Transporter would definitely not run at the server occurs when a non-Windows server, such as Novell, holds the replica. In this case, the Transporter must run on another computer running either Microsoft Windows 95 or Microsoft Windows NT 3.51.

The Transporter is configured through the Replication Manager user interface. When the Replication Manager is first configured on a computer, the user is asked for the network and folders to be used by the Transporter and whether the Transporter should be started automatically each time the computer is started. If the user selects automatic startup, a shortcut to the Transporter program is placed in the Start menu. To change the Transporter startup to manual mode, you should move the Transporter icon to the Microsoft Access folder.

The status of the Transporter is reported through the Replication Manager user interface. At the lower-right corner of the map of the replica set, there is an image of two computers with a connection. The image between the computers changes as the status of the Transporter changes, and a legend explains the status of the Transporter. For information about restarting the Transporter if it has stopped, see the online Help in Replication Manager.

Planning for Replication

Implementing and managing database replication can be challenging, but careful planning can prevent problems and improve the efficiency of the replication system. This section discusses two questions that database administrators need to address while planning their use of replication. These questions are:

- What schedule do you want to follow for synchronizing replicas?
- Do you want single or multiple data masters?

Each of these questions is explored in this section.

When Do You Want to Synchronize Members in the Replica Set?

In planning the design and consistency of your database, you should give careful consideration to both the order in which updates are routed among members in the replica set and the schedule for initiating updates. If you are using Briefcase or Microsoft Access commands only, then synchronization is always done on demand and only between the current replica and the replica specified by the user. If you are using Replication Manager, you have greater control over the sequence and timetable for synchronization.

Replica Topology

The physical layout of your network can interact with the number and location of replicas to make your database more complex. If all members in the replica set exist on the same network and can be updated simultaneously, the order in which they update one another is less significant. Under database replication, all members ultimately update one another, but the latency in the chaining can be important. If A updates B, which updates C, which updates B, which updates A, then the time lag between B and C can be important. On the other hand, if A updates both B and C, and then B updates C, A is provided with the more current information sooner. The developer and database administrator need to work together to determine the order in which updates are propagated throughout the database.

A second aspect of topology is whether the members being synchronized are directly or indirectly connected. If two members are directly connected, then the Transporter performing the synchronization is able to open both members simultaneously. Even though each members might be located on a separate computer, it is possible for a Transporter to connect to each member through the network. If the Transporter cannot simultaneously open both members—either because there is no common network or the member is temporarily removed from the network—then the members are indirectly connected.

For a replica set member to synchronize with another, indirectly connected member, the Transporter for the first member must leave a message for the Transporter of the second member and wait for the second member to process the message. The return message to the first Transporter may take a few minutes, hours, or days, depending upon how often the second member connects to the network. Synchronizing a directly connected member bypasses the second Transporter completely. Direct exchanges are processed much faster than indirect exchanges. To determine whether an exchange is direct, look at the Exchange details in the Synch History.

Scheduled Updates

Synchronizing members in a replica set means that one member sends another member its changes, and then the second member sends its changes back to the first one. In Replication Manager, scheduled updates are programmed ahead of time so they occur at anticipated times and can be completed unattended. However, under certain circumstances, the user might want to synchronize all members immediately, or on demand. If you are using Briefcase or Microsoft Access commands, synchronization can only be done on demand.

The schedule for updating all the members has important consequences for the accuracy of the data and the overhead cost of the system. When planning the exchange schedule, keep in mind any differences in time zones, office hours, and telecommunication rates. For example, scheduling an update for midnight in New York means the update arrives a few minutes later in Rome at 5:00 AM local time. Also, with the presence of dispersed end users and dispersed offices, the scheduled update might not occur right away. Although the start of the update is triggered at the time specified, the update might have to sit on a server for hours or days until the target Transporter picks up the update. The target Transporter may or may not initiate the return exchange right away, adding further delays to the completion of the synchronization process.

Interacting Features Result in Increasing Replica Complexity

Generating and managing replicas is easier for some databases than others. Certain characteristics of the database—for example, whether it has a single data master rather than multiple data masters—have a major impact on the exchange process and the likelihood that there will be conflicts during an exchange. The overall combination of characteristics may make for increasingly complex databases and increase the likelihood of conflicts during updates.

Listed in order of increasing complexity, these include:

- Single data master
- Single data master with attached tables
- Single data master with attached tables and a large number of replicas
- Multiple data master
- Multiple data masters with attached tables
- Multiple data masters with attached tables and a large number of replicas
- Multiple data masters using Briefcase
- Multiple data master with automatic cascading and a large number of replicas

When planning your application, be sure to carefully consider how the characteristics of your database interact to increase its complexity. For additional technical information on how the Microsoft Jet database engine implements replication, see Chapter 7, "Replication" in the *Microsoft Jet Engine Programmer's Guide*.

Managing Replicas

After users have created replicas, the synchronization process is fairly automatic and requires little administrator involvement. Two issues that often arise at this point are the steps to maintain database security and elimination of routine backups of the database. This section discusses both of these issues.

Database Security

Replicated databases use the same security model as non-replicable databases: a user's permissions for the database are determined at the time he or she starts Microsoft Access and logs on. It is up to you as the database administrator to ensure that the same security information is available at each location where a replica is used. There are two methods to achieve this. First, the identical security file, System.mdw, can be made available to users at each location where a replica is used. The security file cannot be replicated but can be physically copied to each location. Second, you can re-create the entries for users and groups at each location in the local security file by entering exactly the same user and group names with associated PIDs at each location. Modifications to permissions is a design change and can only be made at the Design Master.

New security permissions have been introduced to control certain aspects of database replication. A new permission—Administrator on the database object—has been defined. By default, this permission is granted to the Users and Admins groups plus the current logged on user when a new database is created or converted from an earlier version of Microsoft Access. It is up to you as the database administrator to restrict this permission to selected users if security is to be enforced.

With the new security permissions, a user must have Administrator permission on the database to:

- Convert a non-replicable database into a replicated database.

- Make a local object replicated or make a replicated object local. These actions can be taken only at the current Design Master.

- Make a replica the new Design Master. This action can be taken at any replica in the set; however, there must never be more than one Design Master in a set at one time.

Avoid Making Backups of Replicas

You should not back up and restore replicas using copy or backup commands as you would with non-replica files. In particular, backing up and restoring the Design Master could result in it becoming irrevocably different in structure from the replicas in the set. If the Design Master becomes corrupted, simply make a replica of the new Design Master. Do not copy or restore an older version of the Design Master. To make a replica of the new Design Master, use the Recover Design Master command on the Microsoft Access Replication submenu.

Warning   A copy of the Design Master created through Copy and Paste commands might not be able to synchronize with the other members of the replica set.

A database can be a member of a replica set only by being replicated from a Design Master or an existing replica. Creating a database externally and then modifying its structure, data, and objects to be identical with the Design Master does not work because the new database still requires unique AutoNumbers which cannot be created by users. Furthermore, the replica would not have the replica-specific system tables necessary for it to synchronize with other replicas.

Troubleshooting Conflicts

Using database replication may result in occasional conflicts that must be resolved by the database administrator. This section helps you troubleshoot one potential source of errors—an incompatibility with earlier versions of Microsoft Access—and two sources of conflicts—synchronization conflicts and manual adjustments to the replica that is not chosen.

Compatibility with Earlier Versions of Microsoft Access

Previous versions of the Microsoft Jet database engine did not have the capability to replicate databases. Therefore, versions of Microsoft Access prior to Microsoft Access for Windows 95 cannot use replicated databases. However, Microsoft Access for Windows 95 can use databases created with earlier versions of Microsoft Access, but it cannot make them replicable in their present form. Version 1.*x* and 2.0 databases must be converted to Microsoft Access for Windows 95 format before they can be made replicable.

Synchronization Conflicts

When you synchronize replicas, conflict between versions is always possible because the same record might be updated at two different locations. If this happens, the Jet database engine cannot determine which of the two changes should take precedence—even if the changes occur in different fields.

The Microsoft Jet database engine accepts the changes from one replica and records the changes of the other in a conflict table at the location where the change occurred. By default, the record with the most changes since the last exchange has priority. The Jet database engine does not look at the content of the data that has changed; instead, it examines the version number of the record. The update with the higher version number is chosen because it is assumed that the replica changed the most is the correct version. Each time a change is made to the data in a record, the version number increases by one. For example, a record with no changes has a version number of 0. A change to data changes the version number to 1. A second change to the same data, or a change to different data in the record, changes the version number to 2. When two replicas give an updated record the same version number, the Jet database engine chooses which update to accept based upon Replica IDs. Because you cannot change the algorithm used, be prepared to manually resolve the conflicts at any member of the replica set. For more information on how Microsoft Jet handles synchronization conflicts, see Chapter 7, "Replication" in the *Microsoft Jet Engine Programmer's Guide*.

Conflict tables derive both their names and fields from the underlying tables. Conflict table names are in the form *table*_Conflict, where *table* is the original table name. For example, if the original table name is Customers, the conflict table name is Customers_Conflict. Because conflicts are reported only to the replica that originated the losing update, conflict tables are not replicated.

Manual Resolution of Conflicts

After synchronizing two members in the replica set, you should review the database for conflicts and determine whether any further action must be taken. If a conflict has occurred for a specific table, you will see a conflict table, *tablename*_Conflict, appear on the list of database tables and a message the next time you open the database at the replica whos data change lost to the other member. The message states that a conflict has occurred and asks if you want Microsoft Access to assist you in resolving these conflicts. If you request assistance, Microsoft Access displays all the tables having conflicts and the number of conflicts in each table. After you select a table having a conflict, Microsoft Access sequentially displays the records where conflicts occurred and gives you the option of copying the field to the database, copying all fields in the record to the database, or deleting the conflicting record.

You can also point to Replication on the Microsoft Access Tools menu and click Resolve Conflicts to display the form showing any conflicts between your replica and the member you synchronized with. You can then examine the conflicts and work through them record by record, fixing whatever is appropriate. Possible actions include:

- Manually entering the data from the conflict table into the database.
- Leaving the database unchanged and delete the record from the conflict table.
- Developing a custom conflict resolution program.
- Conferring with users to determine whether procedural changes are necessary in how replicas are synchronized.

If you have a custom conflict resolution program you want to use in place of the default program in Microsoft Access, you can specify that program as a custom property for the replicated database. To install the custom program, click Database Properties on the Microsoft Access File menu. Click the Custom tab; enter ReplicationConflictFunction as the name of the property and select Text as the Type of property. Enter the name of the custom program, followed by (), as the Value of the property. After the members of the replica set are synchronized again, the custom program will be available to all users.

Summary

This chapter introduced the concept of database replication, the major features of a replicated database, and the situations where replication is likely to be most successful. As you begin to apply the Microsoft Jet database replication capabilities, keep in mind the following:

- Multiple data masters can exist within a replicated database; data can be changed at any of the replicas having read-write access.
- A replicated database has a single Design Master and the design of the replicated objects can be changed only at the Design Master.
- A replicated database can have a mix of read-write and read-only replicas.
- Replicating a database changes the incremental Autonumber field to a random Autonumber field, thereby possibly affecting applications that depend on that counter.
- During the synchronization of two members in a replica set, only changed elements are propagated between the members.
- In a replicated database, the table record, not the field, is the smallest manipulated unit.
- A replicated database doesn't replicate attached tables. Each member of the replica set must attach the tables separately.
- Local objects can be made replicated if they are moved to the Design Master and marked as replicated.
- Whenever possible, synchronize the Design Master and all replicas in the set before making changes to the design of the database.

In addition to these general guidelines, also keep in mind the following as you develop your actual replication applications:

- Your replicated database will be physically larger than the original database because of the addition of extra fields to your tables and extra tables to your database. Set aside the appropriate amount of space on the hard drive. Also, set aside enough disk space to accommodate the optional back up copy of the database made during the conversion process.
- Determine the order in which you want the members to propagate updates across the replica set, recognizing that the exchanges are sequential rather than simultaneous.
- Determine the overall time frame for initiating and completing synchronization, recognizing that a replica set member may be on a laptop computer that is periodically disconnected from the network.

- Establish a procedure or algorithm for examining conflict tables and resolving conflicts.

- Determine which replica will be made the new Design Master if the old Design Master is accidentally erased or otherwise unavailable.

- Identify compatibility issues stemming from earlier versions of Microsoft Access being unable to use replicated databases.

- Determine how the features of your database will interact under replication.

P A R T   5

Switching from Other Applications

Chapter 17, "Switching to Microsoft Access," was written for the person managing the transition to Microsoft Access from another database management system. The chapter describes both the complete transition of organizations to Microsoft Access, and the sharing of database resources between those who have converted to Microsoft Access and those still using another database management system. The products covered include dBASE, FoxPro, and Paradox.

Chapter 18, "Switching to Microsoft Excel," covers the issues that arise when a workgroup is moving to Microsoft Excel from another spreadsheet application. This chapter is intended as a starting point to be used in the transition process, and offers guidance and information specific to that process. The products covered include Lotus 1-2-3, Borland Quattro Pro™ for MS-DOS and Windows, Multiplan®, and Microsoft Works.

Chapter 19, "Switching to Microsoft PowerPoint," includes information about the file translators provided to convert files to PowerPoint from other presentation packages, including Harvard Graphics and Freelance Graphics. Covered in detail are the Harvard Graphics translations features, and how each feature is converted when you open the file in PowerPoint.

Chapter 20, "Switching to Microsoft Word," includes information on converting WordPerfect 5.x-6.x, DisplayWrite®, MultiMate®, Microsoft Write, Word for MS-DOS, RTF, Microsoft Works, Wordstar®, and other document formats to Word for Window 95. This chapter also describes in detail the differences between the user's previous application and Word 7.0.

C H A P T E R   1 7

Switching to Microsoft Access

This chapter was written for the person managing the transition from another database management system to Microsoft Access. The transition to Microsoft Access cannot always be accomplished in one step. Your organization may be so large that you need to convert in phases. This chapter, therefore, describes both the complete transition of organizations to Microsoft Access, and the sharing of database resources between those who have converted to Microsoft Access, and those still using another database management system.

This chapter is a starting point in the transition process, and offers guidance and information specific to the transition. Many references to other sources are included that can provide further assistance. Foremost among these is the Microsoft Access program itself, as well as the printed documentation and online Help that accompanies it.

In This Chapter

Using Microsoft Access

Most likely the users in your organization are already experienced with database management systems. They understand the basic concepts, the steps used to create tables, and how to create databases for different purposes. For users who are converting their files to Microsoft Access, this section introduces Microsoft Access and some of its basic features—such as its single-file architecture, the graphical user interface, and the online Help system.

Single File Architecture

Most database management packages, including dBASE and Paradox, store individual database components, such as database files (tables), reports and forms, in separate MS-DOS–based files. A complete application may consist of hundreds of individual files.

A Microsoft Access database, by contrast, is a collection of objects (tables, forms, reports, queries, macros, and modules) stored in a single file with the extension .mdb. When you open a Microsoft Access database, you're opening all the tools that help you use information stored in the database. If you are converting from an MS-DOS–based database program, or a program that places a similar limitation on the length of filenames that compose a database, note that you can give the tables, reports and other database objects stored in a single Microsoft Access database file longer, descriptive names like "Customers " or "Sales by Month."

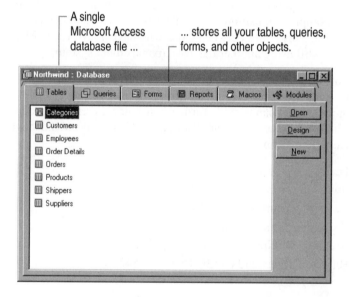

Note   Although a Microsoft Access database can contain all your objects, you can also work with objects that are stored in separate databases. For example, you can store your tables in one database and your forms and reports in another database. For more information, see "Separating the Application from the Data" in Chapter 2.

Like other common database management packages, such as dBASE and Paradox, Microsoft Access is a *relational database management system*. To efficiently and accurately provide you with information, a relational database like Microsoft Access needs facts about different subjects stored in separate tables. For example, you might have one table that stores only facts about employees, and another that stores only facts about orders. Then you define relationships between the tables, and Microsoft Access uses the relationships to find associated information stored in your database. Using the example above, you would define a relationship between the Employees and Orders tables, so that you can associate an employee with each order.

Using the Graphical User Interface

The menus, toolbars, dialog boxes, and other graphical elements in Microsoft Access are similar, if not identical, to other Microsoft Office applications. Microsoft Access can be readily used as an everyday business application, and it also contains many sophisticated features that you can use without programming. For applications that require even more specialized functionality, you can use features available through Visual Basic for applications. The best way for any new user to begin is to open a new database; link, import, or create your first table and see what you can do. Changes are always easy to make.

Database Window

The Database window, like the Northwind: Database window pictured in the "Single File Architecture" section, is how you view all of the objects in your .mdb files; it is your control center for working with your database. Each tab on the top of the window lets you work with a specific type of Microsoft Access object. Microsoft Access allows long names for tables and other objects. For example, you can name a table Order Details instead of ORDERDET, or a field within a table Quarterly Results instead of abbreviating as is required in dBASE and many MS-DOS–based database products.

You can list objects using large or small icons, or by name and details. The details are the object's properties: object description, date modified, date created, object type, and owner. Each detail appears in a separate column that you can resize to hide or show more of that information. Regardless of how you list objects, you can also sort them to display in a different order.

The Database window also supports a number of drag-and-drop features:

- Dragging a table, query, form, report, or macro to the desktop creates a shortcut for opening that object without starting Microsoft Access first.
- Dragging and dropping tables and queries from the Database window to Microsoft Excel or Microsoft Word copies that data into a worksheet or document.
- Dragging and dropping Microsoft Word tables and Microsoft Excel spreadsheet cells to the Database window creates new tables.

Copying and pasting data between applications can also be performed using the Copy and Paste commands on the Edit menu.

Tables

Tables are the basis of any database application. A table is collection of related data or records. Each table column represents a field, and each row represents a record. Unlike most database products, Microsoft Access tables do not exist as separate files but are included in the Microsoft Access .mdb file. You need at least one table in your database. Relating tables to one another is accomplished graphically, with no need for separate index files, such as .ndx in dBASE.

Queries

Queries are used to select a specific subset of data. For example, building the Microsoft Access request "Give me all customers who live in the state of New York" will return New York customers only, instead of customers from every state. Microsoft Access queries return a record set that is actually a view into the underlying tables. These record sets can be updatable or read-only, depending on your preference. If updatable, the resulting data can be added to, changed, or deleted as with any other table. For example, you can run a query with a linked table from dBASE, several native Microsoft Access tables, and a linked table from Paradox (or any other popular database format), and update the result. Microsoft Access will make your changes in all the underlying tables in the query. For information about linked tables, see "Getting Information into Microsoft Access" later in this chapter.

Queries can be incorporated in your application as a substitute for programming. For example, you can use queries to perform any of the following data update tasks:

- Update a field in a specified subset of records to a new value. You can specify the value when designing the query, provide the value using a field on a form, or from a field value from a table or query. This kind of query is called an *update query*.

- Delete a specified subset of records. The scope of records to be deleted can be determined by specifying criteria when designing the query, from the value of a field on a form, or from a table or query. This kind of query is called a *delete query*.

- Add records to a table. This is called an *append query*.

- Create a new table based on another table or a set of related tables. This is called a *make-table query*.

Forms

Microsoft Access Forms are based on tables and/or queries. Using forms you can view, enter, change, and print data. You can display data, pictures, graphs, and documents that you are tracking, in a Microsoft Access form. Using forms to go from one Table (Customers) to another (Orders for that Customer) can be as easy as clicking a button. You can create forms with or without the aid of the Form Wizard. The Form Wizard prompts you with questions and then creates a form based on your answers. You can create a new default form with one click of your mouse using the AutoForm Wizard. With a form you can view all the values for one record, or you can switch to Datasheet view of the form to view multiple records in a tabular format.

Reports

Reports allow you to display information, from tables and queries, in a way that may be more meaningful and readable than just looking at a series of records in a table. Making a quick report is easy in Microsoft Access. You can create most reports by using a Report Wizard. The Groups/Totals Wizard, for example, has the ability to automatically create logical groups of data (for example, orders grouped together by customer number), Totals (for example, total number of orders for all customers), and Subtotals (for example, total number of orders for each customer). You can add text, data, pictures, lines, boxes, and graphs to your reports to make them look the way you want.

Macros

You can use macros to automate repetitive tasks and to extend the capabilities of your database. A macro automatically carries out a command or series of commands called *actions* for you. To create a macro you can select from a list of actions. The macro executes the actions in the order they are listed, using the objects or data you've specified for the action arguments. This is an easy way to do point-and-click programming. You can link a macro to a button or to an event such as the closing of a form or report. You might find that all of the programming needs of your application can be satisfied by using macros.

Modules

You use modules for advanced programming tasks such as creating your own functions, for instance to calculate market projections or mask error messages. Visual Basic for applications code (Procedures, Functions, Global variables, and so on) resides in modules. Use modules when the actions you want your application to perform cannot be carried out by a simple query or macro.

When to Use What Type of Object

Microsoft Access provides several methods of getting information from your database. Use the method that best matches the task:

- To view all of the products that a particular vendor supplies, or that are out of stock or on order, use a query.

- To view all of the information about a particular product, customer, or supplier at once, use a form.

- To organize and print product sales for a formal presentation, use a report.

- For simply automating tasks, for example using a button to open a form or to execute a menu command or series of menu commands each time a database opens, use a macro. Buttons can also be created using the Command Button Wizard.

- To write specialized routines that give your application greater functionality, develop a module using Visual Basic for applications code.

Creating New Objects

To create a new database object, click the appropriate tab in the Database Window (Tables, Queries, Forms, and so on) and then click the New button on the right side of the Database Window. For example, to create a new query, click the Query tab and then click the New button. Or you can use the New Table, New Query, New Form, New Report, New Macro, or New Module buttons from the New Object drop-down button on the toolbar. When creating new tables, queries, forms, and reports, you will be presented with the choice of one or more wizards or to create a blank object from scratch. The wizards are very useful for learning about Microsoft Access and creating anything from simple to very complex objects. As you become more familiar with Microsoft Access and want to customize your tables or other objects, you might want to start from scratch or use a wizard and then make modifications in Design view.

Working with Existing Objects

You work with an existing object using the Database Window. To work with an object, click the appropriate tab in the Database Window, click the object, and then choose how you want to work with that object using the buttons on the right side of the Database Window or a button on the toolbar. The following sections describe the most common actions you will perform on database objects.

Working with Data in Tables, Queries, and Forms

To work with the data in a table, query, or form, double-click the name of the object in the Database Window, or select the object in the Database Window and click Open. You can then view, enter, or modify your data. A table or query always appears as a *Datasheet*, which displays data in rows and columns much like a spreadsheet. When working with data, a form displays by default in Form view, but can be switched to Datasheet view.

Previewing and Printing Reports

To preview a report, double-click the name of the report in the Database Window, or select the report in the Database Window and click Preview. After the report is displayed, you can print the report by clicking the Print button on the toolbar. To print a report directly, select the report in the Database Window and then click the Print button on the toolbar.

Running Macros

Macros are usually linked to a button, to a custom menu option, or triggered by an event in a form or report; however, you can also run a macro directly from the Database Window. To do this, double-click the name of the macro in the Database Window, or select the macro in the Database Window and click Run.

Changing the Design of an Existing Object

To open an object in Design view, select the object name in the Database Window and click the Design button, either in the Database window or on the toolbar. In Design View, you can make changes to the design of your tables, queries, and forms by changing colors, adding sound clips, and adding command buttons, subforms, drop-down list boxes, and so on. You can change reports by adding pictures, changing fonts, sizing column widths, and so on; you can also change macros or modules.

To switch between views of objects, click these buttons:

Other Object-Specific Features

The commands available on the menu bar and toolbar vary depending upon the database object you're working with and the view in which it is displayed. Microsoft Access allows you to have many objects open at once. The menu bar and toolbar commands available correspond to the object that is currently selected. A different set of commands will also be available when the Database Window is selected.

Keyboard Differences

When you're viewing and editing data in a form or datasheet, you'll notice that the navigation keys work differently in Microsoft Access than in some other database applications. For example, in dBASE, pressing the RIGHT ARROW or LEFT ARROW key moves the insertion point one character to the right or left within a field. However, in Microsoft Access, by default the contents of a field are automatically highlighted, and pressing these keys moves to the next or previous field. If you click in the field or press F2 to activate the insertion point, pressing the RIGHT ARROW or LEFT ARROW key will move one character to the right or left within a field.

If you want the navigation keys to work as they do in the application you're used to, you can use the Options command on the Tools menu to set keyboard options. The following table explains the keyboard options you may want to change, and the settings available for each.

Option	Setting	Result
Arrow Key Behavior	Next Field (default)	Pressing RIGHT ARROW or LEFT ARROW moves the selection to the next field. To activate the insertion point and move it within a field, click the field or press F2. To prevent Microsoft Access from selecting the entire field, use the Behavior Entering Field setting.
	Next Character	As in dBASE, pressing RIGHT ARROW or LEFT ARROW always moves to the next character.
Move After Enter	No	Pressing ENTER selects the current field but doesn't move to another field.
	Next Field (default)	Pressing ENTER moves to the next field.
	Next Record	Pressing ENTER moves to the same field in the next record.
Cursor Stops at First/Last Field	No (default)	Pressing RIGHT ARROW or LEFT ARROW moves past the first or last field.
	Yes	Pressing RIGHT ARROW or LEFT ARROW moves no further than the first or last field.
Behavior Entering Field	Select Entire Field (default)	Determines whether Microsoft Access selects the entire contents of a field when moving from field to field with the ENTER, TAB, and arrow keys.
		Selects the entire field. To activate the insertion point and move it within a field, click the field or press F2.
	Go To Start Of Field	Places the insertion point at the start of the field.
	Go To End Of Field	Places the insertion point at the end of the field.

Getting Data into Microsoft Access

If you have data in separate databases, the first step in converting to Microsoft Access is to import or link tables. If you want to leave your data in its current format, you can link the tables to a Microsoft Access database. This way, other users can still use the tables in the original application. On the other hand, if you plan to use your data only in Microsoft Access, you should import the tables.

If you choose to leave your data in another database or data format and create linked tables, you can use this data just as you use tables stored in your Microsoft Access database. For example, you can edit the data in linked tables, and you can create queries, forms, and reports that use the data. You can even combine external data with the data in your Microsoft Access tables.

The icon that represents a linked table remains in the Database window along with tables in the current database, so you can open the table whenever you want. Microsoft Access displays a different icon for tables from each type of source database. If you delete the icon, you delete the link to the table, not the external table itself.

On the other hand, if you know you will use your data only in Microsoft Access, you should import it. Microsoft Access generally works faster with its own tables, and you can customize Microsoft Access tables to meet your needs.

Whether you plan to import or link tables, you start by choosing the New Database command to create your Microsoft Access database. Then use the Import or Link Table command to get your existing data into the new Microsoft Access database. For details on importing and linking tables, see "Importing or Linking External Tables" later in this chapter.

The following tips can help you get the most from tables you import or link:

- Microsoft Access table names aren't limited to MS-DOS file-naming rules. Table names can include spaces as well as uppercase and lowercase letters. For example, after you import or link a table called SLSDAT95, you can use the Rename command on the File menu to rename the table Sales Data for 1995.

- The first time you open a table in Datasheet view, all the columns have the same width. You can adjust the width of the columns using the mouse, and then save the column width settings by choosing Save Table from the File menu. The next time you open the table, the column layout appears the way you left it.

- By setting field properties in a table's Design view, you can make data easier to work with. For example, you can specify display formats or validation rules you want Microsoft Access to use in forms and datasheets.

- For information about optimizing Microsoft Access databases, see "Optimizing Microsoft Access for Windows 95" in Chapter 11.

Tip When you import your data, you can enhance your tables by opening each one in Design view and changing its structure or properties. It's a good idea to make these changes right away, before you create queries, forms, and reports based on the tables.

You can take advantage of the following features with tables you import but not with tables you link:

- **Longer field names**   In Microsoft Access, field names can be up to 64 characters long and can contain spaces. This gives you much more flexibility than dBASE, which allows only ten characters. For example, after importing a table from dBASE, you can change the CUSTADDR field name to Customer Address.

- **More data types**   Microsoft Access provides data types that aren't available in other applications but may be appropriate for your data. For example, the Currency data type is ideal for storing monetary values. After you import a table, you may want to change the data type of such fields from Number to Currency.

- **Primary keys**   You can set a primary key that uniquely identifies each record in the table. If you don't have an appropriate primary key in your table, you can add a field with the AutoNumber data type and the NewValues property set to Increment (this is the default), which automatically assigns a consecutive number for each record you add.

- **Indexes**   To speed up operations in fields that you anticipate searching or sorting on often, you can create indexes. Simply set the field's Indexed property to Yes.

- **AutoNumber**   Microsoft Access gives you an automatic counter field that is a good choice for creating primary keys, indexing, and creating unique relationships if the table doesn't already contain a unique value for each record.

- **Relationships**   If you import related tables, you can add relationships to your database that Microsoft Access uses to relate data in queries, forms, and reports. If you want, Microsoft Access can automatically enforce *referential integrity* when adding or deleting records in related tables. Referential integrity ensures that relationships between records are valid, and that you don't accidentally delete related data.

Deciding Whether to Import or Link an External Table

The decision as to whether or not you should link a table depends on whether you will continue to use the data with the program that originally produced it. As an example, suppose that you have a dBASE file that contains a list of products your company sells. You no longer use dBASE, and you'd like to have this data handy on your computer. In this case, it makes sense to import the dBASE file into a Microsoft Access table. To make the table look and perform better, you could set a primary key and perhaps change field names or set other field properties.

By comparison, suppose that your company keeps its sales figures in a Microsoft SQL Server database on a network. Because you might use software other than Microsoft Access to view or edit this data, you don't want to move it to a Microsoft Access database. In this case, it makes sense to link the Sales table and use Microsoft Access as a front end to your SQL database. After linking the table, you can update the data from Microsoft Access and print weekly sales reports.

In addition, if your staff and applications are gradually moving to Microsoft Access, you will want to first link tables in their current data format, so you can maintain one master set of data during the transition, then import the data after all users and all applications are moved to Microsoft Access.

Even if all users are using Microsoft Access, you may want to maintain your data in a separate database as linked tables and keep your forms, reports, and other objects in their own database. For more information, see "Separating the Application from the Data" in Chapter 2.

Importing or Linking External Tables

Microsoft Access can use data from the following formats and applications:

- Paradox 3.*x* , 4.*x*, and 5.*x*
- Microsoft FoxPro 2.0, 2.5, 2.6, and 3.0 (import only for 3.0)
- dBASE III, dBASE IV, and dBASE 5
- Applications that supply Open Database Connectivity (ODBC) drivers, such as SQL databases, like Microsoft SQL Server, Sybase SQL Server, and Oracle Server
- Microsoft Access 1.*x*, 2.0, and 7.0 (databases other than the open database)
- Microsoft Excel 3.0, 4.0, 5.0, and 7.0
- Lotus 1-2-3 .wk1 and .wk3 formats
- Text (fixed-width and delimited formats)

Tips for Importing and Linking

When you import or link a table from another database application, keep in mind the following tips and considerations:

- If you import or link a table from Paradox or an SQL database, you may need to supply a password. This password is different from a Microsoft Access user password; it is the password set in the other application.

- If you link a table that requires a password, Microsoft Access stores this password in your database so you can open the table later (this is optional for SQL tables). For this reason, you may want to add some form of security to your database to control who can open it. The simplest form of security is requiring a password to open a database, which you can set using the Set Database Password command on the Security submenu of the Tools menu. For more information about database passwords, see "Share-Level Security: Database Password Protection" in Chapter 15.

- To link an external table on a network, you must connect to the network and you must have access to the database file. If you want Microsoft Access to automatically connect to the appropriate file server each time you open a linked table, specify the fully qualified network path for the file. For example, if you use a Microsoft Windows NT Server network, you can enter the path to connect to a dBASE file using the following format: *\\Server\Share\Datadir\Myfile.dbf.*

  This format is called the Universal Naming Convention (UNC) pathname, and is supported by many networks. When using this format, you don't need to map a drive letter to a file, which prevents problems if the drive letter is changed or the database is moved to a different computer with differently mapped drives.

- After you import or link an external table, it's a good idea to set table properties in the table's Design view. If you import a table, it's especially important to set a primary key.

- Although you can use a linked table as if it were a Microsoft Access table, there are a few special considerations. After you link a table from another database, the table icon Microsoft Access displays in the Database window indicates that the data in the table is outside of your database. Microsoft Access stores all the information you supply when linking the table so it can find the external data whenever you need it. When you open a linked table, Microsoft Access opens the appropriate database file or connection and displays the data.

  You can also use linked tables with other database objects, such as queries, forms, and reports. Using a query, you can even join the data in the linked table with data in your Microsoft Access tables. Even though the data may reside on a separate computer, Microsoft Access combines the data to answer your query.

Relationships

You create and edit relationships between tables in Microsoft Access using the Relationships window. To display the Relationships window, choose Relationships from the Tool menu. When you create a relationship in Microsoft Access, you choose the fields you want to use to create the relationship between two tables by dragging a field from one table and dropping it on the appropriate field in another table. Microsoft Access displays what kind of relationship will be created. If only one of the related fields is a primary key or unique index, a one-to-many relationship is created; if both related fields are primary keys or unique indexes, a one-to-one relationship is created. You have the option of choosing referential integrity, cascading updates, and cascading deletes. Choosing referential integrity prevents orphaned records in your database. For example, no one will be able to enter an order for a customer that isn't in the Customers table or delete a customer if orders exist for that customer. Choosing Cascading Updates or Deletes means that editing or deleting records is confirmed among all of the related tables so that your changes are automatically updated. You can control how these relationships are maintained through the Relationships window.

Table Field List

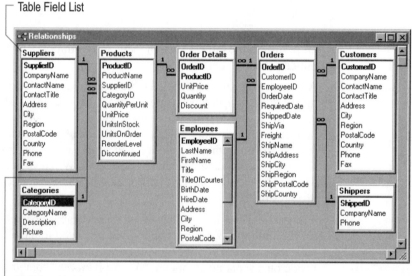

Relationship Line

Double-clicking any of the relationship lines between the tables opens a dialog box in which you can specify the fields used to create the relationship and the degree of integrity it maintains. These relationships are then saved and automatically shown in any query that you build.

Table-Level Validation and Referential Integrity

Many other database systems require you to write validation code for each form and at every other point in your application where data is updated. You may also be required to write additional code to maintain referential integrity. When using Microsoft Access, you can define validation rules when defining tables, and referential integrity when defining relationships. These rules will then carry through all of your forms and queries. In many cases, table-level validation and referential integrity will meet all of your application's validation requirements. If more sophisticated validation rules are required, you can use form-level validation and write user-defined functions or procedures using Visual Basic for applications code.

Programming in Microsoft Access

In many cases, when using Microsoft Access you will not need to use programming to achieve the same results as other systems that do require programming. If you do need to perform programming in Microsoft Access you use Visual Basic for applications code. Visual Basic for applications is very similar to the Microsoft Visual Basic programming system. You use Visual Basic for applications to perform the same kinds of tasks you do with macros: to perform operations on one or more objects, creating a coherent, efficient application. Visual Basic for applications code also provides additional features that aren't available using macros, such as the ability to define user-defined functions, and provide error handling. Visual Basic for applications code exists in blocks called either *procedures* or *functions*. Procedures and functions contain a series of Visual Basic for applications statements that perform an operation necessary in your application. You store your Visual Basic for applications code in modules, or in forms or reports in association with events occurring within a form or report such as clicking a button. For more information about Visual Basic for applications, see *Building Applications with Microsoft Access for Windows 95*.

Using the Sample Applications

One of the easiest ways to produce new database objects is to copy one that resembles what you want. The sample databases provided with Microsoft Access—which you will find in the Samples folder—include several typical business databases. As you browse through the objects in these applications, you can copy any of them by highlighting its name in the Database window and choosing Copy from the Edit menu. Then close the sample database, open your own application, select the appropriate tab in the Database window, and choose Paste from the Edit menu. If it is a table, you can modify the field definitions, remove its data and paste your own data into it. For forms and reports, you can change the Source in the Properties box to point to the table or query you want to use and change the field references.

Online Help

Microsoft Access online Help is extensive. Choosing the Answer Wizard command on the Help menu displays a dialog box into which you can type a search request and Microsoft Access will return a list of the most likely help topics that answer that question. Clicking a text box in a property sheet, or highlighting a Visual Basic keyword in the module window and then pressing the F1 key in Microsoft Access will bring up a screen of context-sensitive Help. You can also get help by searching for a topic using keywords on the Index tab or by browsing the contents on the Contents tab. You can access the online Help system by choosing Microsoft Access Help Topics or Answer Wizard from the Help menu.

Additional Context-sensitive Help

In addition to F1 help, clicking the ▶? button on the toolbar gives you a Help mouse pointer that will display help for whatever object you click. Pointing at a button with your mouse without clicking displays a ToolTip that tells you what the button does. The status bar at the lower left of your screen will offer a quick tip on whatever object is currently selected. You can also determine what will appear on the status bar for your users when you create forms.

Switching from dBASE

Databases created in dBASE are compatible with Microsoft Access. You can either link or import data from .dbf files.

Note A primary difference between Microsoft Access and MS-DOS–based applications is the use of the Microsoft Windows graphical interface. If you're currently using an MS-DOS–based version of dBASE and are new to Microsoft Windows, study your Windows documentation to learn basic techniques.

Terms Your Users Need to Know

Many common database terms are the same across different applications. The following table matches Microsoft Access terms with the equivalent term or command in dBASE. The Microsoft Access term is not necessarily an exact equivalent of the dBASE term, but rather a term you can look up in Microsoft Access Help for information. You don't need to understand all of these terms before you start using Microsoft Access.

dBASE	Microsoft Access
Catalog	Database
Database file	Table
BROWSE command	Datasheet view
MODIFY STRUCTURE command	Table Design view
Character data type	Text data type
Unique index	Primary key
Index	Index
PICTURE/VALID clause	Validation rule
Query, view	Query
Screen	Form
Multiple-file screen	Subform
SET FORMAT TO; EDIT	Open a form
LOCATE and SEEK commands	Find command
APPEND command	Data Entry command
Pick list	List box, combo box
SET EXCLUSIVE mode	Exclusive/Shared access
Program file	Module

Importing or Linking dBASE Files

If you need to leave your data in dBASE .dbf format so that it can continue to be used by dBASE users, you can link this data to your Microsoft Access database. Using Microsoft Access, you can edit the data in linked tables and you can create queries, forms, and reports that use the data. You can even combine data from linked tables with the data from any other tables in your Microsoft Access tables.

If you have no need to maintain your dBASE data in its original format, you can import your .dbf tables into Microsoft Access. Unlike linking to your dBASE file, importing the data creates a copy of the data in Microsoft Access. Importing a table gives you greater flexibility and control of the data, but excludes users not running Microsoft Access from updating the data.

You can import or link .dbf files in dBASE III, dBASE IV, or dBASE 5 format. If you link a .dbf file to your Microsoft Access database, you can view and update data, even if others are using it in dBASE.

If you link a dBASE file, you can also tell Microsoft Access to use one or more dBASE index (.ndx or .mdx) files to improve performance. Microsoft Access keeps track of the indexes in a special information (.inf) file. When you use Microsoft Access to update the data in your .dbf file, Microsoft Access also updates the index files to reflect your changes.

If you link a .dbf file and associate an index (.ndx or .mdx) file, Microsoft Access needs the index file to open the linked table. If you delete or move index files or the information (.inf) file, you won't be able to open the linked table. If you use dBASE to update data, you must update the associated indexes within dBASE as well. Microsoft Access cannot use a linked table if the indexes you specify aren't current.

If your dBASE files are stored on a read-only drive or CD-ROM, Microsoft Access cannot create an .inf file in the same folder as your .dbf files. To link tables on a read-only drive, you must specify the folder path where you want Microsoft Access to create the .inf file. To do so, you need to specify an INFPath value in the Windows registry that points to a location in which the .inf file can be written. This value should be added to the \\Hkey_Local_Machine\Software\Microsoft\Jet\3.0\Engines\Xbase folder of the Windows registry.

▶ **To import or link a dBASE file**

1. Open a database in Microsoft Access or switch to the Database window for the open database.

2. On the File menu, point to Get External Data, and then click Import or Link Tables.

3. In the Files Of Type box, select dBASE III, dBASE IV, or dBASE 5.

4. Use the Look In list to switch to the appropriate folder, select the .dbf file you want, and then click Import or Link.

   If you're importing, Microsoft Access creates a new table named after the file you selected and imports the data from the .dbf file. Go to step 7.

   If you're linking, Microsoft Access displays a dialog box where you can associate dBASE index files. Go to step 5.

5. Select each dBASE index (.ndx or .mdx) file one at a time and click Select. When you finish associating indexes, click Close. If there are no indexes to associate, click Cancel to continue.

   Microsoft Access displays the Select Unique Record Identifier dialog box.

6. If an index you've chosen uniquely identifies each record in the table so that indexed fields don't contain any duplicate values, select the index and click OK. (If you don't select an index that provides a unique identifier, Microsoft Access may not be able to update data in queries with joins to this table because records cannot be uniquely identified to maintain referential integrity.)

   Microsoft Access adds the table name with a linked table icon to the list in the Database window. When you choose a linked table from the list, you open the dBASE database file that contains the table, and the data is available as if it were part of your Microsoft Access database.

7. To import or link another dBASE file, go back to step 4. When you finish importing or linking, click Close.

After you have successfully imported all the tables, a *primary key structure*, a unique identifier used to relate tables, and indexes should be built on all fields on which you want to search or sort. You should also check to see if you want to modify any data types, field properties, or table properties at this time.

For additional tips on using imported or linked tables, see "Getting Data into Microsoft Access" earlier in this chapter.

Data Type Conversions

When you import data from a dBASE file, Microsoft Access translates dBASE data types into the corresponding Microsoft Access data types. The following table lists the data type conversions.

dBASE data type	Microsoft Access data type
Character	Text
Numeric, Float	Number (FieldSize property set to Double)
Logical	Yes/No
Date	Date/Time
Memo	Memo

Note the following differences between dBASE data types and Microsoft Access data types:

- **Number field types**   dBASE supports two number field types, Numeric and Float. In Microsoft Access, a single Number field type lets you specify the accuracy to which the data is to be maintained using the FieldSize property.

- **Fixed-length fields**   As in dBASE, you must specify the length of the character fields for the longest anticipated entry. Data will be truncated if a record exceeds the specified length. However, unlike dBASE, Microsoft Access does not actually store all of the unused space characters for fixed-length fields, so that the size of your files does not have to be a consideration.

- **Additional field types**   Microsoft Access offers the AutoNumber and Currency field types. The most common form of AutoNumber field automatically increments a value by one for each succeeding record so that a unique identifier for each record is generated. This field type is perfect for primary keys and for creating ID numbers. The Currency field type is tailored to the kind of rounding and calculation typical of currency transactions.

Defining Relationships

After you have defined primary keys or unique indexes for each of your tables, you should define the relationships between your tables. For information about how to define relationships with Microsoft Access, see "Relationships" earlier in this chapter.

Queries and Views

You will have to recreate your dBASE queries in Microsoft Access. You can use your mouse to drag tables from the Database window list into the table area of the query output grid, or click the Add Table button on the toolbar to add a table or query to the query you are in the process of creating. If you have defined relationships, they are reflected in your query automatically. You can double-click a relationship line between two tables to change the relationship.

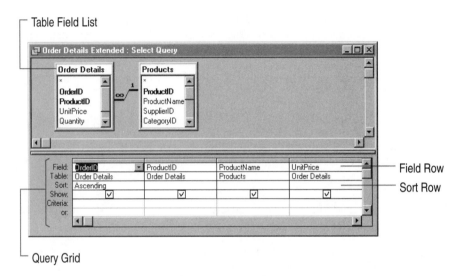

Table Field List

Field Row

Sort Row

Query Grid

Add fields to the query by dragging them from the table field list onto the query grid, or by selecting them from the drop-down list in the Field row of the query grid. To indicate a sort order for those fields you want sorted, choose Ascending or Descending from the drop-down list in the Sort row of the query grid. Enter criteria formulas in the rows directly below the field names. You will find that many of the functions and formulas are similar to their dBASE equivalents.

Microsoft Access also has Query Wizards to help you make the most common complex queries simple. Use the Query Wizards to learn how to build queries in Microsoft Access, and as you build more advanced queries, use the wizards as a starting point for your query design.

Forms

Microsoft Access forms are the equivalent of dBASE screens. The form Design view, provides graphical orientation and direct tools for building edit boxes, drop-down lists, and other form objects. The Form Wizard creates an attractive form from your tables or queries. To use it, click the Forms tab on the Database window, click the New button, and then double-click Form Wizard.

Forms in a Graphical Environment

The dBASE Form Designer tools limit you to using only fields and text. As a result of this limitation, the traditional dBASE approach to adding features to forms is to set function keys in a program that calls procedures related to the form. In dBASE, to make the user aware of these functions, you add text to the form that indicates which function keys to press to invoke certain procedures. You can also write programming code to create a more user-friendly dBASE form.

Microsoft Access presents user-friendly forms that take advantage of the Windows graphical environment by allowing you to easily create controls such as command buttons, check boxes, and drop-down lists. Microsoft Access forms also use visual controls to access built-in features, such as the record navigation buttons at the bottom of each form. There are many things you can do to update the way your current dBASE form works when moving it into Microsoft Access. The Answer Wizard and the Form Wizard will walk you through adding features to your forms, without programming. Here are some tips for updating your forms to take advantage of Microsoft Access features:

- If you are using multiple choice fields, such as Picture @M, on a dBASE form, consider substituting option buttons, toggle buttons, or a combo box on the Microsoft Access version of the form.

- If you have one or more logical fields on a dBASE form, consider replacing them with checkbox controls.

- If your dBASE form is programmed to display detail records in a BROWSE window or screen, consider replacing the separate BROWSE interface with an integrated subform on the Microsoft Access form, like the following illustration.

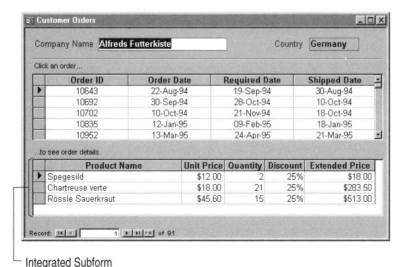

Integrated Subform

- Most Microsoft Access form controls have a Special Effect property, to make controls on your forms look three-dimensional.

- You can have more than one Microsoft Access form open at a time. For example, you may want to link your Inventory form with your Manufacturing Schedule form and display them simultaneously. If having more than one form open at once is confusing or causes a problem, you can set the form's Modal property to Yes to force the user to close the current form before continuing.

- The Microsoft Access equivalent to the dBASE field Picture Functions and the field Template is either the Format property or the Input Mask property. There is also a Microsoft Access field property equivalent for most of the dBASE field Edit Options. You can get status bar hints by highlighting each field property in the property window.

Reports

Microsoft Access uses a banded report designer similar to that in dBASE but with extensive graphical tools and data windows. As with forms, you can choose a Report Wizard as a quick way to get started creating a report. By selecting a table or a query and following the wizard's prompts, Microsoft Access will create a complete report with an attractive and consistent look that you can apply to all of your reports. For most reports, the Report Wizards are all you need; otherwise, you can open the report in Design view and use the Microsoft Access report tools to customize your reports. Like dBASE, the Microsoft Access report tool is banded, meaning that you design the report by specifying what each section should print. You can transfer your experience creating dBASE reports to creating reports in Microsoft Access.

Tip Like dBASE, Microsoft Access supports calculated fields on reports. In addition, Microsoft Access provides a special Running Sum calculated field, which does not exist in dBASE.

Catalogs

The Database window serves the function of uniting all of the objects in your database, much as the Control Center does in dBASE IV. However, in Microsoft Access, all of the objects are incorporated into a single file with an .mdb extension with the exception of linked objects. For linked objects, the links are stored in the .mdb file, but the objects themselves are stored in other files.

Exporting a Table to a dBASE File

If you need to save the data from a table or query that has been created in Microsoft Access so that it can be used by users who are still using dBASE, you can export that data.

▶ **To export a Microsoft Access table or query to a dBASE file**

1. Open a Microsoft Access database, or switch to the Database window for the open database.

2. In the Database window, highlight the table or query you want to export.

3. On the File menu, click Save As/Export.

4. Click To An External File Or Database, and then click OK.

5. In the Save As Type box, select the dBASE format you want, and click OK.

6. In the File Name box, enter a filename for the database file you want to export.

7. In the Save In box, select the folder you want to save in, and then click Export.

If you export a table with table or field names that aren't allowed in the destination database, Microsoft Access adjusts the names. For example, if you export data to a dBASE table, any field names longer than 10 characters are truncated.

Setting Microsoft Access Options for dBASE or FoxPro Tables

Microsoft Access for Windows 95 uses the Microsoft Jet Database engine to read and write data whether it is using its own native tables or linking tables in other data formats. The settings Microsoft Jet uses to initialize the Xbase driver (the driver for both dBASE and FoxPro files) are located in the \\Hkey_Local_Machine\Software\Microsoft\Jet\3.0\Engines\Xbase folder of the Windows registry. Although the Microsoft Access Setup program automatically creates recommended option settings, if you need to, you can modify these settings.

For more information on how to modify Microsoft Access registry settings, see Appendix B, "Registry Keys and Values."

Switching from FoxPro

The following tips and instructions will help you use Microsoft Access for Windows 95 with FoxPro databases.

Importing or Linking FoxPro Files

You can import or link .dbf files in FoxPro 2.0, 2.5, or 2.6 format. You can also import, but not link files in FoxPro 3.0 format. If you link a FoxPro file to your Microsoft Access database, you can view and update data, even if others are using it in FoxPro.

If you link a FoxPro file, you can also tell Microsoft Access to use one or more FoxPro index (.idx or .cdx) files to improve performance. Microsoft Access keeps track of the indexes in a special information (.inf) file. When you use Microsoft Access to update the data in your .dbf file, Microsoft Access also updates the index files to reflect your changes.

If you link a .dbf file and associate an index (.idx or .cdx) file, Microsoft Access needs the index file to open the linked table. If you delete or move index files or the information (.inf) file, you won't be able to open the linked table.

If your FoxPro files are stored on a read-only drive or CD-ROM, Microsoft Access cannot create an .inf file in the same folder as your .dbf or .dbc files. To do so, you need to specify an INFPath value in the Windows registry that points to a location in which the .inf file can be written. This value should be added to the \\Hkey_Local_Machine\Software\Microsoft\Jet\3.0\Engines\Xbase folder of the Windows registry.

▸   **To import or link a FoxPro file**

1. Open a database in Microsoft Access or switch to the Database window for the open database.

2. On the File menu, point to Get External Data, and then click Import or the Link Tables.

3. In the Files Of Type box, select Microsoft FoxPro (.dbf) to import or link versions 2.0, 2.5, or 2.6, or select Microsoftt FoxPro 3.0 (.dbc) to import version 3.0. The Microsoft FoxPro 3.0 (.dbc) option is not available if you selected Link Tables in step 2.

4. Use the Look In list to switch to the appropriate folder, select the file you want, then click Import or Link.

   If you're importing, Microsoft Access creates a new table named after the file you selected and imports the data from the FoxPro file. Go to step 7.

   If you're linking, Microsoft Access displays a dialog box where you can associate FoxPro index files. Go to step 5.

5. Select each FoxPro index (.idx or .cdx) file one at a time and click Select. When you finish associating indexes, click Close. If there are no indexes to associate, click Cancel to continue.

6. If an index you've chosen uniquely identifies each record in the table so that indexed fields don't contain any duplicate values, select the index and click OK. (If you don't select an index that provides a unique identifier, Microsoft Access may not be able to update data in queries with joins to this table because records cannot be uniquely identified to maintain referential integrity.)

    Microsoft Access adds the table name with a linked table icon to the list in the Database window. When you choose a linked table from the list, you open the FoxPro database file that contains the table, and the data is available as if it were part of your Microsoft Access database.

7. To import or link another FoxPro file, go back to step 4. When you finish importing or linking, click Close.

After you have successfully imported all the tables, a *primary key structure*—a unique identifier used to relate tables—and indexes should be built on all fields on which you want to search or sort. You should also check to see if you want to modify any data types, field properties, or table properties at this time.

For additional tips on using imported or linked tables, see "Getting Data into Microsoft Access" earlier in this chapter.

Data Type Conversions

When you import data from a FoxPro file, Microsoft Access translates FoxPro data types into the corresponding Microsoft Access data types. The following table lists the data type conversions.

FoxPro data type	Microsoft Access data type
Character	Text
Numeric, Float	Number (FieldSize property set to Double)
Logical	Yes/No
Date	Date/Time
Memo	Memo
General (FoxPro only)	OLE

Defining Relationships

After you have defined primary keys or unique indexes for each of your tables, you can define the relationships between your tables. For more information about defining relationships using Microsoft Access, see "Relationships" earlier in this chapter.

Using Microsoft FoxPro Version 2.5 Files

Microsoft FoxPro version 2.5 doesn't distinguish between tables created with the MS-DOS version and those created with the Microsoft Windows version. Data in tables created with FoxPro version 2.5 for MS-DOS is stored in OEM format. Data in tables created with FoxPro version 2.5 for Windows is stored in ANSI format. Microsoft Access converts all FoxPro version 2.5 data from an OEM code page to the ANSI 1252 code page when importing or linking FoxPro 2.5 data, and it converts the ANSI code page to an OEM code page when exporting to FoxPro 2.5 tables. The result is that *extended characters* (characters with ASCII and ANSI codes above 128) in tables created with FoxPro version 2.5 for Windows aren't converted properly.

If your FoxPro version 2.5 tables contain extended characters, you should be certain that the tables are stored in OEM format (that is, created by FoxPro version 2.5 for MS-DOS). Releases of FoxPro subsequent to 2.5 (2.5a, 2.5b, and so on) correctly identify the code page format of the data, enabling Microsoft Access to correctly determine how to convert extended characters.

Exporting a Table to a FoxPro File

If you need to save the data from a table or query that has been created in Microsoft Access so that it can be used by users who are still using FoxPro, you can export that data.

▶ **To export a Microsoft Access table or query to a FoxPro file**

1. Open a database, or switch to the Database window for the open database.

2. In the Database window, select the table or query you want to export.

3. On the File menu, click Save As/Export.

4. Click To An External File Or Database, and then click OK.

5. In the Save As Type box, select the FoxPro format you want, then choose OK.

6. In the File Name box, type a filename for the database file you want to export.

7. In the Save In box, select the folder you want to save in, and then click Export.

If you export a table with table or field names that aren't allowed in the destination database, Microsoft Access adjusts the names. For example, if you export data to a FoxPro table, any field names longer than 10 characters are truncated.

Setting Microsoft Access Options for FoxPro

For details on Windows registry settings that you can customize for the Microsoft Access FoxPro database driver, see "Setting Microsoft Access Options for dBASE or FoxPro" earlier in this chapter

Switching from Paradox

This section presents information about switching from Paradox to Microsoft Access. It includes tips for importing or linking your data into a Microsoft Access database, and compares the terms used in Microsoft Access with Paradox terminology.

Note A primary difference between Microsoft Access and MS-DOS–based applications is the use of the Microsoft Windows graphical interface. If you're currently using an MS-DOS–based version of Paradox and are new to Microsoft Windows, study your Windows documentation to learn basic techniques.

Terms Your Users Need to Know

Many common database terms are the same across different applications. The following table matches Microsoft Access terms with the equivalent terms or commands in Paradox. The Microsoft Access term is not necessarily an exact equivalent of the Paradox term, but rather a term you can look up in the Microsoft Access Online Help Topics for more information. You don't need to understand all of these terms before you start using Microsoft Access.

Paradox	Microsoft Access
Folder of related files	Database
Table	Table
View command	Datasheet view
Modify Restructure command	Table Design view
Alphanumeric data type	Text data type
Key field	Primary key
Tools QuerySpeed	Index
ValChecks	Validation rule
Query	Query
Form	Form
Multiple-record section	Subform
Image PickForm	Open a form
Zoom command	Find command
Modify DataEntry	Data Entry command
Lookup	List box, combo box
Edit/Coedit mode	Exclusive/Shared access
Script	Module

Importing or Linking Paradox Tables

With Microsoft Access, you can import or link tables from Paradox or Paradox for Windows (versions 3.x, 4.x, or 5.0). If you provide the correct password, Microsoft Access can open encrypted Paradox tables. If you link a Paradox table to your Microsoft Access database, you can view and update data, even if others are using it in Paradox.

Important Paradox stores important information about a table's primary key in an index (.px) file. If you link a Paradox table that has a primary key, Microsoft Access needs the .px file to open the linked table. If you delete or move this file, you won't be able to open the linked table.

If you link a Paradox table that doesn't have a primary key, you won't be able to update data in the table using Microsoft Access. If you want to be able to update the table, define a primary key for the table in Paradox.

For additional considerations and potential problems when importing and linking Paradox files, see "Using Microsoft Access with Paradox Databases" later in this section.

▸ **To import or link a Paradox table**

1. Open a database in Microsoft Access or switch to the Database window for the open database.

2. On the File menu, point to Get External Data, and then click Import or Link Tables.

3. In the Files Of Type box, select the Paradox format you want to import or link.

4. Use the Look In box to switch to the appropriate folder, select the Paradox.db file you want, and then click Import or Link.

5. If the Paradox table you select is encrypted, Microsoft Access prompts you for the password. Type the password for the Paradox table, and click OK.

   If you're importing, Microsoft Access creates a new table named after the file you selected and imports the data from the .db file. If you're linking, Microsoft Access adds the table name with a linked table icon to the list in the Database window. When you choose a linked table from the list, you open the Paradox database file that contains the table, and the data is available as if it were part of your Microsoft Access database.

6. To import or link another Paradox file, repeat steps 3 through 5. When you finish importing or linking, click Close.

After you have successfully imported all the tables, a primary key structure (unique identifier used to relate tables) and indexes should be built on all fields on which you want to search or sort. You should also check to see if you want to modify any data types, field properties, or table properties at this time.

For additional tips on using imported or linked tables, see "Getting Data into Microsoft Access," earlier in this chapter.

Data Type Conversions

When you import data from a Paradox table, Microsoft Access translates Paradox data types into the corresponding Microsoft Access data types. The following table lists the data type conversions.

Paradox data type	Microsoft Access data type
Alphanumeric	Text
Number	Number (FieldSize property set to Double)
Short number	Number (FieldSize property set to Integer)
Currency	Number (FieldSize property set to Double)
Date	Date/Time
Memo	Memo
OLE	OLE Object

Note Although Paradox tables containing OLE fields can be imported or linked into Microsoft Access, the OLE objects cannot be opened in Microsoft Access. This is due to differences in the way Microsoft Access and Paradox store OLE object header information. If you add a record to a linked Paradox table with OLE fields, those fields will be null (blank).

If you import or link a Paradox 4.x table that contains memo fields with the Graphic, Binary, or Formatted data types, these fields aren't included in the table in Microsoft Access because it cannot read fields of these formats.

Using Microsoft Access with Paradox Databases

The following tips and instructions will help you use Microsoft Access for Windows 95 with Paradox and Paradox for Windows databases.

Selecting the Paradox Locking Style

You can use the Paradox 4.x locking style to access both Paradox 3.x and 4.x tables. You cannot link Paradox 4.x tables while using the Paradox 3.x locking style.

If a Paradox 3.5 user opens a table, you won't be able to open or import from this table using the 4.*x* locking style. The table will be inaccessible from Microsoft Access until the Paradox 3.5 user closes it.

For information about how to set a Paradox locking style in the Windows registry, see Appendix B.

Paradox Tables on a Read-only Drive

You cannot link or import from Paradox tables on read-only drives. This is because Microsoft Access cannot create the necessary lock files.

Linking Nonkeyed Paradox Tables

If you link an empty Paradox table with no primary key, you will be able to add records the first time you use the table. However, because Microsoft Access cannot update Paradox tables without primary keys, after the table is closed and reopened, it will be read-only.

You can open only one cursor at a time on a nonkeyed Paradox table.

ParadoxNetPaths Must Be Identical

In Microsoft Access, for all users sharing the same Paradox database, the ParadoxNetPath value in the Windows registry must refer to the full path to the folder containing the Paradox.net file (for Paradox 3.x) or the Pdoxusrs.net file (for Paradox 4.x). This parameter is located in the \\Hkey_Local_Machine\Software\Microsoft\Jet\3.0\Engines\Paradox folder of the Windows registry. For information about how to set the Paradox NetPath in the Windows registry, see Appendix B.

In Paradox, you can do this either by running Nupdate.exe or by using the **-net** command-line option (Paradox 4.*x* versions only). If you use the **-net** command-line option, be sure to include a backslash (\) at the end of the path. This is because both Microsoft Access and the Paradox Nupdate.exe program place the backslash at the end automatically. The **-net** command-line option was not available in Paradox prior to version 4.0. For more information, see the *Paradox Network Administrator's Guide*.

Paradox .lck Files

Occasionally the Paradox .lck file is inadvertently left in a folder. This prevents either Microsoft Access or Paradox from accessing files in that folder. To fix this, delete the .lck file.

Potential Paradox for Windows Restructure Problem

Problems occasionally occur when using the Paradox for Windows table restructure routine. If you are having difficulty getting Microsoft Access to open your Paradox 4.*x* table properly, consider restructuring it in Paradox for DOS version 4.0 or 4.5 and trying again.

Linking or Opening Paradox Tables on a Network

Microsoft Access for Windows 95 is unable to link or open Paradox tables in the private folder of an active Paradox session. While you have a linked Paradox table open in Microsoft Access, records added by other users will not be visible to you until you close and reopen the table. However, records added by you in Microsoft Access will be visible to the Paradox user when their screen is refreshed, if they have Auto Refresh turned on.

Primary Key Greater Than 255 Bytes

If a multifield primary key is greater than 255 bytes, the table can only be opened read-only. If you have a table with a two-plus field primary index, and the sum of the bytes used by the index exceeds 255 bytes (characters), you are limited to read-only access to the table.

Encrypted Tables

Microsoft Access doesn't support auxiliary passwords on Paradox tables. To use the table with Microsoft Access, open the table in Paradox and remove the auxiliary password.

Paradox Referential Integrity

Microsoft Access referential integrity doesn't work with linked Paradox tables. Linked Paradox tables cannot be used to trigger cascading deletes or updates, or prevent *orphaning of records* (deleting a master record when related detail records still exist in other tables).

Specifying a User Name in the ParadoxUserName Entry in the Windows Registry

You must specify a user name in the ParadoxUserName entry in the \\Hkey_Local_Machine\Software\Microsoft\Jet\3.0\Engines\Paradox folder of the Windows registry. There must also not be more than one user registered with the same name on the same network, which can occur if you ran Microsoft Access Setup, and didn't specify a name when prompted, or if you ran Setup with the **/q** option and didn't specify a name using the **/n** *username* option. When you don't specify a name, Setup uses the company name in the ParadoxUserName entry. This works for a single user, but if more than one person on a network did not specify a name, there will be duplicate names.

To avoid this problem, make sure you specify a user name when you set up Microsoft Access, or use the **/n** option when using the **/q** option. If you've already run Setup, edit the ParadoxUserName entry manually and add a user name.

Defining Relationships

After you have defined primary keys or unique indexes for each of your tables, you should define the relationships between your tables. For more information about defining relationships using Microsoft Access, see "Relationships" earlier in this chapter.

Exporting a Table to a Paradox File

If you need to save the data from a table or query that has been created in Microsoft Access so that it can be used by users who are still using Paradox, you can export that data.

▸ **To export a Microsoft Access table or query to a Paradox file**

1. Open a database, or switch to the Database window for the open database.

2. In the Database window, highlight the table or query you want to export.

3. On the File menu, click Save As/Export.

4. Click To An External File Or Database, and then click OK.

5. In the Save As Type box, select the Paradox format you want, and click OK.

6. In the File Name box, type a filename for the database file you want to export.

7. In the Save In box, select the folder you want to save in, and then click Export.

If you export a table with table or field names that don't fit the requirements in the destination database, Microsoft Access adjusts the names. For example, if you export data to a Paradox table, any field names longer than 10 characters are truncated.

If you attempt to export a Microsoft Access table containing long field names to Paradox, and the first 25 characters are identical to an existing field name, Microsoft Access will generate a unique field name.

When Microsoft Access exports a table with a field name containing a number sign (#), it is converted to a period. An opening or closing parenthesis, curly bracket, or quotation mark—that is, (,), {, }, or "—is converted to an underscore character (_).

Exporting Microsoft Access Memo fields to Paradox format results in extra carriage return characters.

When using Visual Basic for applications to create Paradox tables, text columns default to 255 characters if you do not specify a field width using the FieldSize property. Wide columns such as these make it easy for the new table to exceed the 1350 character maximum width of a Paradox table with a primary key. If you attempt to append a primary index to a Paradox table wider than 1350 characters, you will get an error message.

Setting Microsoft Access Options for Paradox

Microsoft Access for Windows 95 uses the Microsoft Jet 3.0 database engine to read and write data whether it is using its own native tables or linking tables in other data formats. The settings Microsoft Jet 3.0 uses to initialize the Paradox driver are located in the \\Hkey_Local_Machine\Software\Microsoft\Jet\3.0\Engines\Paradox folder of the Windows registry. Although the Microsoft Access Setup program automatically creates recommended option settings, if you need to, you can modify these settings.

For more information on Microsoft Access registry settings, see Appendix B, "Registry Keys and Values."

Running Multiple Data Access Applications

Microsoft Access for Windows 95, Microsoft Excel for Windows 95, Microsoft Visual Basic 4.0, and custom applications developed using these programs all use the Microsoft Jet 3.0 database engine to perform their database-related operations. If you are running one or more of these applications on the same computer, they will all be initializing the Microsoft Jet 3.0 database engine using the Windows registry settings below the \\Hkey_Local_Machine\Software\Microsoft\Jet\3.0 key. If you modify any of these settings, these changes will apply to all applications using the Microsoft Jet 3.0 database engine on the same computer. It is possible to avoid this in two ways.

- Any settings defined in the \\Hkey_Local_Machine\Software\Microsoft\Access\7.0\Jet\3.0\Engines key will override settings in the \\Hkey_Local_Machine\Software\Microsoft\Jet\3.0\Engines key and will apply only to Microsoft Access for Windows 95.

- If you have the Access Developers Toolkit for Microsoft Access for Windows 95, you can use the Setup Wizard to create an installation program for a custom Microsoft Access application that will set up a *user profile*. A user profile is an alternative set of registry keys containing settings that override the standard Microsoft Access and Microsoft Jet 3.0 settings when running that application. User profiles are analogous to *Appname*.ini files that are used in previous versions of Microsoft Access.

For more information on Microsoft Access registry settings, see Appendix B, "Registry Keys and Values."

These considerations do not apply to previous versions of Microsoft Access and Visual Basic, which use .ini files for initialization information. The following table shows where each of these previous version applications looks for its initialization information.

Application	INI file
Microsoft Access version 2.0	Msacc20.ini
Microsoft Access version 1.x	Msaccess.ini
Microsoft Access 1.x or 2.0 application	*Appname*.ini
Visual Basic 3.0 at design time	Vb.ini
Visual Basic 3.0 at run time	Vb.ini
Visual Basic 3.0 .exe application	*Appname*.ini

Built-in Drivers and ODBC Drivers

In Microsoft Access, you can import, export, and link data in a number of different database formats as well as spreadsheets and text files. To connect to a particular type of data, Microsoft Access uses either a built-in driver or an ODBC (Open Database Connectivity) driver. A driver is a dynamic link library (.dll) used to connect a specific data source with another client application, in this case, Microsoft Access.

Built-in Drivers

You can use built-in drivers to import, export, or link the following types of data:

- Other Microsoft Access databases, versions 1.x, 2.0, and 7.0.
- Microsoft FoxPro version 2.0, 2.5, 2.6 database files. Import and export, but not link, 3.0 database files.
- Paradox version 3.x, 4.x, and 5.x tables.
- dBASE III, IV, and 5 files.
- Microsoft Excel and Lotus 1-2-3 spreadsheets.
- Text (fixed-width and delimited text files).
- Microsoft Word for Windows mail merge data files (export only).

If you chose Typical or Compact when you first installed Microsoft Access, the FoxPro, Paradox, and dBASE drivers are not installed. If you need to use these drivers, re-run the Microsoft Access or Office Setup program to install them. Microsoft Access supports Microsoft Excel, Lotus 1-2-3, Text, and Microsoft Word for Windows without installing drivers.

Products from other vendors and other Microsoft products also contain ODBC drivers, including drivers for the applications in the previous list. These drivers may have been installed on your computer. If you want to know whether these drivers have been tested and verified for use with Microsoft Access, contact the driver vendor.

ODBC Drivers

The Microsoft SQL Server ODBC driver has been tested and verified for use with Microsoft Access. This driver is supplied with Microsoft Access and Microsoft Office Pro. If it is not installed on your computer, re-run Setup, choose Add/Remove, and make sure that the SQL Server Driver option is selected.

After you've installed the Microsoft SQL Server driver from Microsoft Office Setup, use the ODBC Manager (or the ODBC Administrator if you are running under Windows NT) to add, modify, and delete ODBC drivers and data sources.

▷ **To set up ODBC data sources using the ODBC Manager**

1. In Microsoft Windows, click the Windows Start button, point to Settings, and then click Control Panel.

   In Microsoft Windows NT, double-click the ODBC Administrator icon in the ODBC program group.

2. Double-click the icon 32-bit ODBC.

3. Do one of the following:

   - To define a new data source for a currently installed driver, click Add.

   - To modify the definition of a current data source, click a name in the Data Sources list, and then click Setup.

   - To install or delete an ODBC driver, click Drivers.

You must use specific network protocols and network configurations when you connect a Microsoft Access database to an SQL database using an ODBC driver.

The following protocols and configurations have been tested for use with Microsoft Access and the Microsoft SQL Server driver.

Server platform	Network protocol
Microsoft SQL Server version 4.2a (OS/2)	Microsoft Named Pipes
Microsoft SQL Server NT	Microsoft Named Pipes
Microsoft SQL Server 6.0	Microsoft Named Pipes

For other supported platforms, see your Microsoft SQL Server documentation including the SQL Server Driver Help file.

For more information about ODBC and how it works, see "ODBC and Client/Server Operations" in Chapter 15, "Using Workgroup Features and Applications with Office."

CHAPTER 18

Switching to Microsoft Excel

This chapter places particular emphasis on issues that arise when a workgroup is moving to Microsoft Excel from another spreadsheet application. This chapter is intended as a starting point to be used in the transition process, and offers guidance and information specific to that process.

In This Chapter

Converting File Formats

File formats determine the way information in a workbook is stored in a file. Different spreadsheet applications use different file formats. Microsoft Excel enables you to open and save files in many different formats, using the Open and Save As commands on the File menu. This section examines these data exchange formats in detail.

Data Exchange Specifications

Microsoft Excel can both open and save many different file formats. The list of formats that appears in the Save As dialog box varies depending on what kind of sheet is active. When saving, some file formats save the entire workbook and others save only the active worksheet. (When saving the latter file type, you need to activate and save each sheet in the workbook individually.) See the following lists for a comprehensive summary of formats based on how they can be used.

Formats for Opening and Saving Files

File Formats That Save the Entire Workbook:

Version	File format
Microsoft Excel 5.0 Workbook	XLS
Microsoft Excel 5.0 Template	XLT
Microsoft Excel 5.0 Workspace	XLW
Microsoft Excel version 4.0 Workspace (saves worksheets, chart sheets, and Microsoft Excel version 4.0 macro sheets only)	XLW, XLA, XLT, XLB, XLL
Lotus 1-2-3 Release 5 for Windows	WK4
Lotus 1-2-3 Release 4.*x* for Windows	WK4
Lotus 1-2-3 Release 3.*x* (saves worksheets and chart sheets only)	WK3, FM3

Note A supplemental converter exists to allow users of Microsoft Excel 5.0c for Windows (16-bit) to open, but not save, WK4 files. You can obtain this converter from the Office Resource Kit CD, or by calling Microsoft Product Support Services.

File Formats That Save the Active Sheet Only

Version	File format
Formatted Text (space delimited Lotus PRN format)	PRN
Text (Windows, tab delimited)	TXT, Text (Macintosh, OS/2, or MS-DOS)
CSV (Windows, comma delimited)	CSV (Macintosh, OS/2, or MS-DOS)
Microsoft Excel Version 4.0 formats	XLS, XLC, XLM, XLT, XLA, XLB, XLW
Microsoft Excel Version 3.0 formats	XLS, XLC, XLM, XLW, XLA, XLT
Microsoft Excel Version 2.*x* formats	XLS, XLC, XLM, XLW
Microsoft Excel Macro (Microsoft Excel versions 2.1, 3.0, 4.0)	XLM
Lotus 1-2-3	WKS, WK1, (ALL, FMT)
Quattro/Pro (DOS)	WQ1
dBASE II, III, IV	DBF
CSV (Macintosh, OS/2, or MS-DOS; comma delimited)	CSV
DIF (data interchange format)	DIF
SYLK (symbolic link format)	SLK

Formats for Opening Files

File Formats That Microsoft Excel Can Open But Not Save:

Version	File format
Microsoft Works (MS-DOS and Windows only)	WKS
Lotus 1-2-3 Releases 3.0, 3.1+, and 1-2-3/W	PIC (when included in an ALL file)
Lotus 1-2-3 Release 5 for Windows Templates	WT4
Novell Quattro Pro for Windows Versions 5.0	WB1

Clipboard Formats

You can paste the following formats in Microsoft Excel with the Paste or Paste Special command:

Format	Clipboard type identifier
Picture	Picture (also known as Windows metafile) for Windows; PICT for the Macintosh
Bitmap	Bitmap for Windows
Microsoft Excel file formats	BIFF, BIFF3, BIFF4
Symbolic link format	SYLK
Lotus 1-2-3 Release 2.x format	WK1
Data interchange format	DIF
Text (tab delimited) format	Text
Comma-separated values format	CSV
Formatted text*	Rich Text Format (RTF)
Embedded object	Native, OwnerLink, and Picture for Windows; NATV, OLNK, and PICT for the Macintosh; or other presentation format
Linked object	OwnerLink, ObjectLink, Link, and Picture for Windows; OLNK, OJLK, LINK, and PICT for the Macintosh; or other format
Text	Display Text, OEM Text
Values	VALU for the Macintosh

*From Microsoft Excel only

Importing Text Files

If you want to open a text file in Microsoft Excel, click the Open button or choose Open from the File menu, select the filename, and click OK. The file is loaded and the Text Import Wizard appears. The Text Import Wizard guides you through the steps you need to import the text file and distribute the text across columns.

Switching from Lotus 1-2-3

All of your Lotus 1-2-3 worksheets are compatible with Microsoft Excel, allowing you to open them, work on them, and then save them either as Lotus 1-2-3 worksheets or Microsoft Excel worksheets. With Microsoft Excel for Windows 95, you can run Lotus 1-2-3 Release 2.01-compatible macros, and you can import formatting files created using Allways or the WYSIWYG add-in. You can also use the skills you developed while using Lotus 1-2-3 to help you learn Microsoft Excel for Windows. With Help for Lotus 1-2-3 Users, you can enter a Lotus 1-2-3 command and then choose either to watch as Microsoft Excel performs the equivalent Microsoft Excel commands or to read a set of detailed written instructions.

The simple act of opening a Lotus 1-2-3 worksheet into Microsoft Excel converts both formulas and formatting automatically. After the worksheet is opened (or loaded, in Lotus 1-2-3 terms), you can start working with it immediately.

Note If you open any Lotus 1-2-3 .WK? file in Microsoft Excel, the Transition Formula Evaluation option is automatically activated, which causes Microsoft Excel to use Lotus 1-2-3 rules for calculating formulas. For more information about Transition Formula Evaluation, see "Using the Transition Tab" later in this chapter.

Using Your Knowledge of Lotus 1-2-3 to Learn Microsoft Excel

Although the set of commands and rules for entering data in Lotus 1-2-3 differs from those of Microsoft Excel, there are several features built into Microsoft Excel that allow you to use what you know about working with Lotus 1-2-3 to learn Microsoft Excel. By using some or all of these options, you can be immediately productive and learn Microsoft Excel at the same time.

If you want	Do this
To use Lotus 1-2-3 commands to learn equivalent Microsoft Excel commands	Click Options on the Tools menu, click the Transition tab, type a menu-activation character in the Microsoft Excel Menu Or Help Key box (the slash character is entered there for you), and select the Lotus 1-2-3 Help option button. (You type the menu activation character to activate the menu bar using the keyboard.)
To navigate through Microsoft Excel worksheets using an alternate command set	Click Options on the Tools menu, click the Transition tab, and select the Transition Navigation Keys check box.
To learn Microsoft Excel formula syntax by using Lotus 1-2-3 function syntax	Click Options on the Tools menu, click the Transition tab, and select the Transition Formula Entry check box.
To assist file conversion to Microsoft Excel by using Lotus 1-2-3 rules for evaluating text fields and database criteria	Click Options on the Tools menu, click the Transition tab, and select the Transition Formula Evaluation check box.
To run your Lotus 1-2-3 macros	Open the Lotus 1-2-3 file containing the macros you want to use, hold down CTRL and press the macro letter.

Help for Lotus 1-2-3 Users

You can use your knowledge of 1-2-3 to learn Microsoft Excel. In the Help for Lotus 1-2-3 dialog box, you can type a 1-2-3 command and Microsoft Excel either displays a set of instructions or performs an interactive demonstration of the equivalent Microsoft Excel command. If you select the Instructions option button, the instructions for the task are placed on your worksheet so that you can view them conveniently while you finish the task.

Choose a 1-2-3 command you want help with.

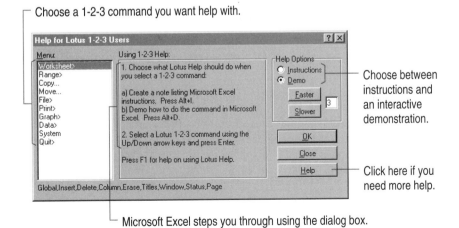

Choose between instructions and an interactive demonstration.

Click here if you need more help.

Microsoft Excel steps you through using the dialog box.

There are two ways to open the Help For Lotus 1-2-3 Users dialog box:

- On the Help menu, click Lotus 1-2-3 Help.
- On the Tools menu, click the Options command, click the Transition tab. In the Excel Menu Or Help Key box, make sure the / (slash) character appears, and select the Lotus 1-2-3 Help option button. With these settings, pressing the SLASH key (/) displays the Help For Lotus 1-2-3 Users dialog box.

The following paragraphs describe each section of the Help for Lotus 1-2-3 Users dialog box.

Menu   Displays a list of Lotus 1-2-3 menu items. Type the Lotus 1-2-3 keystrokes you would use to choose a command, depending on the type of help you select in Help Options, as described below. For multilevel Lotus 1-2-3 menus, Microsoft Excel displays the next submenu on a status line at the bottom of the dialog box. To move down to a lower menu level, select the menu item and press ENTER or type the first letter of the menu item.

Using 1-2-3 Help   The Using 1-2-3 Help box initially displays instructions for using Help for Lotus 1-2-3 Users. If you select a Lotus 1-2-3 command, this box displays instructions for performing the equivalent command in Microsoft Excel. The title of this box changes depending on the menu item currently selected. If you select the Instructions option under Help Options and then press ENTER when the command is selected and the procedure is visible, the dialog box disappears but the procedure remains posted on your sheet for reference as you carry out the command. (This also occurs if you select the last item in a keystroke sequence, such as the "r" in \fr.)To remove the text box containing the procedure, press ESC.

Help Options   You can choose to either display a text box containing the Microsoft Excel equivalent procedure for carrying out a Lotus 1-2-3 command (the Instructions option), or to watch Microsoft Excel demonstrate the equivalent steps for you (the Demo option). To select the Instructions option with the keyboard, press ALT+I. To select the Demo option with the keyboard, press ALT+D.

For commands requiring additional information, such as cell references, you are prompted for the necessary information at the top of the Microsoft Excel window before the demonstration starts.

The Faster and Slower buttons enable you to choose from among five demonstration speeds, with 5 being the fastest and 1 being the slowest. The current speed is displayed in the box to the right of the two buttons. To select speeds with the keyboard, press ALT+F for faster, or press ALT+S for slower.

Using the Transition Tab

Some Microsoft Excel spreadsheet operations such as calculating formulas, using the keyboard, and entering dates work differently from those in other spreadsheet applications. Fortunately, Microsoft Excel lets you decide how you want these features to work. You can select either the standard Microsoft Excel operation or the operation that matches 1-2-3 and other 1-2-3–compatible spreadsheet applications.

To specify how you want Microsoft Excel to operate, choose the Options command from the Tools menu and select the Transition tab. This tab contains options to help you in your transition to Microsoft Excel.

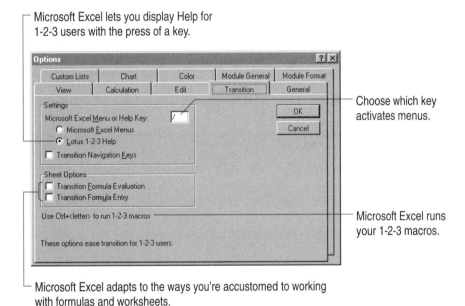

Microsoft Excel lets you display Help for 1-2-3 users with the press of a key.

Choose which key activates menus.

Microsoft Excel runs your 1-2-3 macros.

Microsoft Excel adapts to the ways you're accustomed to working with formulas and worksheets.

Transition Navigation Keys

Microsoft Excel for Windows provides an alternate set of keyboard commands for navigating around spreadsheets. To activate this alternate set of commands, choose the Options command from the Tools menu, select the Transition tab, and then select the Transition Navigation Keys check box. For example, in Lotus 1-2-3, pressing HOME moves the active cell highlight to cell A1. In Microsoft Excel, pressing HOME moves the active cell highlight to the first cell in the current row. When you activate the Transition Navigation Keys option, pressing HOME moves the active cell to cell A1.

The following tables list the keyboard shortcuts that are in effect when you select the Transition Navigation Keys check box.

Navigation Keys	Description
CTRL+LEFT ARROW	Left one page
CTRL+RIGHT ARROW	Right one page
CTRL+PAGE UP	In a workbook, next sheet
CTRL+PAGE DOWN	In a workbook, previous sheet
TAB	Right one page
SHIFT+TAB	Left one page
HOME	Selects cell in the upper-left corner of the sheet

Function Keys	Description
F5	Edit menu, Go To command
F6	Next window of the same workbook
SHIFT+F6	Previous pane of the same window

In Data Find Mode

LEFT ARROW	Moves to the previous field of the current record
RIGHT ARROW	Moves to the next field of the current record
HOME	Moves to the first record
END	Moves to the last record

When the Transition Navigation Keys check box is selected, use the following text-alignment prefix characters to assign alignment formats as you enter data into cells.

Text-Alignment Prefix Characters

' (apostrophe)	Aligns data in the cell to the left
" (quotation mark)	Aligns data in the cell to the right
^ (caret)	Centers data in the cell
\ (backslash)	Repeats characters across the cell

When in Point mode, hidden columns unhide themselves temporarily.

Transition Formula Entry

Microsoft Excel uses a different syntax than Lotus 1-2-3 in formulas and functions. Using Transition Formula Entry to learn the Microsoft Excel syntax, you can enter any formula or function exactly as you would in Lotus 1-2-3, and you will be shown how it is entered Microsoft Excel.

With the Transition tab of the Options command on the Tools menu, you can select the Transition Formula Entry check box to enter any formula or function or range name according to Lotus 1-2-3 syntax. Microsoft Excel does not automatically turn on Transition Formula Entry for Microsoft Excel worksheets or Lotus 1-2-3 worksheets.

When Transition Formula Entry is turned on, you can:

- Enter any formula or function as you would in Lotus 1-2-3. Microsoft Excel automatically translates the formula into a Microsoft Excel formula when you click the enter box (the checked box) in the formula bar or press ENTER. For example, if you enter the formula @AVG(A1..A5), Microsoft Excel changes it to =AVERAGE(A1:A5).

- Enter a reference that corresponds to a defined range name. The range name appears in the formula after you click the enter box (the checked box) or press ENTER.

- Edit the reference of a range name in the formula bar by clicking the formula bar, which automatically displays the reference. The range name reappears when you click the enter box (the checked box) or press ENTER.

- Delete a range name. All formulas that contain that range name change to display the reference instead of the range name.

- Use a dollar sign ($) before a range name to make the range name absolute.

When you turn Transition Formula Entry on or off, formulas don't automatically reapply names or revert names to references. Therefore, decide whether you want to turn Transition Formula Entry on of off before you begin working on a worksheet.

After you turn on Transition Formula Entry, it remains turned on for that worksheet until you turn it off, even if you save the Lotus 1-2-3 worksheet as a Microsoft Excel worksheet.

Transition formula entry affects only range names that are simple and absolute, and does not affect range names that refer to nonadjacent selections. All Lotus 1-2-3 range names created in Lotus 1-2-3 are affected by Transition Formula Entry.

Transition Formula Evaluation

Microsoft Excel and Lotus 1-2-3 evaluate certain formulas and expressions differently. The Transition Formula Evaluation option allows Microsoft Excel to calculate formulas and database criteria according to Lotus 1-2-3 rules.

The following types of expressions are evaluated differently in Excel than in Lotus:

- Cells that contain text in Lotus 1-2-3 are considered to have a value of zero (0) when the cell is used in a formula. In Microsoft Excel, you cannot combine text and numeric entries in the same formula. For example, suppose you want to calculate an average using a range of cells containing numeric entries and cells containing text. In Microsoft Excel, the cells containing text are ignored rather than included in the calculation as zero entries.

- Boolean expressions in Lotus 1-2-3 are evaluated to 0 or 1 and display 0 or 1 in the cell. For example, 2<3 shows a 1 in the cell to represent true. Microsoft Excel also calculates them as 0 and 1, but displays FALSE or TRUE, respectively, in the cell.

- In Microsoft Excel, database criteria ranges are evaluated differently when you are extracting data, finding data, and using database functions. For example, computed criteria can use existing field names.

- Certain functions, including @MOD, @VLOOKUP, and @HLOOKUP, are evaluated differently than the equivalent Microsoft Excel functions. For example, the Lotus 1-2-3 @VLOOKUP function performs literal matches on text, whereas Microsoft Excel's VLOOKUP function returns a lookup value for nonliteral text, using the nearest entry in alphabetic order.

When you open a Lotus 1-2-3 worksheet in Microsoft Excel, Transition Formula Evaluation is turned on for that sheet. This ensures that the formulas are calculated according to the preceding Lotus 1-2-3 rules.

If your save the Lotus 1-2-3 worksheet as a Microsoft Excel worksheet, Transition Formula Evaluation remains turned on until you turn it off. Transition Formula Evaluation is not turned on automatically for Microsoft Excel worksheets.

Warning Avoid turning Transition Formula Evaluation on and off; otherwise, the values calculated on your worksheet might change. If you leave Transition Formula Evaluation turned off, your worksheet will adhere to Microsoft Excel rules. If you leave the option turned on, your worksheet will adhere to Lotus 1-2-3 rules.

Consolidating Multiple Worksheets

Using the Consolidate command, you can easily select data from other files, on your computer or on the network. The addresses of these data sources are stored in the worksheet, and you can call them whenever an update is needed by using the Consolidate command on the Data menu. You can also construct dynamic links to the source data that will update the figures in the consolidation worksheet automatically.

For example, suppose you have a departmental budget that consists of monthly data from several different sources throughout the department. The source sheets can be a variety of Microsoft Excel and Lotus 1-2-3 files. Each source might have a set of daily, weekly, or monthly worksheets itemizing actual and projected budgets. Each source can use consolidation to collect specific data from the set of worksheets in order to create a summary worksheet. The person responsible for the overall budget can use consolidation formulas to collect this summary information from each source across the network and, in turn, create a master departmental summary worksheet.

Using 3-Dimensional Formulas in Workbooks

If you store a group of worksheets with identical layouts, such as monthly reports, in the same workbook, you can use 3-dimensional formulas to consolidate data into summary worksheets. 3-dimensional formulas allow you to specify sheet ranges in a workbook, which are similar to cell ranges on a worksheet. You can apply a number of different functions, such as SUM and AVERAGE, to the resulting 3-dimensional range.

While you can create summary reports for identical sheets in a workbook using the Consolidate command, 3-dimensional formulas offer several advantages. 3-dimensional formulas are dynamic. Like other Microsoft Excel formulas, the results are automatically updated to reflect changes in subordinate data. Using linked consolidation instead of 3-dimensional formulas adds an outline to the summary worksheet, inserting hidden rows and columns to store the linking formulas. 3-dimensional formulas are also easier to create and modify than linked consolidations.

Transition Terminology

The following table lists Lotus 1-2-3 terms and their Microsoft Excel counterparts. The Microsoft Excel term is not necessarily an exact equivalent of the Lotus 1-2-3 term, but rather a term you can look up in the online help system for more information. You don't need to understand all of these terms before you start using Microsoft Excel.

Lotus 1-2-3 term	Microsoft Excel term
@Function	Function
Address	Reference
Anchor cell	Selecting a range of cells
Border	Row and column headings
CALC indicator	Status bar
Cell pointer	Active cell
Column labels	Column headings

Lotus 1-2-3 term	Microsoft Excel term
Command prompt	Dialog box
Control panel	Menu bar, formula bar, status bar
Copy	Copy, and then paste
Crosshatching	Chart patterns
Current cell	Active cell
Current worksheet	Active worksheet, chart, or macro sheet
Cursor	Insertion point
Data labels	Data marker labels
Data range	Data series
Data table 1	One-input table
Data table 2	Two-input table
Date format	Number format
Erase	Clear
Formula criteria	Computed criteria
Global	Workspace
Graph	Chart
Graph labels	Chart text
Graph titles	Chart titles
Highlight	Select or selection
Indicator	Status bar
Input range	Database range
Label	Text
Label-prefix	Alignment
Label/matching criteria	Comparison criteria
Logical 0	FALSE
Logical 1	TRUE
Menu pointer	Menu selection
Mode indicator	Status bar
Move	Cut, and then paste
Number/matching criteria	Comparison criteria
Numeric format	Number format
Output range	Extract range
Picture file	Chart document
Pointer movement keys	Arrow keys
Print range	Print area

Lotus 1-2-3 term	Microsoft Excel term
PrintGraph	Printing a chart
Prompt	Dialog box
Protected cell	Locked/protected cell
Range highlight	Selected range
Repeating label	Fill alignment
Retrieve a file	Open a file
Row numbers	Row headings
Stacked bar graph	Column chart, bar chart
Status indicator, status line	Status bar
String	Text
Target cell	Dependent cell
Target file	Dependent document
Time format	Number format
Titles	Split worksheet window with frozen panes
Translate utility	Open and Save As commands on the File menu
Value	Number
Window	Multiple windows, pane

File Conversions

You can use Microsoft Excel with your existing Lotus 1-2-3 worksheets by simply opening your Lotus 1-2-3 worksheet in Microsoft Excel the same way you open any Microsoft Excel worksheet—using the Open toolbar button or the Open command on the File menu. When you finish editing the worksheet, you can save it as either a Microsoft Excel worksheet or a Lotus 1-2-3 worksheet.

Similarly, it's easy to save a Microsoft Excel worksheet in a Lotus 1-2-3 format and then open it in Lotus 1-2-3. After you export a Microsoft Excel worksheet to Lotus 1-2-3 format, you can edit it using Lotus 1-2-3.

When you open a WK3 file in Microsoft Excel, it is opened as a workbook. The associated FM3 formatting file is also opened and its formatting information is applied. Similarly, when you save Microsoft Excel workbooks in WK3 format, the associated FM3 file is created automatically.

Microsoft Excel opens and saves the following Lotus 1-2-3 file formats:

Lotus 1-2-3 release	File format
1, 1A	WKS
2.0, 2.01, 2.2	WK1, ALL
2.3, 2.4	WK1, FMT
3.0	WK3
3.1, 3.1+, 1-2-3/W, R1.1	WK3, FM3
4.0, 5.0	WK4, WT4

Note In WK3 and WK4 formats, Microsoft Excel can read and write both 2-dimensional and 3-dimensional worksheets.

When you open a Lotus 1-2-3 worksheet in Microsoft Excel, Microsoft Excel automatically opens the corresponding ALL, FMT, or FM3 file. Drop shadows and objects drawn on top of charts are not imported to Microsoft Excel. Also, double underlines and wide underlines appear as a single underline in Microsoft Excel. When you save a Lotus 1-2-3 worksheet in Microsoft Excel, an FMT or FM3 file is automatically saved. However, because of the limitations of the Impress add-in, you can save only the first eight styles you create and the first eight fonts you use.

For more information about Impress, see "WYSIWYG (Impress) Formatting" later in this chapter.

Unsupported Lotus 1-2-3 Release 4 and Release 5 Features

Features without direct equivalents in Microsoft Excel will not be imported:

- No direct equivalent exists in Microsoft Excel for range versions created with the Lotus 1-2-3 Version Manager. Therefore, Microsoft Excel will import only the data from the version that is currently displayed (the last time the file was saved). However, you can use the Microsoft Excel Scenario Manager to create, store, and retrieve what-if assumptions for multiple sets of up to 32 changing cells.

- Database Records in Lotus 1-2-3 Release 4 are not compatible with either ODBC or Microsoft Query, so they are not imported.

- Embedded OLE objects are not imported. This includes the Lotus Maps objects from Release 5.

- Rotated text or drawing objects are imported, but displayed with normal horizontal alignment.

- Designer Frames are not imported.

- For gradient fills, the cell or object is formatted using only the primary color from the fill.

Importing and Exporting References

When exporting Microsoft Excel files to Lotus 1-2-3, the following occur due to the lack of equivalent functionality in Lotus 1-2-3.

- Microsoft Excel cannot export formulas containing references to nonadjacent selections, unless they are arguments to translatable functions.

- Functions that produce references as a result are not exported to WKS.

- The Microsoft Excel intersection (blank space) and union (comma) operators are not exported to Lotus 1-2-3.

In these cases, Microsoft Excel substitutes the value of the formula for the formula itself. When you save a document in a Lotus 1-2-3 file format, any references in a Microsoft Excel worksheet to rows beyond 2048 (for WKS file format) or 8192 (for WK1 and WK3 file formats) wrap around the edges of the worksheet. For example, when you save a reference to cell A8193 in WK1 format, the reference changes to A1 in Microsoft Excel.

Importing and Exporting External References

Lotus 1-2-3 Releases 1a and 2.01 don't support external references (file linking) to other worksheets, so any Microsoft Excel formulas containing external references are not exported to WKS or WK1 file formats. In these cases, Microsoft Excel substitutes the value of the formula for the formula itself.

Opening and Saving a Lotus 1-2-3 Worksheet

The majority of your Lotus 1-2-3 worksheets can easily be converted to Microsoft Excel format by opening them and saving them with Microsoft Excel.

▶ **To open and save a Lotus 1-2-3 worksheet in Microsoft Excel**

1. In Microsoft Excel, click the Open button on the Standard toolbar or choose the Open command from the File menu.

2. In the Files Of Type list box, select Lotus 1-2-3 Files.

3. Switch to the appropriate folder and select the Lotus 1-2-3 worksheet that you want to convert, or type the complete filename in the File Name box.

   If the Lotus 1-2-3 worksheet you want to convert has graphs associated with it, Microsoft Excel converts the Lotus 1-2-3 graphs to Microsoft Excel charts, and places them on a separate chart sheet in the workbook. Charts created using Impress or Allways are embedded on the corresponding worksheet.

4. On the File menu, click Save As to save each converted Lotus 1-2-3 worksheet as a Microsoft Excel workbook. Make sure the Microsoft Excel Workbook option is selected in the Save As Type list box.

If you have any formulas in cells that cannot be converted, Microsoft Excel displays another dialog box asking you if it should continue to alert you each time a cell does not convert. Microsoft Excel attaches a note to any cell that does not convert. Formulas that do not convert are discarded, but the result of the formula is preserved in the cell. Keep a copy of the original Lotus 1-2-3 worksheet in case there are formulas that do not convert, so that you can refer to the original Lotus 1-2-3 formula in order to rebuild it using the equivalent Microsoft Excel method. The most common conversion problems are formulas that have over eight levels of nesting in one formula, as is common with formulas that use multiple @IF functions. (For more information, see "Nested Formulas" later in this chapter.)

Auditing Your Lotus 1-2-3 Worksheet Before Conversion

Audits conducted by the industry on corporate MS-DOS–based worksheets found that approximately 30 percent of all worksheets contain serious errors. In some cases, major decisions have been made using worksheets that have been incorrect for years.

The only way to catch these errors is with a worksheet audit. You can do the audit while the worksheet is in Lotus 1-2-3 or after it is converted to Microsoft Excel. We recommend a partial audit on both sides. Each audit catches different problems. Auditing before conversion catches problems inherent to the original worksheet, such as values that have replaced formulas, circular errors, error results, and bad range names. Auditing after conversion catches problems introduced by the conversion process or by reorganization and linking.

Auditing Your Converted Worksheet

Auditing the worksheets in Microsoft Excel helps you find formulas that did not convert, links that are incorrect, or unexpected problems for which you might need additional help. The three Microsoft Excel features that are useful for auditing are the Auditing commands on the Tools menu, the Find command on the Edit menu, and the Special button in the dialog box that appears when you choose the Go To command on the Edit menu.

Note If Microsoft Excel encounters formulas that it cannot convert when you open a Lotus 1-2-3 worksheet, only the resulting values are displayed and the original formula is discarded. Microsoft Excel indicates this by displaying a cell note (and cell note indicator) in the cell, containing the message "Formula failed to convert." For more information, see "Translating Lotus 1-2-3 Formulas," later in this chapter.

▶ **To search for cells containing formulas that did not convert correctly**

1. On the Edit menu, click Find.

2. In the Find dialog box, select Notes from the Look In list.

3. In the Find What box, type **formula failed to convert**

4. Choose the Find Next button.

   The first cell containing the text you entered is selected. A message appears if the text cannot be found.

5. Choose the Find Next button again to go to the next cell with a note containing the text.

To select all cells with cell notes after you've loaded the file, click the Go To command on the Edit menu, click the Special button, and then select the Notes option button. This will select all cells with notes, allowing you to see where your formulas did not convert. You can also click the Page Setup command on the File menu, click the Sheet tab, and then select the Notes check box to print the notes along with the sheet. You can then use this printed document as a reference for troubleshooting. These cell notes will consist of all notes inserted by Microsoft Excel during the conversion process, as well as all cells converted from WK3 files that contain Lotus 1-2-3–style text notes in their formulas.

The Go To Special dialog box is a powerful tool. Using various Go To Special options, you can find:

- Cells supplying values to the active cell (Precedents option).

- Cells that use the value in the active cell (Dependents option).

- Cells containing only values (Constants option).

- Cells containing only formulas (Formulas option).

- Cells containing error values (Errors option).

- Cells containing notes (Notes option).

- Cells containing different reference patterns in a row or column (Row Differences or Column Differences options).

Auditing Using Cell Tracers

Another powerful auditing feature included with Microsoft Excel are *cell tracers*. Cell tracers are arrows drawn on a worksheet that point to the precedents or dependents of a selected cell, or trace the error path of a cell containing an error value. You use the Auditing command on the Tools menu to display tracer arrows. Alternatively, you can choose the Auditing command and then choose the Show Auditing Toolbar command to display the Auditing toolbar, which you can use to trace the flow of data between cells on your worksheet.

In the following figure, cell J8 was selected and the Trace Dependents button was clicked twice. The first click added arrows pointing to the first level of precedent cells, J5:J7; the second click indicated the second level of precedent cells, C2:C4 and C8:C10.

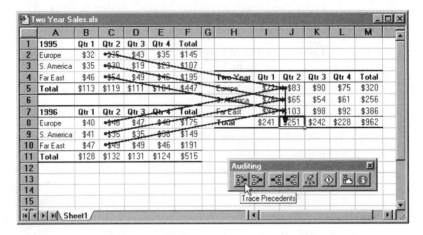

The auditing tools trace precedents and dependents of a selected formula using arrows.

Microsoft Excel Equivalents for Frequently Used Lotus 1-2-3 Commands

The following table lists Lotus 1-2-3 commands and the equivalent commands in Microsoft Excel.

Note In Microsoft Excel you select the range you want to work with before you choose a command. Many common commands can be carried out by clicking a button on a toolbar.

Lotus 1-2-3 command	Microsoft Excel command
/c	Edit menu, Copy and Paste command
/fd	File menu, Open command
/few	File menu, Find File command
/fr	File menu, Open command
/fs	File menu, Save As command
/gv	File menu, Open command is used when chart is in a separate file

Lotus 1-2-3 command	Microsoft Excel command
/m	Edit menu, Cut and Paste command
/ppg	File menu, Print command
/ppr	File menu, Set Print Area command, Print Area submenu
/qy	File menu, Exit command
/re	Edit menu, Clear command
/rf,	Format menu, Number tab, Cells command
/rfc	Format menu, Number tab, Cells command
/rfp	Format menu, Number tab, Cells command
/rnl	Insert menu, Create command, Name submenu
/rnc	Insert menu, Define command, Name submenu
/wcs	Format menu, Width command, Column submenu
/wdc	Edit menu, Delete command
/wdr	Edit menu, Delete command
/wey	File menu, Close and New commands
/wic	Insert menu, Columns command
/wir	Insert menu, Rows command
/wtc	Window menu, Unfreeze Panes command
/wth	Window menu, Freeze Panes command
/wtv	Window menu, Freeze Panes command

Lotus 1-2-3 Keyboard Equivalents

Microsoft Excel default keyboard equivalents to Lotus 1-2-3 keys are listed in the following tables. If you have not activated the Transition Navigation Keys option, these Lotus 1-2-3 keyboard equivalents will be in effect.

Function Keys

The following table compares function key assignments in Lotus 1-2-3 and their equivalents in Microsoft Excel.

Lotus 1-2-3	Microsoft Excel	Meaning
F1	F1	Help
F2	F2	Edit
F3	F3	Name
F4	F4	Absolute/Relative
F5	F5	Goto
F6	CTRL+F6	Next window

Lotus 1-2-3	Microsoft Excel	Meaning
F7	ALT, D, F	Query (first time)
	DOWN ARROW	Query (thereafter)
F8	Automatic	Table
F9	F9	Calculate
F10	F11 or ALT+F1	Graph

Navigation Keys

The default Microsoft Excel navigation keys are listed below. You can also turn on Microsoft Excel's transition navigation keys, which are equivalent to many of the Lotus 1-2-3 navigation keys.

Lotus 1-2-3	Microsoft Excel
Up, Down	UP ARROW, DOWN ARROW
Left, Right	LEFT ARROW, RIGHT ARROW
End, Up	CTRL+UP ARROW or END+UP ARROW
End, Down	CTRL+DOWN ARROW or END+DOWN ARROW
End, Left	CTRL+LEFT ARROW or END+LEFT ARROW
End, Right	CTRL+RIGHT ARROW or END+RIGHT ARROW
Home	CTRL+HOME
Tab	CTRL+PAGE DOWN
Shift+Tab	CTRL+PAGE UP
PgUp	PAGE UP
PgDn	PAGE DOWN

Translating Lotus 1-2-3 Formatting

Many Lotus 1-2-3 users have used add-ins to assist in the formatting of their worksheets. Lotus 1-2-3 Release 2.01 and 2.2 use the Allways add-in (which produces files with filenames that end with the .all extension), while Releases 2.3 and later use the WYSIWYG or Impress add-in (which produces files with filenames that end with .fmt or .fm3). In Lotus 1-2-3, after formatting is applied to a worksheet, a separate file is created and saved along with the worksheet. In Microsoft Excel, formatting information is saved in the workbook file.

WYSIWYG (Impress) Formatting

When you open a Lotus 1-2-3 worksheet that has a corresponding FMT (WK1) or FM3 (WK3) file created with the WYSIWYG add-in in the same folder, Microsoft Excel opens the WYSIWYG file automatically and applies the equivalent formats in Microsoft Excel. Conversely, when you use Microsoft Excel to save a Lotus 1-2-3 worksheet in Lotus 1-2-3 format, an FMT or FM3 file is automatically saved along with it, if one existed originally. You can also create an FMT or FM3 file when you save a WK1 or WK3 file, even if none existed originally.

Allways Formatting

Microsoft Excel offers full support of Allways files (.all). When you import a Lotus 1-2-3 worksheet that has a corresponding ALL file (with the same name, in the same folder), Microsoft Excel opens the Allways file automatically. When you use Microsoft Excel to save the same Lotus 1-2-3 file, Microsoft Excel will save both the WK1 file and a separate ALL file, if one existed originally. You can also create an ALL file when you save a WK1 file, even if none existed originally.

Underlining

When you open in Microsoft Excel a Lotus 1-2-3 worksheet that contains double underlines, the double underlines are converted to single underlines. Many underlining tasks, such as double underlining or single underlining at the bottom of summed columns, will be better accomplished in Microsoft Excel with the Cells command on the Format menu, using the text underlining options in the Font tab or the cell border options in the Border tab.

Objects Drawn Over WYSIWYG Graphs

The Lotus 1-2-3 WYSIWYG add-in creates embedded graphs, and also draws arrows, ovals, and other objects on top of these graphs. In Microsoft Excel, when you import a Lotus 1-2-3 worksheet and its associated WYSIWYG file, the embedded graph appears, but any overlaid drawings do not. However, after the worksheet and graph are imported, you can easily use any of the Microsoft Excel drawing tools to enhance them, as long as you save the worksheet in Microsoft Excel format.

Formatting in Microsoft Excel

This section describes the general procedure used to apply formatting in Microsoft Excel, and describes how formatting in Microsoft Excel equates to formatting in Lotus 1-2-3.

▶   **To format numbers**

1. Select the cells you want to format.

2. On the Format menu, click Cells.

3. Select the Number tab.

4. Select a format.

    Refer to the table below for Microsoft Excel equivalents to Lotus 1-2-3 formats.

    You can create other fixed decimal number formats by editing the displayed format in the Code box or by typing an entirely new one.

5. Click OK.

You use the same general procedure as described above to apply other types of formatting, using the other tabs in the Cells dialog box.

The following table lists Microsoft Excel equivalents to Lotus 1-2-3 formats, as shown on the Number tab in the Cells dialog box on the Format menu. The Microsoft Excel column indicates the category and selected options of the format.

Lotus 1-2-3	Microsoft Excel
Fixed	Number category, with default settings
Scientific	Scientific category, with default setting
Currency	Currency category, with the Use $ option turned off and the ($1,234.10) option selected in the Negative Numbers list
Comma	Number category, with the Use 1000 Separator (,) option selected
General	General category
+/-	No equivalent
Percent	Percentage category, with default setting
Date	Date category, with the 04-Mar-95 format selected in the Type list
Time	Time category, with the 1:30:55 PM format selected in the Type list
Text	You can choose to display either formulas or values for the entire worksheet, but not just in selected ranges. To display formulas or values, click Options on the Tools menu, click the View tab, and click the Formulas box in Window Options.
Hidden	Custom category, type ;;; in the Type edit box. Or use the Hide command on the Row submenu or Column submenu of the Format menu to hide entire rows or columns.
Reset	General

Translating Lotus 1-2-3 Formulas

Most Lotus 1-2-3 formulas and functions will convert to their Microsoft Excel equivalents when the worksheet is opened. If Microsoft Excel finds formulas that it cannot convert when you open a Lotus 1-2-3 worksheet, then only the resulting values will be present and the original formula will be lost. Microsoft Excel indicates this in two ways: first, a message that notifies the user that Excel cannot read the record appears when a formula is encountered that it cannot convert, and second, a cell note (and cell note indicator) appears in the cell, containing the message "Formula failed to convert."

Note For more information about converting formulas, see "Transition Formula Entry" and "Transition Formula Evaluation" earlier in this chapter.

Nested Formulas

Perhaps the most common reason that the "Cannot read record" message appears when loading Lotus 1-2-3 files is that a formula in your Lotus 1-2-3 worksheet uses more than eight levels of nesting. To get around this, you can break the formula in sections of less than eight nested segments each before conversion. However, many such nested formulas exist in order to construct elaborate alternative calculations based on a range of current conditions, such as @IF statements. In this case, a better workaround is to create a formula using @VLOOKUP and refer to a table on the side. Then there is no nesting needed, and you end up with a more readable and structured formula.

For example, suppose that in one cell you have the following Lotus 1-2-3 formula that arrives at a value, based on the name of a month from January to September:

```
@IF(a1="Jan",12,@IF(a1="Feb",2,@IF(a1="Mar",4,@IF(a1="Apr",34,
@IF(a1="May",32,@IF(a1="Jun",8,@IF(a1="Jul",43,@IF(a1="Aug",3,
@IF(a1="Sep",67,0)))))))))
```

The above formula has eight levels of nesting. To fix the problem, rewrite the formula like this in Lotus 1-2-3:

```
@VLOOKUP(a1,table,1)
```

where *table* is a range name that refers to the following two-column table, located anywhere on the worksheet:

```
Jan    12
Feb    2
Mar    4
Apr    34
May    32
Jun    8
Jul    43
Aug    3
Sep    67
```

When you then load the file in Microsoft Excel, it will convert without problems, and the formula will work properly (the offset argument 1 will be automatically converted to 2, because Microsoft Excel starts counting at 1, not 0). Using a table in this way is not only easier to read than the original formula, but it is also easy to modify by changing or adding new values.

Lotus 1-2-3 Functions

Most Lotus 1-2-3 functions have an equivalent in Microsoft Excel. When Transition Formula Entry is activated, you can type most Lotus 1-2-3 functions directly into the formula bar, where they are automatically converted to their Microsoft Excel equivalents. The functions you cannot enter in this way are specific to Lotus 1-2-3 Release 3 and later. To turn on Transition Formula Entry, select the Transition tab of the Options command on the Tools menu. Then select the Transition Formula Entry check box under Sheet Options.

Microsoft Excel uses different rules than Lotus 1-2-3 does when evaluating text in formulas, certain database criteria, and the value of certain logical operators. When Transition Formula Evaluation is activated, some functions are interpreted as they would be in Lotus 1-2-3, and are listed in the following table. To turn on Transition Formula Evaluation, select the Transition tab in the Options dialog box. See also "Entering Lotus 1-2-3 Formulas," earlier in this chapter.

The following table is an alphabetic list of Lotus 1-2-3 functions that have Microsoft Excel equivalents. For a list of Microsoft Excel functions without Lotus 1-2-3 equivalents, see the following section.

Lotus 1-2-3 function	Microsoft Excel equivalent	Comments
@@	INDIRECT	
@ABS	ABS	
@ACOS	ACOS	
@ASIN	ASIN	
@ATAN	ATAN	
@ATAN2	ATAN2	
@AVG	AVERAGE	
@CELL	CELL	
@CELLPOINTER	CELL	When used without a second argument, returns information about the current selection.
@CHAR	CHAR	
@CHOOSE	CHOOSE	
@CLEAN	CLEAN	

Lotus 1-2-3 function	Microsoft Excel equivalent	Comments
@CODE	CODE	
@COLS	COLUMNS	
@COS	COS	
@COUNT	COUNTA	
@CTERM	NPER	Requires periodic payment instead of future value.
@DATE	DATE	
@DATEVALUE	DATEVALUE	
@DAVG	DAVERAGE	
@DAY	DAY	
@D360	DAYS360	Lotus 1-2-3 Release 3 and later.
@DCOUNT	DCOUNTA	
@DDB	DDB	
@DGET	DGET	
@DMAX	DMAX	
@DMIN	DMIN	
@DSTD	DSTDEVP	
@DSTDS	DSTDEV	Lotus 1-2-3 Release 3 and later.
@DSUM	DSUM	
@DVAR	DVARP	
@DVARS	DVAR	Lotus 1-2-3 Release 3 and later.
@ERR	-	No equivalent is necessary, because Microsoft Excel lets you type error values directly into cells and formulas.
@EXACT	EXACT	
@EXP	EXP	
@FALSE	FALSE	
@FIND	FIND	
@FV	FV	
@HLOOKUP	HLOOKUP	Turn on Transition Formula Evaluation to use the Lotus 1-2-3 evaluation rules.
@HOUR	HOUR	
@IF	IF	Last two arguments can be any value, not just numbers or strings, as in @IF.
@INDEX	INDEX	Also has form for selecting values from an array.

Lotus 1-2-3 function	Microsoft Excel equivalent	Comments
@INT	TRUNC	
@IRR	IRR	Arguments are given in reverse order.
@ISERR	ISERR	Detects any of six Microsoft Excel error values.
@ISNA	ISNA	
@ISNUMBER	ISNONTEXT	
@ISRANGE	ISREF	Lotus 1-2-3 Release 3 and later.
@ISSTRING	ISTEXT	
@LEFT	LEFT	
@LENGTH	LEN	
@LN	LN	
@LOWER	LOWER	
@LOG	LOG	
@MAX	MAX	
@MID	MID	
@MIN	MIN	
@MINUTE	MINUTE	
@MOD	MOD	Turn on Transition Formula Evaluation to use the Lotus 1-2-3 evaluation rules.
@MONTH	MONTH	
@N	N	
@NA	NA	
@NOW	NOW	
@NPV	NPV	
@PI	PI	
@PMT	PMT	Arguments are in different order than in @PMT.
@PROPER	PROPER	
@PV	PV	Arguments are in different order than in @PV.
@RAND	RAND	Calculates values randomly each time it is recalculated (@RAND calculates the same values in each work session).
@RATE	RATE	Arguments are in different order than in @RATE.
@REPEAT	REPT	

Lotus 1-2-3 function	Microsoft Excel equivalent	Comments
@REPLACE	REPLACE	
@RIGHT	RIGHT	
@ROUND	ROUND	
@ROWS	ROWS	
@S	T	
@SECOND	SECOND	
@SIN	SIN	
@SLN	SLN	
@SQRT	SQRT	
@STD	STDEVP	
@STDS	STDEV	Lotus 1-2-3 Release 3 and later.
@STRING	FIXED	
@SUM	SUM	
@SYD	SYD	
@TAN	TAN	
@TERM	NPER	Arguments are in different order than in @TERM
@TIME	TIME	
@TIMEVALUE	TIMEVALUE	
@TODAY	TODAY	
@TRIM	TRIM	
@TRUE	TRUE	
@UPPER	UPPER	
@VALUE	VALUE	
@VAR	VARP	
@VARS	VAR	Lotus 1-2-3 Release 3 and later.
@VDB	VDB	
@VLOOKUP	VLOOKUP	Turn on Transition Formula Evaluation to use the Lotus 1-2-3 evaluation rules.
@YEAR	YEAR	

Excel Functions Without Lotus 1-2-3 Equivalents

Many Microsoft Excel functions are equivalent to Lotus 1-2-3 functions. However, The following Microsoft Excel functions have no equivalents in Lotus 1-2-3 Release 3.1 or earlier, or Lotus 1-2-3/W Release 1.0. Microsoft Excel also provides many add-in functions and statistical functions in the Analysis ToolPak that don't have Lotus 1-2-3 equivalents; these are not included in this list.

AREAS	MATCH
DOLLAR	MDETERM
DPRODUCT	MINVERSE
FACT	MIRR
FREQUENCY	MMULT
GROWTH	PPMT
INT	PRODUCT
IPMT	SEARCH
ISBLANK	SUBSTITUTE
ISERROR	TEXT
ISLOGICAL	TRANSPOSE
LINEST	TREND
LOGEST	TYPE
LOOKUP	WEEKDAY

WK3 Functions That Do Not Convert

A number of WK3 functions—nonaggregate functions that use 3-dimensional references—will not properly convert. An *aggregate* function is one that is always used with a range of values, such as SUM, AVERAGE, MIN, and MAX. A *nonaggregate* function is one that is not commonly used with a range of values. For example, the nonaggregate @INDEX function will not convert if it uses references that encompass more than one ply of a 3-dimensional worksheet. (It converts properly if no 3-dimensional reference is used.) Unsupported WK3 functions are shown in the following list. These functions are unsupported when they include a 3-dimensional argument, so if a normal argument is used, it may work.

Nonaggregate Functions with 3-Dimensional References

@CELL	@IRR	@ROWS
@COLS	@ISRANGE	@S
@COORD	@N	@SHEETS
@INDEX	@NPV	@SUMPRODUCT

Other Functions That Present Conversion Problems Microsoft Excel cannot convert formulas with more than one table argument using @DSUM, @DAVG, @DMIN, @DMAX, @DSTD, @DVAR, @DSTDS, or @DVARS. Other functions that present conversion problems include @DQUERY when using the DataLens add-in, and @CELLPOINTER, when using the sheet argument.

Invalid Characters Converted to Underscores

Microsoft Excel converts invalid characters in names to the underscore character (_) when reading Lotus 1-2-3 worksheets. Microsoft Excel notifies the user that Excel cannot read the record if two or more defined names on the worksheet contain special characters that cause them to resolve to the same name. Because Microsoft Excel doesn't allow all of the special characters in names that Lotus 1-2-3 does, names that contain different special characters but are otherwise identical will be converted to an identical name, resulting in an error. Besides letters and numbers, Microsoft Excel allows only underscore and backslash (\) characters to be used in names.

For example, if you have defined the names TOTAL$ and TOTAL# on a Lotus 1-2-3 worksheet and you open the worksheet in Microsoft Excel, both names will be converted to TOTAL_ (underscore). This results in two different ranges defined with the same name. You can work around this by checking for invalid characters in your Lotus 1-2-3 worksheets before converting them to Microsoft Excel.

Lotus 1-2-3 System Command

There is no direct equivalent for the Lotus 1-2-3 System command in Microsoft Excel, but you can activate MS-DOS from the Microsoft Windows Start menu (or the Windows NT Program Manager).

▷ **To activate MS-DOS**

- Click the Windows Start button, point to Programs, and then click MS-DOS Prompt.

Lotus 1-2-3 Data Distribution Command

There is no equivalent command in Microsoft Excel for the Lotus 1-2-3 Data Distribution command. Instead, Microsoft Excel provides the FREQUENCY function, which calculates a data distribution. You can also choose the Data Analysis command on the Tools menu and select the Histogram tool to calculate frequencies for a range of data.

Note If the Data Analysis command does not appear on the Tools menu, you need to install the Analysis ToolPak add-in. To do so, click the Add-Ins command on the Tools menu, and then click the Analysis ToolPak option. If the Analysis ToolPak option does not appear in the Add-ins dialog box, you need to rerun Setup to install it. For information about Setup, see Chapter 8, "Installing Microsoft Office."

Lotus 1-2-3 Data Matrix Commands

The Microsoft Excel equivalents to the Data Matrix commands are array functions, rather than commands.

Lotus 1-2-3	Microsoft Excel function
Invert	MINVERSE
Multiply	MMULT

Lotus 1-2-3 Data Regression Commands

The Microsoft Excel equivalents to the Data Regression commands are array functions rather than commands and do not translate directly. Instead, Microsoft Excel includes the LINEST, TREND, LOGEST, and GROWTH functions for performing regression analysis.

You can also choose the Data Analysis command on the Tools menu and select the Regression tool to perform regression analysis.

Note If the Data Analysis command does not appear on the Tools menu, you need to install the Analysis ToolPak add-in. To do so, choose the Add-Ins command on the Tools menu and click the Analysis ToolPak option. If the Analysis ToolPak option does not appear in the Add-ins dialog box, you need to rerun Setup to install it. For information about Setup, see Chapter 8, "Installing Microsoft Office."

Getting Help About Microsoft Excel Functions

For details about Microsoft Excel functions, click the Function Wizard button on the Standard toolbar, select the function you want, and click the Help button. Functions are divided into categories in the Function Wizard dialog box. For example, the FREQUENCY, LINEST, LOGEST, GROWTH, and TREND functions are located in the Statistical category, while the MINVERSE and MMULT functions are located in the Math & Trig category. Help for the Analysis ToolPak is available by clicking the Help button in any Analysis ToolPak dialog box.

Mathematical Operator Evaluation in Lotus 1-2-3 and Microsoft Excel

The following table shows the mathematical operators used by Microsoft Excel and Lotus 1-2-3, in descending order of evaluation.

Lotus 1-2-3 order of operators	Microsoft Excel order of operators
^	AND, OR, NOT functions
+ or – (unary)	+ or – (unary)
* or /	^
+ or –	* or /
= < > <= >= <>	+ or –
#not# (unary)	&
#and# #or#	= < > <= >= <>
& (Release 2.0 or later only)	

In Lotus 1-2-3, the exponentiation operator (^) is evaluated before the negation operator (–); in Microsoft Excel, negation is evaluated first. Thus, the formula

```
=-2^4
```

produces the value –16 in Lotus 1-2-3, and 16 in Microsoft Excel. To fix this, use parentheses to force the correct order of evaluation, for example:

```
=-(2^4)
```

Linking Lotus 1-2-3 Worksheets and Microsoft Excel Worksheets

You can use values from a Lotus 1-2-3 worksheet without exporting the worksheet to Microsoft Excel by linking cells. Then, when you change the date in the Lotus 1-2-3 worksheet, the Microsoft Excel worksheet is automatically updated. For example, you can link sales figures from various Lotus 1-2-3 worksheets to a single Microsoft Excel worksheet and then use the formatting and printing features of Microsoft Excel to create a summary report of sales.

▶ **To link from a Lotus 1-2-3 worksheet to a Microsoft Excel worksheet**

1. In Microsoft Excel, open both the Lotus 1-2-3 worksheet and the Microsoft Excel worksheet you want to link.

2. Switch to the Lotus 1-2-3 worksheet (ALT, W, worksheet number.)

3. Select the cell or range containing the data you want to link to the Microsoft Excel worksheet (SHIFT+arrow keys).

4. On the Edit Menu or the shortcut menu, click Copy (ALT, E, C or CTRL+C).

    A moving border appears around the selected cell or range.

5. Switch to the Microsoft Excel worksheet (ALT, W, worksheet number).

6. Select the cell or the upper-left corner of the range that you want linked to the Lotus 1-2-3 worksheet (arrow keys).

7. On the Edit menu, click Paste Special (ALT, E, S).

8. Click the Paste Link button (ALT+L).

Microsoft Excel enters a formula in each cell that links the worksheets.

Note If the linked data from Lotus 1-2-3 is pasted into more than one cell, Microsoft Excel enters the formula that links the worksheets as an array formula. You cannot clear, delete, or move individual cells that contain an array formula. If you want to be able to edit individual cells, copy and link each cell individually.

You can link Microsoft Excel worksheets to files saved in any of the following Lotus 1-2-3 formats:

-   WKS
-   WK1
-   WK3
-   WK4

If you use Lotus 1-2-3 to edit a Lotus 1-2-3 worksheet linked to a Microsoft Excel worksheet, the linked cells are updated when you open the Microsoft Excel worksheet.

You can use the Links command on the Edit menu to open the Lotus 1-2-3 worksheet that contains the source data for the Microsoft Excel worksheet you're editing. You can also redirect links to refer to another worksheet.

Working with Charts

Microsoft Excel and Lotus 1-2-3 take different approaches to formatting charts. This section discusses Microsoft Excel equivalents for Lotus 1-2-3 chart Format commands.

Lotus 1-2-3 Graph Options Format Commands

The Lotus 1-2-3 Graph Options Format commands apply to line and xy (scatter) charts only.

▶ **To format a line or xy (scatter) chart in Microsoft Excel**

1. Select a data series.

2. On the Format menu, click Selected Series.

3. Click the Patterns tab.

4. Under Line, select a line style, color, and weight.

   If you don't want any lines, click the None option button.

5. Under Marker, select a marker style, foreground color, and background color.

   If you don't want any markers, click the None option button.

Lotus 1-2-3 Graph Options Grid Commands

The Lotus 1-2-3 Graph Options Format commands apply to all graph types with axes.

▶ **To add and delete axes in a chart in Microsoft Excel**

1. On the Insert menu, click Axes.

2. Turn axes off or on.

Lotus 1-2-3 Graph Type Commands

In Microsoft Excel, you change the chart (graph) type after you create the chart (graph). Use the Chart Type command on the Format menu when a chart window is active. It also offers additional chart types, such as 3-dimensional charts.

Lotus 1-2-3 Graph View Command

After you create a chart (graph) in Microsoft Excel, it remains visible on a worksheet as a embedded chart, or as a separate chart sheet in the workbook. Therefore, the procedure for creating a chart in Microsoft Excel is the closest equivalent to the Lotus 1-2-3 Graph View command.

Lotus 1-2-3 Graph Options Color Command

There is no direct equivalent in Microsoft Excel for the Lotus 1-2-3 Graph Options Color command. However, you can change the color of individual chart items by clicking the chart item you want to format, clicking the Format menu and pointing to the Selected (Item) command on the Format menu. Note that the name of the command changes, depending on the chart item selected.

Lotus 1-2-3 Graph Options Scale Commands

This section discusses Microsoft Excel equivalents for the Scale commands in Lotus 1-2-3.

Auto

Microsoft Excel creates the scale automatically. If you designated any aspect of the scale as manual, you can return it to automatic by following these steps:

▶ **To set the axis scale to automatic**

1. Select the x (category) or y (value) axis.

2. On the Format menu, click the Selected Axis command.

3. Click the Scale tab.

   The options are different for the x-axis and the y-axis.

4. Select the Auto check box for any option you want to return to automatic.

5. Click OK.

Manual, Lower, Upper

▶ **To control the scale manually**

1. Click the x (category) or y (value) axis.

2. On the Format menu, click the Selected Axis command.

3. Click the Scale tab.

   The options are different for the x-axis and the y-axis.

4. Change any options you want.

Format

▶ **To change the number format on the scale**

1. On the source worksheet, select the numbers you want to format.

2. On the Format menu, click Cells.

3. Click the Number tab.

   Select the number format you want to use on the chart.

4. Click OK.

Indicator

▶ **To select or clear scale indicators**

1. Select the chart.

2. On the Insert menu, click Axes.

3. Select the Category (X) Axis or Value (Y) Axis check box.

4. Click OK.

Working With Printers

This section describes the differences in printer setup and printing procedures between Lotus 1-2-3 and Microsoft Excel.

Lotus 1-2-3 Worksheet Global Default Printer Commands

Lotus 1-2-3	Microsoft Excel
Interface	Setting up a printer and port
Auto-LF	Not necessary; handled by printer driver
Left	File menu, Page Setup command
Right	File menu, Page Setup command
Top	File menu, Page Setup command
Bottom	File menu, Page Setup command
Pg-Length	File menu, Page Setup command
Wait	File menu, Page Setup command
Setup	Not necessary; handled by printer driver
Name	File menu, Page Setup command
Quit	ESC key

Lotus 1-2-3 Line Print Command

There is no command in Microsoft Excel that is equivalent to the Lotus 1-2-3 Line Print command. To provide the same functionality, Microsoft Excel includes a LINE.PRINT macro function that provides compatibility with Lotus 1-2-3. However, the LINE.PRINT macro function does not use the Microsoft Windows printer drivers. Unless you have a specific need for the LINE.PRINT macro function, use the Print command on the File menu or the PRINT function instead.

Note The LINE.PRINT macro function is only available from a Microsoft Excel 4.0 macro sheet. To insert one, choose the Macro command on the Insert menu, and click the MS Excel 4.0 Macro command.

The LINE.PRINT macro function has three forms:

Syntax 1: Go, Line, Page, Align, and Clear

LINE.PRINT(command, file, append)

Syntax 2: Worksheet settings

LINE.PRINT(command, setup_text, leftmarg, rightmarg, topmarg, botmarg, pglen, formatted)

Syntax 3: Global settings

LINE.PRINT(command, setup_text, leftmarg, rightmarg, topmarg, botmarg, pglen, wait, autolf, port, update)

The following macro formula prints the currently defined print area to the currently defined printer port:

```
LINE.PRINT(1)
```

Command

A number corresponding to the command you want LINE.PRINT to carry out. For syntax 2 of the LINE.PRINT function, the command argument must be 5. For syntax 3, the command argument must be 6.

Command	Command that is carried out
1	Go
2	Line
3	Page
4	Align
5	Worksheet settings
6	Global settings (saved in the Windows registry)
7	Clear (change to current global settings)

File

The name of a file to which you want to print. If omitted, Microsoft Excel prints to the printer port determined by the current global settings.

Append

A logical value specifying whether to append text to file. If TRUE, the file you are printing is appended to file; if FALSE or omitted, the file you are printing overwrites the contents of file.

Setup_text

Text that includes a printer initialization sequence or other control codes to prepare your printer for printing. If omitted, no setup text is used.

Leftmarg

The size of the left margin measured in characters from the left side of the page. If omitted, it is assumed to be 4.

Rightmarg

The size of the right margin measured in characters from the left side of the page. If omitted, it is assumed to be 76.

Topmarg

The size of the top margin measured in lines from the top of the page. If omitted, it is assumed to be 2.

Botmarg

The size of the bottom margin measured in lines from the bottom of the page. If omitted, it is assumed to be 2.

Pglen

The number of lines on one page. If omitted, it is assumed to be 66 (11 inches with 6 lines per inch). If you're using an HP® LaserJet or compatible printer, set pglen to 60 (the printer reserves six lines).

Formatted

A logical value specifying whether to format the output. If TRUE or omitted, the output is formatted; if FALSE, it is not formatted.

Wait

A logical value specifying whether to wait after printing a page. If TRUE, Microsoft Excel waits; if FALSE or omitted, Microsoft Excel continues printing.

Autolf

A logical value specifying whether your printer has automatic line feeding. If TRUE, Microsoft Excel prints lines normally; if FALSE or omitted, Microsoft Excel sends an additional line feed character after printing each line.

Port

A number from 1 to 8 specifying which port to use when printing.

Port	Port used when printing
1 or omitted	LPT1
2	COM1
3	LPT2
4	COM2
5	LPT1
6	LPT2
7	LPT3
8	LPT4

Update

A logical value specifying whether to update and save global settings. If TRUE, the settings are saved in the Windows registry; if FALSE or omitted, the global settings are not saved.

Note The default values for print settings on your worksheet are determined by the current global settings.

Lotus 1-2-3 Print Printer Commands

Lotus 1-2-3	Microsoft Excel
Range	Use the Set Print Area button.
Line	Use the LINE.PRINT macro function.
Page	Not applicable in Microsoft Excel.
Options	
Header	On the File menu, click Page Setup.
Footer	On the File menu, click Page Setup.
Margins	On the File menu, click Page Setup.
Borders	Use the Sheet tab of the Page Setup command, File menu.
Setup	Select cells, choose the Cells command from the Format menu, and choose the Font tab.
Pg-Length	On the File menu, click Page Setup.
Other	Worksheet is printed as displayed. To display values or formulas, select the View tab from the Tools menu, Options command. To add or remove headers and footers, choose Page Setup from the File menu. To add or remove page breaks, choose Set Page Break or Remove Page Break from the Insert menu.
Quit	Press ESC.
Clear	
All	Reset individual settings.
Range	On the Insert menu, click the Name submenu, Define command and delete Print_Area.
Borders	On the Insert menu, click the Name submenu, Define command and delete Print_Titles.
Format	On the File menu, click Page Setup to reset margins. Page Length and Setup String are handled by the printer driver.
Align	Not applicable in Microsoft Excel.
Go	On the File menu, click Print.
Quit	Press ESC.

Lotus 1-2-3 Macros

Most Lotus 1-2-3 users are concerned with how Microsoft Excel works with the multitude of macros that they have invested their time in building over the years.

The Macro Interpreter

The Macro Interpreter for Lotus 1-2-3 Users will run your large Lotus 1-2-3 macro applications, including custom menus, without modification. With the Macro Interpreter, you can run 1-2-3 macros that are compatible with Lotus 1-2-3 Release 2.01.

To run a macro on a Lotus 1-2-3 worksheet, hold down the CTRL key and press the macro letter name that is normally used with the backslash (\) key to define the macro in Lotus 1-2-3. The name assigned to a macro in Lotus 1-2-3, such as \a, is defined in Microsoft Excel as a Lotus 1-2-3 macro name when you open a Lotus 1-2-3 worksheet in Microsoft Excel. You can run any macro that is assigned to a macro name consisting of a backslash (\) followed by a single letter. Microsoft Excel assigns a lowercase letter to each macro name. You can only run your existing Lotus 1-2-3 macros and cannot create new Lotus 1-2-3 macros in Microsoft Excel.

Note If you have any Lotus 1-2-3 macros on the Lotus 1-2-3 worksheet and you save the worksheet as a Microsoft Excel worksheet, you can continue to run the macros on the Microsoft Excel worksheet. Some commands, such as /File Combine, work only when applied to WK1 files.

Macros Created Using Lotus 1-2-3 Release 2.2

Microsoft Excel can run macros that contain any Lotus 1-2-3 Release 2.2 advanced macro commands, such as {BORDERSON}, {BORDERSOFF}, {FRAMEON}, {FRAMEOFF}, {GRAPHON}, and {GRAPHOFF}. Microsoft Excel also reads linking formulas created by Release 2.2. However, Microsoft Excel cannot run macros that use slash menu commands that are specific to Release 2.2.

Converting Lotus 1-2-3 Release 2.2 Macro Library Files

If you have Lotus 1-2-3 macros in 1-2-3 macro libraries (macros in Lotus 1-2-3 Release 2.2 MLB file format), convert the macro library files to a Lotus 1-2-3 WK1 format. Then open the worksheet in Microsoft Excel to run the macro.

Running Autoexec Macros

If you have a Lotus 1-2-3 autoexec macro (named \0) on your worksheet, the macro runs automatically when you open the worksheet in Microsoft Excel. To open a worksheet without running the autoexec macro, click the Open button or choose Open from the File menu, select the filename, and then hold down SHIFT and click OK. If you have both a Microsoft Excel name Auto_Open that refers to a macro sheet and a \0 macro on the same worksheet, the Auto_Open macro runs first, and then the \0 macro runs.

Lotus 1-2-3 Add-ins Are Not Supported

Be sure to remove any occurrence of keystrokes or command names that attach, start, or use a Lotus 1-2-3 add-in, such as the Allways add-in and its menu structure. For example, remove statements such as /a and {app1}.

1-2-3 Macros Cannot End in a Menu

When you run a Lotus 1-2-3 macro in Microsoft Excel, the Lotus 1-2-3 macro cannot end in a menu, such as the keystrokes /PP (Print Printer). If a macro does end in a menu, a message appears stating that macros cannot end in a menu. Then the macro terminates. The macro can, however, end in a prompt for more information, such as the keystrokes /PPR (Print Printer Range), so that you can specify the print range.

Getting Help Within Macro Prompts

When you run a Lotus 1-2-3 macro that contains a command for user input, such as /XN, /XL, {GETLABEL}, or {GETNUMBER}, Microsoft Excel displays a dialog box requesting user input. Enter the information and then click OK.

If a Lotus 1-2-3 macro contains custom menu commands, such as /XM, {MENUBRANCH}, or {MENUCALL}, a Menu dialog box appears displaying your menu choices.

To get Help with macro prompt dialog boxes, press F1.

Verifying Options Before Running 1-2-3 Macros

When you run a Lotus 1-2-3 macro, the Transition Formula Entry and Transition Navigation Keys options, on the Transition tab of the Options command on the Tools menu, are temporarily turned on and the Move Selection After Enter Check Box option on the Edit tab is temporarily turned off. However, Transition Formula Evaluation is not automatically turned on when you run a Lotus 1-2-3 macro. For more information, see "Transition Formula Entry" and "Transition Formula Evaluation," earlier in this chapter.

Adjusting Screen Size Before Running Lotus 1-2-3 Macros

For best visual results, you can maximize the Microsoft Excel window, as well as the active document window. Note that the {PGUP}, {PGDN}, {BIGRIGHT}, and {BIGLEFT} commands work with the current page size, not with the 20-row page size that is standard in Lotus 1-2-3.

Macros That Don't Need to Be Converted

Approximately half of all Lotus 1-2-3 macros do not need to be converted. They were built to aid the user with formatting or printing from Lotus 1-2-3 and are replaced by the standard features of Microsoft Excel. Some of the most common Lotus 1-2-3 macros and the features that replace them are in the table below.

Lotus 1-2-3 macro action	Use the Microsoft Excel feature
Inputs printer setup strings	Cells command, Font tab and Page Setup dialog box
Accepts dates, parses into YY,MM,DD, then re-enters with @Date and formats	Automatic date acceptance and formatting
Prompts to select ranges for chart data	ChartWizard button on the Standard toolbar
Formats anything quickly	Style command
Adjusts column width	Drag the heading separator bar, or double-click for best fit
Adjusts multiple column widths simultaneously	Drag across column headers, and then drag or double-click heading separator bar
Sums column or row	AutoSum button on the Standard toolbar
Aligns text with Range Label Align	Left, Right, or Center icons on the Formatting toolbar
Underlines	Cells command, Border and Font tabs
Shifts a block of cells	Drag-and-drop editing, or the Insert and Delete buttons or commands
Enters commonly used formulas	Workbook containing a Microsoft Excel Visual Basic module containing function procedures to share among users
Redefines and updates multiple data tables (Lotus 1-2-3 can have only one data table active at a time)	Multiple data tables available in worksheet without redefinition
Requests data by line item or builds a data entry form on the worksheet	Data Form command for data entry and editing that automatically creates a custom data form without macros

Lotus 1-2-3 macro action	Use the Microsoft Excel feature
Changes to commonly used directories using the File Dir command because the File Dir command is a separate command from the File Retrieve	Folder changing and file opening all in the same dialog box
Splits horizontal or vertical windows	Drag window split bar
Inserts monthly, quarterly or weekly headers	Use the AutoFill feature by dragging the fill handle or by using the Fill commands

Macros That Don't Convert

The Macro Interpreter runs your Lotus 1-2-3 macros with a few exceptions:

- Macros that are not compatible with Lotus 1-2-3 Release 2.01, or that contain keystrokes for Release 2.2-specific menu commands.

- Macros that call a Lotus 1-2-3 add-in.

When a macro does not run, a dialog box appears that identifies the cell address where the error occurred. It is a good idea to make a note of this cell reference. Also, the dialog box contains a Help button that you can use to see more information about possible causes of the error. If you have macros that call Lotus 1-2-3 add-ins, you will need to remove these macro statements from your Lotus 1-2-3 macros.

Calling Microsoft Excel Procedures from Lotus 1-2-3 Macros

Two Microsoft Excel macro commands allow you to call or branch to Visual Basic procedures or Microsoft Excel 4.0 macros written in Microsoft Excel from within a Lotus 1-2-3 macro: {XLCALL} and {XLBRANCH}. These functions take the form:

```
{XLCALL xl_name}
{XLBRANCH xl_name}
```

Substitute the procedure name for the placeholder *xl_name* shown above. One use of these commands might be to replace calls to Lotus 1-2-3 add-ins with calls to Microsoft Excel add-ins or Visual Basic procedures. Using XLCALL, you can run a Microsoft Excel procedure, after which control returns to the Lotus 1-2-3 macro. Using XLBRANCH, Microsoft Excel takes over and control does not return to the original Lotus 1-2-3 macro.

With these two commands, you can rebuild part or all of complex Lotus 1-2-3 macro statements with more concise Visual Basic code; it is not necessary to rewrite the entire macro.

Erasing the Active Worksheet and Starting a New One

Microsoft Excel files are called *workbooks*, and each can contain multiple worksheets. You can have more than one workbook open at once, so you can keep the active workbook open while starting a new one. The following procedure corresponds to the Lotus 1-2-3 Worksheet Erase command, which removes the active worksheet from memory, but not from your disk, so you can start a new one.

▸ **To remove the active workbook from memory**

1. On the File menu, click Close.

   If you made unsaved changes to the active worksheet, a dialog box appears asking if you want to save your changes.

2. To erase the active worksheet without saving changes, choose the No button.

3. On the File menu, click New to open a new worksheet.

Borland Quattro Pro for MS-DOS Compatibility

Microsoft Excel for Windows 95 lets you use your existing Quattro Pro for MS-DOS files while taking advantage of the ease and power of Microsoft Excel. You can open Quattro Pro for MS-DOS files in Microsoft Excel and run Quattro Pro macros that are compatible with Lotus 1-2-3 release 2.01.

Opening Quattro Pro for MS-DOS Files in Microsoft Excel

▸ **To open Microsoft Excel worksheet files from Quattro Pro for MS-DOS**

1. On the File menu, click Open.

2. In the Files Of Type box, select Quattro Pro/DOS.

3. Select the Quattro Pro worksheet you want to open or type the complete filename in the File Name box.

4. Click OK.

Microsoft Excel opens the worksheet. If for some reason Microsoft Excel cannot read a formula in the worksheet, it substitutes the value of the formula for the formula itself.

Running Quattro Pro for MS-DOS Macros in Microsoft Excel

Microsoft Excel for Windows runs Lotus 1-2-3 macros that are compatible with Lotus 1-2-3 Release 2.01. If your Quattro Pro for MS-DOS macro is compatible with Lotus 1-2-3 Release 2.01, then you can run it in Microsoft Excel. For more information, see the Lotus 1-2-3 macro information earlier in this chapter.

▶ **To run a Quattro Pro for MS-DOS macro**

1. On the File menu, click Open.
2. In the Files Of Type box, select Quattro Pro.
3. Select the Quattro Pro worksheet you want to open or type the complete filename in the File Name box.
4. Click OK.
5. On the Tools menu, click Macro.
6. In the Macro Name/Reference box, type or select the name of the Quattro Pro macro you want to run.
7. Click OK.

Borland Quattro Pro for Windows Compatibility

You can use Microsoft Excel with your existing Quattro Pro for Windows Notebooks by simply opening your Notebook in Microsoft Excel the same way you open any Microsoft Excel workbook—using the Open button on the Standard toolbar, or the Open command on the File menu. When you finish editing the workbook, you can save it as either a Microsoft Excel workbook or a Quattro Pro for Windows Notebook.

Unsupported Borland Quattro Pro for Windows Version 5 Features

Features without direct equivalents in Microsoft Excel will not be imported.

- Quattro Pro for Windows graphs are stored in a very different manner than Microsoft Excel stores its charts. Therefore, graphs are not imported.

- The Microsoft Excel Scenario Manager is not directly equivalent to the Quattro Pro for Windows Scenario Manager. Therefore, Microsoft Excel will import only the data from the scenario that is currently displayed (the last time the file was saved). You can use the Microsoft Excel Scenario Manager to create, store, and retrieve what-if assumptions for multiple sets of up to 32 changing cells.

- Hot Links to external database tables or to the Data Modeling Desktop are not compatible with ODBC, Microsoft Query, nor Microsoft Excel Pivot Tables, so they are not imported.

- Embedded OLE objects are not imported.

- For gradient fills, the object is formatted using the primary color from the fill.

Multiplan Compatibility

To transfer Multiplan files to Microsoft Excel, you must save the Multiplan worksheet in SYLK format.

▶ **To open a worksheet in Microsoft Excel that was created with Multiplan version 3.04 and earlier and saved in SYLK format:**

1. On the File menu, click Open.

2. In the Files of Type list box, select SYLK Files.

3. In the list box, locate and select the Multiplan worksheet.

4. Click OK.

You can save your Microsoft Excel workbooks so that you can open them in Multiplan. When you do this, Microsoft Excel saves only the first worksheet in the workbook, so you'll need to save each sheet separately.

▶ **To save a Microsoft Excel workbook so you can open it in Multiplan version 3.04 and earlier**

1. On the File menu, click Save As.

2. In the Save As Type list box, select SYLK (Symbolic Link).

3. Click OK.

   A dialog box informs you that only the active sheet will be saved.

4. Click OK.

Repeat this procedure for each sheet in the workbook you want to open in Multiplan.

▶ **To save a Microsoft Excel workbook so you can open it in Multiplan version 4.0 and later.**

1. On the File menu, click Save As.

2. In the Save File As Type box, select Microsoft Excel 2.1 Worksheet.

3. Click OK.

   A dialog box informs you that only the active sheet will be saved.

5. Click OK.

Multiplan version 4.0 and later can open and save files in a Microsoft Excel file format.

Multiplan Format Options Command

Multiplan option	Microsoft Excel equivalent
Commas (Multiplan version 3.04 and earlier)	Format menu, Cells command, Number tab
Decimal separator (Multiplan version 4.0 and later)	Changing the decimal separator
Error messages (Multiplan version 4.0 and later)	No equivalent
Formulas	Tools menu, Options command, View tab()

Multiplan Function and Special Keys

Selecting and Carrying Out Commands

Multiplan key	Microsoft Excel command or action
F1, SEMICOLON (;) or CTRL+W	On the Window menu, select the number of he window you want
F2 or CTRL+F	With worksheet protection turned on, press TAB
SHIFT+F2 or CTRL+R, CTRL+F	With worksheet protection turned on, press SHIFT+TAB
F4 or EXCLAMATION POINT (!)	F9 or Tools menu, Options dialog box, Calculation tab, Calc Now button
F6 or COLON (:)	Extend the selection by dragging with the mouse
ALT+H or QUESTION MARK (?)	Help

Editing Cells and Commands

Multiplan key	Microsoft Excel command or action
F3 or @	F4
F5 or CTRL+V	Edit cells on macro sheet
SHIFT+F1, SHIFT+F6	On the Window menu, select the number of the window you want
SHIFT+F3, ARROW KEY or @),@,ARROW KEY	Insert menu, Function command
F3, ARROW KEY or @, ARROW KEY	Insert menu, Name submenu, Paste command
SHIFT+F5 or CTRL+T	Step Macro button
SHIFT+F6 or CTRL+R, CTRL+U	Recalculate links

Multiplan key	Microsoft Excel command or action
SHIFT+F9 or SHIFT+F7 or CTRL+R, CTRL+R	Tools menu, Record Macro submenu, Record New Macro and Stop Recording command
SHIFT+F10 or CTRL+R, CTRL+P	Edit end
F7 or CTRL+O	Word left
F8 or CTRL+P	Word right
F9 or CTRL+K	Character left
F10 or CTRL+L	Character right

Multiplan Options Command

Multiplan option	Microsoft Excel equivalent
Recalc	Calculation tab (Options command, Tools menu)
Iteration	Calculation tab (Options command, Tools menu)
Test at	Calculation tab (Options command, Tools menu)
Alpha/value	You don't need to specify alpha or value; Microsoft Excel accepts any type of valid data in the selected cell.
Learn	Select all the cells in which you want to enter data. The ENTER, TAB, and arrow keys move the active cell within the selection.
Mute	In the Windows Control Panel, double-click the Sounds icon to manage the system sounds.
Old menus (Multiplan version 4.0 and later)	No equivalent
Hold Alpha (Multiplan version 4.0 and later)	You don't need to hold the Alpha command; Microsoft Excel is always ready to accept data in the selected cell.

Multiplan Print File Command

There is no procedure in Microsoft Excel for the Multiplan Print File command. For information about printing to a text file, see your Windows documentation.

Multiplan Print Options Command

Multiplan option	Microsoft Excel equivalent
Area	Set Print Area button
Setup (Multiplan version 3.04 and earlier)	File menu, Page Setup command
Formulas	Tools menu, Options command, View tab
Row-col numbers	File menu, Page Setup command
Printer (Multiplan version 4.0 and earlier)	File menu, Page Setup command
Model (Multiplan version 4.0 and earlier)	File menu, Page Setup command
Draft (Multiplan version 4.0 and earlier)	File menu, Print command
Number of copies (Multiplan version 4.2)	File menu, Print command

Multiplan Run Command Command

There is no direct equivalent to the Multiplan Run Command command in Microsoft Excel, but you can activate an MS-DOS window by using the Microsoft Windows Start menu.

▸ **To activate an MS-DOS window**

1. Click the Windows Start button.

2. On the Programs menu, click the MS-DOS Prompt command.

▸ **To return to Microsoft Excel**

1. Type **exit**

2. Click the Microsoft Excel button on the Windows taskbar.

Multiplan Run Report Commands

Multiplan option	Microsoft Excel equivalent
Cross-ref	No direct equivalent. You can trace formula precedents and dependents using the Auditing commands on the Tools menu.
Names	To get a list of defined names in a worksheet, select an empty area of the worksheet, choose the Name command on the Insert menu, click Paste, and click the Paste List button.
Summary	No direct equivalent. This command prints a report of the conditions in a worksheet that are likely to cause errors. Use the Auditing commands on the Tools menu.

Multiplan Transfer Clear Window Command

There is no direct equivalent to the Multiplan Transfer Clear Window command in Microsoft Excel.

- To create a new workbook, choose New from the File menu.

- To close the active workbook, choose Close from the File menu.

- To clear cell contents from the active worksheet, select the cells you want to clear, then choose the Clear command on the Edit menu. (To select an entire worksheet, click the button located at the intersection of the row headers and column headers.)

Microsoft Works Compatibility

Microsoft Excel lets you open files created with Microsoft Works 2.0. Now you can easily move up to Microsoft Excel or just use its analytical and presentation abilities to finish work you started in Microsoft Works.

▸ **To open Microsoft Works worksheet files in Microsoft Excel**

1. On the File menu, click Open.

2. In the Files Of Type box, select Microsoft Works 2.0 Files.

3. Select the Works worksheet you want to open or type the complete filename in the File Name box.

4. Click OK.

Microsoft Excel opens the worksheet. If for some reason Microsoft Excel cannot read a formula in the worksheet, it substitutes the value of the formula for the formula itself.

CHAPTER 19

Switching to Microsoft PowerPoint

This chapter includes information about file translators used by Microsoft PowerPoint to convert files created in other presentation packages. Table show exactly how features in various versions of Harvard Graphics and Freelance Graphics are converted in PowerPoint, so you can help your users understand what happened in their files when they opened them in PowerPoint.

In this Chapter

Translating Presentations Created in Other Programs

The file translators provide PowerPoint users a mechanism to convert files from other presentation packages into PowerPoint presentations that can be changed and edited. When a file is translated, the result will be a new untitled PowerPoint presentation.

The translators are listed in the Files Of Type drop-down list box in the Open command dialog box (File menu). The following translators are available:

- Harvard Graphics 3.0 for DOS charts (.ch3)
- Harvard Graphics 3.0 for DOS shows (.sh3)
- Harvard Graphics 2.3 for DOS charts (.cht)
- Harvard Graphics 2.3 for DOS shows (.shw)
- Freelance Graphics 4.0 for DOS (.drw)
- Freelance Graphics 4.0 for DOS shows (.shw)
- Freelance Graphics 1.0 to 2.1 for Windows (.pre)

> **Note** Installation of the translators is an option in the Office Setup program. If the translators do not appear in the Files Of Type list in the Open dialog box, you need to rerun Office Setup to install them. For custom installation scripts, make sure the PowerPoint translators are specified for installation on computers where files from other presentation programs will be opened.

Translating Multiple Files

You can select multiple files in the Open dialog box by pressing SHIFT and clicking on filenames in the list. If multiple files are selected, PowerPoint translates them one by one, with each file creating a separate PowerPoint presentation.

If you have to convert a large number of files to PowerPoint 7.0 format, the Microsoft Office Resource Kit CD includes a conversion utility called BatchConvert.exe that you can use to convert multiple files at once. If you want to move the files as you convert them, you can specify a new destination and extension for the converted files.

Harvard Graphics Translation Features

The following table indicates special cases where Harvard Graphics features might not be translated as expected.

Harvard Graphics feature	PowerPoint translation
Tables	Tables are converted to PowerPoint text retaining row and column position and creating lines and borders graphically.
Templates and background objects	Template options are applied to associated charts and background objects are applied to individual slides rather than to the slide master.
Shaded objects and backgrounds	Harvard Graphics supports only vertical shading and only when printing to film recorders. Shading will be translated to PowerPoint shading, which can be previewed and printed on all devices supported.
Transitions	Terminology is different in some cases, but the effects are essentially the same. Some effects (overlay, keep, weave, and rain) have no equivalent; these will be assigned as None.
Sequential AutoBuilds	No equivalent, become text builds.

Harvard Graphics feature	PowerPoint translation
Highlight AutoBuilds	No equivalent, become text builds.
AutoBuilds that are both Sequential and Highlight	Become text builds where previous highlighted text turns gray.
HyperLinks	Not translated, but can be implemented using drawn objects and the Interactive Settings command.
HyperShow®	Not translated, but can be implemented using drawn objects and the Interactive Settings command.
Build slides	Harvard Graphics creates multiple slides for builds, so these will be translated to multiple slides in PowerPoint. User can remove extra slides and use the PowerPoint Build feature on one slide.
QuickSlides	Not supported.

Harvard Graphics 2.3 for DOS

Objects are translated as closely as possible to PowerPoint objects. The following tables list translation details.

File Types

Harvard Graphics 2.3	PowerPoint	Comments
.tpl - Template file	N/A	When referenced in .shw, converted to slide. Background items such as company logos are placed in Slide Masters.
.cht - Chart file	.ppt	Converted to presentation with one slide.
.cbk - Chartbook file	N/A	Not supported.
.shw - Show file	.ppt	Converted to presentation with multiple slides, complete with notes (translated from Practice Cards) and Slide Masters.
.pal - palette file	N/A	Not read in directly, but when referenced, the colors are used in PowerPoint color scheme. Palette is handled as follows: 1. Look in explicit path for .pal file. 2. Look in current folder for .pal file. 3. Use built-in default palette if .pal file is not found

Fonts

Harvard Graphics 2.3	PowerPoint (True Type)
Executive	Arial
Traditional	Times New Roman
Square Serif	Courier New
Roman	Times New Roman
Sans Serif	Arial
Script	Monotype Corsiva
Gothic	Century Gothic

Note For fonts which are not in the table, the Windows typeface mapping mechanism replaces the fonts automatically. The original font name shows up in the Font list box. Windows substitutes the appropriate TrueType font for display.

Speedo Fonts

For Speedo and hardware fonts, Speedo names will be named Speedo[*number*] and hardware fonts will be named LP[*number*]. Use the Replace Fonts feature in PowerPoint to assign to the appropriate TrueType font.

Text Attributes

Harvard Graphics 2.3	Converts to PowerPoint	Comments
Filled	No	Plain text.
Skewed	No	Plain text.
Table	Yes	PowerPoint objects of text and lines, not table. Each text object is separate item.
Colors - palette of 16 colors	Yes	Colors are maintained and added to Color scheme if palette file found.
Kerning	No	
Organization Chart	Yes	Converted to Microsoft Organization Chart object, size not always maintained. Only five levels are supported. Levels greater than five are converted to Level five.
Bitmap fills	No	All bitmap filled objects translated to single-color filled objects.

Charts

Harvard Graphics 2.3	Converts to PowerPoint	Comments
Charts	As Microsoft Graph 5.0 objects	Maintain all data in the datasheet, Graph type converted as closely as possible.
Linked charts	No	Multiple graphs created with same datasheet, not linked in Microsoft Graph.
Pie chart - Sort slices option	No	Ignored.
3-dimensional combination charts	No	Maintain combination chart (overlay), turn into 2-dimensional charts.
Pyramid chart	No	Column chart.
Cylinder chart	No	Column chart.
Charts with datasheet (table)	No	Maintain chart, data is retained in datasheet but is not displayed.
XY Line and Point Curved	No	Translated to a Line chart; the user may change to a Curved line.
XY Line and Point Best Fit	Yes	Translated to Line chart; the user may change to a Regression Line.
Charts plotted along Y axis horizontally	No	Plotted along X-axis vertically in Microsoft Graph.
XY Bar (Horizontal)	No	Paired Bar, series overlay 100%.
Pie chart with both data labels and values	No	Microsoft Graph allows only labels, or values, or percentage and label. Displays labels only.
More than 4 overlay charts	No	Data is retained in the datasheet, but rows are excluded so only first 4 charts are plotted.
Hyperlinks, HyperShow	No	

Other Chart Information

Text in Title Charts

- First, second, and third lines of Top field will translate into the PowerPoint title.

- Middle field and Bottom fields will translate into PowerPoint text blocks.

Text in Simple List Charts

- Title and subtitles will translate into one PowerPoint title, using title alignment.

- Footnotes will be translated into one PowerPoint text block.

- Text will be translated into one PowerPoint text body object, maintaining alignment.

Text in Bullet List Charts

- Title and subtitles will be translated into PowerPoint titles.

- Footnotes will be translated into one PowerPoint text block.

- Text will be translated one PowerPoint text body object.

Text in Column Charts

- Title and subtitles will be translated into the PowerPoint title.

- Footnotes will be translated into one PowerPoint text block.

- Multicolumn text—the first column will become the body, and the remaining columns will be translated into text objects.

Slide Show Transitions

PowerPoint and Harvard Graphics provide different types of fades, dissolves, and other transitions between slides in slide shows. This table describes how different slide transitions are translated.

Harvard Graphics 2.3	PowerPoint
Replace	Cut
Overlay	No Transition
Keep	No Transition
Wipe Right	Wipe Right
Wipe Left	Wipe Left
Wipe Up	Wipe Up
Wipe Down	Wipe Down
Scroll Right	Cover Right
Scroll Left	Cover Left
Scroll Up	Cover Up
Scroll Down	Cover Down
Fade	Dissolve
Fade Down	Dissolve
Open Right	Split Vertical Out
Open Left	Split Vertical Out

Harvard Graphics 2.3	PowerPoint
Open Up	Split Vertical Out
Open Down	Split Vertical Out
Close Right	Split Vertical In
Close Left	Split Vertical In
Close Up	Split Vertical In
Close Down	Split Vertical In
Blinds Right	Blinds Vertical
Blinds Left	Blinds Vertical
Blinds Up	Blinds Horizontal
Blinds Down	Blinds Horizontal
Iris In	Box In
Iris Out	Box Out
Weave	No Transition (not supported)
Rain	No Transition (not supported)

Drawing Objects

PowerPoint and Harvard Graphics provide different types of drawing objects. This table describes how different objects are translated.

Harvard Graphics 2.3	PowerPoint
Rectangle	Rectangle
Frame (two rectangles)	Freeform and rectangle
Octagon frame (rectangle + octagon)	Polygon
Rounded rectangle	Rounded rectangle
Shadowed rectangle (four directions)	Shadowed rectangle
3-D rectangle (four directions)	3-D rectangle
Page (four directions)	2 objects: rectangle + polygon
Caption (four directions)	Polygon
Octagon	Polygon
Buttons	Emulated with set of polygons
Circle/oval	Circle/oval
Line	Line
Angled polylines	Polygon
Curved polylines	Freeform
Symbols (clip art)	PowerPoint objects

Other Drawing Information

- The maximum number of intersection points available for drawing objects converted to freeform objects is 2048 points.

- Freeform and Draw/Annotation Text will translate into separate PowerPoint text blocks.

Harvard Graphics 3.0 for DOS

Objects are translated as closely as possible to PowerPoint objects. The following tables list translation details.

File Types

Harvard Graphics 3.0	PowerPoint	Comments
.ch3 - Chart file	.ppt	Converted to presentation with one slide.
.sh3 - Show file	.ppt	Converted to presentation with multiple slides, complete with notes (translated from Practice Cards) and slide masters.
.tp3 - Template file	Not supported	Chart attributes are applied to associated charts. Objects are placed on associated slides.
.pc3 - custom palette file	Not supported	Ignored.
.pl3 - chart palette file	N/A	.pl3 palettes are translated to PowerPoint color scheme if found. Palette is handled as follows: 1. Look in explicit path for .pl3 file. 2. Look in current folder for .pl3 file. 3. Use built-in default palette if .pl3 file is not found.

Fonts

Harvard Graphics 3.0	PowerPoint (TrueType)
Swiss	Arial
Dutch	Times New Roman
Geo Slab	Courier New
HG Roman	Times New Roman
HG Sans Serif	Arial
HG Script	Monotype Corsiva
HG Gothic	Century Gothic
Monospace	Arial

Note For fonts which are not in the preceding list, the Windows typeface mapping mechanism replaces the fonts automatically. The original font name shows up in the Font list box. Windows substitutes the appropriate TrueType font for display.

Speedo Fonts

For Speedo and hardware fonts, Speedo names will be named Speedo[*number*] and hardware fonts will be named LP[*number*]. Use the Replace Fonts feature in PowerPoint to apply the appropriate TrueType font.

Text Attributes

Harvard Graphics 3.0	Converted to PowerPoint	Comments
Filled	No	Plain text.
Rotated	Yes	Rotated to closest possible position.
Skewed	No	Plain text.
Evolved	No	Look maintained, converted to objects.
Connected to an object	No	Plain text, each character is individual text item.
Stretched vertically and horizontally	No	As close as possible.
Outline	No	Bold text.
Color	Yes	Color.
Regular	Yes	Plain text.
Bold	Yes	Bold.
Drop shadow	Yes	Drop shadow.
Slant	Yes	Italic.
Underline	Yes	Underline.
Table	Yes	PowerPoint objects of text and lines, not table. Each text object is separate item.
Top, Center, Bottom	Yes	Top, Center, Bottom.
Superscript	Yes	Superscript.
Subscript	Yes	Subscript.
Left, Center, Right, Justify	Yes	Left, Center, Right, Justify.
Colors – palette of 64 colors defined by .pc3 file	Yes	Colors are maintained and added to Color scheme if palette file found.

Harvard Graphics 3.0	Converted to PowerPoint	Comments
Organization chart	Yes	Converted to Microsoft Organization Chart object, size not always maintained. Only five levels are supported. Levels greater than five are converted to Level 5.
Gradient fill (rectangle behind text)	No	Ignored.
Bitmap fills	No	All bitmap filled objects translated to single-color filled objects (use object fill color).
Bezier curve	No	Freeform curve.

Charts

Harvard Graphics 3.0	Converted to PowerPoint	Comments
Charts	Converted to Microsoft Graph objects	Maintain all data in the datasheet, Graph type converted as closely as possible.
Linked charts	No	Multiple graphs created with same datasheet, not linked in Microsoft Graph.
Pie chart - Sort slices option	No	Ignored.
3-dimensional combination charts	No	Maintain combination chart (overlay), turn into 2-dimensional charts.
Pyramid chart	No	Column chart.
Cylinder chart	No	Column chart.
Charts with datasheet (table)	No	Maintain chart, data is retained in datasheet but is not displayed.
XY Line and Point Curved (option 2 in Gallery)	No	Translated to a Line chart; the user may change to a Curved Line.
XY Line and Point Best Fit (option 3 in Gallery)	Yes	Translated to Line chart; the user may change to a Regression Line.
Charts plotted along Y-axis horizontally (for example, Horizontal Line Gallery)	No	Plotted along X-axis vertically in Microsoft Graph.
XY Bar (Horizontal) (Gallery option 6)	No	Paired Bar, series overlay 100%

Harvard Graphics 3.0	Converted to PowerPoint	Comments
Pie chart with both data labels and values	No	Microsoft Graph allows only labels, or values, or percentage and label. Displays labels only.
More than 4 overlay charts	No	Data is retained in the datasheet, but rows are excluded so only first 4 charts are plotted.
Pictures - .tif, .pcx, .pcc	.tif, .pcx supported .pcc not supported	.pcc will be ignored, .pcx and .tif files will be converted if they are located in explicit path, or in the current folder and if appropriate graphics filter is installed by PowerPoint Setup.

Other Chart Information

Text in Title Charts

- First, second, and third lines of Top field will translate into the PowerPoint title.
- Middle field and Bottom fields will translate into PowerPoint text blocks.

Text in Simple List Charts

- Title and subtitles will translate into one PowerPoint title, using title alignment.
- Footnotes will be translated into one PowerPoint text block.
- Text will be translated into one PowerPoint text body object, maintaining alignment.

Text in Bullet List Charts

- Title and subtitles will be translated into PowerPoint titles.
- Footnotes will be translated into one PowerPoint text block.
- Text will be translated one PowerPoint text body object.

Text in Column Charts

- Title and subtitles will be translated into the PowerPoint title.
- Footnotes will be translated into one PowerPoint text block.
- The first column of multicolumn text will become the body, and the remaining columns will be translated into text objects.

Slide Show Transitions

PowerPoint and Harvard Graphics provide different types of fades, dissolves, and other transitions between slides in slide shows. This table describes how different slide transitions are translated.

Harvard Graphics 3.0	PowerPoint
Replace	Cut
Overlay	No Transition (not supported)
Keep	No Transition (not supported)
Wipe Right	Wipe Right
Wipe Left	Wipe Left
Wipe Up	Wipe Up
Wipe Down	Wipe Down
Wipe In	Box In
Wipe Out	Box Out
Scroll Right	Cover Right
Scroll Left	Cover Left
Scroll Up	Cover Up
Scroll Down	Cover Down
Scroll In	Cover Up
Scroll Out	Cover Down
Fade	Dissolve
Fade Right	Dissolve
Fade Left	Dissolve
Fade Up	Dissolve
Fade Down	Dissolve
Fade In	Dissolve
Fade Out	Dissolve
Open Right	Split Vertical Out
Open Left	Split Vertical Out
Open Up	Split Vertical Out
Open Down	Split Vertical Out
Open In	Box Out
Open Out	Box Out
Close Right	Split Vertical In
Close Left	Split Vertical In
Close Up	Split Vertical In

Harvard Graphics 3.0	PowerPoint
Close Down	Split Vertical In
Close In	Box In
Close Out	Box In
Blinds Right	Blinds Vertical
Blinds Left	Blinds Vertical
Blinds Up	Blinds Horizontal
Blinds Down	Blinds Horizontal
Blinds In	Blinds Vertical
Blinds Out	Blinds Horizontal
Iris In	Box In
Iris Out	Box Out

Drawing Objects

PowerPoint and Harvard Graphics provide different types of drawing objects. This table describes how different objects are translated.

Harvard Graphics 3.0	PowerPoint
Rectangle	Rectangle
Frame (two rectangles)	Freeform and rectangle
Octagon frame (rectangle + octagon)	Polygon
Rounded rectangle	Rounded rectangle
Shadowed rectangle (four directions)	Shadowed rectangle
3-D rectangle (four directions)	3-D rectangle
Page (four directions)	Two objects: rectangle + polygon
Caption (four directions)	Polygon
Octagon	Polygon
Buttons	Emulated with set of polygons
Circle/oval	Circle/oval
Line	Line
Angled polylines	Polygon
Curved polylines	Freeform
Symbols (clip art)	PowerPoint objects

Other Drawing Information

- The maximum number of intersection points available for drawing objects converted to freeform objects is 2048 points.

- Freeform and Draw/Annotation Text will translate into separate PowerPoint text blocks.

Drawing Object Attributes

Drawing object attributes are converted as follows.

Harvard Graphics 3.0	PowerPoint
Fill Style: Solid Color	Fill Style: Solid Color
Fill Style: Pattern	Fill Style: Pattern (patterns may differ)
Fill Style: Gradient	Fill Style: Shaded (one color to gray)
Fill Style: Bitmap	Fill Style: Solid (object fill color). Can be changed to bitmap fill after translation.
Line Style: Solid, Dotted, Dashed	Line Style: Solid or Dashed
Line Width: 1 to 25	Line
Arrowhead: Double-tipped	Arrowhead: Double-tipped
Arrowhead: Single-tipped	Arrowhead: Single-tipped
Layering (front, middle, back)	Preserve layering
Grouped and ungrouped	Preserve grouping

Note Harvard Graphics Animation is not supported.

Lotus Freelance Translation Features

The following tables explain what happens when a file created in Lotus Freelance 4.0 for DOS or Freelance Graphics 1.0 through 2.1 for Windows is converted to PowerPoint.

Freelance 4.0 for DOS

Objects are translated as closely as possible to PowerPoint objects.

Note Lotus Freelance for DOS 3.0 files are not translated. To convert Lotus Freelance for DOS 3.0 files, they first be upgraded to Lotus Freelance for DOS 4.0 format.

In translating Freelance files, VGA defaults are used in many cases where the original information cannot be determined. For example, fonts, background objects, pattern fills, and color palettes are referenced in a system table device file, whose information is not stored in the .drw file. A set of VGA defaults is used in the case where the information is not available. In the case of the color palette, it is also dependent on the target output device (VGA, plotter, and so on) for which there is a set of default colors for each output device.

The following tables provide translation details.

File Types

Freelance 4.0	PowerPoint	Comments
.drw	.ppt	Converted to presentation with one slide.
.shw - Show file	.ppt	Converted to presentation with multiple slides.
.pfl - Portfolio file	Not supported	

Fonts

Freelance 4.0	PowerPoint (True Type)
Swiss	Arial
B-Swiss	Arial bold
I-Swiss	Arial italic
B, I-Swiss	Arial bold italic
Dutch	Times New Roman
B-Dutch	Times New Roman bold
I-Dutch	Times New Roman italic
B, I-Dutch	Times New Roman bold italic

Note If the font table is not located, the translator will use a built-in default table that matches the Freelance default configuration.

Drawing Objects

Freelance 4.0	PowerPoint
Line	Line
Arrow: one-head	Line + Arrowhead
Arrow: two-heads	Line + Arrowheads
Rectangle	Rectangle
Polygon	Polygon
Circle	Circle
Slice	Freehand
Bow	Arc
Freehand	Freehand

Drawing Object Attributes

Freelance 4.0	PowerPoint
Line width: single	1 pixel width line
Line width: narrow	2 pixel width line
Line width: medium	3 pixel width line
Line width: wide	4 pixel width line
Line width: very wide	6 pixel width line
Line style: solid	Solid
Line style: dashed	Dashed
Line style: long dash	Dashed
Line style: chain, dotted	Dashed
Line style: chain, dashed	Dashed
Fill: solid (A)	Fill with color
Fill: narrow crosshatch (B)	Pattern 36
Fill: narrow right hatch (C)	Pattern 10
Fill: narrow left hatch (D)	Pattern 14
Fill: wide crosshatch (E)	Pattern 36
Fill: wide right hatch (F)	Pattern 11
Fill: wide left hatch (G)	Pattern 15
Fill: empty (H)	None
Fill: solid (I)	Fill with color
Fill: 75% shade (J)	Pattern 3
Fill: 50% shade (K)	Pattern 4
Fill: 25% shade (L)	Pattern 8
Fill: 12% shade (M)	Pattern 7
Fill: 6% shade (N)	Pattern 6
Fill: 3% shade (O)	Pattern 5
Table	PowerPoint objects of text and lines, not table. Each text object is separate item.
Colors - palette of 16 colors	Default values are used depending on the target output device.
Pattern fills	Default VGA values used.

Charts

Freelance charts are converted to Microsoft Graph charts, maintaining all data in the datasheet, with the graph type converted as follows:

Freelance 4.0	Conversion to PowerPoint	Comments
Bar-Vertical	Yes	Column
3-D Bar - Vertical	Yes	3-D Column with 2.5-D gridlines
Bar-Horizontal	Yes	Bar
Stacked Bar-Vertical	Yes	Stacked Column
Stacked Bar-Horizontal	Yes	Stacked Bar
Line	Yes	Line
Pie	Yes	Pie
XY (Scatter)	Yes	XY Scatter
Scatter with regression lines	Yes	Scatter
High-Low-Close-Open	Yes	Line (Hi-Low-Open-Close)
Area	Yes	Area
Bar-Line	Yes	Combination
3-D Bar (XYZ)	Yes	3-D Bar, 3-D Column
Text chart	No equivalent	Text becomes PowerPoint body text objects

Slide Transitions

Freelance 4.0	PowerPoint
Replace	No Transition (not supported)
Wipe up	Wipe up
Wipe down	Wipe down
Wipe right	Wipe right
Wipe left	Wipe left
H-Split in	Split Horizontal Out
H-Split out	Split Horizontal In
V-Split in	Split Vertical In
V-Split out	Split Vertical Out
Scroll up	Cover Up
Scroll down	Cover Down
Scroll right	Cover Right
Scroll left	Cover Left

Freelance 4.0	PowerPoint
Fade	Dissolve
Box in	Box in
Box out	Box out
Diagonal up-left	Strips Up-Left
Diagonal up-right	Strips Up-Right
Diagonal down-left	Strips Down-Left
Diagonal down-right	Strips Down-Right
Weave	Random Bars Vertical
Shake	No Transition
Drip up	Build - Fly From Bottom
Drip down	Build - Fly From Top
Spiral clockwise	Box Out
Spiral cntrclock	Box Out
Half up	Cover Up
Half down	Cover Down
Half right	Cover Right
Half left	Cover Left
Quad up-left	Cover Up
Quad up-right	Cover Down
Quad down-left	Cover Right
Quad down-right	Cover Left

Freelance Graphics for Windows

The translator reads files created by Freelance Graphics 1.0 through 2.1 for Windows.

Freelance	PowerPoint	Comments
.pre - Presentation File	.ppt	Converted to presentation with multiple slides.

Text and Fonts

- The StrikeOut font type is converted to normal text in PowerPoint.
- Curved text is not translated. Curved text is translated to normal text.
- Line spacing of text is not maintained. All text will be translated to single-spaced text in PowerPoint. The line spacing can be adjusted in PowerPoint after translation.

- Text in Number Grids is not preserved.

- In PowerPoint, text indentation for a level of text can not be set to a value less than the previous level. Text indentation will not be fully preserved when translated with text boxes that that have this property in Freelance.

- Fully justified text is not maintained. Text can be fully justified in PowerPoint after translation.

Bullets

In Freelance, enumerated bullets and symbol bullets are translated to dash bullets in PowerPoint. Also, any clip art symbol can be a bullet. This is not supported in PowerPoint, and is translated as a simple dashed bullet.

Tables

Freelance table objects are translated to tab-delimited PowerPoint text, retaining row and column position and creating lines and borders as appropriate. Columns can be aligned by adjusting the tab locations for the text box in PowerPoint after translation.

Organization Charts

Organization charts are translated to Microsoft Organization Chart 2.0 objects.

- Formatting of organization charts including box layout, box style, box color, and line style is not preserved when translated to PowerPoint.

- Only five organization chart levels are supported. Levels greater than five are converted to level five.

Layouts

Text that is entered in the page layout of a Freelance presentation will not be preserved when translated to a PowerPoint presentation. The page layout contains text such as the "Click Here" messages that should not appear in the translated presentation. The text can be restored in the PowerPoint presentation by adding it to the master slide.

Drawing Objects

Because of differences in the coordinate systems used by Freelance and PowerPoint, there may be slight differences in the scaling and placement of objects relative to the slide boundaries.

- In Freelance, the slide area represents the entire printed page, whereas in PowerPoint the slide area represents the printable area of a printed page.

- The roundness of corners in a rounded rectangle is not maintained when translated from Freelance to PowerPoint. The roundness of the corners can be changed using the adjust handle on the rounded rectangle in PowerPoint after translation.

- Colors of all objects may not be preserved for Freelance 1.0 files.

This table describes how different objects are translated.

Freelance for Windows	PowerPoint
Line	Line
Arrow: one-head	Line + Arrowhead
Arrow: two-heads	Line + Arrowheads
Rectangle	Rectangle
Rectangle with Round (low, medium, high)	Rounded Rectangle shape
Polygon	Polygon
Circle	Circle
Curve	Freehand
Arc	Arc
Freehand	Freehand

Charts

All charts are translated into Microsoft Graph 5.0 objects. The appearance of a chart may change slightly when translated, due to differences in the two charting components.

Axes

- When minimum and maximum values for Y-axis values are set to automatic, the actual values may differ slightly in the original Freelance chart and the translated PowerPoint chart.

- When tick marks are set to automatic, the number of tick marks used may differ slightly in the original Freelance chart and the translated PowerPoint chart.

- The location of axis labels is not maintained. Axis labels appear in their default location in the translated chart, and can be changed after translation.

- The axis label on/off setting is not maintained. Axis labels are turned on in the translated chart, and can be turned off after translation.

- Tick mark color is not maintained. Tick marks have the same color as the axis in the translated chart.

Pie Charts

- In PowerPoint, each slice in a 3-dimensional pie chart can only have one color. If different side and top face colors are set in Freelance, these will not be preserved when translated.

- Multiple pie charts appear as single pie charts when translated to PowerPoint. The data for all series is preserved in the datasheet, but only the data for the first series is displayed.

Legends

- Only one line of legend text per data series is preserved.

- The legend on/off setting is not translated. The legend will appear in the translated chart, and can be turned off after translation.

Graph Types

The following table shows how different types of graphs are translated.

Freelance for Windows	PowerPoint
Bar (2-D and 3-D)	Column (2-D and 3-D)
Stacked Bar	Stacked Column
Horizontal Bar	Bar
Horizontal Stacked Bar	Stacked Bar
Line (2-D and 3-D)	Line (2-D and 3-D)
Bar-Line	Combination
Single Pie	Pie
Multiple Pie	Only one pie chart is displayed, but all data is preserved in the datasheet
XY (Scatter)	XY Scatter
Radar	Radar
High-Low-Close-Open	Line (Hi-Low-Open-Close)
Area (2-D and 3-D)	Area (2-D and 3-D)
3-D Bar (XYZ)	3-D Bar, 3-D Column
Number Grid	Simulated table using text box and lines

Other Chart Information

- The frame area that is used as the background of a chart is slightly different for Freelance graphs and PowerPoint graphs.

- Notes attached to charts are not preserved.

- Series that are hidden in a Freelance chart are displayed after translation, and can be hidden after translation.

Slide Show Transitions

PowerPoint and Freelance provide different types of fades, dissolves, and other transitions between slides in slide shows. This table describes how different slide transitions are translated.

Freelance for Windows	PowerPoint
Blinds	Blinds Horizontal
Bottom	Wipe Up
Box In	Box In
Box Out	Box Out
Center	Box Out
Checkboard	Checkboard Across
Curtains	Split Vertical Out
Diagonal Left	Strips Down Right
Diagonal Right	Strips Down Left
Draw	Cover Down
Fade	Dissolve
Hsplit In	Split Horizontal In
Hsplit Out	Split Horizontal Out
Leftside	Wipe Right
Louvers	Blinds Vertical
Paint Brush	Cover Left
Pan Left	Uncover Right
Pan Right	Uncover Left
Rain	Random Bars Vertical
Replace	Cut
RightSide	Wipe Left
Scroll Top	Cover Down
Scroll Bottom	Cover Up
Shade	Cover Left

Freelance for Windows	PowerPoint
Text Top	Uncover Down
Text Bottom	Uncover Up
Text Left	Uncover Left
Text Right	Uncover Right
Top	Wipe Down
Use Bitmap Colors	Cut
Vsplit In	Split Vertical In
Vsplit Out	Split Vertical Out
Zigzag	Strips Right Down

Other Items

- For some Freelance files, the translator can not determine the number of slides in the presentation, so the "Slide Total" will be "???" in the progress dialog box.

- For each slide in the Freelance presentation, objects in the master slide are placed in the slide foreground in PowerPoint rather than the master slide. PowerPoint supports only a single master slide per presentation.

Switching to Microsoft Word

Word 7.0 recognizes the file formats of common word-processing, spreadsheet, database, and page-layout programs. When these types of documents are opened, Word automatically converts them to Word format, preserving the original content and formatting. Users can also save Word documents in other file formats and preserve as much formatting as the other application can support.

In This Chapter

If users need to transfer documents between Word and applications for which specific converters aren't available, they can import and export documents in one of several plain-text formats. Plain-text formats retain the text of a document without most of the formatting. Plain text formats are also useful for transferring text when using electronic mail systems.

You can use this chapter as a tutorial on the conversion process, and as a reference to the differences between the user's old word processing application and Word. This chapter explains the process of opening and saving documents created by other word-processing applications. In addition, it contains detailed instructions on converting WordPerfect 5.*x*-6.*x*, Word for MS-DOS, RTF and other document formats to Word 7.0. Once the documents have been converted, this chapter describes in detail the differences between the user's previous application and Word 7.0.

Using Microsoft Word

Most of your users will already be experienced with word processing. They understand the basic concepts, the steps used to create documents, and how to create different types of documents for different purposes. Users who are new to Windows or Word can use the printed and online assistance that is included with these products.

To use Word effectively, users need a few basic skills—choosing a command from a menu, filling out a dialog box, and working with document windows. There are a number of sources for information on these skills:

If users want	Refer them to
Information about Windows	Windows Help (on the Start menu, click Help)
Printed information about Word	*Getting Results with Microsoft Office for Windows 95*
Online information about Word	The Answer Wizard (on the Help menu in Word, click Answer Wizard)

Working with Proportional Fonts

For users accustomed to the MS-DOS environment, one of the big changes in moving to the Windows operating system is the use of proportional fonts. Proportional fonts are fonts in which letters are of varying size. For example, in a proportional font, an *i* is narrower than an *m*. Many MS-DOS–based applications use fixed-width fonts, in which each letter is the same width.

The proportional fonts are much more attractive than fixed-width fonts. They look like the typeset text in books and magazines. However, they do require users to change how they position text. Users can no longer use spaces to align characters at margins or in tables, because the space character has a width that may or may not be identical to a particular letter. When using proportional fonts, users must use tabs and tables to make text line up correctly.

Converting File Formats

When a document created in another application is opened, Word converts it to Word format but preserves as much of its original content and formatting as possible. Users can also save a Word document in another file format and preserve as much formatting as the other application can support.

Converters change the file format of a document. If a document includes graphics, Word uses *graphics filters* to import and export graphics that are within, or linked to, the document. To convert documents to and from different file formats, you must install the appropriate converters. To import and export graphics contained in documents, you must install graphics filters. If you performed a complete installation when you installed Word, converters and graphics filters were also installed. If not, you can run the Microsoft Office Setup program again.

To convert several documents at once, use the batch conversion macro BatchConversion in the Convert7.dot template. For information about using this macro, see "Converting Several Documents at Once," later in this chapter.

If you need to move a document between Word and an application for which a specific converter is not available, you can import and export the document in plain-text format. Plain-text format retains the text of a document without most of the formatting. This format is also useful for sending and receiving text on an electronic mail system that cannot use the Word document format.

Text Converters

Word provides converters for documents created by the following applications and for several plain-text file formats.

- Enable 3.0, 4.0, and 4.5 (obtain a free Office Enabler Kit by calling (800) 626-8622, Department TNF)
- Lotus 1-2-3 versions 2.*x*-5.0 (import only)
- Microsoft Excel 3.0-7.0 (import only)
- Microsoft FoxPro/Borland dBase II, III, and IV
- Microsoft Word for MS-DOS versions 3.*x*, 4.0, 5.0, 5.5, and 6.0
- Microsoft Word for the Macintosh versions 4.0, 5.0, and 5.1 (only required for export)
- Microsoft Word for Windows versions 2.*x* and 6.0 (only required for export)
- Microsoft Works 3.0-4.0.
- RFT-DCA
- Rich Text format (RTF)

- Text Only / MS-DOS Text Only
- Text with Layout / MS-DOS Text with Layout
- Windows Write version 3.*x*
- WordPad 1.0
- WordPerfect 5.*x*-6.*x* for MS-DOS and Windows
- WordPerfect Secondary Files (mail merge) versions 5.0, 5.1, and 5.2

WordStar Versions for DOS 3.3–7.0 and for Windows 1.0–2.0 (import only) Graphics Filters

The graphics filters supplied by Word support files in the following formats. All supplied filters support only conversion (importing) into Word, except DrawPerfect, which can be used for both importing and exporting.

- AutoCAD® Format 2-D (DXF)
- CompuServe GIF (GIF)
- Computer Graphics Metafile (CGM)
- CorelDRAW 3.0, 4.0, and 5.0 (CDR)
- Encapsulated PostScript™ (EPS)
- HP Graphics Language (HPGL) / HP Plotter Print File (PLT)
- JPEG File Interchange Format (JPG)
- Kodak Photo CD (PCD)
- Macintosh PICT (PCT)
- Micrografx Designer/Draw (DRW)
- PC Paintbrush® (PCX)
- Tagged Image File Format (TIF)
- Truevision Targa (TGA)
- Windows Bitmap (BMP)
- Windows Metafile (WMF)
- WordPerfect Graphics/DrawPerfect (WPG) (import and export)

Not all converters are installed with Word in a Typical Office installation. To ensure that you get the converters you need, run a Complete/Custom Office installation and select the converters you want. Additional converters for older versions of Word are available on the Office Resource Kit CD-ROM. For more information, see Appendix D, "Contents of the Office Resource Kit CD."

Importing and Exporting Graphics

When you convert a file that contains graphics, Word tries to import the graphics as the file is converted. When the graphics are in the *native format*, or most common format supported by the application that created the file (for example, Metafile format for Windows applications or PICT format for Macintosh applications), Word can import the graphics automatically.

If the graphics are in another common format, such as TIFF, Word inserts a field such as an IMPORT or INCLUDEPICTURE field and imports the original graphics file into your document. To view the graphics instead of the fields, click Options on the Tools menu, click the View tab, then clear the Field Codes check box.

If you still cannot see the graphics, the graphics file may no longer exist at the location specified in the field. For example, this could happen if you got the converted file from another computer and did not get the graphics file as well.

When you save a document in a different format such as Word for the Macintosh or WordPerfect format, Word 7.0 uses the graphics filters to export graphics in your document while it converts the text.

Opening a Document in Another File Format

To convert most types of documents, open them using the File Open command in Word. If Word recognizes the file format, it converts the document, and then displays it in a Word window. If Word cannot recognize the format, it displays the Convert File dialog box. Select the appropriate file format, and click OK. Word then converts and opens the document.

If you don't see the document you want to open in the Open dialog box, try selecting one of the options in the Files Of Type box. If you don't know the extension of the document you're looking for, or if it doesn't have an extension, select All Files.

Note   The file format does not necessarily correspond to the filename extension. For example, a WordPerfect document may have a .doc or .wpd extension, or no extension at all. When you open a file in another format, Word first looks at the contents of the file to determine the file format. If Word doesn't recognize the file format, it tries to use the converters that correspond to the filename extension. If Word is still unable to recognize the file format, it asks you to choose a converter and suggests Text Only.

If a document isn't converted correctly, close it without saving the document and then try opening the document again with a different converter. The original document remains unchanged until you save it in Word format or in some other format. You can also change the way Word converts some formats. For more information, see "Customizing Conversions and Improving Compatibility," later in this chapter.

If the converter you need was not installed when you installed Word, you need to run the Microsoft Office Setup program again to install it.

If you want Word to ask which converter to use before performing any conversion, click the Options command on the Tools menu, then click the General tab. Under General Options check the Confirm Conversion at Open box.

Saving a Word Document in Another File Format

You can save Word documents in file formats that can be read by other applications or by earlier versions of Word. To save a Word document in another file format, use the Save As command. For a list of the available file formats, see the "Text Converters" section, earlier in this chapter.

When you save a Word document in another file format, it's a good idea to save it with a different name; this way, you still have the document in Word format as a backup.

Saving and Closing Converted Documents

After you convert a document to or from another file format, you must confirm the file format when you save or close the document or quit Word. This precaution ensures that you have an opportunity to save all formatting. Other file formats may not support all of the features and formatting available in Word.

When you save a converted document, Word displays the Save Format dialog box. Click the button for the format in which you want to save the document.

Converting Several Documents at Once

To convert several documents at once, you can use the BatchConversion macro, which is supplied with Word. This macro converts the files as described earlier in this chapter. The appropriate converters and graphics filters must have been previously installed to run the macro.

The BatchConversion macro is stored in the template \Winword\Macros\Convert7.dot. If you want to make the BatchConversion macro readily accessible, you can load this template as a global template.

Customizing Conversions and Improving Compatibility

When you convert a document, Word preserves the document's original content and formatting as much as possible. However, other applications might have similar features that work slightly differently, so you might not always get the results that you expect. For example, the converted document may look different from the original document if text was aligned using spaces instead of tab stops; or line and page breaks may occur in different places due to differences in fonts or printer drivers. You can choose how Word handles some of these differences.

Customizing Conversions

If a document isn't converted the way you'd like it to be, you may be able to change some aspects of the conversion with the EditConversionOptions macro. This macro is stored in the template \Winword\Macros\Convert7.dot. Depending on the converter you're using, you may be able to specify such things as the preferred line length or how you want certain fields to be converted. For example, when converting documents from Word 7.0 to Word for the Macintosh, you can control how INCLUDETEXT fields are handled.

If you want to make the EditConversionOptions macro readily accessible, you can load this template as a global template.

▷ **To run the BatchConversions or EditConversionsOptions Macro**

1. On the Tools menu, click Macro.

2. Select BatchConversion or EditConversionsOptions in the Macro Name list.

3. Click the Run button.

4. Follow the instructions on the screen.

Improving Compatibility with Other Word Processors

Word provides special compatibility options that allow you to alter the behavior of Word so that it more closely matches the behavior of another application. For example, in WordPerfect 5.x, blank spaces at the end of a line are wrapped to the next line, but in Word, the spaces extend beyond the right margin. These compatibility options change the way Word behaves without changing the document itself. Using compatibility options in Word is especially useful when you plan to convert a document back and forth between Word and another word processor.

When you convert a document, Word selects the options that are applicable to the original format of the document. You can turn the compatibility options on or off at any time. When you save a converted document, Word saves the compatibility options with it. Keep in mind that these options affect the document only while you're working with it in Word. If you later convert the document back to its original format, it will work in the other word processor just as it did before you converted it to Word.

To turn these options on or off, click Options on the Tools menu, and then click the Compatibility tab.

Select WordPerfect in this box.

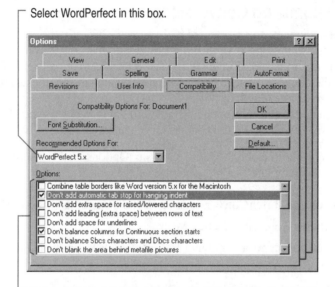

To turn individual options on or off, select or clear these check boxes.

If you want to use the compatibility options for all new documents that you create using Word, click the Default button on the Compatibility tab. Doing so saves the options in the Normal.dot template.

Specifying Fonts for Converted Documents

When you open a converted document on a different computer from the one used to create it, you may find that its line breaks, page breaks, and length don't correspond to the original. If a converted document contains fonts that aren't available on your computer or printer, Word automatically substitutes similar fonts. However, when converting documents between Word for the Macintosh and Word 7.0, or between Word and certain MS-DOS–based applications, you can specify the fonts that you want Word to substitute.

Substituting Fonts for Documents Converted to Word Format

To substitute fonts, click Options on the Tools menu, click the Compatibility tab, then click the Font Substitution button. The fonts used in the document that aren't available in Word are in the Missing Document Font list. If all fonts used in the document are available, Word displays a message.

Under Substituted Font, Word lists the font that will be substituted for each missing font. When the substituted font is listed as Default, Word uses a font suggested by the system that best matches the missing font. To see which font will be substituted, select a listed font and read the message near the bottom of the dialog box. The indicated font is substituted unless Default is specified. In that case other fonts may be used that more closely match individual occurrences of formatted text.

To specify another font to substitute, select a font in the Missing Document Font list and then select a font in the Substituted Font box. If you want Word to replace the fonts in the converted document permanently, click the Convert Permanently button.

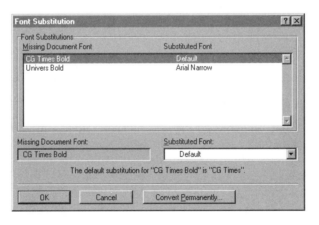

Word lets users specify font mappings for text formatted with fonts not available on their computer or printer. A user can use the default mapping or create a custom mapping. Also, the user can permanently convert to these mappings, or choose to retain the original font information for better round-trip conversion.

Keep in mind that you're substituting fonts for the document while you work with it in Word. If you later convert the document back to its original format, the document will retain its original fonts, unless you converted them by clicking the Convert Permanently button.

Word saves your font substitution settings with the converted document. It also saves these settings in the Msfntmap.ini file in the Windows folder, so the next time you convert a document from the same file format, Word knows which fonts to substitute. Sometimes the font substitution settings saved with a document may differ from the settings in your Msfntmap.ini file. For example, if you open a document that was converted on another computer with a different Msfntmap.ini file, your Msfntmap.ini settings override the settings in the document.

Substituting Fonts for Documents Converted from Word to Another Format

You can also specify which fonts you want to use when converting a document from Word format to another format. To do this, you modify a font-mapping file that is supplied with Word. Doing so overrides the default font mapping performed by the converters.

The font-mapping files that Word supplies are listed in a table later in this section. To customize a file, open it in Word and follow the instructions contained in the file itself. Save the customized file with the same filename and the .dat filename extension in the folder where the text converter is located, which is usually the Program Files\Common Files\Microsoft Shared\Textconv folder or the Windows\Msapps\Textconv folder.

Alternately, you can copy the font-mapping file and the file to be converted into the same folder.

To convert from Word 7 into this format	Modify this file
Word for MS-DOS	RTF_PCW.TXT
Word for the Macintosh 5.x	RTF_MW5.TXT
RFT-DCA	RTF_DCA.TXT
WordPerfect 5.x	RTF_WP5.TXT

Substituting Fonts for Documents Converted from Word for the Macintosh 4.0

Font mapping for Word for the Macintosh 4.0 files is different from font mapping for Word for the Macintosh 5.x and other converters. Macintosh Word version 4.0 stores font information in document files by the Macintosh System font numbers. These numbers can be assigned by the user to arbitrary fonts installed in the Macintosh System by the user. This means that character font information in the converted Word for the Macintosh files can be different for every user and the converter may not make the correct font conversion.

Note An application note titled "Mac Font Font-Mapping Utility," which enables identification of the Macintosh System font numbers and matching font names on your Macintosh computer, is available from Product Support Services. For information on contacting Product Support Services, see Appendix F, "Resources."

When opening Word for Macintosh 4.0 documents in Word 7, fonts with numbers greater than 128 are mapped to font names with the following syntax: "Font<font number>", so font number 2000 and 2001 would become "Font2000" and "Font2001" respectively.

Font Mapping Dialog Box

The Word for the Macintosh converter has an option to determine whether a dialog box will be displayed to locate the font-mapping file. This behavior is controlled using the Font Dialog= setting in the [MacWordConv] section in the Mstxtcnv.ini file. To use the dialog boxes for user defined font-mapping files for Word for the Macintosh 4.0, set Font Dialog to Yes, or leave it blank. If you don't want to use the dialog boxes, set Font Dialog to No.

For more information on changing these options, see "Customizing Conversions" earlier in this chapter.

Format of a Word for the Macintosh 4.0 Font-Mapping File

The font-mapping file, MAC_FONT.DAT, should consist of a series of entries in the following format:

```
Winfontname;MacFont#[FontFamilyID]
```

The semicolon is required. There can be an arbitrary number of spaces between Winfontname, the semicolon, MacFont#, and FontFamilyID. Each entry must appear on its own line. There can be an arbitrary number of blank lines between entries.

Winfontname

The Winfontname is the name of the Windows font that will be replaced in Word for the Macintosh by the associated MacFont# when converting to a Word for the Macintosh 4.0 document from Word 7. If a Winfontname has more than one associated MacFont#, then the last MacFont# to be associated with the Winfontname will be used when converting from RTF to Word for the Macintosh 4.0 document.

For example, if the following entries appear in the font-mapping file being used in the conversion from Word 7 to Word for the Macintosh:

```
Arial;2
Arial;3
```

then all characters in the Arial font will be given font number 3.

If a Word 7 font isn't specified in the font-mapping file, then font number 2 (New York) will be used in the Word for the Macintosh document.

MacFont#

The MacFont# is the number of the font that will appear in the Word for the Macintosh document in place of the associated Winfontname when converting from Word 7 to Word for the Macintosh 4.0. If a MacFont# has more than one associated Winfontname, the last Winfontname to be associated with the MacFont# will be used when converting from Word 7 to a Word for the Macintosh 4.0 document.

For example, if the following entries appear in the font-mapping file being used in the conversion from Word 7 to Word for the Macintosh:

```
Arial;3
Arial-Narrow;3
```

then all characters in the Arial or Arial-Narrow font will be given font number 3.

Opening or Saving a Plain-Text File

If you need to exchange documents between Word and an application for which there is no converter available, you can save your document in a plain-text file format, which most applications can read, and then open the document in the other application. Most plain-text file formats do not include formatting codes, which maintain the layout and appearance of text. Therefore, most formatting will be lost when you convert a document to a plain-text format. The Rich Text Format (RTF) format is an exception to this, as detailed in the following table.

When you save a Word document in a plain-text file format, it's a good idea to save it with a different name so that you can keep a copy of the original document in Word format as a backup.

Word can open or save text files in many formats. To open a document in one of these formats, select the format from the Files Of Type box in the Open dialog box (File menu, Open command). To save a document in one of these formats, select the format from the Save As Type box in the Save As dialog box. The following text file formats can be used to open or save files.

Text file format	Suggested uses	What it does
Text Only	Use to share documents between MS-DOS–based, Windows–based, and Macintosh applications. Use only if the destination application is unable to read any of the other available file formats.	Saves text without formatting. Converts all line break characters, section breaks, and page breaks to paragraph marks. Uses either the ANSI (Windows) character set or the Macintosh character set (which includes ASCII).
MS-DOS Text Only	Use to share documents between Word 7.0 and MS-DOS–based applications not designed for Windows.	Converts files the same way as Text Only format. Uses the extended ASCII character set (the standard for MS-DOS–based applications).
Text Only With Line Breaks, MS-DOS Text Only With Line Breaks	Use when you want to maintain line breaks —for example, when transferring text to an electronic mail system.	Saves text without formatting. Converts all line breaks, section breaks, and page breaks to paragraph marks.
Text With Layout, MS-DOS Text With Layout	Use to convert a document to a text file format while maintaining the page layout. You can then reformat the document in the new application, using the converted layout as a guide.	Preserves the length of lines. Inserts spaces in the document to approximate indents, tables, spacing between lines, spacing between paragraphs, and tab stops. Converts section breaks and page breaks to paragraph marks.
Rich Text Format (RTF)	Use to convert documents from one Microsoft application to another, or to transfer documents between a Macintosh and an MS-DOS–based system. You can also use RTF to transfer fully formatted documents by using communications software that accepts only text files.	Saves all formatting. Converts formatting to text instructions that other applications (including compatible Microsoft applications) can read.

Switching from Word for MS-DOS

You already know how to create, edit, format, and print documents using Microsoft Word for MS-DOS. This section explains how to use Word 7.0 to accomplish the same tasks and many more.

A Glossary of Word for MS-DOS Terms Versus Word 7.0 Terms

This section includes a glossary of Word for MS-DOS terms and the corresponding Word 7.0 terms or features. The Word terms in *italic* can be looked up in the index or in online Help.

Version numbers in parentheses—for example, (5.0)—refer to the version or versions of Word for MS-DOS in which the term is used. No version number is given if the term is used in version 5.0 and all later versions.

Word for MS-DOS term	Description of Word 7.0 term or feature
command fields (5.0)	You communicate with Word 7.0 (as with Word for MS-DOS 5.5 and 6.0) by using *dialog boxes.* A dialog box contains controls and options that you fill in similarly to command fields in a Word for MS-DOS 5.0 menu.
division (5.0)	A *section* in Word 7.0 is similar to a division.
format character command	In Word 7.0, the equivalent is the Font command. It is located on the Format menu.
gallery (5.0)	There is no equivalent to this menu in Word 7.0. You do not need special editing commands to edit styles. In Word 7.0, styles are controlled by the Style command on the Format menu and by toolbar buttons.
outline edit and outline organize modes (5.0, 5.5)	Word 7.0 does not have two outlining modes; you do the work of both modes in outline view.
queued printing	To be able to continue working in Word 7.0 while you print a document, click Options on the Tools menu, click the Print tab, and then click the Background Printing check box. To control your system's connection to a network printer, use Printers, on the Control Panel, in Windows. For more information about the Printers, see your Windows documentation.
scrap	The Clipboard, a Windows feature, provides an enhanced equivalent of the Word for MS-DOS scrap feature. The Clipboard is a temporary storage location that you can use for moving and copying text and graphics between Word 7.0 documents and different Windows applications.
side-by-side paragraphs (5.0, 5.5)	You can easily create side-by-side paragraphs by using the Word 7.0 tables feature.
style sheet	In Word 7.0, styles are not contained in separate style sheet documents. Instead, a style becomes part of the active document or the template in which you define the style.
table (5.0, 5.5)	In Word 7.0, as in Word for MS-DOS 6.0, you do not need to use tabs and paragraph settings to create a table; Word 7.0 creates tables for you. You specify the number and width of the columns you want in the table by using the Insert command on the Table menu or the Table button on the Standard toolbar. You can use a wizard to help you set up a table, or you can choose the Table AutoFormat command on the Table menu to design a table.
usage-variant label (5.0)	Usage and variant identifiers are not used in Word 7.0. Instead, styles are identified by style names. The style defines the format of the paragraphs to which it is applied and the character formatting of the text within the paragraphs.

Opening and Saving a Word for MS-DOS Document in Word 7.0

You can open a Word for MS-DOS document in Word 7.0 by using the Open command on the File menu and selecting a Word for MS-DOS filename. Word 7.0 automatically converts a Word for MS-DOS document to the Word 7.0 file format.

To save a document in Word for MS-DOS file format, use the Save As command on the File menu and, under Save File as Type, select either Word for MS-DOS 3.*x* - 5.*x* or Word for MS-DOS 6.0.

Converting between Word 7.0 and Word for MS-DOS

In the following table, "Yes" means the feature exists in both products and is converted from one product to the other. "No" means it exists in both products but is not completely converted between the two. "Not supported" means the feature is not supported in one of the products or is not converted completely between products.

Feature	Word 7.0 to Word for MS-DOS	Word for MS-DOS to Word 7.0	Comments
Character Formatting			
Color	Yes	Yes	If the same colors are not present in both word processors, the closest color or pattern is used.
Underline (word)	No	Not supported	Word 7.0 word and dotted underlining become single underlining in Word for MS-DOS.
Spacing (condensed, expanded)	No	Not supported	Word 7.0 condensed and expanded characters become normal characters in Word for MS-DOS.
Subscript/ superscript	Yes	Yes	Word for MS-DOS superscript and subscript are automatically offset above or below the character baseline by 3 points.
Columns			
Line Between	No	Not supported	Line Between formatting in Word for Windows is not converted to Word for MS-DOS.
Uneven columns	See comment	See comment	Word for MS-DOS only supports even-width columns so Word 7.0 uneven columns become even when converted to Word for MS-DOS.

Feature	Word 7.0 to Word for MS-DOS	Word for MS-DOS to Word 7.0	Comments
Document Formatting			
Default tab stops	No	Yes	See the information on the MWINI parameter in [Conversion Options] in the Mstxtcnv.ini file located in your Windows folder. You can change conversion options using the EditConversionOptions macro included in the Convert7.dot template. This template is located in the Macros folder in the Word 7.0 program folder (for example, C:\Winword\ Macros). For more information, see "Converting Several Documents at Once," earlier in this chapter.
Footnote position	See comment	Yes	Word for MS-DOS does not support footnotes beneath text; those are converted to end-of-page footnotes. Endnotes become footnotes in Word for MS-DOS.
Summary Info	Yes	Yes	Word for MS-DOS has no SUBJECT field. Word for Windows has no OPERATOR field.
Widow control	No	Yes	See the information about the MWINI switch in [Conversion Options] in the Mstxtcnv.ini file located in your Windows folder. You can change conversion options using the EditConversionOptions macro included in the Convert7.dot template. This template is located in the Macros folder in the Word 7.0 program folder (for example, C:\Winword\ Macros).
Page Formatting			
Page orientation	Yes	Yes	Word for MS-DOS supports portrait and landscape orientation in the same document only for printers that support autorotation.
Paper source	Not supported	No	
Paragraph Formatting			
Page break before	Yes	Not supported	Word 7.0 Page Break Before formatting is converted to manual page breaks in Word for MS-DOS.
Line spacing	Yes	Yes	

Feature	Word 7.0 to Word for MS-DOS	Word for MS-DOS to Word 7.0	Comments
Section Formatting			
Line numbering (Start At #)	No	Not supported	Word for MS-DOS line numbers always start at 1.
Vertical alignment (top, centered, justified)	Yes	No	
Page numbers	Yes	Yes	Word for MS-DOS page numbers are put in a header or footer in Word 7.0.
Tables			
Tables	Yes	Yes	Word 7.0 tables become side-by-side paragraphs in Word for MS-DOS version 5.5 and earlier, and vice versa. Multiple conversions of the document may result in changes to the left and right indents.
Other Features			
Bookmarks	See comment	Yes	Word 7.0 bookmark names longer than 20 characters are not converted in Word for MS-DOS.
Fields (DATE, TIME, FILENAME)	Yes	Yes	Word 7.0 supports more date and time formats than Word for MS-DOS. The FILENAME field is not supported in Word for MS-DOS.
Page number format	Yes	Yes	Word 7.0 supports more page number formats than Word for MS-DOS.
Footnotes (separators, continuation notices)	See comment	See comment	Word for MS-DOS footnote separators cannot be modified. Continuation notices are not supported in Word for MS-DOS.
Graphics (scaling, cropping)	See comment	See comment	Links to graphics in Word 7.0 are converted to Word for MS-DOS if the graphic format is supported in Word for MS-DOS. For more information, see "Converting Graphics," later in this section.
Language	Yes	Yes	Legal, medical, and user-defined dictionaries will convert to the default language.

Feature	Word 7.0 to Word for MS-DOS	Word for MS-DOS to Word 7.0	Comments
Other Features *(continued)*			
Underline (word)	No	Not supported	Word 7.0 word and dotted underlining become single underlining in Word for MS-DOS.
Spacing (condensed, expanded)	No	Not supported	Word 7.0 condensed and expanded characters become normal characters in Word for MS-DOS.
Subscript/ superscript	Yes	Yes	Word for MS-DOS superscript and subscript are automatically offset above or below the character baseline by 6 points.

Using Word for MS-DOS Styles in Word 7.0

In Word for MS-DOS, styles are stored in a style sheet file that is attached to the Word file. When you convert a document from Word for MS-DOS to Word 7.0 format, the conversion filter looks for the style sheet file that is attached to the original document. If that style sheet file is found, paragraph and character styles used in the Word for MS-DOS document are stored in the Word 7.0 document; the Word for MS-DOS Style ID becomes the Word 7.0 style name. If the style sheet file is not found, the converter prompts you for the file's location. You can either specify the location or choose not to. If you choose not to specify the style sheet file location, all formatting applied with styles in the Word for MS-DOS document is converted to direct formatting.

You can add the styles in the converted document to a Word 7.0 template and use the template to create other Word 7.0 documents. If a style with the same name as the Word for MS-DOS style already exists in the active template in Word 7.0, the Word for MS-DOS style overrides the Windows style.

If you do not wish to be prompted for missing style sheet files, you can modify the functionality of the Word for MS-DOS converter so that this message is not displayed. For more information, see the description of the Word for MS-DOS StyleDialog option in the EditConversionOptions macro stored in the Convert7.dot template. The Word 7.0 Setup program installs Convert7.dot in the Macros folder of the Word program folder.

You can add the styles in the converted document to a Word 7.0 template in the same way that you can add styles from a Word 7.0 document and use the template to create other Word 7.0 documents.

Using Word 7.0 Styles in Word for MS-DOS

To convert style formatting in a Word 7.0 document into a Word for MS-DOS style sheet, use the Save As command on the File menu to save the file in Word for MS-DOS format. When you save the document in Word for MS-DOS, you are asked if you want to attach a style sheet to the document. You can do one of the following:

- Create a new Word for MS-DOS style sheet to contain the styles from the Word 7.0 document template.

- Ignore all styles. If you ignore styles, the style formatting from the original Word 7.0 document is converted to direct formatting in the Word for MS-DOS document.

- Attach an existing Word for MS-DOS style sheet.

If you attach an existing Word for MS-DOS style sheet, text formatted with a standard style retains the formatting of a Word for MS-DOS style with the same name. If no Word for MS-DOS style with the same name exists, standard styles are converted as direct formatting.

If the style does not exist in the Word for MS-DOS document, the converter merges the style.

Converting Word for MS-DOS Glossaries

Word 7.0 does not convert Word for MS-DOS glossary entries when opening a Word for MS-DOS document. Word for MS-DOS glossary files must be converted separately, using a two-part macro conversion described in the following procedure. The macro conversion files are included on the Office Resource Kit CD-ROM. For more information, see Appendix D, "Contents of the Office Resource Kit CD."

▶ **To convert a Word for MS-DOS glossary**

1. Open a glossary file in Word for MS-DOS. Because you cannot use the mouse during the macro, you should copy the conversion glossary files (60convrt.gly, 55convrt.gly, and 50convrt.gly) from the Office Resource Kit CD-ROM into the same folder as the glossary file you intend to convert; this will make keyboard input easier. Do one of the following, depending on which version of Word for MS-DOS you are using:

   - In Word for MS-DOS version 6.0, click Glossary on the Edit menu, and then click Open Glossary. Select the glossary file 60convrt.gly, and then click OK. Click Close to close the Glossary dialog box.

- In Word for MS-DOS version 5.5, click Glossary on the Edit menu, and then click Open Glossary. Select the glossary file 55convrt.gly, and then click OK. Click Close to close the Glossary dialog box.

- In Word for MS-DOS version 5.0, click Glossary Load on the Transfer menu, select the glossary file 50convrt.gly, and then press ENTER.

2. In an empty Word for MS-DOS document, type **convert_glossary** and then press F3.

3. In the Merge Glossary dialog box, type the drive, folder, and filename of the glossary file you want to convert in the File Name box, and then press ENTER.

4. In the Glossary dialog box, type the filename of the glossary file you want to convert in the Glossary Name box, and then press ENTER.

   Word converts the glossary file, and then stores it in the same folder as the glossary file you converted. The file is stored with the same name as the original glossary file, with the filename extension .cvt.

   When prompted to end the macro, press ENTER.

   When you quit Word for MS-DOS, be sure to click No when prompted to save the Convrt.gly file.

5. Start Word 7.0.

6. On the File menu, click New.

7. On the General tab, click the Msword template; or, if you have a shortcut to an old template folder containing Msword.dot, click it and then click OK.

8. On the File menu, click Open, and then specify the location and name of the file with the .cvt extension. To list files with a .cvt extension, type *.cvt in the File Name box, and then press ENTER.

9. Word 7.0 asks if you want the converted AutoText (glossary) entries to be available globally to all documents or only to documents based on a particular template. Select the option you want, and then click OK.

   If you choose to make the AutoText entries available only to documents based on a specific template, the macro asks you for a template filename. Type a new name, or type or select an existing template name, and then click OK. Word prompts you to supply document summary information. Click OK; the Word for MS-DOS glossary entries are transferred to the Word 7.0 template you specified.

Converting Graphics

Word 7.0 and Word for MS-DOS both support TIFF, HPGL, EPS, PCX, and Lotus PIC graphic file formats. Links to any of these graphics contained in a Word for MS-DOS document are automatically converted to Word 7.0 INCLUDEPICTURE fields, and vice versa. Links are lost for formats not supported by Word for MS-DOS.

Word for MS-DOS includes graphics by specifying a tag that consists of the path and filename of the graphics file to be included in the document. For example, a tag may look like the following:

```
.G.C:\WINWORD\FILENAME.PCX;6";1.158";PCX
```

These tags are converted to Word 7.0 graphics fields. For example:

```
{includepicture C:\\WINWORD\\FILENAME.PCX \* mergeformat}
```

For a graphic to appear in a converted document, the appropriate graphics filter must be installed in Word 7.0, and the original graphic file must remain in the path specified in the converted document's INCLUDEPICTURE field.

Additional Graphics Considerations

Word 7.0 may not recognize graphics created using the Word for MS-DOS Capture.com utility. These files have a .scr filename extension by default. (Capture.com also creates ASCII text files which have a .lst extension by default.)

Linked graphics in PageView file format become bitmaps. These files have a filename extension such as .po1, .po2, .po3, and so on.

Commands for Word for MS-DOS Features

The following tables show the Word 7.0 equivalents for Word for MS-DOS commands.

Throughout the rest of this section, Word 5.0 menus, commands, and shortcut keys are presented in tables that show their equivalents in Word. As you read the tables, please note the following conventions:

- "Not applicable" means that the Word 5.0 command has no equivalent in Word.

- Italicized text after a key combination means that you type variable information. For example, "ALT+SHIFT+*number*" means that you hold down the ALT and SHIFT keys while typing a number.

Commands for Opening, Creating, and Saving Documents

Word 5.0	Word 5.5, Word 6.0	Word 7.0
Transfer Load	File menu, Open command	File menu, Open command
Transfer Save	File menu, Save command	File menu, Save command
Formatted	File menu, Save As command	File menu, Save As command
Transfer Clear All	File menu, Close All command	SHIFT+File menu, Close All command

Word 5.0	Word 5.5, Word 6.0	Word 7.0
Transfer Clear Windows	Window Close command	File menu, Close command
Transfer Delete	File menu, File Management command	File menu, Open command, Advanced button
Transfer Merge	Insert menu, File command	Insert menu, File command
Transfer Options	File menu, Save As command	File menu, Save As command
Transfer Rename	File menu, Save As command	File menu, Save As command
Transfer Glossary	Edit menu, Glossary command	Edit menu, AutoText command

Commands for Document Display

Word 5.0	Word 5.5, Word 6.0	Word 7.0
Options Non-printing symbols	View menu, Preferences command	Tools menu, Options command, View tab
Printer display	View menu, Preferences command	(Not applicable)
Menu	(Not applicable)	(Not applicable)
Mute	View menu, Preferences command	Control Panel (Windows Start menu)
Display	View menu, Preferences command	Tools menu, Options command, View tab
Default tab width	Utilities menu, Customize command (5.5) Tools menu, Customize command (6.0)	Format menu, Tabs command
Measure	Utilities menu, Customize command (5.5) Tools menu, Customize command (6.0)	Tools menu, Options command, General tab

Commands for Window Control

Word 5.0	Word 5.5, Word 6.0	Word 7.0
Window Split		
Horizontal	Window menu, Split command	Window menu, New Window command, Window menu, Arrange All command
Vertical	Window menu, New Window command (and drag borders with the mouse)	Window menu, New Window command (and drag borders with the mouse)
Footnote	View menu, Footnotes/ Annotations command	View menu, Footnotes command

Word 5.0	Word 5.5, Word 6.0	Word 7.0
Window Close	Window menu, Close command	File menu, Close command, CTRL+W, or CTRL+F4
Options		
Window number	Window menu, *document number*	Window menu, *document number*
Outline	View menu, Outline command	View menu, Outline command
Show hidden text	View menu, Preferences command	Tools menu, Options command, View tab
Background color	View menu, Preferences command	Control Panel (Windows Start menu)
Style bar	View menu, Preferences command	Formatting toolbar
Ruler	View menu, Ruler command	View menu, Ruler command (horizontal ruler)

Commands for Copying, Deleting, and Moving

Word 5.0	Word 5.5, Word 6.0	Word 7.0
Edit Copy		
To Scrap	Edit menu, Copy command	Edit menu, Copy command
To Glossary	Edit menu, Glossary command	Edit menu, AutoText command
Macro	Macro menu, Record command (5.5)	Tools menu, Macro command
	Tools menu, Record Macro command (6.0)	
Edit Delete	Edit menu, Cut command	Edit menu, Clear command
To Scrap	Edit menu, Cut command	Edit menu, Cut command or Edit menu, Clear command
To Glossary	(Not applicable)	(Not applicable)
Help	Help menu	Help menu
Quit	File menu, Exit Word command	File menu, Exit command
Insert		
From Scrap	Edit menu, Paste command	Edit menu, Paste command
From Glossary	Edit menu, Glossary command	Edit menu, AutoText command
Replace	Edit menu, Replace command	Edit menu, Replace command
Search	Edit menu, Search command	Edit menu, Find command
Undo	Edit menu, Undo command	Edit menu, Undo command

Commands for Formatting

Word 5.0	Word 5.5, Word 6.0	Word 7.0
Format Character	Format menu, Character command	Format menu, Font command
Strikethrough	Format menu, Character command	Format menu, Font command
Paragraph	Format menu, Paragraph command	Format menu, Paragraph command
Side-by-side	Format menu, Paragraph command or Attach menu, Style Sheet command (5.5) Table menu, Insert Table command (6.0)	Table menu, Insert Table command
Tab	Format menu, Tabs command	Format menu, Tabs command
Border	Format menu, Borders command (5.5) Format menu, Border command (6.0)	Format menu, Borders and Shading command
Footnote	Insert menu, Footnote command	Insert menu, Footnote command
Division		
Margins	Format menu, Margins command	File menu, Page Setup command
Running head position	Format menu, Header/Footer command	View menu, Header and Footer command
Page numbers	Insert menu, Page Numbers command	Insert menu, Page Numbers command
Layout	Format menu, Section command	File menu, Page Setup command
Footnote location	Format menu, Section command	Insert menu, Footnote command
Line numbers	Format menu, Section command	File menu, Page Setup command
Running head	Format menu, Header/Footer command	View menu, Header and Footer command

The Gallery Menu (Word for MS-DOS 5.0 only)

The following table shows the commands that are equivalent to those of the Gallery menu in Word for MS-DOS 5.0.

Word 5.0	Word 5.5, Word 6.0	Word 7.0
Copy	Format menu, Define Styles command, Format menu, Record Style command	Format menu, Style command
Delete	Format menu, Attach Style Sheet command	Format menu, Style command
Exit	(Not applicable)	(Not applicable)
Format	Format menu, Define Style command	Format menu, Style command
Division	Format menu, Section command	File menu, Page Setup command
Help	F1	F1
Insert	Format menu, Attach Style Sheet command	Format menu, Style command
Name	Format menu, Attach Style Sheet command	Format menu, Style command
Print	File menu, Print command	File menu, Print command
Transfer	Format menu, Attach Style Sheet command	Format menu, Style command
Undo	Edit menu, Undo command	Edit menu, Undo command

Note   You do not need the special editing commands found in the Gallery menu to create and edit styles in Word 7.0. Use the Style command on the Format menu to create or modify your styles in Word 7.0.

Differences in Outlining

The basic features of outlining in Word 7.0 are similar to those in Word for MS-DOS, but there are some differences:

- You can see character formatting in outline view.

- You can view all of the body text or only the first line of body text.

- Unlike Word for MS-DOS 5.0 and 5.5, you can assign heading levels, collapse and expand subordinate levels, and reorganize headings with the Outlining toolbar as well as with key combinations and heading level styles.

- Unlike Word for MS-DOS 5.0 and 5.5, you can use drag-and-drop editing to move headings together with their subordinate text.

Commands for Inserting Text

Word 5.0	Word 5.5, Word 6.0	Word 7.0
{ } (scrap)	Edit menu, Paste command	Edit menu, Paste command
Glossary entry	Edit menu, Glossary command	Edit menu, AutoText command or *AutoText entry,* F3
Page	Insert menu, Page Numbers command	Insert menu, Page Numbers command
Date	Edit menu, Glossary command	Insert menu, Date and Time command
Time	Edit menu, Glossary command	Insert menu, Date and Time command
Footnote	Insert menu, Footnote command	Insert menu, Footnote command
Timeprint	Edit menu, Glossary command	Insert menu, Field command
Dateprint	Edit menu, Glossary command	Insert menu, Field command
Macro	Macro menu, Run command (5.5) Tools menu, Macro command (6.0)	Tools menu, Macro command

Commands for Printing

Word 5.0	Word 5.5, Word 6.0	Word 7.0
Printer	File menu, Print command	File menu, Print command
Direct	File menu, Print command	(Not applicable)
File	File menu, Print command	File menu, Print command
Glossary	File menu, Print command	File menu, Print command
Merge	File menu, Print Merge command	Tools menu, Mail Merge command
Printer	File menu, Printer Setup command	File menu, Print command, Printer button
Widow/Orphan control	Utilities menu, Customize command (5.5) Tools menu, Customize command (6.0)	Format menu, Paragraph command, Text Flow tab
Feed	File menu, Print command	Print Manager (Windows)
Setup	File menu, Printer Setup command	File menu, Print command, Printer button

Word 5.0	Word 5.5, Word 6.0	Word 7.0
Merge *(continued)*		
Queued	File menu, Printer Setup command (5.5)	Print Manager (Windows)
	File menu, Print command (6.0)	
Queue	File menu, Print command	Tools menu, Options command, Print tab, Background Printing, option
Repaginate	Utilities menu, Repaginate Now command (5.5)	(Not applicable)
	Tools menu, Repaginate Now command (6.0)	
Confirm page breaks	Utilities menu, Repaginate Now command (5.5)	(Not applicable)
	Tools menu, Repaginate Now command (6.0)	

Library, Utilities, and Tools Commands

Word 5.0	Word 5.5, Word 6.0	Word 7.0
Library AutoSort	Utilities menu, Sort command (5.5)	Table menu, Sort Text command
	Tools menu, Sort command (6.0)	
Library Document Retrieval	File menu, File Management command	File menu, Open command, Advanced button
Library Update	File menu, File Management command	File menu, Summary Info command
Library Hyphenate	Utilities menu, Hyphenate command (5.5)	Tools menu, Hyphenation command
	Tools menu, Hyphenate command (6.0)	
Library Index	Insert menu, Index command	Insert menu, Index and Tables command
Entry/page separator	Insert menu, Index command	Insert menu, Index and Tables command
Cap main entries	Insert menu, Index command	Insert menu, Index and Tables command
Indent each level	Insert menu, Index command	Insert menu, Index and Tables command
Use style sheet	Insert menu, Index command	(Done automatically)

Word 5.0	Word 5.5, Word 6.0	Word 7.0
Link	Insert menu, File command	Edit menu, Links command
Number	Utilities menu, Renumber command (5.5)	(Not applicable)
	Tools menu, Sort command (6.0)	
Run	File menu, MS-DOS commands command	Windows Start Menu, Run command
Spell	Utilities menu, Spelling command (5.5)	Tools menu, Spelling command
	Tools menu, Spelling command (6.0)	
Table	Insert menu, Table of Contents command	Insert menu, Index and Tables command
Thesaurus	Utilities menu, Thesaurus command (5.5)	Tools menu, Thesaurus command
	Tools menu, Thesaurus command (6.0)	

Shortcut Keys

If you are familiar with the shortcut-key assignments in Word for MS-DOS 5.0, you will find many differences between them and those in Word 7.0. The following tables present the Word for MS-DOS 5.0 key assignments (middle column) together with their Word for MS-DOS commands or functions (left column) and the equivalent Word 7.0 commands or key assignments (right column).

Note The shortcut-key assignments in Word for MS-DOS 6.0 closely match those in Word 7.0, and are not listed here.

Word for MS-DOS 5.0 Function Keys and Their Equivalents

Word 5.0 command	Word 5.0 keys	Word 7.0
Calculate expression	F2	Table menu, Formula command or Insert menu, Field command
Change font	ALT+F8	Format menu, Font command (CTRL+D)
Check spelling	ALT+F6	Tools menu, Spelling command (F7)
Column selection on/off	SHIFT+F6	CTRL+SHIFT+F8
Copy to scrap	ALT+F3	Edit menu, Copy command (CTRL+C)
Create footer	ALT+F2	View menu, Header and Footer command

Word 5.0 command	Word 5.0 keys	Word 7.0
Create header	CTRL+F2	View menu, Header and Footer command
Display summary sheet	F1	File menu, Summary Info command
Expand glossary name	F3	Edit menu, AutoText command (F3)
Extend selection	F6	F8
Go To page	ALT+F5	Edit menu, Go To command (F5)
Graphics/text mode	ALT+F9	(Use View menu commands)
Insert an index code	F3	Insert menu, Index and Tables command
Insert macro text	F3	Tools menu, Macro command
Line drawing on/off	CTRL+F5	(Not applicable)
List glossaries	F1	Edit menu, AutoText command
List macros	F1	Tools menu, Macro command
List style variant names	F1	Format menu, Style command
Load (open) a document	CTRL+F7	File menu, Open command (CTRL+F12 or CTRL+O)
Next window	F1	Window menu, *number* (CTRL+F6)
Open thesaurus	CTRL+F6	Tools menu, Thesaurus command (SHIFT+F7)
Outline organize	SHIFT+F5	View menu, Outline command (CTRL+ALT+O)
Outline view on/off	SHIFT+F2	View menu, Outline command (CTRL+ALT+O)
Overtype mode	F5	INS
Print a document	CTRL+F8	File menu, Print command (CTRL+P)
Record a macro	SHIFT+F3	Tools menu, Macro command
Record a style	ALT+F10	Click the Format Painter button on the Standard toolbar
Repaginate	CTRL+F9	(Not applicable)
Repeat command	F4	Edit menu, Repeat command (F4)
Repeat search	SHIFT+F4	Edit menu, Find command (SHIFT+F4)
Resize a window	F1	CTRL+F8
Run a macro	F3	Tools menu, Macro command
Save a document	CTRL+F10	File menu, Save command (SHIFT+F12)
Select current line	SHIFT+F9	HOME, SHIFT+END
Select next paragraph	F10	CTRL+SHIFT+DOWN ARROW
Select next word	F8	CTRL+SHIFT+RIGHT ARROW
Select preceding sentence	SHIFT+F7	(Not applicable)

Word 5.0 command	Word 5.0 keys	Word 7.0
Select previous paragraph	F9	CTRL+SHIFT+UP ARROW
Select previous word	F7	CTRL+SHIFT+LEFT ARROW
Select to the next period	SHIFT+F8	F8, PERIOD
Select whole document	SHIFT+F10	CTRL+A or CTRL+5 (on numeric keypad)
Set margins	ALT+F4	File menu, Page Setup command
Set tab	ALT+F1	Format menu, Tabs command
Step through a macro	CTRL+F3	Tools menu, Macro command
Turn printer display on/off	ALT+F7	(Done automatically)
Undo	SHIFT+F1	Edit menu, Undo command (CTRL+Z)
Zoom/restore	CTRL+F1	CTRL+F10/CTRL+F5

If you do not have the F11 and F12 keys

If your keyboard has only ten function keys, you can use the following alternative keystrokes.

Instead of these keystrokes	You can press
F11	ALT+F1
SHIFT+F11	SHIFT+ALT+F1
CTRL+F11	CTRL+ALT+F1
F12	ALT+F2
SHIFT+F12	SHIFT+ALT+F2
CTRL+F12	CTRL+ALT+F2

Keys for Character Formatting

Word 5.0 command	Word 5.0 keys	Word 7.0
Normal style	ALT+SPACEBAR	CTRL+SPACEBAR
Bold	ALT+B	CTRL+B
Italic	ALT+I	CTRL+I
Text underline	ALT+U	CTRL+U
Double underline	ALT+D	CTRL+SHIFT+D
Hidden text	ALT+E	CTRL+SHIFT+H
Small caps	ALT+K	CTRL+SHIFT+K
Strikethrough	ALT+S	Format menu, Font command
Subscript	ALT+MINUS SIGN	CTRL+EQUAL SIGN
Superscript	ALT+PLUS SIGN	CTRL+SHIFT+EQUAL SIGN

Keys for Paragraph Formatting

Word 5.0 command	Word 5.0 keys	Word 7.0
Normal paragraph style	ALT+P	Format menu, Paragraph command
Right alignment	ALT+R	CTRL+R
Left alignment	ALT+L	CTRL+L
Center alignment	ALT+C	CTRL+E
Justify	ALT+J	CTRL+J
Hanging indent	ALT+T	CTRL+T
First line indent	ALT+F	Format menu, Paragraph command
Increase left indent	ALT+N	CTRL+M
Decrease left indent	ALT+M	CTRL+SHIFT+M
Increase space between paragraphs	ALT+O	Format menu, Paragraph command
Double space	ALT+2	CTRL+2
Side-by-side paragraphs	ALT+2L or 2R or EL or #C or 3R	Table menu, Insert Table command or Table menu, Convert Table to Text command
Graphics/text mode	ALT+F9	(Use commands on View menu)
Remove paragraph style	ALT+XP	CTRL+Q

Keys for Outlining

Outlining action	Word 5.0 keys	Word 7.0
Switch to or from outline view	SHIFT+F2	(No shortcut keys; click View menu, Outline command)
Switch to or from outline edit or outline organize	SHIFT+F5	(Not applicable)
Promote heading level	ALT+9	ALT+SHIFT+LEFT ARROW
Demote heading level	ALT+0	ALT+SHIFT+RIGHT ARROW
Demote heading to body text	ALT+P	ALT+SHIFT+5 (on numeric keypad with NUM LOCK turned off)
Expand text under a heading	PLUS SIGN (on numeric keypad)	ALT+SHIFT+PLUS SIGN
Collapse body text under a heading	SHIFT+MINUS SIGN (on numeric keypad)	ALT+SHIFT+MINUS SIGN
Display headings to specified level	CTRL+PLUS SIGN+*number*	ALT+SHIFT+*number*

Special Characters

Word 5.0 command	Word 5.0 keys	Word 7.0
Hard page break	CTRL+SHIFT+ENTER	CTRL+ENTER
Optional hyphen	CTRL+HYPHEN	CTRL+HYPHEN
Nonbreaking hyphen	CTRL+SHIFT+HYPHEN	CTRL+SHIFT+HYPHEN
Nonbreaking space	CTRL+SPACEBAR	CTRL+SHIFT+SPACEBAR
Symbols and special characters	ALT+*code*	ALT+*ANSI code* (with NUM LOCK turned on)

Miscellaneous Keys

Word 5.0 command	Word 5.0 keys	Word 7.0
Style sheet help	ALT+XH	F1 (Help)
Insert field markers	CTRL+LEFT BRACKET or CTRL+RIGHT BRACKET	CTRL+F9
Next field	CTRL+>	F11
Previous field	CTRL+<	SHIFT+F11
Cancel command	CTRL+ESC	ESC

Switching from WordPerfect

Word 7.0 continues Word's strong support for WordPerfect transition. Our first concern is to protect a user's existing investment in WordPerfect knowledge and experience. We want to help WordPerfect users leverage their existing word processing knowledge as they learn about Word and still get their work done. Second, it is imperative that WordPerfect users be able to bring along their existing files as they make the move to Word. Word includes several features and learning aids designed exclusively for former WordPerfect users.

A Comfortable Environment for WordPerfect Users

Several features added to Word are specifically designed to make Word more comfortable for people moving from any WordPerfect environment.

ToolTips Just pause the mouse pointer over any toolbar button, and the name of the button automatically appears.

    ToolTips appear when the user pauses over a toolbar button.

100-Level Undo/Redo   Word 7.0 offers 100 levels of undo and redo. This, in essence, shows you a history of your document while you work, allowing you to reverse any action you take.

Word lets you undo and redo up to 100 actions.

Full Screen view   If you want to maximize the screen space that's available for displaying documents, you can clear the screen of elements such as toolbars, rulers, the status bar, the menu bar, and scroll bars. Click Full Screen on the View menu. To choose commands in full-screen view, use shortcut keys, or choose menu commands by pressing ALT to activate the menu bar and then pressing the letter underlined in the menu name. (The menu bar doesn't actually appear on the screen, but the individual pull-down menus do.) While in Full Screen view, Word's pull-down menus are hidden but accessible by clicking at the top of the screen. To restore the regular Word screen, click the Full Screen button or press ESC.

Blue Background, White Text   Users of WordPerfect can view their Word document with the familiar blue background and white text. To select this, from Word's Tools menu click Options, click the General tab, and select the Blue Background, White Text option. If this is combined with other Word customization options like Full Screen and Draft views, the view the user sees in Word can be made to appear similar to WordPerfect for DOS.

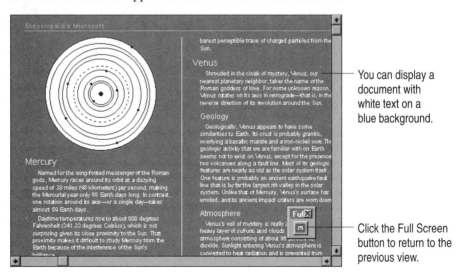

You can display a document with white text on a blue background.

Click the Full Screen button to return to the previous view.

Full screen view gives you more room for typing and editing.

Reveal Formats Reveal Formats is a graphical way to troubleshoot document formatting, similar to using reveal codes in WordPerfect. In Word, choosing the Help toolbar button and clicking on your document displays a pop-up window describing the formatting at the cursor location. Also, WordPerfect Help demonstrates this for the user when they press ALT+F3, the equivalent WordPerfect keyboard command.

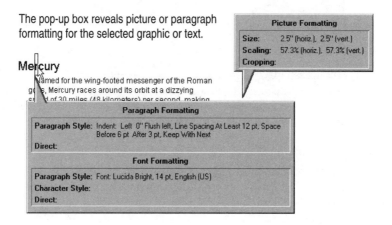

The pop-up box reveals picture or paragraph formatting for the selected graphic or text.

Online Help for WordPerfect Users

Note The WordPerfect Help feature in Word 7.0 provides help topics for users switching from WordPerfect 5.1 for DOS.

In Word, the WordPerfect Help feature allows you to use familiar WordPerfect keys and commands while you learn how to use Word. For example, you can choose a WordPerfect key or command and have Word display step-by-step instructions for the corresponding action in Word. Or Word can demonstrate and actually carry out the corresponding action. You can also set the navigation keys (such as PAGE UP and ESC) to function as they do in WordPerfect.

Have you installed Help for WordPerfect users?

If you performed a Complete installation during setup, Help For WordPerfect Users was installed automatically. If you performed a Typical or Compact installation, you need to run the Microsoft Office Setup program again to install Help For WordPerfect Users. Choose the Custom installation option, then select Microsoft Word, Online Help, Help for WordPerfect Users.

Navigation Keys for WordPerfect Users

You can set the navigation keys PAGE UP, PAGE DOWN, HOME, END, and ESC to function as they do in WordPerfect. For example, if you press ESC, you can repeat the previous keystroke a specific number of times as in WordPerfect; ESC doesn't cancel a dialog box as it normally does in Word.

There are two ways to turn on WordPerfect Navigation Keys:

- Double-click WPH on the status bar, or click WordPerfect Help on the Help menu. Then click the Options button, and select the Navigation Keys For WordPerfect Users check box. Click the OK button, and then click the Close button.

- On the Tools menu, click Options. Click the General tab, and then select the Navigation Keys For WordPerfect Users check box. Then click OK.

To indicate that WordPerfect navigation keys are on, WPH appears undimmed on the status bar.

Automatic Help for WordPerfect Keys and Commands

You can press a WordPerfect key and have Word either automatically demonstrate the corresponding feature or list the steps you need to perform in Word. If you're not sure which WordPerfect key to press, you can choose from a list of WordPerfect commands instead.

There are two ways to turn on Automatic Help for WordPerfect Keys:

- Double-click WPH on the status bar, or click WordPerfect Help on the Help menu. Then click the Options button, and select the Help For WordPerfect Users check box. Click the OK button, and then click the Close button.

- On the Tools menu, click Options. Click the General tab, and select the Help For WordPerfect Users check box. Then click OK.

To indicate that Help for WordPerfect keys is on, WPH appears undimmed on the status bar. If you've also turned on WordPerfect navigation keys, WP appears instead.

Displaying Step-by-Step Instructions or Demonstrations

You need to indicate whether you want to see step-by-step instructions or demonstrations whenever you press WordPerfect keys. To do this, double-click WPH on the status bar or click WordPerfect Help on the Help menu. Click the Options button, select either the Help Text or Demo option button under Help Type, click the OK button, and then click the Close button.

Then press a WordPerfect key to see the instructions or demonstrations. If you press a WordPerfect key combination—such as CTRL+F8 to change the point size of selected text—a dialog box appears. Just press the number or underlined letter of the command you want, or select a command and then click either the Help Text or Demo button.

If you select a command followed by an ellipsis (...), a submenu of commands appears. (You can press F1 to return to the previous menu.)

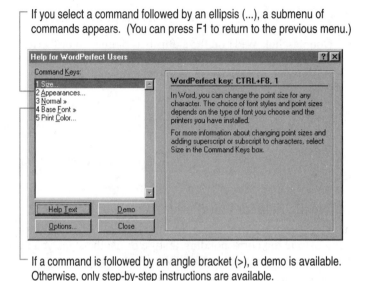

If a command is followed by an angle bracket (>), a demo is available. Otherwise, only step-by-step instructions are available.

If you chose to display step-by-step instructions, a dialog box appears. The instructions remain on the screen while you work in the document. If the dialog box covers part of the document, you can drag the title bar of the dialog box to move it out of your way.

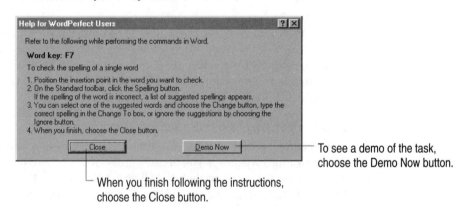

To see a demo of the task, choose the Demo Now button.

When you finish following the instructions, choose the Close button.

If you chose to display a demonstration, Word demonstrates the actions necessary to complete the command. If Word needs some input from you, such as a filename, a message tells you what to do.

For example, if you choose the Bold command,
the demo shows you how to click the Bold
button on the Formatting toolbar.

The following illustration shows WordPerfect Help when a user presses F2, the WordPerfect equivalent for searching forward.

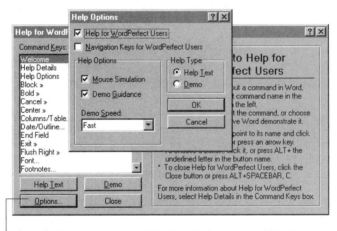

Click Options to specify how WordPerfect demos should be run.

After you type F2 (Search →), Word starts
the multi-step demonstration. Word pulls
down the Edit menu and selects the Find
command for the user.

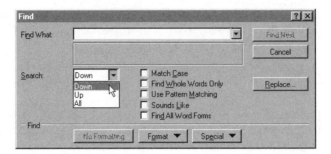

Since you typed F2 which searches forward from the current location in WordPerfect, Word automatically changes from its default behavior of searching the entire document to searching down from the current location. An animated cursor shows Word actually changing the setting.

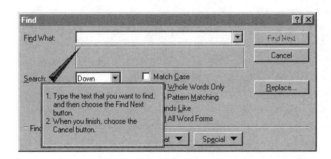

If you don't type anything within a few seconds, Word automatically provides a tip that describes the necessary steps to finish executing the command.

To customize the way demonstrations work, you can set the demonstration speed, turn off the mouse simulation, and turn off the display of messages that ask for user input. For more information, see "Customizing Help for WordPerfect Users," later in this chapter.

Getting Help on WordPerfect Commands

First, indicate whether you want to see instructions or demonstrations when you select a WordPerfect command. For more information, see "Displaying Step-by-Step Instructions or Demonstrations," earlier in this chapter.

To select a WordPerfect command, double-click WPH on the status bar or click WordPerfect Help on the Help menu. In the Help For WordPerfect Users dialog box, select a command, and then press ENTER. Or select a command, and then click either the Help Text or Demo button.

Customizing Help for WordPerfect Users

You can customize the Help for WordPerfect users. Just double-click WPH on the status bar, or click WordPerfect Help on the Help menu. Click the Options button, and then select the options you want in the Help Options dialog box.

Clear these check boxes to turn off Help for WordPerfect
users and WordPerfect navigation keys.

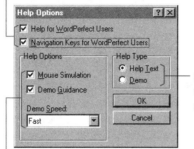

Select the type of help you want displayed
when you press a WordPerfect key or select
a WordPerfect command.

Use the options under Help Options to change the demo
speed, turn off simulated mouse actions, or turn off the
display of messages that ask for user input.

Key Concepts for WordPerfect Users

Research conducted by Microsoft has shown that there are a few key concepts that
separate successful from unsuccessful users in their attempts to become
productive using Word.

- **Selecting Text** The single most important concept that differentiates
  successful from unsuccessful users is their ability to select or block text and
  then perform an action on that selection. Users who don't grasp the concept of
  selecting text fail to complete most of the tasks of the usability test. This is
  because the notion of a "select, then do" model is at the heart of Word. In
  contrast, many WordPerfect for DOS users are initially more comfortable
  choosing an action and then specifying the object of that action.

- **Editing and Formatting Text** Another key concept is a user's ability to
  understand the differences between the editing and formatting models found in
  Word and WordPerfect. WordPerfect for DOS uses a text stream formatting
  model, where the user inserts formatting codes to toggle different states. For
  example, text is marked as bold in WordPerfect by inserting a [BOLD] code to
  signify that bold is turned on. From that point on, the document text will be
  formatted as bold until a [bold] code is encountered to signify that bold
  should be turned off. Because of this, Reveal Codes become a necessary
  formatting tool.

  This approach differs widely from Word's paragraph-based formatting model,
  which associates formatting properties with objects. The formatting
  information for a paragraph is stored at the end of a paragraph in the paragraph
  marker ¶, and text in Word is WYSIWYG (what you see is what you get). This
  means formatting displays on screen exactly as it will print. Users who grasp
  the differences between the formatting models are much more successful at
  becoming productive using the formatting features found in Word.

- **Undo** The last characteristic shared by successful transitioners is an understanding of where to turn and what tools to use for troubleshooting when mistakes occur. One key feature of Word is Undo, which is similar to the WordPerfect Restore command. Awareness of this feature is enough to make most users more willing to explore Word, and this allows them to learn more quickly as a result.

Understanding "Select, Then Do"

"Select, then do" is a rule that applies to almost every action in Word. You select the object you want to work on and then choose the action you want to perform. For example, you select text and then delete it.

In this way, selecting in Word 7.0 is similar to blocking in WordPerfect for DOS. In WordPerfect, you block text before you can move it or delete it. However, many formatting actions in WordPerfect require users to insert codes in front of the text, type the text, and then insert codes after the text. In Word 7.0, you simply select the text and then choose the formatting command.

To WordPerfect for DOS users, typing and then formatting may seem an unusual procedure, but it is an efficient way to work with Word; it gives users the opportunity to focus on content—to get important ideas down quickly first and work with formatting later.

Because editing documents enforces the "select, then do" model, encourage users to practice with the sample documents included with Word before they create their own documents.

Note Many Word formatting commands can also be used in the same way as WordPerfect commands. For example, in Word you can select italic formatting, type a word, and then select italic formatting again to continue typing with normally formatted text. Users should become familiar with both ways of working and use the method that suits them best or that works best for a particular task.

Selecting Text

Users can select text and graphics with the mouse or keys.

To	Do this
Select any text or graphic using the mouse	Position the mouse pointer (I-beam) at one end of the text or graphic, hold down the left mouse button, and drag over the text or graphic.
Select any text or graphic using the keyboard	Press the ARROW keys until the insertion point is in front of the text or graphic. Hold down the SHIFT key and press the RIGHT ARROW key until you've selected the item.
Cancel a selection	Click elsewhere with the mouse or press the ESC key.

Selected text appears highlighted on the screen.

This paragraph is selected.

• Mercury¶

> Named·for·the·wing-footed·messenger·of·the·Roman·
> gods,·Mercury·races·around·its·orbit·at·a·dizzying·
> speed·of·30·miles·(48·kilometers)·per·second,·making·
> the·Mercurial·year·only·88·Earth·days·long.·In·contrast,·
> one·rotation·around·its·axis—or·a·single·day—takes·
> almost·59·Earth·days.¶

Daytime·temperatures·rise·to·about·800·degrees·
Fahrenheit·(341.33·degrees·Celsius),·which·is·not·
surprising·given·its·close·proximity·to·the·Sun.·That·
proximity·makes·it·difficult·to·study·Mercury·from·the·
Earth·because·of·the·interference·of·the·Sun's·
brilliance.¶

About Word Key Combinations

Users can accomplish many tasks in Word without moving their hands from the keyboard. For example, they can select, delete, and insert text, format characters and paragraphs, and move the insertion point in the document.

WordPerfect 5.1 and Word 7.0 use different keystrokes to carry out similar actions. For example, WordPerfect 5.1 uses ALT-F4, DEL to select and delete a block of text, while Word 7.0 uses F8, arrow keys (UP ARROW, DOWN ARROW, LEFT ARROW, or RIGHT ARROW), DEL.

Note WordPerfect 5.1 and Word documentation represent key combinations differently. Word uses a plus sign (+) to indicate keys that are pressed simultaneously, while WordPerfect uses a minus sign (-). For example, SHIFT+F1 in Word means to hold down the SHIFT key while pressing F1. A sequence of keys is represented in Word by commas; for example, ALT, F, A means to press and release each key in sequence.

Understanding Paragraph-Based Word Processing

WordPerfect 5.1, like most MS-DOS–based word processors, treats a document as a stream of text. The text has no formatting associated with it; formatting is applied by inserting codes into the text stream.

Word 7.0 also treats a document as a stream of text, but formatting is applied directly to the text. Word does not rely on codes in the text stream.

In WordPerfect, if a base font code is inserted into the text stream, all the text after the code will be formatted in the specified font until another base font code is inserted. If a word from the middle of the text stream is cut and pasted elsewhere, it will not take the formatting with it unless the font codes are correctly duplicated and inserted in the new location.

In Word 7.0, if text is cut and pasted in a new location, its attributes move with it; codes do not have to be duplicated and placed before and after the text.

Character formatting, such as bold, italic, and underline, is attached directly to the text characters to which it is applied. Paragraph formatting, such as indentation and tab stop locations, is stored in a nonprinting paragraph mark (¶) at the end of each paragraph. Any paragraph formats apply to the paragraph as a whole.

Working with Paragraphs in Word

When a user presses ENTER to end a paragraph, Word automatically inserts a paragraph mark and applies the current formats to the next paragraph. If the user deletes a paragraph mark, the text from the following paragraph will merge with the previous paragraph and take on the previous paragraph formatting.

If a user moves text from one paragraph to another and leaves the paragraph mark behind, the original paragraph formatting is lost, unless the new paragraph has the same formats as the original. To retain the paragraph formatting when moving or copying text, users should include the paragraph mark in the selection.

¶

Show/Hide ¶ button

It's a good idea for new users to work with paragraph marks displayed. To display paragraph marks, tabs, and other nonprinting characters, click the Show/Hide ¶ button on the Standard toolbar.

WordPerfect 5.1 users are accustomed to thinking of a paragraph as a series of lines. In WordPerfect, they can center or right-align a single line in a paragraph or a portion of text in a multiline paragraph using the [Center] or [Flsh Rgt] codes. In Word, to center a single line of text, users must put it in a separate paragraph. Tab stops and tabs are used to center or right-align a portion of a line.

Like most actions in Word, the "select, then do" idea can be applied to formatting paragraphs. Instead of using the WordPerfect 5.1 method of choosing an action—such as indenting, then typing the text, and then pressing ENTER to end the indentation—Word users can select a paragraph and then choose a command to apply the formats they want. Users can apply formats by clicking buttons on the toolbars, using key combinations, or choosing the Paragraph command on the Format menu.

To quickly apply a group of formats, such as indentation and spacing, you can apply a style that contains those formats. By default, the Normal style is applied to all paragraphs in Word. If you frequently use formats that are different from the defaults in the Normal style, you can save time by redefining the Normal style.

Tip You can format a single paragraph simply by placing the insertion point in the paragraph and choosing a style; you don't need to highlight all the text in a paragraph before formatting it.

Remind your users to follow these guidelines:

- Use the SPACEBAR to insert spaces between words. Do not use it to move the insertion point or to align text.

- Use the paragraph formatting options to align and indent text.

To use the formatting options, select the text and choose any of the following: the Increase Indent and Decrease Indent buttons on the Formatting toolbar, the alignment buttons on the Formatting toolbar, the indent markers on the ruler, or the Paragraph command on the Formatting menu.

Correcting Mistakes

WordPerfect 5.1 users often correct mistakes and troubleshoot by displaying reveal codes and making adjustments to them. There is no need for reveal codes in Word 7.0. Word is WYSIWYG—what you see is what you get. You can see what your document looks like right on screen.

In Word, you can correct formatting errors by using the Undo command on the Edit menu. You can also troubleshoot formatting errors by displaying a list of the formatting applied to text.

Correcting Errors Using Undo and Redo

If you choose the wrong command or delete something by mistake, you can often correct the error by selecting the Undo command on the Edit menu or the Undo button on the Standard toolbar. Undo is similar to the WordPerfect 5.1 Restore command, but it can reverse the effect of commands as well as restore text. If you decide to do the action after all, you can redo it by using the Redo command or button.

Undo button

Redo button

To use Undo, click the Undo command on the Edit menu. The last change made to the file is undone. If you click the down arrow next to the Undo button, you can select an entire string of commands to undo. Some actions, such as saving a document, cannot be reversed. To indicate that the command is unavailable, Undo changes to Can't Undo and appears dimmed on the Edit menu.

Troubleshooting Without Reveal Codes

Use the following techniques when working with text formatting.

Checking the Formatting toolbar and dialog boxes

You can check formatting information of characters and paragraphs in two locations: the Formatting toolbar and the Formatting dialog boxes. Select a character or string of text. Next, check the settings on the Formatting toolbar. For example, if text is bold, the Bold button on the toolbar appears pressed down when that text is selected. You can also click Character on the Format menu. The Bold option in the Character dialog box will be selected.

The Formatting toolbar also shows paragraph formatting. For example, if a paragraph is centered and has a hanging indent, the Centered button on the toolbar appears pressed down and the indent markers on the left end of the ruler show the indent. You can also click the Paragraph command on the Format menu and look at the Paragraph dialog box. It provides the same information as the toolbar. In addition, it gives exact measurements for the hanging indent.

If you select several characters or paragraphs that have different formats, the toolbar buttons will be grayed and the affected fields in the dialog boxes will be blank. Word cannot show more than one format at a time. You can still apply settings even if the buttons or options are grayed. For example, if a selection includes some text that is bold and some that is not bold, the Bold button on the Formatting toolbar will be grayed. Clicking the Bold button will make all of the text in the selection bold. In a dialog box, clicking a grayed check box will select the option and format all of the selected text with the selected formatting. Clicking it a second time will remove the option from all of the selected text.

Viewing Word's Formatting Codes

Help button

You can also check formatting by clicking the Help button on the Standard toolbar or pressing SHIFT+F1. When the pointer becomes a question mark, click the text you want to check.

After clicking the text, you can click the Help button again or press ESC to clear the formatting information.

Most commands for viewing documents are on the View menu.

Changing the view

You can also get information about formatting in documents by displaying Word in different views. The default view is Normal. It is usually the fastest view to work in, but it does not show how the page will look when it is printed. When you need to see the layout of text and graphics on the page, you may want to switch to page layout view.

Page layout is a fully editable, WYSIWYG view that shows all page elements as they will print, including columns, graphics, margins, headers, footers, footnotes, and page numbers. For a full-page representation of the document, switch to Print Preview.

Displaying nonprinting characters

You can display the invisible characters you type, such as paragraph marks (¶) and spaces (·), by clicking the Hide/Show ¶ button. It's a good idea to display these characters to see if there are extra spaces between words, typed spaces instead of a tab character, or accidentally placed hard returns. As the name implies, nonprinting characters appear on the screen but are never printed.

Terms Your Users Should Know

This section provides a glossary of WordPerfect terms and the corresponding Word terms or features. The Word terms in *italics* can be looked up in the index or in online Help.

WordPerfect term	Description of Word term or feature
advance	To position text in an exact location on a page, use the ADVANCE *field*.
append	To add text to the end of another document, use the Edit menu, *Cut* or *Copy* and the *Paste* commands; or use the *drag-and-drop editing* feature.
attribute	Attributes such as bold, italic, underline, superscript, and text size are called *character formats*.
base font	When you first start typing, Word uses a plain font that doesn't have attributes such as bold or underline. However, you can change the *default font* that Word uses.
binding offset	To add extra space to the inside margins so that text isn't hidden when you bind the document, set a *gutter margin*.
block	To highlight an area of text so that you can modify it, *select* the text. The highlighted text is called the *selection*.
block, copy or move	To copy or move text, select it and then use the *Cut* or *Copy* and the *Paste* commands (Edit menu); or use the *drag-and-drop editing* feature.
block protect	To prevent page breaks from occurring in the middle of a paragraph or between specific paragraphs, use the Keep Lines Together or Keep With Next option (*keeping together*).
box	See "graphics box," later in this glossary.
center line	To align text on a line, use a *center tab*.
center page	To center paragraphs vertically on a page, use the *vertical alignment* feature.
clean screen	To maximize the screen space that's available for displaying documents, use *full screen view*.
codes	Word is WYSIWYG (what you see is what you get), which means that text appears on the screen as it will appear in the printed document. Word does not display formatting codes on the screen. See "Correcting Mistakes," earlier in this chapter.
compose	Use the *symbols* available in a font such as Symbol or Wingdings®. To include mathematical symbols or equations, use the *Equation Editor*.
conditional end of page	To prevent page breaks from occurring in the middle of a paragraph or between specific paragraphs, use the Keep Lines Together or Keep With Next option (*keeping together*).

WordPerfect term	Description of Word term or feature
cursor	The *insertion point* is the blinking vertical line that indicates where the text you type will appear.
document comments	To add comments to a document, use *annotations*.
document compare	To compare two versions of a document, use the *Compare Versions* feature.
document summary	You can include *summary information* for a document, such as author and date.
dot leader	The solid, dashed, or dotted line in the space filled by a tab character is called the *tab stop leader*.
edit-screen options	To change the way a document appears on the screen, switch to a different *view* or display the *nonprinting characters*.
environment setup	To set options such as the unit of measurement or the interval between automatic saves, use the *Options* command (Tools menu). You can also use the Windows 95 Control Panel (on the Windows Start menu, point to Settings, then click Control Panel) to set other options, such as the speed at which the pointer moves across the screen.
flush right	To align text flush with the right margin (or with the right indent), you *right align* it.
generate	After you mark items for an index, table of contents, or table of authorities, you *compile* the index or table. To update cross-references, you *update fields*.
graphics box	To create a box of text or graphics, use a *frame*. For example, you can wrap text around a frame.
graphics lines	To draw lines, use *drawing objects* on the Drawing toolbar.
hard hyphen	A *nonbreaking hyphen* prevents hyphenated words from breaking if they fall at the end of a line.
hard return	When you press ENTER to end a paragraph, a nonprinting *paragraph mark* (¶) appears.
hard space	A *nonbreaking space* prevents multiple words, such as a proper name or a date, from breaking if they fall at the end of a line.
justification	You can horizontally *align* text on the left, centered, on the right, or justified (aligned both left and right).
leading adjustment	To adjust the space between lines, change the *line spacing*. To add space between paragraphs, adjust the *paragraph spacing*.
line draw	To draw circles, squares, polygons, and other shapes, use the *Drawing toolbar*.
line formats	To set options such as justification, line spacing, and tab stops, use *paragraph formats*. To set the left and right *margins,* use the horizontal *ruler* or the *Page Setup* command (File menu). To set *hyphenation* options, use the Hyphenation command (Tools menu).

WordPerfect term	Description of Word term or feature
list	To create an equivalent list in Word, use a *Table of Figures*.
list files	You can see a list of the files in a folder whenever you *open* or *save* a document. To change the *default folders* for documents or templates, use the File Locations tab in the Options dialog box (Tools menu). To copy or rename files, use the *Save As* command (File menu).
locked documents	To prevent other users from opening or changing a document, you can *protect* it with a *password*.
look	To preview a document before you open, copy, print or delete it, use the File menu, *Open* command, Advanced button.
margin release	Create a *hanging indent*.
mark text	You can mark text to be included in an *index, table of contents,* or *table of authorities*.
math	To perform *math calculations,* use a *formula*.
merge codes	Use *merge fields* to insert variable text and merge instructions into merge documents.
page formats	To set margins and paper size, center text vertically, and set up facing pages, use the *Page Setup* command (File menu). To create headers and footers, use the *Header And Footer toolbar*. To add page numbers, use the *Page Numbers* command (Insert menu).
parallel columns	Use a *table* to create side-by-side paragraphs of text.
pitch	Text size is measured in *points,* which determine the height of characters. To convert points to pitch, divide 120 by the number of points.
redline	To identify text that has been added to a document, use *revision marks*.
restore	To restore deleted text and reverse many commands, use the *Undo* command. If you change your mind, use the *Redo* command.
retrieve	You can *open* a document and display it on the screen. To insert a document within another document, use the *File* command (Insert menu).
reveal codes	See "codes," earlier in this glossary.
rewrite	To update page breaks whenever you pause while typing or editing, use *background repagination*.
search	To search for specific text or formatting, use the *Find* command (Edit menu).
soft hyphen	An *optional hyphen* tells Word where to hyphenate a word if it falls at the end of a line.
strikeout	To identify text that has been deleted from a document, use *revision marks*. You can also use the *strikethrough* character format to mark revisions manually.

WordPerfect term	Description of Word term or feature
style	In Word, a *style* is a collection of formats you name and save. To save boilerplate text for reuse, use the *AutoText* feature.
switch	To switch between open documents, use the Window menu. To change uppercase text to lowercase, or vice versa, use the *Change Case* command (Format menu).
text in/out	To *convert* a text only file to Word format, just *open* the document. To convert a Word document to text only format, save the document as plain text.
typeover	Use *overtype mode* when you want to type over existing text.
undelete	If you accidentally delete text, you can restore it by using the *Undo* command.

Converting WordPerfect Documents

This section describes how to convert WordPerfect documents to Word format, or vice versa. You can also use a macro to quickly convert multiple WordPerfect documents to Word format. If a document isn't converted the way you want, you can customize the conversion process. This section also includes troubleshooting tips for the most common conversion problems.

Have you installed the WordPerfect converter?   Before you can convert documents, the WordPerfect converter and graphics filters must be installed on your computer. If you performed a Typical or Complete installation during setup, the converter and filters for WordPerfect 5.*x* and 6.*x* for DOS and Windows are installed automatically. If you performed a Compact installation, you need to run the Microsoft Office Setup program again to install the converter and graphics filters.

Additional fonts and templates for smoother conversion   The Office Resource Kit CD-ROM includes fonts and templates for better conversions of WordPerfect documents. For more information, see Appendix D, "Contents of the Office Resource Kit CD."

Converting a WordPerfect Document to Word Format

To convert a WordPerfect document to a Word document, you simply open (retrieve) the document. Word handles the conversion automatically. To complete the conversion, you save the document to a Word format.

Open button

▶ **To open and convert a WordPerfect document**

1. Click the Open button on the Standard toolbar

2. In the List Files Of Type box, select All Files.

3. If necessary, select the drive and folder where the document is located.

4. In the File Name box, type or select the name of the document. (If you prefer, you can type the full path—for example, c:\wp51\work\letter.doc—in the File Name box.)

5. Click OK.

First, select All Files from the list.

Then, select the drive and folder in which the WordPerfect document is stored.

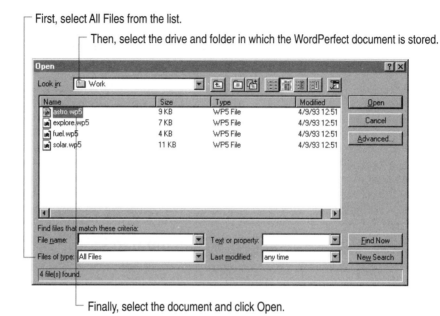

Finally, select the document and click Open.

Word converts the WordPerfect document and opens it. If the WordPerfect converter isn't installed or if Word cannot identify the format of the document, Word displays the Convert File dialog box.

Saving the Converted Document

After you convert a WordPerfect document to a Word document, the converted document exists only in your computer's memory; the original document remains unchanged on disk. To complete the conversion, you need to save the converted document in Word format.

Save button

If you want to keep the original WordPerfect document as a backup, click Save As on the File menu and give the converted document a new name. Otherwise, click the Save button on the Standard toolbar, or click Save on the File menu. When Word displays the Save Format dialog box, click the Word button.

When you close the document or quit Word, Word may ask if you want to save changes to the document. Click the Yes button.

Converting Multiple WordPerfect Documents to Word Format

To convert multiple WordPerfect documents, you can open multiple documents at the same time in the Open dialog box. To select a contiguous group of documents in the list, click the name of the first document you want to convert, and then hold down SHIFT and click the name of the last document you want to convert. Or hold down CTRL and click the names of the individual documents you want to convert. When you click the OK button, Word converts and opens each document you've selected. When you finish editing the documents, you need to save each document as described in the previous section, "Saving the Converted Document."

Using the BatchConversion Macro

If you want to convert multiple documents to or from WordPerfect format, use the BatchConversion macro. The BatchConversion macro is stored in the Convert7.dot template. This template is located in the Macros folder of the Word 7.0 program folder (for example, C:\Winword\ Macros) For more information, see "Converting File Formats" in Chapter 21.

Converting a Word Document to WordPerfect Format

To convert a Word document to WordPerfect format, you simply use the Save As command.

▶ **To convert a Word Document to WordPerfect format**

1. Click Save As on the File menu.

2. In the Save File As Type box, select either WordPerfect 5.0 or 5.1. Both WordPerfect 5.*x* and WordPerfect 6.0 can open a document saved in WordPerfect 5.0 or 5.1 format directly.

3. If necessary, specify the drive or folder where you want to store the converted document.

4. In the File Name box, type a name for the converted document. (If you save the document with a different name you will still have the document in Word format as a backup.)

5. Click OK.

When you close the document or quit Word, Word asks if you want to save changes to the document. Click the Yes button. This message appears even if you have not changed the document since converting it.

Customizing WordPerfect Conversions

When you convert a WordPerfect document to Word format, Word preserves the document's original content and formatting. However, Word and WordPerfect have different sets of features—and even similar features work differently—so you might not always get the results you expect. For example, the converted document may look different from the original document if text was aligned using spaces instead of tab stops; or line and page breaks may occur in different locations due to differences in fonts or printer drivers.

Improving Compatibility with WordPerfect

Word provides special compatibility options that allow you to change options in Word so that it more closely matches WordPerfect. For example, in Word, blank spaces at the end of a line extend beyond the right margin; however, you can set a compatibility option to wrap the blank spaces to the next line, as in WordPerfect.

When you convert a WordPerfect document, Word automatically sets the compatibility options that are applicable to the type or format of the document. If you want to change these settings, click Options on the Tools menu, and then Click the Compatibility tab. For more information, see "Customizing Conversions and Improving Compatibility" earlier in this chapter.

Specifying Fonts for a Converted Document

The fonts originally used to format a converted WordPerfect document may not be available on your computer or printer. In this case, Word automatically substitutes similar available fonts to display and print the document. The substituted fonts aren't actually applied to the text; if you later convert the document back to WordPerfect format, the document will retain the original fonts it had in WordPerfect.

If you want, you can specify the fonts Word substitutes for each missing font in the converted WordPerfect document. Or you can permanently replace the missing fonts. For more information, see "Specifying Fonts for Converted Documents" earlier in this chapter.

Converting Between Word 7.0 and WordPerfect 5.0, 5.1, or 5.2

The WordPerfect 5.x converter shipped with Word 7.0 is designed to take advantage of features and conversion capabilities specifically available in Word 7.0.

Note Converting a file from Word format to WordPerfect format and back again may cause the loss of some formatting, for example, fonts, justification, styles, and mail merge, unless you load, paginate, and save the converted file in WordPerfect before converting back to Word.

In the following table, "Yes" means the feature exists in both products and is converted from one product to the other. "No" means it exists in both products but is not completely converted between the two. "Not supported" means the feature is not supported in one of the products or is not converted completely between products.

Feature	Word 7.0 to WordPerfect 5.x	WordPerfect 5.x to Word 7.0	Comments
Character Formatting			
All caps	Yes	Not supported	All caps formatting becomes all capital letters.
Hidden	Yes	Not supported	Hidden text in Word becomes WordPerfect Comment text.
Strikethrough	See comment	See comment	WordPerfect strikeout becomes strikethrough formatting in Word; WordPerfect redlining becomes revision marking in Word. Word strikethrough formatting converts to strikeout in WordPerfect; Word revision marking converts to WordPerfect redlining.
Underlining	Yes	Yes	Underlining format is preserved, but the type of underlining may be changed.
Spacing (condensed, expanded)	Not supported	Not supported	
Kerning	Yes	Yes	
Paragraph Formatting			
Alignment	Yes	Yes	Centering codes may have to be individually repositioned in WordPerfect after conversion.
First-line indents	Yes	Yes	First-line indents are created with tabs in WordPerfect.
Page Break Before	Yes	Not supported	Approximated with a page break in WordPerfect.
Space before/ after paragraphs	Yes	Not supported	Approximated with blank lines in WordPerfect.
Tab leaders	See comment	Yes	All Word tab leaders become dot leaders in WordPerfect.

Feature	Word 7.0 to WordPerfect 5.x	WordPerfect 5.x to Word 7.0	Comments
Paragraph Formatting *(continued)*			
Leading/baselines, Lines/baselines	Not supported	Not supported	
[Center]/ [Flsh Rgt] codes	Not supported	See comment	From WordPerfect to Word, Center and Flush Right codes convert to center and right-aligned tab stops.
Section Formatting			
Margins	Yes	Yes	Word margins are measured from the paper's edge to body text; WordPerfect margins are measured from the edge to the header. The conversion adjusts the margins as needed to preserve page layout. If problems are experienced with margins (for example, if they are set outside the printable range in Word), click Page Setup on the File menu, select the Margins tab and click OK. If margins need to be adjusted, Word will ask to fix them.
Newspaper Columns	Yes	Yes	Line Between formatting is not supported by WordPerfect.
Parallel Columns	Not supported	See comment	From WordPerfect to Word, parallel columns convert to tables. If a parallel column layout contains a page-anchored box, the entire parallel column converts to newspaper columns.
Tables			
Tables	Yes	Yes	Vertical merging of cells is not converted.
Table Formulas/Math	Not supported	Not supported	
Decimal table cell alignment	Not supported	See comment	Converted to right paragraph alignment.
Document Formatting			
Default tab stops	Not supported	Yes	
Footnotes	Yes	Yes	Footnotes placed at end of sections are converted to endnotes, because WordPerfect doesn't have sections. Starting number and separators are not converted. Custom footnote marks are added to automatic numbering.

Feature	Word 7.0 to WordPerfect 5.x	WordPerfect 5.x to Word 7.0	Comments
Document Formatting *(continued)*			
Gutter Margins, Widow Control, Mirror Even/Odd Pages, Paper Size	Yes	Yes	Widow Control is a document property in Word; Even/Odd pages is not converted.
Other Features			
Annotations	Yes	Not supported	Annotations become WordPerfect Comment text.
Outlining/ Paragraph Numbers/ Word 7.0 Lists	Yes	Yes	Word Lists and paragraph numbers convert to sequence fields when present in Tables, Footnotes, and other non-body text locations.
Print merge commands	Yes	Yes	Word data source documents can be either tab or comma delimited or in table format to convert to WordPerfect. Word automatically converts WordPerfect secondary files to Word data source document format. Conditional print merge constructs and macros are lost when converting to Word.
Date/time stamps	Yes	Yes	Default formats only.
Subdocuments (INCLUDE field)	Yes	See comment	WordPerfect master documents and subdocuments convert to Word master documents and subdocuments. Word master documents and subdocuments convert to WordPerfect master documents and subdocuments.
Equations	See comment	See comment	From Word to WordPerfect, equation objects are converted as editable equation boxes. Equation fields are not converted from Word to WordPerfect. From WordPerfect to Word, equations are converted as editable equation objects.
Extended characters	Yes	Yes	Extended characters that are available in both products are converted.
Text Boxes/Lines	Yes	Yes	Some text boxes and lines convert to Word drawing layer objects. Drawing layer objects are only visible in page layout view, print preview, and when printing. Drawing layer objects will not appear in normal view.

Feature	Word 7.0 to WordPerfect 5.x	WordPerfect 5.x to Word 7.0	Comments
Other Features *(continued)*			
Line Draw	Yes	Yes	Line Draw characters are converted; however, Word's line spacing causes gaps to appear between line draw characters on successive lines. This can be corrected for printing by setting line spacing to the exact current font size in points. Click the Paragraph command on the Format menu to change line spacing.
PRIVATE field codes	Not supported	See comment	PRIVATE fields are inserted by the WordPerfect converter to preserve information needed to accurately save the file back to WordPerfect format. These fields should not be edited and have no effect on the document in Word.
Styles	Yes	See comment	From WordPerfect to Word, styles containing paragraph formatting codes convert to paragraph styles. WordPerfect styles containing only character formatting convert to character styles in Word, text contained in a style is converted as normal text.

Converting Between Word 7.0 and WordPerfect 6.0 or 6.1

The WordPerfect 6.x converter included in your Word 7.0 package converts documents from WordPerfect 6.0 for DOS and Windows and WordPerfect 6.1 for Windows to Word 7.0. This converter cannot be used to save a Word document in WordPerfect 6.x format.

Note If the document being converted was originally created in WordPerfect 5.x and a font does not seem to be mapped correctly after conversion, try the following: if you have access to WordPerfect 6.x, reopen the document in WordPerfect 6.x, press CTRL+END or scroll to the end of the document, and resave the document in WordPerfect 6.x format before again converting to Word 7.0.

If the document being converted was originally created in WordPerfect 6.x and a font does not seem to be mapped correctly after conversion, try the following: reopen the document in WordPerfect 6.x to confirm the original font. If the original font in the document is not on the system, WordPerfect 6.0 displays in the status bar the name of the font it is mapped to, followed by the name of the original font, in parentheses. WordPerfect 6.1 displays only the name of the font it is mapped it to, when the original font is not available.

In the following table, "Yes" means the feature exists in both products and is converted from one product to the other. "No" means it exists in both products but is not completely converted between the two. "Not supported" means the feature is not supported in one of the products or is not converted completely between products.

Feature	WordPerfect 6.x to Word 7.0	Comments
Character Formatting		
Strikethrough and Redlining	Yes	WordPerfect strikeout becomes strikethrough formatting in Word; WordPerfect redlining becomes deletion revision marking in Word.
Kerning	Not supported	
Word and Letter Spacing	Not supported	
Paragraph Formatting		
[Center]/ [Flsh Rgt] codes	Yes	Center and Flush Right codes convert to center and right-aligned tab stops and tabs.
Back Tabs	See comment	Back tabs that are preceded by text are not converted.
Default tabs	See comment	Trailing default tabs at ends of lines are not converted.
Tab leaders	See comment	Dot tab leaders, minus sign tab leaders, and underscore tab leaders are converted to the same tab leaders in Word. All other WordPerfect tab leaders become dot leaders in Word.
Keep Text Together properties	Not supported	
Leading adjustment between lines/baselines	Not supported	
Paragraph Margins	Yes	WordPerfect paragraph margins are converted to left and right paragraph indents in Word.
Spacing between Paragraphs	Yes	Spacing between Paragraphs in WordPerfect is converted to Spacing After paragraph format in Word.
Styles	Not supported	Style contents are converted as direct formatting in Word.
Other Features		
Advance	Yes	Advance codes are converted to ADVANCE fields in Word. Advance codes that have the effect of advancing text upward on a page cannot be fully emulated in Word. Absolute vertical advance codes in headers are not converted.
Bookmarks	Not supported	

Feature	WordPerfect 6.x to Word 7.0	Comments
Other Features (*continued*)		
Borders and Fill (for column, page and paragraph)	Not supported	
Captions	Not supported	
Chapter and Volume numbers	Not supported	
Comments	Yes	Comments become annotations in Word. Comments in headers, footers, footnotes and endnote text are not retained in Word.
Contour Wrap for graphics boxes	See comment	Contour wrap is converted to square wrap (wrap around property) in Word, as Word does not support Contour wrap.
Cross-references and Hypertext Links	Not supported	They are retained as plain text in Word.
Drop Cap	Not supported	
Equations	Yes	Equations are converted as editable equation objects.
Footnotes	Yes	Custom footnote marks are converted to automatic numbered marks. If the numbering format of notes is changed in a document, the notes numbered with the new format are converted as custom notes.
Index and Lists	Not supported	They are retained as plain text in Word.
Insert Filename	Not supported	
Labels and Bar codes	Not supported	Text of labels is retained in Word.
Line Numbers	Not supported	
Macros	Not supported	
Margins	Yes	Word margins are measured from the paper's edge to body text; WordPerfect margins are measured from the top and bottom edge of page to the top of the header and bottom of footer, respectively. The conversion adjusts the margins as needed to preserve page layout. If problems are experienced with margins (for example, if they are set outside the printable range in Word), click Page Setup on the File menu, select the Margins tab and click OK. If margins need to be adjusted, Word will ask to fix them.
Merge codes	Not supported	Merge constructs and macros are lost when converting to Word.
Outlining/ Paragraph Numbers/ Counters	Yes	All are converted to SEQUENCE fields in Word.

Feature	WordPerfect 6.x to Word 7.0	Comments
Other Features *(continued)*		
Page features (center page, page binding, and subdivide pages)	Not supported	
Parallel Columns	See comment	Parallel columns convert to tables.
Table vertical cell merge, and cell alignment	Not supported	
Text Boxes/ Lines	Yes	Some text boxes and lines convert to Word drawing layer objects. Drawing layer objects are only visible in page layout view, print preview, and when printing. Drawing layer objects will not appear in normal view.
		Graphics boxes in tables, parallel columns, and headers/footers, that are anchored to page or paragraph, and have wrap around text in the original document, are converted to boxes with wrap through in Word. In most cases these boxes are converted to drawing layer objects in Word.
		All graphics lines are converted as solid lines.
Watermarks	Not supported	
WordPerfect characters	Yes	If the WordPerfect fonts containing the characters are available on the system, all the characters are converted. If one or more of these fonts is not available, some characters may not be converted.

WordPerfect Conversion Features Supported

Below are detailed descriptions of several WordPerfect conversion features.

Variable-width Columns

Because of its support for variable-width columns, as shown in the following illustration, Word 7.0 fully supports conversion of WordPerfect variable-width column layouts. Variable width columns allow successful conversion of newsletters and many other documents that commonly use this feature.

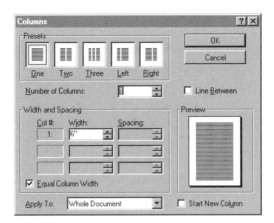

Word is very flexible in its support of columns, which greatly improves WordPerfect file conversions.

Layered Drawing

Through the use of its drawing layer, Word 7.0 fully supports the conversion of WordPerfect boxes that have been set as transparent to overlay text. These are converted to Word text boxes that can be placed above or below document text with no text wrapping. This method of formatting is commonly seen in WordPerfect documents, because transparent overlay boxes are the primary method of creating page borders. Transparent overlay boxes are also used in all WordPerfect legal pleading documents, which can be easily converted to Word 7.0.

Compatibility Options

Word 7.0 includes options, shown in the following illustration, to modify certain layout and pagination behaviors to more closely mimic WordPerfect behavior. When a document is converted from WordPerfect, several of these options are automatically triggered by the converter so that Word can make converted documents closely retain their original appearance.

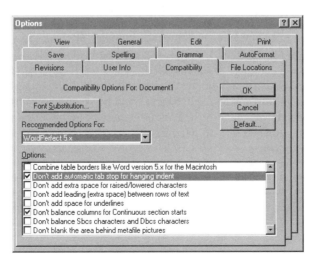

To improve the appearance of converted WordPerfect files, you can configure Word to closely mimic WordPerfect layout and pagination behavior.

Following is an explanation of some of these options.

Don't add automatic tab stop for hanging indent   When a Word paragraph is set with a hanging indent, it normally acts as if an automatic tab stop is set to the level of the indent. WordPerfect does not act this way, so the converter turns this behavior off. This helps to retain tab settings in all documents.

Don't balance columns for Continuous section starts   Word automatically balances columns preceding a Continuous section break. Because WordPerfect does not behave like this, the converter deactivates this feature of Word. This ensures that documents with column layouts more closely match their original unconverted appearance.

Don't blank the area behind metafile pictures   WordPerfect treats pictures with white backgrounds in overlay frames as if they are transparent, so the converter toggles an option in Word to make it act similarly.

Wrap trailing spaces to next line   The converter configures Word to be consistent with WordPerfect in the way it treats trailing space characters: they wrap like hard characters, underline like hard characters, and can be used to add space from a right-aligned paragraph or right-aligned tab. This option allows direct conversion of form-like documents with underlined spaces.

Substitute fonts based on font size   This option is used by the WordPerfect 6.*x* converter to make a font request based on font size first, and if a match is not found, to actually map the font. Word only maps fonts based on the font name. For example, if you have a line of text formatted as the Courier printer font and you format the line to be 24 points, WordPerfect dynamically maps the font request to Courier New 24-type because the Courier printer font is not available in 24 points. In Word, the font would remain Courier with the closest matching point size, in this case, 12 points. This option is turned on for WordPerfect 6.*x* for Windows and WordPerfect 6.0 for DOS.

Suppress extra line spacing like WordPerfect version 5.*x*   Word adds internal leading to the line height of text. The leading is obtained from the font, and the amount of leading depends on the font and size. WordPerfect does not include internal leading in the line height. Instead, WordPerfect adds 2 points to the line height of proportionately spaced fonts and does not add anything extra to monospaced fonts. This ensures that the layout of converted WordPerfect documents formatted with Automatic line height closely matches that of the original documents.

Truncate font height   WordPerfect rounds down the font size to the next lower number, whereas Word rounds up to the next higher number. This results in the font size in WordPerfect documents being slightly smaller than in Word documents. This option is turned on for WordPerfect 6.*x* for Windows.

Advance Codes

Using the Advance field, Word successfully converts most of the cases where advance codes are used in WordPerfect documents.

Styles

Word converts WordPerfect style definitions into Word styles containing the formatting of the WordPerfect style. Word also converts styled text with the proper styles assigned, making it easier to edit converted WordPerfect documents.

Private Field

For greater fidelity in repeated conversion of documents between Word and WordPerfect, Word includes a PRIVATE field. The converter makes use of this field to store binary information about how the document was constructed before it was originally converted. This allows the converter to use this information later to reconstruct features accurately that would otherwise change or be lost in conversion. The PRIVATE field is used in over a dozen locations by the converter. Some examples of features that are preserved by this field include tables of contents, figure captions, and paragraph numbering.

Parallel Column Conversion

Because of its two-pass conversion architecture and key improvements to tables, in most cases Word converts WordPerfect parallel columns into Word tables with rows that break across pages. If a parallel column layout itself contains a box or exists on a page containing a paragraph-anchored box, it is instead converted to a newspaper column layout because Word tables cannot contain frames.

WordPerfect Mail Merge (Secondary Merge Files)

Word automatically detects and converts WordPerfect 5.x secondary merge files to Word data source document format. Secondary files containing 32 fields or less become tables, and those with more than 32 fields become tab-delimited. Likewise, if you choose to save a Word data source document as a WordPerfect 5.0 Secondary File or WordPerfect 5.1 or 5.2 Secondary File, the document is converted to a secondary merge file delimited with the appropriate merge commands for that version of WordPerfect.

Keyboard Input Fields

Word converts WordPerfect INPUT, PROMPT/KEYBOARD, and STATUSPROMPT/KEYBOARD combination merge fields into FILLIN fields in Word. This is useful for converting WordPerfect merge documents.

Table Row Heights

Word maps WordPerfect table row top and bottom cell margins to equivalent space before and space after paragraph margin settings. The length and pagination of documents with tables convert more accurately as a result of this mapping.

Table Headers

Because of its ability to define table header rows, Word successfully converts tables from WordPerfect that contain header definitions. Because table headers are a commonly used feature, this affects many WordPerfect documents.

Dashed and Dotted Borders

Because of its ability to create dashed and dotted borders around paragraphs, frames, and table cells, Word can accurately convert WordPerfect borders.

Master Documents

Word converts WordPerfect master documents to the Word master documents feature. This improves conversion of long documents where the master document feature is used.

Table of Authorities

Because of its support for tables of authorities (TOAs), Word converts WordPerfect short- and long-form TOA entries and TOAs. Word accomplishes this by converting WordPerfect short- and long-form entries to Word Table of Contents (TC) fields and by converting WordPerfect TOAs to TOA fields. This improves conversion of most legal documents, because Word TOAs are linked, updating as the document changes.

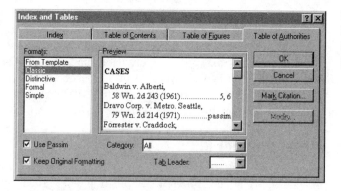

Word directly supports legal Tables of Authorities, so they can be converted directly from WordPerfect.

Cross-Reference Targets

Word converts WordPerfect cross-reference targets to bookmarks and vice versa.

Caption Conversion

Word converts WordPerfect figure captions into Word captions.

Footnotes and Endnotes

Because of its ability to have both footnotes and endnotes in the same document, Word supports the conversion of WordPerfect endnotes and footnotes. This ensures accurate conversion of academic documents that often include both endnotes and footnotes.

Cross-references

Word converts WordPerfect endnote, footnote, page, figure box, text box, user box, and equation box cross-references to Word cross-references. This means that documents that incorporate cross-references to these objects will remain linked.

Paragraph Numbering

Word converts WordPerfect paragraph numbering into numbered paragraphs or SEQ fields in Word. This means that numbering will continue to update automatically as these documents are edited after conversion. Word also stores information in its PRIVATE field for accurate conversion back to WordPerfect.

Line Numbering

Word converts WordPerfect line numbering. This is useful for legal documents.

Equations

Word imports and exports equations between Word's Equation Editor and WordPerfect equation format. This allows converted WordPerfect equations to be easily edited in Word and also transferred to WordPerfect, which is useful for converting scientific and mathematical documents.

WordPerfect for Windows Support

Word fully supports the conversion of WordPerfect for Windows documents containing Dynamic Data Exchange (DDE) links and OLE objects. To facilitate the proper export of these features, the converter also offers separate options to convert to WordPerfect 5.0, WordPerfect 5.1 for DOS, and WordPerfect 5.x for Windows. Selecting WordPerfect 5.x for Windows will ensure that OLE objects remain as objects and retain all of the necessary binary data, whereas choosing WordPerfect 5.0 or WordPerfect 5.1 for DOS will convert OLE objects to pictures that can be understood by WordPerfect for MS-DOS.

Suppress Code Conversion

Word converts WordPerfect suppress codes into the appropriate Word section definitions.

Text-based Linedraw

Word can convert WordPerfect text-based linedraw characters to a TrueTypeLinedraw font. This is useful for manuals and other documents containing embedded MS-DOS screen captures.

Vertical and Horizontal Line Positioning

Through the use of its drawing layer, Word can convert and position WordPerfect linedraw graphics.

Round-trip Frame Reassembly

Word improves coexistence with WordPerfect through round-trip disassembly and reassembly of framed objects. This is necessary because Word allows mixed text and graphics to appear inside of frames, but WordPerfect does not allow similar functionality in its boxes. On export from Word, Word converts such a frame to a WordPerfect text box with separate WordPerfect figure boxes for each graphic. Then, on returning to Word, Word reassembles such collections of boxes into the original mixed text-and-graphics frame.

Hyphenation Zone

Word converts WordPerfect's Left Hyphenation Zone percentage to an appropriate hyphenation zone measure in Word.

Label Definitions

Word detects the WordPerfect Label page type and creates a Word document with table definitions and margin settings to print onto the same type of labels.

Conditional End-of-Page

Word converts WordPerfect Conditional End-of-Page settings to the closest possible equivalent Keep With Next paragraph format.

Block Protect

Word converts WordPerfect Block Protect to the closest equivalent paragraph protection via Keep With Next and Keep Lines Together paragraph formats. WordPerfect Block Protect is a character/line protection property. Word's Keep With Next and Keep Lines Together paragraph formats are converted to Block Protect when saving in WordPerfect format.

Color Optimization

When you choose to save as WordPerfect 5.1 for DOS, Word maps Word 7.0 font colors to the standard colors that WordPerfect 5.1 for DOS understands, for example, [Color:Blue]. If you instead choose to save as WordPerfect 5.x for Windows, font colors are mapped to RGB color codes understood by WordPerfect for Windows, for example, [Color:0%,0%,100%].

Comments/Annotations

Word converts WordPerfect Comments to Word Annotations, and vice versa.

Underline Formatting

Word converts underline formatting to ensure consistency with the original WordPerfect document. For example, WordPerfect allows double underlining to be applied only to words and tabs, whereas double underlining is applied continuously in Word. Word 7.0 detects this underline format in conversion and turns the double underline format on and off in Word to retain the document's original appearance.

In addition, if WordPerfect underlining starts at the beginning of a line with any combination of tabs or indents, WordPerfect by default underlines only the text that follows. Word correctly interprets this layout, except for the dotted underline format, which is converted to single underline. This has no equivalent in Word. All other underline combinations are retained in conversion to and from WordPerfect.

Graphics on Disk

Word converts WordPerfect Figure Boxes containing a link to graphics on disk by dynamically calling the WPG Graphic import filter to process the graphic file. If the graphic file is not available in the location specified in the WordPerfect Figure Box, Word prompts you with the option to specify the location of the graphic, ignore the graphic and continue conversion, or cancel conversion. If you choose to ignore the graphic, an IMPORT field is created and a frame placeholder appears in the converted document.

Language Code Conversion

Word converts WordPerfect language codes into Word's equivalent settings. This is useful for documents that contain passages of foreign language text.

Automatic Pair and Manual Kerning

Word supports automatic pair kerning. WordPerfect manual kerning is applied using advance codes, which are converted to Word ADVANCE fields, thus maintaining the proper kerning effect. Kerning conversion allows Word to maintain the original appearance of documents such as newsletters, that use kerning.

Commands for WordPerfect Features

The following tables show the Word equivalents for WordPerfect commands.

Throughout the rest of this section, WordPerfect menus, commands, and shortcut keys are presented in tables that show their equivalents in Word. As you read the tables, please note the following conventions:

- "Not applicable" means that the WordPerfect command has no equivalent in Word.

- Italicized text after a key combination means that you type variable information. For example, "ALT+SHIFT+*number*" means that you hold down the ALT and SHIFT keys while typing a number.

WordPerfect List Files Commands

The following tables show the Word command equivalents for the WordPerfect commands and keystrokes listed.

WordPerfect command	WordPerfect 5.0 keys	WordPerfect 5.1 menu	Word 7.0 command or keys
List files	F5	File menu, List command	File menu, Open command
Retrieve		File Retrieve	File menu, Open command
Delete directory		File menu, List command	File menu, Open command
Rename		File menu, List command	File menu, Save As command
Print		File menu, List command	File menu, Open command
Text in		File menu, Text In command	File menu, Open command
Look		File menu, List command	File menu, Open command
Change directory		File menu, List command	File menu, Open command
Copy		File menu, List command	File menu, Save As command
Word search		File menu, List command	File menu, Open command
Name search		File menu, List command	File menu, Open command
Switch	SHIFT+F3	Edit Switch Document	CTRL+F6

Warning You cannot delete a document with the Open command if the document is open. Use the Open command to delete closed files only. Nor should you use the Windows Explorer to delete a file while you are running Word, because damage to Word and your document may occur.

WordPerfect Exit, Save, and Retrieve Commands

WordPerfect command	WordPerfect 5.0 keys	WordPerfect 5.1 menu	Word 7.0 command or keys
Save	F10	File menu, Save command	File menu, Save command
Retrieve	SHIFT+F10	File menu, Retrieve command	File menu, Open command
Exit	F7	File menu, Exit command	File menu, Exit command
Save a document		If yes	**y** (at prompt)
Do not save document		If no	**n** (at prompt)
Exit WP		Exit WP	Not applicable
If no		If no	File menu, New command
If yes		If yes	File menu, Exit command
Go to DOS	CTRL+F1	File Go to DOS	Windows Start menu, MS-DOS prompt

Note Word does not create backup copies (.bak) by default. If you want Word to make a backup copy every time a document is saved, click the Options command on the Tools menu, Click the Save tab, and then select the Always Create Backup Copy check box.

WordPerfect Text In/Out Commands

WordPerfect command	WordPerfect 5.0 keys	WordPerfect 5.1 menu	Word 7.0 command or keys
Text in/out	CTRL+F5		
DOS text		File menu, Text In command	File menu, Open command or File menu, Save As command
Password		File menu, Password command	File menu, Save As command, Options button
Save generic		File menu, Text Out command	File menu, Save As command
Document summary	SHIFT+F8	File menu, Summary command	File menu, Properties command

WordPerfect Delete Commands

WordPerfect command	WordPerfect 5.0 or 5.1 keys	Word 7.0 command or keys
Delete		
Word	CTRL+BACKSPACE	CTRL+BACKSPACE or CTRL+DEL
To end of line	CTRL+END	SHIFT+END, DEL
To end of page	CTRL+PAGE DOWN	SHIFT+DOWN ARROW (to end of page), DEL
To left word boundary	HOME, BACKSPACE	CTRL+BACKSPACE
To right word boundary	HOME, DEL	CTRL+DEL
Delete block	ALT+F4, DEL	F8, *arrow key*, DEL

WordPerfect Move Text Commands

WordPerfect 5.0 command	WordPerfect 5.0 keys	WordPerfect 5.1 command	Word 7.0 command or keys
Move text	CTRL+F4	Edit menu, Move command (Cut)	Edit menu, Cut command, and then Edit menu, Paste command
Cut block		Edit menu, Move command (Cut) or CTRL+DEL	Edit menu, Cut command

WordPerfect 5.0 command	WordPerfect 5.0 keys	WordPerfect 5.1 command	Word 7.0 command or keys
Copy block		Edit menu, Move command (Cut) or CTRL+INS	Edit menu, Copy command, and then Edit menu, Paste command
Delete		Edit menu, Delete command	Edit menu, Cut command or BACKSPACE
Append block		Edit menu, Append command	Edit menu, Cut command, and then Edit menu, Paste command
Cut/copy column		Edit menu, Move command (Cut)	Select the column, Edit menu, Cut command; Select the column, Edit menu, Copy command, and then Edit menu, Paste command
Cut/copy rectangle		Edit menu, Move command (Cut)	Select text, Edit menu, Cut command, and then Edit menu, Paste command
Move sentence		Edit menu, Move command (Cut)	Select text, Edit menu, Cut command, and then Edit menu, Paste command
Move paragraph		Edit menu, Move command (Cut)	Select text, Edit menu, Cut command, and then Edit menu, Paste command
Move page		Edit menu, Move command (Cut)	Select text, Edit menu, Cut command, and then Edit menu, Paste command
Retrieve column, text, rectangle		Edit menu, Move command (Cut)	Edit menu, Paste command

WordPerfect Page Format Commands

WordPerfect command	WordPerfect 5.0 keys	WordPerfect 5.1 menu	Word 7.0 command
Format page	SHIFT+F8	Layout Page	File menu, Page Setup command
Page numbering		Page Numbering	Insert menu, Page Numbers command or View menu, Header and Footer command
Center page		Center	File menu, Page Setup command, Layout tab
Paper size		PaperSize	File menu, Page Setup command

WordPerfect command	WordPerfect 5.0 keys	WordPerfect 5.1 menu	Word 7.0 command
Format page *(continued)*		Layout Page	
Margins top/bottom		Margins Top/Bottom	File menu, Page Setup command
Headers and footers		Headers and Footers	View menu, Header and Footer command
Suppress		Suppress	File menu, Page Setup command, Layout and Margins tabs
Format other		Layout Other	
Conditional end of page		Conditional end of page	Format menu, Paragraph command, Text Flow tab
Language		Language	Tools menu, Language command
		Border Options	Format menu, Borders and Shading command

Line Format Commands

WordPerfect command	WordPerfect 5.0 keys	WordPerfect 5.1 menu	Word 7.0 command or keys
Format line	SHIFT+F8	Layout Line	
Tab set		Tab set	Format menu, Tabs command
Margins—left, right		Margins—left right	Format menu, Page Setup command
Justification		Justification	Format menu, Paragraph command
Line height		Line Height	Format menu, Paragraph command
Line numbering		Line Numbering	File menu, Page Setup command, Layout tab
Line spacing		Line Spacing	Format menu, Paragraph command
Hyphenation		Hyphenation zone	Tools menu, Hyphenation command
Widow/Orphan		Widow/Orphan	Format menu, Paragraph command, Text Flow tab
Format other		Layout Other	
Advance		Advance	Format menu, Paragraph command

WordPerfect command	WordPerfect 5.0 keys	WordPerfect 5.1 menu	Word 7.0 command or keys
Format other *(continued)*		Layout Other	
Overstrike character		Overstrike character	Format menu, Font command
Underline (spaces and tabs)		Underline (spaces and tabs)	Format menu, Font command
Decimal character		Decimal character	Control Panel (Windows 95)

Text Layout Functions

WordPerfect command	WordPerfect 5.0 keys	WordPerfect 5.1 command/keys	Word 7.0 command or keys
Center text	SHIFT+F6	SHIFT+F6	Format menu, Paragraph
Flush right	ALT+F6	Layout Align	Format menu, Paragraph command
Hard space	HOME, SPACEBAR	HOME, SPACEBAR	CTRL+SHIFT+SPACEBAR
Margin release	SHIFT+TAB	SHIFT+TAB	Format menu, Paragraph command, Indents and Spacing tab
Page break	CTRL+ENTER	CTRL+ENTER	Insert menu, Break command
Indent			Format menu, Paragraph command
Hanging indent	F4	F4	Format menu, Paragraph command or Format menu, Bullets and Numbering command
Indent left and right	SHIFT+F4	SHIFT+F4	Format menu, Paragraph command
Columns	ALT+F7		Table menu, Insert Table command or Format menu, Columns command
Math on		Layout Math	Table menu, Formula command or Insert menu, Field command= *Formula*
Math def		Layout Math	Table menu, Formula command
Column on/off		Layout Columns or Layout Tables	Format menu, Columns command or Table menu, Insert Table command

WordPerfect command	WordPerfect 5.0 keys	WordPerfect 5.1 command/keys	Word 7.0 command or keys
Columns *(continued)*			
Column define		Layout Columns or Layout Tables	Format menu, Columns command or Table menu, Insert Table command
Footnotes/endnotes	CTRL+F7		
Footnote		Layout Footnote	Insert menu, Footnote and Endnote command
Endnote		Layout Endnote	Insert menu, Footnote and Endnote command
Endnote placement		Layout Endnote	Insert menu, Footnote and Endnote command

Font Attributes

WordPerfect command	WordPerfect 5.0 keys	WordPerfect 5.1 menu	Word 7.0 command or keys
Font	CTRL+F8		
Size			
Superscript		Font Superscript	Format menu, Font command
Subscript		Font Subscript	Format menu, Font command
Fine to extra		Font Fine to Extra	Format menu, Font command
Large		Large	Format menu, Font command
Appearance		Font Appearance	
Bold		Bold	Format menu, Font command
Underline		Underline	Format menu, Font command
Double underline		Double Underline	Format menu, Font command
Italics		Italics	Format menu, Font command
Outline		Outline	Insert Object, Microsoft WordArt 2.0
Shadow		Shadow	Insert Object, Microsoft WordArt 2.0

WordPerfect command	WordPerfect 5.0 keys	WordPerfect 5.1 menu	Word 7.0 command or keys
Appearance *(continued)*		Font Appearance	
Small caps		Small Caps	Format menu, Font command
Redline		Redline	Format menu, Border command
Strikeout		Strikeout	Format menu, Font command
Normal		Font Normal	CTRL+SPACEBAR
Base font		Font Base Font	Format menu, Font command
Print color		Font Print Color	Format menu, Color command

WordPerfect Print Commands

WordPerfect command	WordPerfect 5.0 keys	WordPerfect 5.1 menu	Word 7.0 command
Print	SHIFT+F7	File Print	
Full document		Full document	File menu, Print command
Page		Page	File menu, Print command
Document on disk		Document on disk	File menu, Open command, Commands and settings button
Control printer		Control Printer	File menu, Print command
		Multiple pages	File menu, Print command
View document		View document	File Menu, Print Preview command
Initialize printer		Initialize Printer	(Not applicable)
Select printer		Select Printer	File menu, Print command
Binding		Binding	File menu, Page Setup command
Number of copies		Number of copies	File menu, Print command
Graphic quality		Graphic quality	Tools menu, Options command, Print button
Text quality		Text quality	Tools menu, Options command, Print button

Commands for Advanced WordPerfect Features

The following tables show the Word equivalents for WordPerfect Mark Text, automating features, and graphics commands.

WordPerfect Mark Text Commands

WordPerfect command	WordPerfect 5.0 keys	WordPerfect 5.1 menu	Word 7.0 command
Mark text	ALT+F5		
Cross-ref			Edit menu, Bookmark command or Insert menu, Cross-reference command
Subdoc		Mark Subdocument	View menu, Master Document command
Index		Mark Index	Insert menu, Index and Tables command, Index tab
Short form		Mark Table of Authorities	Insert menu, Index and Tables command, Table of Authorities tab
Define		Mark Define	
Table of contents		Table of Contents	Insert menu, Index and Tables command
List		List	Format menu, Bullets and Numbering command
Index		Index	Insert menu, Index and Tables command
Table of authorities		Table of Authorities	Insert menu, Index and Tables command
Generate		Mark Generate	Insert menu, Index and Tables command
Outline	SHIFT+F5	Tools Outline	View menu, Outline command
Para num		Tools Page Number	Tools menu, Bullets and Numbering command
Define		Tools Define	Tools menu, Bullets and Numbering command

Other Automating Features

WordPerfect command	WordPerfect 5.0 keys	WordPerfect 5.1 menu	Word 7.0 command or keys
Date	SHIFT+F5		
Date text		Tools Date Text	Insert menu, Date and Time command or ALT+SHIFT+D
Date code		Tools Date Code	Insert menu, Date and Time command, Update Automatically (Insert As Field) check box
Date format		Tools Date Format	Insert menu, Date and Time command
Merge/Sort	CTRL+F9		
Merge		Tools Merge	Tools menu, Mail Merge command
Sort		Tools Sort	Tools menu, Mail Merge command, Query Options button
Merge codes	SHIFT+F9	Tools Merge Codes	Insert menu, Field command, MergeField (or use Mail Merge toolbar)
End field	F9	Tools Merge Codes	(Not applicable)
Macro			
Define	CTRL+F10	Tools Macro	Tools menu, Macro command, Record button
Start	ALT+F10	Tools Macro	Tools menu, Macro command, Run button
Replace	ALT+F2	Search Replace	Edit menu, Replace command
Search	F2 or SHIFT+F2	Search Forward/ Backward	Edit menu, Find command
Spell/word count	CTRL+F2	Tools Spell	Tools menu, Spelling command or File menu, Properties command
Thesaurus	ALT+F1	Tools Thesaurus	Tools menu, Thesaurus command
Undelete	F1	Edit Undelete	Edit menu, Undo command

WordPerfect Graphics Commands

WordPerfect command	WordPerfect 5.0 keys	WordPerfect 5.1 menu	Word 7.0 command
Graphics	ALT+F9		
Figure		Graphics Figure	Insert menu, Picture command
Table		Graphics Table Box	Insert menu, Picture or Frame or Object command, or Table menu, Insert Table command
Text box		Graphics Text Box	Insert menu, Picture or Frame or Object command
User-defined box		Graphics User-Defined Box	Insert menu, Picture or Frame or Object command, or Format menu, Borders and Shading command or View Toolbars, Forms
Line		Graphics Line	Format menu, Borders and Shading command or View Toolbars, Drawing
		Graphics Equation	Insert menu, Object command

WordPerfect Graphics Export

When you convert a Word 7.0 document to WordPerfect 5.x or 6.x format, this export filter converts Windows Metafiles to the WordPerfect Graphic format. When you want to convert a Word document containing graphics to WordPerfect format, the WordPerfect text converter runs this filter for each graphic in the Word document and embeds each converted graphic in the WordPerfect document.

When exporting Word documents containing graphics, the default behavior is to not display the progress meter for each graphic. This behavior can also be changed by editing a setting in Mstxtcnv.ini. Word provides the EditConversionOptions macro to facilitate editing Mstxtcnv.ini.

WordPerfect Graphics Import

The WPG import filter is used by the WordPerfect document converter to convert graphics embedded in a WordPerfect document.

The filter uses the size of the picture frame stored in the WPG file to determine the size of the picture to import. The picture-frame size of WPG graphics created by DrawPerfect is the size of the screen.

WPG images often contain a background color that may impair the fidelity of the image when imported into Word. By default, the filter will remove this background color to improve clarity. This behavior can be changed by editing the Mstxtcnv.ini file located in your Windows folder. The [WPGImport] section of this file includes a RetainBackground setting. By assigning a value of 1 to this setting, all background color will be retained upon import. Word provides the EditConversionOptions macro to facilitate editing Mstxtcnv.ini.

When importing WordPerfect documents containing graphics, the progress meter is not displayed for each graphic, by default. This default can be changed by editing a setting in Mstxtcnv.ini. Word provides the EditConversionOptions macro to facilitate editing Mstxtcnv.ini.

Switching from DisplayWrite

You already know how to create, edit, format, and print documents using DisplayWrite version 4 or 5. This section explains how to use Word to accomplish the same tasks, and many more.

Opening and Saving a DisplayWrite Document in Word

You can open a DisplayWrite document in Word as long as it has been saved in RFT-DCA format. On the File menu in Word, click Open. In the Files of Type box, select All Files. In the File Name box, select the document's filename. Word detects the RFT-DCA file format and converts it to a Word file format.

It is just as easy to convert a Word file to an RFT-DCA file, which you can then open in DisplayWrite. In Word, click the Save As command on the File menu and then select RFT-DCA as the file format.

For information about attributes that are supported when opening or saving documents in RFT-DCA format, see "Switching from RFT-DCA Format Documents" later in this chapter.

A Glossary of DisplayWrite Terms Versus Word Terms

This section provides a glossary of DisplayWrite terms and the corresponding Word terms or features. The Word terms are *italic* so that you can look them up in the index or in the online Answer Wizard.

DisplayWrite term	Description of Word term or feature
auto page end	By default, Word paginates or *repaginates* documents automatically. If this is not happening, click Options on the Tools menu, click the General tab, and then select the Background Repagination check box.
carrier return	As you type, Word automatically wraps text to the next line. When you press ENTER, Word ends the current paragraph and inserts a paragraph mark.
codes	Word displays your document as it will be printed, depending on the capabilities of your printer and display monitor. You can display symbols representing line breaks, paragraphs, spaces, and tab stops by clicking the Show/Hide ¶ button on the Standard toolbar, or you can display the symbols you prefer to see by clicking Options on the Tools menu and selecting the appropriate check boxes on the View tab. Also on the View tab, you can display field codes by selecting the Field Codes check box.
data file	Data files can be created in Word for mail merge and other document-merging purposes. You can also create a simple database in Word, independent of the mail merge feature. In addition, you can import data from a database application and link the data in Word to the source file.
document assembly	Word provides several powerful *mail merge* features to help you create personalized documents and form letters.
field	In a DisplayWrite data file, this is a specific category of variable information in a record. In a Word data file, this is referred to as a data field, and when it is inserted into a mail merge main document it is called a merge field. Word also uses the term fields to mean special codes that enable you to insert various types of information into documents—including the time, the date, a table of contents, mathematical calculations, or data from another Windows application (such as Microsoft Excel).
footnote library	Footnotes and other frequently used text can be stored as Word AutoText entries for subsequent use.
keystroke programming	A series of repeatable keystrokes and command operations is called a *macro* in Word.
menu cursor	In Word, you can choose a command or select an option from a menu or list box by clicking the item.

DisplayWrite term	Description of Word term or feature
notepad	The Windows Clipboard provides a temporary storage area for moving and copying text. You can store frequently used text and graphics as *AutoText* entries.
paper clip	In Word, you can use *bookmarks* not only to locate places in your document but also to identify ranges of text. Inserting a bookmark name in a field enables you to refer to, move, or copy the text represented by the bookmark.
profile	In Word, you standardize document formats by using templates. You can control the defaults for many editing and formatting functions by choosing the applicable Word commands. You can change the default printer by clicking Print on the File menu and then clicking a printer in the Name box. Other defaults related to the screen display—such as colors—and the console are controlled from the Windows Control Panel.
scale line	In DisplayWrite, the scale line displays the margins and tab stops for the portion of text containing the text cursor. In Word, the horizontal ruler performs this function. The ruler, together with the Formatting toolbar, also displays a graphical representation of some paragraph formats applied to the paragraph or paragraphs containing the insertion point. In addition, the horizontal ruler displays a graphical representation of some table formats, and the vertical ruler (visible in page layout view) displays top and bottom margins. You can change formats directly on the rulers and on the Formatting toolbar.
syllable hyphen	In Word, this is called an *optional hyphen.* You can insert an optional hyphen by pressing CTRL+HYPHEN.
text cursor	In Word, this is called the *insertion point.* It is displayed as a blinking vertical line.
type style	You choose a type style in Word by selecting the name of the font and then specifying the point size.
typing line	In Word, margins are measured from the edges of the page to the text boundary in inches, centimeters, points, or picas.

Commands for DisplayWrite Features

Throughout the rest of this section, DisplayWrite menus, commands, and shortcut keys are presented in tables that show their equivalents in Word. As you read the tables, note the following conventions:

- In the Word command column, the menu names precede the command names. For example, the Open command on the File menu is given in the tables as "File menu, Open command."

- "Not applicable" means that the DisplayWrite command has no equivalent in Word.

- Italicized text after a key combination means that you type variable information. For example, "ALT+SHIFT+*number*" means that you hold down the ALT and SHIFT keys while typing a number.

DisplayWrite Main Menu, Creating a Document

The following table shows the Word equivalents of the DisplayWrite main menu options for creating a document.

DisplayWrite menu option	Word command
Create a document	File menu, New command
Revise a document	File menu, Open command
View a document	File menu, Open command, Read Only check box

DisplayWrite Function Keys and Menu Options for Help, Saving, Document Retrieval (List Services), and Editing

The following tables show the Word command equivalents for the DisplayWrite menu options listed.

DisplayWrite function key	DisplayWrite menu option	Word command or key
F1, Help key	Help	Help menu, Answer Wizard command
F2, END/SAVE	End and save	File menu, Close command
	Save and continue	File menu, Save command
	Quit without saving	File menu, Exit command, **n** at prompt
	Paginate, end, save	File menu, Exit command, **y** at prompt
F3, LIST	List services	File menu, Open command
F4, BLOCK	Move	Edit menu, Cut command, and then Edit menu, Paste command
	Copy	Edit menu, Copy command, and then Edit menu, Paste command

DisplayWrite function key	DisplayWrite menu option	Word command or key
	Delete	Edit menu, Cut command or DEL
	Restore delete	Edit menu, Undo command
	Set style	
	Plain	Format menu, Font command
	Underline	Format menu, Font command
	Bold	Format menu, Font command
	Overstrike	Format menu, Font command
	Mark	Tools menu, Revisions command
F6, Search key	Repeat	Edit menu, Repeat command
	Find	Edit menu, Find command
	Search/replace	Edit menu, Replace command
	Go to page	Edit menu, Go To command, Page option

DisplayWrite F5 Functions Key

DisplayWrite menu option	Word command or keys
Notepad	
Move to notepad	Edit menu, Cut command (to Clipboard)
Copy to notepad	Edit menu, Copy command (to Clipboard)
Recall	Edit menu, Paste command
ASCII copy to file	File menu, Save As command, Text Only option
Get file	Insert menu, File command
Spell	Tools menu, Spelling command
View/revise	
Footnote	View menu, Footnotes command
Formats	View menu, Page Layout command or File menu, Print Preview command
Math instructions	Tools menu, Options command, View tab, Field Codes check box or Insert menu, Field command
Outlines	View menu, Outline command
Revise variables	Tools menu, Options command, View tab, Field Codes check box or Insert menu, Field command
Document options	
Document format	Format menu (various commands)
Alternate format	Format menu (various commands)
Document comment	File menu, Summary Info command
Paginate document	(Done automatically)

DisplayWrite menu option	Word command or keys
Edit options	
Display all codes	Tools menu, Options command, View tab
Auto carrier return	(By default)
Auto page end	(Done automatically)
Return to paper clip	Edit menu, Go To command, Bookmark option
Keyboard extension	ALT+*ANSI code* (with NUM LOCK on)
Overstrike character	Tools menu, Revisions command
Notepad choice	(Done automatically)
Table	Table menu, Insert Table command (and other commands on the Table menu)
Math	Table menu, Formula command or Insert menu, Field command, =Formula option

Notes By default, Word paginates or repaginates documents automatically. If this is not happening, click Options on the Tools menu, click the General tab, and then select the Background Repagination check box.

When you use the revision marks feature, Word automatically applies the strike-through format to any text you delete.

DisplayWrite F8 Instructions Key

DisplayWrite menu option	Word command or keys
Begin/end keep	Format menu, Paragraph command
Begin/end spell	Tools menu, Spelling command
Footnote	Insert menu, Footnote command
Merge instructions	
Variable	Insert menu, Field command, MergeField option or Tools menu, Mail Merge command
Include	Insert menu, Field command, Include Picture option or Insert menu, Field command, Include Text option
Skip to line number	(Not applicable)
Math	Insert menu, Field command, *expression*
If variable empty, not empty	Insert menu, Field command, If
End Iftest	(Done automatically)
User-defined control	ALT+*ANSI code* (with NUM LOCK on)
Voice note	Insert menu, Annotation command

DisplayWrite F7 Format Key

DisplayWrite menu option	Word command
Margins	File menu, Page Setup command
Tabs	Format menu, Tabs command
Line spacing	Format menu, Paragraph command
Justification	Format menu, Paragraph command
Type style	Format menu, Font command
Page layout/paper options	File menu, Page Setup command
Header/footer	View menu, Header and Footer command
Even/odd headers	View menu, Header and Footer command
Reset format	(Not applicable)

DisplayWrite Main Menu, Features

DisplayWrite menu option	Word command
Spell	Tools menu, Spelling command
Utilities	
Copy a file	Windows Explorer
Erase a file	Windows Explorer
Rename a file	File menu, Save As command
Compress	(Done automatically)
Recover	(Not applicable)
Document conversion	File menu, Save As command or File menu, Open command
Merge	Tools menu, Mail Merge command
DOS commands	MS-DOS Prompt (Windows Start menu)
Profiles	
Textdefault settings	File menu, New command, Template option
Margins	File menu, Page Setup command
Tabs	Format menu, Tabs command
Line spacing	Format menu, Paragraph command
Justification	Format menu, Paragraph command
Type style	Format menu, Font command
Page layout options	File menu, Page Setup command
Footnote format	Insert menu, Footnote command or Format menu, Style command
Outline format	View menu, Outline command or Format menu, Style command, Modify button

DisplayWrite menu option	Word command
Page layout options *(continued)*	
Edit copy of document	File menu, Save As command (to make a second copy)
Workstation default	(Not applicable)
Default system paths	Tools menu, Options command, File Locations tab
Revisable-form text (RFT) conversion defaults	File menu, Save As command

DisplayWrite Main Menu, Printing a Document

DisplayWrite menu option	Word command or key
Print	
Active document	File menu, Print command
Other document	File menu, Open command, Commands and Settings button, Print command
Printer options	File menu, Print command, Printer button
List or reorder print jobs	Printers (Windows Start menu)
Cancel print jobs	ESC

DisplayWrite F9 Table Key

DisplayWrite menu option	Word command
Layout new table	
Tabular columns	Table menu, Insert Table command
Text columns	Table menu, Insert Table command
Define text as table	Table menu, Convert Text to Table command
Revise table	
Move column	Edit menu, Cut command, and then Edit menu, Paste command
Copy column	Edit menu, Copy command, and then Edit menu, Paste command
Delete column	Table menu, Delete Columns command
Revise column	Table menu, Cell Height and Width command
Insert new column	Table menu, Insert Columns command
Revise table layout	Table menu, AutoFormat command or Cell Height and Width command
Set up reference areas	(Not applicable)

DisplayWrite F10, F11, and F12 Function Keys (Spelling and Drawing)

DisplayWrite function keys	DisplayWrite menu option	Word command
F10, Spell key	Spell	Tools menu, Spelling command
	Word	(Select word first) Tools menu, Spelling command
	Page	(Select page first) Tools menu, Spelling command
F11 or ALT+F1, Draw key	Cursor draw	View menu, Toolbars command, Drawing or Borders toolbars
F12 or ALT+F2, Adjust Line key	Line adjust	(Done automatically)

Note   There is no cursor draw equivalent in Word. However, the tools available on the Drawing toolbar provide the ability to draw lines and a wide range of other drawing options. You can also draw borders quickly and easily around paragraphs and table cells by using the Format menu, Borders and Shading command.

Function Key Combinations

DisplayWrite menu option	DisplayWrite keys	Word command or keys
Application change	ALT+7	ALT+ESC or CTRL+ESC or use the toolbar
Cursor draw	ALT+1	View menu, Toolbars command, Drawing or Borders toolbars
Line adjust	ALT+2	(Done automatically)
Erase end of line	ALT+8	DEL or BACKSPACE
Document options	CTRL+F7	(Not applicable)
Edit options	CTRL+F5	See table under "DisplayWrite F5 Functions Key," earlier in this section
Get	CTRL+F6	Insert menu, File command
Key program	CTRL+F1	Tools menu, Macro command
Playback auto		Tools menu, Macro command, Run button
Playback single		Tools menu, Macro command, Edit button
Capture		Tools menu, Macro command, Record button

DisplayWrite menu option	DisplayWrite keys	Word command or keys
Pause		Tools menu, Macro command, Edit button
Save		Tools menu, Macro command, Stop Recording button
Recall		Tools menu, Macro command, Run button
End playback		ESC
Math	CTRL+F9	Table menu, Formula command or Insert menu, Field command, =*Formula*
Menu restore	CTRL+F2	(Not applicable)
Notepad	CTRL+F4	See table under "DisplayWrite F5 Functions Key," earlier in this section
View/revise	CTRL+F8	See table under "DisplayWrite F5 Functions Key," earlier in this section

Switching from MultiMate

You already know how to create, edit, format, and print documents using MultiMate version 3.3, Advantage (hereafter referred to as MultiMate 3.6), Advantage II, or MultiMate version 4.0. This section explains how to use Word to accomplish the same tasks, and many more.

Opening and Saving a MultiMate Document in Word

You can open a MultiMate document in Word as long as it has been saved in a compatible format. For MultiMate version 4.0 documents, use RTF format. For documents created in earlier versions of MultiMate, use RFT-DCA format. On the File menu in Word, click Open. In the Files of Type box, select All Files. In the File Name box, select the document's filename. Word detects the RTF or RFT-DCA file format and converts it to a Word file format.

It is just as easy to convert a Word file to an RTF or RFT-DCA file, which you can then open in MultiMate. In Word, click the Save As command on the File menu and then select RTF or RFT-DCA as the file format.

For information about attributes that are supported when opening or saving documents in RFT-DCA format, see "Switching from RFT-DCA Format Documents" later in this chapter.

A Glossary of MultiMate Terms Versus Word Terms

This section includes a glossary of MutliMate terms and the corresponding Word terms or features. The Word terms in *italic* can be looked up in the index or in online Help.

MultiMate term	Description of Word term or feature
bound columns	This type of column layout is created in Word as a *table*.
cursor	The *insertion point* is the blinking vertical line that indicates where the text you type will appear.
external copy	You use the Windows Clipboard to copy or move text or graphics from one Word document to another or from one Windows application to another.
format line	Similar to the Word ruler. In Word, however, the tab stops and other paragraph formats controlled by the ruler are specific to the text selection or the paragraph that contains the insertion point. As you move the insertion point through the document, the ruler reflects the formatting of the currently selected paragraph.
highlight	Similar to *selecting* in Word. Text that is selected appears highlighted in the document.
key procedure	Similar to a *macro* in Word. Macros can record keystrokes and play them back. Macros can also contain detailed programming instructions written in WordBasic.
library	Similar to *AutoText* in Word. You can create AutoText entries composed of text or graphics and reuse them. AutoText entries can be stored in either the Normal template or a custom template.
placemark	Similar to a *bookmark* in Word. A bookmark can also identify a range of text, not just a position within a document.
print modes	In Word, emphasizing text with bold, underlining, and other formats is called *character formatting,* or font formatting.
required page break	A mandatory page break that you insert in a Word document is called a *hard page break.* It remains in the document until you delete it.
snaking columns	You can create snaking, or *newspaper-style,* columns on any page by selecting the text you want to organize in columns, clicking the Columns command on the Format menu and designating the number of columns you want. A section break will appear before and after the selected text. Insert a continuous section break to have a different column format on the same page.

MultiMate term	Description of Word term or feature
system print commands	Date, time, page numbers, and total page count are inserted in Word documents as fields.
template	In Word, templates define the format and content of all types of routine documents—not just data files for merge documents. You can also use templates to create blank forms.

Commands for MultiMate Features

Throughout the rest of this section, MultiMate menus, commands, and options are presented in tables that show their equivalents in Word. As you read the tables, please note the following conventions:

- Version numbers in parentheses—for example, (3.6)— refer to the version or versions of MultiMate in which the term is used.

- In the Word column, the menu names precede the command names. For example, the Open command on the File menu is given in the tables as "File menu, Open command."

- "Not applicable" means that the MultiMate command has no equivalent in Word.

- Italicized text after a key combination means that you type variable information. For example, "ALT+SHIFT+*number*" means that you hold down the ALT and SHIFT keys while typing a number.

MultiMate Main Menu Options

The following tables show the Word command equivalents for the MultiMate main menu options listed.

MultiMate menu option	Word command or keys
Edit a document Edit an old document (3.6)	File menu, Open command
Create a document Create a new document (3.6)	File menu, New command
Print a document Print document utility (3.6) Print/Preview a document (4.0)	File menu, Print command File menu, Print Preview command
Additional print functions	File menu, Print command
Printer control utility (3.6)	File menu, Print command, Properties button
Merge print a document Merge print utilities (3.6)	Tools menu, Mail Merge command
Document management Document handling utilities (3.6) Document management tools (4.0)	File menu, Open command, Advanced button

MultiMate menu option	Word command or keys
System and document defaults Other utilities (3.6)	File menu, Save As command, Commands and Settings button, Properties command
Spell check a document	Tools menu, Spelling command
Exit word processor Return to DOS (3.6) Exit MultiMate (4.0)	File menu, Exit command (to quit Word) ALT+TAB (to switch to Windows and leave Word running)

MultiMate Modify Document Defaults

MultiMate menu option	Word command
Allow widows and orphans?	Format menu, Paragraph command, Text Flow tab
Automatic page breaks?	(Done automatically)
Back up before editing document?	File menu, Save As command, Options button
Text- or page-associated headers and footers?	View menu, Header and Footer command
Acceptable decimal tab character?	Control Panel (Windows Start menu)
Number of lines per page?	(Not applicable)
Repagination page/text? (4.0)	(Done automatically)
Display document startup screens? (II, 4.0)	(Not applicable)
Print data standard (II)	Control Panel (Windows Start menu)
Currency symbol?	Control Panel (Windows Start menu)
Footnotes or endnotes?	Insert menu, Footnote command
Section numbering style?	Format menu, Heading Numbering command

MultiMate System and Document Defaults and Other Utilities

MultiMate menu option	Word command
Edit system format line	File menu, Page Setup command and Format menu, Paragraph command
Edit drive defaults Edit drive/path defaults (4.0)	(Windows)

MultiMate Edit/Modify System Defaults

MultiMate menu option	Word command
Insert mode drop down/push?	(Not applicable)
Allow widows and orphans?	Format menu, Paragraph command, Text Flow tab
Automatic page breaks?	(Done automatically)
Destructive backspace	(Not applicable)
Back up before editing document?	Tools menu, Options command, Save tab
Display directory	(Done automatically)
Display document	(Not applicable)
Display document startup screens (4.0)	(Not applicable)
File type extension (4.0)	(Not applicable)
Document or page mode	(Done automatically)
Text or page associated headers and footers?	View menu, Header and Footer command
Number of lines per page?	(Not Applicable)
Repagination page/text (4.0)	(Done automatically)
Acceptable decimal tab	Control Panel (Windows Start menu)
Display spaces as dots?	Tools menu, Options command, View tab
Speed up movement between pages	(Not applicable)
Keep document closed for safety?	(Not applicable)
Compact document after saving (4.0)	(Done automatically)
Strike out character?	(Not applicable)
System date standard	Control Panel (Windows Start menu)
Print date standard?	Control Panel (Windows Start menu)
Section numbering style	Format menu, Heading Numbering command
Currency symbol	Control Panel (Windows Start menu)
Footnotes or endnotes	Insert menu, Footnote command
Acceleration rate	(Not applicable)
Acceleration responsiveness	(Not applicable)
Main dictionary language	Tools menu, Options command, Spelling tab
Custom dictionary	Tools menu, Options command, Spelling tab

MultiMate Document Management/Document Handling Utilities and Document Handling Tools

MultiMate menu option	Word command
Copy a document	Windows Explorer
Move a document	Windows Explorer
Delete a document	File menu, Open command, shortcut menu, Delete command
Undelete a document (4.0)	(Not applicable)
Rename a document (4.0)	File menu, Save As command
Print document summary	File menu, Print command, Print What box
Search document summary	File menu, Open command, Advanced button
Spell check a document (4.0)	Tools menu, Spelling command
Compare two documents (4.0)	Tools menu, Revisions command, Compare Versions button
Restore a backup document	(Done automatically)

MultiMate Editing Functions

MultiMate menu option	MultiMate keys	Word command or keys
Center	F3	Format menu, Paragraph command
Comments	CTRL+[	Insert menu, Annotation command
Copy		
From a document	SHIFT+F8	Edit menu, Copy command, and then Edit menu, Paste command
Within a document	F8	Edit menu, Copy command, and then Edit menu, Paste command
Delete		
Text	DEL	DEL or BACKSPACE or Edit menu, Cut command
Character	MINUS SIGN (keypad)	DEL or BACKSPACE
Undo delete	ASTERISK (keypad)	Edit menu, Undo command
Endnote/footnote	ALT+V	Insert menu, Footnote command, Endnote option
Grammar checker (4.0)	ALT+L, CTRL+E, N, ENTER, G, ENTER	Tools menu, Grammar command
Graphics (4.0)	ALT+L, CTRL+O, G, ENTER, I, ENTER	Insert menu, Picture command

MultiMate menu option	MultiMate keys	Word command or keys
Hard space	ALT+S	CTRL+SHIFT+SPACEBAR
Hyphen (soft)	SHIFT+F7	CTRL+HYPHEN
Hyphenation (auto)	CTRL+F2	Tools menu, Hyphenation command
Indent	F4	Format menu, Paragraph command
Insert		
Character	PLUS SIGN (keypad)	(Not applicable)
Text	INS	INS key
Line and box draw	ALT+E	View menu, Toolbars command, Drawing or Borders toolbars
Move	F7	Edit menu, Cut command, then Edit menu, Paste command
Paging		
Page break	F2	(Done automatically)
Page break (required)	ALT+B	Insert menu, Break command
Page combine	SHIFT+F2	(Not applicable)
Page length		File menu, Page Setup command, Paper Size tab
Page numbering	ALT+F2	Insert menu, Page Numbers command
Repaginate	CTRL+F2	(Done automatically)
Placemarks		
Set Placemark	ALT+F1	Edit menu, Bookmark command
Clear Placemark	ALT+Y	Edit menu, Bookmark command
Replace	SHIFT+F6	Edit menu, Replace command
Save	SHIFT+F10	File menu, Save command
Save and exit	F10	File menu, Exit command, **y** (at prompt)
Save as 4.0	ALT+F10	File menu, Save As command
Search	F6	Edit menu, Find command
Section numbers	CTRL+F2	View menu, Outline command
Spell check	CTRL+F10	Tools menu, Spelling command
Spell edit	ALT+F10	(Not applicable)
Spell check document (4.0)	ALT+L	Tools menu, Spelling command
Strikeout	ALT+O	Format menu, Character command

MultiMate menu option	MultiMate keys	Word command or keys
TOC, create	CTRL+F2	Insert menu, Index and Tables command
Thesaurus	ALT+T	Tools menu, Thesaurus command
Underline		
Alphanumeric	ALT+EQUAL SIGN	Format menu, Character command
Alphanumeric (4.0)	ALT+PLUS SIGN	Format menu, Character command
Double	CTRL+HYPHEN	Format menu, Character command
Manual	SHIFT+HYPHEN	(Not applicable)
Text	ALT+HYPHEN	Format menu, Character command

Note By default, Word paginates or repaginates documents automatically. If this is not happening, click Options on the Tools menu, click the General tab, and then select the Background Repagination check box.

MultiMate Formatting Functions

MultiMate menu option	MultiMate keys	Word command or key
Change format line	F9	(Not applicable)
Tabs	TAB	Format menu, Tabs command
Line length	ENTER	File menu, Page Setup command, Page Size tab
Line spacing	F9, BACKSPACE	Format menu, Paragraph command
Single spacing	1	Format menu, Paragraph command
Double spacing	2	Format menu, Paragraph command
1½ spacing	PLUS SIGN	Format menu, Paragraph command
All other spacing		Format menu, Paragraph command
Column format line	F9, COMMA	(Not applicable)
Snake columns		Format menu, Columns command
Bound columns		Table menu, Insert Table command

MultiMate menu option	MultiMate keys	Word command or key
Delete format line	DEL, F9, DEL	(Delete the paragraph mark)
Insert format line		(Not applicable)
Current	SHIFT+F9	Format menu, Style command
Page	ALT+F9	Format menu, Style command
System	ALT+F9	Format menu, Style command
Replace format line	SHIFT+F6	Edit menu, Replace command
Search format line	F6, F9	Edit menu, Find command

MultiMate Printing Functions

MultiMate menu option	Word command or keys
Bold print	Format menu, Font command
Draft print	File menu, Print command, Options button
Enhanced print	File menu, Print command, Properties button or Options button
Endnote positioning	Insert menu, Footnote command, Options button
Header/footer	View menu, Header and Footer command
Hot print	File menu, Print command
Page numbering	Insert menu, Page Numbers command
Pause printer	Printers (Windows Start menu)
Print font/pitch	Format menu, Font command
Printer control codes	ALT+*ANSI code* (with NUM LOCK on)
Shadow print	(Not applicable)
Subscript	Format menu, Font command
Superscript	Format menu, Font command
Stop printing	ESC

MultiMate Additional Print Functions and Print Control Utilities (Version 3.6 only)

MultiMate menu option	Word command
Printer queue control	Printers (Windows Start menu)
Edit printer defaults	File menu, Print command, Properties button
Typewriter mode (Char)	(Not applicable)
Typewriter mode (Line)	(Not applicable)

MultiMate Modify Printer Defaults and Print Parameters for Document (Version 3.6 only)

MultiMate menu option	Word command
Start print at page number	File menu, Print command
Stop print after page number	File menu, Print command
Left margin	File menu, Page Setup command
Top margin	File menu, Page Setup command
Pause between pages	(Not applicable)
Draft print	File menu, Print command, Options button
Default print	Format menu, Font command
Printer action table	(Not applicable)
Lines per inch	Format menu, Paragraph command
Justification	Format menu, Paragraph command
Proportional spacing	Format menu, Font command
Character translate/width table	(Done automatically)
Header/footer first page number	View menu, Header and Footer command
Starting footnote number	Insert menu, Footnote command
Number of original copies	File menu, Print command
Document page length	File menu, Page Setup command, Paper Size tab
Sheet feeder action table	File menu, Page Setup command, Paper Source tab

Sheet feeder bin numbers
    First page, middle, last page
    Parallel/serial/list/auxiliary file
	File menu, Page Setup command, Paper Source tab

Device number	Control Panel (Windows Start menu)
Print document summary screen	File menu, Print command, Print What box
Print printer parameters	(Not applicable)
Background/foreground	(Not applicable)
Remove queue entry when done	(Done automatically)
Delay print until time is	(Not applicable)
Delay print until date is	(Not applicable)
Creating a print file or ASCII file	File menu, Save As command

MultiMate Document Print Options and Edit Printer Defaults

MultiMate menu option	Word command
Start print at page number	File menu, Print command
Stop print after page number	File menu, Print command
Enhanced/draft print	File menu, Print command, Options button
Number of original copies	File menu, Print command
Printer action table	File menu, Print command, Properties button
Use: Parallel/serial/file/list/auxiliary Console	Control Panel (Windows Start menu)
Device number	Control Panel (Windows Start menu)
Pause between pages	(Not applicable)
Print comments	File menu, Print command, Print What box
Print document summary screen	File menu, Print command, Print What box
Print this screen	File menu, Print command
Header/footer first page number	File menu, Page Setup command, Layout tab
Starting footnote number	Insert menu, Footnote command, Options button
Number lines (4.0)	File menu, Page Setup command, Layout tab
Left margin	File menu, Page Setup command
Top margin	File menu, Page Setup command
Double-space the document	Format menu, Paragraph command
Default pitch	Format menu, Font command
Sheet feeder action table	File menu, Page Setup command, Paper Source tab
Sheet feeder bin numbers First, middle, last page	File menu, Page Setup command, Paper Source tab
Character translate/width table	(Done automatically)
Background/foreground	(Not applicable)
Justification	Format menu, Paragraph command
Proportional spacing	Format menu, Font command
Lines per inch	Format menu, Paragraph command
Paper length (lines per page)	(Not applicable)
Default font	Format menu, Font command
Download font (4.0)	Control Panel (Windows Start menu)
Eject last page (4.0)	(Not applicable)
Remove queue entry when done	(Done automatically)
Delay print until time is	(Not applicable)
Delay print until date is	(Not applicable)

Advanced MultiMate Functions

MultiMate menu option	MultiMate keys	Word command or keys
Alternate keyboard	ALT+K	ALT+*ANSI code* (with NUM LOCK on)
Column (bound)	F9, COMMA	Table menu, Insert Table command
Column (snaking)	F9, COMMA	Format menu, Columns command
Column manipulation	SHIFT+F3	Table menu (various commands)
Copy	F8	Edit menu, Copy command, then Edit menu, Paste command
Delete	DEL	Edit menu, Cut command
Insert	INS	Table menu, Insert Columns command
Move	F7	Edit menu, Cut command, then Edit menu, Paste command
Sort	SHIFT+F3, F5	Table menu, Sort command
Decimal tab	SHIFT+F4	Format menu, Tabs command
DOS access	CTRL+F2	ALT+ESC or CTRL+ESC
Import ASCII file	CTRL+F6	File menu, Open command
Key procedures		
Build	CTRL+F5	Tools menu, Macro command, Record button
Execute	CTRL+F8	Tools menu, Macro command, Run button
Pause	CTRL+F6	Tools menu, Macro command, Edit button
Prompt	CTRL+F7	(Not applicable)
Replay	ALT+R	Tools menu, Macro command, Run button
Libraries		
Attach	SHIFT+F5	Edit menu, AutoText command
Create	F5	Edit menu, AutoText command
Copy	ALT+J	Edit menu, Copy command
Insert	F5	Edit menu, AutoText command
Line/box drawing	ALT+E	View menu, Toolbars command, Drawing or Borders toolbars
Math		
Horizontal	CTRL+F3	Table menu, Formula command
Vertical	CTRL+F4	Table menu, Formula command

MultiMate menu option	MultiMate keys	Word command or keys
Merge code	ALT+M	Insert menu, Field command, MergeField or Tools menu, Mail Merge command
Sort (4.0)	SHIFT+F3, F5	Table menu, Sort command
Sort mode	F5	Table menu, Sort command

MultiMate 4.0 and MultiMate Advantage II Pull-Down Menus

The following tables show the Word command equivalents for the MultiMate menu options listed.

Layout Functions

MultiMate menu option	Word command
Modify current format line	File menu, Page Setup command or Format menu, Paragraph command
Insert copy of current format line	Format menu, Style command
Insert copy of page format line	Format menu, Style command
Insert copy of system format line	Format menu, Style command
Insert current format line (4.0)	Format menu, Style command
Decimal align	Format menu, Tabs command
Center on a page	(Not applicable)
Center (4.0)	Format menu, Paragraph command
Indent	Format menu, Paragraph command
Page break	(Done automatically)
Page combine	(Not applicable)
Required page break (4.0)	Insert menu, Break command
Repagination	(Done automatically)
Hyphenation	Tools menu, Hyphenation command
Section numbering	View menu, Outline command
Create a TOC	Insert menu, Index and Tables command
Create an index (4.0)	Insert menu, Index and Tables command
Column breaks (4.0)	Insert menu, Break command, Column Break option
Preview/preview document (4.0)	File menu, Print Preview command
Preview current page (4.0)	File menu, Print Preview command

Type Style Functions

MultiMate menu option	Word command
Superscript	Format menu, Font command
Subscript	Format menu, Font command
Font (4.0)	Format menu, Font command
Pitch (4.0)	Format menu, Font command
Strikeout	Format menu, Font command
Draft	Tools menu, Options command, View tab
Enhanced	File menu, Print command, Properties or Options buttons
Bold	Format menu, Font command
Double-strike (4.0)	Format menu, Font command, Bold check box
Shadow	(Not applicable)
Underline text	Format menu, Font command
Underline alpha	Format menu, Font command
Underline double	Format menu, Font command

Editing Functions

MultiMate menu option	Word command or key
Move	Edit menu, Cut command, then Edit menu, Paste command
Copy	Edit menu, Copy command, then Edit menu, Paste command
Delete (4.0)	Edit menu, Cut command or DEL or BACKSPACE
Undo delete (4.0)	Edit menu, Undo command
Move a column of text	Edit menu, Cut command, then Edit menu, Paste command
Copy a column of text	Edit menu, Copy command, then Edit menu, Paste command
Insert a column of text	Table menu, Insert Columns command
Delete a column of text	Table menu, Delete Columns command
External copy (4.0)	Edit menu, Copy command, then Edit menu, Paste command
Go to page (4.0)	Edit menu, Go To command
Search/replace (4.0)	Edit menu, Find command, or Edit menu, Replace command
Comment begin/end (4.0)	Insert menu, Annotation command
Header/footer (4.0)	View menu, Header and Footer command
Place mark (4.0)	Edit menu, Bookmark command

Library Functions

MultiMate menu option	Word command
Attach	Edit menu, AutoText command
Copy text to a library	Edit menu, AutoText command
Insert library entry into a document	Edit menu, AutoText command

Special Functions

MultiMate menu option	Word command
Sort	Table menu, Sort command
Import ASCII file	File menu, Open command
Line and box drawing	View menu, Toolbars command, Drawing or Borders toolbars
Graphics (4.0)	Insert menu, Picture command
Footnotes/endnotes (4.0)	Insert menu, Footnote and Endnote command
Thesaurus	Tools menu, Thesaurus command
Grammar check document (4.0)	Tools menu, Grammar command
Spell check an entire document	Tools menu, Spelling command
Spell check portion of document/Spell check block (4.0)	Select text, then Tools menu, Spelling command
Spell edit flagged word	Select word, then Tools menu, Spelling command
Math (4.0)	Table menu, Formula command or Insert menu, Field command, =Formula
Macro (4.0)	Tools menu, Macro command

Print Functions

MultiMate menu option	Word command
Current document	File menu, Print command
Current page/Hot print page (4.0)	File menu, Print command
Print document (4.0)	File menu, Print command
Change printer setup (4.0)	File Print Setup or Printers (Windows Start menu, Settings menu)
Additional functions (4.0)	
Merge print (4.0)	File menu, Print Merge command
Queue control (4.0)	Printers (Windows Start menu, Settings menu)

Exit Functions

MultiMate menu option	Word command or keys
Save text	File menu, Save command
Save text/exit	File menu, Exit command, **y** (at prompt)
Exit without saving text	File menu, Exit command, **n** (at prompt)
Save as (4.0)	File menu, Save As command
Save as other file type (4.0)	File menu, Save As command
Save, exit, and compact (4.0)	(Not applicable)
Edit another document/ Edit document (4.0)	File menu, Open command
Create a new document/ Create document (4.0)	File menu, New command
Modify document summary (4.0)	File menu, Summary Info command
Exit word processor/Exit MultiMate (4.0)	File menu, Exit command
DOS access/Access DOS (4.0)	ALT+ESC or CTRL+ESC

Switching from Microsoft Write for Windows

After converting a Write 3.*x* document to Word 7.0 and back, it may appear that objects were lost in the conversion. If this happens, simply repaginate the final document within Write, and the objects should reappear.

Switching from RFT-DCA Format Documents

In the following table, "Yes" means the feature exists in both products and is converted from one product to the other. "No" means it exists in both products but is not completely converted between the two. "Not supported" means the feature is not supported in one of the products or is not converted completely between products.

Feature	Word 7.0 to RFT-DCA	RFT-DCA to Word 7.0	Comments
Character Formatting			
Size	See comment	See comment	Pitch is converted to points in Word, and vice versa.
Language	No	Not supported	
Color	No	Yes	

Feature	Word 7.0 to RFT-DCA	RFT-DCA to Word 7.0	Comments
Character Formatting *(continued)*			
Hidden	See comment	Not supported	Hidden text is converted to RFT-DCA underline.
Small caps	See comment	Not supported	Small caps are converted to all caps in RFT-DCA.
Strikethrough	See comment	See comment	When converting to RFT-DCA, the Strikethrough option is used to specify the overstrike character used.
Revision marks	No	No	When converting to Word, strikethrough formatting is converted, whereas overstrike characters are ignored.
Underline (double, single, word)	See comment	Yes	All underlining options are converted to single underlining in RFT-DCA.
Spacing (condensed, expanded)	No	Not supported	
Paragraph Formatting			
Alignment	Yes	Yes	RFT-DCA handles alignment of text line by line, not by paragraph.
Borders (double, single, shadow, and shading)	No	Not supported	
Keep With Next	Yes	Yes	Word 7.0 Keep With Next formatting is converted to RFT-DCA "keep" property.
Paragraph/break before	Yes		Page Break Before formatting is converted to separate hard page breaks before the paragraph in RFT-DCA.
Space before/after para	See comment		Space before and after is simulated with blank lines.
Tab (decimal)	See comment	See comment	RFT-DCA can align any characters with a period or a comma. Word 7.0 can decimal align only with numeric characters and periods.

Feature	Word 7.0 to RFT-DCA	RFT-DCA to Word 7.0	Comments
Section Formatting			
Section			RFT-DCA has no section formats.
Columns	See comment	See comment	The only column conversion supported is RFT-DCA fixed columns of equal length to Word 7.0 columns.
			RFT-DCA Flowing Balanced columns convert to Word 7.0 columns followed by a continuous section break (balances the length of the columns). RFT-DCA Flowing, but not Balanced, columns convert to Word 7.0 columns. RFT-DCA Related Text Columns convert to Word 7.0 Tables.
Headers/footers	See comment	Yes	Different First Page is not converted.
Line numbering	No	No	
Vertical alignment	No	Not supported	
Document Formatting			
Footnotes	See comment	Yes	All footnotes are positioned at bottom of page when converting from Word 7.0 to RFT-DCA.
Margins	Yes	Yes	Margins are emulated as closely as possible, but may not convert exactly due to font differences and differences in the layout options of Word 7.0 and RFT-DCA.
Widow control	No	No	Widow control is always set to "on" during conversion.
Mirror Margins, Even/Odd Pages	No	Not supported	Even and odd headers and footers are supported.
Page size	Yes	Yes	
Other Features			
Absolute-positioned objects	No	Not supported	
Annotations	No	Not supported	
Styles	See comment	Not supported	Styles are converted to direct formatting.
Outlining	See comment	See comment	Appearance is preserved.
Tables	See comment	Not supported	Tabular columns and word-wrap columns convert to Word 7.0. Word Tables convert to RFT-DCA Related Text Columns.

Feature	Word 7.0 to RFT-DCA	RFT-DCA to Word 7.0	Comments
Other Features *(continued)*			
Indexes/Tables of Contents	See comment	See comment	Appearance is preserved.
Print Merge commands	No	No	
Date/time stamps	Yes	Yes	TIME fields are ignored by RFT-DCA.
Page number	Yes	Yes	Page numbers are converted, but not page number formatting.
Subdocuments (INCLUDETEXT field)	See comment	No	The latest result is inserted and the INCLUDETEXT field is lost.
Cross-references and bookmarks	No	Not supported	
Formulas	No	Not supported	
Graphics	No	No	If you encounter difficulties saving a file containing graphics as RFT-DCA format, try double-clicking the graphics, then returning to the document before saving.
Extended characters	Yes	Yes	Converted when available in EBCDIC character sets 256 and 259 and ANSI. ANSI publishing characters are not converted back and forth.
Stop Codes and Prompted Stop Codes	Not supported	No	
Auto Text	No	Not supported	
Linedraw	See comment	Yes	In Word 7.0, line spacing causes vertical gaps in converted line-drawn objects that span multiple lines. To eliminate the gaps for printing, change the line draw paragraph's line spacing to exactly the current font size in points. To set line spacing, choose Paragraph from the Format menu.
Font Mapping	See comment	Yes	Fonts convert to Courier New by default in Word 7.0, but the original font names are preserved and exported to the correct font when saved again as RFT-DCA.

Switching from Text with Layout Format Documents

In the following table, "Yes" means the feature exists in both products and is converted from one product to the other. "No" means it exists in both products but is not completely converted between the two. "Not supported" means the feature is not supported in one of the products or is not converted completely between products.

Feature	Word 7.0 to Text with Layout	Text with Layout to Word 7.0	Comments
Character Formatting			
Character	No	No	Character formatting is not converted. This includes font, font size, color, bold, italic, small caps, hidden, underline, word underline, double underline, subscript, superscript, expanded, and condensed character formats. When saving to or reading from an MS-DOS-based application, the MS-DOS Text with Layout format should be used.
Columns			
Columns	See comment		Line Between formatting is not converted.
Document Formatting			
Document	See comment		Widow control is not converted.
Page Formatting			
Page			Page dimensions are not converted. Page breaks are not preserved.
Paragraph Formatting			
Borders, Keep Lines Together, Keep With Next, Page Break Before	No	Not supported	
Tab Leaders	No	No	
Section Formatting			
Section breaks (even, odd, continuous, next page)	No	Not supported	
Headers/footers	See comment	Not supported	The text of a header/footer is placed at the beginning of the document.

Feature	Word 7.0 to Text with Layout	Text with Layout to Word 7.0	Comments
Section Formatting (continued)			
Different Odd and Even Pages	See comment	Not supported	When different odd/even headers are defined in the document, the text of the even header is placed at the start of the converted document, and the text of the odd header is lost. If only an odd header is defined in the document, the text of the odd header is placed at the start of the converted document.
Different First Page	See comment	Not supported	If a first-page and other header are defined, the text of the non-first-page header is placed at the beginning of the converted document, and the text of the first-page header is lost.
Position	See comment	Not supported	Header/footer distance from the page edge is not preserved. Footers are placed at the beginning of the page.
Line numbering	No		
Page numbering (Start At)	No		
Tables			
Borders, row formatting, row height	See comment	Not supported	Borders are not converted. Justified text alignment is not converted. Minimum row height is not converted.
Indents	See comment	Not supported	Right indents and hanging indents applied within table cells are not retained.
Tables			Table text and structure are preserved in conversion to text.
Other Features			
Annotations	See comment	No	Annotations are inserted at the end of the document in the order they appear in the document.
Fields (DATE, TIME)	See comment		Fields are converted to the text of the last result.
Footnotes			Footnotes are inserted at the end of the document in the order they appear in the document. Footnotes are numbered sequentially throughout the whole document. Text of custom separators is inserted at the beginning of the document.
Graphics	See comment		Bitmaps and metafiles are not converted.

Feature	Word 7.0 to Text with Layout	Text with Layout to Word 7.0	Comments
Tables *(continued)*			
Formulas	No		
Hard space	See comment		Converted to normal space.
Nonbreaking hyphen	See comment		Converted to normal hyphen.
Optional hyphen	No		

Switching from Microsoft Works

You already know how to create, edit, format, and print documents using Microsoft Works version 3.0 for MS-DOS or Windows. This section explains what happens to various document attributes when documents are converted from or to Word 7.0.

Converting Between Microsoft Word 7.0 and Microsoft Works for MS-DOS

In the following table, "Yes" means the feature exists in both products and is converted from one product to the other. "No" means it exists in both products but is not completely converted between the two. "Not supported" means the feature is not supported in one of the products or is not converted completely between products.

Feature	Word 7.0 to Works for MS-DOS	Works for MS-DOS to Word 7.0	Comments
Paragraph Formatting			
Tabs			Tab leaders for default tabs in Works are not converted in Word.
Bullets and Numbering	See comment	Not supported	Bullets and numbering are converted to plain text.
Section Formatting			
Headers/footers	See comment	See comment	To be converted, headers and footers must be located at the beginning of the Works document. Works headers are converted to a single paragraph in Word.

Feature	Word 7.0 to Works for MS-DOS	Works for MS-DOS to Word 7.0	Comments
Section Formatting (*continued*)			
Even/odd special	See comment	See comment	Works does not have different right and left headers. If one of the two is present in a Word document, it is preserved in the Works document. If right and left headers are both present, the latter of the two is preserved.
Tables	See comment	Not supported	Table cells in Word are converted to sequential paragraphs in Works.
Other Features			
Frames	See comment	Not supported	Framed objects are vertically positioned when converted to Works.
Annotations	See comment	Not supported	Annotations are converted to footnotes in Works.
Footnotes (manual reference marks)	See comment	See comment	Only the first character of a user-defined footnote reference mark is converted to Works. Automatic footnotes are converted.
Graphics	No	No	
Styles	See comment	Not supported	Styles are converted to direct formatting in Works.
Outlining	No	Not supported	Outline structure is lost when converting to Works.
Tables of contents, indices, tables of authority	See comment	See comment	Generated tables of contents and indexes are converted. TC (Table of Contents Entry) fields are not converted.

Converting Between Microsoft Word 7.0 and Microsoft Works for Windows 3.0

Note You can open Works for Windows 3.0 files directly in Word. When opening Works for Windows 3.0 files in Word, first make sure that the Confirm Conversions checkbox is selected in the Word Open dialog box on the File menu. When you open the Works for Windows 3.0 file, the Convert From dialog box is displayed. Select Works For Windows 3.0 in the list of file formats and click OK.

In the following table, "Yes" means the feature exists in both products and is converted from one product to the other. "No" means it exists in both products but is not completely converted between the two. "Not supported" means the feature is not supported in one of the products or is not converted completely between products.

Feature	Word 7.0 to Works for Windows	Works for Windows to Word 7.0	Comments
Character Formatting			Changed to plain text format in Works for Windows if format is not supported.
All caps, small caps, hidden, and color	No	Not supported	
Outline, shadow	Not supported	Not supported	
Underline (dotted, double, word)	See comment	Not supported	Works for Windows supports only single, continuous underlining.
Spacing (condensed, expanded)	No	Not supported	
Columns	No	Not supported	
Document Formatting			
Footnotes	See comment	See comment	Footnotes are always at the end of the document in Works for Windows.
Summary info	No	Not supported	
Widow control	No	See comment	This feature is automatic in Works for Windows.

Feature	Word 7.0 to Works for Windows	Works for Windows to Word 7.0	Comments
Page Formatting			
Margin (gutter), mirror even/odd pages, page orientation, paper source	No	Not supported	
Paragraph Formatting			
Background shading, numbering	No	Not supported	
Borders	Yes	Yes	Thin, thick, and double borders are converted properly. Unsupported border styles become thin line borders.
Page break before	See comment	Not supported	This format is converted to hard page breaks in Works for Windows.
Tabs	See comment	Yes	Negative tabs are not allowed in Works for Windows.
Section Formatting			Works for Windows does not have section formatting. Many properties related to sections in Word 7.0 become document properties in Works for Windows.
Section breaks (even, odd, continuous, next page)	No	Not supported	Section breaks are converted to page breaks in Works for Windows.
Headers/footers	See comment	See comment	Headers and footers are document properties in Works for Windows. Even/Odd Special is not converted. First Page Special in Works for Windows only offers options of no header or footer on first page.
Line numbering	No	Not supported	
Restart page number at one	No	Not supported	
Vertical alignment (top, centered, justified)	No	Not supported	
Tables	No	Not supported	Tables are converted to tab-delimited text in Works for Windows.

Feature	Word 7.0 to Works for Windows	Works for Windows to Word 7.0	Comments
Other Features			
Frames	No	Not supported	
Annotations	See comment	Not supported	Annotations are converted to footnotes in Works for Windows, retaining the page number reference.
Endnotes	No	Not supported	
Footnotes	See comment	See comment	Numbering of footnotes is different in the two products. Works for Windows counts manual footnote entries in the numbering sequence, whereas Word 7.0 counts these separately.
Footnote starting number, separators, continuation notices, restart each section	No	Not supported	Footnotes always start with 1 in Works for Windows.
Footnote position (end of page, end of document)	No	Not supported	Notes are always endnotes in Works for Windows and appear at the end of the document.
Graphics (cropping)	No	Not supported	
Drawing Layer	No	Not supported	
Styles	No	Not supported	Word 7.0 styles are converted to direct formatting in Works for Windows.
Outlining	No	Not supported	
Revision marks	No	Not supported	
Tables of contents, indexes, tables of authorities	See comment	Not supported	The tables are converted to text-result only in Works for Windows.
Print Merge commands (logic, data files)	No	No	Merge fields are converted, but data documents are not automatically converted.

Feature	Word 7.0 to Works for Windows	Works for Windows to Word 7.0	Comments
Other Features *(continued)*			
Date/time stamps (custom), page number (format, restart), subdocuments (INCLUDE field)	No	Not supported	
Cross-references/ bookmarks	See comment	Yes	Bookmarks are not allowed in a Word 7.0 header or footer. Bookmarks in these areas are lost.
Fields (equations, formulas, links, form fields, bar codes)	No	Not supported	Some fields are converted to the text of the last result when converting from Word 7.0 to Works for Windows. Check your converted documents for conversion results.
Object linking and embedding (OLE)	Yes	Yes	Word 7.0 is a client for Works for Windows charts, MS Draw drawings, and Microsoft Excel charts and worksheets.
Bullets/ Numbering	See comment	Not supported	Automatic bullets and numbering are converted to plain text.

Switching from WordStar

You already know how to create, edit, format, and print documents using WordStar for DOS versions 3.3 through 7.0 or WordStar for Windows versions 1.0 through 2.0. This section explains what happens to various document attributes when documents are converted from or to Word 7.0.

In the following table, "Yes" means the feature exists in both products and is converted from one product to the other. "No" means it exists in both products but is not completely converted between the two. "Not supported" means the feature is not supported in one of the products or is not converted completely between products.

Feature	Word 7.0 to WordStar	WordStar to Word 7.0	Comments
Character Formatting			Changed to plain text format in WordStar if feature is not available.
Small caps	No	Not supported	
Font color	No	Yes	

Feature	Word 7.0 to WordStar	WordStar to Word 7.0	Comments
Character Formatting *(continued)*			
Double-strike format	Not supported	No	
Space Underline	Not supported	No	
Font type styles	Not supported	No	
Document Formatting			
Footnotes	See comment	Yes	Converting to WordStar, custom footnote numbers do not convert, and starting footnote reference numbers do not convert.
Page Formatting			
Margins	See comment	Yes	The first margin setting encountered in the Word document is used for the entire document when converted to WordStar.
Gutter margins	No	No	
Paragraph Formatting			
Tabs	See comment	Yes	Converting to WordStar, vertical tab alignment does not convert.
Right indents	No	Not supported	
Space before and after	See comment	Not supported	Converting to WordStar, space before and after is simulated with blank lines.
Paragraph numbering	No	No	
Paragraph margins	No	No	
Tab leaders and decimal tabs	See comment	See comment	Tab leaders are not converted. Decimal tabs become left tabs.
Keep with next and keep together	No	Not supported	
Section Formatting			
First page special header/footer	No	Not supported	
Date and time entries in footers	No	Not supported	
Even/odd headers/footers	No	No	

Feature	Word 7.0 to WordStar	WordStar to Word 7.0	Comments
Section Formatting *(continued)*			
Headers/Footers general	See comment	See comment	More than 3 lines of header/footer text does not convert to WordStar. Paragraph formatting in headers/footers does not convert.
WordStar default page number in a footer	Not supported	No	
Tables	See comment	Not supported	Tables are converted to tab-delimited text in WordStar.
Other Features			
Styles	See comment	See comment	Styles are converted only for WordStar 5.5 and above, to direct formatting in Word 7.0.
Table of contents	No	See comment	To retain the appearance of a WordStar table of contents, convert the .toc file separately, then insert it into the converted WordStar document that is associated with it.
Index	No	See comment	To retain the appearance of a WordStar index, convert the .idx file separately, then insert it into the converted WordStar document that is associated with it.
Tables of captions, tables of figures, tables of authorities	No		
Outline	No	No	
Page Numbers	See comment	See comment	Non-numeric page numbers and page position are not converted.
Print Merge	No	No	
"Dark" and "Light" colors	Not supported	See comment	Converted to Black.
Printer control codes	Not supported	No	
Orientation	No	No	
Summary info	No	No	
Place markers	Not supported	No	
Overprinting	Not supported	No	

Importing Documents from Microsoft Excel

Use the File command on the Insert menu or the Open command on the File menu to open a Microsoft Excel 3.*x* through 7.0 document in Word. The converter functions in one direction only. Data may be brought in from Microsoft Excel worksheets, but not saved in Microsoft Excel format.

Feature (From Excel to Word only)	Comments
Formatting	
Fill	Specified fill characters become left aligned.
Row height	Each row takes on the height of the cell that contains the most text.
Column width	Most columns retain their width. Hidden columns and zero-width columns become a standard width.
Hidden columns	Converted as regular table columns.
Numeric formatting	
Regular Excel formats	Numbers formatted for general format will try to fit into the current column width. These numbers are brought in at full precision. This may result in more decimal places than are displayed in the worksheet.
User-defined formats	The "?" and "*" characters are not supported when used to define fractional number formats. For example, if the value of a cell is 0.5, and the user-defined number format is "# ?/?," Microsoft Excel displays 1/2; Word displays 0.5.
Worksheet Size	
Less than 32 columns	A table is created in Word.
More than 32 columns or wider than 22 inches	The worksheet is represented in Word as tab-delimited text.

Converting from Excel 4.0

Excel 4.0 allows you to press ALT+ENTER to begin a new line within a text cell. The resulting new line character is translated to a paragraph mark in a table if the original Excel worksheet width is 32 columns or less, or to a new line character in tab-delimited text. These conversions ensure mail-merge compatibility.

Importing Documents from Lotus 1-2-3

The converter functions in one direction only. Data may be brought in from Lotus 1-2-3 files, but not saved in Lotus 1-2-3 format.

Feature (from Lotus 1-2-3 to Word only)	Comments
Formatting	
Font	All Lotus 1-2-3 data becomes 10-point Courier font.
Numeric formatting	Lotus 1-2-3 will try to fit numbers in General format into the current column width. When converted, these numbers are brought in at their full precision. You may see more decimal places in Word 7.0 than you did in your worksheet.
Worksheet Size	
Less than 32 columns	A table is created in Word 7.0.
More than 32 columns or wider than 22 inches	The worksheet is represented in Word 7.0 as tab-delimited text.
Other	
Ranges	The converter displays a dialog box asking you to choose from a list of range names. Type in a Lotus 1-2-3 range (b2..g43) or choose an existing range name (my_data), or press ENTER to convert the entire worksheet. Note that 3-D range names are supported correctly, but explicit 3-D range definitions (e.g., a:a1..c:c5) are not supported.
Password	If the worksheet is password protected, you will be asked to enter the password. Note that you may have to reenter the password when beginning a print merge operation. Password-protected files created in Lotus 1-2-3 version 3.x cannot be converted.
Empty files	Empty worksheets are imported into Word 7.0 as a single empty cell.

Importing PIC Graphic Files

Word can import PIC files created by Lotus 1-2-3 and Borland Quattro Pro. Word cannot import Micrografx PIC or Draw Plus PIC.

Troubleshooting

Word doesn't list the document I'm looking for in the Open dialog box.

Make sure that you selected the correct file type or extension in the Files Of Type box. If the document name you're looking for still doesn't appear, select All Files. Also check to make sure that you have selected the correct drive and folder.

The document I opened has symbols and characters in it that I didn't expect.

If you opened the document and Word prompted you to specify which converter to use, you may have chosen the wrong converter. Try choosing a different one. You can also use the Replace command to quickly delete unwanted characters from the document.

If the unexpected symbols are few and scattered throughout the document, it's possible that you need to specify a different font to substitute for a symbol font used in the original document.

I can't find the converter I need.

The converter you need probably isn't installed. To install converters, run the Microsoft Office Setup program. If you have installed all of the converters that come with Word and you still don't see the one you need, you may be able to obtain it on a supplemental disk.

The text of the document was converted correctly, but the graphics disappeared.

Either the correct graphics filter isn't installed or the graphics are in a format Word cannot import. To install the graphics filter you need, run the Microsoft Office Setup program.

The fonts are different in the converted document.

If the document you're converting contains fonts that aren't installed on your computer, Word automatically substitutes different fonts. However, you can specify the fonts that you want Word to use in the converted document.

Line breaks and page breaks are different, or the document increased in size.

There are two reasons why a converted document may have different line breaks and page breaks—even if you use the same printer. First, various word processors may calculate line spacing, line breaks, and page breaks in slightly different ways. Second, different printer drivers use slightly different fonts and character spacing information when printing to the same printer. You may be able to adjust the line breaks and page breaks by substituting different fonts.

Appendixes

Appendix A, "Setup Command Line Options and File Format" lists the command line options used to change the way Setup runs and describes the internal formats of the Setup table file and the disk information file associated with Setup.

Appendix B, "Registry Keys and Values," covers the registry entries created and used by the Office applications.

Appendix C, "List of Installed Components," lists components installed by Office Setup according to whether the installation is Custom, Typical, Compact, Run From CD, or Run From Server. Information is included on whether or not the component is automatically installed and how much disk space is needed.

Appendix D, "Contents of the Office Resource Kit CD," lists the general categories of software tools, converters, utilities, and sample files on the CD that comes with this book. The CD also includes an online version of this book so you can use full-text search to locate information quickly.

Appendix E, "System Requirements for Office for Windows 95," lists the system requirements for Office Standard, Office Professional, and for each Office application.

Appendix F, "Resources," includes information about the various support resources available to you from Microsoft and others. Support is available directly from Microsoft by telephone and through online services, both domestically and overseas. Also listed in this appendix are various training resources and reference materials available from Microsoft and others.

APPENDIX A

Setup Command Line Options and File Format

This appendix presents specific technical details of the Setup program for Microsoft Office for Windows 95, including all of the possible command line options, the general Setup process flow, and the formats of the Setup table files.

In This Appendix

Setup Command Line Options

The following table shows the command line options recognized by Setup.

Option	Description	Example
/a	Administrative mode; creates an administrative installation point. Only available when running from CD or floppy disks.	/a
/b #	Suppresses the dialog box for choosing installation type by preselecting one of the large buttons: #. = 1 represents the first button, 2 the second one, and so on. This option is ignored if an invalid digit is given.	/b 2
/c "COA"	Specifies the Certificate of Authorization: enters and validates the 20-character Product ID from the OEM Certificate of Authorization, replacing the user dialog box that would appear.	/c "01234567890123456789"
/f	Disables the writing of long filenames.	/f
/g "filename"	Specifies the log file: generates a log file that records details of the setup process.	/g "c:\msoffice\log.txt"
/m #	Specifies the MLP (Multi-License Pak) licensing information needed to activate the MLP for floppy disks. Setup increments the multilicense count on the floppy disks by the number you specify. Setup terminates immediately after setting the count.	/m 50

Option	Description	Example
/n ""	Setup will use the Windows registry Copy Disincentive name if it exists; otherwise, Setup will prompt the user for the name. Ignored with /a option.	/n ""
/n "*name*"	Specifies the user name: Setup will use the Windows registry Copy Disincentive name if it exists; otherwise, Setup will use the user name supplied here. Ignored with /a option.	/n "John Doe"
/o ""	Setup will use the Windows registry Copy Disincentive organization name if it exists; otherwise, Setup will prompt the user for the organization name.	/o ""
/o "*organization*"	Specifies the organization name: Setup will use the Windows registry Copy Disincentive organization name if it exists; otherwise, it will use the organization name supplied here.	/o "Microsoft"
/q[*option*]	Quiet mode: performs a batch mode installation with no user interaction. If present, *option* can be **0**, **1**, or **t**: • /q or /q0 suppresses all dialog boxes except the exit dialog box. • /q1 suppresses all dialog boxes, including the exit dialog box. • /qt suppresses all of the UI, including the blue background and the copy gauge.	/q1
/r	Reinstall the application.	/r
/t *table file*	Specifies the STF filename: the default is *<base>*.stf, where *<base>* is the filename of the Setup executable (for example., Setup.stf is the default file for Setup.exe).	/t newsetup.stf
/u[a]	Uninstall Office: /u removes all application files except shared components; /ua always removes shared components without prompting the user. If /q is also specified with /u, the shared components are not removed because the prompt will not appear.	/ua
/y	Don't copy file: Setup proceeds normally, including setting registry entries, but without actually copying any files. Used for restoring registry entry values or tracking down process problems without copying files.	/y
/?	Displays Setup command line options.	/?

Notes

- All options and arguments are case insensitive (they can be uppercase or lowercase).

- Options can be combined in the command line; for example:

  ```
  setup.exe /n "john doe" /o "megacorp" /g "c:\tmp\offlog.txt"
  ```

- The **/a** and **/q** options are mutually exclusive and result in a usage error message.

- The **/n** option is ignored if **/a** is used.

- The **/u** and **/r** options are mutually exclusive and only make sense when running Setup in Maintenance mode. Using both options results in a usage error message.

Setup Process Flow

This section is a general overview of the process that Setup follows during an installation. The basic actions of a client install are as follows:

1. Determine whether this is a new install or a Maintenance mode install. You can identify Maintenance mode by looking for an entry placed by Setup in the registry to indicate that Setup has been run before. The entry has the following format:

   ```
   HKey_Local_Machine\Software\Microsoft\MS Setup (ACME)\Table Files
   ```

   The values located at this key have a name part, consisting of the product name and version, and a data part, which is the fully qualified path to the .stf file. For example, the Office for Windows 95 value might look like this:

```
Name                           Data
MS Office 95@v95.0.0.0307(1033) "c:\Program Files\Microsoft Office\Setup\setup.stf"
```

   If a value exists that has a matching name portion, Setup is started in Maintenance mode using the .stf file identified by the data portion of the value.

   If no value exists with that pattern, or if the file described here cannot be found or opened, Setup is started in install mode using the .stf file found in the folder in which the Setup program (Setup.exe) resides. The .stf file is found by using the eight-character name portion of the Setup program file, with an .stf extension. For example, if Setup.exe has been renamed to Newsetup.exe, Setup will look for the .stf file under the name Newsetup.stf.

   If the **/t** command line option is used to specifiy a particular .stf file, Setup will start in install mode with the specified .stf file.

2. If Setup is running from disk 1 of a floppy disk set, it will create the Mssetup temporary folder. This is created on the first hard disk drive found (drives are searched starting with drive letter Z and searching to drive letter A) that has sufficient disk space. If no hard disk drive is found, the user's Windows folder is used.

   If Setup is running from a CD, a hard disk, or a network server, the temporary folder is not created.

3. Check the .stf file for syntax errors (this will only fail if the .stf file has been modified in some way and a syntax error is introduced).

4. Check for potentially disruptive active applications. The list of applications to check is given in the Check Modules item in the Header section of the .stf file.

5. Execute the .stf file according to the branching logic defined in the file, and then perform the following steps:

   - Check for duplicate versions of the application being installed.

   - Prompt the user for input regarding corrections and custom configurations.

   - Determine whether there is adequate space on the hard drive.

6. Copy the files into the system- and user-specified folders according to the instructions in the .stf file and the .inf file. The .inf file specifies the characteristics of each file or group of files in the product (including size, date, and so on), as well as instructions to be used when copying the files (including whether to decompress the file, whether to overwrite the destination file if it exists, and so on). The .stf file determines which files or groups of files are copied and the destinations they are copied to.

7. Delete or replace existing files as indicated.

8. Make appropriate changes to the registry and .ini files.

9. Remove the Mssetup folder, if one was created.

Setup File Formats

Microsoft Office for Windows 95 Setup is a general-purpose installation tool that uses application-specific information in support files to control the way it performs the installation. This section describes the internal formats of the key files associated with Setup. The information provided here is for your reference and will help you understand how Setup works and how you can use the Network Installation Wizard to modify the behavior of Setup.

> **Warning**   The table files associated with Office Setup have been carefully built and tested. The behavior of Setup and the successful installation of Office depend on the internal integrity of these files. These files are tab-delimited and rely on positional parameters. It is not recommended that you modify these files directly; instead, use the Network Installation Wizard to customize the setup process. For more information about the Network Installation Wizard and about using it to customize the Office installation process, see Chapter 9, "Customizing Client Installations."

Setup Support Files

Office Setup relies on a set of files that work together to describe the installation process for Office. The following tables identifies some of these Setup installation files.

Filename	Description
Setup.exe	Primary executable file for Setup
Off95Std.inf—Office Standard Off95Pro.inf—Office Pro	Disk information file (.inf file); provides detailed information about the files to be installed
Setup.stf	Setup table file (.stf file); specifies the logic of the installation process
Admin.inf	Application information file used by Setup to run installations in Network mode
*.dll	DLL library files containing custom action procedures
Setup.lst, Setup.ini	Information files for Setup

Because the .inf and .stf files control the behavior of Setup, and because they are the files modified by the Network Installation Wizard, it is the internal format of these files that will be described in detail in this appendix.

Using long filenames   To support long filenames, the following construct is used for specifying filenames and folder names in the .stf and .inf files:

short_filename<long_filename>

This format is used anywhere filenames or folder names are specified in the .stf file or the .inf file. Short filenames always accompany long filenames. Setup assumes that everything enclosed within the < and > symbols is the long filename, and all characters supported by Windows 95 are allowed within these symbols. Setup determines on the fly which filename to use by checking the registry. When creating an Admin image, Setup always uses short filenames regardless of whether or not the server supports long filenames.

The Setup Disk Information File (.inf)

The Setup .inf file is a text file that contains extensive information regarding all the files involved in an installation. This information includes the following:

- A file's location and its default attributes
- Whether a file is to be appended to an existing copy
- Whether a file is to be backed up, renamed, or copied
- Which language a file is to support

There are two Setup .inf files:

- Off95Std.inf (Office Standard) or Off95Pro.inf (Office Professional), used in all installation modes except Network mode.
- Admin.inf, used in Network mode only when the application is installed to a workstation from a network image. In general, there are no disk number references, no split files, and no files requiring compression.

The Setup .inf file consists of sections, lines, and fields. Sections are groups of lines preceded by a short description of the grouping. A line consists of comma-delimited fields. A single carriage return delimits the lines themselves. A field is a data item in a line.

Section headings are always enclosed in square brackets and placed at the left margin of the file. An example of a section heading is **[ClipArt]**.

The Setup .inf file has three main parts:

- **[Source Media Descriptions]** This part is a section that describes each of the disks in the application installation set.
- **[Default File Settings]** This part is a section that describes the default attributes Setup uses to install a file.
- **File Properties** This part consists of the remaining sections. These sections describe the properties of each file to be installed by Setup, as well as any files that must be modified or removed during the installation process. There can be as many sections for file properties as are needed. Comment lines are indicated with a semicolon at the left margin.

Source Media Descriptions

The **[Source Media Description]** section of a Setup .inf file contains one line for each of the disks you use to install the product. Source Media Description lines are indented and contain four strings, each of which is enclosed in quotation marks and separated by a comma.

Data Format   *"DiskID", "Disk Label", "Tag Filename", "Relative Path"*

String	Description
DiskID	Disk identification number. A unique integer between 1 and 999.
Disk label	Name on the paper label of the shipped disk.
Tag filename	Name of a file residing on the specified disk. Setup uses this filename to confirm that the correct floppy disk is in the drive. If the field is empty (" "), Setup uses the name of the file to be copied at that moment.
Relative path	Relative path for the disk from the folder from which Setup.exe is running. The quotation marks are mandatory. A string is included in this field only if the installable files are on a network disk drive. The relative path for the disk from Setup.exe is used when Setup is run from the network image. If the string is empty, Setup uses the folder where Setup.exe currently resides.

Example
```
"1", "My Disk Label 1", "SETUP.exe", ""
```

Default File Settings

This section contains default values that Setup uses when a field in a file description line in the .inf file is empty. A line in the **[Default Fail Settings]** section consists of a symbol name for a specific installation action, an equal-sign (=), and the value to assign to the symbol. These lines always begin at the left margin, and symbols and values are always enclosed in quotation marks; even null fields are enclosed in quotation marks.

Data Format   *"Symbol" = "value"*

Example
```
"STF_COPY" = "YES"
```

The following tables show the symbol names and possible values for the **[Default File Settings]** section.

STF_BACKUP

Possible value	Meaning
null	Do not create a .bak file (default).
*	Create a .bak file.

STF_COPY

Possible value	Meaning
YES	Copy (default).
null	Do not copy.

STF_DECOMPRESS

Possible value	Meaning
YES	Decompress (default).
null	Do not decompress.

STF_OVERWRITE

Possible value	Meaning
ALWAYS	Always overwrite an existing version of the file when there is no version information (default).
NEVER	Never overwrite an existing version of the file.
OLDER	Overwrite the existing version of the file if it is older.
UNPROTECTED	Overwrite the existing version of the file if it is not write-protected.
QUERY	If a copy of the file exists, display a dialog box asking the user whether to overwrite it.

STF_READONLY

Possible value	Meaning
null	Do not set the read-only file attribute (default).
YES	When the file is copied, set the read-only file attribute.

STF_ROOT

Possible value	Meaning
null	Use the entire path for the file in the .inf file description line (default).
YES	When copying the file, strip any subfolders from the path of the file in the .inf file description line.

STF_SETTIME

Possible value	Meaning
YES	Use the contents of the DATE file property in the .inf file description line to set the creation date of the copied file (default).
null	Leave the creation date as it is (the date on which the file was copied onto the user's hard disk).

STF_TIME

Possible value	Meaning
null	Setup uses the value provided for the Size file property in the .inf file description (default).
n	Size of file expressed as a non-zero positive integer. Setup uses this number to calculate the percentage complete on the copy gauge.

STF_VITAL

Possible value	Meaning
YES	This is a vital file that must be successfully copied to the user's hard disk if the installation is to succeed (default).
null	The file is not vital to the success of the installation.

STF_DATE

Possible value	Meaning
null	Uses the default setting.
YYYY-MM-DD	Specify a date between 1980-01-01 and 2099-12-13

File Properties

The File Properties portion of the .inf file consists of lines describing how each file is to be handled during an installation.

These lines are formatted in either of two ways. For both formats, the disk's identification number has a description line in the **[Source Media Descriptions]** section, and each field is delimited by a comma. The two possible formats are as follows:

- **Format A (with reference key)**   This format is used if a Setup table file object that's being defined refers to a specific file. The line begins immediately at the left margin with a short reference name (called a "key") enclosed in quotation marks. Quotation marks are not used for any of the remaining fields. The key is followed by an equal sign (=) and a disk identification number. The filename is followed with a sequence of 19 file property fields separated by commas.

  Data Format   *"Reference key" = DiskID, short_filename<long_filename>,*
  ↪ *Append, Backup, Copy, Date, Decompress, Language, Overwrite,*
  ↪ *ReadOnly, Remove Rename, Root, SetTimeStamp, Shared, Size, System,*
  ↪ *TimeToCopy, Reserved, Version, Vital*

Example

The following example describes a shared file having the reference key "CustDict" (Custom Dictionary):

```
"CustDict" = 1,custom.dic,,,,1993-01-13,,,OLDER,,,,,,SHARED,69632,,,,
↪ 0.2.0.2,
```

- **Format B (without reference key)** This format is used if a Setup table file object that's being defined does not require a reference to a specific file. Each line is indented from the left margin, either with spaces or with a tab. The line begins with the disk identification number for the disk on which the file resides. This is followed by the filename and the 19 file property fields. Fields are not enclosed in quotation marks.

   Data Format *DiskID, , short_filename<long_filename>, Append, Backup,*
   ↪ *Copy, Date, Decompress, Language, Overwrite, ReadOnly,*
   ↪ *Remove Rename, Root, SetTimeStamp, Shared, Size, System, TimeToCopy,*
   ↪ *Reserved, Version, Vital*

   ### Example

   ```
   1,bldcui\dialogs.res,,,,1993-01-30,,,,,,,ROOT,,,13839,,6,,,
   ```

The following tables show the 19 file properties of a file-properties description line, along with their possible values.

Append

Possible value	Meaning
null	Do not append to an existing file; overwrite it.
filename	Append to the specified file. You cannot append the installable file to an existing file if you have specified *Rename, Root,* or *Backup.*

Backup

Possible value	Meaning
null	Use the default setting.
*	Back up the file to the same filename with a .bak extension.
filename	Filename you want to use for the backup copy.

Copy

Possible value	Meaning
null	Use the default setting.
COPY	Copy the file onto the user's hard disk or network server.
!COPY	Do not copy the file.

Date

Possible value	Meaning
null	Use the default setting.
YYYY-MM-DD	Specify a date between 1980-01-01 and 2099-12-31.

Decompress

Possible value	Meaning
null	Use the default setting.
DECOMPRESS	Decompress the file.
!DECOMPRESS	Do not decompress the file.

Language

Possible value	Meaning
null	Supports all language versions.
country code(s)	Supports specified language version(s) only.

Overwrite

Possible value	Meaning
null	Use the default setting.
ALWAYS	Always overwrite when there is no version information or when version is older.
NEVER	Never overwrite.
OLDER	Overwrite older versions only.
UNPROTECTED	Do not overwrite files with write privileges.
QUERY	Query user as to whether to overwrite.

ReadOnly

Possible value	Meaning
null	Use the default setting.
READONLY	Set read-only attributes on the file after it has been installed.
!READONLY	Do not set read-only attributes.

Remove

Possible value	Meaning
null	Copy the file using other properties.
!REMOVE	Copy the file using other properties.
REMOVE	Remove the file from the user's hard disk or network server.

Rename

Possible value	Meaning
null	Use the source filename when the file is copied.
filename	Use the specified filename when the file is copied. You cannot specify a filename for this property if you have also specified *Root* or *Append*.

Root

Possible value	Meaning
null	Use the default setting.
ROOT	Strip any subfolders from the filename when the file is copied.
!ROOT	Do not strip subfolders from the filename when the file is copied. You cannot specify *Root* if you have specified *Rename* or *Append*.

SetTimeStamp

Possible value	Meaning
null	Use the default setting.
SETTIME	Use the DATE property..
!SETTIME	Use the current system time.

Shared

Possible value	Meaning
null	Do not treat the file as a shared file.
SHARED	Treat the file as a shared file—an existing copy of the file might be in use during installation.
!SHARED	Do not treat the file as a shared file.

Size

Possible value	Meaning
integer	Size of the file in bytes (uncompressed).

System

Possible value	Meaning
null	Treat this file as a non-system file.
SYSTEM	Treat this file as a system file that is to be replaced during system restart.
!SYSTEM	Treat this file as a non-system file.

TimeToCopy

Possible value	Meaning
null	Use default setting.
integer	When a file is copied, the copy progress indicator advances one increment of *a/b*, where *a* = TimeToCopy value for the file and *b* = total of all TimeToCopy values for all files in copy list.

Reserved

Possible value	Meaning
null	This is a reserved field and must be empty.

Version

Possible value	Meaning
null	There is no version resource in the source file.
w.x or *w.x.y.z*	Version of the file. For more information about this format, see the Microsoft Windows SDK documentation.

Vital

Possible value	Meaning
null	Use the default setting.
VITAL	Installation fails if this file cannot be successfully installed.
!VITAL	Installation does not fail if this file cannot be successfully installed.

The Setup Table File (.stf)

The Setup table file is the primary tool for configuring a Setup installation for an application. It specifies the installation process for each of the modes, determining the nature, sequence, and extent of all user input. It determines which options to install, where to install the options, and how to respond to current configurations and user input.

The Setup table file is a text file with data fields delimited by tabs. Subfields are delimited by characters as specified by the data format.

If a subfield contains a character that Setup can interpret incorrectly as a delimiter (such as a space, comma, period, or tab), the entire subfield is enclosed in quotation marks. If a subfield contains a quotation mark character (") that Setup can interpret incorrectly as a subfield delimiter, another quotation mark is added. Thus, the sub-field value

```
"Type the word ""Yes"" here."
```

appears in the user interface as

```
Type the word "Yes" here.
```

Each data field contains a maximum of 255 characters, and each line contains a maximum of 1024 characters.

The Setup table file contains two basic sections:

- **Header section**   The Header section of the table file contains the basic information of the Setup protocol—for example, the location of the .inf file, dialog box text strings, and references to the second section of the table. There are only two columns in this section: one for the parameter name and one for the parameter data. Blank lines are ignored, but they are added for clarity.

- **Object section**   The Object section of the table file contains the sequence and options of the installation process as well as specific configuration information on a line-by-line, object-by-object basis. Each line designates an object and consists of 15 columns. Each line provides specific data and instructions for the Setup installation. This information is arranged in a hierarchical fashion— that is, a given object can be a specific installation action, an object branching to other objects and groups of objects, or both.

Of the 15 columns, the last three are for internal use by Setup.

About Table Design

The entire table can be viewed as a tree structure, and any given piece of the tree can be referenced by any of several paths through the tree. In many cases, multiple references are preferable to duplicating the lines for these pieces, but there are consequences to overusing this feature.

The major advantage of using multiple references is that when the actual installation steps are performed by Setup, each line is performed only once, regardless of how many tree paths activate the line. This is appropriate for common components.

The major consequence of using multiple references is that the disk space cost for the common component is accumulated when displayed in the UI. When possible, references to common components are moved high on the tree. For example, suppose that the dialog box for the Custom option has a "converters" line that leads to an Option dialog box with 20 different converters, and each converter requires a shared system component. Rather than reference the common component in each converter line, it can be referenced just once as a hidden reference for the converter's Option dialog box. The common component will be installed if any converter is selected. If such a solution is not possible, a complicated set of Depend objects can be used to produce the appropriate result. Components that require little or no disk space (such as billboards and .ini modifications) are left at a low level on the tree to make the table easier to read.

Log of Actions

A log file can be generated that keeps track of everything Setup does: what files it copies, where it copies them, what ini/reg modifications it makes, and any errors it encounters. The **/g** command line argument causes the log to be generated. For a description of this Setup command line option, see "Setup Command Line Options" at the beginning of this chapter.

Header Section

The following paragraphs describe the data required for each of the items in the Header section.

App Name

This is the name of the application's executable file.

Example

```
WINWORD.exe
```

App Version

This is the version designation of the application.

Example

```
4.0.1.000
```

Frame Bitmap (optional)

This is the reference to the .dll containing the bitmap to display in the Setup screen. The first bitmap ID is used unless the second bitmap ID is specified and the monitor is EGA.

Data Format *dll, id [[,id]]*

Example

```
WW30STP.dll, 246, 247
```

Frame Caption

This is the text string to appear at the top of the Setup screen. This text typically identifies the Setup program by application name.

Example

```
Microsoft Excel 3.0 Setup
```

Help File Name

This line specifies which online Help file should be used with Setup. The Help filename does not include a path, and it is assumed to exist in the same folder as other support files, such as the .inf file. If this key is not provided, the default filename Acmsetup.hlp is used.

Example

```
SETUP.HLP
```

Dialog Caption Base

This is the text string that appears as the standard part of the title for most of the dialog boxes. This is typically the name and version number of the application being installed. Other strings that are specific to individual dialog boxes are concatenated with the Dialog Caption Base string. Thus, if the Dialog Caption Base is "Microsoft Word 7.0," the complete heading for a specific dialog box might be something like "Microsoft Word 7.0—Custom Options."

Example

```
Microsoft Word 7.0
```

Usage String (optional)

This is the text that appears when the user types **/?** at the command line. If the data field is left blank, Setup provides the default.

Example

```
Usage: Setup or Setup /A\nSetup /A runs the setup in Administrator mode.
```

Default

```
Usage: Setup [1A]\n\nUse the /A switch to run in Administrator mode.
```

About Box String

This is the text that appears in the About box.

Example

```
Microsoft Word 7.0 for Windows\n\nCopyright (C) 1995 Microsoft
↪ Corporation
```

Check Modules, Check Modules2 (Optional)

This is a list of module-name/module-text pairs representing applications and .dll modules that could cause problems if they are running during the installation process—especially those modules that Setup modifies. Setup checks for running instances of the designated applications and, if it finds any, displays a dialog box to warn the user and suggest that the application be closed. The module name for an application can be found in the application .def file, or it can be displayed by typing the MS-DOS command **exehdr** *path\filename* for the application .exe or .dll file.

The module text is the terminology that Setup is to use when identifying the application to the user; typically, this is the name of the application. Each element is separated with a comma. If there are no entries in this field, Setup omits the check for running applications.

Data Format *module-name1, module-text1, module-name2, module-text2*

Example

```
msword, MS Word, winoldap, MS-DOS
```

Source Folder

This field is left blank. Setup provides data to this field for use during Maintenance mode. Setup detects the folder from which Setup is being run and then automatically provides a source folder designation into this field.

In Admin mode installations, this field remains blank. This line is not included in the Table file in the version that ships on a floppy disk.

MSAPPS Location

This field is left blank. MSAPPS are components (such as spelling utilities) that other applications can share and that should be installed in a separate folder. Setup provides a universal naming convention (UNC) folder name to identify where shared components were installed during an Admin mode setup. It can be useful later to refer to this field to determine whether a source image is an Admin or Network installation. In Network mode installations, Setup specifies the appropriate values. This line is not included in the Table file in the version that ships on a floppy disk.

MSAPPS Mode

This indicates whether MSAPPS mode is *local*, *shared*, or *user-choice*. This, in turn, determines whether Setup creates private copies of a shared application or points to copies of the application on the network. This is always specified as "local" for applications shipped on floppy disks.

Inf Filename

This is the name of the corresponding .inf file. If this field is left blank, Setup uses the Setup table filename and replaces its extension with the .inf extension.

Inf Parser (optional)

This is the compliance-checking hook. This object checks the user's compliance with restrictions that are specified in the .dll hook procedure.

Data Format *DLL-name, Proc-name, Other-Data*

Parameter	Description
DLL-name	Name of the compliance-checking .dll file included with the product.
Proc-name	Name of the procedure being called from the .dll file.
Other-Data	String value to pass to the .dll file. This field is mandatory, but it can be null.

Example

```
Sampapp.dll, FParseData, "2.0.3.0"
```

Setup Status

This field stores encrypted CD information, which is updated only by Setup for use in Maintenance mode. The field does not exist in a new Table file.

Maximum Object ID

This is a number only slightly larger than the largest **ObjID** number in the .stf file. Setup uses this field to operate more efficiently.

Admin Mode Root Object ID

This indicates the point in the Object section at which an Admin mode installation begins.

Data Format *obj_ref_root* [[: *list_AppSearch_obj_ref*]]

Parameter	Description
obj_ref_root	**ObjID** number at which Setup begins an Admin mode installation.
list_AppSearch_obj_ref	Optional. The **ObjID** number of a line containing an **AppSearch** object. More than one **AppSearch** object can be specified; each one is separated by a colon. No application search is actually performed, but Setup needs to know the names of the specified default folders.

Example

```
3:01
```

Floppy Mode Root Object ID

This is the point in the Object section of the Setup table at which Setup begins a Floppy mode installation. This the default Setup mode.

Data Format   *obj_ref_root* [[: *list_AppSearch_obj_ref*]]

Parameter	Description
obj_ref_root	**ObjID** number at which Setup begins a Floppy mode installation.
list_AppSearch_obj_ref	Optional. The **ObjID** number of a line containing an **AppSearch** object. More than one **AppSearch** object can be specified; each one is separated by a colon. **AppSearch** objects are activated first, followed by the root object.

Example

```
4:01
```

Network Mode Root Object ID

This is the point in the Object section of the Setup table at which Setup begins a Network mode installation.

Data Format   *obj_ref_root* [[: *list_AppSearch_obj_ref*]]

Parameter	Description
obj_ref_root	**ObjID** number at which Setup begins a Network mode installation.
list_AppSearch_obj_ref	Optional. The **ObjID** number of a line containing an **AppSearch** object. More than one **AppSearch** object can be specified; each one is separated by a colon. No application search is actually performed, but Setup needs to know the names of the specified default folders. **AppSearch** objects are activated first, followed by the root object.

Example

```
5:1
```

Network Maintenance Mode Root Object ID

This is the point in the Object section of the Setup table at which Setup begins a Network maintenance mode installation, that is, Maintenance mode Setup following a Network mode installation.

Data Format *obj_ref_root* [[: *list_AppSearch_obj_ref*]]

Parameter	Description
obj_ref_root	**ObjID** number at which Setup begins a Network mode installation.
list_AppSearch_obj_ref	Optional. The **ObjID** number of a line containing an **AppSearch** object. More than one **AppSearch** object can be specified; each one is separated by a colon. No application search is actually performed, but Setup needs to know the names of the specified default folders. **AppSearch** objects are activated first, followed by the root object.

Example

5:1

Maintenance Mode Root Object ID

This is the point in the Object section of the Setup table at which Setup begins a Maintenance mode installation (that is, setups run after the initial installation).

Data Format *obj_ref_root* [[: *list_AppSearch_obj_ref*]]

Parameter	Description
obj_ref_root	**ObjID** number at which Setup begins Maintenance mode installation.
list_AppSearch_obj_ref	Optional. The **ObjID** number of a line containing an **AppSearch** object. More than one **AppSearch** object can be specified; each one is separated by a colon. No application search is actually performed, but Setup needs to know the names of the specified default folders.

Example

6:1

Batch Mode Root Object ID

This is the point in the Object section of the Setup table at which Setup begins a Batch mode installation (that is, an installation with minimal user interaction).

Data Format   *obj_ref_root* [[: *list_AppSearch_obj_ref*]]

Parameter	Description
obj_ref_root	**ObjID** number at which Setup begins a Batch mode installation.
list_AppSearch_obj_ref	Optional. The **ObjID** number of a line containing an **AppSearch** object. More than one **AppSearch** object can be specified; each one is separated by a colon. No application search is actually performed, but Setup needs to know the names of the specified default folders.

Example

7:1

Suppress Copy Disincentive Dialogs

If present, this line prevents the display of the copy disincentive dialog boxes.

Suppress Serial Number Dialog

If present, this line prevents the display of the serial number dialog box.

Setup Version

This is the version number of the current Setup. Setup uses this value to identify the version of the setup tool for which the current table file has been generated. Setup will not run with .stf files created for an old version of Setup.

If you are creating a new version 1.2 Setup for an application that was previously released using Setup 1.0, be sure that you increment the application version number on the App Version line in the new .stf file. If you don't do this, Setup may attempt to run in Maintenance mode using the old application Setup files.

Disable OODS Install Now Button

If present, this will disable the "Install Now" button on the Out Of Disk Space dialog (the button will be greyed-out and unavaible to the user).

This switch is used if it is necessary to prohibit the user from proceeding with the installation when Setup detects that insufficient disk space is available. Normally, Setup allows the user the option to continue with the installation anyway, to allow for possible disk space calculation inaccuracies due to disk compression, and other factors.

Launch Registration Wizard

If present, this line changes the format of the "Setup was successful" dialog to include an "Online Registration" button (as long as the conditions outlined below are also true). If the user clicks this button, Setup will launch the Registration Wizard to allow the user to automatically register the product that was just installed.

Note: If the user elects not to perform online registration at this time, or cancels the Registration Wizard before completing registration, the "Online Registration" button will be presented again on the Maintenance Mode Welcome dialog.

In addition to the presence of the "Launch Registration Wizard" header line, the following conditions must also be true in order for the "Online Registration" button to appear:

1. Setup must be running under Windows 95 (the Registration Wizard runs only under Windows 95, due to TAPI and Signup.exe requirements).

2. An InstallComplianceFile action must be used in your active install tree, in order to install the compliance/product inventory DLL that the Registration Wizard needs. See the file "actions.txt" for more information about InstallComplianceFile.

> **Note** The file installed by your InstallComplianceFile action must be a valid product inventory DLL (i.e. it must export an API named "RegProductSearch"). If not, the "Online Registration" button will be suppressed.

3. The Registration Wizard itself must be properly installed and registered (the Registration Wizard is considered to be a part of the Windows 95 system, so this should have been done as a part of Windows 95 Setup). Setup locates the Registration Wizard by looking for the following key:

```
HKEY_LOCAL_MACHINE\Software\Microsoft\Shared Tools\Registration
↪ Wizard\1.0
```

The directory in which the Registration Wizard is located is then retrieved from the "Location" named value under that key. If this key and value are not present, or if an application named "regwiz.exe" is not found at the specified location, the "Online Registration" button will be suppressed.

4. Online registration has NOT already been completed for this product. Setup determines this by checking for value of "1" in a special registry entry named "RegDone", which is a named value under the registry key that Setup passes to the Registration Wizard before launching it, as detailed below. This value is written by the "signup.exe" application only after that application has been launched itself by the Registration Wizard, and then only if and when all registration information has been successfully transmitted via modem.

5. Setup is running in Floppy mode or Workstation mode. During Maintenance mode, the "Online Registration" button appears only on the Welcome dialog (as long as all the other conditions are true), and it never appears during Admin mode.

Before launching the Registration Wizard, Setup creates a special registry key and writes information to several named values under that key. The name of this key is passed as a command line parameter to the Registration Wizard, and the values serve as registration "input parameters". The name for the key is constructed as follows:

```
HKEY_LOCAL_MACHINE\Software\Microsoft\<App Name>\<App Version>\
↪ Registration
```

where <App Name> and <App Version> refer to the contents of the correspondingly named top-level header lines in your .stf file. The values that are written to this key are as follows:

Value Name	Value String
InventoryPath	Path to the file installed by InstallComplianceFile.
ProductID	The Product ID associated with your installation.
ProductName	Value specified for the <App Name> header line.
RegDone	"1" if registration has been completed for this product (not written by Setup; see comments above).

Note: If the "Online Registration" button does not appear on the "Setup was successful" exit dialog, and you were expecting it to, check the Setup log (make sure you have logging enabled). If any of the conditions specified above are not met, Setup will write one or more entries to the log detailing the problem.

No Long File Names

Normally used only for Maintenance mode installs. The item is present if the file system does not support long file names. It also may be explicitly entered to force long file names to be disabled.

Object Section

This section describes the object fields in the Setup table file, reading from left to right.

ObjID

Object identification number. The **ObjID** is a unique number, greater than 0 (zero), that identifies the object. Typically, the numbers in this column begin at 1 and increase incrementally. Setup tolerates gaps in the numbering sequence or even larger numbers preceding smaller numbers, but for clarity's sake the numbers are given an increasing sequence.

Note Objects that reference other objects (such as **Group**, **CustomDlg**, and **AppMainDlg**) can only reference objects with **ObjID** numbers higher than their own. This is independent of the position of the line in the table file.

Install During Batch Mode

This specifies whether the applications at this object line should be installed during a Batch mode installation. This option applies only to network installations and to options that are normally selected by a user. Thus, although it is possible to specify the installation of options within the **AppMainDlg**, **CustomDlg**, **OptionDlg**, and **YesNoDlg** objects, certain other objects that do not offer options at all (such as the **InstallProofTool** and **InstallProofLex** selections) cannot be influenced.

If a yes/no value is specified for one option within an object, a yes/no value must also be specified for the remaining options within that object. When you use the Network Installation Wizard to select components to install in Batch mode, it sets this field. When Setup is run with the **/q** command line option ("setup /q"), Setup installs the application with little or no user interaction, using this field to determine what options are installed. Fields can remain blank only for objects that are never controlled by the user.

Value	Meaning
Yes	Install object.
No	Do not install object.
blank	Object not subject to user selection.

Title

This is the text string associated with this object. For an **AppMainDlg** object, Setup displays this text next to a button. For **CustomDlg** and **OptionDlg** objects, Setup displays this text in the list box. This text can also appear within dialog box captions or in the Copy Progress dialog box. For objects with either the Vital or Shared attribute set, this value appears in the warning dialog boxess when the user attempts to remove the object or chooses not to install a component.

Examples

```
Complete Installation
Minimum Installation
Converters
Proofing Tools
```

Description

This is a text string describing this object to the user. This text string is used in dialog boxes to describe specific user-selectable options.

Example

```
Installs all application options. This installation requires a total of
↳ 12 MB of disk space.
```

Object Type

This is the type of object. All object type names are case sensitive.

Examples

```
AppMainDlg
CustomDlg
OptionDlg
Group
CopyFile
CopySection
AddPathToAutoexec
CustomAction
...
```

Object Data

The content of this field is a comma-delimited or space-delimited sequence of subfields specific to the object type. The separator depends on the object type. Setup uses the information in this field to define and run the various automated and user-selectable options.

Dialog Objects Identifies the objects to be displayed in the dialog box. This consists of a space-delimited list of the **ObjID** numbers for these objects.

Example

```
7 11 32 45
```

Group Objects Identifies the objects to be triggered when the user selects the associated option. This consists of a space-delimited list of **ObjID** numbers for these objects.

Example

```
13 486
```

Install Actions Identifies the install action with a list of comma-delimited subfields.

Example
```
WIN.ini, WINWORD.exe, 2, 0, 2, 2, no, yes, 2
```

Bitmap ID

This is a resource ID for a button bitmap. The resources are stored in a separate dll. If a second ID is specified, the first is used unless the second bitmap ID is specified and the monitor is EGA.

Data Format *dll*, *id* [[,*id*]]

Example
```
APP.dll, 101, 102
```

Vital Attribute

This is a value indicating whether a portion of an application is vital to the proper functioning of the application. An empty field indicates a value of "not vital." If the user fails to select a vital portion of the application, Setup displays a warning screen. The warning uses the value in the Title column.

Possible values are *Vital* and *Not vital*.

Shared Attribute

This indicates whether this item is shared or private. An empty field indicates the value "private." If the user attempts to remove a shared item, Setup displays a warning. The warning uses the value in the Title column.

Possible values are *Shared* and *Private*.

Configurable Folder

This determines whether the folder text box is an edit control or not. If the value in this field is *yes*, the user can edit the folder. If the value is *no*, editing is not permitted; an empty field indicates the value no. The value *YesNoSource* allows the user to change the destination folder; in post-Admin mode, however, the Use Source button is not displayed.

Destination Folder

This identifies the destination folder for the files controlled by this object. Each time a destination folder is identified, it applies to all objects downward in the table's hierarchical structure. Therefore, the destination folder is typically specified only at the lines where the folders change.

Value	Meaning
%obj_id	Use the destination folder of a specified object. Example: **%1**
%D	Use the destination folder of the parent.
null	Same as **%D**.
%S	Use the source folder.
%W	Use the Windows folder.
%M	Use the Windows system folder.
%D*subdir*	Use a subfolder of the parent. Example: %D\WINWORD
%S*subdir*	Use a subfolder of the source folder.
%W*subdir*	Use a subfolder of the Windows folder.
%M*subdir*	Use a subfolder of the Windows system folder.
%obj_id\subdir	Use a subfolder of the specified object.

Note The values **%W** and **%M** are necessary for Admin mode. In other modes, the values can be implied by the action, and Setup automatically determines the proper folder.

Check Folder

This indicates whether Setup is to check a user-selectable folder for previous versions of the file(s) specified at this line. To do this, the **ObjID** number of an **AppSearch** object is specified. This applies only to objects for which the user can change the default folder—that is, where the **Configurable Folder** field has been set to yes.

Data Format *obj_id* (Note that there is no preceding percent sign (%))

Example

25

Installed By

This field is left blank. Setup inserts the necessary data into this field. The information is used during Maintenance mode. If Setup encounters any previously installed files that are preferable versions (for example, more recent versions than those being installed), it marks this field "se" (somebody else). If Setup successfully installs the files specified at this object line of the table, it marks this field "us." Otherwise, this field is marked "nyi" (not yet installed), indicating that no files were installed. An empty field indicates "nyi."

Possible values are *us*, *se*, *nyi*, and *null* (same as *nyi*)

Install Data

This field is left blank. Setup provides the necessary data for this field. The information is used during Maintenance mode. The content is specific to the object type.

Install Dest Dir

This field is left blank. Setup provides the necessary data for this field. The information is used during Maintenance mode. The content is specific to the object yype. For objects whose Installed By value is *us*, Setup writes out the object's destination folder. All internal objects use this value for subsequent setting of their DestDir.

STF Object Types Reference

This section describes the object types that can be called from within the Setup table file. They are listed alphabetically by category. The names are case sensitive.

Field values are enclosed in quotation marks whenever the value is a string or whenever it contains spaces, tabs, or any punctuation or symbols that Setup can understand as a field delimiter. If the potential for confusion exists, quotation marks are used.

The following are the main types of objects:

- Directory Searching
- Dialog boxes
- Groupings
- Detection Operation
- Installation Action
- Miscellaneous

Folder Searching Operations

The following object search specified folders on the user's system for instances of specified files. The application destination folder is specified using one or more of these objects in the Header section of the Setup table file.

AppSearch

Searches for previously installed versions of your application.

Data Format   *defaultDir, filename, version, num_sub_dirs_needed,*
↳ *extended_chars_allowed, dialog_if_using_default, obj_list_of_search_types*

Parameter	Description
defaultDir	Must contain either a complete path (for example, C:\winword) or a relative path from another **AppSearch** object (for example, %12\winword).
filename	Determines whether a path (either found by searching or typed by the user) contains a previous or current version of the search object. If no filename is provided, Setup does not look for a previous or existing version and proceeds as if no version was found.
version	Differentiates between previous and current or newer versions of your application. An empty *version* field value indicates that any existing file that is found is considered a previous version.
num_sub_dirs_needed	Can contain any non-negative integer to specify the number of subfolders (in the maximum depth subfolder tree) created off this folder (MS-DOS limits the depth of a path to five levels). Do not confuse this number with the number of folders created off that folder; it specifies only the depth of the deepest one. Thus, in the path C:\dir_A\dir_B\dir_C, dir_C is the third subfolder.
extended_chars_allowed	Specifies whether to allow any ANSI characters in the path selected by the user that do not map to the same character in the OEM character set. Typically, these are extended characters, because not all extended characters are part of the OEM set. A yes in this field allows these characters; a no or a null value does not allow these characters.
dialog_if_using_default	Specifies whether Setup displays a dialog box to confirm the default folder if no previous version of the application is found during a search. Dialog boxes always appear whenever Setup finds a previous, current, or newer version of the application specified in the *filename* field.
obj_list_of_search_types	List of **ObjID** numbers representing search objects (**SearchIni**, **SearchReg**, **SearchOpen**, **SearchEnv**, or **Search Drives**) that **AppSearch** checks in sequential order until one returns a find. Typically, **AppSearch** objects are at the top of the second section of the Setup table file, followed by their referenced search objects. Dialog boxes generated by **AppSearch** use the Title table file string in the body of their messages

Example

```
C:\WINWORD, WINWORD.exe, 2.0.2.0,2, NO, YES, 2
```

SearchIni

Searches for a file as specified within the .ini file.

Data Format *file, section, key, field*

Parameter	Description
file	Name of the .ini file.
section	Section identifier.
key	Line identifier.
field	Number indicating the position of a field that contains a full path to the file that Setup is to locate. In the example, "3" indicates the third comma-delimited field on the key line.

Example

```
WIN.ini, Embedding, WordDocument, 3
```

SearchReg

Searches for the registration database.

Data Format *rootkey, regkey, name, inifield*

Parameter	Description
rootkey	Registry root key
regkey	Registry key
name	Registry entry name
inifield	Field identifier; default is 1

Example

```
CLASSES,MSToolbar\MSOffice
```

SearchOpen

Calls the MS Windows API **OpenFile( )** using the filename from the **AppSearch** object. No argument is required.

SearchEnv

Searches for the specified MS-DOS environment variable.

Data Format *env_var_name*

Parameter	Description
env_var_namy	The name of the environmental variable.

Example

`"PATH"`

SearchDrives

Searches a particular set of nonremovable drives.

Data Format *type*

Parameter	Description
type	The *type* field value can be "all," "fixed," or "remote."

Example

`"all "`

Dialog Operations

The following objects present the dialog boxes for actions permitting user interaction.

AppMainDlg

Displays the Main Options dialog box with bitmap push buttons for selecting a mode (for example, Complete, Custom, Minimum, or Server).

Note The **Configurable Directory** field must always be set to "Yes."

Data Format *obj_list* : *obj_list_always*

Parameter	Description
obj_list	Contains the **ObjID** numbers for each of the big buttons in the Main Options dialog box. Each of the **ObjID** numbers in the *obj_list* field must be greater than the **ObjID** number identifying the **AppMainDlg** object itself.
obj_list_always	Contains items that do not appear in the dialog box but are always installed whenever **AppMainDlg** is called. Typically, this object is not in the Maintenance tree, so references in *obj_list_always* cannot be uninstalled. This may be acceptable for system components, but for the reference it can be moved down to the next level (that is, added to the group for Complete/Typical/Minimum/Workstation and as an *obj_list_always* reference for CustomDlg, as described in the following section).

Example

`7 8 9 : 990`

CustomDlg

Displays the Custom Options dialog box. Setup replaces the Continue button with an OK button if **CustomDlg** is called by another **CustomDlg** object.

Data Format   *obj_list : obj_list_always*

Parameter	Description
obj_list	Contains the **ObjID** numbers for each of the options offered to the user in the Custom Options dialog box. Each of the **ObjID** numbers in the *obj_list* field must be greater than the **ObjID** number identifying the AppMainDlg object itself. Setup uses the **Install During Batch Mode** column to set the initial state of check boxes for options.
obj_list_always	Items in the *obj_list_always* field do not appear in the list box but are always installed.

Example

```
14 15 16 17 18 19 20 21 22 : 990
```

OptionDlg

Same as **CustomDlg** except that it does not call suboption dialog boxes.

Data Format   *obj_list : obj_list_always*

Parameter	Description
obj_list	Contains the **ObjID** numbers for each of the suboptions to be displayed in the Custom Options dialog box. Each of the **ObjID** numbers in the *obj_list* field must be greater than the **ObjID** number identifying the **OptionDlg** object itself. Setup uses the **Install During Batch Mode** column to set the initial state of check boxes for options.
obj_list_always	Items in the *obj_list_always* field do not appear in the list box but are always installed.

Example

```
26 27 28 29 : 990
```

YesNoDlg

Displays a basic dialog box with a single query and Yes and No buttons. The *obj_id* value resulting from the Yes/No choice must be used as the trigger with a later **Depend** object. Setup uses the **Install During Batch Mode** column to set the button default value. If the entry in the **Install During Batch Mode** column is "no," the default button will be "No." Otherwise, the default button will be "Yes."

Data Format *dialog text*

Example
```
"Do you want WordPerfect Help?"
```

Grouping Operations

Grouping operations accumulate a list of application components to be installed.

Group

Propagates activation down through the *obj_list* objects. **ObjID** numbers in this field must be greater than this object's own **ObjID** number.

Data Format *obj_list*

Parameter	Description
obj_list	A list of **ObjID** numbers designating components to be installed. Use spaces to delimit numbers.

Example
```
13 478 495
```

Depend

Reads the value returned by the object designated in the *obj_id ("trigger")* field. If the *obj_id* returns a TRUE value, each of the table objects in the *obj_list1* field (if any) is activated. If FALSE, each of the objects in the *obj_list2* field (if any) is activated. This object can be useful for **CopyFile** or **AddIni** dependencies. The object reference numbers in the *obj_list1* and *obj_list2* fields must be greater than this object's own object reference number, and obj_id must be less than this object's reference number.

Data Format *obj_id ? [[obj_list1]] [[:obj_list2]]*

Parameter	Description
obj_id	**ObjID** number of the object
obj_list1	**ObjID** numbers designating application components
obj_list2	**ObjID** numbers designating application components

Example
```
76 ? 134 : 146
```

DependAsk

Same as **Depend** except when Setup does a reinstall in Maintenance mode, at which time Setup will always reask its question of the *obj_id ("trigger")* field.

Detection Operations

Detection Operations objects detect information about the user's system.

DetectIniLine

Detects a specified line in a specified .ini file. Returns a value of TRUE if the specified file and section contain a line with the specified key—even if the field is empty. You must use this function as a trigger with a later **Depend** object.

Data Format *file, inisect, inikey*

Parameter	Description
file	Name of the .ini file.
inisect	Section identifier of the .ini file.
inikey	Line identifier of the .ini file.

Example
```
"WIN.ini", "Extensions", "doc"
```

DetectOlderFile

Detects older versions of a specified file. Returns the value TRUE to the **Depend** action if an older version of the specified file exists in the Dst folder; otherwise, it returns the value FALSE. If no version is specified, the function checks only for any version of the specified file. This function is used as a trigger with a later **Depend** object.

Data Format *file* [[, *version*]]

Parameter	Description
file	Name of the .ini file.
version	Differentiates between previous versions and current or newer versions of the application. Valid version values can be expressed in either two or four integers ("7.0" or "7.0.1.0"). An empty *version* field indicates that any existing file detected is considered a previous version

Example
```
"WINWORD.exe", "7.0.1.0"
```

Installation Action

Installation Action objects, as the name implies, designate specific actions to be performed by Setup. There is a **CustomAction** object available for adding installation actions that are not available from the predefined list of Setup Installation Action objects.

The following is a list of the different groups of Installation Action objects:

- Normal File Operations
- Shared File Operations (MSAPPS)
- Proofing Tools File Operations
- ODBC File Operations
- System File Operations
- File Modifications

Normal File Operations

The following objects perform the basic file-handling operations.

CopyFile

Copies specified components of an .inf file.

Data Format *infsect*, *infkey*

Parameter	Description
infsect	Section identifier of the .inf file
infkey	Line identifier of the .inf file

Example

```
"MSGraph", "oldhelp"
```

CopySection

Copies all files in the specified .inf-defined section.

Data Format *infsect*

Parameter	Description
infsect	A section identifier of the .inf file.

Example

```
"WinWord"
```

RemoveFile

Removes the specified .inf-defined file. This is the same as **CopyFile** with the REMOVE flag set in the .inf file.

Data Format *infsect, infkey*

Parameter	Description
infsect	Section identifier of the .inf file
infkey	Line identifier of the .inf file

Example
```
"MSGraph", "oldhelp"
```

RemoveSection

Removes all files in the specified .inf-defined section. This is the same as **CopyGroup** with REMOVE flags set in the .inf file.

Data Format *infsect*

Parameter	Description
infsect	A section identifier of the .inf file.

Example
```
"MSGraph", "oldhelp"
```

CreateDir

Creates the specified folder if it does not exist.

Data Format *dir*

Parameter	Description
dir	The *dir* value is not a full path, but rather a subfolder (or multiple subfolder) location that Setup adds to the object's normal destination folder.

Example
```
"\WINWORD"
```

RemoveDir

Removes the specified folder if it exists and is empty.

Data Format *dir*

Parameter	Description
dir	The *dir* value is not a full path, but rather a subfolder (or multiple subfolder) location that Setup adds to the object's normal destination folder.

Example

`"\WINWORD"`

Shared File Operations (MSAPPS)

The following objects install or activate files that can be shared with other Microsoft applications. The objects implicitly use the ROOT attribute when processing the .inf filename information, which results in the removal of the source subfolders.

Setup maintains both a usage count and a dependency list in the registry so that it is possible to know which applications as well as how many applications depend on a shared component.

Before copying a shared component to a local hard disk, Setup checks to see whether the component already exists (as determined by filename, size, and date). If it does exist, or if the local version is greater than the one being installed, Setup does not copy the component, but instead increments the corresponding usage counter in the registry for that shared component and adds a dependency to the list. If the shared component does not exist, Setup copies it locally, writes the initial usage count string to the registry and sets it to 1, and then adds a dependency to the list.

When uninstalling an application with a shared component, Setup follows a related scheme in determining whether to delete or decrement. Setup checks the registry usage count and dependency list for the shared component. If the count is greater than 1 and the application is in the dependency list, Setup decrements the count and removes the dependency from the list. If the count is 1 and the only item in the dependency list is the application, Setup removes the component from the file system and removes the usage count entry and the dependency list entry from the registry.

CompanionFile

Uses the destination folder specified in the *obj_id* field to install this file if *obj_id* is actually copied or if the companion file is missing in the destination folder. This action is intended for use with shared components such as .hlp files. The **ObjID** number must be less than the ObjID number for this object.

Data Format *obj_id* : *infsect, infkey*

Parameter	Description
obj_id	**ObjID** number of the object specifying the destination folder
infsect	Section identifier of the .inf file
infkey	Line identifier of the .inf file

Example

```
79 : "PrintDrv", "printdrv"
```

Proofing Tools File Operations

The following objects install proofing tools and their relevant data files.

InstallProofTool

Installs the specified .inf-defined proofing tool file, with a full Msapps search using the **[MS Proofing Tools]** Win.ini section. For example, for a speller, the *tool_ini_key* argument is "Spelling"; for a thesaurus, the argument is "Thesaurus."

Note The *tool_ini_key* field must contain a value and cannot begin with white space.

Data Format *infsect, infkey, tool_ini_key, dict_obj_list*

Parameter	Description
infsect	Section identifier of the .inf file.
infkey	Line identifier of the .inf file.
tool_ini_key	Line identifier within the MS Proofing Tools section. This field must contain a value and cannot begin with white space.
dict_obj_list	**ObjID** numbers designating the **InstallProofLex** lines in the .stf table file. The **ObjID** numbers in the *dict_obj_list* must be greater than this object's own **ObjID** number. If the dictionary set (Lex) to be installed is incompatible with a currently installed set, this object's **Title** value is used in the body of the resulting error message.

Example

```
"Speller", "speller", "SPELLING", 276
```

InstallProofLex

Installs a dictionary file or other proofing tool data file.

Note An **InstallProofLex** action can be initiated only by an **InstallProofTool** action. In Admin mode, the DestDir is determined by the parent InstallProofTool action.

Data Format *infsect, infkey, filename, sCountry, sLexType, szLanguage*

Parameter	Description
infsect	Section identifier of the .inf file.
infkey	Line identifier of the .inf file.
filename	Source file specified in the .inf source file is copied and renamed *filename*.
sCountry	Used for matching and generating Win.ini line entries.
sLexType	Used for matching and generating Win.ini line entries. The *sLexType* field is a string, typically NORMAL. Each special lex (lexicon) file, such as a legal or medical dictionary, is designated by a string (for example., MEDICAL).
szLanguage	Displayed in a dialog box if Lex format incompatibilities prevent installing this component.

Example

```
"Dictionaries", "USA", "MSSP2_EN.LEX", 1033, 0, "US English"
```

InstallComplianceFile

This object has the same data syntax and functionality as CopyFile, but in addition it writes the location of the file it installed to a special location in the Registration Database, for later reference by the Registration Wizard.

This action is used for installing the compliance checking DLL, for example, Complinc.dll, if the table file script uses the "Launch Registration Wizard" header line.

Data Format *infsect, infkey*

Parameter	Description
infsect	Section identifier of the .inf file
infkey	Line identifier of the .inf file

System File Operations

The following objects install Microsoft Windows operating system files. Because of potential damage to other Windows-based applications or to Windows itself, Setup does not permit the user to use Maintenance mode to remove any system files installed by these objects.

InstallSysFile

Installs the specified .inf-defined file to the Windows system folder, with full Shared-Windows support.

Data Format *infsect*, *infkey*

Parameter	Description
infsect	Section identifier of the .inf file
infkey	Line identifier of the .inf file

Example

```
"PrintDrv", "prntdrv"
```

InstallFontFile

Installs the specified .inf-defined font file in the Windows system folder with full Shared-Windows support. Setup creates the *inikey* value in the [fonts] section of the Win.ini file.

Note This action does not install screen fonts based on video mode.

Data Format *infsect*, *infkey*, *inikey*

Parameter	Description
infsect	Section identifier of the .inf file
infkey	Line identifier of the .inf file
inikey	Line identifier of the .ini file

Example

```
"LDFont", "ldfont", "MS LineDraw (All res)"
```

InstallTTFFile

Installs the specified .inf-defined TrueType font file. Setup creates the *inikey* value in the [fonts] section of the Win.ini file.

Data Format   *infsect, infkey, inikey*

Parameter	Description
infsect	Section identifier of the .inf file
infkey	Line identifier of the .inf file
inikey	Line identifier of the .ini file

Example

```
"EqFonts", "fences", "Fences Plain (TrueType)"
```

File Modifications

The following objects perform internal modifications to files already installed on the user's system.

AddIniLine

Adds the specified line to the specified .ini file, or replaces that line, whether or not the line is already present.

Data Format   *file, inisect, inikey, value*

Parameter	Description
File	Contains a fully qualified path and a reference to an **ObjId** number with a value less than itself whose destination path it should use (for example, *%obj_id*\Filename.ini) or contains no path at all, relying on the standard Windows .ini file search mechanism.
inisect	Section identifier of the .ini file.
inikey	Line identifier of the .ini file.
value	Can contain embedded **%s** sequences ("s" must be lowercase) that are replaced with the object's calculated **Destination Directory** value.

Example

```
"WIN.ini", "Extensions", "reg", "regedit.exe ^.reg"
```

CreateIniLine

Adds the specified line to the specified .ini file only if the line does not already exist.

Data Format *file, inisect, inikey, value*

Parameter	Description
file	Contains a fully qualified path and a reference to an **ObjID** number with a value less than itself whose destination path it should use (for example, *%obj_id*\Filename.ini) or contains no path at all, relying on the standard Windows .ini file search mechanism.
inisect	Section identifier of the .ini file.
inikey	Line identifier of the .ini file.
value	Can contain embedded **%s** sequences (the "s" must be lowercase) that are replaced with the objects' calculated **Destination Directory** value.

Example

```
"WIN.ini", "Microsoft Word 6.0", "autosave-path", "%s"
```

RemoveIniLine

Removes the specified line from the specified .ini file.

Data Format *file, inisect, inikey*

Parameter	Description
file	Contains a fully qualified path and a reference to an **ObjId** number with a value less than itself whose destination path it should use (for example, *%object_id*\FILENAME.ini) or contains no path at all, relying on the standard Windows .ini file search mechanism.
inisect	Section identifier of the .ini file.
inikey	Line identifier of the .ini file.

Example

```
"WIN.ini", "Microsoft Word 2.0", "autosave-path"
```

CopyIniValue

Copies an .ini field value from one file-section-key to another.

Data Format *file1, inisect1, inikey1, file2, inisect2, inikey2*

Parameter	Description
file	Contains a fully qualified path and a reference to an **ObjID** number with a value less than itself whose destination path it should use (for example, *%object_id*\FILENAME.ini) or contains no path at all, relying on the standard Windows .ini file search mechanism.
inisect	Section identifier of the .ini file.
inikey	Line identifier of the .ini file.

CopyIniValueToReg

Copies an .ini field value from one file-section-key to the registry.

Data Format *file1, inisect1, inikey1, file2, rootkey, regkey, value*

Parameter	Description
file	Contains a fully qualified path and a reference to an **ObjID** number with a value less than itself whose destination path it should use (for example, *%object_id*\FILENAME.ini) or contains no path at all, relying on the standard Windows .ini file search mechanism.
inisect	Section identifier of the .ini file.
inikey	Line identifier of the .ini file.
rootkey	Registry root key.
regkey	Registry key.
value	Key value.

Example

```
win.ini,MS Proofing Tools,Custom Dict 1,LOCAL,Software\Microsoft\
↳ Shared Tools\Proofing Tools\Custom Dictionaries,1
```

AppendIniLine

Appends the specified value as a new comma-delimited field to a specified line in the .ini file. If the specified value is a substring of the current .ini line value, no action occurs. If the specified line does not exist, the line is created.

Data Format *file, inisect, inikey, value*

Parameter	Description
file	Contains a fully qualified path and a reference to an **ObjID** number with a value less than itself whose destination path it should use (for example, *%obj_id*\Filename.ini) or contains no path at all, relying on the standard Windows .ini file search mechanism.
inisect	Section identifier of the .ini file.
inikey	Line identifier of the .ini file.
value	Can contain embedded **%s** sequences (the "s" must be lowercase) that are replaced with the objects' calculated **Destination Directory** value.

Example

```
"WIN.ini", "MS Word 6.0", "autosave-path", "%s"
```

AddIncKeyIniLine

Adds the specified line to the specified .ini file. Unlike **AddIniLine**, the **AddIncKeyIniLine** object increments a specified key if it already exists in a line, until a new, unique key is generated. If, for example, the specified key is "open" and an "open" line already exists, subsequent keys are "open1," "open2," "open3," and so on. On the other hand, if the specified key is "open1," subsequent keys are "open11," "open12," "open13," and so on.

Note If the content of the *value* field is a legitimate full-path filename, the **AddIncKeyIniLine** object does not generate a new key but instead replaces any existing key (or its increment) having the same root filename in its *value* field.

Data Format *file, inisect, inikey, value*

Parameter	Description
file	Contains a fully qualified path and a reference to an **ObjId** number with a value less than itself whose destination path it should use (for example, *%obj_id*\Filename.ini) or contains no path at all, relying on the standard Windows .ini file search mechanism.
inisect	Section identifier of the .ini file.

Parameter	Description
inikey	Line identifier of the .ini file.
value	Can contain embedded **%s** sequences (the "s" must be lowercase) that are replaced with the objects' calculated **Destination Directory** value.

Example

```
"WIN.ini", "MS Word 6.0-MRV List", "open", "readme.doc"
```

AddRegData

Adds specified data to the registration database (Reg.dat). If only the first two fields are specified, the key is created in Reg.dat, but no values are added to it.

Data Format   *rootkey, regkey, name, value, type*

Parameter	Description
rootkey	Can be one of the following: Hkey_Classes_Root, Hkey_Current_User, Hkey_Local_Machine, or Hkey_Users (abbreviated as Classes, Current, LocaL, or Users). If the field is left empty, it defaults to Hkey_Classes_Root.
regkey	Registry key.
name	Registry entry name.
value	Key value.
type	Can be one of the following: REG_SZ or REG_DWORD (abbreviated as SZ or DWORD). If the field is left empty or is omitted, it defaults to REG_SZ.

Example

```
"LOCAL","Software\Microsoft\Shared Tools\Proofing Tools\
↪ Custom Dictionaries","1","%s\CUSTOM.DIC",""
```

SelfReg

Launches a function or application that performs all the work needed to update the registry. The SelfReg action has a built-in dependency on the referenced action, so the two actions do not need to be explicitly linked using a **Depend**.

The *infsect* and *infkey* parameters identify the name of the library to pass to **LoadLibrary()**. This action assumes that the library was successfully installed by a previous action to the folder specified by the SelfReg object's **DestDir** field.

The SelfReg action calls **OleInitialize()** before calling the register/unregister entry point and then calling **OleUninitialize()**. This condition is necessary to properly register OLE servers. However, this feature can also be used for registering any component, not just OLE servers. When used with components that are not OLE servers, the OLE initialization and uninitialization functions are still called, but there should be no adverse consequences.

Data Format   *infsect, infkey* [*reg_proc, unreg_proc*]

Parameter	Description
infsect	Section identifier in the .inf file.
infkey	Line identifier in the .inf file.
reg_proc	Optional. By default, the name of the function for which GetProcAddress() is called during an installation pass is DllRegisterServer. The *reg_proc* parameter is used to specify a different name.
unreg_proc	Optional. By default, the name of the function for which GetProcAddress() is called during a maintenance mode remove pass is DllUnRegisterServer. The *unreg_proc* parameter is used to specify a different name.

Example

```
"Schdplus","msspc32_dll","","","10000"
```

SelfUnreg

Launches a function or application that performs all the work needed to clean up the registry for that component. The SelfUnreg action has a built-in dependency on the referenced action, so the two actions do not need to be explicitly linked using a **Depend**.

The *infsect* and *infkey* parameters identify the name of the library to pass to **LoadLibrary()**. This action assumes that the library was successfully installed by a previous action to the folder specified by the SelfReg object's **DestDir** field.

The SelfUnreg action calls **OleInitialize()** before calling the register/unregister entry point and then calling **OleUninitialize()**. This condition is necessary to properly register OLE servers. However, this feature can also be used for registering any component, not just OLE servers. When used with components that are not OLE servers, the OLE initialization and uninitialization functions are still called, but there should be no adverse consequences.

Data Format   *infsect, infkey* [*unreg_proc*]

Parameter	Description
infsect	Section identifier in the .inf file.
infkey	Line identifier in the .inf file.
unreg_proc	Optional. By default, the name of the function for which GetProcAddress() is called during a maintenance mode remove pass is DllUnRegisterServer. The *unreg_proc* parameter is used to specify a different name.

RemoveRegEntry

Removes the specified entry from the registration database (Reg.dat file).

If the *name* field is removed, the entire key is removed. (This is possible only if the key has no subkeys.) Note the important difference between the following:

rootkey, regkey	This removes the entire key.
rootkey, regkey,	This removes the value with no name from the key *regkey*.

Data Format *rootkey, regkey, name*

Parameter	Description
rootkey	Registry root key
regkey	Registry key
name	Registry entry name

Example

```
CLASSES,Equation,
```

AddProgmanItem

Adds the specified item to a specified Windows Program Manager group, creating the group if necessary. The *cmd* and *other* fields can contain embedded **%s** sequences (the "s" must be lowercase) that are replaced with the object's calculated **Destination Directory** value.

Data Format *group, item, cmd, other*

Parameter	Description
group	Name of the Program Manager group.
item	Name of the product.
cmd	Product .exe file.
other	Used to specify items such as an accelerator or a different icon. The *other* field can also be an empty string. For more information, see the Windows SDK documentation.

Example

```
"Word for Windows 95", "Word for Windows 95", "%s\WINWORD.exe", ""
```

AddProgmanItemQuiet

Adds the specified item to a specified Windows Program Manager group, creating the group, if necessary; it does not, however, display the Program Group dialog box, so the user cannot change the group. The *cmd* and *other* fields can contain embedded **%s** sequences (the "s" must be lowercase) that are replaced with the object's calculated **Destination Directory** value.

Data Format *group*, *item*, *cmd*, *other*

Parameter	Description
group	Name of the Program Manager group.
item	Name of the product.
Cmd	Product .exe file.
other	Used to specify items such as an accelerator or a different icon. The *other* field can also be an empty string. For more information, see the Windows SDK documentation.

Example

```
"Word for Windows 95", "Word for Windows 95", "%s\WINWORD.exe", ""
```

StampCDInfo

Stamps **Copy Disincentive** information into the specified resource of the specified file.

Data Format *file_copy_id*, *resource_type*, *resource_id*

Parameter	Description
file_copy_id	The **ObjID** number designating a **CopyFile** object. This **ObjID** number must be less than the **ObjID** number of the **StampCDInfo** object itself.
resource_type	Designates the type identifier within the specified resource file.
resource_id	Designates the identifier of the resource.

Example

```
126, 106, 196
```

StampRes

Stamps specified data into a specified resource of a specified file.

Data Format   *file_copy_id*, *resource_type*, *resource_id*, *hex_val*

Parameter	Description
file_copy_id	The **ObjID** number designating a **CopyFile** object. This **ObjID** number must be less than the **ObjID** number of the **StampRes** object itself.
resource_type	Designates the type identifier within the specified resource file.
resource_id	Designates the identifier of the resource.
hex_val	Binary data represented as a string of hex characters (0–9, A–F).

Example

```
126, 106, 196, 0107A3FF
```

AddPathToAutoexec

Adds the destination path to the PATH environment variable in the Autoexec.bat file if it is not already there. No argument in Data is necessary.

Miscellaneous Operations

Miscellaneous Operations objects perform specific installation and configuration actions.

AddBillboard

Adds a specified billboard to the billboard list for display during file copy actions. Billboards are displayed in the order indicated by their **ObjID** numbers.

Data Format   *dll*, *dlg_id*, *dlg_proc*

Parameter	Description
dll	Name of the .dll file.
dlg_id	Identifier of the billboard's dialog template resource.
dlg_proc	Dialog procedure (exported from the .dll).

Example

```
"sampapp.dll", 990, "FBillbrdDlgProc"
```

CustomAction

Executes a custom installation action.

Data Format *dll*, *function*, *custom_data*

Parameter	Description
dll	Name of the .dll file
function	Name of the **CustomAction** Handler procedure exported from the .dll file
custom_data	Any parameters the **CustomAction** requires

Example

```
"sampapp.dll", "InstallWinPermFile", "Section,Key"
```

WriteTableFile

Names the output Setup table tile created by Setup. If there is no **WriteTableFile** object in the input table file, Setup uses the name of the product to be installed, adding an .stf extension.

Data Format *file*

Parameter	Description
file	The full filename of the output .stf file.

Example

```
acmeword.stf
```

APPENDIX   B

Registry Keys and Values

This appendix contains information about registry entries created in and used by the various Microsoft Office for Windows 95 applications.

Microsoft Office and the various Office applications store initialization information as part of the Windows registry. The Windows registry is a centralized database that Windows uses to set up and configure the software and hardware running in your Windows environment. The registry is analogous to the .ini files used in Windows 3.*x*; each key in the registry is similar to a bracketed heading in an .ini file, and values under a registry key are similar to entries under an .ini file heading.

Caution Many registry settings are added automatically when you install Microsoft Office. Changing the installed settings can produce unexpected results, which may make it necessary for you to reinstall Microsoft Office. It is strongly recommended that you do not change settings in the Windows registry. However, if you must change settings and options, use the Registry Editor, and only change those settings or options that are explicitly documented in the topics below. The revised settings take effect the next time you start Microsoft Office.

In This Appendix

Note In future versions of Office, the locations and values of any of these registry keys may change without notice and without being backward compatible.

Using the Registry Editor

To edit registry settings in either Microsoft Windows 95 or Microsoft Windows NT, use the Registry Editor.

If there is a plus sign (+) to the left of the folder, that registry key contains additional keys. To edit a registry key's values, double-click the key's folder in the left pane of the Registry Editor window to open it, and then double-click the value you want to edit in the right pane of the Registry Editor window. In some cases, you may need to add new keys or values. For more information, use the Help menu on the Registry Editor menu bar.

Always make a backup of the Windows registry before you modify any settings. You can back up the entire registry by copying System.dat and User.dat, or you can back up only a portion of it by exporting that portion using REGEDIT.

▶ **To start the Registry Editor in Windows 95**

1. Click the Windows Start button, and then click Run.
2. Type **regedit** and then click OK.
3. Double-click the folder icons to navigate to the appropriate registry folder.

▶ **To start the Registry Editor in Windows NT**

1. Open or switch to either Program Manager or File Manager.
2. On the File menu, click Run.
3. Type **regedt32** and then click OK.
4. Double-click folder names to navigate to the appropriate registry folder.

Microsoft Access Registry Keys and Values

As is true for all the other Office applications, Microsoft Access stores its initialization information as part of the Windows registry.

Instead of editing the registry, if you have the Access Developers Toolkit for Microsoft Access for Windows 95, you can use the Setup Wizard included with it to create an installation program for a custom Microsoft Access application and create a *user profile*. A user profile is an alternative set of registry keys containing settings that override the standard Microsoft Access and Microsoft Jet 3.0 settings when running that application. User profiles are analogous to *Appname*.ini files that are used in previous versions of Microsoft Access. User profiles are invoked by issuing the /profile command-line option when starting Microsoft Access.

Customizing Builders, Wizards, and Add-ins

Instead of editing registry settings, in most cases you can customize builders, wizards, and other add-ins using options available in their dialog boxes. For more information, see Chapter 12, "Using Library Databases and Dynamic-Link Libraries," and Chapter 16, "Creating Wizards, Builders, and Add-ins," in *Building Applications with Microsoft Access for Windows 95.*

Using the Registry Editor

The main subtrees containing settings that affect Microsoft Access are as follows:

- \\Hkey_Current_User\Software\Microsoft\Access\7.0
- \\Hkey_Local_Machine\Software\Microsoft\Access\7.0
- \\Hkey_Local_Machine\Software\Microsoft\Jet\3.0

The folders that are displayed below the \Microsoft\Access\7.0 folders apply specifically to Microsoft Access 7.0. The folders that are displayed below the \Microsoft\Jet\3.0 folder apply to the Microsoft Jet database engine that Microsoft Access uses for data access. Other programs, such as Microsoft Excel for Windows 95 and Visual Basic 4.0, may also use the Jet database engine.

Microsoft Access Hkey_Current_User Settings

The following sections describe the values contained in the \\Hkey_Current_User\Software\Microsoft\Access\7.0\Settings key. The Hkey_Current_User key points to a branch of Hkey_Users for the user who is currently logged on.

Entry	Type	Description
LastUser	String	Records the user name of the last user who logged on to Microsoft Access. If the Logon dialog box has not been activated, this value is always the default user "Admin."
Maximized	DWORD	Indicates whether or not the application fills the screen. 0 = Application window size and position are set by the WindowTop, WindowLeft, WindowHeight, and Window Width values. 1 = Application window fills the screen.
WindowHeight	DWORD	Sets the height (in points) of the application window; when maximized, it is 0.
WindowLeft	DWORD	Sets the distance (in points) from the left edge of the application window to the left edge of the screen; when maximized, it is 0.
WindowTop	DWORD	Sets the distance (in points) from the top of the application window to the top of the screen; when maximized, it is 0.
WindowWidth	DWORD	Sets the width (in points) of the application window; when maximized, it is 0.

Specifying Whether OLE Links Are Saved in OLE 1.0 or 2.0 Format

You can specify whether Microsoft Access saves OLE links in OLE 2.0 format, which saves both *relative* and *absolute* link source references, or OLE 1.0 format, which saves only absolute references. An absolute link source reference obtains data from an object that's stored as a file. A relative link source reference obtains data from an object that may be embedded within a document. Set this option to 1 to ensure consistency of OLE linking operations in Microsoft Access 1.*x* databases in an environment where both versions 1.*x* and 7.0 of Microsoft Access are used.

▶ **To specify how OLE links are saved**

1. Start the Registry Editor, and then navigate to the \Hkey_Local_Machine\Software\Microsoft\Access\7.0 key in the registry.

2. Double-click the icon for the Options folder. If AllowOLE1LinkFormat is already listed in the Name column in the right pane of the Registry Editor, skip to step 5.

3. On the Edit menu, point to New, and then click DWORD Value.

4. Type **AllowOLE1LinkFormat** and then press ENTER.

5. Double-click AllowOLE1LinkFormat, and then type **1** in the Value Data box to save in OLE 1.0 link format, or type **0** to save in OLE 2.0 link format.

6. Quit the Registry Editor.

The next time you start Microsoft Access, it will use the OLE link settings you specified in step 5.

Microsoft Jet Database Engine Initialization Settings

The following sections describe the values used to initialize the Microsoft Jet database engine. These include settings that control how native Jet (Microsoft Access) .mdb files are accessed, as well as settings for other file types, such as dBASE, FoxPro, and Paradox file types.

Global Settings Versus Microsoft Access-Specific Settings

Microsoft Jet database engine settings can be specified in two places:

- \\Hkey_Local_Machine\Software\Microsoft\Jet\3.0
- \\Hkey_Local_Machine\Software\Microsoft\Access\7.0\Jet\3.0

The settings below the \\Hkey_Local_Machine\Software\Microsoft\Jet\3.0 key affect all programs using the Jet database engine, such as Microsoft Access 7.0, Microsoft Excel 7.0, and Visual Basic 4.0. These settings are called *global settings*.

A setting in the \\Hkey_Local_Machine\Software\Microsoft\Access\7.0\Jet\3.0 key overrides the corresponding global setting and affects only Microsoft Access. These settings are called *Microsoft Access-specific settings*.

If you want to change settings to affect all programs using the Jet database engine, change the global settings. However, if you do this, keep in mind that you may be affecting more than just Microsoft Access. If you want changes to Jet database engine settings to affect only Microsoft Access, change the Microsoft Access-specific settings.

The installation process does not write default values for most Jet database engine settings to the registry. No Jet keys or values are written for global Jet database engine settings.

▶ **To change global Jet database engine settings**

1. Start the Registry Editor.

2. Open the \\Hkey_Local_Machine\Software\Microsoft\Jet\3.0\Engines subkey.

3. If a folder for the key exists below the subkey, open that folder.

   If a folder for the key doesn't exist below the subkey, add a new key below the subkey and name it appropriately. For example, by default, Setup does not create a folder for Jet\3.0\Engines\Jet global settings. In this case, you need to add a key below the subkey and name it "Jet."

4. If a value that you want to change is specified, double-click the value and then type the new setting.

   If a value that you want to change isn't specified, do the following for each default value that you want to specify:

   ▪ Add a new value of the specified type (String, DWORD, or Binary).

   ▪ Type the name of the value.

   ▪ Double-click the new value, and then specify its value.

▶ **To change Microsoft Access-specific Jet database engine settings**

1. Start the Registry Editor

2. Open the \\Hkey_Local_Machine\Software\Microsoft\Access\7.0\Jet\3.0\Engines subkey.

3. If a folder for the key exists below the subkey, open that folder.

   If a folder for the key doesn't exist below the subkey, add a new key below the subkey and name it appropriately. For example, by default, Setup does not create a folder for Jet\3.0\Engines\Xbase Microsoft Access-specific settings. In this case, you need to add a key below the subkey and name it "Xbase."

4. If a value that you want to change is specified, double-click the value and then type the new setting.

   If a value that you want to change isn't specified, do the following for each default value that you want to specify:

   - Add a new value of the specified type (String, DWORD, or Binary).

   - Type the name of the value.

   - Double-click the new value, and then specify its value.

Caution Do not delete the SystemDB value in \\Hkey_Local_Machine\Software\Microsoft\Access\7.0\Jet\3.0\Engines\Jet. If you delete this value, Microsoft Access will not work properly; you may not be able to log on to Microsoft Access, and you will not be able to create new databases or perform any security-related actions.

For information about how to add keys or how to create and specify values, see the appropriate Help topics in the Registry Editor.

Microsoft Jet 3.0 Engine Initialization Settings

These settings can be specified in one of the following places, depending on what you want the settings to apply to:

- To specify settings that apply only to Microsoft Access, use \\Hkey_Local_Machine\Software\Microsoft\Access\7.0\Jet\3.0\Engines\Jet.

- To specify settings that apply to all programs using Microsoft Jet format databases (*.mdb), use \\Hkey_Local_Machine\Software\Microsoft\Jet\3.0\Engines\Jet.

The Setup program does not create the \\Hkey_Local_Machine\Software\Microsoft\Jet\3.0\Engines\Jet folder, and it does not write default values for these settings. You must add this folder and then add and specify values if you want to change default values in this location. Only the SystemDB value is written by the Setup program to the \\Hkey_Local_Machine\Software\Microsoft\Access\7.0\Jet\3.0\Engines\Jet folder. You must add and specify values if you want to change default values in this location.

Entry	Type	Description
ExclusiveAsyncDelay	DWORD	Specifies the length of time (in milliseconds) to defer an asynchronous flush of an exclusive database. The default value is 2000, or 2 seconds.
ImplicitCommitSync	String	Specifies whether the system waits for a commit to finish. "No" instructs the system to proceed without waiting for the commit to finish; "Yes" instructs the system to wait for the commit to finish. The default is No.
LockRetry	DWORD	Number of times to repeat attempts to access a locked page before returning a lock conflict message. The default is 20.

MaxBufferSize	DWORD	Size of the database engine internal cache, measured in kilobytes (K). MaxBufferSize must be an integer value greater than or equal to 512. The default is based on the following formula:
		
		`((TotalRAM in MB - 12 MB) / 4) + 512 KB`
		
		For example, on a system with 32 MB of RAM, the default buffer size is ((32 MB - 12 MB) / 4) + 512 K or 5632 K. To set the value to the default, set the registry key to the following:
		
		`MaxBufferSize=`

PageTimeout	DWORD	Length of time between when data that is not read-locked is placed in an internal cache and when it is invalidated, expressed in milliseconds. The default is 5000 milliseconds, or 5 seconds.
SharedAsyncDelay	DWORD	Specifies the length of time (in milliseconds) to defer an asynchronous flush of a shared database. The default value is 0.
SystemDB	String	Specifies the full path and filename of the workgroup information file. The default is the appropriate path followed by the filename System.mdw.
Threads	DWORD	Number of background threads available to the Jet database engine. The default is 3.
UserCommitSync	String	Specifies whether the system waits for a commit to finish. "Yes" instructs the system to wait; "No" instructs the system to perform the commit asynchronously. The default is Yes.

Microsoft Jet 3.0 Engine ISAM Formats

The \\Hkey_Local_Machine\Software\Microsoft\Access\7.0\Jet\3.0\
ISAM Formats\Microsoft Access folder contains the entries listed in the
following table.

Entry	Type	Value
CanLink	Binary	00
CreateDBOnExport	Binary	00
Engine	String	Jet 3.0
ExportFilter	String	Microsoft Access (*.mdb)
ImportFilter	String	Microsoft Access (*.mdb)
IndexDialog	Binary	00
OneTablePerFile	Binary	00
ResultTextExport	String	Export data from the current database to a Microsoft Access database. This process will overwrite the data if it is exported to an existing file.
ResultTextImport	String	Import data from the external file into the current database. Changing data in the current database will not change data in the external file.
ResultTextLink	String	Create a table in the database that is currently linked to the external file. Changing data in the current database will change data in the external file.

Microsoft Jet 2.x Engine Initialization Settings

These settings are used by the Microsoft Jet database engine when you access
database files from Microsoft Access 1.x and 2.0.

When the Microsoft Jet 2.x Engine database driver is installed, the Setup program
writes a set of default values to the Windows registry in the Engines and ISAM
Formats subkeys. You must use the Registry Editor to add, remove, or change
these settings. The following sections describe initialization and ISAM Format
settings for the Jet 2.x Engine database driver.

Note The installation procedure writes only one setting (win32) to the
Jet\3.0\Engines\Jet 2.x folder; you must add all other engine settings manually.

To modify Jet 2.x Engine driver settings, you must add a folder named ISAM
below the Jet\3.0\Engines\Jet2.x folder and add and specify initialization settings
using the following names and types.

Entry	Type	Description
CommitLockRetry	DWORD	Number of times Jet attempts to acquire a lock on data to commit changes to that data. If Jet cannot acquire a commit lock, changes to the data will be unsuccessful.
		The number of attempts Jet makes to get a *commit* lock is directly related to the LockRetry value. For each attempt made to acquire a commit lock, Jet will make as many attempts as specified by the LockRetry value to acquire a lock. For example, if CommitLockRetry is set to 20 and LockRetry is set to 20, Jet will try to acquire a commit lock as many as 20 times; for each of those attempts, Jet will try to acquire a lock as many as 20 times, for a total of 400 attempts.
		The default value for CommitLockRetry is 20.
CursorTimeout	DWORD	Length of time a reference to a page will remain on that page, expressed in 100-millisecond units. The default is 5 units, or 0.5 seconds. This setting applies only to databases created with version 1.*x* of the Microsoft Jet database engine.
IdleFrequency	DWORD	Amount of time, in 100-millisecond units, that Jet will wait before releasing a read lock. The default is 10 units, or 1 second.
LockedPageTimeout	DWORD	Length of time between when data that is read-locked is placed in an internal cache and when it is invalidated, expressed in 100-millisecond units. The default is 5 units, or 0.5 seconds.
LockRetry	DWORD	Number of times to repeat attempts to access a locked page before returning a lock conflict message. The default is 20 times; LockRetry is related to CommitLockRetry, which is described in the following table entry.
MaxBufferSize	DWORD	Size of the database engine internal cache, measured in kilobytes (K). MaxBufferSize must be a whole number value between 9 and 4096, inclusive. The default is 512.
PageTimeout	DWORD	Length of time between when data that is not read-locked is placed in an internal cache and when it is invalidated, expressed in 100-millisecond units. The default is 5 units, or 0.5 seconds.
ReadAheadPages	DWORD	Number of pages to read ahead when performing sequential scans. The default is 16.
win32	String	Location of the database engine driver (.dll). The path is determined at the time of installation.

Microsoft Jet 2.*x* Engine ISAM Settings

The Jet\3.0\ISAM Formats\Jet 2.*x* folder contains the entries listed in the following table.

Entry	Type	Value
CreateDBOnExport	Binary	00
Engine	String	Jet 2.*x*
IndexDialog	Binary	00
IsamType	DWORD	0
OneTablePerFile	Binary	00

Microsoft Excel Initialization Settings

The Jet\3.0\Engines\Excel folder includes initialization settings for the Msxl3032.dll driver, used for external access to Microsoft Excel worksheets.

The Microsoft Jet database engine uses the Excel folder entries listed in the following table.

Entry	Type	Description
AppendBlankRows	DWORD	Number of blank rows to be appended to the end of a Microsoft Excel 3.0 or 4.0 worksheet before new data is added. For example, if AppendBlankRows is set to 4, Jet will append four blank rows to the end of the worksheet before appending rows that contain data. Integer values for this setting can range from 0 to 16; the default is 0 (no additional rows appended).
ImportMixedTypes	String	Can be set to MajorityType or Text. If set to MajorityType, columns of mixed data types will be cast to the predominant data type on import. If set to Text, columns of mixed data types will be cast to Text on import. The default is Text.
TypeGuessRows	DWORD	Number of rows to be checked for the data type. The data type is determined based on the maximum number of data types found. If there is a tie, the data type is determined in the following order: Number, Currency, Date, Text, Boolean. If data is encountered that does not match the data type guessed for the column, it is returned as a **Null** value. On import, if a column has mixed data types, the entire column will be cast according to the ImportMixedTypes setting. The default number of rows to be checked is 8.
win32	String	Location of Msxl3032.dll. The full path is determined at the time of installation.

Entry	Type	Description
FirstRowHasNames	Binary	Indicates whether the first row of the table contains column names. A value of 01 indicates that, during import, column names are taken from the first row. A value of 00 indicates that there are no column names in the first row; column names appear as F1, F2, F3, and so on. The default is 01.

Microsoft Excel ISAM Formats

The Jet\3.0\ISAM Formats\Excel 3.0 folder contains the entries listed in the following table.

Entry	Type	Value
CanLink	Binary	01
CreateDBOnExport	Binary	01
Engine	String	Excel
ExportFilter	String	Microsoft Excel 3 (*.xls)
IndexDialog	Binary	00
IsamType	DWORD	1
OneTablePerFile	Binary	00
ResultTextExport	String	Export data from the current database into a Microsoft Excel 3.0 file. This process will overwrite the data if it is exported to an existing file.

The Jet\3.0\ISAM Formats\Excel 4.0 folder contains the entries listed in the following table.

Entry	Type	Value
CanLink	Binary	01
CreateDBOnExport	Binary	01
Engine	String	Excel
ExportFilter	String	Microsoft Excel 4 (*.xls)
IndexDialog	Binary	00
IsamType	DWORD	1
OneTablePerFile	Binary	00
ResultTextExport	String	Export data from the current database to a Microsoft Excel 4.0 file. This process will overwrite the data if it is exported to an existing file.

The Jet\3.0\ISAM Formats\Excel 5.0 folder contains the entries listed in the following table, which apply to Microsoft Excel 5.0 and 7.0.

Entry	Type	Value
CanLink	Binary	01
CreateDBOnExport	Binary	01
Engine	String	Excel
ExportFilter	String	Microsoft Excel 5-7 (*.xls)
ImportFilter	String	Microsoft Excel (*.xls)
IndexDialog	Binary	00
IsamType	DWORD	1
OneTablePerFile	Binary	00
ResultTextExport	String	Export data from the current database to a Microsoft Excel 5.0 file. This process will overwrite the data if it is exported to an existing file.
ResultTextImport	String	Import data from the external file into the current database. Changing data in the current database will not change data in the external file.
ResultTextLink	String	Create a table in the current database that is linked to the external file. Changing data in the current database will change data in the external file.

Microsoft FoxPro Initialization Settings

The Jet\3.0\Engines\Xbase folder includes initialization settings for the Msxb3032.dll driver, which is used for access to external FoxPro data sources.

The Microsoft Jet database engine uses the Xbase folder entries listed in the following table.

Entry	Type	Description
NetworkAccess	Binary	Binary indicator for file locking preference. If NetworkAccess is set to 00, tables are opened for exclusive access, regardless of the settings of the *exclusive* argument for the **OpenDatabase** and **OpenRecordset** methods. The default value is 01.
PageTimeout	DWORD	Length of time between when data is placed in an internal cache and when it is invalidated. The value is specified in 100-millisecond units. The default is 600 units, or 60 seconds.
win32	String	Location of Msxb3032.dll. The full path is determined at the time of installation.

Entry	Type	Description
Century	Binary	Binary indicator for formatting the century component of dates in cases where date-to-string functions are used in index expressions. A value of 01 corresponds to the Microsoft FoxPro command SET CENTURY ON, and a value of 00 corresponds to the Microsoft FoxPro command SET CENTURY OFF. The default is 00.
CollatingSequence	String	Collating sequence for all Microsoft FoxPro tables created or opened using Microsoft Jet. Possible values are ASCII and International. The default is ASCII.
DataCodePage	String	Indicator of how text pages are stored. Possible settings are as follows: ■ OEM = OemToAnsi and AnsiToOem conversions done. ■ ANSI = OemToAnsi and AnsiToOem conversions not done. The default is OEM.
Date	String	Date formatting style to use in cases where date-to-string functions are used in index expressions. The possible settings, which correspond to the Microsoft FoxPro SET DATE command, are American, ANSI, British, French, DMY, German, Italian, Japan, MDY, USA, and YMD. The default is MDY.
Deleted	Binary	Binary indicator that determines how records marked for deletion are handled by the Microsoft Jet database engine. A value of 01 corresponds to the Microsoft FoxPro command SET DELETED ON and indicates never to retrieve or position on a deleted record. A value of 00 corresponds to the Microsoft FoxPro command SET DELETED OFF and indicates to treat a deleted record like any other record. The default is 00.
INFPath	String	Full path to the .inf file folder. The Microsoft Jet database engine first looks for an .inf file in the folder containing the table. If the .inf file is not in the database folder, the engine looks in the INFPath. If there is no INFPath, it uses whatever index files (.cdx or .mdx) it finds in the database folder. This entry is not written by the installation procedure.

Entry	Type	Description
Exact	Binary	Binary indicator for string comparisons. A value of 01 corresponds to the Microsoft FoxPro command SET EXACT ON. A value of 00 corresponds to the Microsoft FoxPro command SET EXACT OFF. The default is 00.
Mark	DWORD	Decimal value of the ASCII character used to separate date parts. The default depends on the Date setting as follows: ■ "/" (American, MDY) ■ "." (ANSI) ■ "/" (British, French, DMY) ■ "." (German) ■ "-" (Italian) ■ "/" (Japan, YMD) ■ "-" (USA) A value of 0 specifies that the system should use the separator usually associated with the selected date format. The default is 0.

Microsoft FoxPro ISAM Formats

The Jet\3.0\ISAM Formats\FoxPro 2.0 folder contains the entries listed in the following table.

Entry	Type	Value
CanLink	Binary	01
CreateDBOnExport	Binary	00
Engine	String	Xbase
ExportFilter	String	Microsoft FoxPro 2.0 (*.dbf)
ImportFilter	String	Microsoft FoxPro (*.dbf)
IndexDialog	Binary	01
IndexFilter	String	Microsoft FoxPro Index (*.idx; *.cdx)
IsamType	DWORD	0
OneTablePerFile	Binary	01
ResultTextExport	String	Export data from the current database to a Microsoft FoxPro 2.0 file. This process will overwrite the data if it is exported to an existing file.
ResultTextImport	String	Import data from the external file into the current database. Changing data in the current database will not change data in the external file.
ResultTextLink	String	Create a table in the current database that is linked to the external file. Changing data in the current database will change data in the external file.

The Jet\3.0\ISAM Formats\FoxPro 2.5 folder contains the entries listed in the following table.

Entry	Type	Value
CanLink	Binary	01
CreateDBOnExport	Binary	00
Engine	String	Xbase
ExportFilter	String	Microsoft FoxPro 2.5 (*.dbf)
IndexDialog	Binary	01
IndexFilter	String	Microsoft FoxPro Index (*.idx; *.cdx)
IsamType	DWORD	0
OneTablePerFile	Binary	01
ResultTextExport	String	Export data from the current database to a Microsoft FoxPro 2.5 file. This process will overwrite the data if it is exported to an existing file.

The Jet\3.0\ISAM Formats\FoxPro 2.6 folder contains the entries listed in the following table.

Entry	Type	Value
CanLink	Binary	01
CreateDBOnExport	Binary	00
Engine	String	Xbase
ExportFilter	String	Microsoft FoxPro 2.6 (*.dbf)
IndexDialog	Binary	01
IndexFilter	String	Microsoft FoxPro Index (*.idx; *.cdx)
IsamType	DWORD	0
OneTablePerFile	Binary	01
ResultTextExport	String	Export data from the current database to a Microsoft FoxPro 2.6 file. This process will overwrite the data if it is exported to an existing file.

The Jet\3.0\ISAM Formats\FoxPro 3.0 folder contains the entries listed in the following table.

Entry	Type	Value
CanLink	Binary	00
CreateDBOnExport	Binary	00
Engine	String	Xbase
ExportFilter	String	Microsoft FoxPro 3.0 (*.dbf)
IndexDialog	Binary	01

Entry	Type	Value
IsamType	DWORD	0
OneTablePerFile	Binary	01
ResultTextExport	String	Export data from the current database to a Microsoft FoxPro 3.0 file. This process will overwrite the data if it is exported to an existing file.

The Jet\3.0\ISAM Formats\FoxPro 3.0 folder contains the entries listed in the following table.

Entry	Type	Value
CanLink	Binary	00
CreateDBOnExport	Binary	00
Engine	String	Xbase
ExportFilter	String	Microsoft FoxPro 3.0 (*.dbc)
IndexDialog	Binary	00
IsamType	DWORD	0
OneTablePerFile	Binary	00
ResultTextImport	String	Import data from the external file into the current database. Changing data in the current database will not change data in the external file.

dBASE Initialization Settings

The Jet\3.0\Engines\Xbase folder includes initialization settings for the Msxb3032.dll driver, which is used for access to external dBASE data sources.

The Microsoft Jet database engine uses the Xbase folder entries listed in the following table.

Entry	Type	Description
NetworkAccess	Binary	Binary indicator for file-locking preference. If NetworkAccess is set to 00, tables are opened for exclusive access, regardless of the settings of the *exclusive* argument for the **OpenDatabase** and **OpenRecordset** methods. The default value is 01.
PageTimeout	DWORD	Length of time between when data is placed in an internal cache and when it is invalidated. The value is specified in 100-millisecond units. The default is 600 units, or 60 seconds.
win32	String	Location of Msxb3032.dll. The full path is determined at the time of installation.

Entry	Type	Description
Century	Binary	Binary indicator for formatting the century component of dates in cases where date-to-string functions are used in index expressions. A value of 01 corresponds to the dBASE command SET CENTURY ON, and a value of 00 corresponds to the dBASE command SET CENTURY OFF. The default is 00.
CollatingSequence	String	Collating sequence for all dBASE tables created or opened using Microsoft Jet. Possible values are ASCII and International. The default is ASCII.
DataCodePage	String	Indicator of how text pages are stored. Possible settings are as follows: • OEM = OemToAnsi and AnsiToOem conversions done. • ANSI = OemToAnsi and AnsiToOem conversions not done. The default is OEM.
Date	String	Date formatting style to use in cases where date-to-string functions are used in index expressions. The possible settings for this entry, which corresponds to the dBASE SET DATE command, are American, ANSI, British, French, DMY, German, Italian, Japan, MDY, USA, and YMD. The default is MDY.
Deleted	Binary	Binary indicator that determines how records marked for deletion are handled by the Microsoft Jet database engine. A value of 01 corresponds to the dBASE command SET DELETED ON and indicates never to retrieve or position on a deleted record. A value of 00 corresponds to the dBASE command SET DELETED OFF and indicates to treat a deleted record like any other record. The default is 00.
INFPath	String	Full path to the .inf file folder. The Microsoft Jet database engine first looks for an .inf file in the folder containing the table. If the .inf file isn't in the database folder, the engine looks in the INFPath. If there is no INFPath, it uses whatever index files (.cdx or .mdx) it finds in the database folder. This entry is not written by the installation procedure.

Entry	Type	Description
Exact	Binary	Binary indicator for string comparisons. A value of 01 corresponds to the dBASE command SET EXACT ON. A value of 00 corresponds to the dBASE command SET EXACT OFF. The default is 00.
Mark	DWORD	Decimal value of the ASCII character used to separate date parts. The default depends on the Date setting as follows: • "/" (American, MDY) • "." (ANSI) • "/" (British, French, DMY) • "." (German) • "-" (Italian) • "/" (Japan, YMD) • "-" (USA) A value of 0 specifies that the system should use the separator usually associated with the selected date format. The default is 0.

dBASE ISAM Formats

The Jet\3.0\ISAM Formats\dBASE III folder contains the entries listed in the following table.

Entry	Type	Value
CanLink	Binary	01
CreateDBOnExport	Binary	00
Engine	String	Xbase
ExportFilter	String	dBASE III (*.dbf)
ImportFilter	String	dBASE III (*.dbf)
IndexDialog	Binary	01
IndexFilter	String	dBASE Index (*.ndx)
IsamType	DWORD	0
OneTablePerFile	Binary	01
ResultTextExport	String	Export data from the current database to a dBASE III file. This process will overwrite the data if it is exported to an existing file.
ResultTextImport	String	Import data from the external file to the current database. Changing data in the current database will not change data in the external file.
ResultTextLink	String	Create a table in the current database that is linked to the external file. Changing data in the current database will change data in the external file.

The Jet\3.0\ISAM Formats\dBASE IV folder contains the entries listed in the following table.

Entry	Type	Value
CanLink	Binary	01
CreateDBOnExport	Binary	00
Engine	String	Xbase
ExportFilter	String	dBASE IV (*.dbf)
ImportFilter	String	dBASE IV (*.dbf)
IndexDialog	Binary	01
IndexFilter	String	dBASE Index (*.ndx; *.mdx)
IsamType	DWORD	0
OneTablePerFile	Binary	01
ResultTextExport	String	Export data from the current database to a dBASE IV file. This process will overwrite the data if it is exported to an existing file.
ResultTextImport	String	Import data from the external file to the current database. Changing data in the current database will not change data in the external file.
ResultTextLink	String	Create a table in the current database that is linked to the external file. Changing data in the current database will change data in the external file.

The Jet\3.0\ISAM Formats\dBASE 5.*x* folder contains the entries listed in the following table.

Entry	Type	Value
CanLink	Binary	01
CreateDBOnExport	Binary	00
Engine	String	Xbase
ExportFilter	String	dBASE 5.0 (*.dbf)
ImportFilter	String	dBASE 5.0 (*.dbf)
IndexDialog	Binary	01
IndexFilter	String	dBASE Index (*.ndx; *.mdx)
IsamType	DWORD	0
OneTablePerFile	Binary	01
ResultTextExport	String	Export data from the current database to a dBASE 5 file. This process will overwrite the data if it is exported to an existing file.

Entry	Type	Value
ResultTextImport	String	Import data from the external file to the current database. Changing data in the current database will not change data in the external file.
ResultTextLink	String	Create a table in the current database that is linked to the external file. Changing data in the current database will change data in the external file.

Paradox Initialization Settings

The Jet\3.0\Engines\Paradox folder includes initialization settings for the Mspx3032.dll driver, which is used for access to external Paradox data.

The Microsoft Jet database engine uses the Paradox folder entries listed in the following table.

Entry	Type	Description
CollatingSequence	String	Collating sequence for all Paradox tables created or opened using Microsoft Jet. Possible values are ASCII, International, Norwegian-Danish, and Swedish-Finnish. The CollatingSequence entry must match the collating sequence used when the Paradox table was built. The default is ASCII.
DataCodePage	String	Indicator of how text pages are stored. Possible settings are as follows: • OEM = OemToAnsi and AnsiToOem conversions done. • ANSI = OemToAnsi and AnsiToOem conversions not done. The default is OEM.
PageTimeout	DWORD	Length of time between when data is placed in an internal cache and when it is invalidated. The value is specified in 100-millisecond units. The default is 600 units, or 60 seconds.
ParadoxNetPath	String	Full path to the folder containing the Paradox.net file (for Paradox 3.x) or the Pdoxusrs.net file (for Paradox 4.x). This entry isn't added if the computer isn't on a network. Usually, you need to change the initial setting (added by the Setup program), which is a best guess at where the file might be. The full ParadoxNetPath (including the drive letter) must be consistent for all users sharing a particular database (folder). **Note:** If you indicate a ParadoxNetPath, you must also specify a ParadoxUserName and a ParadoxNetStyle or you'll receive an error when you try to access external Paradox data.

Entry	Type	Description
ParadoxNetStyle	String	The network access style to use when accessing Paradox data. Possible values are 3.*x* and 4.*x*.
		Paradox 3.*x* users cannot set this to 4.*x*; if they do, the driver will use the wrong locking method. Paradox 5.0 users must use the 4.*x* ParadoxNetStyle setting to ensure proper locking behavior.
		This entry isn't added if the computer isn't on a network. This entry should correspond to whatever version of Paradox the users in the group are using. It must be consistent for all users sharing a particular database (folder). The default is 4.*x*.
		Note: If you indicate a ParadoxNetStyle, you must also specify a ParadoxUserName and a ParadoxNetPath or you'll receive an error when you try to access external Paradox data.
ParadoxUserName	String	Name to be displayed by Paradox if a table is locked by the Paradox ISAM and an interactive user accessing the data from Paradox (rather than from Microsoft Access) attempts to place an incompatible lock. This entry isn't added if the computer isn't on a network.
		Note: If you indicate a ParadoxUserName, you must also specify a ParadoxNetPath and a ParadoxNetStyle or you'll receive an error when you try to access external Paradox data.
win32	String	Location of Mspx3032.dll. The full path is determined at the time of installation.

Network Paths for Paradox

When you link or open a Paradox table that resides on a server and is shared by multiple users, you must set the ParadoxNetPath option in the Jet\3.0\Engines\Paradox directory of the Windows registry to the path for either the Paradox.net file (for Paradox 3.*x*) or the Pdoxusrs.net file (for Paradox 4.*x*).

Important The ParadoxNetPath, including the drive letter, must be consistent for all users sharing a particular database (folder). For example, if the Paradox.net file is in the Wrkgrp folder on drive Q for one user of the database, it must be in the Wrkgrp folder on drive Q for all other users of the database.

Paradox ISAM Formats

The Jet\3.0\ISAM Formats\Paradox 3.*x* folder contains the entries listed in the following table.

Entry	Type	Value
CanLink	Binary	01
CreateDBOnExport	Binary	00
Engine	String	Paradox
ExportFilter	String	Paradox 3 (*.db)
ImportFilter	String	Paradox (*.db)
IndexDialog	Binary	00
IsamType	DWORD	0
OneTablePerFile	Binary	01
ResultTextExport	String	Export data from the current database to a Paradox 3 file. This process will overwrite the data if it is exported to an existing file.
ResultTextImport	String	Import data from the external file to the current database. Changing data in the current database will not change data in the external file.
ResultTextLink	String	Create a table in the current database that is linked to the external file. Changing data in the current database will change data in the external file.

The Jet\3.0\ISAM Formats\Paradox 4.*x* folder contains the entries listed in the following table.

Entry	Type	Value
CanLink	Binary	01
CreateDBOnExport	Binary	00
Engine	String	Paradox
ExportFilter	String	Paradox 4 (*.db)
IndexDialog	Binary	00
IsamType	DWORD	0
OneTablePerFile	Binary	01
ResultTextExport	String	Export data from the current database to a Paradox 4 file. This process will overwrite the data if it is exported to an existing file.

The Jet\3.0\ISAM Formats\Paradox 5.*x* folder contains the entries listed in the following table.

Entry	Type	Value
CanLink	Binary	01
CreateDBOnExport	Binary	00
Engine	String	Paradox
ExportFilter	String	Paradox 5 (*.db)
IndexDialog	Binary	00
IsamType	DWORD	0
OneTablePerFile	Binary	01
ResultTextExport	String	Export data from the current database to a Paradox 5 file. This process will overwrite the data if it is exported to an existing file.

Lotus Initialization Settings

The Jet\3.0\Engines\Lotus folder includes initialization settings for the Mslt3032.dll driver, which is used for external access to Lotus spreadsheets.

The Microsoft Jet database engine uses the Lotus folder entries listed in the following table.

Entry	Type	Description
AppendBlankRows	DWORD	Number of blank rows to be appended to the end of a WK1 worksheet before new data is added. For example, if AppendBlankRows is set to 4, Microsoft Jet will append four blank rows to the end of the worksheet before appending rows that contain data. Integer values for this setting can range from 0 to 16; the default is 0 (no additional rows appended).
FirstRowHasNames	Binary	Indicates whether the first row of the table contains column names. A value of 01 indicates that, during import, column names are taken from the first row. A value of 00 indicates that there are no column names in the first row; column names appear as F1, F2, F3, and so on. The default is 01.
ImportMixedTypes	String	Can be set to MajorityType or Text. If set to MajorityType, columns of mixed data types will be cast to the predominant data type on import. If set to Text, columns of mixed data types will be cast to Text on import. The default is Text.

Entry	Type	Description
TypeGuessRows	DWORD	Number of rows to be checked for the data type. The data type is determined based on the most frequently found data type in the selection. If there is a tie, the data type is determined in the following order: Number, Currency, Date, Text, Long Text. If data is encountered that does not match the data type guessed for the column, it is returned as a **Null** value. On import, if a column has mixed data types, the entire column will be converted according to the ImportMixedTypes setting. The default number of rows to be checked is 8.
win32	String	Location of Mslt032.dll. The full path is determined at the time of installation.

Lotus ISAM Formats

The Jet\3.0\ISAM Formats\Lotus WK1 folder contains the entries listed in the following table.

Entry	Type	Value
CanLink	Binary	00
CreateDBOnExport	Binary	01
Engine	String	Lotus
ExportFilter	String	Lotus 1-2-3 WK1 (*.wk1)
ImportFilter	String	Lotus 1-2-3 WK1 (*.wk*)
IndexDialog	Binary	00
IsamType	DWORD	1
OneTablePerFile	Binary	00
ResultTextExport	String	Export data from the current database to a Lotus 1-2-3 version 2 file. This process will overwrite the data if it is exported to an existing file.
ResultTextImport	String	Import data from the external file to the current database. Changing data in the current database will not change data in the external file.

The Jet\3.0\ISAM Formats\Lotus WK3 folder contains the entries listed in the following table.

Entry	Type	Value
CanLink	Binary	00
CreateDBOnExport	Binary	01
Engine	String	Lotus

Entry	Type	Value
ExportFilter	String	Lotus 1-2-3 WK3 (*.wk3)
IndexDialog	Binary	00
IsamType	DWORD	1
OneTablePerFile	Binary	00
ResultTextExport	String	Export data from the current database to a Lotus 1-2-3 version 3 file. This process will overwrite the data if it is exported to an existing file.

The Jet\3.0\ISAM Formats\Lotus WK4 folder contains the entries listed in the following table.

Entry	Type	Value
CanLink	Binary	00
CreateDBOnExport	Binary	01
Engine	String	Lotus
IndexDialog	Binary	00
IsamType	DWORD	1
OneTablePerFile	Binary	00

Text Data Source Initialization Settings

The Jet\3.0\Engines\Text folder includes initialization settings for the Mstx3032.dll driver, which is used for external access to text data files.

The Microsoft Jet database engine uses the Text folder entries listed in the following table.

Entry	Type	Description
FirstRowHas Names	Binary	Indicates whether the first row of the table contains column names. A value of 01 indicates that, during import, column names are taken from the first row. A value of 00 indicates that there are no column names in the first row. The default is 01.
MaxScanRows	DWORD	Number of rows to be scanned when guessing the column types. If set to 0, the entire file will be searched. The default is 25.
win32	String	Location of Mstx3032.dll. The full path is determined at the time of installation.

Entry	Type	Description
CharacterSet	String	Indicator of how text pages are stored. Possible settings are as follows: • OEM = OemToAnsi and AnsiToOem conversions done. • ANSI = OemToAnsi and AnsiToOem conversions not done. The default is OEM.
ExportCurrencySymbols	Binary	Indicates whether the appropriate currency symbol is included when currency fields are exported. A value of 01 indicates that the symbol is included. A value of 00 indicates that only the numeric data is exported. The default is 01.
Extensions	String	Extension of whatever files are to be browsed when you're looking for text-based data. The default is .txt, .csv, .tab, or .asc.
Format	String	Can be any of the following: TabDelimited, CSVDelimited, Delimited (<single character >). The single-character delimiter in the Delimited format can be any single character except a double quotation mark ("). The default is CSVDelimited.

Text Data Source ISAM Formats

The Jet\3.0\ISAM Formats\Text folder contains the entries listed in the following table.

Entry	Type	Value
CanLink	Binary	01
CreateDBOnExport	Binary	00
Engine	String	Text
ExportFilter	String	Text Files (*.txt; *.csv; *.tab; *.asc)
ImportFilter	String	Text Files (*.txt; *.csv; *.tab; *.asc)
IndexDialog	Binary	00
IsamType	DWORD	2
OneTablePerFile	Binary	01
ResultTextExport	String	Export data from the current database to a text file. This process will overwrite the data if it is exported to an existing file.

Entry	Type	Value
ResultTextImport	String	Import data from the external file into the current database. Changing data in the current database will not change data in the external file.
ResultTextLink	String	Create a table in the current database that is linked to the external file. Changing data in the current database will change data in the external file.

Microsoft ODBC Driver Initialization Settings

The following section describes initialization settings for the Microsoft ODBC database driver. These registry settings must be added manually; the Setup program does not write default values to the \Hkey_Local_Machine\Software\Microsoft\Access\7.0\Jet\3.0\Engines\ODBC folder.

The \Hkey_Local_Machine\Software\Microsoft\Access\7.0\Jet\3.0\Engines\ODBC folder stores initialization settings for the Microsoft Jet database engine.

The Jet database engine uses the ODBC entries listed in the following table.

Entry	Type	Description
AsyncRetryInterval	DWORD	Number of milliseconds between polls to determine whether the server is finished processing a query. This entry is used only for asynchronous processing. The default is 500.
AttachableObjects	String	List of server object types to which linking will be allowed. The default is: 'TABLE', 'VIEW', 'SYSTEM TABLE', 'ALIAS', 'SYNONYM'.
AttachCaseSensitive	DWORD	Indicator of whether to match table names exactly when linking. Values are 0 (link the first table matching the specified name, regardless of case) and 1 (link a table only if the name matches exactly). The default is 0.
ConnectionTimeout	DWORD	Number of seconds a cached connection can remain idle before timing out. The default is 600.
DisableAsync	DWORD	Indicator of whether to force synchronous query execution. Values are 0 (use asynchronous query execution if possible) and 1 (force synchronous query execution). The default is 0.
FastRequery	DWORD	Indicator of whether to use a prepared SELECT statement for parameterized queries. Values are 0 (no) and 1 (yes). The default is 0.

Entry	Type	Description
JetTryAuth	DWORD	Indicator of whether to try using the Microsoft Access user name and password to log on to the server before prompting. Values are 0 (no) and 1 (yes). The default is 1.
LoginTimeout	DWORD	Number of seconds a logon attempt can continue before timing out. The default is 20.
PreparedInsert	DWORD	Indicator of whether to use a prepared INSERT statement that inserts data in all columns. Values are 0 (use a custom INSERT statement that inserts only non-**Null** values) and 1 (use a prepared INSERT statement). The default is 0. Using prepared INSERT statements can cause **Nulls** to overwrite server defaults and can cause triggers to execute on columns that weren't inserted explicitly.
PreparedUpdate	DWORD	Indicator of whether to use a prepared UPDATE statement that updates data in all columns. Values are 0 (use a custom UPDATE statement that sets only columns that have changed) and 1 (use a prepared UPDATE statement). The default is 0. Using prepared UPDATE statements can cause triggers to execute on unchanged columns.
QueryTimeout	DWORD	Number of seconds (total processing time) a query can run before timing out. The default is 60.
SnapshotOnly	DWORD	Indicator of whether **Recordset** objects are forced to be of the snapshot type. Values are 0 (allow dynasets) and 1 (force snapshots only). The default is 0.
TraceODBCAPI	DWORD	Indicator of whether to trace ODBC API calls in Odbcapi.txt. Values are 0 (no) and 1 (yes). The default is 0.
TraceSQLMode	DWORD	Indicator of whether the Jet database engine will trace SQL statements sent to an ODBC data source in Sqlout.txt. Values are 0 (no) and 1 (yes). The default is 0. This entry is interchangeable with SQLTraceMode.

Microsoft Excel Registry Keys and Values

This section covers the registry keys and values for Microsoft Excel. If you need to change these values, use the Registry Editor (follow the procedure given earlier in this chapter).

Microsoft Excel Key

The following sections describe the values contained in the Microsoft Excel key.

AltStartup

The AltStartup value is a string that specifies the alternate startup folder. When you start Microsoft Excel, files located in the Xlstart folder are loaded automatically, followed by files located in the alternate startup folder.

AutoCalculate (new for version 7.0)

This value is a DWORD that stores an index to the AutoCalculation function. The values are as listed in the following table.

Value	Function
0	Count Nums
4	Sum
5	Average
6	Min
7	Max
169	Count

AutoFormat and AutoFormat Options

The AutoFormat and AutoFormat Options values are DWORD values that specify the default formatting choice to be used when the AutoFormat toolbar button is clicked.

The AutoFormat value stores an index number that points to a format. The format indexes are numbered 1 through 14, corresponding to the order in which they appear in the list in the AutoFormat dialog box.

The AutoFormat Options value controls which formatting attributes are applied for the format specified in the AutoFormat value. The formatting attributes correspond to the options in the AutoFormat dialog box. The values for the formatting attributes are listed in the following table.

AutoFormat option	Indicates
1	Number
2	Font
4	Alignment
8	Border
16	Patterns
32	Width/Height

For example, if the AutoFormat Options value is 10, the font and border properties of a format are applied. The number 10 is the sum of 2 (font) and 8 (border). The default value for AutoFormat Options is 63—the sum of all of the numbers—indicating that all of the formatting properties are applied.

AutoDec

Auto Decimal places.

Basics (new for version 7.0)

The Setup program writes a 0 (zero) to this DWORD value, which tells Microsoft Excel to display the What's New topic the first time you start the application. When you dismiss the What's New topic, Microsoft Excel writes a 1 to this value, which prevents the What's New topic from being displayed again.

CFDDELink

The CFDDELink value is a DWORD. If the CFDDELink value is set to 1, Microsoft Excel remembers the last clipboard format used for a successful DDE operation; this is used to reduce the time required for future DDE operations.

Default Chart

The Default Chart value is a string that specifies the name of the default chart format. This value stores the setting from the Chart tab in the Options dialog box. The actual default chart formats are saved as chart sheets in a workbook called Xl5galry.xls, in the Xlstart folder.

DefaultPath

The DefaultPath value is a string that specifies the fully qualified path to the default file location. This value stores the Default File Location setting from the General tab in the Options dialog box.

DefSheets

The DefSheets value is a DWORD that specifies the number of new worksheets in each new workbook. For example, if DefSheets is 1, then when you create a new workbook it will contain one worksheet. This value stores the setting from the General tab in the Options dialog box.

Font

The Font value is a string that stores the default font and font size for new worksheets. For example, to specify that the default font is 10-point Arial, the value would be as follows:

```
Arial,10
```

The font name must be the name of the font spelled exactly as it appears in the Font box on the Font tab in the Format Cells dialog box. The FONT value sets the default font used for the Normal style and for row and column headings.

G1Dft-DemoSpd and G1Dft-HelpType

These two values are DWORD values that correspond to options on the Transition tab in the Options dialog box.

If G1Dft-HelpType is 0, this indicates that you want Help for Lotus 1-2-3 Users to display a set of instructions. If G1Dft-HelpType is 1, this indicates that you want Help for Lotus 1-2-3 Users to give a demonstration for the Lotus 1-2-3 commands that the user types.

The G1Dft-DemoSpd value controls the speed of the demonstration when the G1Dft-HelpType option is 1. This can be a number from 1 to 5, where 1 is slow and 5 is fast.

Maximized and Pos

The Maximized value is a DWORD that indicates the size of the application window and the size of the workbook window when you start Microsoft Excel. Bit 0 controls the size of the application window, and bit 1 controls the size of the workbook window, as shown in the following table.

Maximized	Indicates
0	Application window size and position are set by the Pos value; workbook window is slightly smaller than the available space.
1	Application window fills the screen; workbook window is slightly smaller than the available space.
2	Application window size and position are set by the Pos value; workbook window fills the available space below the toolbars.
3	Application window fills the screen; workbook window fills the available space below the toolbars.

The Pos value is a string that contains window coordinates for the application window when it is not maximized. The first two coordinates set the distance from the left and top of the screen to the top-left corner of the window, respectively. The third coordinate is the window width, and the fourth coordinate is the window height. All coordinates are in points.

The following tables show typical values for Maximized and Pos as they would appear in the Registry Editor. In this example, the application window is not maximized and the workbook window is maximized.

Name	Data
Maximized	0x00000002 (2)
Pos	"28,22,480,321"

MenuKey

The MenuKey value is a DWORD that indicates the ASCII value corresponding to the character used to activate Microsoft Excel menus or help. The default is the forward slash (/), which corresponds to the menu key for Lotus 1-2-3. For example, if you changed the menu key on the Transition tab in the Options dialog box to the backslash (\) key, the MenuKey value would be 92.

MoveEnterDir (new for version 7.0)

This value is a DWORD that stores the setting of the Move Selection After Enter Direction option on the Edit tab in the Options dialog box. The values are shown in the following table.

Value	Indicates
0	Down
1	Right
2	Up
3	Left

MRUFuncs

The MRUFuncs value specifies the functions that appear in the most recently used list in the Function Wizard. The functions are stored as their function index number (iftab).

OPEN

You can use OPEN string values to specify workbooks that you want opened automatically at startup. The first OPEN name is OPEN, the second is OPEN1, the third is OPEN2, and so on. The OPEN string contains the full path to the file to open, and the filename must be enclosed in double quotation marks. When you view the OPEN value in the Registry Editor, the filename will have two sets of double quotation marks.

The Add-In Manager (the Add-Ins command on the Tools menu) reads and writes OPEN values. For example, when you select the check box to the left of the Analysis ToolPak add-in, Microsoft Excel writes a string in an OPEN value when it quits; this string h is similar to the following:

```
/R "C:\OFFICE95\EXCEL\LIBRARY\ANALYSIS\ANALYS32.XLL"
```

The /R switch is described in the following section.

Option Switches for the OPEN Value

You can use the /R and /F option switches, alone or together, to modify the behavior of the OPEN value. The /R option switch opens the file as read-only. The /F (fast load) option switch places template workbooks in the New dialog box (File menu).

When you install an add-in that contains demand-loaded custom functions, there will be an OPEN value that points to the add-in workbook, and it will contain the /F switch. Demand loading means that when Microsoft Excel starts, it reads only enough information from the add-in workbook file to establish references to the custom functions in the add-in. These functions are added to the list in the Function Wizard and can be entered on a worksheet. However, the add-in is not fully loaded until one of its custom functions is recalculated.

The /F switch is added to the filename string when the name __DemandLoad (the string "DemandLoad" preceded by two underscores) is defined somewhere in the add-in workbook. For more information about add-ins, see the *Microsoft Excel Visual Basic for Windows 95 Programmer's Guide,* available from Microsoft Press. You can order any Microsoft Press book by calling Microsoft Press at 1-800-MSPRESS (1-800-677-7377).

Options, Options3, Options5, and Options95

Each of these four values contains 16 flag bits that are expressed as a DWORD in the registry. After a new installation of Microsoft Excel, the Options value does not appear in the registry. When you change one of the default settings stored in the Options value, Microsoft Excel will write the value to the registry. The flag bits are used as shown in the following table.

Options

Options	Indicates
bit 0	Show scroll bars.
bit 1	Show formula bar.
bit 2	Show status bar.
bit 3	(Reserved.)
bit 4	Use A1-style references.
bit 5	(Reserved.)

Options	Indicates
bit 6	DDE is enabled.
bits 7 and 8	Apple Macintosh command underlines.
bits 9–15	(Reserved.)

Options3

Options3	Indicates
bit 0	(Reserved.)
bit 1	Alternate navigation keys are on.
bit 2	Lotus 1-2-3 Help is on.
bit 3	Cell note indicators are off.
bit 4	(Reserved.)
bit 5	Macros are saved in the Personal Macro Workbook.
bits 6–13	(Reserved.)
bit 14	Gridlines in new sheets are off.
bit 15	(Reserved.)

Options5

Options5	Indicates
bit 0	Tip Wizard is on.
bit 1	Prompt for Summary Info.
bit 2	Editing directly in cells is not allowed.
bit 3	Status bar is visible in full-screen mode.
bit 4	Formula bar is visible in full-screen mode.
bit 5	Full-screen mode.
bit 6	Most recently used file list is not displayed.
bit 7	Cut, copy, and sort objects with cells.
bit 8	Tool tips are off.
bit 9	Small toolbar buttons.
bit 10	Toolbar autosensing.
bit 11	Do not move to next cell after ENTER is pressed.
bit 12	Do not warn before drag-and-drop copy or paste.
bit 13	Use black-and-white toolbar buttons.
bit 14	Ask to update automatic links.

Options95 (new for version 7.0)

Options95	Indicates
bit 0	AutoComplete is on.
bit 1	Cell animation is on.
bits 2–15	(Reserved.)

Randomize

If you want Microsoft Excel to generate a unique set of random numbers each time you use the RAND function, set Randomize to 1.

StickyPtX and StickyPtY

StickyPtX and StickyPtY indicate the preferred location where you want dialog boxes to appear on the screen: They are updated every time you quit Microsoft Excel.

User

The User value is a string that stores the User Name option on the General tab in the Options dialog box.

Summary of the Values in the Microsoft Excel Key

The following table contains a summary list of the values described in this section.

Entry	Type
AltStartup	String
AutoCalculate	DWORD
AutoDec	
AutoFormat	DWORD
AutoFormat Options	DWORD
CFDDELink	DWORD
Default Chart	String
DefaultPath	String
DefSheets	DWORD
Font	String
G1Dft-DemoSpd	DWORD
G1Dft-HelpType	DWORD
Maximized	DWORD
MenuKey	DWORD
MoveEnterDir	DWORD

Entry	Type
MRUFuncs	String
OPEN	String
Options	DWORD
Options3	DWORD
Options5	DWORD
Options95	DWORD
Pos	String
Randomize	DWORD
StickyPtX	DWORD
StickyPtY	DWORD
User	String

Spell Checker Key

The Spell Checker key contains the values listed in the following table.

Entry	Type	Description
Custom Dict	String	Path to custom dictionaries (there can be more than one custom dictionary). For Windows NT, all custom dictionaries must be placed in the Msapps\Proof subfolder of your Windows folder. For Windows 95 (with long filename support), all custom dictionaries must be placed in the \Program Files\Microsoft Shared\Proof folder.
Ignore Caps	DWORD	State of the Ignore Caps check box; 1 = checked.
Speller	String	See the following section.
Suggest Always	DWORD	State of the Suggest check box; 1 = checked.

The Speller value is a string that includes two arguments—Country Code and Dictionary Type—separated by a backslash. Country Code specifies the proper spelling tool to use with the corresponding language version of Microsoft Excel. The following table shows the various country codes.

Country code	Language
1030	Danish
1031	German
1033	U.S. English
1034	Spanish
1036	French
1040	Italian

Country code	Language
1043	Dutch
1044	Norwegian
1054	Swedish
2057	British English
2070	Portuguese
3081	Australian English

The Dictionary Type argument refers to five possible types of dictionaries that can be used by the speller. Microsoft Excel always uses type 0 (Normal). The five dictionary types are Normal, Concise (subset of Normal), Complete (includes Medical and Legal), Medical, and Legal.

Init Menus Key

The Init Menus key contains one string value for each menu that is added to a built-in menu bar. Each value name is a unique tag that identifies the added menu. The string has the following form:

menu_bar_num,menu_name,menu_position

Argument	Description
menu_bar_num	Number of the built-in menu bar to which you want to add the menu. The menu bars change, depending on the type of sheet that is active in the workbook. The menu bar numbers are as follows: 3 Nil menu bar (no open workbooks) 10 Worksheet, dialog sheet, version 4.0 macro sheet 11 Chart sheet 12 Visual Basic module
menu_name	Name of the new menu.
menu_position	Position of the new menu on the menu bar. This may be the name of the menu after which you want to place the new menu, or a number indicating the menu's position from the left end of the menu bar.

Init Commands Key

The Init Menus key contains one string value for each command that is added to a menu. Each value name is a unique tag that identifies the added command. The string has the following form:

menu_bar_num,menu_name,command_name,macro,command_position,
↳ *macro_key,status_text,help_reference*

Argument	Description
menu_bar_num	Number of the built-in menu bar to which you want to add the new menu. The menu bars change, depending on the type of sheet that is active in the workbook. The menu bar numbers are as follows:
	3 Nil menu bar (no open workbooks) 10 Worksheet, dialog sheet, version 4 0 macro sheet 11 Chart sheet 12 Visual Basic module
menu_name	Name of the new menu.
command_name	Name of the new command.
macro	Reference to a procedure in an add-in workbook. Choosing the command opens the add-in and runs this procedure. The procedure should delete the command added by this registry key and then replace it with a command that runs a procedure that performs the command actions.
command_position	Position of the command on the menu. This may be the name of the command after which you want to place the new command, or a number indicating the command's position on the menu. If omitted, the command appears at the end of the menu.
macro_key	Key assigned to the procedure, if any.
status_text	Message to be displayed in the status bar when the command is selected.
help_reference	Filename and topic number for a custom Help topic for the command.

Delete Commands Key

You can use the Delete Commands key to delete commands from built-in menus. The Add-In Manager (Add-Ins command on the Tools menu) reads and writes values in the Delete Commands key. The key contains one string value for each command that is deleted from a menu. Each value name is a unique tag that identifies the deleted command. The string has the following form:

menu_bar_num,menu_name,command_position

Argument	Description
menu_bar_num	Number of the built-in menu bar that contains the menu from which you want to delete the command. The menu bars change, depending on the type of sheet that is active in the workbook. The menu bar numbers are as follows:
	3 Nil menu bar (no open workbooks)
	10 Worksheet, dialog sheet, version 4.0 macro sheet
	11 Chart sheet
	12 Visual Basic module
menu_name	Name of the menu.
command_position	Position of the command on the menu. This may be the name of the command or a number indicating the command's position on the menu.

Caution Don't delete the Exit command from the File menu unless you've created another way to quit Microsoft Excel!

Recent File List Key

The Recent File List key contains a string value for each of the four most recently used files, which are listed at the bottom of the File menu. The list is updated each time the user quits Microsoft Excel. The string values appear in the Registry Editor, as shown in the following table.

Value name	Data
File1	"C:\Accounting\Closing statement.xls"
File2	"D:\Monthly\January Sales.xls"
File3	"C:\Office95\Excel\scratch.xls"
File4	"\\Corp\public\assets\real\1995 depreciation.xls"

Add-In Manager Key

This key contains one string value for each add-in that the user installed but later disabled. The string value is the full path and filename of the add-in. When an add-in is installed and enabled, the add-in name appears in the Add-Ins dialog box, and the check box to the left of the name is checked. When the user clears the check box, the add-in is considered to be installed but disabled.

Installed and enabled add-ins cause Microsoft Excel to write an OPEN value to the Microsoft Excel key when the program quits (see "Microsoft Excel Key" in the preceding section). If an add-in is installed and disabled, the OPEN value is removed, and then a corresponding string value is written in the Add-In Manager key.

Converters Key

This key contains the description and .dll location of external file converters, such as the Microsoft Multiplan converter. Each value name is a unique tag that identifies the converter, and each string value has the following form:

Friendly description,DLL filename and path,search filter

Token	Description
Friendly description	Text that appears in the List Files Of Type box in the Open dialog box.
DLL filename and path	Filename and path of the converter DLL. If you omit the path, the .dll file must be in the same folder as Excel.exe.
Search filter	File filter string—for example, *.xl*.

WK? Settings Key

This key contains values that control settings for opening and saving Lotus 1-2-3 files; these values are listed in the following table.

Name	Type	Description
AFE	String	Controls whether Transition Formula Entry (AFE) is on. A value of 2 is used as the default, indicating that AFE is turned on only if a macro name exists on the Lotus 1-2-3 worksheet. Otherwise, a value of 1 causes AFE to always be turned on, whereas a value of 0 causes AFE to be never turned on.
Gridlines	String	If Gridlines=1, gridlines are displayed when a Lotus 1-2-3 worksheet is opened. If Gridlines=0, gridlines are not displayed.

Name	Type	Description
Load_Chart_Wnd	String	If Load_Chart_Wnd=1, Lotus 1-2-3 graphs are converted into Microsoft Excel chart sheets. If Load_Chart_Wnd=0, Lotus 1-2-3 graphs are converted into embedded charts.
Monospace	String	If Monospace=1, Lotus 1-2-3 worksheets are displayed in Microsoft Excel using a monospace font (10-point Courier). If Monospace=0, the Normal style is used.

Line Print Key

This key contains values that control settings used in Lotus 1-2-3 macro line printing. These settings are defined using the various Lotus 1-2-3 Worksheet Global Default Printer (/wgdp) commands and are updated in the registry whenever Microsoft Excel encounters a Lotus 1-2-3 Worksheet Global Default Update (/wgdu) command.

The LeftMarg, RightMarg, TopMarg, and BotMarg values are strings that contain the respective margin settings. The data for LeftMarg and RightMarg refers to numbers of characters. While these two values can be from 0 to 1000, a standard page is 80 characters wide. The data for TopMarg and BotMarg refers to numbers of lines. Although these two values can be from 0 to 240, standard 11-inch-high paper can accommodate a maximum of 66 lines. The number of lines on the page is given by the PgLen string value.

The Setup value is equivalent to the Lotus 1-2-3 Worksheet Global Default Printer Settings (/wgdps) command; it specifies the printer setup string.

The Options value contains 6 bits cast to a decimal number, and it is stored as a string. The following table lists the bits used in the Options value.

Bit	Lotus 1-2-3 /wgdp command
0	Wait
1	Formatted
2	AutoLf
3-5	Port (0 through 7)

The best way to determine the appropriate decimal number to use with the Options value is to construct the binary number first and then convert it to a decimal value. The default value is Options=2—or, in binary, 0000 0010— meaning that bit 1 is set but all the others are cleared.

Bits 3, 4, and 5 indicate the setting used by Lotus 1-2-3 to specify the hardware port used for printing. Microsoft Excel interprets this value as a logical port. The default port setting is LPT1:, which corresponds to bits 3, 4, and 5 being equal to 0 (zero). These port settings are listed in the following table.

Bits 3–5	Port
000	LPT1:
001	COM1:
010	LPT2:
011	COM2:
100	LPT1:
101	LPT2:
110	LPT3:
111	LPT4:

Note that LPT1: and LPT2: are each represented twice. Either combination of bits can be used; the results will be the same.

Microsoft Office Registry Keys and Values

This section includes the registry keys and values for mail support, WordMail, Notes/FX support, Office Shortcut Bar settings, and template settings.

Office Mail Support Settings in the Windows Registry

The following section describes the registry values that support Office mail capabilities.

MapiDLL

This key, located in Hkey_Local_Machine\Software\Microsoft\Microsoft Office\95, determines which e-mail system the Office applications use. You can set this key from an .stf file. Change this setting if you upgrade to a new e-mail system.

This key has a single value, DLL32, which is a string that specifies the path of the DLL that provides MAPI support. Some possible settings are given in the following table.

Setting	Function
Mapi32.dll (or entry missing from registry)	Support for Microsoft Exchange, provided with Windows 95. Use this setting with any 32-bit simple MAPI or MAPI 1.0-based e-mail system.
Mapivi32.dll	Support for 16-bit VIM mail systems, including cc:Mail and Lotus Notes Mail.

WordMail Support Settings in the Windows Registry

The following section describes the registry values that support Office mail capabilities.

Stationery

The Stationery keyword in Hkey_Current_User\Software\Microsoft\Word\7.0 has the settings shown in the following table. All settings can be modified from an .stf file and must be present for the WordMail Options dialog box to work correctly.

Setting	Function
Cfg File Location	Provides the path to the WordMail configuration file.
Default Template	Provides the path to the default template to use for WordMail messages, email.dot.
DlgDefTpl	Records the default template setting made using the WordMail Options dialog box.
Option	Index number of the last template used to compose a message, or the default template Email.lnk in the WordMail folder, if present.

Options

The Wordmail-Path setting under the Options keyword in Hkey_Current_User\Software\Microsoft\Word\7.0 provides the path to the WordMail program folder, a subfolder of the Word folder. This setting can be modified from an .stf file. Other settings in this keyword do not apply to WordMail. For information about these settings, see "Microsoft Word Registry Keys and Values" later in this appendix.

WordMail

The WordMail keyword in Hkey_Current_User\Software\Microsoft\Word\7.0 provides a Window setting that records the size and position of the WordMail window. This setting is self-registering.

Extensions

Two settings under the Extensions keyword in Hkey_Local_Machine\Software\Microsoft\Exchange\Client provide information that the Microsoft Exchange client needs to run WordMail. These settings are shown in the following table.

Setting	Function
Stationery	Provides the version, path, and other information about Station.dll, which provides the WordMail stationery (template).
Wordmail	Provides the version, path, and other information about Wordmail.dll, which provides WordMail capability to the Microsoft Exchange client software.

Other settings in this keyword do not apply to WordMail. For information about these settings, see the Microsoft Exchange documentation.

Notes/FX Support Settings in the Windows Registry

The following settings are provided for Notes/FX support. The Office Setup program enters them automatically. They can be set from an .stf file.

NoteshNote

This setting supports the NoteshNote clipboard format for each Office application, as in the following:

```
Hkey_Classes_Root\Clsid\<ID>\DataFormats\GetSet\<n> = NoteshNote,-1,1,1
```

In the above entry, <ID> is the class ID number for the application, and <n> is the next available number.

RequestDataFormats

This setting enables the NoteshNote clipboard format, as in the following:

```
Hkey_Classes_Root\<Object>\Protocol\StdFileEditing\
↳ RequestDataFormats=NoteshNote
```

In this entry, <Object> is the version-dependent program ID.

Office Shortcut Bar Settings in the Windows Registry

Office 95 no longer uses .ini files. When previous versions of Office are updated, buttons included in Msoffice.ini are migrated to the Old Office toolbar, as described in "Upgrading Previous Versions of Microsoft Office Manager" in Chapter 10. After the upgrade is complete, the older .ini file has no further effect on Office 95.

The following sections describe the keys contained under Office Shortcut Bar in the Windows 95 registry. These settings are all self-registering except for the toolbar root, which is established by Office Setup.

Position

The key Hkey_Current_User\Software\Microsoft\Office Shortcut Bar\Position has subkeys that represent the different coordinates for the Office Shortcut Bar when it is undocked (when the user double-clicks in the title bar). This key is self-registering.

Toolbar Root

The key Hkey_Current_User\Software\Microsoft\Office Shortcut Bar\Toolbar Root contains the path to the root folder for the toolbars. By default, this is the Msoffice\Office\Shortcut Bar folder. This key is set by the Setup program and is not self-registering.

Toolbars

To allow easy addition of applications to the Office Shortcut Bar, the Windows 95 registry contains the folder location for toolbars. Each toolbar is described by a set of values under the Hkey_Current_User\Software\Microsoft\Office Shortcut Bar\Toolbars key.

Each toolbar has the settings listed in the following table.

Setting	Values
Default	Not used.
Buttons	Binary data defining the buttons on the toolbar.
Face	String providing the path to a file containing an icon to use for the selector button and the icon number within that file to use. The path can be relative or fully qualified—for example, "msow.exe", 2
Path	A string providing the path to the underlying folder containing the files and folders to be displayed as buttons on the toolbar. The path can be fully qualified or can contain the special strings [Office] to indicate that the path is rooted below the Msoffice\Office\Shortcut Bar folder.

The value for the Buttons setting is data that has the following format:

```
[RGB][%][button][NULL][%][separator][NULL][%][button2][NULL][NULL]
↳ [Position][Rows][Hidden]
```

The elements of this data are listed in the following table.

Element	Contains
RGB	A 3-byte color value for the toolbar.
%	Either an * for hidden buttons or a space for visible buttons.
buttons	For each button, the exact name of the file it represents, including the .lnk extension for shortcuts.
separator	The \ character, always preceded by a space.
NULL	The ASCII 0 character, which follows each button string. Two NULLs follow the last button string.

Element	Contains
Position	A word indicating the position of this toolbar within the list of toolbars. Note that this is in little-endian ordering; to specify position, enter 04 00 as the word value.
Rows	A word indicating the default number of rows for the toolbar when not docked. Rows is optional, the default value is 04 00 (four rows).
Hidden	A word: 01 00 for hidden, 00 00 for visible.

When you add buttons to toolbars or add new toolbars to the Office Shortcut Bar, consider the user's need for access to the default buttons and toolbars. You might want to make any new toolbars hidden. Users can then turn the toolbar on when they are ready to use its functionality.

▶ **To create a new toolbar**

1. Make sure that the Office Shortcut Bar (Msoffice.exe) is not running: using the right mouse button, click the background of any toolbar, and then click Exit.

2. Create a toolbar folder in the file system. The recommended location is under the Toolbar Root folder. The Toolbar Root location is specified in Hkey_Current_User\Software\Microsoft\Office Shortcut Bar\Toolbar Root.

3. Add a new key under Hkey_Current_User\Software\Microsoft\Office Shortcut Bar\Toolbars with the same name as your toolbar folder.

4. Add the registry values for the toolbar as described earlier in this "Toolbars" section.

5. Restart the Office Shortcut Bar.

Template Settings in the Windows Registry

The location of the local template directory is specified by Hkey_Current_User\Software\Microsoft\Microsoft Office\95\Filenew\ LocalTemplates. The value for this setting is the fully-qualified path to the root template directory on the user's local system. For information about adding templates and tabs to the New dialog box, see "Supporting Custom Templates" in the Office section of Chapter 12, "Support and Troubleshooting."

The file types recognized in the New dialog box are specified by Hkey_Local_Machine\Software\Microsoft\Microsoft Office\95\Wrapper\ NewTypes. Modify this setting to add extensions for files created by applications other than the Office applications. The value for this setting is a list of extensions separated by semicolons and ending with two semicolons. The default value is:

```
*.doc;*.dot;*.wiz;*.ppt;*.pot;*.pwz;*.mdb;*.xlt;*.xls;*.obd;*.obt;*.obz;;
```

Important Be careful to retain any existing settings whenever you modify this key.

Ghosting Message Setting for the Answer Wizard

For each Office application, the Answer Wizard pauses and displays a message the first few times the user selects a ghosted Help topic. In ghosted Help topics, the Answer Wizard selects the command or option for the user. After the user has selected six ghosted Help topics, the message is no longer displayed and the ghosting starts without a pause.

To reset the Answer Wizard so that display of the message is restored for a particular Microsoft Office for Windows 95 application, delete the key that's stored in Hkey_Current_User\Software\Microsoft\Microsoft Office\95\IntelliSearch\ *application.* This key is self-registering. By deleting this key, you also delete the list of the last few questions that the user asked the Answer Wizard.

Microsoft PowerPoint Registry Keys and Values

This section lists registry entries that can be found in the following Registry Editor location:

```
HKEY_CURRENT_USER\Software\Microsoft\Office\PowerPoint\7.0
```

The Addins Key

The Addins key contains settings for PowerPoint features that are implemented using add-ins. Note that, unlike most keys, these keys are case-sensitive, and they always appear in all caps.

The Answer Wizard Key

The Answer Wizard key stores the location of the Answer Wizard database files. The value "Database1" is the default. Any additional databases appear as "Database2," "Database3," and so on. The key's "Default" value contains the path to the Answer Wizard data file, such as "C:\Office\Powerpnt\powerpnt.aw."

The AutoClipArt Key

The AutoClipArt key contains the locations of all the clip-art packages that are indexed for use with AutoClipArt. For more information about the ClipArt Gallery, see "ClipArt Gallery Registry Keys" later in this appendix. For more information about AutoClipArt, see "Clip Art in PowerPoint" in Chapter 12, "Support and Troubleshooting."

The Content Templates Key

This key is used by the AutoContent Wizard. It stores the locations of the templates in the Office\Templates\Presentations folder—for example, "C:\MSOffice\Templates\Presentations\Training.pot." For more information, see "The AutoContent Wizard," in Chapter 12.

The Design Templates Key

This key is used by the AutoContent Wizard. It stores the locations of the design templates in the Office\Templates\Presentation Designs folder that correspond to the "Professional" and "Contemporary" visual style options in the AutoContent Wizard—for example, "C:\MSOffice\Templates\Presentation Designs\Professional.pot."

For more information about PowerPoint templates, see Chapter 4, "Microsoft PowerPoint Architecture."

The DLL Addins Key

The DLL Addins Key contains settings for PowerPoint features that are implemented using DLLs.

The Document Routing Key

The Document Routing Key stores the state of the "Track Status" check box in the Add Routing Slip dialog box (File menu): 1 = Yes, 0 = No.

The OLE Play Options Key

The OLE Play Options key contains the values listed in the following table.

Value name	Type	Value
AddImpact	String	"Movie"
AIPlayer	String	"Movie"
AVIFile	String	"Movie,1,1"
LotusMedia	String	"Movie"
LotusSound	String	"Sound"
MIDFile	String	"Sound,1,1"
MPlayer	String	"Movie,1,1"
PlayerFrameClass	String	"Movie"
SoundRec	String	"Sound"

In the values, the first number represents the first OLE verb for Media Player, which is "Play." The second number is either 1 or 2; 1 means that the object cannot be played across multiple slides. Both numbers are optional.

The Powerpnt.ini File

Almost all of the settings that used to be controlled using .ini files in previous versions of Windows are now handled by the registry. One of the few remaining .ini files is \Windows\Powerpnt.ini.

The registry's AVIFile and MIDFile keys are also included in the OLE Play Options section of the \Windows\Powerpnt.ini file, which is necessary to share files with PowerPoint 4.0.

The Options Key

The Options Key contains the values listed in the following table.

Name	Type	Description
Always render high-quality 24-bit images	DWORD	1 = Yes, 0 = No.
AlwaysSuggest	DWORD	Suggest words in the Spelling dialog box: 1 = Yes, 0 = No.
AppMaximized	DWORD	1 = Yes, 0 = No.
AutoRegistration	DWORD	1 = Yes, 0 = No.
BackgroundPrint	DWORD	1 = Yes, 0 = No.
Bottom	DWORD	Screen position of application window when not maximized, in pixels.
DocMaximized	DWORD	1 = Yes, 0 = No.
DragAndDrop	DWORD	Allow drag-and-drop text editing 1 = Yes, 0 = No.
FullTextSearch	DWORD	Save information used for full-text searches: 1 = Yes, 0 = No.
GuidesVisible	DWORD	1 = Yes, 0 = No.
Left	DWORD	Screen position of application window when not maximized, in pixels.
NewSlideDialog	DWORD	Show Slide Layout dialog when inserting new slides: 1 = Yes, 0 = No.
NoEditTime	DWORD	1 = Yes, 0 = No. 1 indicates that total editing time will not be tracked and will show up as 0 minutes in the Properties dialog box. The total editing statistic is also 0 (zero) in files that are saved. The default is 0, except in the German version of PowerPoint.

Name	Type	Description
NoStyledTitleBar	DWORD	Changes the format of text in the PowerPoint title bar: 1 = Not Styled, 0 = Styled.
Number of Undos	DWORD	Maximum number possible: 150.
Options dialog current tab	DWORD	1 through 4.
Produce 8-bit metafiles	DWORD	1 = Yes, 0 = No. Turning off this option allows metafiles to display better on 24-bit systems.
PromptForAutoShape	DWORD	Not used.
Right	DWORD	Screen position of application window when not maximized, in pixels.
RulersVisible	DWORD	1 = Yes, 0 = No.
Save Text Content Stream	DWORD	Copies all slide text to a Text_Content index stream for use by Find File. Corresponds to the "Save Full Text Search Information" option. 1 = Yes, 0 = No.
Share one IME context	DWORD	Not used.
Show Preview	DWORD	Indicates whether the Slide Miniature (View menu) window is visible: 1 = Yes, 0 = No.
ShowStatusBar	DWORD	1 = Yes, 0 = No.
SizeOfMRUList	DWORD	Most recently used files listed on the File menu; the maximum is nine.
SmartCutPaste	DWORD	1 = Yes, 0 = No.
SmartQuotes	DWORD	1 = Yes, 0 = No.
SSEndOnBlankSlide	DWORD	1 = Yes, 0 = No.
SSMenuButton	DWORD	Show menu button during slide shows: 1 = Yes, 0 = No.
SSRightMouse	DWORD	Display right-click menu during slide shows: 1 = Yes, 0 = No.
StartupDialog	DWORD	1 = Yes, 0 = No.
StartupDialogDefault	DWORD	Indicates the last setting chosen in the Startup dialog box: 6 = AutoContent Wizard (default), 7 = Template, 8 = Blank Presentation, 9 = Open Existing Presentation.
SummaryInfo	DWORD	Display Properties dialog box on save: 1 = Yes, 0 = No.
TipOfDay	DWORD	1 = Yes, 0 = No.
TipOfDayId	DWORD	ID Number of last Tip of the Day displayed.
Top	DWORD	Screen position of application window when not maximized, in pixels.

Name	Type	Description
True Inline Conversion	DWORD	1 = Yes, 0 = No. Applies only to Far East software versions. Chooses type of IME conversion to be used.
Use Fast OLE Save	DWORD	1 = Yes, 0 = No. 1 results in faster saves but slightly larger file sizes.
VerticalRuler	DWORD	1 = Yes, 0 = No.
WordSelection	DWORD	1 = Yes, 0 = No.

The PowerPoint Font Substitutions Key

The PowerPoint Font Substitutions key is not used.

The Ttembed.ini File

Almost all of the settings that used to be controlled using .ini files in previous versions of Windows are now handled by the registry. One of the few remaining .ini files is \Windows\Ttembed.ini.

The PowerPoint Font Substitutions key contains a list of default fonts that are shipped with Windows. These are fonts for which substitutions do not need to be made when True Type fonts are embedded in presentations. For example, Arial=0 indicates that Arial is a default Windows font and does not need to be embedded.

The Quick Preview Section Key

The Quick Preview Section key contains the values listed in the following table:

Name	Type	Description
FirstTime	DWORD	A "What's New" screen appears the first time PowerPoint is started. This key changes to 0 (zero) after What's New is first run. Enter any non-zero number to reset.
QuickPreview	String	Filename, such as "Ppvisex.exe."

You can view the "What's New" screen at any time by typing **what's new** in the Answer Wizard.

The More Info Key

The More Info key keeps track of how many times a message is displayed that explains how to get more information about topics in the Quick Preview window.

The Recent Typeface List Key

The Recent Typeface List key becomes active only after a font is applied; it contains the names of the most recently used typefaces.

The Recent File List Key

The Recent File List key contains a string value for each of the most recently used files, as listed at the bottom of the File menu. The list is updated each time the user quits PowerPoint. The values appear as strings such as [Path]\[Filename1]. The number of entries in the recent file list depends on the SizeOfMRUList setting in the Options key and the number of files opened or created since the initial installation of PowerPoint. The user can specify the size of the MRU list (and thus the setting in the Options key) on the General tab in the Options dialog box.

Note If you want your users to have easy access to particular network locations at the time of installation, use the STF editor to populate the Recent File List and Recent Folder List keys with paths to important folders. For more information about the STF editor, see Chapter 9, "Customizing Client Installations."

The Recent Folder List Key

The Recent Folder List key contains the path and names of the folders most recently used in particular dialog boxes. This key keeps track of folders selected in the Look In drop-down box in the dialog boxes listed in the following table.

Dialog box	Menu	Key
Insert Picture	Insert	PictureDir
Insert Movie	Insert	MultimediaDir
Insert Outline	Insert (Slides From Outline command)	OutlineDir
Apply Design Template	Format	TemplateDir
Options, Advanced Tab	Tools	Default (My Documents, if not otherwise specified)
Select Presentation Template	None (click the Other button in the AutoContent Wizard)	ACOtherCurrentDir

The Default key records the path specified in the Default File Location box on the Advanced tab in the Options dialog box. When there is a value for this key (when the user enters a Default File Location in the Options dialog box), the Open and Save As dialog boxes default to the specified location.

The Sound Key

The Sound key contains a list of MS-DOS file extensions indicating valid sound file types. The default is ".wav."

The Sound Effects Key

The Sound Effects key contains a list of sound effects that are available for use by the Animation Settings command on the Tools menu, along with strings indicating their paths and filenames—for example, "C:\MSOffice\Sounds\drum.wav." To add sounds, the value name of the new sound must start with a unique number followed by a colon and then the name of the sound—for example, "120:Door Slam." The name you type for the sound appears in the Sound Effects drop-down box in the Animation Settings dialog box.

The StyleChecker Key

The Style Checker key becomes active only when any Style Checker options are changed. This key contains the values listed in the following table.

Name	Type	Description
BodyAddlPuncChr	String	Character, other than a period, that is designated as the preferred end punctuation character for body text.
BodyCase	String	Case selected for body text: 1= Sentence case, 2= lowercase, 3= UPPERCASE, 4= Title Case, 5= tOGGLE cASE.
BodyMaxBullets	String	Maximum number of bullets per slide.
BodyMinFontSize	String	Smallest font size for body text.
BodyPeriods	String	"Remove," "Add," or "Ignore" periods in body text.
BulletsMaxLines	String	Maximum lines of text in bulleted items.
CheckBodyMaxBullets	String	Activate checking for number of bullets per slide.
CheckBodyMin FontSize	String	Activate checking for minimum font size in body text.
CheckBodyStyle	String	Activate checking for case of body text.
CheckBulletsMaxLines	String	Activate checking for maximum lines of text per bullet.
CheckSlideMax FontNum	String	Activate checking for maximum number of fonts per slide.
CheckTitleMaxLines	String	Activate checking for maximum lines of text per slide title.

Name	Type	Description
CheckTitleMin FontSize	String	Activate checking for minimum font size for slide title.
CheckTitleStyle	String	Activate checking for case of slide titles.
LargeBlocksOfText	String	Unused.
SlideMaxFontNum	String	Maximum number of fonts per slide.
TextOffSlide	String	Check for text that extends beyond slide borders.
TitleAddlPuncChar	String	Character, other than a period, that is designated as the preferred end punctuation character for slide titles.
TitleCase	String	Case selected for slide titles: 1= Sentence case, 2= lowercase, 3= UPPERCASE, 4= Title Case, 5= tOGGLE cASE.
TitleMaxLines	String	Maximum lines of text in slide titles.
TitleMinFontSize	String	Smallest font size for slide titles.
TitlePeriods	String	"Remove," "Add," or "Ignore" periods in slide titles.

The Spelling Key

The Spelling key contains the Speller key, whose value includes two arguments—Country Code and Dictionary Type—separated by a backslash; for example, "1033\Normal." Country Code specifies the proper spelling tool to use with the corresponding language version of Microsoft PowerPoint. The following table lists the various country codes.

Country code	Language
1030	Danish
1031	German
1033	U.S. English
1034	Spanish
1036	French
1040	Italian
1043	Dutch
1044	Norwegian
1054	Swedish
2057	British English
2070	Portuguese
3081	Australian English

The Dictionary Type argument refers to five possible types of dictionaries that can be used by the speller. The five dictionary types are Normal, Concise (subset of Normal), Complete (includes Medical and Legal), Medical, and Legal. PowerPoint always uses Normal.

The Toolbar Configuration Key

The Toolbar Configuration key contains the values listed in the following table.

Name	Type	Description
ColorButtons	DWORD	1 = Yes, 0 = No.
Large Buttons	DWORD	1 = Yes, 0 = No.
Number	DWORD	Indicates the number of custom toolbar configurations created by the user.
StateN	String	Indicates visible toolbars and their positions. One key listed (State1, State2, and so on) for each toolbar not included in the default toolbar configuration.
ToolTips	DWORD	1 = Yes, 0 = No.

The Translators Key

The Translators key contains the description and location of external file converters shipped with PowerPoint, such as the Harvard Graphics converter. Each translator has a separate key, with one of the formats listed in the following table.

Name	Description
Extensions	MS-DOS file extension string—for example, ".SHW"
Path	Filename and path of the translator
Title	Text that appears in the List Files Of Type box in the Open dialog box
Translator Type	1 = PowerPoint translator, 0 = non-PowerPoint translator

Note Translator keys pertaining to sharing PowerPoint files between versions are also included in the MS PowerPoint Translators section of the \Windows\Powerpnt.ini file, which is necessary to share files with PowerPoint 4.0.

ClipArt Gallery Registry Keys

This section discusses registry entries that can be found in the following Registry Editor path:

```
HKEY_LOCAL_MACHINE\Software\Microsoft\ClipArt Gallery\2.0\
```

The Import Key

When new clip-art packages are installed on the computer (but not installed in the ClipArt Gallery) and registered, they appear under the Import key. Each Import key entry includes a string indicating the location of the ClipArt Gallery file (with the extension .cag) for each ClipArt Gallery category installed for PowerPoint, such as "PowerPoint Popular ClipArt." These files contain information used by the ClipArt Gallery to locate, index, and display thumbnail sketches of the Picture Store files (with a .pcs extension) used by the ClipArt Gallery.

The first time it is started, the ClipArt Gallery creates a master database file named *artgalry.cag* (using the entries listed in the Import key), stores it in the location specified in the 2.0 key's Database value, and moves entries in the Import key to the Installed key. After the ClipArt Gallery is run for the first time, anything listed in the Import key that is not specifically installed is automatically moved to the Postponed key. The default location for the artgalry.cag file is the Windows folder. The string value for each key is a path to the .cag file, such as in the following example:

```
<Office path>\clipart\pcsfiles\<package name>.CAG
```

Note In earlier versions of PowerPoint, two files were installed for each clip-art category: an index (.idx) file containing information about the art files, and a "thumbnail" file (.thm) containing thumbnail images of each piece of art. In Office 95, these two files are replaced by a single .cag file.

Almost all of the settings that used to be controlled using .ini files in previous versions of Windows are now handled by the Windows registry. When installing PowerPoint 7.0 over an earlier version of PowerPoint, the settings stored in the powerpnt.ini file regarding the status of .idx and .thm files are transferred to the registry.

The Installed and Postponed Keys

The Import key contains entries when the ClipArt Gallery is started for the first time or when new clip-art packages are installed and registered on the computer. When the Import key contains entries and the ClipArt Gallery is started, the Add New Pictures dialog box appears, listing the items that have not yet been added to the ClipArt Gallery—that is, the items listed in the Import key. When a user selects one or more entries in this list and adds them to the ClipArt Gallery, those entries are moved from the Import key to the Installed key. Any entries not imported are removed from the Import key and placed in the Postponed key. Entries in the Postponed key can be imported by clicking the Organize button in the ClipArt Gallery and then clicking Add Pictures.

The MRUDescription, MRUName, and Settings Keys

These keys, which are related to the ClipArt Gallery, can be found in the following Registry Editor path:

```
HKEY_CURRENT_USER\Software\Microsoft\ClipArt Gallery\2.0\
```

The Find button in the ClipArt Gallery displays the Find ClipArt dialog box. This dialog box contains edit boxes for name and description, in which a user can enter text to search for clip art with matching names and/or descriptions. The two "MRU" (most recently used) keys store the latest text entries used in these edit boxes.

The Settings key stores the WindowPos value, indicating the most recent screen position and size coordinates of the ClipArt Gallery application window.

Graphics Filter Registry Keys

The Graphics Filters key stores strings indicating types of graphic import and export filters for all Microsoft Office applications. This key is located in the following path in the registry:

```
HKEY_LOCAL_MACHINE\Software\Microsoft\Shared Tools\
➥ Graphics Filters\Import
```

Each key entry includes strings indicating the name, path, and three-character MS-DOS filename extension for the filter. The string values for each key are listed in the following table.

Name	Description
Extensions	MS-DOS filename extension string—for example, ".bmp".
Name	Name of the filter, such as "Windows bitmap".
Path	The path to the filter, such as "C:\Windows\MSApps\Grphflt\Bmpimp32.Flt".

Schedule+ Registry Keys and Values

This section describes the registry keys and values for Schedule+ 7.0.

HKEY_CURRENT_USER Registry Entries

If MAPI is installed and Schedule+ is being used in group-enabled mode, some information about Schedule+ is stored in the Software\Microsoft\Windows Messaging Subsystem\Profiles section of Hkey_Current_User. This information can be modified only by the Schedule+ program itself, not by an administrator or user.

Warning Changing Schedule+ registry entries in the Hkey_Current_User\Software\Microsoft\Windows Messaging Subsystem\Profiles section of the Windows registry can result in damage to the Schedule+ installation and possible loss of Schedule+ functionality.

This remainder of this section describes Schedule+ registry entries in Hkey_Current_User\Software\Microsoft\Schedule+.

Note Binary values are specified using a DWORD unless otherwise noted.

Application Key

Entry	Type	Description
ApptBookLinesColor	Binary	Index to color used to draw the lines in the appointment book.
ArchiveFile	String	Full path of archive file.
BackupFile	String	Full path of backup file.
CoverBitmap	String	Full path to the bitmap file that is displayed on the Cover Page tab.
DefaultPrinter	Binary	Flag to indicate whether the user is printing to the default system printer: 0 = Not printing to the default system printer. 1 = Printing to the default system printer.
ExportFile	String	Full path of the Schedule+ export (.sc2) file.
GridAutoFit	Binary	Flag to indicate whether the grid used to display columns of data in the user interface should always automatically fit columns, based on available space.
GridLinesColor	Binary	Index to color used to draw the lines in every grid view.

Entry	Type	Description
GridTextColor	Binary	Index to color used to draw the text in every grid view.
InitialAccess	Binary	Determines what the default access for the schedule (.scd) file will be. Applies only to version 7.0. 0 = Read-minimal (default) 1 = No access privileges 2 = Read-only
LocalPath	String	Full path of schedule file; used only if the user is not mail-enabled. If the user is mail-enabled, this information is stored in the Windows Messaging System\Profile section of the registry.
LocalUser	String	Default display name of the user currently logged on. Used to determine the base name of the schedule file when it is first created.
MailDisabled	Binary	Mail-disabled flag. This flag is set to "1" if the user elects not to be mail-enabled in the "Group Enabling" dialog box and never wants to be queried again. 0 = Possibly group enabled 1 = Never group enabled
MessageHideStatus	Binary	Indicates whether the status bar will be shown for Schedule+ meeting forms: 0 = Don't hide status bar. 1 = Hide status bar.
MessageHideToolbar	Binary	Indicates whether the toolbar will be shown for Schedule+ meeting forms: 0 = Don't hide toolbar. 1 = Hide toolbar.
NoAutoScan	Binary	Determines whether Schedule+ will scan the user's Inbox for Schedule+ messages and automatically process them. Applies only if the user is working in group-enabled mode. 0 = Automatically scan inbox for Schedule+ messages. 1 = Don't scan inbox for Schedule+ messages.
NoScaleCoverBitmap	Binary	Determines whether or not the Cover Page bitmap is scaled to fit the window: 0 = Scale to fit window. 1 = Don't scale to fit window.
NoStatusBar	Binary	Indicates whether Schedule+ should not show the status bar for opened schedules.

Entry	Type	Description
NoToolbar	Binary	Indicates whether Schedule+ should not show the toolbar for opened schedules.
OptionsFilePath	String	Full path to the user options (.vue) file. If no value is specified, the user options file is created in the Windows folder.
OptionsTab	Binary	Indicates which tab was active in the Options dialog box when the user clicked OK.
ReminderToTop	Binary	Interval to bring popped-up reminders to the top, in minutes. If not specified, the default value is 5 minutes. The range is from 0 to 60 minutes.
ShowRecurInstances	Binary	Number of instances of recurring objects to show. The range is from 1 to 32.
SyncStartIdle	Binary	Length of idle time (in hundredths of a second) before the synchronization routine starts. The default value is 6000, or 60 seconds.
TentativeApptColor	Binary	Index of color used as background for tentative appointments in appointment views.
UpdateCover	Binary	Indicates how often to update the Cover Page bitmap, in minutes. If this entry is not present, the default is 120 minutes.

Custom Menus Key

Adds menu items to the Schedule+ user interface. The general form of an add menu entry is as follows:

```
version;menu;new_menu_item;reserved;command_string;help_file;help_id
```

The fields are listed and described in the following table.

Field	Description
Version	Identifies the version of Schedule+ with which the command is compatible; 7.0 is the current version.
Menu	Specifies the menu and the location on the menu where the new menu item is to be placed. The new item is placed just above the existing one on the menu. Provide the menu name, the submenu (if appropriate), and the menu item, separated by commas. The name is case insensitive, and ampersands are ignored. To specify an absolute menu position, use "#" followed by the number for the position. If -1 is specified for the position, the new menu will be added at the end of the menu specified.
New Menu Item	Menu name to be added to the menu bar. Include an ampersand just before the letter that is to serve as an ALT+*key* accelerator. If no name is provided, a separator is added to the menu.

Field	Description
Reserved	This position is reserved for future use.
Command String	Command string used to call WinExec. If no command string is provided, a new popup menu is added.
Status Bar Text	Text string shown in the status bar when the menu item is selected.
Help File	Windows Help file to be invoked when the user presses F1 while the command is selected. Passed to the Windows Help program.
Help ID	Passed to the Windows Help program along with the Help filename. Use -1 (Help file index) if there is no specific entry in the Help file for this command.

Custom Popup Menus Key

Adds entries to one of the context menus that appear when a user clicks with the secondary mouse button on an area of the user interface. Follows the format described in the preceding section. The menu field can have one of the following values: edit, appts, events, tabs, toolbar, tasks, projects, contacts, columns, or navigator.

Deleted Menus Key

Deletes menu items from the Schedule+ user interface. The general form is as follows:

```
version;menu
```

The fields are described in the following table.

Field	Description
Version	Identifies the version of Schedule+; 7.0 is the current version.
Menu	Specifies the menu and the location on the menu of the item to delete. Provide the menu name, the submenu (if appropriate), and the menu item, separated by commas. The name is case insensitive, and ampersands are ignored. To specify an absolute menu position, use "#" followed by the number for the position.

Deleted Popup Menus Key

Deletes an entry from a context-sensitive pop-up menu. The format is the same as that described in the preceding section.

Meeting Wizard Key

Entry	Type	Description
AskLocation	Binary	Indicates whether Schedule+ will prompt the user to select locations for the meeting.
AskOptional	Binary	Indicates whether Schedule+ will prompt the user to select optional attendees for the meeting.
AskRequired	Binary	Indicates whether Schedule+ will prompt the user to select required attendees for the meeting.
AskResource	Binary	Indicates whether Schedule+ will prompt the user to select resources for the meeting.
Duration	Binary	Length of the meeting, in minutes. The valid range is from one minute to one day minus one minute.
IncludeOptional	Binary	Indicates whether Schedule+ should check the free time of optional attendees: "0" means don't check optional attendees' free time; "1" means check optional attendees' free time.
Locations	String	List of locations that will be used when the meeting wizard is run. Locations in the list are separated by semicolons. The list of locations from the previous run of the meeting wizard are saved here.
MeetAfter	Binary	Time of the day where Schedule+ begins searching for a valid meeting time. The valid range is from 0 minutes to 1439 minutes (11:59 P.M.). Default value is the user's start-of-day preference.
MeetBefore	Binary	Time of the day when Schedule+ stops searching for a valid meeting time. The valid range is from 0 minutes to 1439 minutes (11:59 P.M.). The default value is the user's end-of-day preference.
Optional	String	List of optional attendees that will be used when the meeting wizard is run. Attendees in the list are separated by semicolons. The list of optional attendees from the previous run of the meeting wizard are saved in this location.
Required	String	List of required attendees that will be used when the meeting wizard is run. Attendees in the list are separated by semicolons. The list of required attendees from the previous run of the meeting wizard are saved here.
Resources	String	List of resources that will be used when the meeting wizard is run. Resources in the list are separated by semicolons. The list of resources from the previous run of the meeting wizard is saved in this location.

Entry	Type	Description
TravelFrom	Binary	Length of time allotted to travel from the meeting after the meeting has finished. The valid range is from 0 minutes to 99 minutes. The default is 0 minutes.
TravelTo	Binary	Length of time allotted to travel to the meeting. The valid range is from 0 minutes to 99 minutes. The default is 5 minutes.
ValidDays	String	Specifies which days to search for a valid meeting time. The string consists of 1's and 0's (zeros); 1 specifies a valid meeting day. Sunday is the first day in the string, followed by Monday, and so on.

Microsoft Schedule+ Key

This registry key is not used by Schedule+ 7.0.

Text Export Wizard Key

Entry	Type	Description
Appt Fields	String	Comma-separated string giving the number of each of the exported Schedule+ appointment fields.
Event Fields	String	Comma-separated string giving the number of each of the exported Schedule+ event fields.
Contact Fields	String	Comma-separated string giving the number of each of the exported Schedule+ contact fields.
Filename	String	Name of the export file. Default: <Windows directory>\Desktop\Export.csv.
NoFieldNames	Binary	Flag to indicate whether the data is to be exported with field names. Default: 0. Possible values: 0 - 3 (Appts, Tasks, Events, Contacts).
QualifierChar	Binary	ASCII value of string delimiter character + 1. The + 1 is necessary to distinguish a NULL delimiter. Default: quotation mark + 1 (0x00000023, 35 decimal).
SeparatorChar		ASCII value of field separator character. Default: comma (0x0000002C, 44 decimal).
SingleLine	Binary	Indicates whether export fields containing strings can have carriage-return and line-feed characters. If this flag is set to 1, string fields spanning multiple lines are truncated at the end of the first line during the exporting.

Entry	Type	Description
Task Fields	String	Comma-separated string giving the number of each of the exported Schedule+ task fields.
Type	Binary	Index of the radio button for the default export type. Default: 0. Possible values: 0 - 3 (Appts, Tasks, Events, Contacts).

Text Import Wizard Key

The registry entries for this key are the same as those for the Text Export Wizard key.

Watch Wizard Key

AlarmData1 through AlarmData5

Encoded information about each alarm. Type: String-encoded ULONG. The formats for Alarm On are listed in the following table.

Position in ULONG	Meaning
26-27	Type
21-25	Hour
15-20	Minute
10-14	Day of monthly reminder
5-9	Month of yearly reminder
0-4	Day of yearly reminder

The formats for Alarm Off are listed in the following table.

Position in ULONG	Meaning
11-12	Type
6-10	Hour
0-5	Minute

The formats for Alarm Type are listed in the following table.

Position in ULONG	Meaning
0	Daily
1	Monthly
2	Yearly

ApptsDays

Number of days of appointments to export. Type: Binary. Default: 7.

ApptsReminderAmt

Number of minutes before the appointment to ring the watch alarm. Type: Binary. Default: 2.

TasksDays

Number of days of tasks to export. Type: Binary. Default: 7.

TasksPriority

Indicates minimum task priority for tasks to be downloaded. Type: Binary. Possible values are as follows: the high byte of the word is ASCII code for one of SPACE, 'A', 'B', 'C', 'D', 'E', or 'F'; the low byte of the word is ASCII code for one of the 10 digits.

TmzIndex0

Primary time zone. Type: String-encoded integer. Possible values: 0–51. For a mapping of indexes to time zone names, see the Time Zone tab in the Schedule+ Options dialog box.

TmzIndex1

Secondary time zone. Type: String-encoded integer. Possible values: 0–51.

WatchFlags

Control flags for radio buttons and check boxes in the Watch Wizard. Type: String-encoded WORD. These flags are listed in the following table.

Position in WORD	Label	Values
0	UserModified	1 – This word exists because the user has used the wizard before.
1	ApptsAtLeast	1 – Send at least as many as N days of the appointment.
		0 – Send exactly N days of the appointment.
2	ApptsTentative	1 – Send tentative appointments.
		0 – Do not send tentative appointments.
3	ApptsReminder	1 – Ring an alarm before each appointment.
4	TasksAll	1 – Send all tasks.
		0 – Send filtered set of tasks.
5	TmzDefault	1 – Use the system time zone setting for a watch.
6	Tmz24Hr0	1 – Time zone 0 is in 24-hour format.
7	Tmz24Hr1	1 – Time zone 1 is in 24-hour format.
8	Alarm1	1 – Alarm 1 is enabled.
9	Alarm2	1 – Alarm 2 is enabled.

Position in WORD	Label	Values
10	Alarm3	1 – Alarm 3 is enabled.
11	Alarm4	1 – Alarm 4 is enabled.
12	Alarm5	1 – Alarm 5 is enabled.
13	ApptsLocation	1 – Download the meeting location with appointment text.

WatchFormsWanted

Flag set for which panes of the wizard to display. Type: String-encoded WORD. These flags are listed in the following table.

Position in WORD	Label	Value
0	All	1 – Show all panes.
1	Appts	1 – Show the Appointments pane(s).
2	Tasks	1 – Show the Task pane(s).
3	Phone	1 – Show the contact phone number pane.
4	Anniv	1 – Show the contact anniversary pane.
5	Alarms	1 – Show the alarm pane.

HKEY_LOCAL_MACHINE Registry Entries

The following information about Schedule+ is found in the registry under HKEY_LOCAL_MACHINE\SOFTWARE\Microsoft\Schedule+\Application.

Application Key

Entry	Type	Description
AppPath	String	Path to the Schedule+ executable files on the local machine.
CDPath	String	Path to Schedule+ DLLs. The installation path may be different if installed from CD ROM.
DefaultLocalPath	String	Path pointing to where new schedules files will be created.
DemosEnabled	Binary	Indicates whether to show the Microsoft Schedule+ Demos menu item.
FormsRegistered	Binary	Indicates whether the Schedule+ message forms have been registered with the MAPI Forms registry.
GrayShade	Binary	Makes the level of gray shading for printing lighter or darker. Default value: 230. Possible values: 0 to 255.

Entry	Type	Description
LocalPrintFileDir	String	Points to the path where the application can find .prt and .fmt files for printing. If this entry is not present, the default is CDPath.
MailPath	String	Location of Exchange mail client.
MAPIPresent	Binary	Indicates whether or not Schedule+ brings up the Group Enabling dialog box at startup time. If this flag is 0 and MAPI is detected, the user is queried about being group-enabled.
OfficeInstalled	Binary	Set to 1 if Office for Windows 95 is installed; set to 0 if it is not. If this flag is 1, Schedule+ attempts to load the Office 95 DLLs for Office-specific features such as the Answer Wizard.
PrimaryServer	Binary	Indicates whether the user wishes to work primarily with the server copy of the schedule.
ScheduleFinders	String	Identifies the DLLs to load to find server schedules for any user. Multiple DLLs can be specified if they are separated by a space. Schedule+ automatically appends "32.dll" at the end of each entry when searching for the DLL.
ScheduleInterfaces	String	Identifies which DLLs to load to provide the interface between the application and schedule storage. Multiple DLLs can be specified if they are separated by a space. Schedule+ automatically appends a "32.dll" at the end of each entry when searching for the DLL.
ServerPath	String	Identifies the server where files for the file mstrs32.dll can be found.
TimexWatchInterface	String	Identifies which DLL to load for the Timex Data Link watch Export Wizard. Schedule+ automatically appends a "32.dll" at the end of the entry when searching for the DLL.
WatchInstalled	Binary	Indicates whether the software drivers for exporting to the Timex Data Link watch are installed.

Microsoft Word Registry Keys and Values

This section describes the registry keys and values for Word 7.0.

Data Key

Settings

The binary value that stores the Winword.opt file information in binary format.

Help Key

Files

The string values that store the locations and filenames for various Word Help files.

Value	Description
Winword.hlp	Word's primary Help file
Wphelp.hlp	Help for WordPerfect users upgrading to Word
Wrdbasic.hlp	Help for users working with WordBasic

Options Key

Entry	Type	Description
Autosave-Path	String	Default folder in which Word locates the temporary files it automatically saves. The default refers to the folder referenced by the TEMP environment variable.
AutoSpell	Integer	Specifies whether to use background spell checking: 0 = Do not use background spell checking. 1 = Use background spell checking.
Picture-Path	String	Default folder where the clip-art pictures supplied with Word are located. The default refers to the Clipart folder where Word was installed—for example, C:\Office95\Clipart.
NoEditTime	Integer	One document property that Word can track is Total Editing Time. This appears on the Statistics tab in the Properties dialog box (File menu, Properties command). 0 = Track editing time. 1 = Do not track editing time.
Programdir	String	Folder in which the Word executable program is located—for example, C:\Office95\Winword.
Startup-Path	String	Startup folder used by Word. The default refers to the Startup folder where Word was installed—for example, C:\Office95\Winword\Startup.
StartWhatIsNew	Integer	Indicates whether Word will automatically start the "What's New in Word 95" online demo when Word is first started. Be default, Word starts this online demo only once. 0 = Word will not start the online demo. 1 = Word will start the online demo.

Entry	Type	Description
Tools-Path	String	Default folder where Word tools (such as dictionaries) are located. The default for Tools-Path refers to the folder where Word was installed—for example, C:\Office95\Winword.
Wordmail-Path	String	Default folder where files needed to use Word as an e-mail editor are located.
WPHelp	Integer	Specifies whether to use WordPerfect commands. 0 = Do not use WordPerfect commands. 1 = Use WordPerfect commands.

Proofing Tools Key

Entry	Type	Description
Grammar*language*\\Normal\Dictionary	String	Names the dictionary for a given language and grammar-checking engine.
Grammar*language*\\Normal\Engine	String	Names the DLL for a given language and grammar-checking engine.
Hyphenate*language*\\Normal\Dictionary	String	Names the dictionary for a given language and hyphenation engine.
Hyphenate*language*\\Normal\Engine	String	Names the DLL for a given language and hyphenation engine

Stationery Key

Entry	Type	Description
Cfg File Location	String	Applies when using Word as an e-mail editor (WordMail). Specifies the folder where WordMail configuration files are located.
Default Template	String	Applies when using Word as an e-mail editor (WordMail). Specifies the Word template to use for WordMail.

Text Converters Key

Entry	Type	Description
Export*converter export classname*\Name	String	Name of the export text converter.
Export*converter export classname*\Path	String	Location of the export text converter.
Export*converter export classname*\Extensions	String	Lists the extensions for document files supported by this export text converter. Extensions are space-separated and not preceded by a period.
Import*converter import classname*\Name	String	Name of the import text converter.
Import*converter import classname*\Path	String	Location of the import text converter.
Import*converter import classname*\Extensions	String	List of the extensions for document files supported by this import text converter. Extensions are space-separated and not preceded by a period.

Find Fast Registry Keys and Values

The following registry entries apply to the Find Fast utility. You can edit most values directly in the Registry Editor, or through the Find Fast control panel.

95\Index List\Index *nn*

Entry	Type	Description
Automatic	Binary	Specifies whether the current index should be automatically updated. The value is in binary format, followed by a decimal value enclosed in parentheses. 0 = Index will not be updated automatically. 1 = Index will be updated automatically.
Folder	String	Drive and folder (including all subfolders) indexed in the current index key.
Index Operation	Integer	Specifies the updating option of the current index. The value is in binary format, followed by a decimal value enclosed in parentheses. 1 = Create the index. 2 = Update the index one time only. 3 = Update the index continuously.
LogFilePath	String	Path to the hidden log file maintained by Find Fast —for example, C:\Windows\System\Ffastlog.txt.

Entry	Type	Description
Size Limit	Binary	Limits the maximum size of the current index. The value is in binary format, followed by a decimal value enclosed in parentheses. The decimal value represents bytes.
Proximity Search	Integer	Specifies whether the current index should support faster phrase or proximity searching. When proximity searching is enabled, entire phrases and quoted strings are included in the index. Enabling proximity searching greatly increases the size of the index file. When proximity searching is disabled, the Find Fast utility can accomplish the same searches, but they will take longer. 0 = Proximity searching is disabled. 1 = Proximity searching is enabled.
Type	Integer	Specifies the type of documents indexed in the current index. The value is in binary format, followed by a decimal value enclosed in parentheses. 0 = Microsoft Office documents 1 = Microsoft Word documents 2 = Microsoft Excel documents 3 = Microsoft PowerPoint documents 4 = Microsoft Project documents 5 = All indexable file types (excludes .exe, and so on)

APPENDIX C

List of Installed Components

This appendix lists components installed by Office Setup according to whether the installation is Custom, Typical, Compact, Run From CD, or Run From Server. Information on whether or not the component is automatically installed and how much disk space is needed is included.

Note The tables in this appendix do not include the components installed with Microsoft Access in Microsoft Office for Windows 95 Professional. This data was not available at the time of printing. Where possible, total disk space used by Office Professional is estimated below.

In This Appendix

Custom Installation

During a Custom installation, components that are marked in the following tables as being installed automatically will be installed if you run the installation in batch mode. In the Setup dialog box, these options are enabled by default. Components marked as not being installed automatically will not be installed if you run the installation in batch mode, and they are disabled by default in the Setup dialog box. The complete installation of Office for Windows 95 takes approximately 89 MB of disk space for Office Standard, and approximately 130 MB for Office Professional.

Microsoft Office Binder and Shortcut Bar

Option Component	Sub-component	Auto install?	Space (K)	Description
Office Binder and Shortcut Bar		Yes	3,246	Files required for the Office Binder and Shortcut Bar utilities.
Microsoft Office Shortcut Bar		Yes	517	Complete set of files for the Microsoft Office Shortcut Bar.
Office Help		Yes	681	Office Help Files.
Microsoft Binder		Yes	497	Microsoft Office Binder.
Microsoft Binder Help Files		Yes	713	Help files for Microsoft Binder.
Office Binder Templates		Yes	840	Collections of pre-formatted documents for business tasks.
	Report	Yes	128	Documents for organizing reports.
	Client Billing	Yes	360	Fax cover sheet, cover letter, and billing documents.
	Proposal and Marketing Plan	Yes	168	Documents related to bids or marketing proposals.
	Meeting Organizer	Yes	184	Documents for organizing and recording the results of meetings.

Office Tools

Option Component	Sub-component	Auto install?	Space (K)	Description
Office Tools		Yes	12,727	Tools for use with Microsoft Office.
Spelling Checker		Yes	570	Checks the spelling of text in documents.
WordArt		No	597	Creates special effects for text, such as rotation and shading.
Organizational Chart		No	1,535	Application to create organization charts.
Microsoft Graph 5.0		Yes	1,791	Use to create charts and graphs with your data.
Microsoft Graph 5.0 Help		No	513	Online Help files for Microsoft Graph 5.0
Equation Editor		No	741	Equation Editor.
MS Info		Yes	401	Troubleshooting tool used to gather system configuration information.

Option Component	Sub-component	Auto install?	Space (K)	Description
Clip Art Gallery		Yes	956	Microsoft ClipArt Gallery indexes your clip art, letting you browse and search your collection.
Clip Art		Yes	2,793	Clip art that can be added to documents.
	Popular Clip Art	Yes	1513	Collection of the most popular clip art from Microsoft PowerPoint.
	Word Clip Art	No	1,281	Clip art that can be added to documents.
Find Fast		Yes	153	Feature in the Control Panel that makes finding and opening documents much faster from within any Microsoft Office 95 application.
Animation Effects Sounds		Yes	57	Sounds used for built-in animation effects in PowerPoint.
Additional Sounds		No	354	Sounds that can be used to add sizzle to your presentation.
Microsoft TrueType fonts		Yes	1,906	Collection of Microsoft TrueType fonts.
	Font Algerian	No	73	
	Font Arial Narrow	Yes	65	
	Font Arial Black	Yes	49	
	Arial Rounded MT Bold	No	41	
	Font Book Antiqua	Yes	257	
	Font Bookman Old Style	Yes	281	
	Font Braggadocio	No	41	
	Font Britannic	No	41	
	Font Brush Script	No	49	
	Font Century Gothic	No	65	
	Font Century Schoolbook	Yes	289	
	Font Colonna	No	57	
	Font Desdemona	No	57	
	Font Footlight	No	81	
	Font Garamond	Yes	257	

Option Component	Sub-component	Auto install?	Space (K)	Description
Microsoft TrueType fonts *(continued)*	Font Impact	No	57	
	Fontino	No	33	
	Font Matura	No	49	
	Font Playbill	No	41	
	Font Wide Latin	No	41	
Find All Word Forms		No	369	Find and replace noun forms or verb tenses.

Microsoft Excel

Option Component	Sub-component	Auto install?	Space (K)	Description
Microsoft Excel		Yes	25,048	Microsoft Excel will be installed with only the selected options.
Microsoft Excel program files		Yes	6,489	Complete set of Microsoft Excel program files.
Online Help and sample files		Yes	8,115	Step-by-step procedures, reference information, and a collection of sample files for Microsoft Excel.
	Online Help for Microsoft Excel	Yes	3,585	Step-by-step procedures, reference information, and a collection of sample files for Microsoft Excel.
	Online Help for Visual Basic	No	3,850	Comprehensive help for Visual Basic for applications for Microsoft Excel.
	Sample files	Yes	112	Sample files for Microsoft Excel that you can use to make your work easier.
Microsoft Data Map		No	5,435	Analyzes and charts data by geographical regions.
Spreadsheet Templates		Yes	2,913	Professionally designed templates that help you create the most common types of spreadsheets.
	Car Lease Template	No	280	Helps you decide how to negotiate a car lease.
	Change Request Template	No	240	Helps you create Change Request forms and a log to track them.
	Expense Report Template	No	256	Helps you create Expense Report forms and a log to track them.
	Financial Planner Template	No	304	Helps you create financial documents, such as Income Statements and Balance Sheets.

Option Component	Sub-component	Auto install?	Space (K)	Description
Spreadsheet Templates (*continued*)	Invoice Template	Yes	249	Helps you create professional looking invoices for billing.
	Loan Amortization Template	Yes	288	Helps you understand the cost of borrowing money.
	Personal Budget Template	No	272	Helps you create a personal budget that tracks expenses and savings.
	Purchase Order Template	Yes	248	Helps you create professional looking Purchase Orders to send to your vendors.
	Sales Quote Template	No	296	Helps you create professional looking sales quotes for prospective customers.
	Timecard Template	No	288	Helps you track time spent working on various projects.
Add-ins		Yes	2,002	A collection of Microsoft Excel macros that can assist you with common spreadsheet tasks.
	Access Links	Yes	121	Lets you use Microsoft Access Forms and Reports on Microsoft Excel data tables.
	Analysis ToolPak	Yes	568	Tools that help you apply statistical and engineering analysis to data.
	AutoSave	Yes	56	Automatically saves documents at a specified interval to prevent data loss.
	Report Manager	No	137	Prints reports with a set sequence of views and scenarios.
	Solver	No	481	Helps you use a variety of numeric methods for equation solving and optimization.
	Template Wizard with Data Tracking	Yes	497	Automatically records the contents of data entry fields in workbooks to a database for tracking and analysis.
	View Manager	No	121	Creates, stores, and displays different views of a worksheet.
Spreadsheet Converters		No	97	Utilities for importing other spreadsheet formats. (Many formats are built into Microsoft Excel and are not listed here.)
	Quattro Pro for Windows	No	97	Converts spreadsheets from Quattro Pro for Windows format.

Microsoft PowerPoint

Option Component	Sub-component	Auto install?	Space (K)	Description
Microsoft PowerPoint		Yes	18,446	Microsoft PowerPoint will be installed with only the selected options.
Microsoft PowerPoint Program Files		Yes	9,336	Microsoft PowerPoint and required system components.
Online Help for Microsoft PowerPoint		Yes	2,426	Complete online reference for Microsoft PowerPoint.
Design templates		Yes	1,336	Used with the AutoContent Wizard.
Genigraphics Wizard and Graphics Link		No	1,234	Genigraphics Wizard lets you send presentations to Genigraphics to create 35mm slides, posters, color overheads, prints, and more.
Presentation Translators		No	996	Utilities for reading presentations.
	Lotus Freelance 4.0 for DOS	No	209	Allows PowerPoint to open presentations created by Lotus Freelance 4.0 for DOS.
	Lotus Freelance 1.0-2.1 for Windows	No	297	Allows PowerPoint to open presentations created by Lotus Freelance 1.0–2.1 for Windows.
	Harvard Graphics 3.0 for DOS	No	273	Allows PowerPoint to open presentations created by Harvard Graphics 3.0 for DOS.
	Harvard Graphics 2.3 for DOS	No	217	Allows PowerPoint to open presentations created by Harvard Graphics 2.3 for DOS.
PowerPoint Viewer		Yes	1,640	Lets you present PowerPoint slide shows without PowerPoint. You may freely distribute copies of the PowerPoint Viewer disks.

Microsoft Schedule+

Option Component	Sub-component	Auto install?	Space (K)	Description
Microsoft Schedule+		Yes	6,033	Microsoft Schedule+ will be installed with only the options selected.
Microsoft Schedule+ Program Files		Yes	2,312	Installs the Schedule+ executable and other required files.
Print Layouts and Paper Formats		Yes	161	Installs the Print Layouts and Paper Formats.

Option Component	Sub-component	Auto install?	Space (K)	Description
Additional Importers and Exporters		No	1,465	Installs custom import and export utilities for data exchange with hand-held devices and other applications.
Seven Habits Tools		Yes	1,369	Installs the Seven Habits of Highly Effective People module.
Timex Data Link Utilities		Yes	81	Installs data download utilities for the Timex Data Link watch.
Help		Yes	649	Installs the Schedule+ Help files.

Microsoft Word

Option Component	Sub-component	Auto install?	Space (K)	Description
Microsoft Word		Yes	20,327	Microsoft Word will be installed with only the selected options.
Microsoft Word Program Files		Yes	5,761	Microsoft Word will be installed with only the selected options.
Online Help		Yes	6,050	Word procedures, reference information, and tips.
	Online Help for Microsoft Word	Yes	2,913	Word procedures, reference information, and tips.
	WordBasic Help	No	2,409	Complete reference information about the WordBasic macro language.
	Help for WordPerfect Users	No	169	Online Help and demonstrations for WordPerfect users.
Wizards, Templates, and Letters		Yes	4,905	Wizards help you create documents; Templates give you document layouts; Letters provide standard text for commonly used documents.
	Faxes	Yes	264	Contemporary, elegant and professional faxes.
	Letters	Yes	240	Contemporary, elegant and professional letters.
	Memos	Yes	208	Contemporary, elegant and professional memos.
	Reports	Yes	136	Contemporary, elegant and professional reports.
	Forms	No	208	Invoice, purchase order and weektime.
	More wizards	No	1,272	Agenda, award, calendar and pleading wizards.
	Newsletters	No	576	Newsletter template and wizard.

Option Component	Sub-component	Auto install?	Space (K)	Description
Wizards, Templates, and Letters (continued)	Press Releases	No	128	Contemporary, elegant and professional press releases.
	Publications	No	216	Brochure, directory, manual and thesis publications.
	Resumes	No	216	Contemporary, elegant and professional resumes.
	Table Wizard	No	160	Wizard to help you create tables.
	Sample Letters	No	360	Commonly used sample business letters.
	Macro Templates	No	600	Templates with sample macros.
Proofing Tools		Yes	2,323	Thesaurus, hyphenation, and grammar utilities.
	Hyphenation	Yes	82	Changes the hyphenation settings for the active document.
	Grammar	No	1,561	Checks grammar.
	Thesaurus	Yes	681	Suggests word alternatives.
Address Book		Yes	186	Tools for integrating with the Microsoft Exchange Personal Address Book and the Microsoft Schedule+ Contact List.
WordMail		No	596	Replaces Exchange's Standard Read/Compose Note with Microsoft Word.
Dialog Editor		No	104	Application to visually create code for dialogs that can be used in WordBasic macros.
Text Converters		No	309	Utilities for converting documents to and from other file formats.
	Lotus 1-2-3 Converter	No	114	Converts files from Lotus 1-2-3 versions 2.x and 3.x. (can be used to open Lotus 1-2-3 files, but not to save them).
	Text with Layout Converter	No	195	Converts documents to and from text files, while preserving the original page layout.

Converters, Filters, and Data Access

Option Component	Sub-component	Auto install?	Space (K)	Description
Converters, Filters, and Data Access		Yes	15,303	Text converters, Graphics filters, and ODBC drivers.
Converters		Yes	3,060	Utilities for converting documents to and from other file formats.
	Word for Windows 2.0 Converter	No	186	Converts documents to and from Word for Windows 2.0 (not necessary for opening Word for Windows 2.0 files).
	Word for the Macintosh 4.0–5.1 Converter	No	203	Converts documents to and from Word for the Macintosh versions 4.0, 5.0, and 5.1 (not necessary for opening Word files).
	Microsoft Excel Converter	Yes	138	Converts documents from Microsoft Excel versions 2.x, 3.0, 4.0, and 5.0 (can only be used to open files, but not to save them).
	Word for MS-DOS 3.0–6.0 Converter	No	226	Converts documents to and from Word for MS-DOS versions 3.0, 4.0, 5.0, 5.5, and 6.0.
	RFT-DCA Converter	No	178	Converts documents to and from IBM Revisable Form Text-Document Content Architecture format.
	Write for Windows Converter	No	82	Converts documents to and from Write for Windows versions 3.0 and 3.1.
	Word 6.0 for Windows and the Macintosh	Yes	145	Converts documents from Word 6.0 for Windows/Macintosh format.
	WordPerfect 6.x Converter	Yes	554	Converts documents from WordPerfect 6.0 for DOS and WordPerfect 6.0 and 6.1 for Windows.
	WordPerfect 5.x Converter	Yes	836	Converts documents to and from WordPerfect 5.0 and 5.1 for DOS and WordPerfect for Windows.
	Works for Windows 3.0	No	122	Converts documents to and from Works 3.0 for Windows and DOS.
	Works for Windows 4.0	No	121	Converts documents to and from Works 4.0.
	WordStar for DOS/Windows Converter	No	274	Converts documents from WordStar 3.3, 3.45, 4.0, 5.0, 6.0, 7.0, and WordStar for Windows 1.0 and 2.0. Also converts to WordStar.

Option Component	Sub-component	Auto install?	Space (K)	Description
Graphics Filters		Yes	2,081	Utilities for converting graphics to a format that Word can use.
	Tag Image File Format Import	Yes	113	Imports graphics from the Tag Image File Format (TIFF).
	Encapsulated Postscript Import	No	49	Imports graphics from the Encapsulated PostScript (EPS) format.
	Windows Bitmap Import	Yes	73	Imports graphics from the Windows Bitmap (BMP and DIB) formats.
	Truevision Targa Import	No	65	Imports graphics from the Truevision Targa (TGA) format.
	AutoCAD DXF Import	No	281	Imports graphics from the AutoCAD (DXF) format.
	Computer Graphics Metafile Import	No	65	Imports graphics from Computer Graphics Metafile (CGM) format.
	PC Paintbrush PCX Import	No	73	Imports graphics from the PC Paintbrush (PCX) format.
	Micrografx Designer/Draw Import	No	273	Imports graphics from the Micrografx Designer/Draw (DRW) format.
	CorelDRAW Import	No	137	Imports graphics from the CorelDRAW (CDR 3.0, 4.0, and 5.0) formats.
	WordPerfect Graphic Import	Yes	153	Imports graphics from the WordPerfect Graphic (WPG 1.0, 1.0e and 2.0) formats. Also used by the WordPerfect converter.
	DrawPerfect Export	Yes	73	Exports graphics to the WordPerfect Graphic (WPG) format (This file is only used with the WordPerfect converter).
	HP Graphics Language Import	No	241	Imports graphics from the HP Graphics Language (HPGL) format.
	Macintosh PICT Import	Yes	57	Imports graphics from the Macintosh (PICT) format.
	Windows Metafile Import	Yes	17	Imports graphics from the Windows Metafile (WMF) format.
	CompuServe GIF Import	No	81	Imports graphics from the CompuServe (GIF) format.
	Kodak Photo CD Import	No	201	Imports graphics from the Kodak Photo CD format.

		Yes	137	Imports graphics from the standard JPEG File Interchange Format.
Graphics Filters *(continued)*	JPEG File Interchange Format Import			
Data Access		No	10,076	Utilities and add-ins that let you use external databases with Microsoft Excel.
	Microsoft Query	Yes	1,042	Application you can use to retrieve data from external data sources and analyze it in Microsoft Excel.
	Microsoft Query Help and Cue Cards	No	1,457	Step-by-step procedures that help you learn how to use Microsoft Query.
	Data Access Objects for Visual Basic	Yes	477	Objects used to access external data from Visual Basic for applications code and from custom applications.
	Online Help for Data Access Objects	No	1,513	Comprehensive help for Data Access Objects.
	Microsoft Access Driver	Yes	0	Lets you analyze and import data from Microsoft Access databases.
	dBase and Microsoft FoxPro Drivers	No	292	Lets you analyze and import data from dBase and Microsoft FoxPro databases.
	Microsoft Excel Driver	Yes	225	Lets you analyze and import data from Microsoft Excel databases.
	Paradox Driver	No	252	Lets you analyze and import data from Paradox databases.
	Microsoft SQL Server Driver	No	352	Lets you analyze and import data from Microsoft SQL Server databases.
	Text Driver	No	129	Lets you analyze and import data from text databases.

Getting Results Book

Option	Sub-component	Auto install?	Space (K)	Description
Getting Results Book		Yes	16	Online version of the book, *Getting Results with Microsoft Office*. Selecting this option places a button on the Office Shortcut Bar.

Typical Installation

Typical installation is recommended for most users. This installation installs all Office applications and popular components. It takes approximately 55 MB of disk space for Office Standard, and approximately 85 MB for Microsoft Access.

During a Typical installation, components listed in the following tables will be installed.

Microsoft Office

Option Component	Sub-component	Space (K)	Description
Microsoft Office		2,574	Microsoft Office Typical.
Microsoft Office Shortcut Bar		517	Complete set of files for the Microsoft Office Shortcut Bar.
Office Help		681	Office Help files.
Microsoft Binder		497	Microsoft Office Binder.
Microsoft Binder Help Files		713	Help files for Microsoft Binder.
Office Binder Templates		168	Collections of pre-formatted documents for business tasks.
	Proposal and Marketing Plan	168	Documents related to bids or marketing proposals.

Office Tools

Option Component	Sub-component	Space (K)	Description
Office Tools		7,855	Tools for use with Microsoft Office.
Spelling Checker		570	Checks the spelling of text in documents.
Microsoft Graph 5.0		1,791	Use to create charts and graphs with your data.
Microsoft Graph 5.0 Help		513	Online Help files for Microsoft Graph 5.0.
MS Info		401	
Clip Art Gallery		956	Microsoft ClipArt Gallery indexes your clip art, letting you browse and search your collection.
Clip Art		1,513	Microsoft ClipArt Gallery indexes your ClipArt, allowing you to browse and search your ClipArt collection.
	Popular Clip Art	1,513	Collection of the most popular clip art from Microsoft PowerPoint.

Option Component	Sub-component	Space (K)	Description
Find Fast		153	Feature in the Control Panel that makes finding and opening documents much faster from within any Microsoft Office 95 application.
Animation Effects Sounds		57	Sounds used for built-in animation effects in PowerPoint.
Microsoft TrueType fonts		1,906	Collection of Microsoft TrueType fonts.
	Font Algerian	73	
	Font Arial Narrow	65	
	Font Arial Black	49	
	Arial Rounded MT Bold	41	
	Font Book Antiqua	257	
	Font Bookman Old Style	281	
	Font Braggadocio	41	
	Font Britannic	41	
	Font Brush Script	49	
	Font Century Gothic	65	
	Font Century Schoolbook	289	
	Font Colonna	57	
	Font Desdemona	57	
	Font Footlight	81	
	Font Garamond	257	
	Font Impact	57	
	Fontino	33	
	Font Matura	49	
	Font Playbill	41	
	Font Wide Latin	41	

Microsoft Excel

Option Component	Sub-component	Space (K)	Description
Microsoft Excel		12,995	Microsoft Excel will be installed with the most commonly used options.
Microsoft Excel program files		6,489	Complete set of Microsoft Excel program files.
Online Help and sample files		4,265	
	Online Help for Microsoft Excel	3,585	Step-by-step producers, reference information, and a collection of sample files for Microsoft Excel.
	Sample files	112	Sample files for Microsoft Excel that you can use to make your work easier.
Spreadsheet Templates		977	
	Invoice Template	248	Helps you create professional looking invoices for billing.
	Loan Amortization Template	288	Helps you understand the cost of borrowing money.
	Purchase Order Template	248	Helps you create professional looking Purchase Orders to send to your vendors.
Add-ins		1,266	
	Access Links	121	Lets you use Microsoft Access Forms and Reports on Microsoft Excel data tables.
	Analysis ToolPak	568	Tools that help you apply statistical and engineering analysis to data.
	AutoSave	56	Automatically saves documents at a specified interval to prevent data loss.
	Template Wizard with Data Tracking	497	Automatically records the contents of data entry fields in workbooks to a database for tracking and analysis.

Microsoft PowerPoint

Option Component	Sub-component	Space (K)	Description
Microsoft PowerPoint		16,217	Microsoft PowerPoint will be installed with only the selected options.
Microsoft PowerPoint Program Files		9,336	Microsoft PowerPoint and required system components.
Online Help for Microsoft PowerPoint		2,426	Complete online reference for Microsoft PowerPoint.

Option Component	Sub-component	Space (K)	Description
Design templates		1,336	Used with the AutoContent Wizard.
PowerPoint Viewer		1,640	Lets you present PowerPoint slide shows without PowerPoint. You may freely distribute copies of the PowerPoint Viewer disks.

Microsoft Schedule+

Option Component	Sub-component	Space (K)	Description
Microsoft Schedule+		4,569	Microsoft Schedule+ will be installed with the most common options.
Microsoft Schedule+ Program Files		2,312	Installs the Schedule+ executable and other required files.
Print Layouts and Paper Formats		161	Installs the Print Layouts and Paper Formats.
Seven Habits Tools		1,369	Installs the Seven Habits of Highly Effective People module.
Timex Data Link Utilities		81	Installs data download utilities for the Timex Data Link watch.
Help		649	Installs the Schedule+ Help files.

Microsoft Word

Option Component	Sub-component	Space (K)	Description
Microsoft Word		10,684	Components required for a Typical install of Microsoft Word.
Microsoft Word Program Files		5,761	Microsoft Word will be installed with only the selected options.
Online Help		3,474	
	Online Help for Microsoft Word	2,913	Word procedures, reference information, and tips.
Wizards, Templates, and Letters		1,169	
	Faxes	264	Contemporary, elegant and professional faxes.
	Letters	240	Contemporary, Elegant and Professional Letters.
	Memos	208	Contemporary, Elegant and Professional Memos.
	Reports	136	Contemporary, Elegant and Professional Reports.
Address Book		186	Tools for integrating with the Microsoft Exchange Personal Address Book and the Microsoft Schedule+ Contact List.

Converters

Option Component	Sub-component	Space (K)	Description
Converters		1,672	Utilities for converting documents to and from other file formats.
Microsoft Excel Converter		138	Converts documents from Microsoft Excel versions 2.*x*, 3.0, 4.0, and 5.0 (can be used to open Excel files, but not to save them).
Word 6.0 for Windows/Macintosh		145	Converts documents from Word 6.0 for Windows/Macintosh format.
WordPerfect 6.*x* Converter		554	Converts documents from WordPerfect 6.0 for DOS, and WordPerfect 6.0 and 6.1 for Windows.
WordPerfect 5.*x* Converter		836	Converts documents to and from WordPerfect 5.0 and 5.1 for DOS and WordPerfect 5.1 and 5.2 for Windows.

Graphics Filters

Option Component	Sub-component	Space (K)	Description
Graphics Filters		620	Utilities for converting graphics to a format that Word can use.
Tag Image File Format Import		113	Imports graphics from the Tag Image File Format (TIFF).
Windows Bitmap Import		73	Imports graphics from the Windows Bitmap (BMP and DIB) formats.
WordPerfect Graphic Import		153	Imports graphics from the WordPerfect Graphic (WPG 1.0, 1.0e and 2.0) formats. Also used by the WordPerfect converter.
DrawPerfect Export		73	Exports graphics to the WordPerfect Graphic (WPG) format (This file is only used with the WordPerfect converter).
Macintosh PICT Import		57	Imports graphics from the Macintosh (PICT) format.
Windows Metafile Import		17	Imports graphics from the Windows Metafile (WMF) format.
JPEG File Interchange Format Import		137	Imports graphics from the standard JPEG File Interchange Format.

Getting Results Book

Option	Sub-component	Space (K)	Description
Getting Results Book		16	Online version of the book, *Getting Results with Microsoft Office*. Selecting this option places a button on the Office Shortcut Bar.

Compact Installation

Compact installation is for computers with minimum available hard disk space. It includes all Office applications, and takes approximately 28 MB of disk space for Office Standard, and approximately 45 MB for Office Professional. During a Compact installation, components listed in the following tables will be installed.

Option Component	Sub-component	Space (K)	Description
Office Binder and Shortcut Bar		1,013	Files required for the Office Binder and Shortcut Bar utilities.
Microsoft Office Shortcut Bar		517	Complete set of files for the Microsoft Office Shortcut Bar.
Microsoft Binder		497	Microsoft Office Binder.
Microsoft Excel		6,489	Microsoft Excel will be installed with the minimum necessary options.
Microsoft Excel program files		6,489	Complete set of Microsoft Excel program files.
Microsoft Word		6,043	Microsoft Word will be installed with the minimum necessary options.
Microsoft Word Program Files		5,761	Microsoft Word will be installed with only the selected options.
Address Book		186	Tools for integrating with the Microsoft Exchange Personal Address Book and the Microsoft Schedule+ Contact List.
Microsoft PowerPoint		13,792	Microsoft PowerPoint will be installed with the minimum necessary options.
Microsoft PowerPoint Program Files		9,336	Microsoft PowerPoint and required system components.
Design templates		1,336	Used with the AutoContent Wizard.
PowerPoint Viewer		1,640	Lets you present PowerPoint slide shows without PowerPoint. You may freely distribute copies of the PowerPoint Viewer disks.

Option Component	Sub-component	Space (K)	Description
Microsoft Schedule+		2,312	Microsoft Schedule+ will be installed with the minimum necessary options.
Microsoft Schedule+ Program Files		2,312	Installs the Schedule+ executable and other required files.
Getting Results Book		16	Online version of the book, *Getting Results with Microsoft Office*. Selecting this option places a button on the Office Shortcut Bar.

Run from Network Server

Install Office to run from the network server. Some components will be copied to your local hard disk. Installing Office to run from the network server requires a minimum of 13 MB disk space on the local computer for Office Standard.

During a network server installation, components listed in the following tables will be installed on the user's local hard disk.

Option	Component	Space (K)
Converters, Filters, and Data Access		4,071
	Data Access	3,954
	Graphics filters	117
Microsoft Excel		2,442
	Microsoft Excel program files	2,303
	Online Help	139
Microsoft PowerPoint		139
	Genigraphics Wizard & Graphics Link	820
	Microsoft PowerPoint Program Files	1,811
Microsoft Schedule+		164
	Microsoft Schedule+ Program Files	100
	Timex Data Link Utilities	64
Microsoft Word		1,173
	Microsoft Word Program Files	1,108
	WordMail	65
Office Binder and Shortcut Bar		3,133
	Microsoft Binder	422
	Microsoft Binder Help Files	695
	Microsoft Office Shortcut Bar	768
	Office Help	665
	Office Setup	584

Option	Component	Space (K)
Office Tools		356
	Clip Art Gallery	50
	Find Fast	121
	Microsoft Graph 5.0	112
	WordArt	73

Run from CD

Install Office to run from the CD-ROM. Shared components will be installed on the hard disk. Installing Office to run from the network server requires approximately 30 MB disk space on the local computer for Office Standard.

During a network server installation, components listed in the following tables will be installed on the user's local hard disk.

Option	Component	Space (K)
Converters, Filters, and Data Access		11,517
	Converters	2,661
	Data Access	6,875
	Graphics Filters	1,981
Microsoft Excel		7,402
	Microsoft Data Map	3,846
	Microsoft Excel Program Files	2,303
	Online Help	1,253
Microsoft PowerPoint		207
	Program Files	207
Microsoft Schedule+		237
	Program Files	173
	Timex Data Link Utilities	64
Microsoft Word		5,435
	Program Files	883
	Proofing Tools	4,111
	Templates	376
	WordMail	65

Option	Component	Space (K)
Office Binder and Shortcut Bar		4,682
	Microsoft Binder	475
	Microsoft Binder Help Files	647
	Microsoft Office Shortcut Bar	2,072
	Office Help	486
	Office Setup	575
	Online Help	427
Office Tools		8,543
	Clip Art Gallery	543
	Equation Editor	712
	Find Fast	121
	Microsoft Graph 5.0	1789
	Microsoft Graph 5.0 Help	516
	Microsoft TrueType Fonts	2,039
	MS Info	384
	Organizational Chart	1,533
	Spelling Checker	351
	WordArt	555

APPENDIX D

Contents of the Office Resource Kit CD

The CD-ROM that comes with the *Office Resource Kit* includes this book and a variety of software tools, converters, utilities, and sample files to assist you in supporting your users and maintaining Office for Windows 95. The CD runs automatically. Insert it in your CD-ROM drive, and follow the instructions on your screen to browse the contents of the CD, copy files, or install software.

The contents of the Office Resource Kit CD are presented in the following categories:

Coexistence This category includes tools to support coexistence among Office applications on the Macintosh, Windows 3.*x,* Windows NT, and Windows 95 platforms. For example, there is a 16-bit Binder Explode application that allows Macintosh and Windows 3.1 users to disassemble Office Binders created on the Windows 95 platform. A version of the Find Fast utility that runs on Windows NT is also included.

Conversions This category includes converters used to migrate files from other platforms and other versions to be compatible with Office for Windows 95 applications. There are converters for both the Macintosh and Windows 3.*x* versions of Microsoft Excel, PowerPoint, and Word. A converter for migrating Windows WordPerfect files to Word 7.0 files is also included.

Administration Administrative tools include the Network Installation Wizard, for customizing and automating the installation of Office on a network, and the System Management Server, which allows you to support client workstations from a remote computer.

Office Resource Kit An online version of this book is included on the Office Resource Kit CD. For another online source of this book, consult the Microsoft Office Resource Kit forum on the Microsoft Network (MSN). The contents of this book will be updated as new information becomes available, making this reference work a living document. For information about accessing MSN, see Appendix F, "Resources."

Programmability This category includes utilities and documentation to assist you in developing your own Office-based software solutions. For example, it includes a help file for Data Access Objects (DAO) coding; it also includes technical information about writing custom applications for Schedule+.

Sample Setup Files This category includes information and tools for customizing setup. For example, information about registry settings and file locations is included, along with setup scripts and Windows 95 Policy files, to be used with the Windows 95 Policy Editor.

Support This category includes utilities for accessing support resources and performing your own troubleshooting. A folder containing Microsoft Network (MSN) shortcuts to Office support forums is included, as is a troubleshooter for printing problems and a PSS KnowledgeBase help file.

Tools In this category, you are provided with a variety of administrative utilities, such as WinDiff, which compares files and folders, and WinExtract, a utility for extracting files from Setup.inf.

A P P E N D I X   E

System Requirements for Office for Windows 95

This appendix lists system requirements for Microsoft Office and for the individual Office applications.

In This Appendix

Microsoft Office Standard

To use Microsoft Office Standard, you need:

- Personal computer with a 386DX or higher processor (486 recommended).
- Microsoft Windows 95 operating system or Microsoft Windows NT Workstation operating system version 3.51 or later (will not run on earlier versions of Windows).
- 8 MB of memory to run two applications on Windows 95; 16 MB of memory to run two applications on Windows NT Workstation; more memory recommended to run three or more applications simultaneously on Windows 95 or Windows NT Workstation.
- Hard disk space required: 28 MB for a compact installation; 55 MB for a typical installation; 89 MB for a custom installation (maximum).
- One 3.5" high-density disk drive.
- One CD-ROM drive, if you purchased Office on CD-ROM.
- VGA or higher-resolution video adapter (SVGA 256-color recommended).
- Microsoft Mouse or compatible pointing device.

Any or all of the following, though not required, can be used with Microsoft Office for Windows 95:

- Windows-compatible network required for workgroup functionality and WordMail.
- Microsoft Exchange client required for workgroup functionality and WordMail on Windows NT.
- 2400-baud or higher modem (9600-baud modem recommended).
- Audio board with headphones or speakers.

Microsoft Office Professional

To use Microsoft Office Professional, you need:

- Personal computer with a 386DX or higher processor (486 recommended).
- Microsoft Windows 95 operating system or Microsoft Windows NT Workstation operating system version 3.51 or later (will not run on earlier versions of Windows).
- 8 MB of memory to run two applications on Windows 95; 12 MB required to run Microsoft Access or to run additional programs simultaneously on Windows 95; 16 MB of memory to run two applications on Windows NT Workstation; more memory is recommended to run three or more applications simultaneously on Windows 95 or Windows NT Workstation.
- 40 MB of hard disk space for a compact installation; 87 MB for a typical installation; 126 MB for a custom installation (maximum).
- One 3.5-inch high-density disk drive.
- One CD-ROM drive, if you purchased Office on CD-ROM.
- VGA or higher-resolution video adapter (SVGA 256-color recommended).
- Microsoft Mouse or compatible pointing device.

Any or all of the following, though not required, can be used with Microsoft Office for Windows 95:

- Windows-compatible network; required for workgroup functionality and WordMail.
- Microsoft Exchange client; required for workgroup functionality and WordMail on Windows NT.
- 2400-baud or higher modem (9600-baud modem recommended).
- Audio board with headphones or speakers.

Individual Office Applications

This section lists each of the individual Office applications and the system requirements necessary for installing and running each application from disk.

Microsoft Access

To use Microsoft Access, you need:

- Personal computer with a 386DX or higher processor (486 recommended).
- Microsoft Windows 95 operating system or Microsoft Windows NT Workstation operating system version 3.51 or later (Access for Windows 95 will not run on earlier versions of Windows).
- 12 MB of memory available for Windows 95 and for Windows NT Workstation.
- 14 MB of hard disk space for a compact installation; 35 MB for a typical installation; 48 MB for a custom installation (maximum).
- One 3.5-inch high-density disk drive.
- VGA or higher-resolution video adapter (SVGA 256-color recommended).
- Microsoft Mouse or compatible pointing device.

Any or all of the following, though not required, can be used with Microsoft Access for Windows 95:

- Windows-compatible network.
- Windows-compatible printer.
- 2400-baud or higher modem (9600-baud modem recommended).
- Audio board with headphones or speakers.

Microsoft Excel

To use Microsoft Excel, you need:

- Personal computer with a 386DX or higher processor (486 recommended).
- Microsoft Windows 95 operating system or Microsoft Windows NT Workstation operating system version 3.51 or later (Microsoft Excel for Windows 95 will not run on earlier versions of Windows).
- 6 MB of memory available for Windows 95; 12 MB of memory available for Windows NT Workstation.
- 8 MB of hard disk space for a compact installation; 18 MB for a typical installation; 38 MB for a custom installation (maximum).

- One 3.5-inch high-density disk drive.
- VGA or higher-resolution video adapter (SVGA 256-color recommended).
- Microsoft Mouse or compatible pointing device.

Any or all of the following, though not required, can be used with Microsoft Excel for Windows 95:

- Windows-compatible network.
- Windows-compatible printer.
- 2400-baud or higher modem (9600-baud modem recommended).
- Audio board with headphones or speakers.

Microsoft PowerPoint

To use Microsoft PowerPoint, you need:

- Personal computer with a 386DX or higher processor (486 recommended).
- Microsoft Windows 95 operating system or Microsoft Windows NT Workstation operating system version 3.51 or later (PowerPoint for Windows 95 will not run on earlier versions of Windows).
- 6 MB of memory available for Windows 95; 12 MB of memory available for Windows NT Workstation.
- 14 MB of hard disk space for a compact installation; 24 MB for a typical installation; 35 MB for a custom installation (maximum).
- One CD-ROM drive or 3.5-inch high-density disk drive.
- VGA or higher-resolution video adapter (SVGA 256-color recommended).
- Microsoft Mouse or compatible pointing device.

Any or all of the following, though not required, can be used with PowerPoint for Windows 95:

- Audio board with headphones or speakers required for sound functionality.
- Network with TCP/IP protocols running required for Presentation Conferencing.
- Windows-compatible network.
- Windows-compatible printer.
- 2400-baud or higher modem (9600-baud modem recommended).

Microsoft Schedule+

To use Microsoft Schedule+, you need:

- Personal computer with a 386DX or higher processor (486 recommended).
- Microsoft Windows 95 operating system or Microsoft Windows NT Workstation operating system version 3.51 or later (Schedule+ for Windows 95 will not run on earlier versions of Windows).
- 6 MB of memory available for Windows 95; 12 MB of memory available for Windows NT Workstation.
- 2 MB of hard disk space for a compact installation; 6 MB for a typical installation; 6 MB for a custom installation (maximum).
- One 3.5-inch high-density disk drive.
- VGA or higher-resolution video adapter (SVGA 256-color recommended).
- Microsoft Mouse or compatible pointing device.

Any or all of the following, though not required, can be used with Microsoft Schedule+ for Windows 95:

- Windows-compatible network; required for workgroup functionality.
- Microsoft Exchange client; required for workgroup functionality on Windows NT.
- Windows-compatible printer.
- 2400-baud or higher modem (9600-baud modem recommended).
- Audio board with headphones or speakers.

Microsoft Word

To use Microsoft Word, you need:

- Personal computer with a 386DX or higher processor (486 recommended).
- Microsoft Windows 95 operating system or Microsoft Windows NT Workstation operating system version 3.51 or later (Word for Windows 95 will not run on earlier versions of Windows).
- 6 MB of memory available for Windows 95; 12 MB of memory available for Windows NT Workstation; additional memory needed for WordMail.
- 8 MB of hard disk space for a compact installation; 16 MB for a typical installation; 35 MB for a custom installation (maximum).
- One 3.5-inch high-density disk drive.
- VGA or higher-resolution video adapter (SVGA 256-color recommended).
- Microsoft Mouse or compatible pointing device.

Any or all of the following, though not required, can be used with Word:

- Windows-compatible network.
- Microsoft Exchange client; required to run WordMail on Windows NT.
- Windows-compatible printer.
- 2400-baud or higher modem (9600-baud modem recommended).
- Audio board with headphones or speakers.

APPENDIX F

Resources

This appendix contains listings of resources to help you support your users in Office for Windows 95. Support is available directly from Microsoft by telephone and through online services, both domestically and overseas.

In This Appendix

Getting Support from Microsoft

If you have a question about Office for Windows 95, first look in the Office product documentation, the *Office Developer's Kit,* or the *Microsoft Windows 95 Resource Kit,* or consult online Help. You can also find late-breaking updates and technical information in the Readme file that came with Office for Windows 95, and in forums on the Microsoft Network, as explained later in this section. If you cannot find the answer, contact the Microsoft Product Support Services (PSS).

In the United States and Canada, you have many options for getting answers to your questions through the Microsoft Support Network, which is explained later in this appendix. Outside the United States and Canada, contact Microsoft Product Support Services at the Microsoft subsidiary office that serves your area.

▶ **For information about Microsoft subsidiary offices**

1. On the Help menu in any Office application, click About.

2. Click Tech Support.

3. Click Product Support Worldwide.

When you call Microsoft Product Support Services, you can use the System Info feature to provide technical support engineers with information they may need about your system. The System Info feature examines your computer and displays information about Office for Windows 95 and your operating system.

▶ **To see information with the System Info feature**

1. On the Help menu, click About.

2. Click System Info.

3. From the System Info tree, select a category for the type of information you want.

You can also save or print information and run programs from the System Info dialog box.

Using the Microsoft Network from Office

If you have the Microsoft Network (MSN) installed on your system, you can access a number of Microsoft forums directly from the Microsoft Office Shortcut Bar. Office for Windows 95 comes with an MSN toolbar, which you can add to your Microsoft Office Shortcut Bar by clicking the Shortcut Bar with the right mouse button, clicking Customize, and then clicking the Toolbars tab. By clicking one of the buttons on this MSN toolbar, you can go directly to one of many Microsoft forums. The toolbar comes with buttons for the following forums:

- Microsoft Access 95
- Microsoft Excel 95
- Microsoft Office 95
- Microsoft Office Family
- Microsoft Office Resource Kit
- Microsoft PowerPoint 95
- Microsoft Schedule+ 95
- Microsoft Word 95
- Microsoft Forum

These forums are continually updated, so you should consult them for the most up-to-date information about the Office applications. Consult the Office Resource Kit forum for late-breaking news and updates to this book.

The Microsoft Support Network

The Microsoft Support Network offers high-quality technical support options that allow you to get what you need: the right answers right now.

Services and prices may vary outside the United States and Canada. The Microsoft Support Network is subject to current Microsoft pricing, terms, and conditions, and may change without notice.

Customer Service

The Microsoft Customer Service telephone number in the United States is (800) 426-9400 between 6:30 A.M. and 5:30 P.M. Pacific time, Monday through Friday, excluding holidays. In Canada, call (800) 563-9048 between 8:00 A.M. and 8:00 P.M. Eastern time, Monday through Friday, excluding holidays. Call this number for information about Microsoft Solution Providers and for Business Value Reports for Windows 95 and Office for Windows 95. This is not a technical support number.

Information Services

No-cost and low-cost electronic information services are available 24 hours a day, 7 days a week, including holidays.

Microsoft FastTips

For Microsoft FastTips, call (800) 936-4100 on a touch-tone telephone. Receive automated answers to common technical problems, and access popular articles from the Microsoft Knowledge Base, all delivered by recording or fax. You can use the following keys on your touch-tone telephone after you reach FastTips:

To	Press
Advance to the next message	*
Repeat the current message	7
Return to the beginning of FastTips	#

Microsoft Download Service (MSDL)

Over a modem, download sample programs, device drivers, patches, software updates and programming aides (1200, 2400, or 9600 baud; no parity; 8 data bits; 1 stop bit). In the United States, call (206) 936-6735. In Canada, call (905) 507-3022. For more information about using this service, see the Microsoft Download Service section later in this appendix.

Internet

Access the Microsoft Knowledge Base and Software Library. The Microsoft World Wide Web site is located at http://www.microsoft.com. The Microsoft Gopher site is located at gopher.microsoft.com. The Microsoft FTP site is located at ftp.microsoft.com and can be accessed via anonymous logon. For more information about accessing the Knowledge Base and Software Library, see "Accessing KB Articles on the Internet" later in this appendix.

CompuServe, MSN, America Online, and GEnie

Access the Microsoft Knowledge Base, the Microsoft Software Library, and participate in MS forums. On CompuServe, at any ! prompt, type **go mskb** to access the Microsoft Knowledge Base, **go msl** to access the Microsoft Software Library, **go microsoft** to access Microsoft application forums, and **go msoffice** to access the Office forum.

To access Microsoft forums through the Microsoft Network (MSN), use the MSN toolbar supplied with the Microsoft Office Shortcut Bar. For information about the MSN toolbar, see "Using the Microsoft Network from Office" earlier in this appendix.

To access the Microsoft Knowledge Base on America Online®, click the Go To menu, type **microsoft** in the Keyword box, and then click Knowledge Base in the Microsoft Resource Center.

To access the Microsoft Knowledge Base on GEnie, type **m505** at the GEnie system prompt.

Standard Support

In the United States, no-charge support from Microsoft support engineers is available via a toll call between 6:00 A.M. and 6:00 P.M. Pacific time, Monday through Friday, excluding holidays.

For technical support for:

Product	Call
Microsoft Office for Windows 95	(206) 635-7056
Microsoft Office for Windows 95—Switcher Line	(206) 635-7041
Microsoft Access for Windows 95	(206) 635-7050
Microsoft Excel for Windows 95	(206) 635-7070
Microsoft PowerPoint for Windows 95	(206) 635-7145
Microsoft Schedule+ for Windows 95	(206) 635-7049
Microsoft Word for Windows 95	(206) 462-9673

In Canada, support engineers are available via a toll call between 8:00 A.M. and 8:00 P.M. Eastern time, Monday through Friday, excluding holidays. Call (905) 568-2294 for Microsoft Office and Office components, or (905) 568-4494 for Microsoft Windows 95.

When you call, you should be at your computer and have the appropriate product documentation at hand. Be prepared to give the following information:

- Version number of the Microsoft product that you are using.
- Type of hardware that you are using.
- Exact wording of any messages that appeared on your screen.
- Description of what happened and what you were doing when the problem occurred.
- Description of how you tried to solve the problem.

Priority Support

The Microsoft Support Network offers priority telephone access to Microsoft support engineers 24 hours a day, 7 days a week, except holidays in the U.S. In Canada, the hours are from 6:00 A.M. to midnight Eastern time, 7 days a week, excluding holidays.

- In the United States, call (900) 555-2000; $1.95 (U.S.) per minute, $25 (U.S.) maximum. Charges appear on your telephone bill. Not available in Canada.
- In the United States, call (800) 936-5700; $25 (U.S.) per incident; in Canada, call (800) 668-7975, at $30 (CDN) per incident. These services are billed to your VISA card, MasterCard, or American Express card.

Text Telephone

Microsoft text telephone (TT/TDD) services are available for the deaf or hard-of-hearing. In the United States, using a TT/TDD modem, dial (206) 635-4948 between 6:00 A.M. and 6:00 P.M. Pacific time, Monday through Friday, excluding holidays. In Canada, using a TT/TDD modem, dial (905) 568-9641 between 8:00 A.M. and 8:00 P.M. Eastern time, Monday through Friday, excluding holidays.

Other Support Options

The Microsoft Support Network offers annual fee-based support plans. For information in the United States, contact the Microsoft Support Network Sales Group at (800) 936-3500 between 6:00 A.M. and 6:00 P.M. Pacific time, Monday through Friday, excluding holidays. In Canada, call (800) 563-9048 between 8:30 A.M. and 6:30 P.M. Eastern time, Monday through Friday, excluding holidays. Technical support is not available through these sales numbers. Please refer to the Standard Support phone number for technical support.

Other Microsoft Services

In addition to telephone and online support, Microsoft offers other resources to help you support your users. These resources include Microsoft Authorized Support Centers, Microsoft Solution Providers, and Microsoft TechNet.

Microsoft Authorized Support Centers

Microsoft Authorized Support Centers (ASCs) are a select group of strategic support providers who offer high quality customized support services that span the complete systems life cycle of planning, implementation and maintenance of your multivendor environment. Services include: on-site support, integration and implementation services, help desk services, hardware support, development resources, and others. Choosing an ASC allows you to work with one vendor for all of your technical support and service needs. You can also combine ASC services with your in-house help desk or the Microsoft support service option to best fit your information technology support needs.

For more information about the ASC program, in the U.S. call (800) 936-3500 between 6:00 A.M. and 6:00 P.M. Pacific time, Monday through Friday, excluding holidays. In Canada, call (800) 563-9048 between 8:00 A.M. and 8:00 P.M. Eastern time, Monday through Friday, excluding holidays.

Microsoft Solution Providers Program

Microsoft Solution Providers are independent developers, consultants, and systems analysts that offer fee-based technical training and support, industry knowledge, objective advice, and a range of value-added services to companies of all sizes. Solution Providers work with organizations to help implement computing systems that take advantage of today's powerful new technologies.

For the name of a Microsoft Solution Provider near you, in the U.S. call (800) 426-9400 between 6:30 A.M. and 5:30 P.M. Pacific time, Monday through Friday, excluding holidays. In Canada, call (800) 563-9048 between 8:00 A.M. and 8:00 P.M. Eastern time, Monday through Friday, excluding holidays.

Microsoft TechNet

Microsoft TechNet is the front-line resource for fast, complete answers to technical questions on Microsoft systems and desktop products. Information available on TechNet ranges from crucial data on client-server and workgroup computing, systems platforms, and database products, to the latest on support for Microsoft Windows and Macintosh-based applications.

As a TechNet user you receive:

- Twelve monthly compact discs containing the Microsoft Knowledge Base, Microsoft operating systems product resource kits, customer solutions, key Microsoft conference session notes, and other valuable information.

- Twelve monthly supplemental (drivers and patches) compact discs containing the Microsoft Software Library.

- A dedicated Microsoft TechNet forum on CompuServe (GO TECHNET).

- WinCIM, a Windows-based application for accessing CompuServe.

- A 20% discount on Microsoft Press books.

For more information about Microsoft TechNet, in the United States and Canada, call (800) 344-2121, between 7:00 A.M. and 7:00 P.M. Central time, Monday through Friday. Outside of the U.S. and Canada, contact your Microsoft Subsidiary, or call (303) 684-0914.

Microsoft Download Service (MSDL)

Microsoft Download Service (MSDL) operates in the same way as any MS-DOS–based computer bulletin board system (BBS). The MSDL contains Application Notes from Microsoft Product Support Services (PSS), and driver files and other types of support files for download. To use the MSDL, you must have a computer with a modem and a terminal package. Any terminal package, such as Microsoft Works, Windows Terminal, Procomm, or Crosstalk, will work with the MSDL. If you experience difficulty while you are working with the MSDL, try calling a local BBS so you can avoid paying long-distance charges while trying to determine the cause of the problem.

Please note that technical support is not available on the MSDL.

The MSDL supports 1200, 2400, 9600, and 14400 baud rates (V.32 and V.42), with 8 data bits, 1 stop bit, and no parity. Make sure that the terminal software is configured to operate with these settings. After you have chosen these settings, you can begin the session as follows:

▶ **To connect to the MSDL**

1. Call the MSDL at (206) 936-MSDL (936-6735).

2. Enter your full name and the location you are calling from.

The MSDL will list some basic instructions and information and then display the Main menu:

```
*******************************************
****    Microsoft Download Service    ****
****              Main Menu            ****
*******************************************
[D]ownload File
[F]ile Index
[I]nstructions on Using This Service
[W]indows Driver Library Update
[N]ew Files & Complete File Listing
[M]icrosoft Information
[A]lter User Settings
[U]tilities - Comments
[L]ength of Call
[E]xit - Logoff the System
[H]elp - System Instructions
Command:
```

If you already know the exact name of the file to download, perform the following steps. If you do not know the filename, see "To search for files" following this procedure.

▶ **To download files**

1. At the Main menu, press D for Download.

2. Press D again and press ENTER.

3. When asked for the filename, type the name of the file you want to download. Be sure to include the correct extension (usually .exe); also be sure to differentiate between the letter O and the number 0 (zero) in filenames.

   If you see a -More- prompt at the bottom of the screen, you can press the SPACEBAR to see more files.

4. When asked which protocol you would like to use, enter any protocol supported by your terminal package (check your software manual for more information). If you are unsure, press X for Xmodem.

5. The MSDL will then display the Awaiting Start Signal message. When you see this message, start the download process with your terminal software. For example, if you are using Windows Terminal, click Receive Binary File on the Transfers menu.

   If you don't start the process, the transfer will fail, and you'll need to start again at step 2.

6. After your transfer is complete and you want to exit the MSDL, choose Exit from the menu by pressing E.

If you do not know the exact name of the file to download or you simply want to find out what files are available, do the following:

▶ **To search for files**

1. At the Main menu, press F for the File Index.

2. Press F for File Search.

3. You will be prompted to enter the text to search on. For example, if you want to search for a Hewlett-Packard LaserJet printer driver, type **hp laserjet** and press ENTER.

   The matching filenames will be displayed in a list.

   If you see a -More- prompt at the bottom of the screen, press the SPACEBAR to see more files.

   If you don't find what you are looking for, see the following procedure "To use the file index."

4. When you see the file that you want, write down the filename so you can download the file later.

5. Press ENTER to quit the search option.

▶ **To use the file index**

1. At the Main menu, press F for File Index.

2. In the next screen (the File menu), choose the number that matches the application you are looking for.

3. Continue to select the appropriate number from the menus that appear until you see a list of files displayed on-screen.

   For example, if you are looking for a Windows 3.1 printer driver, do the following:

   - Press F at the Main menu.
   - Press 1 for Windows and MS-DOS.
   - Press 2 for Windows 3.1 Driver Library.
   - Press 2 for Windows 3.1 Printer Drivers.

4. A list of files will be displayed on the screen. Read through the list to see if the file you need is displayed.

   If you see a -More- prompt at the bottom of the screen, you can press the SPACEBAR to see more files.

5. When you locate the file, write down the name. Press the SPACEBAR until you see the following at the bottom of the screen:

   ```
   <D>ownload, <P>rotocol, <E>xamine, <N>ew, <L>ist, or <H>elp
   Selection or <CR> to exit:
   ```

6. To download the file, press D, then follow steps 3-6 in the procedure "To download files" earlier in this section.

▶ **To use the file after it is downloaded**

- If the file has an .exe extension, run the file by typing its name at the MS-DOS command prompt. The .exe file will extract its contents and the resulting files are then ready to be installed. Refer to any text files that have been extracted for exact instructions on using the downloaded file or files.

Microsoft Knowledge Base

The Microsoft Knowledge Base (KB) is a primary source of product information for Microsoft support engineers and customers. This comprehensive collection of articles contains more than 56,000 detailed how-to articles, answers to technical support questions, bug lists, fix lists, and documentation errors. Over 600 Visual Basic articles are available in the KB.

In addition, the Microsoft Software Library (MSL) is a collection of files for all Microsoft products. Both KB articles and MSL files are available from several electronic services. For information about accessing KB articles and MSL files, see "Information Services" earlier in this appendix.

A collection of KB articles is included on the *Office Resource Kit* CD. However, KB articles are updated daily online. For the latest, most up-to-date information about Office, Office applications, and Windows 95, you should consult the online KB articles.

At the top of each KB article, you will find information about the product, version, and operating system the article applies to. For example, the article below contains information about the version 3.0 of the Standard and Professional Editions of Microsoft Visual Basic, running under Microsoft Windows:

```
Visual Basic 3.0 Common Questions & Answers             [B_VBasic]
ID: Q92545    CREATED: 04-AUG-1993   MODIFIED: 22-JUL-1994
3.00
WINDOWS
ENDUSER |


- - - - - - - - - - - - - - - - - - - - - - - - - - - - - - - - - - - - - - - -

The information in this article applies to:

- Standard and Professional Editions of Microsoft Visual Basic
  programming system for Windows, version 3.0
- - - - - - - - - - - - - - - - - - - - - - - - - - - - - - - - - - - - - - - -
```

Accessing KB Articles on the Internet

To access KB articles on the Internet, you must connect to the Microsoft Internet server, and know how to find the articles you are searching for. This section explains how to connect to the server, how to find the files you want, and how to download files, using the GET command.

Connecting to the Microsoft Internet Server

Connection to the Microsoft Internet server requires a live session to the Internet through a file transfer program (FTP) service provider.

▶ **To connect to the Microsoft Internet Server**

1. Log on to your Internet account.

2. At the Internet prompt, type

   open ftp.microsoft.com

   or use the following IP address:

   open 198.105.232.1

3. When prompted for a user name, type:

   anonymous

4. When asked for a password, type your full electronic mail address (for example, johndoe@test.com).

How to Find KB Articles on the Internet Server

KB articles are organized by many levels of folders. The first level divides Microsoft products into the following groups:

Group	Topics
Advsys	LAN Manager, Windows NT, SQL Server, Open Data Base Connectivity (ODBC), and Microsoft Mail
Deskapps	Desktop applications, including Microsoft Excel, Word for Windows, and Office
Developer	Development tools and languages
Peropsys	Personal operating systems, including Microsoft Windows, Windows for Workgroups, MS-DOS, and Microsoft Mouse

Each group is then divided by product. For example, to access the personal operating systems area, change to the Peropsys folder by typing the following at the FTP prompt:

cd /peropsys

Each group area contains subfolders for each product contained in the group area. Under the Peropsys folder, the following subfolders are available:

Subfolder	Topics
WINDOWS	Microsoft Windows versions 3.0 and later, Windows for Workgroups, and Windows Multimedia
MSDOS	Microsoft MS-DOS
HARDWARE	Microsoft Mouse

Use the CD command from the FTP prompt to select the subfolder you are interested in. Each product subfolder contains a KB subfolder in which the actual KB articles are stored.

Index of Articles

While in the KB folder, download the Readme.txt and Index.txt files. Readme.txt contains important information about Knowledge Base articles. Index.txt contains a list of article titles and KB article IDs for each article. You must determine the KB article ID before you can download the article because there is no search mechanism on the FTP server.

▶ **To download Readme.txt and Index.txt**

- Type the following at the FTP prompt:

    get readme.txt

    get index.txt

After you review Readme.txt and Index.txt and determine the article ID you are interested in, you are ready to download a Knowledge Base article.

Downloading KB Articles with the GET Command

KB articles are stored in a tree structure, with each KB article ID translated into a two-digit filename and stored two subfolders under the KB folder. This method avoids storing thousands of articles in one subfolder, which would slow server performance.

You do not need to change to the folder that contains the KB article you want to download; the folder structure is consistent and the GET command can be used to obtain an article from the KB folder.

The following steps show you how to download a KB article about Windows for Workgroups, How to Troubleshoot WFWG Network Connection Problems. From the Index.txt file, you can find this article listed as having a KB article ID of Q104322.

▶ **To download a KB article**

1. After logging on to the FTP server, change to the Peropsys folder:

   cd /peropsys

2. Change to the Windows folder:

   cd windows

3. Change to the KB folder:

   cd kb

4. Translate the article ID into a GET command. There are three parts of the KB article ID to be divided before using the GET command. The filename of the KB article is the last two digits plus the .txt extension (22.txt). The subarea is the third digit from the right of the ID (3). The primary area is the remaining characters to the left, including the "Q." To use the GET command, place a slash mark (/) between the primary area, subarea, and filename (primary/sub/filename).

   For Q104322, the filename translates to:

   Q104322 = Q104/3/22.txt

5. Use the GET command at the FTP prompt to transfer the article to your system as follows:

   get q104/3/22.txt q104322.txt

   The "Q104322.txt" part of the command above is the destination name for the file. The destination name is the name of the file as it appears on your hard disk drive.

6. To close the connection with the server for most FTP clients, type the following from the FTP prompt:

   bye

Searching with Keywords

All KB articles are categorized and contain keywords describing their content. You can navigate within the KB more effectively if you add keywords to your text searches. Below are the keywords and their meanings:

Keyword	Description
kb3rdparty	Interactions with third-party products
kbappnote	Application Notes
kbatwork	Microsoft At Work
kbbuglist	List of all bugs for a particular version of a product
kbcode	Sample code
kbdocerr	Documentation errors

Keyword	Description
kbenv	Environment and configuration
kberrmsg	Error message followup information
kbfasttip	FastTip scripts or maps
kbfile	Binary file information located in the MSL: sample code, drivers, macros
kbfixlist	List of all fixed bugs for a particular version of a product
kbgraphic	Graphics
kbhw	Hardware
kbinterop	Interoperability with other Microsoft products
kbmacro	Sample macros
kbmm	Multimedia
kbnetwork	Networking
kbole	OLE technology
kbother	Other - any subject not covered in other categories
kbpolicy	Support boundaries, policies, processes, and procedures
kbprb	Problems not classified as bugs
kbprg	Programming
kbprint	Printing
kbreadme	Readme files
kbref	References and lists (phone numbers, folders, and so on)
kbsetup	Setup and installation
kbtlc	FastTip Technical Library Catalog (TLC) items
kbtool	Tools and utilities such as Print Manager or Write
kbtshoot	Troubleshooting information
kbui	User Interface
kbusage	How to use product functionality

Note New keywords may be added to this list over time. A list of the current keywords is available in the KB in article Q94671, KB Categories and Keywords for All KB Articles. You can use "Q94671" as a keyword to find this article.

Visual Basic Articles

Microsoft Visual Basic article contains a keyword that applies to the type of information in the article. You can use these keywords to quickly find the information you need. A list of these keywords is available in the KB in article Q108753, Category Keywords for All Visual Basic KB Articles. You can use "Q108753" as a keyword to find this article.

There more than 600 categorized articles in the Visual Basic for Windows collection. The VB articles have been split up into two help files that you can download from several different electronic services. To obtain these help files, download either Vbkb_ft.exe or Vbkb.exe.

The Help files in Vbkb_ft.exe have an additional Find button that allows full-text search. The Help files in Vbkb.exe do not have the Find button and do not allow full-text search. The technical content in Vbkb.exe is identical to that in Vbkb_ft.exe. Vbkb.exe is 1.5 MB in size while Vbkb_ft.exe is approximately 4 MB. Vbkb_ft.exe is larger because it includes the index and DLLs needed for full-text search.

Both of these files are available from the Microsoft Software Library (MSL). After you download either Vbkb.exe or Vbkb_ft.exe, run it to extract the files it contains.

Finding Fixes to Known Bugs

To list the corrections to known bugs for a given product version number, search on the version of the product in which the problem occurs. For example, to find the list of problems corrected in version 4.50, search on the previous version number (4.00b) and choose the Fixes To Known Bugs menu item.

▸ **To find bug fixes**

1. From any CompuServe prompt type:

   go mskb

   –Or–

   go mdkb

2. Select "4. Search the Knowledge Base."

3. To find problems corrected in version 4.50 of a product, search as follows:

   a. Select the Product Name menu item and specify a product, such as QuickBasic for MS-DOS.

   b. Select the Fixes to Known Bugs menu item.

   c. Select the Product Version menu item and type a version number previous to the version that contains the Fixes to Known Bugs. For example, if you want the list of bugs that were corrected in version 4.50, type 4.00b. Note that if the version number has no letter as a suffix, then typing tenths or hundredths, such as 3.0 or 3.00, will both work. Searching for a number in the form 4.0b won't find any articles if the version is 4.00b; the version you search for must be an exact match.

How to Contribute to the Knowledge Base

You don't have to be a writer to contribute to the KB. The Developer Support Knowledge Base team can rewrite your material for you. All that is needed is complete, well-tested technical information.

When submitting an article, please ensure that it is fully tested and includes all the following information:

- Names of the authors or contributors
- Names of the people who technically reviewed the information
- Product names
- Product version numbers
- Operating systems
- Short summary of the information
- Your phone number

On the Internet, please send mail to:

y-kbfeed@microsoft.com

In CompuServe Mail, put the following on the TO: line of your message:

>internet: y-kbfeed@microsoft.com

Microsoft Software Library (MSL)

The MSL contains files for all Microsoft products, including drivers, utilities, Help files, and Application Notes. To find out what files are available for the product you are interested in, you can query the KB for MSL files.

MSL files are provided on many electronic services, including the Internet, CompuServe, and MSN. The MSL is also available on the Microsoft Download Service. To obtain MSL files from the Internet, go to the Softlib\Mslfiles folder. For information about connecting to the Microsoft Internet server, see "Accessing KB Articles on the Internet" earlier in this appendix. For information about accessing MSL files through CompuServe, MSN, or Microsoft Download Service, see "Information Services" earlier in this appendix.

Microsoft Consulting Services

Microsoft Consulting Services (MCS) has helped hundreds of organizations worldwide to build information technology solutions. With over 400 consultants based in 13 countries, MCS provides services that enable both user organizations and third-party software developers to design and build client-server applications that fully leverage Microsoft technology.

MCS consultants are systems architects with experience and expertise in Microsoft technology, methodologies, and tools, who are chartered to help organizations capitalize on the benefits of client-server computing. MCS consultants focus primarily on transferring their knowledge and skills to corporations, government organizations, Microsoft Solution Providers, and other third parties worldwide. Through its commitment to capabilities transfer, MCS empowers organizations to best meet information technology challenges and, in turn, to achieve maximum results from their enterprise solutions on the Microsoft platform.

Through partnering with Microsoft Solution Providers and other third parties, MCS is able to ensure that organizations are offered effective and solid planning, design, development, integration, and implementation customized for their unique information technology environment. These services are designed to build solutions that yield significant results for clients in a wide variety of industries.

MCS consultants are experienced in designing custom solutions such as order entry, executive information systems, payroll systems, document management, investment bank trading systems, and sales force automation. These solutions draw on the latest and most powerful technologies available, including the Microsoft Windows and Windows NT operating systems, client-server computing, graphical user interface, 32-bit computing, object oriented programming, and messaging. For more information, please call (800) 426-9400 or see the following page for the number of the Microsoft Consulting office nearest you.

Programs—Microsoft Consulting Services

Contact Information

MCS U.S. West

Los Angeles Practice
Santa Monica 310-449-7300

Northern California Practices
Foster City 415-571-7737 (Regional HQ)
San Francisco 415-905-0235

Paific Northwest Practices
Bellevue 206-635-1900
Portland 503-452-6400

Rocky Mountain Practice
Denver 303-843-6224

Southwest Practices
Irvine 714-263-0200
Phoenix 602-266-0302

MCS U.S. Central

Detroit Practice
Southfield 810-827-2000

Windows 95 Practice
Oak Terrace 708-495-5550 (Regional HQ)

Minneapolis Practice
Bloomington 612-896-1001

Dallas Practice
Dallas 214-458-1739

Houston Practice
Houston 713-986-4300

St. Louis Practice
St. Louis 314-432-7772

MCS U.S. East

Atlanta Practice
Atlanta 404-392-7400

Boston Practice
Waltham 617-487-6500 (Regional HQ)

Connecticut Practice
Farmington 203-678-3134

Greater Philadelphia Practice
Wilmington 302-791-9400

New Jersey Practice
Edison 908-632-3300

New York Metro Practice
New York 212-245-2100

Washington D.C. Practice
Washington D.C. 202-364-4266

MCS International

Australia: (2) 870-2200
Brazil: (11) 530-4455
Canada: (905) 712-0333
France: (1) 6986-4480
Germany: (89) 3176-3019
Hong Kong: (852) 804-4200
Italy: (39)2-703-921
Mexico: (5) 325-09-10
New Zealand: (64) (9) 358-3724
Singapore: (65) 329-9435
South Africa: (27) 11-444-0520
United Kingdom: (734) 270-001

Microsoft Developer Network

The Microsoft Developer Network (MSDN) is an annual membership program designed especially for developers targeting the Microsoft Windows, Windows NT, or Microsoft BackOffice platforms. MSDN ensures that developers are kept up-to-date with the latest and most comprehensive programming information, development toolkits, and testing platforms from Microsoft.

Developer Network Membership Benefits

Three levels of MSDN membership are available: Level 1, Level 2, and Level 3.

Level 1 Membership

Level 1 membership in MSDN provides a base level of benefits (including the Development Library and the *Developer Network News*) designed to connect Windows-based developers to all the development-related technical, strategic, and resource information available from Microsoft. MSDN also gives developers the opportunity to provide feedback to Microsoft via CompuServe, the Internet, fax, and mail.

Level 1 members receive the following benefits:

- Four quarterly updates of the Development Library CD
- Six bimonthly issues of the Developer Network News
- Two free phone-support incidents
- A 20% discount on Microsoft Press books
- Invitations to MSDN special events at shows

Level 2 Membership

Level 2 membership in MSDN provides developers with all the software development kits (SDKs), device driver kits (DDKs), and operating systems from Microsoft, in addition to the information resources of a Level 1 membership.

Level 2 delivers all Level 1 benefits plus:

- Four quarterly updates to the Development Platform CDs
- Special premium shipments of important systems releases that fall in between quarterly Development Platform updates

Level 3 Membership

Level 3 membership in MSDN provides developers with an integrated development and testing environment for Microsoft BackOffice: the comprehensive information offered with Level 1 *plus* the client- and server-side toolkits found on the Development Platform *plus* the most current versions of the BackOffice server products.

Level 3 delivers all Level 2 benefits plus:

- Four quarterly updates of the BackOffice Test Platform CDs
- Special premium shipments of important BackOffice releases that fall in between quarterly BackOffice Test Platform updates

Development Library

The Development Library, which is delivered every quarter to Level 1, Level 2, and Level 3 MSDN members, contains more than 150,000 pages of information about programming for Windows, Windows NT, and BackOffice. It's all on one searchable CD: comprehensive product documentation, exclusive technical articles, reusable sample code, the complete Developer Knowledge Base, and much more. And you can be sure you have the latest information because with every edition roughly 50,000 pages are either updated or contain completely new material.

The Development Library includes:

- All documentation for Microsoft development products, such as the Microsoft Solutions Development Kit, the Win32 SDK, Visual Basic, Microsoft Access, Visual FoxPro, and Visual C++.
- Over 1800 sample applications, fully documented and tested, written in Visual Basic and C/C++, that demonstrate development techniques.
- Hundreds of technical articles—more than 200 written exclusively for the Development Library—on topics such as "Porting Your 16-Bit Office-Based Solutions to 32-Bit Office" and "Using the Common Dialogs Under Windows 95." These technical articles discuss complex Windows programming topics in great detail, helping developers solve complex programming problems.
- The latest specifications, covering technologies such as Plug and Play, TrueType, and OLE 2.0.
- Entire Microsoft Press books, such as Jeffrey Richter's *Advanced Windows NT*, Charles Petzold's *Programming Windows 3.1*, Craig Brockschmidt's *Inside OLE 2*, and Nancy Cluts' *Programming the Windows 95 User Interface*.

- Complete issues of the *Microsoft Systems Journal* with source code, plus selected articles from *Inside Visual Basic*, *Visual Basic Programmer's Journal*, *Dr. Dobb's Journal*, *FoxTalk*, *Visual Basic Developer*, and *Smart Access*.

- The complete Developer Knowledge Base, containing over 13,000 articles, with bug reports and workarounds on all Microsoft development products.

- Tools and utilities such as the Windows Help Authoring Tools, the WinG SDK, and the WinToon SDK.

- Papers, presentations, and sample code from conferences, such as Tech•Ed 95.

Each edition of the Development Library contains 1.5 GB of information, but many ease-of-use features have been added to enable MSDN members to quickly find the exact piece of information they need. A Windows-based interface makes the Library easy to read, annotate, search, and browse. Customizable subsets allow you to view only the new and updated content on the Library, or only content relating to specific subsets, such as Office or Visual Basic. And the Library's full-text search engine helps you define sophisticated Boolean queries and then ranks the search results according to the topics with the greatest relative density of the search words.

The Development Platform

The Development Platform, which goes to both Developer Network Level 2 and Level 3 members, is a set of CDs that delivers the latest released versions of Microsoft SDKs, DDKs, and Windows and Windows NT Workstation operating systems, both domestic and international versions. It's an easy way to stay current with the latest systems technology because it's all delivered to you in a single package every three months. And if an important systems release occurs between quarterly Platform updates, it will come to you immediately at no extra charge.

The Development Platform July 1995 edition contains the following:

Development Kits and Tools

- Common Messaging Calls SDK
- Embedded SQL for C Toolkit
- Mail Format File API (FFAPI) SDK 3.0 for Gateways and Applications
- MAPI 1.0 PDK (Beta versions for Windows 3.1, Windows for Workgroups 3.11, Windows 95, Windows NT)
- Microsoft MediaView 1.2 Development Toolkit
- MIGRATE: Source Code Migration Tool
- Open Database Connectivity (ODBC) SDK 2.10
- ODBC 2.0 16-bit Windows and Windows NT Libraries (Danish, Dutch, Finnish, French, German, Italian, Norwegian, Portuguese, Spanish, Swedish)

- ODBC Desktop Database Drivers 2.0 for Windows and for Windows NT
- OLE 2.01 SDK
- OLE Control API for C
- OLE Test Tools (Beta)
- Schedule+ Libraries Version 1.0a2
- Simple MAPI SDK
- SNA Server 2.1 SDK
- TCP/IP-32 for Windows for Workgroups 3.11b (Beta)
- Video for Windows 1.1e Development Kit and the Run-Time Extension
- Win32 SDK Version 3.5 (Japanese)
- Win32 SDK (Final Windows NT 3.51 Components)
- Win32s® 1.25 extension for Windows 3.1 (Japanese)
- Win32s 1.25A extension for Windows 3.1
- Win32s Far East
- Windows 3.1 Driver Library
- Windows 3.1 SDK and DDK
- Windows 3.1 DDK (Chinese Extension, Japanese Extension, Hangeul Extension)
- Windows 3.1 SDK (Arabic Supplement, Chinese Extension, Hangeul Extension, Hebrew Supplement, Japanese)
- Windows 95 Resource Kit
- Windows for Workgroups 3.11 Resource Kit
- Windows for Workgroups SDK and Remote Access Service API (RASAPI) Kit
- Windows Help Compiler 3.10.505
- Windows NT Driver Library
- Windows NT 3.5 DDK (Japanese)
- Windows NT 3.51 DDK
- Windows NT 3.5 Resource Kit
- Windows NT 3.5 Service Pack 2 for Intel, Alpha AXP, and MIPS (Danish, Dutch, French, German, Italian, Norwegian, Spanish, Swedish, U.S.)
- Windows Telephony API (TAPI) 1.0 SDK
- Windows Version 3.1 Resource Kit

Operating Systems

- MS-DOS 6.22 and MS-DOS 6.2/V

- Windows for Workgroups 3.11 (Arabic, Danish, Dutch, English-Arabic, Finnish, France [complies with France's encryption regulations], French, French-Arabic, German, Hebrew, Italian, Norwegian, Portuguese, Spanish, Swedish, Thai, U.S.)

- Windows 3.11 (Dutch, French, German, Italian, Portuguese, Spanish, Swedish, Thai, U.S.)

- Windows 3.1 (Arabic-English, Catalan, Central and Eastern European, Chinese Simplified, Chinese Traditional, Czech, Danish, Finnish, French-Arabic, Greek, Hebrew-English, Hungarian, Japanese [NEC 9800 and Intel], Korean, Norwegian, Polish, Russian, Turkish)

- Windows 3.2 (Chinese Simplified)

- Windows 95 Beta (Danish, Dutch, Finnish, French, German, Italian, Norwegian, Pan-European, Spanish, Swedish)

- Windows NT 3.5 Workstation on Intel, Alpha AXP, and MIPS (Chinese, Danish, Dutch, Finnish, French, German, Italian, Japanese, Norwegian, Portuguese, Spanish, Swedish)

- Windows NT 3.5 Workstation Checked Build on Intel, Alpha AXP, and MIPS (Japanese)

- Windows NT 3.51 Workstation on Intel, Alpha AXP, MIPS, and PowerPC

- Windows NT 3.51 Workstation Checked Build on Intel, Alpha AXP, MIPS, and PowerPC

BackOffice Test Platform

The BackOffice Test Platform is a set of CDs updated each quarter that ships to only Level 3 MSDN members. It contains the latest released versions of the five server components of Microsoft BackOffice: Windows NT Server, Microsoft SQL Server, Microsoft SNA Server, Microsoft Systems Management Server, and Microsoft Mail Server (to be replaced with Microsoft Exchange). A Level 3 membership is the most cost-effective way for any developer writing applications for BackOffice to stay current with the latest programming information (via the Development Library and *Developer Network News*), client- and server-side toolkits (via the Development Platform), and BackOffice products (via the BackOffice Test Platform).

The first BackOffice Test Platform was shipped in August 1995 (concurrent with the release of BackOffice 1.5) and delivered:

- Windows NT Server 3.51
- SQL Server 6.0
- SNA Server 2.11
- Systems Management Server (SMS) 1.1
- Mail Server 3.5
- BackOffice 1.5 SDK

Level 3 members will also receive important BackOffice releases—such as Microsoft Exchange and "Cairo," the next version of Windows NT—as premium shipments if they fall in between the quarterly BackOffice Test Platform release cycle. The Test Platform also allows for up to five simultaneous connections to each server product so you can easily develop and test your client-server applications before deploying them.

Developer Network News

The *Developer Network News*, the bimonthly MSDN newspaper, delivers up-to-the-minute information about Microsoft's systems strategy and development products to all MSDN members. Here you'll find case studies detailing successful implementations of Microsoft Office solutions, the future direction of Windows and Office strategy, new development products, updates to current products (and how to get them), programming tips, the lively Backtalk column where readers' questions are answered, and key phone numbers for Microsoft development information, services, and support.

Online Access to MSDN

MSDN has a significant online presence and will continue to take advantage of the online medium to provide rich, timely, interactive information and a place to contribute to the growing community of Windows-based developers who participate in online forums, chats, and conferences.

MSDN has three online offerings:

- The Developer Network OffRamp can be found on Microsoft's World Wide Web site (http://www.microsoft.com). The OffRamp contains an expanded, online version of the *Developer Network News* that is updated weekly. You'll also find announcements about events, product releases, and overview articles. The OffRamp also includes some of the latest technical articles from MSDN's own developers, as well as selected sample code, backgrounders, and white papers from the Development Library. Information about Microsoft's developer-related products and a link to the Microsoft Knowledge Base are also included in the OffRamp.

- The MSDN area on The Microsoft Network contains an expanded, online version of the *Developer Network News*. Developers can go to the MSDN area on The Microsoft Network for a one-stop source of information about development for Windows, including papers on technology and strategy, case studies, online chat groups and member-to-member forums, and pre-sales information about Microsoft's development-related products.

- Microsoft has a number of Windows development-related forums on CompuServe (GO MSDS). The Knowledge Base (GO MSKB) and Software Library (GO MSL) provide thousands of articles, samples, patches, and fixes for Microsoft's systems and development tools. The MSDN Forum (GO MSDN) is an active area for discussion of development-related issues, with message sections for peer-to-peer support, a place to ask questions about the MSDN program and member benefits, and libraries for downloading technical information.

How to Enroll in MSDN

A one-year Level 1 membership is $195 ($275 CAN) plus tax and shipping and handling. A one-year Level 2 membership is $495 ($695 CAN) plus tax and shipping and handling. The Level 3 annual membership fee is $1495 ($2095 CAN) plus tax and shipping and handling. (Special introductory pricing may be in effect on Level 3 memberships—call for details.) Upgrade pricing (to Level 2 or Level 3) is available for current MSDN members.

To join MSDN in the U.S. and Canada, please call (800) 759-5474, from 6:30 A.M. to 5:30 P.M. (Pacific time), Monday through Friday. Outside North America, call the appropriate number from the following table; for countries not listed, call (303) 684-0914 in the U.S. to obtain local contact information. (Please note that pricing and membership benefits may vary by country.)

Asia

Hong Kong	(852) 2756 5560
India and Central Asia	91 11 646 0694
Japan	03 5600 5033
Korea	(080) 022-7337
Taiwan	886 2 504 3122

Caribbean

Caribbean (same as U.S. and Canada)	(800) 759-5474 or (402) 691-0173

Europe

Austria, Belgium, Channel Islands, Czech Republic, Denmark, Finland, Greece, Greenland, Hungary, Iceland, Ireland, Italy, Luxembourg, Norway, Poland, Portugal, Slovak Republic, Slovenia, Spain, Sweden	+31 10 258 88 64 (European Subscription Centre in the Netherlands) + 31 10 258 88 63
France	05 90 59 04 (toll-free)
Germany	0130 81 02 11 (toll-free)
Netherlands	06 022 24 80 (toll-free)
Russia and neighboring countries	7 095 244 3474
Switzerland	144-9491 (French), 155-9492 (German)
United Kingdom	0800 96 02 79 (toll-free)

Latin America

Argentina	54-1-814-0356
Brazil	(55) 011-251-0299
Chile	56-2-204 2084
Colombia	(57) (1) 618-2225
Mexico and Central America	(915) 325-0911

Middle East and Africa

Israel	(972) (3) 575-7034
South Africa and Sub-Saharan Africa	27 11 445 0000
Turkey	90-212-258 59 98
United Arab Emirates and the Middle East	971 4 827497

Southeast Asia and Australia

Australia	61 2 870 2100
Malaysia	800-1108 (toll-free)
New Zealand	0800 800 004 or 64 9 308 9318
Singapore, Indonesia, Philippines	(65) 2207380

Licensing Options for Development Library

Level 1 membership includes a single-user license for the Development Library. In the U.S. and Canada you can purchase licenses to share a single CD over a network for $40 ($55 Canadian) per additional user. Each additional license allows one designated user to install the Development Library Viewer software on a single workstation to access the CD contents.

For large workgroups, Level 1 memberships with concurrent-user licenses are available in two configurations: a five-user license is $595 ($835 Canadian), and a 25-user license in $2495 ($3495 Canadian). Concurrent-user licenses permit the members of a large group to install the Development Library Viewer software on their workstations, but allow no more than five (or 25) users to run the application at a given time. The number of developers supported by concurrent-user license depends primarily on their usage patterns and network performance. Developers who expect to make heavy use of the Development Library should consider individual memberships. Call (800) 759-5474 for more information about licensing in North America. (Level 1 licensing options are being developed for European members as well; please consult the table above for the appropriate phone number.)

Level 2 membership includes a single-user license for both the Development Library and the Development Platform. Because Microsoft operating systems can be licensed only to a single user, additional licenses are not available for Level 2 memberships.

The BackOffice applications included with each Level 3 membership come with a license for five simultaneous connections to be used exclusively for development and testing purposes (i.e., not to be used as a production server that is accessible to non-development or non-testing clients). Each BackOffice application is hard-coded to accept no more than five connections at any one time. Also, the BackOffice products delivered via the BackOffice Test Platform can only be installed on a single computer.

Training Resources

Microsoft offers training services to help you become an expert in Microsoft solutions. These services include the Microsoft Certified Professional Program and Microsoft Technical Education courses.

Microsoft Certified Professional Program

The Microsoft Certified Professional program offers an excellent way to show employers and clients that you have proven knowledge and skills to help them build, implement, and support effective solutions and that you have the validated expertise to help them get the most out of their technology investment. As a Microsoft Certified Professional you are recognized and promoted by Microsoft as an expert with the technical skills and knowledge to implement and support solutions with Microsoft products.

To become a Microsoft Certified Professional, you must pass a series of rigorous standardized certification exams. When you become a Microsoft Certified Professional, you receive benefits including access to technical information, use of the Microsoft Certified Professional logo, and special invitations to Microsoft conferences and technical events.

For more information about the Microsoft Certified Professional program, call Microsoft at (800) 636-7544 in the United States and Canada. In other countries, contact your local Microsoft subsidiary office. Ask for the Microsoft Education and Certification Roadmap, an online guide to Microsoft Education and Certification. Or see E&CMAP.ZIP from Library 5 of the Solution Provider forum on CompuServe (GO MSEDCERT).

Microsoft Technical Education

Microsoft technical education materials provide computer professionals with the knowledge required to expertly install and support Microsoft solutions. Courses are developed straight from the source—by the Microsoft product and technical support groups. They include in-depth, accurate information and hands-on labs based on real-world experience. Microsoft courses are designed to effectively help you prepare for Microsoft Certified Professional exams.

Microsoft curriculum is developed in two forms:

- Instructor-led classes are delivered by Microsoft Certified Trainers at Microsoft Authorized Technical Education Centers (ATECs). As members for the Solution Provider program, the ATECs are independent businesses that have been evaluated as qualified to deliver official Microsoft curriculum.

- Microsoft develops self-paced curriculum materials that enable you to learn at your convenience. Hands-on lab exercises are included.

For full course descriptions and referral to an ATEC, call (800) SOLPROV (800-765-7768) in the United States and Canada. In other countries, contact your local Microsoft subsidiary office. Ask for the Microsoft Education and Certification Roadmap, an online guide to Microsoft Education and Certification. Or see E&CMAP.ZIP from Library 5 of the Solution Provider forum on CompuServe (GO MSEDCERT).

To find out the location of the Authorized Academic Training Program (AATP) nearest you, call the Microsoft Fax Server at (800) 727-3351 in the United States and Canada, and request document number 10000256. Microsoft ATECs and Microsoft AATPs offer Microsoft Official Curriculum delivered by Microsoft Certified Trainers to educate computer professionals on Microsoft technology.

Reference Materials

Following is a list of publications to consult for additional information about Office, the individual applications of Office, and the Windows operating system. These books are available at many bookstores and software stores. In addition, for Microsoft Press books, in the United States you can place a credit card order directly with Microsoft Press by calling (800) MS PRESS and referring to source code BBK. In Canada, call (800) 667-1115 for direct ordering information. Outside the United States and Canada, fax (206) 936-7329.

Microsoft Windows 95 Resource Kit   Microsoft Press

This book is a guide for administrators and MIS professionals to help them support users at their worksite. It is a technical resource for installing and supporting Windows 95 workstations, and includes sections on system management, system configuration, Microsoft Exchange, the Windows registry, and more.

Microsoft Office Evaluation Guide   Microsoft Corporation

This document provides an overview of Office features and is a guide to evaluating Office in terms of your company's productivity. For a copy of the *Evaluation Guide*, contact Microsoft Customer Service at (800) 426-9400. Ask for part number 098-60004.

Microsoft Solutions Development Kit   Microsoft Corporation

This kit presents a low cost, high value method for delivering the information required for developers to build integrated solutions with Office, BackOffice, and Visual Tools. The kit is provided on a CD, and includes Office and BackOffice developments Kits and information, documentation, integrated sample code and utilities, and other useful information for developers on how to utilize third party components in custom solutions (especially Office Compatible applications).

Step by Step series; editions for Microsoft Office, Microsoft Access, Microsoft Excel, PowerPoint, Word, and Windows 95   Microsoft Press

These books provide a quick, easy way to get users started in Office applications. This series of books presents tutorials and self-paced training for the busy businessperson. Each lesson is modular, example-rich, and fully integrated with a timesaving practice file on an enclosed disk.

Field Guide series; editions for Microsoft Office Microsoft Access, Microsoft Excel, PowerPoint, Word, and Windows 95   Microsoft Press

This series provides concise, easy-to-follow quick-reference material for Microsoft Office for Windows 95 applications.

Microsoft Excel/Visual Basic for Windows 95 Step by Step   Microsoft Press

This guide teaches how to customize Microsoft Excel: how to create macros to streamline routine tasks and how to build custom spreadsheet applications.

Word Developer's Kit, third edition   Microsoft Press

This book teaches how to customize Word: how to create macros to streamline routine tasks and how to build custom applications.

Microsoft Excel Developer's Kit, third edition   Microsoft Press

This book presents technical information and sample code for software developers who want to use Microsoft Excel as an application development platform.

Developing Applications with Microsoft Office for Windows 95   Microsoft Press

This guide provides corporate developers, consultants, and managers with the concepts and techniques they need to plan, develop, and implement customized business applications using Microsoft Office and related technologies, such as OLE, ODBC, and Visual Basic for applications.

Index

Contributors

Writing and Editing Contributors

Catherin Alpert
Peter Bateman
Roxanne Blair
Carl Chatfield
Mark Dodge
Gary Ericson

Patrick Kelley
Ann Laporte
Ken Lassesen
Mark Roberts
Tom Ware

Technical Contributors

Peggy Angevine
Michael Angiulo
Paul Balle
Ed Barnes
Craig Beilinson
Jeff Brown
Kevin Browne
John Budig
Charles Carney
Gordon Church
Jim Cochran
Jennifer Cockrill
Noah Edelstein
Holly Eggleston
Jackie Elleker
Kristin Fresch
David Gonzalez
Dave Gorbet
Susan Grabau
AnneMarie Heaney
Adam Hecktman
Kevin Horst
Dennis Hutchinson

Heikki Kanerva
Eric Levine
Robin Lyle
Michael Mathieu
Michael Maxey
Tom Pizzato
Skip Purdy
Christopher Rimple
Michael Risse
Kit Scruggs
Kevin Shaughnessy
George Snelling
Paul Steckler
Daren Stegelmeier
Nick Stillings
John Tafoya
Martin Thorsen
Kevin Unangst
Tom Vukovic
Ryan Waite
Jim Walsh
Michael Weiss
David Wohlferd

Project Team

Steve Bush
Bryna Hebert
Gwen Lowery

WELCOME TO THE WORLD OF WINDOWS® 95

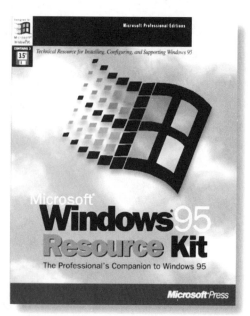

The MICROSOFT® WINDOWS® 95 RESOURCE KIT provides you with all of the information necessary to plan for and implement Windows 95 in your organization.

ISBN 1-55615-678-2
1376 pages, $49.95 ($67.95 Canada)
Three 3.5" disks

Details on how to install, configure, and support Windows 95 will save you hours of time and help ensure that you get the most from your computing investment. This exclusive Microsoft publication, written in cooperation with the Windows 95 development team, is the perfect technical companion for network administrators, support professionals, systems integrators, and computer professionals.

The MICROSOFT WINDOWS 95 RESOURCE KIT contains important information that will help you get the most out of Windows 95. Whether you support Windows 95 in your company or just want to know more about it, the MICROSOFT WINDOWS 95 RESOURCE KIT is a valuable addition to your reference library.

TOUGH DECISIONS
TO MAKE?
TURN TO MICROSOFT® TECHNET.

Microsoft TechNet is designed for technical professionals who evaluate and decide on new technology directions, integrate products and platforms, administer enterprise applications and networks, support and train users. Microsoft TechNet is the leading resource for fast, complete answers to technical questions on Microsoft desktop and system products.

Updated monthly, TechNet provides the most complete collection of technical information on Microsoft products anywhere. In one place, you get everything from crucial data on client-server and workgroup computing, systems platforms, and database products to the latest applications support for Microsoft® Windows® and the Macintosh®. Benefits include:

- Twelve monthly Microsoft TechNet CDs containing the complete Microsoft Knowledge Base, product resource kits, datasheets and whitepapers, customer case studies and other valuable technical and strategic information.

- Twelve monthly Microsoft TechNet Supplemental (Drivers and Patches) CDs containing the complete Microsoft Software Library, with drivers for the entire line of Microsoft software products, code samples and patches for many Microsoft products.
- A dedicated Microsoft TechNet CompuServe® forum (GO TECHNET).
- 20% discount on Microsoft Press® books.

Microsoft TechNet is $299 annually for a single-user license, and $699 annually for a single server-unlimited users license. To order Microsoft TechNet, call (800) 344-2121 dept. 3092. Outside of the US and Canada, contact your Microsoft subsidiary, or call (303) 684-0914.

WHO KNOWS MORE ABOUT WINDOWS® 95 THAN MICROSOFT® PRESS?

ISBN 1-55615-816-5
224 pages
$19.95 ($26.95 Canada)

ISBN 1-55615-683-9
320 pages
$29.95 ($39.95 Canada)

These books are essential if you are a newcomer to Microsoft® Windows® or an upgrader wanting to capitalize on your knowledge of Windows 3.1. Both are written in a straightforward, no-nonsense way, with well-illustrated step-by-step examples, and both include practice files on disk. Learn to use Microsoft's newest operating system quickly and easily with MICROSOFT WINDOWS 95 STEP BY STEP and UPGRADING TO MICROSOFT WINDOWS 95 STEP BY STEP, both from Microsoft Press.

Register Today!

Return this
Microsoft® Office for Windows® 95 Resource Kit
registration card for:

✔ a Microsoft Press® catalog

✔ special offers on
Microsoft Press books

U.S. and Canada addresses only. Fill in information below and mail postage-free. Please mail only the bottom half of this page.

1-55615-818-1A   *Microsoft Office for Windows 95 Resource Kit*   *Owner Registration Card*

NAME

INSTITUTION OR COMPANY NAME

ADDRESS

CITY   STATE   ZIP

Microsoft®Press
Quality Computer Books

**For a free catalog of
Microsoft Press® products, call
1-800-MSPRESS**

BUSINESS REPLY MAIL
FIRST-CLASS MAIL   PERMIT NO. 53   BOTHELL, WA

POSTAGE WILL BE PAID BY ADDRESSEE

MICROSOFT PRESS REGISTRATION
MICROSOFT OFFICE FOR WINDOWS 95
RESOURCE KIT
PO BOX 3019
BOTHELL WA   98041-9946

NO POSTAGE
NECESSARY
IF MAILED
IN THE
UNITED STATES